*

The La Guardia Years

*

The La Guardia Years,

*Machine and reform politics
in New York City*

CHARLES GARRETT

Rutgers University Press   *New Brunswick, New Jersey*

to Mom and Dad

Preface

IT WAS FIVE MINUTES PAST MIDNIGHT, New Year's Day, 1934. Fiorello
H. La Guardia, his wife at his side, faced Supreme Court Justice Philip J.
McCook in the home of Samuel Seabury to take the oath of office for
Mayor. Gathered around them was a handful of spectators including
W. Arthur Cunningham, Bernard S. Deutsch, Charles Tuttle, Roy Howard,
Charles C. Burlingham, Adolf A. Berle, Jr., William M. Chadbourne, Paul
Windels and W. Kingsland Macy. As La Guardia uttered, "I do solemnly
swear," he turned to Mrs. La Guardia and kissed her. From the group in
the background, Seabury exclaimed: "Now we have a Mayor of New
York!" [1]

The ordinary citizen shared his enthusiasm. The crowds that cheered
the new Mayor at his first businesslike, early morning arrival at City Hall
resembled in spirit the ones that had celebrated the arrival of the New
Year and the repeal of Prohibition with the greatest outpouring of rejoic-
ing, hoping, believing, feeling that Broadway had seen in fifteen years. On
both occasions it was felt and said by thoughtful observers that there was
something new and magical in the air, a quickening of confidence and
energy, a new pulsing of the life-stream. [2] Repeal had registered as another
manifestation of a new deal in the nation. In La Guardia's assumption of
office New Yorkers saw the promise of a new deal in the city.

A new era for New York had indeed dawned. After more than fifteen
years of rule by the political machine, an anti-machine Fusion movement
had come to power on the wave of a political upheaval. For a dozen years,
for a longer period than the most enthusiastic Fusion partisan could have
imagined, Fusion was to govern the city. It was to be a great age of municipal reform and progress. At the heart of the reform movement were

Fiorello La Guardia and his administration. From 1934 to 1945 the colorful, dynamic and extremely capable La Guardia dominated the city's political stage, drawing the attention of the nation and, at times, foreign countries. His antics amused and fascinated his generation, and he is remembered partly because of them. His real contribution, however, was the administrative, financial, physical, social and moral rehabilitation he helped to bring about in America's greatest city and the political and governmental legacy he left to its citizens. And the achievements of the reform era take in more than those of the La Guardia administration. Altogether the La Guardia years made an indelible imprint on politics and government in New York City.

This is the story of the reform movement of those years—its development, record and passing and its significance for the City of New York. Of course the book deals with La Guardia and his administration, but its emphasis is upon the reform movement in the broadest sense. The political history of many American cities can be examined in terms of two conflicting traditions—a tradition of machine rule and a reform tradition. Certainly this has been true of New York City, where since the nineteenth century professional politicians have encountered opposition from reformers and periods of machine government have oscillated with periods of reform government. Though there was much that was special about the reform movement of the La Guardia years, essentially it did not constitute a unique experience for New York. Because the reform movement of the 1930's and early 40's can really be understood only within the context of the city's political history, I have devoted not a small number of pages to discussing the machine and reform traditions of New York. Chapters 1 and 2 deal with these traditions before the main part of the story. Chapters 15 and 16 discuss developments involving these traditions in the La Guardia and post-La Guardia years. This book then is also, to a degree, a study of New York's political history. Finally, I have attempted to place the New York story within the wider framework of the political history of American cities. In doing so I have said something in general about the battle for good municipal government in this country.

I should like to thank all those who gave me help or encouragement in connection with this work. At the risk of neglecting to mention people who deserve better of me, I especially should like to express my gratitude to Professor Joseph D. McGoldrick for giving me freely of his time answering questions and for undertaking to read portions of the manuscript; Messrs. I. D. Robbins and Seymour Graubard for examining parts of the manuscript; Professor Arthur M. Schlesinger, Jr. for his valuable editorial criticism; Professor Emeritus Harry J. Carman for his wonderful support throughout. I am also particularly obligated to the librarians of the New York Public Library and Municipal Reference Library for their assistance and to Mrs. Helen Robbins, Mrs. Anne J. Thomson and my aunt, Mrs. Ruth Rhodes, for their skillful secretarial help. None, but myself, of course, is responsible for whatever shortcomings there may be in the following pages.

Without the understanding and co-operation of my mother and father, this book could never have been written. To them I owe a debt that I can never adequately repay.

C.G.

New York City
January, 1961

Contents

PART IV / FROM YESTERDAY TO TOMORROW

*

Part I
Traditions

The machine tradition

AT THE HEART of American politics is the political machine. The machine is composed of committees which represent the framework of a party and the people who run them, the people usually referred to as the professional politicians. Ordinarily the term machine covers, not the entire party organization from the precinct to the national committee, but rather the local organization, in particular, the organization in the cities. Most of the time there is another element in the concept: the machine is viewed as the dominant party organization in a place.

Particularly in politics, things are not always what they seem—or all they seem. In theory, the city political party is a perfectly democratic organization, power flowing upward from individual party members through precinct committeemen and ward chairmen to a city central committee and a city chairman. This structure has variations, to be sure, and the political units and party officers are sometimes known by different titles. But in practice, party power has seldom followed this democratic model. Although the wishes of the party voters have usually not been without some influence, the real power in the party has traditionally been in the hands of the officers of the party. Power has emanated from the top, from the middle, or from some interaction between the two— but not from the bottom. The flow has been downward from the boss, or downward from the boss together with the ward leaders, or upward and downward from the ward leaders. Moreover, this power has not always been exercised entirely within the party structure as set up by law. Extralegal, unofficial committees and officials enmeshed with the formal system may represent the real seat of power. The boss, the actual leader of the machine, might be the same person as the city or county chairman, or he might be a man with no official party position. The small group of men who run and are themselves part of the party machinery, are tied together, not so much by any system created by statute, as by an informal association based upon mutual interest and friendship. Not only do they control the party; for the most part, they *are* the party.

This is not the only way in which theory has been modified by practice. Look at a civics textbook and you may read that the party has an important role in the American democracy: to reflect attitudes and interests and help crystallize public opinion on issues; to nominate candidates and wage campaigns for their election, something ordinary citizens do not usually have time to do; to provide a means by which the legislative and executive branches of government may be co-ordinated; in general, to bridge the gap between the people and the structure of government. It is true that the party does have this role—these functions justify party existence. Of course how well the party discharges its responsibilities, whether its recognized functions are carried out in the public interest or in the interest of party members, is another matter.

But the core of the party, the machine, has, with the exception of some credo parties, fulfilled in practice another, and for professional politicians more important role, which your textbook is unlikely to describe clearly, if mention at all. It is an un-enunciated role, one certainly never given as a rationalization for political organizations. It is an un-political role, one which is, at best, questionable by American standards. In fact, it has traditionally stood in the way of the party's best fulfillment of its political and recognized role and obligations. Nevertheless, it is quite real and its importance can hardly be overemphasized in talking about American city politics. Historically the machine has functioned as a means by which the men who have been part of the machine, their associates and friends, have attempted to achieve the great American goal of individual success.

Through the machine men have obtained power, fame, prestige and, especially, money—probably the most important element in the American success concept. The city machine has provided a ladder whereby people, particularly lower- and lower-middle-class people, often immigrants or their sons, have been able to rise, to improve their circumstances. The immigrants, unlike older stock Americans, have generally not had the advantages of inherited capital or family connections. But in politics, particularly at the lower level, the immigrant or the son of the immigrant has only been required to command numbers, and this is something he has been able to do, if anything, more easily than an older American because of his connection with a community of the foreign-born.[1] No one will really understand municipal political history in this country who does not see the machine's role as an escalator for self-advancement.

The machine has controlled the government of American cities, especially the bigger cities; normally municipal government has been machine government. Usually control has been exercised by one party in a given city, as the Republican Party in Philadelphia or the Democratic Party in Boston; that is why the term machine can take on the connotation of the chief party organization in a city. But regardless of which party or city, the operations and activities of the machine and the consequences of machine rule for city government have been, in the broad view, quite similar.

In New York City the most powerful political organization came to be the Democratic Party. This was not so true in the period before the Civil War. Then the Whigs and the Know-Nothings gave the Democrats a good deal of competition; between 1834 and 1843 the Whigs and Democrats were nearly equal in political strength, and during the next ten years, though the city was generally in Democratic hands, the opposition was anything but weak.[2] But after the Civil War the picture changed. The Democrats ran away with the field, and the Republicans by themselves never constituted a serious threat.

As for the Democratic organization, until events to be described later, it generally has been synonymous with Tammany Hall. That does not mean Tammany has been free of rivals. In the first place, Democratic groups like Mozart Hall, Irving Hall, the County Democracy, arose in Manhattan from time to time to challenge Tammany's leadership. Though Tammany was often forced to compromise with these contenders for a time, in the end, the sarcasm of George Washington Plunkitt, self-appointed Tammany sage, was justified:

I've seen more than one hundred "Democracies" rise and fall in New York City in the last quarter of a century. At least a half dozen new so-called Democratic organizations are formed every year. All of them go in to down Tammany and take its place, but they seldom last more than a year or two, while Tammany's like the everlastin' rocks, the eternal hills and the blockades on the "L" road—it goes on forever.[3]

Then when New York City became more than Manhattan Island, when in 1898 Greater New York was created by the union of Brooklyn, Queens, Richmond, and Manhattan—the Bronx was later carved out of Manhattan and added to the city as a fifth county or borough—Tammany was confronted with the fact that other county organizations were now part of the Democratic Party in the city. Still Tammany retained its dominance in Democratic affairs. Manhattan, the home of most of the city's immigrants, presented a compact population which made it easy for politicians to deliver the vote. Here, too, was the big money. Tammany enjoyed a prestige based in part on its long history. The other Democratic county organizations, though jealous and suspicious of it, became the allies of the stronger Manhattan machine; for years Tammany ruled the Democratic organization in the Bronx as a fief. This did not mean that Tammany's rule was absolute. It could not afford entirely to ignore the aspirations of the other machines.[4] Democratic politics was characterized by bargaining; nevertheless, this game of political give and take was not played by equals, and Tammany took more than it gave.

Generally speaking, in the nineteenth century—especially after the Civil War—and in the early twentieth, the machine in New York City was Tammany Hall; for New Yorkers the machine tradition was the Tammany tradition. Let us consider that organization.

The Society of Saint Tammany or Columbian Order was founded in 1789, the year the Constitution went into operation, as a fraternal and patriotic organization by democratic elements in New York City interested in combatting what they regarded as a dangerous "foreign" drift towards aristocracy.[5] But it did not long remain just a fraternal society. As political polarization in the new nation developed, it became closely identified with the party of Thomas Jefferson; Aaron Burr and his lieutenants in organizing the Jeffersonian Party in New York used the Tammany Society as their political nucleus.[6] Tammany, while remaining a fraternal group, thus also became a political club and one that was strong enough to control the Democratic-Republican Party and, later, the Democratic Party in New York City. About 1805 Tammany leaders adopted for public consumption the fiction, later perpetuated by their successors, that the Society was a group distinct from the political organization.[7] Superficially, it was true, the two groups were divorced. The Society, with a ritual of Indian analogy—the governors who ruled the association were called Sachems, and the head a Grand Sachem—mainly concerned itself with patriotic rallies, and its membership was not limited to Democrats.[8] The party was a separate hierarchical organization of Democrats. Actually, however, the leaders of the Society as a rule controlled the various political committees in the hierarchy, and those who became important in Democratic politics joined the Society, so that Tammany and the Democratic Party in Manhattan became inextricably interwoven. On this point the public was never fooled: it always considered Society and political organization as one.

The Tammany political structure evolved through the years. Up to the 1860's the real power in Tammany was exercised by the General Committee which consisted of constantly changing cliques of various numbers of men. The members of the General Committee were elected by ward committees, but this election was only a matter of form, for the General Committee normally controlled the elections in the wards. Between 1850 and 1863, in the days when Fernando Wood, one of the biggest political manipulators in the city's history, was the leading personality in Tammany, control began to shift from cliques within the General Committee to one man. Wood demonstrated the feasibility of boss rule, but he was never able to centralize power in himself completely because of continual conflicts within the organization. With the emergence of William M. Tweed and his friends, however, the position of boss came into being. Shrewd, unscrupulous, thoroughly skilled in ward politics, Tweed by 1868 was able to gather political power exclusively in his own hands. When the end came for him and his famous Ring, the leadership of the Hall passed to Honest John Kelly (1872–86), who did much to consolidate the position of the boss and systematize what had been a loose relationship among Tammany politicians. Under Kelly what might be called the classic Tammany structure first came into being. Under his successors, Richard Croker (1886–1902) and Charles Murphy (1902–24), the rough edges were polished and the system hardened. In its consummate form this was Tammany's new streamlined machine.

At the head of the organization was the boss. Under him in every assembly district were district leaders (equivalent to ward leaders) who were the rulers in their neighborhoods, but who generally obeyed the big boss. Actually the district leaders elected the boss, but once elected he wielded such power that he was not easily controlled by them, having become for most purposes precisely what the name implies. Beneath the district leaders were the precinct captains, appointed by them, and the ordinary party workers. Neither the position of boss, nor that of district leader, was recognized by law, but both easily meshed with the formal party structure. The district leader was elected along with other delegates from his assembly district to the General Committee or, as it came to be called, the County Committee, which was the officially recognized party committee; but the County Committee really abdicated in favor of a smaller Executive Committee composed mainly of one representative from each assembly district elected by the county committeemen of that district—which person somehow always turned out to be the district leader. The Executive Committee of district leaders then appointed its chairman, who was the boss. The political pyramid was cemented firmly—though not without the possibility of cracks—by the cardinal vows of the professional politician: obedience, regularity, loyalty.[9]

Before and after modernization, always, the main concern of Tammany Hall was what we have suggested was the main concern of machines in general. Obviously the essential requirement for advancing the self-interest of Tammany members, their associates, relatives and friends, was victory at the polls, and victory was always uppermost in the thoughts of precinct workers, district leaders and boss. With keen perception of human nature, Tammany adopted as its main strategy for winning elections—not impressive candidates or platforms, but the practice of catering to voters' personal interests and problems. For immigrant families, businessmen, gamblers, prostitutes, saloon keepers, gangsters and others, Tammany did favors—usually of the kind involving the granting of some special privilege, a dispensation, perhaps, from some law or regulation. In John Kelly's time and after, the district leader was the pivotal figure;

for most people he was the chief point of contact, both with respect to the machine and the government; he was the man to see. About Kelly's time the district club replaced the saloon as the center of political life in each neighborhood, and here, every night in the week, every week in the year, never taking a vacation, the district leader could be found talking to supplicants, often staying late into the night. The next day he would be busy about the courts and the city departments seeing clerks, district attorneys, judges and commissioners—or better still the district leaders responsible for them—in general, carrying out his "contracts" with his constituents.[10]

In return, those who benefited from Tammany's favors helped the organization at election time; the *quid pro quo* might not be vocalized, but it was well understood. The first requirement, of course, for politician as for pushcart peddler, was to vote right—which meant the straight machine ticket. In addition to voting themselves, all were expected to help get out the vote for machine candidates. There were also other ways of contributing, all ultimately reducible to political bullion—votes. From party workers high and low, from the underworld, from businessmen, from, indeed, all who were able—Tammany expected money contributions to pay for the campaign. Under the system inaugurated by Kelly, the Monday before election was known as Dough Day; at that time Tammany distributed the money that was to be spent in the election the next day. Each district leader received as much as he thought he would need to swing his district—to pay for floaters, for carriages to take the lame, the sick and the blind to the polls, for fireworks and orators.[11]

Tammany did not rely only upon the gratitude of voters for whom it had done favors. It was not inclined to leave such a vital thing as political power to chance. It herded unqualified voters to the polls, in many cases illegally naturalized citizens. It bought votes. It encouraged friendly voters to vote more than once. Gangsters and bully boys stuffed ballot boxes and saw to it that the wrong people did not vote. Those who counted the returns arrived at totals which had nothing to do with the real vote cast.

From its beginning, throughout the nineteenth century and in the twentieth, Tammany engaged in such practices, but there were high water marks. As a whole, one can say that in the second half of the nineteenth century, election frauds and violence were more marked than before or after; the nadir in dishonest elections was probably reached in the Tweed era. In the first decade of the twentieth century, Tammany, while still involved in election manipulation, was doing it on a smaller scale, though Lincoln Steffens was exaggerating when he said that Tammany in the 1900's no longer indulged in dishonest election practices, having gained such a hold upon important voting blocs that it no longer felt it had to.[12] In the 1890's, it should be noted, New York obtained the secret ballot which made it a little more difficult for politicians to frustrate the wishes of the voters.[13]

No one should be puzzled as to why the Manhattan machine was able to manipulate the ballot. The source of Tammany's success was its control of the Police Department and the courts. It was estimated that in Tweed's day at least 80 per cent of the policemen were members of the Democratic Party. Croker's Tammany so dominated the department that policemen not only had to obey the orders of Tammany leaders but had to pay money to individual Tammany politicians for their jobs and for promotions; they were "invited" to contribute to the Tammany campaign fund.[14]

Success at the polls opened, or kept open, the golden doors of opportunity. First to be benefited were those elected to public office, but under the dictates of the spoils system, they were quickly joined by others. In the days before civil service, every position was a political plum, and even under the merit system, many city jobs remained political. Under the renovated Tammany developed in the late nineteenth century, the boss would submit a list of names to the Mayor for all vacancies in the city government, and each district leader was provided with places for himself, his captains and his constituents. After Robert Van Wyck won the election of 1897, Plunkitt tells us, "Richard Croker went down to Lakewood [New Jersey] to make up the slate of offices for Mayor Van Wyck to distribute." [15] Not all Mayors were as co-operative as Van Wyck. William R. Grace, Mayor in the 1880's, proved independent of Kelly's dictation, and Charles Murphy had sad experiences with Mayors McClellan—after his re-election in 1905—and Gaynor. Yet it was generally true that the machine was more powerful than its candidates, that most voters voted for the party first and issues and personalities second and that most Mayors, not to mention other local officials, for self-preservation, if for no other reason, were not inclined to act independently of the organization in matters of patronage, or anything else.[16]

Office, elective or appointive, represented the first dividend the machine paid to its own. With office went power, some prestige perhaps, and, most important, the right to draw a salary from the public treasury, often the more attractive for the soft job that went with it. But the sweetest part of victory lay elsewhere. Quite aside from the emoluments of office, control of the government opened up numerous paths to making money, sometimes very big money, for Tammany officeholder and non-officeholder alike. Traditionally, machine politicians profited in four main ways: embezzlements and other frauds on the public treasury, the selling of privileges, extortion and what George Washington Plunkitt labeled "honest graft." The specific variations possible in each method are innumerable and limited only by circumstance and imagination. The selling of privileges has been mentioned. In return for the right to evade certain laws or regulations or to enjoy some special favor at the expense of the public, big businessmen, small businessmen, crooks and prostitutes not only showed their gratitude at election time, but paid continuing indemnity to those responsible for their privileges. Extortion is the squeezing of citizens by those formally or informally in a position of power in the government. Honest graft is money derived from inside knowledge and connections —knowledge, for instance, that a school will be built on a certain site which allows a "far-sighted" politician to make a killing. Some of the money from these sources served as fuel for the machine, going in one way or another for the production of more votes which, in turn, would mean further control of the government and additional opportunities for money-making; the bulk of the intake stayed with and enriched the politicians.

From the earliest days of the organization, Tammany men used all these ways of making money,[17] though at different times in Tammany's history, one or another method was more prevalent, or, at least, more publicized. Thus in the time of Fernando Wood, the New York City Board of Aldermen excelled in the selling of privileges and extortion, as a result of which its members became known as the Forty Thieves. The aldermen sold the city street railway franchises and leases to the highest bidders. They received bribes not only for passing but for suppressing measures, many being introduced for precisely this purpose. Tweed and his Ring cleaned up in many ways, but the most ambitious and famous scheme involved a simple fraud. Working with favored contractors, the Ring instructed them to raise their bills to the city, at first by 55 per cent, and eventually by 65 per cent. The City Auditor, a member of the Ring, paid the contractor the face amount of the bill and received back at the time of payment 55, 60 or 65 per cent of the bill in cash, which he then distributed to members of the Ring. Estimates of what the Tweed Ring made range from more than $30,000,000 to $200,000,000. Not for nothing did the cartoonist Thomas Nast choose as the symbol of Tweed and Tammany Hall the tiger, a symbol that has been identified with the organization ever since. Money-making methods in Kelly's time are obscure. Compared with those who preceded and followed him as boss, John Kelly kept the Hall free from scandal with one unhappy exception: every member of the Board of Aldermen of 1884 except one was accused of accepting bribes to pass a Broadway streetcar franchise. Many of them went to jail, or to Canada, and while Kelly, himself, was not implicated, a number of those accused were members of the Tammany Executive Committee.

During Richard Croker's period, the protection of vice, made possible by the complete political domination of the police force, represented the most notorious form of political enrichment. Both politicians and police were in on the gravy; honest policemen who would not play the game were denied promotion and harassed in other ways. Not only did politicians and policemen allow houses of prostitution and gambling to thrive and saloon keepers to violate the excise laws, but some even had financial interests in houses of prostitution and occasionally suggested to citizens who owned rooming houses that they use them for such purposes. Nor was this the only variety of privilege selling. American capitalism in Croker's day was expanding at a tremendous pace, and Tammany helped along the movement toward economic concentration by favors of one sort or another to big business, favors, of course, which proved profitable, not only to big business, but to Tammany.[18]

Murphy's period saw an increasingly greater emphasis upon honest graft. In the 1900's, George Washington Plunkitt, leader of the Fifteenth Assembly District, boasted that he had made his fortune ("I seen my opportunities and I took 'em") and pointed out that a politician was a fool to deal with dirty business.[19] Plunkitt's sentiment reflected, at least among the bigger politicians, a definite trend. Many Tammany men, for example, became open or secret partners in contracting firms and by using their political influence were able to win big contracts for their companies. This kind of honest graft was not always disassociated from fraud or extortion. Controlled by Tammany politicians such as John J. Murphy, brother of the boss, the New York Contracting and Trucking Company made millions. Once the Board of Aldermen held up a franchise sought by the Pennsylvania Railroad to allow it to use streets for tunnel approaches to its proposed railroad station in Manhattan. Suddenly the Board capitulated, an event which mystified the public. Months later the mystery disappeared; it was discovered that the New York Contracting and Trucking Company, although not the lowest bidder, had been awarded the $2,000,000 contract for digging the station site.[20]

In fairness to Tammany, let us make one point clear: Tammany's techniques and practices were not substantially different from those of other political organizations in the city. The Whigs and Native Americans tried in every way to out-do the Hall in election and fiscal frauds. The Republicans who dominated the legislature at Albany as the Democrats dominated New York City gave evidence of the highest venality in their conduct of that body. Only a few credo parties that cropped up from time to time, such as the Workingmen's Party (1829–31) and its successor, the Equal Rights Party (1834–8), proved exceptions to the rule. The Tiger's distinction, therefore, was not that it was unique in corruption, but that it was, perhaps, more ingenious, and that Tammany's ascendancy gave it opportunities and a tradition not shared by its rivals.[21]

The kind of people who profited from the Tammany machine did not remain the same; both the social and ethnic composition of the Hall changed during the nineteenth century. Tammany began as a middle-class institution, though it contained a smattering of workingmen. From about 1805 to 1837, it was ruled by approximately one-third bankers, one-third merchants, with the remaining third made up of various interests. Even the workingmen had to possess property to vote until the new state constitution in the 1820's created universal male suffrage. The extension of the suffrage and the steady growth of immigration, strengthening the hand of the lower classes, helped produce conflict in the 1830's between lower-class, lower-middle-class radicals and middle-class conservatives for control of the organization. The radical-conservative conflict was an aspect of the class warfare seen elsewhere in the Jacksonian period. The radicals were opposed to corporation privileges, mainly in banking, which gave the conservatives economic advantages. At first the control of the conservatives in Tammany was so complete that the radicals withdrew and under the leadership of certain intellectuals formed the Equal Rights Party. When the Equal Rights Party showed it could hurt Tammany, as it did in the election of 1837, the position of the conservative Democrats began to crumble, and the radicals were able to storm and capture the Hall. The conservative Democrats went over to the Whigs. By 1840 Tammany was clearly in the hands of lower-class, lower-middle-class radicals.

In the beginning many of these radical Democrats were sincere reformers; they hailed their victory as a "purification" of Tammany in which "selfish interest" had been beaten by "the people." But their control did not last long. Other lower-class people, having little interest in reform, moved into the vacuum created by the withdrawal of the middle-class conservatives. In the 1840's Tammany thus became the property of the lower classes, who proceeded to use it precisely as it had been used by their predecessors—to get ahead.[22]

In its early years Tammany was controlled by native Americans; anti-foreignism had been an important reason for the establishment of the organization. But the immigrants, especially those from Southern Ireland, who came to America in increasing hordes in the nineteenth century, brought a challenge to native rule and Tammany dogma. Tammany, always eminently practical, soon adjusted to the trend. Immigrants were admitted into the organization, and from about the middle of the 1820's, the patronage of immigrants became a definite Tammany policy. It is not clear, but it seems likely that the triumph of the lower classes in Tammany was at the same time, at least in part, a triumph of newer Americans. If this was so, it was nevertheless true that the Irish, the most important immigrant bloc in the city, did not really come into their own for a generation. Bigotry probably held them back. In any case, until the Civil War actual control of politics remained in the hands of men of Dutch, English and Scotch-Irish background; the municipal election of 1858 was the first in which Irish Democrats received a full share of the best places on the party's ticket. After the Civil War, at the time of America's great age of economic expansion, the Anglo-Saxons, Dutch and Germans went into industry and finance, leaving practical politics mainly to the Irish. With the rise to leadership of Honest John Kelly, the first Irish Catholic Tammany boss, the Irish took over the Hall. The Irish were in turn pressed somewhat by the Jews and the Italians in the first part of the twentieth century, but the power of the Irish was great, the pressure was not too powerful and by making concessions they were easily able to retain control. In the late nineteenth and early twentieth century Tammany Hall was one of the most powerful Irish Catholic political organizations in the world.[23]

These men who made their way in politics in the last century and early decades of this one were, as a rule, men of a certain mold. Uneducated and unrefined, they were physically powerful, tough and shrewd; and they fought their way upward with any weapon they could lay their hands on, including brass knuckles, clubs, knives and guns. Many of them got their first push ahead in tough neighborhood gangs. In his youth Croker was noted as a slugger and became the leader of the notorious Fourth Avenue Tunnel Gang; once he was arrested for shooting a man to death in a political brawl, but at his trial, the jury could not agree, and he was acquitted.[24] Big Tim Sullivan, political king of the Bowery from the late eighties to around 1909, attributed the beginning of his political career to an exciting battle with a pugilist whom he found beating a woman; by whipping the bully, Sullivan drew around him the most ambitious, aggressive young men of the Bowery, and his gang of young toughs attracted the attention of Tammany politicians.[25]

The old-time district leader was often a big eater and sometimes an open drinker, though Plunkitt maintained that the successful politician did not drink [26] and "he managed his affairs with women so discreetly that only a few hundred people knew about them." [27] The chances are he loved gambling and card playing. He might have been a saloon keeper— many were. Greedy and insensitive to the idea of public welfare as he was, he was not more so than were other Americans outside of politics, many, indeed, with more money and polish and a higher social position. Often, moreover, he was generous, tolerant, genial and humorous. Intensely loyal to his friends, he expected loyalty in return and considered "no crime so mean as ingratitude in politics." [28]

Those who lasted in politics usually climbed the economic and social ladder, and the success story of some is impressive. Son of a chair maker from Scotland, Boss Tweed was worth $2,500,000 to $3,000,000 at the height of his power, though in 1878 after his downfall, he claimed he was worth less than $5,000. Honest John Kelly, born to a poor Irish family on Hester Street in New York, left an estate reputed to be valued around $500,000. (Gustavus Myers notes in his *The History of Tammany Hall* that it was pointed out to Kelly's credit that the fortune he left was "very reasonable" for one who had held real control of New York City for so long.[29]) According to the testimony of his friend Hugh Grant, one-time Mayor of New York City, Richard Croker, who was born in Ireland and very poor when he became boss of Tammany, left a fortune at his death of $5,000,000. He had an estate at Palm Beach, Florida known as the Wigwam, one in England known as the Wantage, and another in Ireland with a magnificent castle, Glencairn. A lover of horse racing, Croker spent huge sums breeding and racing horses, one of which won the famous Newmarket Derby in England in the presence of King Edward and other royal personages. Charlie Murphy, son of an immigrant family in New York, had a country place at Good Ground on Long Island where he played both at golf—on his own course—and at farming; he left an estate of slightly more than $2,000,000. Big Tim Sullivan, born to poverty on New York's East Side in the days when poor Irish immigrants crowded its streets, accumulated between $2,000,000 and $3,000,000 before he died. George Washington Plunkitt, the child of indigent Irish parents in the Fifteenth Assembly District, began as a butcher boy, became a butcher, went into politics and amassed from $500,000 to $1,500,000. The money these and other politicians made often came in good part from legal liquor, contracting or other business, but it would be naive to think of their success in these fields as divorced from their success in politics.[30]

Why, despite its operations and reputation, was Tammany, were city machines in general, able to secure the votes of people not a part of the machine? This is an intriguing question and one to which there is no simple answer. One reason already discussed is very important. Many people outside of politics were interested in Tammany's success for selfish reasons and together with family, relatives and friends, constituted a not inconsequential bloc of voters. To put it another way: there is much to be said for Tammany's view of what we glibly call human nature. At times when civic scandal became too intolerable, some of these people might join in voting against the machine, but normally Tammany—which made it a policy to grant as many favors as possible—could count on them. Then there were others who did not want favors or any part of Tammany, but who feared Tammany's retaliatory power. Also, since Tammany was the local Democratic Party in action, it received the votes of those loyal Democrats who, through habit, apathy, or a standard of values which put party advantage in state and national elections above good municipal government, supported the machine ticket. In New York City the partisan approach to city elections was especially marked in the first two or three decades following the Civil War, though after that somewhat more discriminating voting developed.[31] In control of the government, the Manhattan machine was able, as we pointed out, to dominate the election machinery and the Police Department so as to give itself a big advantage at election time. It was also true that the very difficulty of beating Tammany for these and other reasons gave it a reputation for invincibility which itself was an element in its success.

One aspect of Tammany's success merits special attention. This was the relationship between Tammany, on one hand, and the city's immigrants and poor, on the other. Like other big city machines in America, Tammany's power was built upon a base of the foreign-born poor. In the late nineteenth century and first two decades of the twentieth, Tammany found its chief support among huge blocs of Irish, German, Jewish and

Italian immigrants. These newcomers to America were, for the most part, not intimidated into voting for the Tammany ticket; they did so willingly out of gratitude and self-interest. Basically, they backed Tammany because Tammany aided them and meant something important in their lives.

The help was very real; it involved the humanization of the often difficult process of settlement for the newcomer. To those who had embarked on the great adventure of their lives, had pulled up their roots and crossed the sea to find a better life, often only to arrive in the new country without money or friends, bewildered and anxious, Tammany came with aid—a job, perhaps with the city, and assistance in becoming a citizen and making friends. After the initial settlement, Tammany helped to ease the burdens of a difficult life in other ways. Did the new arrival want some favor from the city—a license, a suspended sentence for an erring son? He turned to the neighborhood district leader. Did he need a hand when out of work? His district leader gave him relief or his personal card which enabled him to get a job shoveling snow or perhaps work with some company which knew that it was not good policy to refuse the requests of Tammany district leaders. To those without funds, Tammany delivered ice in the summer, coal in the winter, and turkey and all the trimmings at Christmas. From a life full of toil and monotony, the immigrant looked forward to the big social events sponsored by his district leader: the clambakes, picnics, dances and free excursions for his wife and children in the summer. For the immigrant, the district leader was often more than a politician; he was a friend who personalized life for him in an America in which life was becoming increasingly impersonal. The foreign-born gave the Democratic machine lifetime fealty—and this often became second and third generation fealty, too.

Tammany also meant something else to the newcomer. In New York City in the nineteenth and early twentieth centuries, there was definite class resentment between the immigrant poor and the "better element," the poor's feeling of economic inferiority being compounded by a sense of inferiority due to foreign birth and often ethnic and religious background. Though the Republican Party contained some Irishmen, a good number of Jews, many Italians, and practically all Negroes and Scandinavians (this last group, however, was politically insignificant in New York), the GOP was dominated by the silk-stocking set which, in addition to being well-to-do, tended to be native and Protestant. In the lower-class mind Tammany became the representative of the "little people," the Republican Party the representative of the wealthy. What added to this impression in Charlie Murphy's time was that GOP legislators invariably opposed important welfare legislation while Tammany legislators—providing it did not inconvenience their money-making—supported such legislation. Naturally Tammany did all it could to capitalize on this voting record as proof Tammany was the champion of—and the Republican Party the enemy of—the "little people."

The "little people" were more justified in their impression of the Republican Party than they ever were about Tammany. Some Tammany politicians, perhaps, felt real empathy for their own kind among whom they lived and whose natural leaders they were, and insofar as it was possible were glad to combine kindness with politics. But politics was the main consideration, and basically Tammany did not have the interests of the immigrants at heart; it had at heart the interests of Tammany—and while the two were sometimes, they were not always, identical. Not naturally inclined to question the order of things, the Manhattan machine during the first part of the nineteenth century originally opposed such reform legislation as universal manhood suffrage, a mechanics' lien law and abolition of imprisonment for debt—all of which would help the lower classes —and only changed its position when it saw the handwriting on the wall, whereupon Tammany jumped on the band wagon and took the credit. More to the point, never would Tammany sacrifice its profits for the lowly. It protected the rich in their privileges, not minding how much the poor had to pay in rotten housing or in excessive charges for gas and electricity. Tammany gave the underworld a free hand to plant vice and crime in the neighborhoods and homes of the poor, and it squeezed hard-earned dollars from pushcart owners and small shopkeepers for tickets to Tammany socials. Tammany cared little about schools, parks and playgrounds, which would greatly benefit the poor, though the push of circumstances would not permit it to entirely ignore these things; besides, there was profit in construction. How deep Tammany's feeling for the lowly really went was dramatically pointed up around the turn of the century in the days of Mayor Van Wyck. The Mazet investigation, one of the periodic inquiries into corruption in New York City by the state legislature, exposed a conspiracy between an ice trust, the American Ice Company, and city officials to maintain a monopoly of New York's ice supply. The investigating committee had proof to show that the arrangement between the company and the city officials was such as to compel the people to pay sixty cents a hundred pounds with the elimination of the sale of five-cent pieces of ice, thus practically cutting off the supply of the very poor. Among the Tammany officials implicated was Mayor Van Wyck, who admitted that he acquired 5,000 shares of company stock worth $500,000. Van Wyck argued that he had paid $57,000 for the stock, but he could not produce proof that he had actually paid anything.

Didn't the people in the downtown tenements see this side of Tammany? Didn't they know the score? Some did, probably, and for some it may have been important. But for the mass of "little people," the benefits were usually more apparent, vital and personally experienced than the disadvantages. However, at times of unusual civic corruption, involving vice and crime in poor neighborhoods, a good number of lower-class people could be persuaded to vote against Tammany and for reform. In general, the

immigrants were too easily led, unaware of their obligations to democracy, too narrowly concerned with self-interest, perhaps ignorant of their
best interests. However, in these respects they were not unique. These
things could have been said of other Americans who had far better opportunities for education and were more acclimated to American civilization.[32]

For in addition to the immigrants, in addition to all the other reasons
we have considered as responsible for Tammany's success, there was
something more basic. The truth is that the vast majority of Americans
were apathetic toward politics, and especially municipal politics. Behind
the indifference lay the dominant drives and values of American civilization. In America, for a complex of reasons, one of which certainly has
been the unparalleled opportunities given to a man to better himself
economically and socially, the highest goal in life has been individual
success, particularly in a monetary sense. Unlike the Greeks in the classical
period, for example, life in America has revolved not around community
activity, but around the individual, and has dealt not mainly with politics
and culture, but with economics. What political interest the American
has felt has usually been absorbed by the national political theater with
its attraction of historical sweep; small town politics has evoked largely
a gossipy kind of interest. But the city—especially the larger city—has
only encouraged political apathy; government is big, complicated, impersonal, and there are economic opportunities for the individual which
work to discourage civic interest. This was particularly true in America
in the second half of the nineteenth and early twentieth centuries. Though,
as we shall see, there have been citizens who have had a strong sense of
civic duty, and there have been times when the majority of voters have
rebelled, normally most citizens, however they might complain about
conditions, have been too preoccupied with the business of advancing
themselves to object to being ruled by professional politicians.

The attitude of the professional politicians and of the majority of citizens toward politics explains why, democratic theory to the contrary, the
real power in political parties has rested with a relative handful of men.
Probably no one has expressed the professional view of politics more
honestly and succinctly than Richard Croker did when testifying before
the Mazet committee. To the committee's counsel, who bluntly asked
him at one point, "Then you are working for your own pocket, are you
not?" the boss snapped, "All the time; the same as you." [33] The professionals have worked politics like a business, have been good at it and
have not been easily defeated by those to whom it has appeared as a secondary interest.

That machine rule entailed serious consequences for New York, as for
other American cities, is obvious from what has been said. Corruption,

disrespect for law and mockery of democracy were not the only consequences. This is how Gustavus Myers in his famous *The History of Tammany Hall* describes New York City in the early 1820's:

> The streets were an abomination of filth. The local authorities long
> refused, despite public pressure, to take steps to have the city furnished
> with pure water. As a result of the bad water of a private corporation
> and the uncleanliness of the streets, yellow fever and cholera had sev-
> eral times devastated the city, and in one year (1822) it was so
> deserted that grass grew in the streets.[34]

M. R. Werner thus portrayed the city during the reign of Boss Tweed:

> Situated as it [New York City] was on an island, it remained with-
> out bridges. The vast produce which came to the city from everywhere
> in the world was landed on rotten wharves. There was no adequate
> means of transportation. Thieves ran riot through the streets. The
> public buildings were dilapidated, and the public places were uncared
> for. Because of defective sewage and unclean streets, the death rate
> was abnormal.[35]

Now Tammany government was often better than these excerpts indicate. But even at best it was inadequate; even at best it was government
marked by waste, inefficiency, shabbiness, mediocrity and a spirit of
standpattism rather than of progress.

How could it be otherwise? What the taxpayer called graft and waste
were to Tammany only political profits. Since much of the public's money
went for such profits, was it surprising that at times the city did not
have adequate funds for new constructions, improvements and the maintenance of existing services? Nor should anyone wonder that what was
done for the community was often not done well; not only were politicians habitually angling for advantage, but the men elected or appointed
to office were, as a whole, not of high calibre. Lacking in ability, imagination and the desire to give the city service, interested only in expending
as little energy as possible except for themselves, successful only because
of their obedience to the machine system—Tammany's public officials
were incompetent and inefficient. Civil service personnel—after they
came into being—tended to be demoralized. Despite the laws, there were
ways of appointing political favorites to the civil service regardless of
merit, as there were ways of rewarding them once in service and of injur-
ing those who inconvenienced others by taking their jobs seriously.
Besides, how honest or efficient could civil service be amid graft and
inertia? In general, the creed was: Let well enough alone, don't create
work, don't work too hard. The tendency was to keep things going but
to avoid tackling problems. Significantly, Tammany rarely instituted

important innovations in the city. And while it is not fair to say that it did nothing, the Hall often found it possible to let big problems drift, and to act, if at all, only as a compulsion from strong public opinion.[36]

Tammany orators were always fond of pointing to the magnificent accomplishments of the city as proof of the Hall's wise leadership, but the truth was something else; the truth was that, for the most part, New York had prospered in spite of this leadership, not because of it. Politics could not abort the healthy, virulent economic forces pushing the city ahead. New York was greater than its politicians.[37]

2

The reform tradition

THERE HAS BEEN another tradition in American cities, a tradition of opposition to machine politics and machine government. The Tammany view of man is only partially valid; men are moved by things other than just narrow self-interest. The goal of individual material success has been the predominant one in American life, but it has not been the only one. Americans have held ideals important: the ideals of morality and ethics, basically of religious origin, the ideals of democracy. Often these have come into conflict with the drive to succeed; all paths upward have not been sanctioned by American mores; despite the cynics, America has really never endorsed success at any price. Besides, there have been those who have realized that real self-interest often lies in the opposite direction from where it might appear to lie at first glance, that real self-interest might be closer to the interest of the community as a whole than to a man's narrower, and perhaps more apparent, interests. By no means divorced from the main temper of America, a handful of men and women in America's cities, more sensitive to the ideals of American civilization than most, quicker to see that self-interest is not always what it might seem to be, have challenged machine government and fought for what they regarded as the interests of the entire city. Under special conditions they have been joined by more citizens, often a majority of the voters, in staging a full scale revolt against machine rule. Those composing the core of the revolt are the people we shall be calling the civic leaders or municipal reformers, though the reader is here cautioned that when we talk about reform movements, reformer will be used in a broader sense too.

The civic leaders mainly came from the professional and business classes. They tended to be native Americans of the older sort, Protestant, well-to-do and well-educated; less obsessed with the struggle for material success than the professional politicians, they were more concerned with the welfare of the community as a whole. Many of those in New York, perhaps the majority, were lawyers, a point which should not be too surprising since lawyers tend to develop a greater interest in government than do most other occupational groups. Generally the New York reformers were native New Yorkers of good families, and often they were graduates of Ivy League colleges.[1]

The reform, or anti-machine, tradition has not been equally strong in every city. For one thing, that vague, but very real element, the civic conscience, has not everywhere been equally sensitive to graft, waste and inefficiency. In some cities civic leadership has been more vigorous, capable, dedicated; a product of the civic conscience, leadership is at the same time a molder of the conscience. It is not easy to say why these differences should be; actually each city, like an individual, has a distinct personality, the product of many complex forces.[2] As American cities go, New York has had a strong reform tradition. In March, 1951, Senator Estes Kefauver, head of the Senate committee investigating crime in the nation, paid New Yorkers a compliment. "The people of this great City," he declared, "have tremendous pride in good government and in keeping the city in good shape . . . I have noticed in New York that always there is an effort to get things better." [3] This may have been laying it on a bit thick, but in good part it has been true.

New York's reform tradition antedates the period of the Civil War, but in the earlier years there does not seem to have been a nucleus of municipal reformers. Leading citizens at times played a prominent part in reform movements, though their role does not come out clearly and they do not appear to have been organized into groups doing continuing work; such organization as there was—and evidence for organization is scanty— seems to have been weak and temporary, concerned only with a particular campaign.[4] The first real civic organization in the city appears to have been the Citizens' Association, organized in 1863 as a nonpartisan body of eminent merchants, lawyers and men of leisure, of people like John Jacob Astor and Peter Cooper, its president for many years. For about a decade the Citizens' Association kept an eye on the administration of the city government and attempted, sometimes successfully, to bring about the passage of important reform legislation at Albany affecting the city.[5]

Tweed's depredations brought about the formation in 1871 of another civic group, the New York City Council of Political Reform, which waged war against the Tweed Ring and thereafter functioned for a few years as the principal group in the city dedicated to the securing of honest, efficient and economical government.[6]

With the object of remedying the evils of an unbridled spoils system, the Civil Service Reform Association came into being in 1877. The leading figures of this organization in its early years were Carl Schurz, general, publicist, politician, George William Curtis, editor of *Harper's Weekly,* E. L. Godkin, editor of the *Nation* and, after 1882, editor also of the *New York Evening Post,* and Dorman B. Eaton, prominent attorney. While the Association was set up primarily to deal, not with the civil service problem in New York City, but with civil service reform in general, and especially with reference to the federal government, it made notable contributions to the establishment of a civil service system in the city government. The New York State Civil Service Law of 1883, which the Association drafted, and a subsequent merit system clause in the state constitution for which it was largely responsible, provided the basis for the merit system in New York City. Moreover, in the last years of the nineteenth century the Association came to shift its interest from the federal field—which it left to the National Civil Service Reform League, an organization created by it in 1881—to that of New York City and State; and from that time to this the Civil Service Reform Association has worked to extend the merit system, maintain the integrity of the State Civil Service Law and, in general, improve the quality of city and state personnel.[7]

Other civic groups appeared in the eighties, fostered by memories of Tweed and the chronic low state of the city's political life. One was the Commonwealth Club, which was founded in 1886 upon a creed of civil service and ballot reform by Carl Schurz and E. L. Godkin. (Characteristic of the reform circle was the tendency of reformers to function through more than one group.) Mainly the organization was a dinner club of four or five hundred people, chiefly substantial and prominent residents of New York City, at which leaders of reform were invited to speak. But it was not all speech-making; once the club sent the legislature a gigantic petition of nearly a million names demanding the adoption of the secret ballot, a petition so enormous a truck had to carry it.[8] Another group was the City Reform Club, formed in 1882 by some young college graduates as a sort of "watchdog" organization. Among those in the inner circle during the heyday of the club were John Jay Chapman, graduate of Harvard College and Harvard Law School, a writer destined to become famous as a brilliant essayist and man of letters, and his cousin William Jay Schieffelin, who had studied chemistry at Columbia College, received a Ph.D. at Munich and at this time was beginning an apprenticeship in the drug company that bears his family name. Both Chapman and Schieffelin were descended on their mothers' side from the first Chief Justice of the United States Supreme Court, John Jay. Here, too, were James W. Pryor and W. Harris Roome, graduates of Columbia College and Columbia Law School, Preble Tucker, another lawyer, educated at the University of Virginia, and Richard Welling, a product of Harvard College and Harvard Law School, whose ancestry went back to Roger Williams; for a while, in the early days of the club, Theodore Roosevelt, one of Welling's Harvard classmates, was a member.[9] A dynamic, exuberant, earnest bunch, the young City Reformers were also somewhat naive about municipal politics. On one occasion, thinking that their success would mean Tammany's doom, they decided to attack election bribery by seeing to it that the saloons which were used by Tammany as pay-off places were closed on election day in accordance with the law, only to discover that somehow nothing could induce the Excise Commissioners to revoke licenses.[10] The City Reform Club, the Commonwealth Club and other civic groups formed in the eighties were short-lived and mainly important, not because of their accomplishments, but because they helped to interest and educate men in the politico-civic life of the city and thus served as valuable training grounds for the development of civic leadership.

The flowering of New York's reform element came in the nineties, a period of great Tammany scandals. Corruption led to an increased interest in municipal affairs and the formation of new reform groups, some blooming only to fade and disappear within a short time, others remaining active into our own day. It was in the nineties that Dr. Charles H. Parkhurst, minister of the Madison Square Presbyterian Church, turned the Society for the Prevention of Crime, from a rather quiet body, which it had been since its inception in 1878, into a civic force to be reckoned with. Intent upon rooting out vice, the Society hired detectives and attorneys to dig up the facts about New York's seamy side which Parkhurst then used in scathing sermons against vice, Tammany and the police. (Often represented as wild-eyed and ridiculous by newspapers, considered a fiend by politicians, policemen and reporters, Parkhurst was described by Lincoln Steffens as quiet, determined, fearless and humorous, a man of strength who was wise in the slangy sense and "never told or preached half of what he knew.") [11]

The City Club of New York was born in 1892. Mainly it was the conception of Edmond Kelly, a graduate of Columbia College and Columbia Law School and Richard Welling's closest friend. A member of the City Reform Club, Kelly, intellectual, dynamic, persuasive, hit upon the idea of creating a new civic club which would have a clubhouse and which would provide a social arena where men specially interested in good government could meet one another, exchange opinions and discuss the city's problems. The new club, Kelly apparently believed, should draw both from the City Reformers, who were young and opposed to a clubhouse for fear that it would take too much money and energy, and the members of the Commonwealth Club, generally older and more sedate. Kelly induced his friends in the City Reform Club—people like Welling, Chapman, Schieffelin, Pryor, Roome and Tucker—to join with Robert Fulton Cutting, officer and director in numerous corporations, James C. Carter, the acknowledged leader of the Bar, and other prominent New Yorkers, some from the Commonwealth Club, to form the new organization. The City Club built its clubhouse and swiftly became an important element in the civic life of the city. In its early years, the club tended to emphasize the need to separate municipal from other elections and to elect good men to city offices, but its concern was as broad as the fight for good government. Other cities copied the New York reformers by setting up city clubs of their own.[12]

Out of the City Club came one of the most interesting politico-civic experiments in New York's history—the Good Government Club movement. Again this was Kelly's idea. With the object of fostering civic education, the City Club, led by Kelly, who had become club secretary, undertook in 1892 to organize in each assembly district Good Government Clubs where citizens interested in municipal reform could meet to discuss city problems—sort of neighborhood City Clubs. All shades of political opinion and religious creed and all nationalities were encouraged to join. In Kelly's mind was the thought that the clubs might serve as a wedge to split workingmen away from Tammany, and he made serious efforts to get them interested. The clubs were given alphabetical designations, and each club had a special job in addition to being concerned with the city government in general; one kept an eye on the Police Department, another was concerned with the Fire Department, another with the District Attorney and so forth. The Goo-Goos, as the *New York Sun* derisively dubbed the clubs' members, were mostly young men. For a few years the clubs were active but the members gradually lost interest. A redistricting of the city in 1903 proved to be the final blow for the movement, for redistricting enabled members to give as an excuse for inactivity that now they did not know to which club they belonged. To Kelly's despair, labor never went along with reform. Not till the days of La Guardia did it become a significant part of the reform camp in New York City. The chief importance of the Good Government Clubs—like the City Reform Club and the Commonwealth Club—was not so much tangible achievements—though, according to shrewd Tammany politicians, the Goo-Goos watched the polls so closely in the election of 1894 that the machine was beaten—as that they made men conscious of the city's problems and of their role as citizens. Though some of the Goo-Goos had been or were members of other reform groups, the Good Government Clubs also attracted others who otherwise might have remained totally uninterested in city government.[13] While some became passive citizens again, something may have rubbed off. And many lost interest in the Good Government Clubs only to join other reform organizations.

It was inevitable that the reformers should experiment with the idea of a nonpartisan city party which could rally all good citizens for good government and run honest and capable candidates for office irrespective of national parties. In the election of 1890 a group of reformers—mainly City Reform Club men—organized the People's Municipal League, but the League was not successful and soon disappeared. In 1897, a mayoral year, circumstances encouraged another try. Many reformers felt that the gains of the reform administration in power at the time would be temporary unless a permanent body was formed to compete with the old political parties. The creation of Greater New York made the election an important one; Tammany could not be allowed to extend its sway beyond Manhattan. The sizable number of independents in Brooklyn encouraged hopes for a city party. The New York State Constitution of 1894, in finally providing for the separation of municipal from state and national elections, also gave impetus to the idea of a city party. The trustees of the City Club, recognizing that the club itself could not become a party, joined with Elihu Root and other prominent Republicans to take the lead in organizing a new group. It was named the Citizens Union. Fulton Cutting was made chairman, and among the first members were many reformers whose names we have seen before. The party formed organizations in the assembly districts, many of those who had been active in the Good Government Clubs going into the district organizations. Active as a party in a few elections, the Citizens Union gradually became transformed in the first decade of its existence into one of the city's outstanding civic groups. Basically, the city party idea failed to work because many people eventually tired or lost interest, and the organization would not give patronage to those who would work only for a price. As time went on, the central body of the Citizens Union was increasingly strengthened at the expense of the district organizations; in 1918 the district units were entirely eliminated. As a civic group, the Citizens Union became interested in city administration, legislation and local candidates. Since 1905 its Committee on Legislation has examined all legislation in the city and all legislation in Albany affecting the city's interest. Its Committee on Local Candidates has investigated and reported on candidates for local offices, certain judicial offices and the state legislature, thus continuing and developing a technique originated by James Pryor, who as a member of the City Reform Club compiled an annual record of assemblymen and senators in Albany. In general, the Citizens Union has attempted to furnish and spotlight information dealing with the city government. In one way or another in the early years of this century, it also played an important role in reform movements.[14]

Other groups came into being after the turn of the century. In 1906 the New York Bureau of Municipal Research, the first of its kind in the United States, developed out of a branch of the Citizens Union, the Bureau of City Betterment. Fulton Cutting, one of the guiding spirits in its formation, soon resigned as chairman of the Citizens Union to devote his time to the new group, his place being taken by Schieffelin. The Bureau of Municipal Research represented a new approach to municipal problems: that the only real way to study and improve city government was to amass the facts "scientifically" and analyze them "objectively" through the use of a paid staff of technical specialists and investigators. This approach resulted from the belief that the greater part of a city's business was technical and that a city's treasury commonly suffered more from inefficiency than dishonesty. The Bureau was largely responsible for the introduction of several important administrative reforms in New York City. The reorganization of the city's general scheme of accounting and of the Water Revenue Bureau (which resulted in an annual $2,000,000 increase in the collection of water rates) and the creation of a Bureau of Child Hygiene in the Department of Health were three. In the 1920's the Bureau of Municipal Research, whose activities had increasingly come to be of a national nature, developed into the Institute of Public Administration, thus disappearing as a New York City organization. The Bureau had left its mark on the city.[15] The Citizens Budget Commission of our own day is somewhat of a spiritual descendant of the old Bureau of Municipal Research.

In 1916, with the help of the City Club, a Women's City Club was organized. In 1920 the League of Women Voters was formed to inform women voters, newly enfranchised, of the techniques of voting, the structure and principles of government and to push for certain social legislation. In time the League's purpose came to be broader, nothing less than the improvement of American democracy, including municipal democracy. Since their establishment both organizations have served as channels through which intelligent, public-spirited women have worked for better city government.[16]

These were the most important, though not the only, groups which helped to develop New York's civic leadership and through which that leadership was expressed in the nineteenth and early twentieth centuries. By the 1920's, New York's reform element was well developed; a rather impressive tradition of civic leadership lay behind the reformers. That leadership in the twenties was associated generally with continuing groups of two kinds. One, which might be called the general purpose type, actually had as its aim the promotion of good government in general; the Citizens Union and the City Club were good examples of this category. The other, which might be called the specific purpose type, exemplified by the Civil Service Reform Association, was concerned with more or less particular areas of government.

Behind the activity of the civic leaders lay a set of assumptions, ideas and feelings about the nature of bad and good city government. In the final analysis, American municipal reformers have generally found the cause of bad government in bad men, or at best incompetent men. When municipal reformers in the nineteenth and early twentieth centuries thought about bad men, however, they had in mind a conception of morality which later generations found difficult to grasp. They did not mean that bad men were bad because they used objectionable means to obtain acceptable ends. They meant that bad men were bad because they violated absolute laws of right and wrong. They usually meant that they were corrupt in a very fundamental and pervasive sense, in a sense that a rotten apple is rotten;

they meant that they were men heavy with sin. This basically religious concept runs through much of the writings of New York's municipal reformers during this period. It comes out most clearly, of course, in the writings of clerics. Read Parkhurst, for example, and you realize that he viewed the famous struggle against Tammany in the period 1892–4, a struggle in which he was the central anti-Tammany figure, as a great battle between right and wrong, between good and evil, indeed between Christ and Satan, the Devil operating through the Tammany politicians and the police.[17]

For the most part, when municipal reformers have talked about bad men they have had in mind simply the politicians who run the government. In the period we are presently concerned with, the reformers generally viewed the trouble as being the result of thieves, brigands, plunderers, "the criminal classes," who, supported by masses of ignorant foreigners, had won power and perverted government to their own selfish purposes. Before the nineties, the businessman was little censured. When municipal reformers criticized him at all it was for nothing more serious than shirking his civic duty, for turning the government over to crooks through apathy; it was not for corruption.[18] But in the 1890's, when it almost took an act of will to remain ignorant on the point, some reformers discovered the corrupt businessman, notably in big business. John Brooks Leavitt, an active Good Government Club member, later prominent in the Citizens Union, writing in *Forum* in August, 1894, tended to expand the term "criminal classes" to include "reputable merchants" who bought privileges from the politicians and who were tied to them by self-interest.[19] And John Jay Chapman in his collection of essays *Causes and Consequences,* published at the end of the century, shifted the main onus for bad government to the shoulders of big business. The big economic interests, he thought, maintained both Tammany Hall and the Republican organization in New York City; the machine boss was but their agent or middle-man.[20] Though Chapman and those of similar views went overboard—corruption was more complicated than they realized—they threw a bright light upon an important part of the story that had been neglected.

Despite these new viewpoints, however, the politician generally remained at the heart of the bad government analysis. Reformers like E. L. Godkin failed to recognize the role of the businessman in causing municipal corruption and tended to think in terms of the Hamiltonian juxtaposition of wealth and virtue and poverty and vice.[21] Americans have long held that the politician has a greater responsibility to be trustworthy than the businessman. Finally, Chapman's diagnosis too much resembled that of the Socialists—its logic pushed toward the Socialists' therapy—and few well-to-do municipal reformers cared for that cure.[22]

As for the remedies for bad government, the municipal reformers approached the problem from two different directions. One approach was mainly in terms of men, the other mainly in terms of mechanisms. Reformers oriented toward the first approach did not believe that mechanisms were of no weight, and reformers inclined toward mechanisms did not hold that they would give good government automatically. In either case, the concern was chiefly with politics and government, not with the businessman and the operations of capitalism. There was one significant exception: a number of reformers, many of whom were not Socialists, advocated the municipal ownership of public utilities.[23]

The men-oriented approach held that the problem was principally one of ferreting out corrupt and incompetent officeholders and bringing about the election of good and competent men. The real trouble, it was felt, lay with the honest citizens. Though in the majority, they were apathetic about politics and government or were divided among themselves by party passions; thus they allowed the crooks and nonentities to take over. As seen by the New York City Council of Political Reform, by Dr. Howard Crosby, pastor of the Fourth Avenue Presbyterian Church, founder and president of the Society for the Prevention of Crime, by Parkhurst and others, the solution was to enlighten good citizens as to the nature of the problem and encourage them to unite and do their civic duty irrespective of party loyalties. What was basically needed was a civic or, as some would have it, a moral awakening. The central task of civic organizations was to stimulate that awakening and serve as instruments for enlightened public opinion.[24]

Though not disagreeing with the desirability or importance of the men-oriented objective, those who took the mechanism approach had a different focus. What was needed, they felt, was a reorganization of city government which would minimize the strength of machine politicians and their opportunity to do harm while maximizing the strength of the majority of citizens and their interest in city government; needed were constitutional amendments, new charters, new systems and devices. But specifically what changes? Here there was trouble. There were plenty of proposals, and not all were acceptable to all reformers; indeed sometimes diametrically opposite ideas were advocated. Nevertheless, as the nineteenth century advanced and turned into the twentieth, one can note in the New York reform circle a tendency toward certain proposals, though there was less agreement on priorities. Because of obvious election dishonesty, there were demands for tighter registration laws and the secret ballot. Because the spoils system produced officeholders of low calibre, corrupt and incompetent, the merit system was advocated. The separation of municipal from other elections was proposed to prevent city issues from becoming a tail to the kite of state and national politics. Home rule for the city was advanced because interference by the legislature undermined the responsibility of city officials as well as the people's interest in local government. Since complicated, cumbersome and poorly unified government with many elective officials made buck-passing easy, encouraged corruption and waste and discouraged popular interest, there were demands for the simplification of government entailing a concentration of responsibility and the reduction of elective (and a corresponding increase in appointive) officers—what came to be called the short ballot idea. The key to streamlined government was usually seen in the mayor, whose powers, especially over the appointment and removal of officials, it was argued, should be increased. Because county government was largely an anachronism, a source of waste, a fountain of patronage, the abolition of county government was proposed, though this was hardly as prevalent in the reformers' repertoire, or as important, as the others.[25] Both the mechanism- and men-oriented approaches were, as they have continued to be, reflected in the work of the civic groups; most civic organizations, though with varying emphasis, have been gadflies to and instruments of the public conscience, as well as champions of changes in system.

Before the 1890's, reformers, as a rule, thought of good government simply as the opposite of bad government. Bad government meant corruption, waste, inefficiency, high taxes, a deteriorating city. Good government meant honest, efficient, economical administration and a low tax rate. It meant government which effectively supplied a minimum of essential services; perhaps it meant government which brought about a beautiful and well-ordered city.[26] In the nineties some reformers arrived at a broader concept of the nature of good government. Good government was not just the reverse of bad government, but involved also an additional element. That element was a concept that went by no one name; sometimes it was referred to as municipal or social betterment; it is what many of us today call welfare in the broad sense. It was the idea that city government must be basically more than a police duty along business principles, must embrace positive efforts to increase the health, safety, convenience, comfort and happiness of its citizens, especially the poorer ones.

It should not be thought that the earlier idea of good government was completely devoid of social concern; a report of the Union League Club in 1867, for instance, listed in addition to other goals for the city government that it should provide for care of the poor, the sick, the intemperate and orphans.[27] But such thinking when it existed was limited, unemphasized and hardly represented a vital part of the good government concept. In the nineties, a time when such problems of urban living as housing, health, recreation, education, and transportation assumed a new seriousness, a belief in more socially-conscious government, in what was sometimes called *municipalism*—the theory of extending the functions of city government—became an important part of reform thinking. It was expressed by people like William Scudamore, the Reverend Leighton Williams, William Howe Tolman, Fulton Cutting and others in the Citizens Union, some of whom appeared to have been influenced by Christian Socialism.[28]

A look at the 1897 and 1901 campaign platforms of the Citizens Union, which became a bastion of the new thinking, gives us a good idea of what the exponents of positive government specifically had in mind. They had in mind adequate school accommodations, an extended library system, extension of the system of small parks, more playgrounds, adequate public baths and lavatories, enforcement of all tenement house laws, enforcement of the eight-hour law for all employees of the city and contractors, and payment of prevailing rate of wages. They had in mind, too, city ownership of its water supply, perhaps of gas and electric utilities as well, and where franchises were granted, the leasing of them only for short periods with stringent supervision over all corporations getting them to insure the public of adequate service at reasonable rates.[29]

By no means did all reformers embrace the new meaning of good government; some were adamantly opposed. When Fulton Cutting in 1900, looking to the mayoral campaign of the following year, suggested that the policy of the Citizens Union must include a great positive program involving the municipal ownership of public utilities and municipal initiative in social betterment, which as we have noted it did—The *New York Times* voiced the sentiments of conservative reform in no uncertain terms. " 'We must remind Mr. Cutting,' " the *Times* admonished, " 'that the campaign will be undertaken for the purpose of electing an honest and capable man mayor of New York. If his Citizens Union wishes to undertake a campaign for the exploitation of fads and the promotion of the raw theories of visionaries, we hope he will give timely notice in order that no time may be lost through misapprehension.' " The serious, practical men of affairs in New York City, the *Times* went on, hope to establish and maintain in City Hall a business office for the management of the New York municipal corporation. " 'They have no intention of setting up an experiment station for socialism.' "[30] Despite this attitude, the viewpoint of those who thought of good government in the larger sense was not without influence on some of the city's reform administrations. The fullest expression of this point of view, however, awaited a different age, a later time—the time of La Guardia.

It is important to say a word about the strength of the civic leaders. Though they were able to advance the cause of good government, the reformers in New York, and in other cities, were from the standpoint of strength not in the same league with the machine politicians. Their fundamental disadvantage, of course, was that they were amateurs indulging what for the most part was a subordinate interest in their lives, whereas the politicians were full-time professionals to whom politics and government were the main business. Well-to-do and educated, the reformers, moreover, found it hard to win the confidence of the lower classes, and in New York Tammany was generally successful in lumping the reform crowd with the Republicans in the lower-class mind.

Other things tended to weaken the reformers. Temperamentally individualistic, they did not find it easy to work together. While all reformers wanted good government, of course, they did not all agree upon what that meant, did not all think the same reforms equally important or agree on the means to bring about the ends. Edmond Kelly, for instance, was poles apart from John Jay Chapman and James Pryor on tactics. Kelly was willing to compromise to gain an objective, whereas Chapman and Pryor, according to Welling, "stuck to principle even when a little deviation might win an election." (To Welling, "they almost resembled the amateur farmer, hard at work cultivating corn in the deep shade of a broad, spreading oak tree. A passing farmer jibed at him: 'Stranger, do you expect anything to grow in that deep shade?' To which the amateur replied: 'I signed to do my duty, and if the Almighty has a mind to flunk, let him flunk.' ")[31] Also in the way of unity were obstacles not unfamiliar to men engaged in other activities—petty rivalries, jealousies, antagonism among groups. Machine politicians, concerned with power rather than principles, were more apt than were the reformers to surmount differences; agreements and under-standings between Democratic and Republican professionals in New York and elsewhere, for example, were common.

While the prestige of the reformers in the community was almost cer-tainly greater than that of the politicians, it was not as great as one might imagine; and for the reformers prestige was more important than for the politicians, who could find compensation in their power. The word reformer often carried—as it still does for some—a connotation of con-tempt. A number of reasons intermingled to account for this. Weakness, some of the reasons for which we noted above, hurt the reputation of the reformers and in turn weakened them further, just as the strength of the machine was, in itself, a factor in its own strength. To some, reform sug-gested denunciation, carping, meddling. In a nation where men of action were valued and visionaries distrusted, some reformers were too much possessed with easy panaceas and pet projects. Others had too narrow a definition of morality, were too much concerned with Prohibition or some kill-joy scheme, identified themselves too closely, perhaps, with God's will. Basically some reformers were temperamentally unattractive people—in direct contrast to the politicians they denounced—too convinced of their own righteousness, goodness and wisdom, too intolerant of life as it is, too unmindful of the human element that must always be considered if anything is to be accomplished at all. Popular feeling against reformers with these and other limitations carried over to the group as a whole. Municipal reformers not thus limited carried a cross, and it was a heavy one.[32]

Normally, despite the opposition of civic leaders, the machine con-tinued to hold political life to its conventional grooves. But something could disrupt normality; almost always that something was too much cor-ruption and bad government, which aroused the civic conscience of the community and evoked a feeling of intense dissatisfaction with the admin-istration in power.[33] But what was "too much?" At what point did the citizens boil over? Why at *that* particular time? "Too much" bad government, of course, is hardly a constant. It takes on meaning only in terms of a host of variables such as the attitude of newspapers, the strength and activity of civic groups, the work of investigating bodies.

The actual development of a reform movement—considered here as the entire effort to throw out the machine—tended to follow a pattern. Often the thing that triggered it was an investigation of one sort or another which uncovered corruption and municipal ills; perhaps the investigation nailed down with concrete details what had only been suspected. As a result, a number of people from the professional and business classes who were not part of the reform set became keenly concerned with city affairs; again many of them were lawyers. They increased the membership of the existing reform groups which under the push of scandals now increased their activity. Together with the reform people they organized one or more committees—new groups—for the purpose of agitation and, perhaps, direct political action.

Political action, the essential part of the reform movement, generally assumed one of three forms: where reform was attempted by means of a regular political party; where the instrument used was an independent citizens' party or committee; where the medium was a fusion of certain groups (generally one or more independent citizens' groups or minor parties) with the machine's nominal chief opposition. In any case, the enlarged group of reformers, people who politically were generally independent Democrats, independent Republicans, or just plain independents, constituted the real moving force behind the movement, though professional politicians—usually from the main opposition party in the city— often played an important part. The key role of the reformers—now in a broader sense than just the nucleus people—though most visible in the second of the three forms noted above, was a fact in all three cases; where a big political party was involved it was usually necessary for the independents first to capture the party or, at least, bring strong pressure to bear on its professional leadership to go along. Indeed, the reformers had to do the driving if the movement was to have a serious chance of success; only independents could give the movement a stamp of legitimacy and encourage what was indispensable for victory—the breakup of traditional voting patterns.

In New York, though all three avenues of political reform were used at one time or another—each successfully—the third form, a fusion movement, became the principle type of reform in the half-century following the Civil War. There were three main components of such a movement in New York. One was the Republican Party. The second was some independent citizens' group or minor party, perhaps more than one, which served mainly to attract the votes of disaffected Democrats, who under no circumstance would vote Republican.[34] The third was a committee formed by the enlarged group of reformers, a committee often called by a number, such as Committee of Seventy. This committee mobilized sentiment for political revolt and in consultation with the leaders of the Republican Party and the leaders of other organizations that were interested, it, or a subcommittee, did the actual job of forging a common ticket, the essence of a fusion movement. Fusion candidates for the big positions—and this was true of reform movements in general—were usually of a higher calibre than the ordinary candidates for the offices. The candidate for Mayor was apt to be the independent kind of Republican or Democrat; if an independent Republican was nominated for Mayor, then the rest of the ticket tended to be weighted in favor of independent Democrats or Democrats, and the reverse was true. Our third component, the citizens' committee, or more likely, a derivative of it, served throughout the campaign as a sort of co-ordinating or steering group.

The campaign of any reform movement was vigorously, bitterly fought; at times it took on the flavor of a crusade. The reform forces mobilized much of the press and the pulpit. They made every effort to stimulate the civic conscience of the mass of voters, to point out how machine rule worked against their self-interest, to induce them to forget party loyalty at the polls. The importance of the last cannot be overestimated. Success depended upon the extent to which the voters—not to mention the leadership of the movement itself—were able to forget national party sympathies and act in a nonpartisan spirit. Unless a good number of Democrats, generally of the independent variety, could be made to support the reform movement in New York, it could not win; and the same was true in other Democratic cities and with respect to Republicans in Republican cities. Success, of course, depended upon other things, too—for example, the quality of the reform leadership, the slate of candidates (especially the choice for mayor), incidents and accidents of the campaign. Victory for reform, if it came, might not be thorough; some positions in the government might remain in machine hands.

If a reform movement was successful, what followed also tended to fall into a pattern. The reform administration began by trying to clean up the Augean stables. Old appointees were swept out, sometimes some were prosecuted. The new appointees were usually of a better breed. The new administration was more honest than the old, and it possessed enthusiasm, energy and imagination. A new spirit pervaded government—old ways of doing things were questioned; there was a tendency toward improvement and innovation. Some reforms might be relatively small, involving more efficient methods of administration. Some might be big, resulting in a new charter with a new form of government. The reform administration sometimes committed serious blunders or failed in other ways; it was far from perfect. But it practically always gave better government than its predecessor and usually much better.

Yet for all its achievements, it was rare for a reform administration to be re-elected; in New York up to the time of La Guardia this had never happened. Why? What happened to a reform movement—now considered in the broadest sense which includes the reform administration as well? [35] In part, the answer could be found in some of the sources of machine strength we noted earlier; but more than this was involved, too, and even with regard to the advantages of the machine a focusing on the reform movement itself makes for a clearer understanding.

In the first place, it was always difficult to maintain solidarity among key reform elements. In a reform movement divergent interests came together under the spur of indignation to achieve a common purpose; but with victory, indignation subsided and unity tended to break up. The non-partisan spirit, indispensable to victory, became a casualty of time; state and national elections, which pushed Democrats and Republicans into opposing camps, did not help. Often, as we have noted, professional political elements took part in the reform movement. Almost always when this happened conflict developed between the professionals, whose orientation was not basically different from that of the politicians who had been beaten, and the independent and "reformist" elements who wanted a genuine reform administration. Where the professionals did not take over the reform movement, their demands and activities were a source of trouble, not to say embarrassment. Sometimes businessmen who had backed reform broke away after the worst abuses had been cleaned up and they came to feel that they had a greater advantage over competitors under the old graft system.

By the time the next election rolled around, lower-class people who had defected from the machine to back the reform movement were usually alienated. Much of the difficulty was the result of class attitudes. An impalpable, but real gap—the product of differing backgrounds, incomes, status—separated the leaders of the reform administration from the poorer people. Always suspicious of the reform camp, cognizant of the help given them by machine politicians, the poor had voted for reform only because of corruption that was too flagrant or manifest; it did not take much to push them back into the other corner. Unintentionally the reform administration leaders were likely to give the shove. At times they made the reform administration too exclusively a property owners' administration—small budget, low tax rate, restricted municipal functions. Even when they did not do this, when they showed an interest in what we have referred to as social betterment or welfare, when they did much for the poor—new parks and enforcement of tenement laws—they often managed to convey the impression, generally grounded in fact, that they had a special deference for men of wealth. Often their efforts on behalf of the poor were not entirely devoid of an air of paternalism which did not sit well with the lower classes. Serving to widen the gap between the administration and the lower classes, moreover, was the fact that a reform mayor seldom possessed or demonstrated a personality that attracted the masses;

often he was the businessman or administrator type, capable and efficient, but lacking in touches of drama and color.

Other things undermined reform. Occasionally opportunistic reform leaders sacrificed the movement to self-advancement. Mistakes and blunders of one sort or another and the failure to keep promises hurt it. No administration is free from mistakes, of course, or can make all dreams come true; but for reform the penalty for falling down was especially high. This was because so much was expected of it—more, much more, than was expected of the machine. People never judged reform by the same standards they used to judge the machine. Sometimes the expectations were reasonable and sometimes unfair in the light of what was possible. In any case, reform administrations always ran a particularly great risk of disillusioning voters, and the disillusioned can be bitter people. And there was this, too—though the point cannot be as clearly demonstrated as the others we have made—there was a tendency for people, sooner or later, to lose interest in civic affairs. Indignation—upon which the reform movement was based—is, after all, ephemeral. No profound change reoriented the people. Actually while most people wanted good government, they were not interested in reorientation, nor could they be. They were satisfied with a revolt which tidied up the house for a time, which served as a catharsis cleansing them from any sense of guilt and allowed them to get back to the main business of life as soon as possible. The citizens' parties—and some had very ambitious plans—almost always declined. Not alone the general public, but reform administration officials themselves, after the days of newness had passed, after the big work had been done, might become tired of public service and turn their eyes elsewhere. The machine never got tired.

Upon reflection, the reader may note that at the heart of much that worked against the reform movement were the strongest drives and deepest values in American life.[36]

We have been speaking in the last few pages in terms of generalities. They will have more meaning for us if we take a brief look at New York City's reform movements. By 1920 many such movements had marked the pages of the city's history,[37] more than even many well-informed people are aware of. The story begins in 1844. New York at the time was pervaded with a deep feeling of disgust for the low character of political life. Both the Democrats and the Whigs were blamed, especially for outrageous election frauds. The Native American Party became the rallying point for those who wanted civic reform, and many people who did not like this party's bigotry against foreigners voted for it in the city elections that year as a means of purifying and improving the city. The Native Americans were swept into office. Almost ten years later, in 1853, revelations about the Forty Thieves led to another successful reform movement. This time the vehicle for reform was an independent party, the City

Reform Party, which nominated certain Whigs and Democrats. 1857 and 1861 saw reactions to the activities of Mayor Fernando Wood. In the first instance, a committee of citizens representing Republicans, Democrats and Native Americans nominated for Mayor Daniel F. Tiemann, a paint dealer (and supposedly one of the nobler members of Tammany Hall) who had made a good record as Governor of the Almshouse. He won, but Wood won re-election two years later, and another reform wave had to sweep him out again in 1861. At that time, the People's Union, a citizens' committee composed of Republicans and Democrats, succeeded, in spite of election frauds, largely because of a conflict between Tammany and a rival group. The main power, however, lay not with the Mayor, but with the Common Council which Tammany controlled; the Hall continued to rule the city in 1862 and 1863, and political life continued to scandalize the citizens. When in 1863 Tammany went too far and nominated an especially obnoxious individual for Mayor, the public reacted again in indignation. In a three-cornered race—the Republican organization put up a candidate—the nominee of a new reform party, C. Godfrey Gunther, was elected.[38]

Aside from the value of political antisepsis which may have resulted from a change in administration at times, these early reform movements accomplished little. (The reform movement which grew out of the scandals of the Forty Thieves indirectly caused Tammany to reorganize the police under a separate department and force the policemen to wear uniforms,[39] but this was an exception.) The lack of results was not surprising. The Mayor's term of office was short, and the new administration had little chance to get going before the next contest. More important, the Mayor's powers were not as significant as they were to become in the years after the Civil War, certainly not anything like we know them to be today; and the politicians, despite the election of a reform Mayor, often continued to control the city's legislative body, which was more important than the Mayor. That reform administrations could not and did not do too much must have been one reason why voters quickly went back to their old voting habits. But often other, more vital, factors limited reform's accomplishments and undermined the movement in other ways. The 1844 movement was taken over by professionals in the Native American Party who interested themselves more in spoils than with real reforms and so sadly disappointed the voters that the electorate returned the Democrats to power the following year.[40] The City Reform Party, which came to power on the reform wave of 1853, quickly disintegrated when Fernando Wood shrewdly encouraged the Whig element to go its own way.[41] Mayor Tiemann was apparently too much concerned with his own future for the good of reform; he tried to please everybody, was accused of conducting the government with an eye on the Tammany nomination for Mayor at the next election and proved incapable.[42]

The first reform movement in the period after the Civil War was directed against the Tweed Ring. In the fall of 1870 a group of Republicans, disaffected Democrats and independents put up a candidate for Mayor. But Tammany was united, and Tweed owned large numbers of Republican officials. Although charges were made that Tweed was a crook, there was as yet no concrete evidence to prove it, and the public had yet to be fully aroused. The reformers lost that election.

By the fall of 1871 the situation had changed. In midsummer, the *New York Times* had begun to publish the damning facts and figures. Tweed had given his classic rejoinder—"What are you going to do about it?"—an unfortunate error on his part, for American voters may accept political dictation, but will not tolerate a questioning of democratic forms. A powerful independent citizens' committee, the Committee of Seventy, investigated the Tweed Ring and put up a ticket which won a smashing victory. This was not a mayoral election, but the following year with reform sentiment still high, the Committee of Seventy elected a Mayor, sugar merchant and former Mayor William F. Havemeyer.[43]

Though in power only two years, Havemeyer's administration fell into a different class than the reform administrations that preceded it. The credit of the city, wrecked by Tweed, was fully restored; a responsible system of accounting was introduced; the public school system was improved; the riffraff were deprived of the run of the city that they had enjoyed in previous years; the streets were kept cleaner than ever before; and serious efforts were made to enforce public health and security ordinances. Though he made mistakes, said the New York City Council of Political Reform, Mayor Havemeyer in general labored like a Trojan to redeem his native city and left a record for economy, integrity and Roman firmness that his successors would do well to imitate.[44]

Despite all this, despite the fact that in 1871 Tammany seemed devastated beyond the hope of recovery, the mayoral election of November, 1874, brought Tammany politicians, now led by Honest John Kelly, back into power. This seems incredible, yet there are understandable reasons why it occurred. Even before Havemeyer's election in 1872, the nonpartisan spirit had begun to evaporate. Some men most conspicuous in the reform movement—men like Samuel J. Tilden, Horatio Seymour, August Belmont—remained or became Sachems of Tammany Hall. As Democrats they may have been motivated by a mixed desire to make Tammany a real reform body, preserve intact the city's Democratic Party and advance their own political fortunes.[45] After 1872 the struggle of the Democratic and Republican parties for control of the state and federal governments—a struggle in which reform Democrats, as a rule, acted with Tammany, and reform Republicans with the Republican Party—completed the destruction of nonpartisan feeling in the Committee of Seventy. National issues such as a third term for President Grant, Washington graft, the tariff, the depression were not without their influences on New York City voters in the mayoral contest of 1874.[46]

Besides, Havemeyer—and hence reform—became unpopular with the masses. The depression of 1873 created a good deal of unemployment. Just at a time when labor would have most welcomed public employment, Havemeyer, because the Ring had looted the city so thoroughly, felt forced to practice economy in public works, a policy which labor either did not understand or cared nothing about. Meanwhile, Tammany declared itself in favor of giving public employment to the workers and scoured the poorer districts during the campaign of 1874, giving aid to the needy. Furthermore, Havemeyer committed the error of making a slurring allusion to John Kelly's humble birth and early occupation—presumably that of grate-setter or stone-cutter—and though Havemeyer died before the end of his term in 1874, his unfortunate allusion served to throw the support of the poor strongly to Kelly and his ticket.[47]

About twenty years after the revolt precipitated by the Tweed scandals came the next reform wave. In 1890, as a result of the findings of the Fassett committee, a committee of the state senate which showed that the city's departments were honeycombed with corruption, a citizens' movement developed in the form of the People's Municipal League. Although the reformers waged a vigorous campaign, Tammany re-elected its mayor largely because of the Democratic tidal wave in the nation that year.[48] Then one Sunday morning in February, 1892, Dr. Charles H. Parkhurst took as his text, "Ye Are the Salt of the Earth," and in a blistering sermon proceeded to point out that, under conditions existing in New York City, the salt had lost a good deal of its savor. "There is not a form under which the devil disguises himself that so perplexes us in our efforts, or so bewilders us in the devising of our schemes," declared the minister, "as the polluted harpies that under the pretense of governing this city, are feeding day and night on its quivering vitals. They are a lying, perjured, rum-soaked and libidinous lot." [49] Other sermons followed. The Lexow committee, another senate investigating body, revealed political and police protection of commercialized vice. The result was a great bustle of civic activity which reached a high point in the election of 1894. At that time, another Committee of Seventy was created which united various civic organizations with the Republicans to form a fusion ticket. The Fusion forces succeeded in electing as mayor William L. Strong, a Republican and a prominent dry goods merchant and banker.[50]

Under Strong's administration, the civil service rules which Tammany had been evading were honestly enforced and the system was extended. Tenement laws were enforced, some of the worst dangers of slum housing abolished, new parks were laid out, new schools built and a City Lodging House for homeless men was created. Theodore Roosevelt, appointed President of the Police Board, somewhat improved the Police Department, and Colonel George E. Waring, Jr. kept the streets clean for the first time since the days of Havemeyer. Administrative corruption during Strong's term was unknown.[51]

But from the start, Strong's administration began to disintegrate; he had trouble with various elements that had figured in the reform victory. Not long after Strong's election, Welling recounts, several businessmen who had been members of the Committee of Seventy began to regret the reform administration and wish for Tammany again on the grounds that then "they could tell with whom to deal." [52] Independents and Republican partisans complained about Strong's handling of patronage, though for different reasons. The former objected to the Mayor's tendency to confuse a multi-partisan government with a nonpartisan one and generously to reward political backers. To Strong's surprise many prominent members of Good Government Clubs declined to take office under him as a matter of principle. The Republicans, whose criticism was more bitter and significant, charged Strong with breaking pre-election pledges given Republican state boss Thomas C. Platt; they never forgave Strong for ousting some of Platt's close friends and hindered him whenever they could.[53]

So unpleasant was Strong's experience as Mayor that he positively refused to consider a renomination in 1897.[54] On the shoals of nominating a successor the Fusion ship went down, though it is hard to see how it would have been otherwise had Strong been of a different mind. The Republicans, who would not have taken him again, steadfastly refused to back Seth Low, the choice of the new Citizens Union, regarding him as another Strong. It is doubtful if the Republicans would have agreed to any man with the slightest streak of independence. Apparently Boss Platt felt the Republicans would do better without a reform administration. The Citizens Union, with an eye, one suspects, toward its own dignity as well as principle, refused to compromise on any candidate but Low. The upshot was that the Citizens Union ran Low alone, the Republicans put up their own man, Henry George also ran—though he died before election day —and in the four-way race, Tammany's Robert Van Wyck walked in. (That anti-Tammany feeling was, nevertheless, still strong and that a fusion movement almost certainly could have won again is seen from the fact that the combined vote of the Republican and Citizens Union candidates for Mayor was almost twenty thousand greater than that received by Van Wyck.) [55] On election night men and women from the Tenderloin section paraded through the city streets carrying toy tigers and shouting, "Well, Well, Reform has gone to Hell!" [56]

So it had. But like Hercules, it came back. The Mazet committee came down from Albany in 1899 and revealed corruption in the city. One scandal, you may recall, involved the famous ice trust. From other sources people learned about the white slave traffic on the lower East Side, where young girls were forced into prostitution. Never did this issue make so deep an impression, particularly on the people of the East Side slums who traditionally voted for Tammany. The year 1901 saw another reform movement, a fusion which this time united the Republicans, the Citizens Union and minor elements behind Seth Low on a ticket which included

William Travers Jerome, candidate for District Attorney of New York County. Low, President of Columbia University, was an independent Republican who had been Mayor of Brooklyn before its merger into Greater New York; he was a businessman and the son of a businessman, rich, educated and honest. William Travers Jerome, a justice of the Court of Special Sessions, had been Assistant District Attorney from 1888 through 1890 and active in various reform groups. Picturesque and dynamic, Jerome's stirring speeches against vice and corruption electrified the campaign and sent Tammany down to defeat.[57]

And so Seth Low moved into City Hall. He appointed to office a number of men of ability radically different from the Tammany type. More money was appropriated for schools in a year and a half of his administration than had been appropriated by the Van Wyck administration in four years, and the supply of schools was brought more abreast of demand. Improvements were made in water supply, in transportation, in the care of the city's health; and, once again, the tenement laws were enforced. Low assessed real estate at full value, instead of at 67 per cent, thus allowing the city to borrow more under state law and increase its public improvements. According to Lincoln Steffens, while some of Low's departments were dishonest and others inefficient, while the administration was not properly co-ordinated, for an American city at that time it was honest and able and was "undeniably one of the best in the whole country." [58]

Low's administration lasted two years. When he ran for re-election in 1903—for a time the Mayor's term was reduced to two years—he went down to defeat before Tammany's George B. McClellan. What was the trouble? Though more was involved, mainly the trouble was Seth Low. Seemingly dignified, aloof and cold, Low was not able to hold the good will of the lower classes. True or not, he gave the impression that he placed himself on an altitude far above them, that he did not and could not understand their lives and their "real personal and civic aspirations." [59] It was possible to cite various acts of Low's administration, such as the enforcement of the peddler's license requirement and the high price for a liquor license as evidence that he was a "silk-stocking." [60] Furthermore, while Low's appointments were generally good, some were politically inspired and did not reflect credit upon him.[61] He was accused of but laxly enforcing the excise (liquor) laws.[62] Police protection of vice had been one of the chief reasons for his election; yet for a year he held on to his Police Commissioner, though that official proved naive and incompetent, ignoring the friendly advice of the press and civic groups until the City Club, completely exasperated, brought the matter to a head and forced the Commissioner to resign.[63] Motivated by partisan feeling, the hope for political advancement, or both, Low, a Republican, committed the cardinal error of angering Democratic and Progressive supporters by speaking for the Republican state ticket in 1902 and by showing favor to the Republicans in other ways.[64] Many of the men who were responsible for his election he offended by his personality. "To them," one influential reformer complained, "the administration owes much; but the Mayor seemingly thinks that the self-delusive magic of his name was the principle means of accomplishment." [65] Stubborn, weak, vacillating, smug and egotistical was the way some of those on the reform side described Seth Low.[66] So dissatisfied were many in the Fusion circle with Low that in 1903 there were efforts to nominate someone else for Mayor, a move that only further weakened reform; William Travers Jerome seems to have been the one the anti-Low people mainly had in mind. Finally, apparently because Fusion had to stand on Low's record, Low was renominated, and McClellan was elected.[67]

There were worse Tammany Mayors than George McClellan. Definitely he was not the usual sort to be Mayor; he had attended Princeton and served five terms in Congress with moderate distinction before Boss Murphy nominated him for the office because the machine needed a "good man" to oppose Low. But when McClellan ran for re-election in 1905, another reform movement developed. The people were incensed at the fortunes Tammany leaders were making from contracting businesses, such as the New York Contracting and Trucking Company, and by revelations of the close connection between big business and the machine which emerged from the muckraking of the period. William Randolph Hearst, in his crusading democratic phase, blasted the "plunderbund" of businessmen as well as the leaders of Tammany Hall in articles, editorials and cartoons in his two New York newspapers; his journalism—sensational, vigorous, understandable to the crudest intelligence—shook the city. The election was especially important for the Mayor's term was again to be four years. But the revolt failed. Partly this was because there was no fusion. Hearst ran for Mayor on the ticket of the Municipal Ownership League, which he had largely founded; the Republicans, who would not back Hearst and could come to no agreement with the Citizens Union, put up their own ticket; the Citizens Union finally did not run a candidate for Mayor but successfully campaigned for Jerome, who was running for re-election as District Attorney. There seems little doubt that reform sentiment was powerful and that most people who wanted reform regarded Hearst's Municipal Ownership League as the vehicle. A fusion of the Republicans with the League would have been unbeatable. As it was, there is good reason to believe that Hearst won the election, but Tammany stole it from him.[68]

After his re-election, McClellan tried hard to steer an independent course and fought Murphy for control of the Hall. But this did not mean good government for the city. McClellan had reasons for keeping some district leaders happy, and Murphy held sway in many administrative and court departments not controlled by the Mayor. City finances were badly confused, vast sums were squandered in the purchasing of city supplies, condemnation proceedings were a source of scandal. During this period,

Governor Charles Evans Hughes removed from office both the Borough President of Manhattan and the Borough President of the Bronx. In 1909 the scene was set for another try to overthrow machine government. The people who wanted reform were confused, however. The chief reform elements led by the Citizens Union and the Republicans nominated a Fusion ticket headed by Otto Bannard, a banker. But Hearst refused to join and ran for Mayor again as the candidate of his organization, now called the Citizens Alliance, after first having it endorse the rest of the Fusion slate, vainly hoping thereby to get Bannard to withdraw in his favor. (Hearst had lost followers but was still strong.) To make matters worse for reform solidarity, Murphy, sniffing the wind, had William J. Gaynor, a justice of the State Supreme Court and a "good man," nominated by Tammany; and some people who wanted reform supported him believing he had the ability to curb the Tiger. Gaynor was elected, but so, with one other exception, was the entire Fusion slate for the Board of Estimate. The election returns made it obvious that if the Hearst organization had come into the Fusion movement behind Bannard, he would have won.[69]

The election was mainly a victory for reform. In addition to controlling the important Board of Estimate, Fusion provided the Acting Mayor for several months during which Gaynor recuperated from a bullet wound inflicted on him by a would-be assassin. Besides, Gaynor, as some reform-minded people had predicted, turned out, generally speaking, to be a creditable Mayor, and one who for a while at least, worked with the Fusion officials.[70] Independent in attitude, cantankerous, belligerent, unsmiling, intransigent, a "character" who said what he thought when he felt like it—there has never been another New York Mayor like Gaynor. (Once, during the campaign of 1909, he addressed a group of Queens voters as "Ye Long Island Clam Diggers."[71]) He had no love for the reformers, though he was somewhat one himself. Partly this was because he found their personalities distasteful and partly because they were for adding to the multiplicity of laws and for putting additional power in the hands of the government; and Gaynor was a passionate Jeffersonian who believed that that government is best which governs least.[72] (To one citizen, annoyed by the clock on the Metropolitan tower striking the hours, Mayor Gaynor, who indulged in slyly humorous and sharp-tongued letters, wrote: "I am sorry for you, but really does the clock make as much noise as Dr. Parkhurst does?"[73]) But if unkind to the reform crowd, he was not the bosom friend of the politicians. He deprecated the Tammany leaders as " 'those fellows up on Fourteenth Street,' "[74] and would not be bossed by Charlie Murphy, who must have rued the day he thought of the nomination. Though Gaynor gave Tammany much patronage, he also went his own way and appointed some good men to office.[75] Moreover, he championed the merit system, abolished long established political sinecures, reduced running expenses and made strides to clean up deplorable conditions in the Magistrates' Courts.[76] "A rare, resourceful character . . . a great Mayor," Henry Curran was later to call Gaynor, and inasmuch as Curran had been a Republican alderman during Gaynor's administration and had violently clashed with him, this was no small compliment.[77]

Still scandals during Gaynor's term as Mayor were forging one of the greatest reform movements in the city's history. Disclosures of vice protection by the police, dramatized by the murder of gambler Herman Rosenthal and the conviction of police lieutenant Charles Becker, as well as the impeachment of Governor William Sulzer by Boss Murphy for insubordination shocked the public. Though the opprobrium for these scandals fell on Tammany and not the Mayor, Gaynor also came in for some criticism, for in the midst of the clamor over the police, his pride kept him from recognizing any criticism of the Police Department but his own. Gaynor, moreover, alienated people on other counts—his idiosyncrasies being one.

In 1913 a citizens' committee called the Committee of One Hundred and Seven was organized with the hope of bringing about reform; and after some difficulty, it succeeded in fusing the Republicans and other groups behind a ticket led by John Purroy Mitchel. Mitchel, an independent Democrat, had been elected President of the Board of Aldermen in 1909 but had resigned in 1913 to become Collector of the Port of New York; he had first achieved fame when as special counsel to the city and as Commissioner of Accounts he carried out investigations of the presidents of the boroughs of Manhattan and the Bronx which led ultimately to their removal. Tammany refused to renominate Gaynor and chose instead Edward McCall, Chairman of the Public Service Commission, First District, a man decidedly more dependable in Murphy's view. A group of citizens, many of them conservative businessmen and merchants, who thought that Gaynor had done a good job and deserved re-election put him up on an independent ticket; and with the reformers split once again, it looked as if Tammany might win after all. But in September Gaynor, who had never fully regained his health after the attempt on his life, died. Most of his supporters joined Fusion, which, under Mitchel, went on to gain a thumping victory in November. In 1914 Fusion controlled the Mayor's office, the Board of Estimate and even the Board of Aldermen.[78]

Straight, just, clean and able, young John Purroy Mitchel (he was only in his thirties) proved to be one of the city's great Mayors. He chose decent, honest, capable subordinates and developed a fine spirit of co-operation among them. His departments were singularly free from scandals of any proportion and were marked by firm discipline, progress, a feeling of pride in the service. Oswald Garrison Villard declared that never before had the Fire Department or the city's charities been so well administered. Neither in Mitchel's time, nor in any other in the city's history, has the administration of the Police Department approached the millennium; the Department has been a headache in practically every administration. But there was generally some improvement during reform administrations (though Low, it is true, had his troubles), and this was particularly the case in Mitchel's administration. Under his Police Commissioner, Arthur Woods, the Department probably reached a higher level of honesty and performance than had been known before; graft was kept down, the laws were fairly well enforced, gamblers and crooks were forced to watch their step. Under Mayor Mitchel, financial honesty was coupled with expert handling of financial problems; improvements were made in the school system; the prisons, for once, were carried on with some semblance of scientific and humanitarian management; the death rate steadily decreased, largely as a result of the efficiency of the Health Department; zoning was instituted.[79]

Mitchel's achievements did not save him any more than they did the city's reform Mayors who had come before him. One big reason was that Mitchel failed to do what a successful Mayor must do—establish intimacy with the whole body of people and stamp the right impression on the public mind. Honest and efficient as his government was, it appeared to lack a quality of humaneness because Mitchel, in that groping for a balance between principle and practicality, was more on the side of "the system," the letter of the law, "what was Right" than on the side of what was reasonable—though this is not to imply he was necessarily wrong. Also, more an administrator than a politician, he refused to cater to the senti- mental and dramatic sense of the masses, though the need to do so has usually been one of the facts of political life. His tendency of hobnobbing with wealthy people did not help endear him to the average voter. (Rabbi Stephen S. Wise, who loved him, grieved that "he chose to see much more of a very limited social and dancing set than he did of the people whose uprising had elected him." [80]) Failure to establish intimacy with the mass of voters hurt Mitchel, not only because he lost a valuable weapon, but because he placed one in the hands of his political enemies. Hearst and the Democrats capitalized on Mitchel's personality, social predilections and certain acts of his administration to picture him as an aristocrat and a tool of the "interests." The impression stuck. Significantly, the New York State Federation of Labor opposed his re-election. Nor may the Mitchel administration have been without some responsibility for the popular image. Leaving aside the debatable question of whether the Fusion administration did not sometimes show favor to wealthy interests, there is this interesting statement made by the pro-Fusion Woman's Municipal League at the time of Mitchel's administration: " 'The claims of Fusion's being the tool of the interests could not have persisted had the city admin- istrators not been confined in their ideas and sympathies by fatal class limitations and lack of popular understanding and needs. There was too much benevolent autocracy about the methods by which reforms were instituted.' " [81]

And Mitchel stepped on various toes, not always to his discredit; he aroused against him and his administration "little hatreds." A Catholic himself, he incurred the enmity of Catholics because the administration firmly insisted on the right to examine the books of Catholic charitable institutions subsidized by the city and because the police tapped the telephone wires of Catholic priests and dignitaries in connection with the charities investigation. Strongly pro-Allied during World War I, Mitchel created resentment among the Germans of the city by his defense preparations and by his outbursts of patriotic fervor; he once attacked State Senator Robert F. Wagner as "the gentleman from Prussia." Since he was not generous with patronage, he alienated the Republican professionals.

Whatever chance Mitchel's administration might have had was lost by a poorly conducted campaign for its re-election in 1917. Mitchel lost the Republican primary for Mayor—the professionals had their revenge—and the event practically eliminated him, although his supporters ran his name on an independent line. Other aspects of the campaign further damaged him, especially the attempt of the Mayor and his ticket to identify themselves with war-time patriotism and smear the Democratic candidate, John F. Hylan, as pro-German. The strategy boomeranged, for many resented the effort, and it tended to solidify against Mitchel those opposed to the war, notably the Germans and the anti-British Irish. In the end Mitchel was decisively repudiated. Hylan's vote exceeded the combined vote of his three biggest rivals, and Mitchel, who had received 57 per cent of the total vote in 1913, got 23 per cent of it in 1917.[82]

By the start of the third decade of the twentieth century these had been the years which signalized reform movements in New York City: 1844, 1853, 1857, 1861, 1863, 1870–2, 1890, 1894, 1901, 1905, 1909, 1913.[83] In their bid for power the reformers were successful in all elections, except that of 1870 (which constituted only a temporary setback to the movement) and those of 1890 and 1905; the results of the 1909 election are ambiguous, though we have tended to view the Gaynor administration as more a reform administration than not. In no case did reform, once in power, stay there after the next mayoral election.

In New York, in American cities generally, the reform tradition—whether referring to the work of the civic leaders or the broader political revolts—was certainly often marked by frustration. But reform was hardly a tradition of futility. Surely it is not without profit for a city to have an eye kept on its public officials and their conduct of the government, to have pressure exerted in the interest of the general welfare, to have the civic conscience educated and stimulated. These things were done for the city by its core of civic leaders. In times of machine rule, they provided the most effective, sometimes the only real, opposition. Though often taking a good deal of time, many of the changes proposed by the reformers to improve government were adopted, and better government did result. New York City, as we have seen, enacted civil service reform, the secret ballot, the separation of city from state and national elections. The trend in New York in the late nineteenth and early twentieth centuries was toward more simplified and unified government; increasingly power came to be concentrated in the hands of the Mayor.[84] Tortuous as the path was, the city moved toward home rule, and in 1923 the voters of the state finally adopted a Home Rule Amendment.[85] Though this amendment has subsequently proven to be less of a boon than had been thought, mainly because the courts have interpreted the amendment against the city,[86] it did give the city more control than before over its own property, affairs and government. Also the pleas of some reformers for a more socially conscious city did not go entirely unheeded.

And the reform movements, despite their short lives, were also not valueless. At the very least, a reform administration usually cleaned house, and this is not to be minimized. "I hope we will never take the position," wrote Rabbi Wise, a great civic reformer, "that because filth comes back to a city after cleaning, no cleaning is to be attempted. It may as well be said that the city sewage system is not worthwhile because it must constantly be renewed." [87] A reform administration, however, often did much more. For a while people had better government, and even when the machine came back, the old ways were not apt to be completely restored; the public had been shown higher standards of government which the machine could not entirely ignore. The reform movement generally had other significant consequences. For one thing, people usually became more interested in city affairs during the time of the reform movement; and for some, it proved to be more than a passing mood. Some of the people who joined reform groups and citizens' committees during the revolt stage—and never was recruitment for civic work so good as when government was "so bad"—were apt to remain actively interested in local affairs after the movement declined. Besides, the movement served to educate the citizens as to machine activities, and the lesson was not likely to be completely forgotten; it tended to become part of the public conscience and worked perhaps to lower the threshold of tolerance of bad government in the future.

All in all, the government of America's biggest city, as well as that of her smaller cities, became increasingly better in the late nineteenth and early twentieth centuries. As dismal as the government of New York was in the 1890's, it was several notches above that which its inhabitants had known in the days of Wood and Tweed. Seth Low, in 1892 comparing the New York of 1890 with that of 1850, declared that in forty years the city had undergone a substantial improvement with respect to its Charter, police conditions, fire control, honesty at the polls, paved streets, the amount of park acreage and the death rate.[88] Gustavus Myers, writing his preface to *The History of Tammany Hall* at the turn of the century, observed that "Tammany today outwardly conforms to ethical demands which would have been scoffed at a half century ago," and noted that this, in itself, was evidence of the growth of higher standards.[89] By the 1920's the improvement, not only in New York, but elsewhere in America, was so marked that Professor William Bennett Munro, noted student of city government in the United States, termed the period 1895–1925 the "Civic Renaissance," distinguishing it from the previous generation which he called the "Dark Ages" of American municipal government.[90] No one is saying that there was not plenty of corruption, graft, waste, inefficiency—in short, bad government—in American cities in the 1920's; that this was true for New York will shortly become obvious. But it is important to keep perspective. The direction with regard to civic conditions was definitely upward. That this was so was mainly due to the reformers—the little band of civic leaders at all times and the enlarged group of active citizens in periods of greater dissatisfaction. Far from paragons, they were, nonetheless, public-spirited, persistent, courageous and sacrificing; refusing to accept what *was,* they kept their eyes on what *might be* and fought hard for it.

*

Part II
The Development of the Reform
Movement of 1933

3

An age of Tammany

MAYOR JOHN F. HYLAN was big-boned and fleshy with heavy features, red hair and a red mustache. His friends called him Honest John, his detractors, Red Mike. The Mayor was a ponderous man, stolid, with a decided lack of wit and humor; when he spoke or walked, he did so slowly and hesitantly. He lacked warmth except when he was denouncing the "traction interests" and insisting upon the maintenance of the five-cent subway fare, his favorite topic. Whatever his cause, he had the fatal gift of putting his audience to sleep. Behind his air of importance, one sensed a man inwardly insecure and uncertain of himself. That, however, did not prevent him, as it has not prevented others, from being either vain or ambitious, and in Hylan's case fortune had done nothing to undermine his presumption.[1]

He had come as a farm boy from Greene County, New York, to live in Brooklyn in the 1880's. For a while he ran a locomotive for the Brooklyn Elevated Railroad, studied law in his free time. Eventually he was admitted to the Bar. Although only a mediocre lawyer, he kept his eye on politics, joined the Democratic organization in the Twentieth Assembly District in Brooklyn and played up to the political leaders. As a result, the machine got behind him: Mayor McClellan appointed him a magistrate in 1906; in 1914 Governor Glynn named him to fill a County Court vacancy in Brooklyn; a year later he was elected to the office for a seven-year term. Hearst's *American* gave him a good deal of publicity, quoting him as a sage on all subjects, even when he said nothing; and the political bosses were shrewd enough to recognize that Hearst, whose support was valuable, had his eye on Hylan. About a year before the election of 1917, Hylan began to work for the mayoral nomination. Three of his friends became the

Allied Boards of Trade and Taxpayers' Associations of Brooklyn and carried on propaganda in his behalf from letter box No. 3 at 1028 Gates Avenue, Brooklyn. Hylan, himself, spoke before taxpayers' groups using facts discreditable to the Mitchel administration which he had obtained from Boss Murphy, only too glad to use any stick to beat a dog; the news-papers covered the talks and gave Hylan publicity. Murphy had another man picked out for Mayor, but when this first choice ran into bankruptcy, thus ruining his chances—for not even Murphy would dare to offer the city a bankrupt to run the huge city budget—the Tammany boss agreed to take Hylan from the Brooklyn machine. Hylan was the sort of man he wanted: a Brooklynite—and Murphy felt that the election called for a man from Brooklyn—a man the voters had heard about and, above all, a man with no independent ideas like Gaynor. Hylan, swept to power in 1917, was re-elected four years later.[2]

Honest John Hylan was miscast as Mayor. He was, indeed, honest, meant well, took his job seriously and worked diligently. But his plodding mind could not cope with the city's problems. He exerted a lot of energy, ran around in circles, and nothing came of the commotion. Habitually he showed lack of tact in dealing with problems which required finesse, and frequently his loud stubbornness created havoc at meetings of the Board of Estimate. His appointments were poor. Had he not possessed such a suspicious mind, which caused him to vigorously denounce the newsmen, he might have received a more favorable press; yet it is also true that any Mayor who received Hearst's support, as he did, would probably have had to endure the enmity of the other newspapers.[3]

As the 1925 election approached, Hylan indicated that he was not yet tired of being Mayor. But many were tired of him, and one of these was Governor Alfred E. Smith. Smith, a product of New York's East Side, had risen to the Executive Mansion by way of the Tammany machine. First elected Governor in 1918, Smith went down to defeat in 1920, the year of a Republican sweep, but was elected Governor again in 1922 and twice in a row after that. As Governor and a Sachem of the Hall, Smith understandably wielded a great deal of influence in Tammany. His oppo-sition to Hylan was strong. Hearst was anathema to Smith and some other leading Tammany Democrats, Hylan was close to Hearst, and this was enough to damn the Mayor. Smith, furthermore, regarded Hylan as intel-lectually unfit for the job. He blamed the Mayor for the failure to build new subways and could not have liked the fact that Hylan had opposed a number of his legislative proposals.[4]

Smith's opposition to Hylan brought about a fight within the Demo-cratic family. George Olvany, former Judge of General Sessions, a friend of Al Smith, had become the boss of Tammany Hall after the death of Charles Murphy in 1924. Olvany and Edward J. Flynn, the young leader of the Democratic organization in the Bronx, joined Smith in opposing Hylan, while John H. McCooey, the Democratic boss in Brooklyn, and

Maurice Connolly and David Rendt, heads of the Democratic machines in Queens and Richmond, decided to stick with the Mayor; according to Flynn, McCooey hoped that if Hylan were re-elected with his backing, the Mayor would be under such obligation to him as to enable him to emerge as leader of the Democratic Party in the city. In this intraparty struggle, Olvany and Flynn, after casting about for a candidate, decided that their strongest one was State Senator James J. Walker, and they submitted his name to Smith for approval.[5]

Al Smith and Jimmy Walker had known each other for years. Both had been protégés of Charles Murphy and were good Tammany men. But while they were outwardly friendly, they were two different personalities and rubbed each other the wrong way. Smith was serious, hard working, a good family man and a devout Catholic. Walker was frivolous and given to play; he treated his marriage vows lightly and for most of his life was not especially concerned with religion. Smith wanted to reform Walker; Walker naturally resented being reformed. Smith did not want Walker as the mayoral candidate, but Olvany and Flynn indicated their determination and the Governor gave in; to beat the existing Mayor in the primary when he has good support is not an easy thing, and Smith, who above all desired to get rid of Hylan, had to go along with the man wanted by the anti-Hylan politicians. Senator Walker made Smith's choice easier by temporarily reforming.[6] Backed by Smith, Walker defeated Hylan in the primary by nearly 100,000 votes and then went on to win the election.[7] Hylan retired to private life, but in 1929, the good-natured Walker appointed the former Mayor to the Children's Court in Queens remarking that "the children now can be tried by their peer." [8] Hylan had other aspirations however. Periodically, as mayoral elections rolled around, he would offer to run again, and once, in 1934, he ran as an independent candidate for Governor; his efforts went unappreciated.[9]

Jimmy Walker had become Mayor as a result of steady promotion by Tammany Hall. His father, William Henry Walker, had been a Tammany alderman, assemblyman, and leader of the old Ninth Ward. Young Walker did not want to follow his father into politics. What he really loved was the life of the theatre and Tin Pan Alley. For a while, in fact, he became a song writer, and his "Will You Love Me In December As You Do In May" became a popular hit. But his father had other ambitions for his son, and to please him, Jimmy agreed to make a career in politics and law. The first rung was the Assembly, which he entered in 1910. After Walker served there four years, Murphy, who liked the young man and predicted a bright future for him, elevated Walker to the Senate, where after a few years he became Democratic floor leader. His bouncing personality, genuine friendliness and personal charm made him a popular figure in the legislature. He won some fame in his lawmaking capacity as the sponsor of bills to legalize boxing in New York and to permit Sunday baseball games.[10]

It is hard to find a man more completely the antithesis of Hylan than Jimmy Walker. Slender, boyish and agile in appearance, he possessed warmth, quick wit, a sense of humor and unusual public speaking ability which won for him a host of admirers. While not a deep thinker, he had a quick and keen mind. He could digest a problem in the time it took to climb the single flight from the Mayor's office to the Board of Estimate chamber. No Mayor in the city's history was as well liked as Walker through most of his administration. Even when the storm finally broke and he was subjected to intense criticism as a public official, there was no hatred for him as a man. William Jay Schieffelin wrote later, "Jimmy Walker had many attractive qualities. Nearly every one who knew him liked him." Rabbi Wise, one of Walker's strongest critics, never had personal feelings against him.[11]

The press treated Walker as it had never treated Hylan. The reporters were friendly because he was "a regular guy," lent them money, as he did practically everybody, and thought of witty things which would make a story. The editorial policies of most papers for many years were more than cordial, and this included Hearst's, which had stood by Hylan in the primary; when the newspapers rapped Walker at all, it was in a kindly, tolerant way.[12]

Yet in one unfortunate respect Walker and Hylan were very similar: though they had different personalities, neither had the personality to make a good Mayor. Some of Jimmy Walker's characteristics that people found most attractive by their very nature prevented his success as the city's chief executive. Walker lived as if life were mainly play instead of work. Deep inside he was a lonely man, and like many lonely people he had to have people around him constantly; and he had to have fun, or at least excitement, all the time—it kept his anxieties down. But a man who holds a job like that of Mayor of New York City cannot live continually in a world of escape. He must discipline himself and work hard. The *New York Times* once observed in an editorial that Walker was too much a part-time Mayor; he worked like a big plant only 35 per cent efficient.[13] Furthermore, he was intensely loyal to his friends, political and other, and he paid for it; too often such loyalty conflicted with his obligations to the city. One gets the feeling that there were times when Walker's civic instincts were good, but that too frequently when he would begin to move he would discover that the execution of an idea would hurt the interest of some friend, and he would defer to him.[14]

Never was a city administration more colorful than Walker's. The Mayor night-clubbed constantly, attended the fights with his sporting friends and the first nights with his Broadway friends, vacationed in Europe, dressed three times a day, courted an actress, spoke at numerous luncheons and dinners, wisecracked his way into the heart of the city and the nation.[15] The relatively drab tasks of policy-making and administration were neglected, and Walker had few people upon whom he could rely to help make up the deficiency. Though his commissioners and assistants should have been excellent, particularly since his own diversions caused him to lean heavily upon them, with one or two exceptions, such as Louis I. Harris in the Health Department and George McLaughlin in Police, both of whom resigned after a short time, they were political mediocrities.[16]

The people had chosen a musical-comedy mayor to head one of the greatest corporations in the world. The interesting fact is that relatively few cared during his first four years. If Walker neglected his responsibilities as Mayor, it was not an age of caring about civic responsibilities. It was a zany, materialistic age in which people wanted to be let alone to grow rich quickly and to have fun. They loved to read about the antics of their dapper little Mayor—how an alligator nipped his trousers in Florida, how he was late for an appointment with President Coolidge, what he said in an interview with Mussolini; they laughed and applauded.[17] In an age bent on revelry and perennial youth, Jimmy Walker was its spirit incarnate. When that age died, the mood of the citizens changed and a different evaluation of Walker and his administration began.

Yet it would be a mistake to overemphasize the personalities of the Mayors in attempting to explain the state of New York City's government in the ten and some odd years following the election of 1917. More important was the predominance of the machine which operated unperturbed behind the changes of mayors and tempers at City Hall; significantly Walker, when he became Mayor, continued twenty of Hylan's twenty-five commissioners.[18] Democratic Mayors with more ability than Hylan and more industry than Walker could have given the city better government, but not substantially better government, unless they had been willing to rebel against the machine system—and even then it is not clear how much they could have accomplished. As it was, neither Hylan nor Walker tried to play Gaynor. Boss Murphy, who had known his man, once remarked that no Tammany Mayor had been more liberal to the Manhattan organization in the way of patronage than Hylan, the man from Brooklyn,[19] and Honest John did not limit his largess to Manhattan. Walker, of course, was completely co-operative.

It was a great age for Tammany. The Democrats ruled the city and, as before, Tammany ruled the Democrats. As we have observed, occasionally rivalry and friction marred the relationship between the Manhattan organization and the other Democratic machines; but in the period we are now considering, the Tiger's hegemony in Democratic politics was never really in jeopardy.[20]

Beneath the surface, however, Tammany's power was being undermined by important economic and social changes. Manhattan was losing the battle of the census to the other boroughs. Families ascending the ladder of success were moving from the congested areas below Fourteenth Street, long Tammany strongholds; and with the reversal of the traditional American immigration policy in the twenties, the borough's chance of making up losses was doomed. Some of those moving went to Brooklyn, but most were attracted to the relatively undeveloped areas of the Bronx and Queens. Between 1920 and 1930, Manhattan lost about 400,000 people and practically all of them from the area south of Fourteenth Street; in the Tammany controlled Fourth Assembly District, for example, the population in this period fell from 95,000 to 54,000.[21] Whereas in 1921 35.6 per cent of those enrolled in the Democratic Party lived in Manhattan and the borough cast 34.8 per cent of the total Democratic vote for Mayor, in 1929 only 24.8 per cent of the city's Democratic enrollees lived in Manhattan and only 26.8 per cent of the Democratic vote for Mayor was cast there.[22] In the 1930's the continuation of these trends, as well as other factors, were to have serious effects on Tammany's power.

Not only did Tammany govern the city in the days of Hylan and Walker, but during much of the time, one of its own members was Governor. While Al Smith threw over Tammany discipline when he went to Albany, he was, nevertheless, a leader in the organization and maintained amicable ties with his old friends; he might not go out of his way to help Tammany, but, at least, he would not hurt it.[23]

The Tammany of the twenties was a slightly different organization from the one we have been discussing: the Tiger became somewhat manicured. Many district leaders were not the rough sort of another generation. The sons of the men who were leaders in the days of Croker had opportunities denied their immigrant fathers. Some had gone to college; George Olvany, for example, was an educated man, an anomaly in the tradition of Tammany leadership. Partly for this reason, perhaps, there was a falling off in election frauds, though the real point was that Tammany did not need them. In profiting from politics these newer district leaders, often lawyers or businessmen, used refinements which were hard to detect or penalize. In particular the tendency toward honest graft which we noticed developing under Murphy was accelerated, and generally Tammany was smoother in its operations than it had been in the early 1900's when "Uncle George" Plunkitt called it "the most perfect political machine on earth." [24] One can easily exaggerate the differences, however. The objectives remained the same. And even with respect to Tammany's means, all the customary methods of self-advancement were still in use.

Following the ancient practice of rewarding the "deserving," Tammany saw to it that the majority of the Mayor's commissioners and deputy commissioners came from the ranks of the district leaders. It extensively broke the spirit and letter of the Civil Service Law. Unfit applicants were exempted from tests or competition for perjured reasons, and, despite the requirements of state law and City Charter, the Civil Service Commission refused to let citizens see the records of such exemptions. Tammany considered few, if any, areas of government immune from politics. It regarded the Health Department as a fertile field for patronage—with disastrous results—and meddled with top school positions, which though exempt from competitive examinations were supposed to be nonpolitical. It notoriously overmanned the departments. The Park Department, for instance, had an amazing number of workers of all kinds from arborists to pruners. The Law Department was chuck-full of corporation counsels and all sorts of assistants. The situation in the five sheriffs' offices gives us a good idea of this kind of machine munificence, although these were county, not city, offices; here there were sheriffs, undersheriffs, deputy sheriffs, assistant deputy sheriffs, special assistant deputy sheriffs and all their secretaries and helpers. The Board of Aldermen, itself a mine of political sinecures, had eleven sergeants-at-arms composed of some of the most competent Tammany captains in the city, each drawing from $2,280 to $3,720.[25]

And Tammany took good care of its appointees. It raised the salaries of politically favored workers whenever there was an opportunity—and to the disadvantage of merit workers. The "salary grab" of 1929, whereby the Mayor's pay was jumped from $25,000 to $40,000, that of the Comptroller and President of the Board of Aldermen from $25,000 to $35,000, while each of the five borough presidents was raised from $15,000 to $20,000, attained notoriety; but it was only a sensational example of a common Tammany practice usually executed without much hubbub.[26]

There is plenty of evidence that the machine boys indulged in other traditional practices in this period. The confession of a foreman of a Street Cleaning Department garage in the Bronx revealed that a group in the Department had been systematically supplementing its income through fraud in the delivery of gasoline to the garages, by payroll padding and in other ways such as the use of Street Cleaning Department trucks to remove refuse which should have been removed by private trucks.[27] A ring of grafters in the Health Department was uncovered; for years it had been conniving in the adulteration of the city's milk supply and the sale of food products below the standards established by the Department. At one time 1,200,000 quarts of impure milk were being distributed daily, and some of it was fed to tubercular children and used in hospitals, homes for the aged and orphanages.[28] Big Tom Foley, one of the most powerful figures in Tammany Hall, was disclosed to be the political protector of a group of "bucketeers," a name given to fraudulent Wall Street operators; and there was much to confirm the belief that he was the protector for other crooked enterprises as well.[29] Market supervisors were revealed to be pressuring pushcart owners into paying graft in order to stay in business.[30] A special committee named by Mayor Walker found that over forty new school buildings, the cream of a $200,000,000 building program, had been badly built; among other things, roofs leaked, ceilings fell and plumbing was defective because construction had been handled by favored contractors and city officials and the Board of Education had allowed them to get away with murder.[31] The head of Tammany's allied machine in Queens, Borough President Maurice Connolly, retired to private life under fire in 1928 for having been involved in an attempt to defraud Queens taxpayers in the building of sewers.[32] Investigations after 1929 were to give a fuller picture of Tammany operations in the twenties.

The result was government characterized, not only by corruption (though one should note that this condition was truer for Walker's administration than for Hylan's), but by inefficiency and extravagance. The cost of government mounted continually, and while some of this was legitimate and the result of a growing city, a good deal was the result of politics.[33] The Board of Aldermen, whose only excuse for existence was its power to slash the budget, was almost entirely Democratic and served as a rubber stamp for the decisions of the Democratic Board of Estimate and Democratic political leaders. Mrs. Ruth Pratt, only woman member on the Board of Aldermen and one of its three Republicans, stated that, instead of cutting expenses, the Board thought constantly of creating new positions, of raising salaries, of spending more money. Its attitude was "Why worry?" [34] In the twenties, Tammany did not worry about the city's finances. Whenever the government needed more money, it raised more. Cleverly Tammany not only did not raise, but actually lowered the tax rate; in an age of prosperity and booming realty values, property was simply assessed at a higher value.[35]

City problems were allowed to drift along. The city administration made no appreciable attempt to solve the city's sewage and garbage problems; the city treated only a small percentage of its sewage chemically and dumped much of its garbage at sea, where it washed back to pollute the beaches.[36] There was a great need for municipal housing, but although Walker claimed credit for a measly block project, his administration accomplished nothing significant in housing.[37] It is true that Tammany undertook a big school building program, but we have already observed that all the consequences did not benefit the city. There was need to simplify and modernize the government which had become clumsy and archaic in many respects. But what machine administration wanted to risk endangering political jobs? Outside of one or two changes, the most notable being the creation of the Department of Hospitals, Tammany did little to remodel the city's government. Walker declared himself in favor of revising the City Charter and at one time appointed a gigantic survey committee composed of distinguished citizens to make recommendations, but there is more than a suspicion that the committee was just a device for warding off criticism; in any case, nothing much ever came of its reports.[38] Walker should be given credit for forcing an appropriation of $16,000,-000 for public hospitals after he was moved by deplorable conditions in a city psychopathic ward and for insisting that the city spend $1,000,000 to improve Central Park; yet these accomplishments, important as they may have been, were trifles in comparison with the larger problems which were neglected.[39]

Yet Tammany's supremacy was not seriously challenged in the twenties. Reformers leveled criticism at the government; the Citizens Union assailed both the administrations of Hylan and Walker, though it certainly tried hard to like Walker's in the beginning;[40] the Civil Service Reform Association took the city's Civil Service Commission to task for its tendency to exempt new jobs from competitive service.[41] But the reformers were crying in the wilderness and, what is more, their voices generally were not as loud or as forceful as one would suppose. Examination of the publications of the City Club and the Women's City Club, for instance, reveal that while these organizations concerned themselves with many important city problems, direct criticism of the city administration was notable by its paucity.[42] As mayoral elections rolled around, some people spoke about the need for a fusion movement, and some even pretended on occasion that there was one; but in the twenties there was no real attempt at reform. In 1921 the Meyer committee, with an eye on tradition, arrived from Albany all set to discover corruption in the Hylan administration; and while nothing came from it, perhaps because of internal troubles,[43] it is doubtful if any but the most serious disclosures would have moved the citizens of the city. The elections of 1921, 1925 and 1929 were essentially straight contests between the Democrats and the Republicans with the outcome never seriously in doubt.

What explains this lack of strong opposition to Tammany, even within the ranks of the anti-machine groups? Largely the fault was in the spirit of the times. If normally the American drive for success has tended to subvert good citizenship, what can be said about the 1920's, an age of excessive individualism and materialism? In a period in which the money-makers were deified, in which the standards of many businessmen were not appreciably higher than those of the machine politicians, people were not inclined to be concerned about Tammany activities and the state of the city government. The new district leaders and an apparent absence of certain activities that had long been associated with the Hall—in particular there was no evidence of the old connection between Tammany and commercial vice which many considered the real test of Tammany misrule—helped to deceive the public. The various scandals were revealed piece-meal; and people seemed to regard them as exceptions, while they overlooked even more the less dramatic evidence of inefficient, costly and muddled government.

And then there was Al Smith. The Happy Warrior was one of the most popular chief executives that New York State has ever had. His record as Governor was impressive: he fought for public waterpower ownership, the preservation of the wild forest lands, the building of new parks and beaches, improved working conditions and gave the state government a much-needed reorganization.[44] The glory Smith attained rubbed off on the Hall; the fact that Tammany legislators backed the Governor's proposals and that George Olvany was Smith's man helped. Some individuals of high calibre were drawn into association with the Manhattan Democratic organization through their attachment to the Governor, and this tended to elevate it in the public mind.[45] Moreover, those hoping for Smith's advancement to the White House, aware that the Tammany label, especially outside of New York City, worked against the fulfillment of his aspirations, were disposed to see the Hall's good points while ignoring those which discredited it.

This friendlier feeling toward Tammany, when coupled with the observation that it had somewhat refined its manners, led to the concept of the "New Tammany," the idea that the contemporary organization was morally improved over that of the past. Smith, who was good, it was thought, had forced the Hall to "reform" and become "good," too (Olvany's leadership was looked upon as significant) even if it was only to prevent it from stymieing his own ambitions.[46] Several political writers of the time voiced this belief that Tammany had become purer,[47] and sometimes with extreme optimism. An editorial in *Collier's* in 1925, which it would be difficult to match for absurdity even when noting that it was written at a time when most of the scandals mentioned above were unknown, attributed Tammany's prosperity to the fact that "idealism rather than private gain is the dominating motive of its effective leaders." [48]

That the New Tammany was a myth should be obvious. Though Smith probably did apply pressure to keep the boys in line, he certainly never reformed the Hall. Some politicos may have become more artful and genteel in exploiting the taxpayers; but these politicians were, nonetheless, very much in business, and there were those, too, who did not share in the new sophistication. When in 1929, after the evaporation of Smith's presidential dream, the anti-Smith forces within Tammany Hall were able to gain the ascendancy, throw out Olvany and elect as boss John F. Curry, an Irish ward politician of the old type, a district leader without distinction or vision, those who had talked "New Tammany" interpreted the events as the beginning of a new age of political racket.[49] But John Curry with considerably more realism declared: "There is no old or new Tammany. There is and has been just one Tammany, one organization. Tammany has always been Tammany." [50]

At the end of the twenties the mayoral election of 1929 dramatically summarized the strength of Tammany and the impotence of the anti-Tammany elements. For this reason and because it presents some interesting contrasts with the election held four years later, we would do well to consider the 1929 election briefly.

The majority of Democrats wanted Walker again. Al Smith did not. He was irritated by Walker's long absences from City Hall, his chronic inability to be on time for an appointment, some of his administration policies and, according to Gene Fowler, mainly Walker's unfaithfulness to his wife.[51] But Smith's opposition, after his presidential defeat and his retirement to private life, was no longer crucial. Walker wanted to run again —to show Smith, in Fowler's opinion [52]—and he held good cards. He had always been a popular figure in the Hall and an influential one as Mayor, and his influence was increasing as Smith's was decreasing. If he did not direct the ousting of Olvany from the leadership, he did not object to it and, in any case, his nod was responsible for the election of John Curry.[53] When in April, 1929, the United States Supreme Court ruled for the city and against the IRT in its suit to raise the five-cent subway fare, a decision which won much good will for the administration, Walker's renomination was assured.[54]

As for the anti-machine forces, some individuals in the early part of 1929 took steps in the direction of a fusion movement. William M. Chadbourne, a lawyer and a Republican who had been conspicuous in the Mitchel elections of 1913 and 1917, was in the center of this activity. Chadbourne and other veterans of past reform movements advocated a bill which would substitute a city convention for the direct primaries in New York with regard to the nomination of Mayor and other elective city and borough officers.[55] The reformers had been sour on the primary system since 1917, when Mitchel had lost the Republican primary. Chadbourne and the others felt that the big leaders of the Republican Party were more responsive to public opinion than the party workers who did most of the voting in the primaries and that a city convention at which independents could negotiate directly with the leaders would make it easier to obtain a fusion ticket containing good candidates.[56] Chadbourne also sponsored a luncheon for members of the 1913 Mitchel Fusion Committee of One Hundred and Seven for the purpose of laying the groundwork for fusion in 1929.[57]

But these efforts got no place. Though the legislature passed the city convention bill, Governor Franklin D. Roosevelt vetoed it, claiming that the bill singled out New York City from the rest of the state for special treatment and that, anyhow, direct primaries were more democratic.[58] More important is what happened to Chadbourne's attempt to start a fusion group going. Joseph M. Price, chairman of the Committee of One Hundred and Seven in 1913 and an independent Democrat, refused to attend the meeting; and his attitude may well explain why only eighteen out of sixty-four people invited showed up, for it seems likely that his view was shared by other independent Democrats. Price hoped that Al Smith would run for Mayor, or that, barring that, the former Governor would back an independent Democrat for the office, and he feared that he might jeopardize this opportunity by allowing Republicans like Chadbourne to assume the leadership in a fusion movement.[59] Consequently

Chadbourne did not initiate anything. The actions of the independent Democrats in 1929 are puzzling. Chadbourne had not set himself against an independent Democrat for Mayor. Besides, even later, in the spring, when the important leaders of the Republican organization in the city came out for a fusion movement and appeared willing to take an independent Democrat, the independent Democrats still held back.[60] Perhaps they never joined because they waited, until it was too late, for some signal from Smith. One point, however, is clear. In 1929, a number of people did not so desperately want a change in the city administration that they were willing to relegate other considerations to the background and somehow find a way; many people acted as if they could afford the luxury of being uncompromising.

So the Republicans went ahead and nominated their own ticket which they called a fusion—because the candidate for President of the Board of Aldermen, Bird S. Coler, had once been a Democratic Comptroller—but which was nothing of the sort. At an unofficial city convention, they selected Fiorello H. La Guardia, popular congressman from East Harlem, political maverick and pepper-pot, as their mayoral candidate. First elected to Congress in 1916 on the Republican ticket from the heavily Democratic Fourteenth Congressional District, La Guardia had been re-elected in 1918 and a year later, in the time of Hylan, had won a special election for President of the Board of Aldermen, an unusual feat for a Republican candidate. Returned to the House in 1922, this time from the Twentieth Congressional District, La Guardia had been continually re-elected. In Congress he had become nationally known as a vociferous champion of progressive causes.[61] Conservative Republicans did not approve of La Guardia, considering him opportunistic, radical, unstable and demagogic, but he received the nomination anyway chiefly because he was determined to be the candidate and threatened a costly primary fight if the convention refused to designate him. His opposition crumbled away for it could not find someone willing to go to the trouble and assume the expense of fighting him. Besides, as strange as it may seem from a later day, the rank and file of Republican Party professionals regarded him with favor.[62]

If anybody had a chance of beating Jimmy Walker, La Guardia did. The congressman, short, swarthy, with fiery dark eyes and black hair, was a scrapper and a showman; he gave the appearance of possessing inexhaustible energy. Like Walker, La Guardia had a warm heart and was master of the crushing retort. A man of the people who spoke the language of the sidewalks of New York, he was a representative of a large Italian minority group yearning for political expression and had many friends among the Jews.[63] Yet he never received adequate support from many elements that one would expect to be fervently on his side. Instead they deplored his "unfitness" for the office. The Citizens Union executive committee called La Guardia an opportunist, declaring that when President of the Board of Aldermen, "he encouraged and echoed Hylan in the output of cheap clap-trap and blatant demagogy that passed for declarations of policy, his voice at times drowning out Hylan's own"; it declared Norman Thomas, the Socialist, the best-qualified candidate for Mayor.[64] Members of the City Club were also cool to La Guardia.[65] The *New York Times,* traditionally anti-Tammany, did not know which candidate to support in a "campaign of dilemmas." [66] The *Evening Post* and the *Herald Tribune* came out for La Guardia, but only after long periods of suffering. The *New York World* refused to support either Walker or La Guardia, but added that if Walker's victory were not inevitable, if the election were really in doubt, it would support Walker, "for the old-time Tammany with all its sins is preferable to the kind of thing which Major La Guardia represents." [67]

La Guardia fought a vigorous campaign. He pounded Walker's admin- istration with charges of graft and misgovernment, some old and some new. He blasted the administration's failure to solve the year-old murder of Arnold Rothstein, the notorious gambler, implying that the failure was due to fear of an exposure of the murdered man's dealings with officials of the government. La Guardia charged that Magistrate Albert H. Vitale had borrowed $20,000 from Rothstein, and outlined a positive program of reform for the city which in a number of respects was very similar to what he was to advocate at a later time. History was shortly to vindicate La Guardia's attack upon Walker's administration; but in 1929 he lacked a bill of particulars, and the charge of "recklessness" that was consequently leveled against La Guardia did not help his cause.[68]

It is probable that had La Guardia been able to document his charges better, it would not have made much difference. As it happened, nothing could touch the popular Jimmy. Walker only ridiculed the charges of graft hurled at his administration and proudly took his stand on his record. He claimed credit for huge school expenditures, park improvements, the "sound" financial condition of the city and, with the straightest face, the cleanup of graft in the Health and Street Cleaning departments.[69] His atti- tude toward the campaign was almost casual; plainly he regarded it as dull.[70] One night during the race, he paid a visit to Tammany Hall and pledged his loyalty to Tammany and its new boss in these terms: "I am the candidate of Tammany Hall and if elected I will be a Tammany Hall Mayor. I never was a charlatan or a faker and I won't be one in politics. Tammany Hall is assisting me and when re-elected I will take my leader- ship and advice from John F. Curry." [71] The voters left no doubt as to their decision. They gave Walker 867,522 votes to La Guardia's 367,675 and more votes than those of all his rivals combined.[72]

4

Investigations and disclosures

EVEN BEFORE THE ELECTION, however, certain events had been set in motion which were destined to shatter Tammany's supremacy. Two weeks before the voters went to the polls, the stock market collapsed. In February, 1929, the City Trust Company, which had been tottering, finally fell, sweeping away the savings of 16,000 depositors, mainly small wage earners. A subsequent inquiry showed that the State Banking Commissioner had accepted about $100,000 in bribes for allowing the enterprise to continue to run, although it was insolvent. Implicated also was General Sessions Judge Francis X. Mancuso, a Tammany stalwart, who had been chairman of the bank's board of directors. The Bar Association of New York began an investigation of the judge's conduct, but before the report could be given to the Governor, Mancuso resigned from the bench. Under pressure, the sixty-nine-year-old Tammany District Attorney, former Supreme Court Justice Thomas C. T. Crain, obtained an indictment against Mancuso, but he was eventually acquitted.[1]

Hard upon the Mancuso affair came the case of Magistrate Albert H. Vitale. La Guardia's charge, made in the fall of 1929, that Vitale had borrowed money from Arnold Rothstein first brought the magistrate under public scrutiny. Then in December, 1929, an incident occurred which dramatized Vitale's connection with underworld characters. The magistrate was guest of honor at a dinner of the Tepicano Democratic Club, of which he was honorary president for life. Some of the diners had police records; chief among them was the notorious Ciro Terranova, called the Artichoke King because of his grip on the artichoke business. Suddenly in the midst of the festivities, masked men, guns in hand, appeared and held up the diners. A detective who was present surrendered his revolver without resistance. The rudeness of the uninvited guests brought the dinner to an end, and Vitale hurried to the clubhouse. Within two hours, he personally returned the detective's gun to him without any explanation as to where he got it. Money and jewelry taken at the holdup were also returned.[2] The motive for the incident is not clear, though the police at the time claimed that the whole thing was the work of Terranova, who used it to recover a certain "murder contract" from one of the guests.[3] The Vitale dinner caused the Bar Association to petition the Appellate Division of the Supreme Court for the magistrate's removal. Early in 1930, after trying Vitale, the Court complied, pointing to the Rothstein loan as sufficient reason. Obviously Vitale was too closely associated with the underworld for any judge. Also brought out in the trial was the curious fact that in four years on the bench, the magistrate had accumulated $165,000, although his total salary during the same period came to only $48,000.[4]

From other quarters in the early part of 1930 came further discoveries. Charles Tuttle, United States District Attorney, began to investigate the income tax returns of certain individuals and to look into some possible mail fraud cases. One person whose income tax returns Tuttle became interested in was Dr. William F. Doyle, a veterinarian, who argued cases before the Board of Standards and Appeals, the agency which had power to permit deviations from zoning and building regulations. Doyle had been extraordinarily successful as a practitioner before the Board; over a nine-year period he had deposited more than $1,000,000. During the course of Tuttle's investigation, Doyle admitted that he split his fees, but he refused to say with whom. Tuttle also made the discovery that William E. Walsh, chairman of the Board of Standards and Appeals, had taken a gratuity; he had accepted a $4,000 apartment for $1,500. The information pertaining to Doyle and Walsh, Tuttle turned over to District Attorney Crain, who for one reason or another was not successful in bringing either man to justice. The disclosures, however, encouraged others, at a later time, to consider the Board of Standards and Appeals more closely and, as we shall see, this examination was not without reward.[5]

Of more immediate importance was what Tuttle found out about Kings County Judge Bernard Vause and Magistrate George F. Ewald. Vause had been president of the Brooklyn Democratic Club at the time of his appointment. He was a good after-dinner speaker, an opponent of easy punishments and a foe of "gross materialism." Tuttle revealed that the judge had lent the influence of his position to help promote a fraudulent bank, the Columbia Finance Corporation, which fleeced thousands of small investors; and Tuttle had Vause indicted on the charge of using the mails to defraud. Vause also was found to have received a fee estimated as high as $190,000 for "negotiations" which gave the United American Lines certain pier leases, a revelation which marked the beginning of some startling discoveries respecting the granting of pier leases. The judge was convicted on the mail fraud charge and sentenced to six years in Atlanta.[6]

Magistrate George Ewald, Vitale's successor, was accused of selling fraudulent stock, and some of it to certain people in his court whose cases had been treated leniently. Tuttle also had Ewald indicted for mail fraud. In the course of this inquiry, the federal district attorney came across evidence that Ewald had bought his position; this new matter quickly overshadowed that of mail fraud. More specifically, it was charged that about the time Ewald was appointed to the bench his wife gave $10,000 to Martin J. Healy, a district leader, through Thomas T. Tommaney, a clerk in the office of the Sheriff of New York County. Tuttle turned this evidence over to Crain. Crain investigated, but made no recommendation to the grand jury, and it refused to indict.[7] The judgeship-buying charge, however, was too explosive to be brushed aside. On August 19 Governor Franklin Roosevelt ordered Republican Attorney General Hamilton Ward to supersede Crain in the Ewald investigation and present his evidence before an extraordinary grand jury.[8] Eventually Healy, Tommaney, Ewald and his wife were indicted on the charge of purchasing and selling public office, but on three different occasions the jury could not agree on a verdict and the indictments were finally dropped.[9] Ewald, incidentally, was not convicted on the charge of mail fraud, the jury in the case also disagreeing on the verdict.[10]

More important than the Ward inquiry was another development which resulted from the Ewald office-buying charge. Segments of the press and the public were thundering for a more thorough probe of the courts. Mancuso, Vitale, Vause, Ewald—too much dirt had been turned up.[11] Under pressure, Roosevelt, on August 21, asked the Appellate Division to investigate the Magistrates' Courts in Manhattan and the Bronx. A few days later, the court ordered the investigation. It appointed as its referee Samuel Seabury who, in turn, named Isidore J. Kresel as special counsel.[12] The first of three famous Seabury investigations was about to get under way.

Samuel Seabury's roots went deep into the past of the city and the nation. He was a direct descendent of the Priscilla-John Alden marriage and of the Reverend Samuel Seabury who became the first Protestant Episcopal bishop in the United States. His grandfather, also called Samuel Seabury, had married a granddaughter of Samuel Jones, "the Father of the New York Bar" and a New York State statesman. Samuel Seabury's father had been an eminent rector in the city and a professor of canon law at the General Theological Seminary. The prominence of the Seabury family was based, not upon wealth, but upon its lineage and achievements.[13]

Seabury was an early bloomer. He graduated from law school at twenty and published a manual on corporation law. At twenty-eight he entered public life by being elected a judge of the City Court. When he was thirty-one he was talked about seriously for Mayor. In 1906, at the age of thirty-three, he became a state supreme court justice. He proved to be a good judge and a glutton for work. In 1913 he ran for the Court of Appeals on the Bull Moose ticket and lost, but he received a big vote and the following year, backed by Democrats and Progressives, he was overwhelmingly elected. The Democrats nominated him for Governor in 1916, but he went down to defeat when Theodore Roosevelt and his Progressives supported Charles Whitman, the Republican candidate, in an effort to help defeat Woodrow Wilson. After that Seabury retired from public life and devoted himself to the practice of law. From this obscurity, the Appellate Divison extracted him in the summer of 1930 when it summoned him to play his most important role.[14]

Few men have been more dedicated to the perpetuation of democracy than Seabury. That is not to say that he was without ambition or did not at times consider his interests. He was human. But more than in most men, idealism played an active part in his life. He had imbibed it in his early years when he listened to the churchmen talking in his father's study and, later, when he read Henry George and was so impressed that he went to see him.[15] To Seabury, democracy meant, among other things, social justice. As a lawyer and a judge, he had championed the causes of the underdog. Throughout its fifteen-year fight in New York, no one had been a more staunch supporter of the principle of employers' liability for workers injured in the line of duty. On the bench, Seabury had upheld the conception of "human rights" as opposed to "liberty of contract." [16]

Democracy to Seabury also meant eternal war against machine rule in New York City. An independent Democrat, he had associated himself with civic activities in the city and had fought Tammany consistently. In 1894 he worked against the machine ticket. He joined a Good Government Club and, when the Citizens Union was formed, accepted the duty of organizing the old Ninth Assembly District. Seabury fought for Low's victory in 1901 and was elected to the City Court on the Fusion ticket in that year. An enthusiast for municipal ownership in those days, he helped to form Hearst's Municipal Ownership League, from which he worked for the publisher's election in 1905. At the time of Seabury's appointment as referee, he was a member of the City Club.[17]

Scrupulous, diligent, thorough, erudite in the law, Seabury was respected as few men were in New York City. His very appearance was imposing. Tall, heavy-set, with the ruddy color of the Briton in his face and beautiful white hair which he combed straight back and parted in the middle, he carried himself with a Jove-like bearing that would have been presumptuous in a lesser man; no one would ever have dreamed of calling him Sam. Seabury was of that type who will not compromise with principle, who takes his stand fervently on the side of morality and righteousness and is convinced he knows what these words mean.[18] Not always have such men given mankind the greatest happiness, but in New York City in 1930 few would argue that such a man was not needed. No single

person was more important in the story of the New York reform movement of the 1930's.

Special Counsel Isidore Kresel, a brilliant lawyer, came from a different
world from that of Seabury. A Jewish immigrant born in Galicia, he was
raised on the lower East Side, where his mother worked in a sweatshop
to support him. An admirable student, Kresel skipped three elementary
grades and then won Pulitzer scholarships to the very special Horace Mann
School and to Columbia University. So impressive were his scholastic
achievements that he attracted the attention of several important people.
One of these was Seth Low, who got him a position as an Assistant District
Attorney under Jerome after Kresel had been admitted to the Bar. When
Jerome retired to private law practice, he took the young immigrant along
as one of his partners, and Kresel made his fortune. Unlike most Americans, particularly of the immigrant generation, Kresel repeatedly put
aside his own affairs to serve the public.[19]

In the history of the Seabury investigations Kresel was extremely important. Although he left the scene of the first investigation before it was over,
he influenced all of them because he created the method which was carried on by others. He did not rely upon confessions, but based his investigations on records and facts. Bank accounts, income tax returns, leases,
brokerage accounts and their like could not be denied; they could only be
explained. It was a "scientific" approach in which no details were overlooked, in which the research on the part of the investigators was pains-
taking.[20]

The investigation into the Magistrates' Courts started slowly. On September 29 Kresel began to take testimony in private, and he continued
to do this throughout October and most of November. Then the volcano
erupted. On November 24, 25, and 26 he held his first public hearings
before Referee Seabury. In three days, he piled up solid evidence showing
that in the Women's Court, a special Magistrates' Court, an infamous ring
of policemen, bondsmen, lawyers and an Assistant District Attorney was
involved in a system of corruption based on extortion from women, most
of whom were prostitutes. The ring operated this way: policemen, members of the Vice Squad, often with the aid of stool pigeons who acted as
agents provocateurs, would inveigle a prostitute into compromising herself
by accepting marked money. Then the police would arrest her and charge
her with prostitution. If the arrested prostitute had no money or decided to
accept punishment, the police would at worst get credit for another arrest.
If she had money and did not want to go to jail, she would accept the help
of a bondsman and a lawyer in the ring, who would bleed her plenty for
their services. The bondsman was the pay-off man who would collect from
the victims and divide the proceeds among the lawyers and the police.
The lawyers and bondsmen would take care of the prosecutor. When the
case would come to court, the defendant would plead not guilty, the
policeman who made the arrest would change his testimony on an essen-

tial point, the prosecutor would weaken his case, and the defendant would be discharged. John C. Weston, the prosecutor in the Women's Court, had collected $20,000 in graft over a period of years for failing to push 600 vice cases involving 900 defendants. More sordid yet was the disclosure that the police and stool pigeons also framed completely innocent women and put them through the mill. Who would accept the word of a defendant as against that of an officer of the law? The investigation showed that certain members of the Vice Squad had grown wealthy and, to believe some of their stories, in remarkable ways.[21]

Hordes of bondsmen and lawyers, it was also discovered, infested other Magistrates' Courts, where they solicited business and did their best to bilk any victim that fell into their hands. Sometimes lawyers worked in collusion with court clerks to have their clients freed. This was possible because of the great influence that the clerks enjoyed. If the court clerk sent a special form to the magistrate, advising him that he had heard the facts in the case and in his opinion did not feel that the drawing of a full complaint was warranted, the magistrate would invariably agree, and the case would be dismissed.[22]

While investigators were unable to prove that any of the magistrates were corrupt, they did succeed in revealing some deplorable behavior. Magistrate Francis X. McQuade was found to have been engaged in a number of business activities, one of which involved the holding of a financial interest in a gambling room. On the morning of his public examination McQuade resigned. Magistrates George Washington Simpson and Henry M. R. Goodman also resigned while their affairs were under scrutiny. Magistrate Louis B. Brodsky testified that he had received his job from his district leader in recognition for his years of party service. He was charged mainly with having speculated on margin in the market and having engaged in many real estate transactions after his appointment. Seabury recommended to the Appellate Division that Brodsky be removed, but although a statute forbade a judge to be engaged in business, the court, with that uncanny insight which comes to men after years in the legal profession, held that Magistrate Brodsky was not "doing business" within the meaning of the statute and refused to remove him.[23]

Two magistrates, Jean H. Norris and Jesse Silbermann, were removed from the bench upon Seabury's recommendation, however. Both had presided for long periods in the Women's Court, but it was not because of the vice ring that they were removed. One would suppose that a judge with even a modicum of intelligence could catch on to what was taking place in his court, especially when glaring instances of perjury abounded and when, as in the case of Silbermann, the magistrate had the advantage of being a close friend of the prosecutor and one of the corrupt lawyers; but complicity could not be shown. Jean Norris, Manhattan's only woman magistrate, was found to be unfit because she callously disregarded the rights of the defendants, distorted the court records so that the higher courts would not find out, held stock in a bonding company whose bonds she was called upon to review and lowered the dignity of the judicial office by endorsing for money a commercial product (Fleischmann's Yeast). Silbermann, who testified that he was appointed to the bench because the Mayor had decided to appoint a Jew from the Bronx, was declared unfit because he decided cases unfairly from considerations outside the record. One such consideration was politics. Silbermann's district leader, James W. Brown, thought the court a wonderful place to enroll Democrats and for this purpose interceded in behalf of prisoners.[24]

The Magistrates' Courts investigation which began in 1930 continued intermittently into the summer of 1931, but Seabury's final report on the investigation was not filed with the Appellate Division until March, 1932. In it he not only reviewed much of what the investigators had found, but advanced certain proposals which he thought would improve the Courts.[25]

The general situation in the Magistrates' Courts disclosed by the Seabury and preceding investigations hardly constituted a new development in New York and was not something of which most people were totally unaware. But the specific disclosures spotlighted the conditions and educated the public as only concrete cases can do. The central fact that the investigations brought out, and which people had tended to forget, was that the lower judiciary was part of the machine system. A man was appointed to the bench, people were once again reminded, not because he was learned in the law or possessed other qualifications a judge is supposed to have, but because he was a party worker. There were indications that the payment of money was in some cases an additional requirement, though the Seabury investigators did not uncover any further evidence of office-buying, and the case against Ewald was never legally proved. Many judges, it was noticed, did not have the faintest conception of judicial dignity or judicial temperament; a number were connected with fast-buck, questionable enterprises of one sort or another; some associated with gamblers and underworld characters; some judged cases with obvious bias. Once in office, the judges, it was evident, did not forget that they were parts of a system. For one thing, they did not ignore the wishes of their district leaders. True, the Silbermann-Brown relationship, documented in black and white, was but one case; but no one was naive enough to believe it was the only one. A later Seabury investigation was to throw more light upon the influence of district leaders in the courts. Secondly, though the magistrates might not actively participate in the schemes of the little people around the bench, they at least shut their eyes to their activities.

The investigators showed, furthermore, that the judiciary was not the only branch of government involved in corruption. An Assistant District Attorney and members of the Police Department, parts of the law-enforcing arm, stood exposed as grafters and worse. It is hardly possible that before the Vice Squad revelations people were completely ignorant of police graft and brutality; there was plenty of it.[26] But the Seabury court disclosures were unusually instructive and they hit home; for the first time in years, people became really aware of police evils.

The Magistrates' Courts scandals, especially those dealing with the Women's Court, led to tremendous demands for further investigations of the city government, and in March, 1931, even before the court inquiry was over, there came into being two new investigations, in each of which Samuel Seabury played a major part. One was an investigation of District Attorney Crain, the other was a traditional city-wide inquiry by a committee of the state legislature. On March 10 Governor Roosevelt appointed Seabury as his commissioner to investigate and report on charges filed against Crain by the City Club. The gist of the charges was that the District Attorney had failed to properly discharge his duties and had shown general incompetency in office; the City Club asked the Governor to remove Crain. Seabury named as counsel John Kirkland Clark, an outstanding member of the New York Bar who had served between 1910 and 1914 as an Assistant District Attorney under Charles Whitman. The investigation took place in April and May, but Seabury did not present his report to the Governor until the last day of August. During the spring and summer of 1931, Seabury was involved in three simultaneous investigations and was obviously a busy man.[27]

It was not surprising that the court probe should encourage an inquiry of Crain, for Weston's behavior had raised grave doubts about the District Attorney's office. These doubts did not stem entirely from the Weston disclosures, however. There had been a growing feeling ever since Crain's election in 1929 that he was not doing his job; the exposure of conditions in the Women's Court, together with certain connecting events, only brought matters to a head. Crain's record was certainly poor. He campaigned upon the promise of solving the Rothstein murder within fifteen days of taking office, but more than a year after he became District Attorney, the mystery was still unsolved. In the City Trust case involving Judge Mancuso, Crain dragged his feet until he was forced to act and finally lost the case. As we have seen, he was singularly ineffective in the Ewald-Healy affair and against Doyle, he failed to prove anything conclusive. Early in 1930, Crain undertook a grand jury investigation of the Magistrates' Courts and found nothing. He dallied in bringing to justice men accused of stock fraud and admitted his inability to effectively curb racketeering, of which there was a good deal. Many of these failures were reflected in the charges against him.[28] Undoubtedly there were those who suspected the worst.

The investigation found that in the matter of racketeering in New York, particularly with respect to the Fulton Fish Market and the millinery industry, Crain had been decidedly incompetent. Before a grand jury looking into racketeering Crain had failed to ask the chief witness the essential question of whether or not he had paid money for protection in the Fulton Fish Market; and Seabury, with more limited power, showed what Crain never did, that there was a regular series of payments to racketeers in the Fulton Fish Market. Crain had failed to prosecute the millinery racketeers on the excusable grounds that witnesses would not testify; but despite this obstacle, Seabury obtained witnesses who testified that they paid as high as $100 a month for protection. The District Attorney had fallen down in other ways. His activities against Doyle, it came out, consisted of writing letters requesting the veterinarian to waive immunity and testify; Doyle refused, and the matter was dropped. Stock fraud cases were allowed to slumber in the District Attorney's office, apparently because the cases were intricate and the papers voluminous.[29]

All in all, what had already been generally felt was now clearly documented: Crain's record was marked by inefficiency and incompetency. Corruption could not be shown. Still those who had preferred charges against Crain had asked that he be removed for incompetency. After wrestling with his conscience, Seabury decided against it. He felt that except where the incompetency had been so general in scope and so gross in character as to require removal, the people's elected officials should not be removed.[30] This is sound democratic doctrine; but after noting Crain's record, one wonders exactly how much more incompetent he was entitled to become before Seabury would allow him into the ranks of the thoroughly incompetent. Roosevelt accepted his commissioner's recommendation and dismissed the charges against the District Attorney.[31]

While the Crain investigation uncovered no evidence that the District Attorney was venal or that he had connived to help others cheat justice, it was not without significance. It served to underscore the miserable way the office was being run. Many doubtlessly were made to wonder why an elderly man like Crain should have been selected for a position requiring an exceptional amount of vigor and assiduity. Furthermore, the inquiry helped to give the public a better insight into racketeering in New York and to call to public attention the fact that, well-meaning or not, the District Attorney was doing little about eradicating racketeering.

The most thorough-going inquiry in this period was that undertaken by a Republican-dominated joint committee of the state legislature composed of twelve senators and assemblymen and headed by Senator Samuel H. Hofstadter. Its aim was to uncover corruption in the city government wherever it could find it. Seabury, who was referee for the Appellate Division and Governor's commissioner, also became counsel to the Hofstadter committee. The legislature voted the investigation on March 23, 1931, but it did not really begin to move until after the Silbermann case was settled early in July. On July 21 the first public hearings were held, and these continued intermittently until December, 1932, when the counsel and committee drew up reports and went out of business.[32]

Around him Seabury gathered a group of bright young lawyers who had not had time to become conservative. They were eager to work under him and ready and willing to undertake the dry-as-dust examination of records that was necessary. Phillip W. Haberman, Jr., who had been one of the group, recalls that they were a nervy bunch and did things to get the facts that he would blush to do today; then, however, it was all for the cause. A number of them had taken part in one or both of the other Seabury investigations. Between Seabury and the young bulls there existed complete frankness and devotion.[33]

Believing that a complete exposure of the city's corruptness would take almost a decade, Seabury set himself to painting an impressionistic picture of the government by showing that venality existed in any department into which he cared to delve. While concerned with the district leaders and the minor officials, he kept his eyes on the bigger boys, and his ultimate strategy was to try to implicate Walker himself.[34]

The work of the committee was not made easy by the attitude and antics of the city's Democrats. They were naturally opposed to any inquiry which might cause Tammany and its political allies embarrassment and went all-out to thwart the investigation in one way or another. John F. Curry made no secret of the fact that he was interested in challenging the committee's power. Walker ridiculed it and declared that its members sought only self-glorification. The Democrats in the legislature fought to prevent a prolongation of the committee's life in January, 1932. Assemblyman Louis Cuvillier and Senator John J. McNaboe, two of the committee's four minority members, tried to sabotage the investigation whenever they could.[35] Yet despite the roadblocks, the investigators could not be derailed.

Their efforts were rewarded. On the level of the district leaders and the run-of-the-mill politicians, they discovered that some of the boys had not kept themselves clean. According to reliable testimony, Thomas M. Farley, Sheriff of New York County, Michael J. Cruise, City Clerk, Harry Perry, Chief Clerk of the City Court of New York, and James A. McQuade, Register of Kings County, all district leaders, had been protecting professional gamblers, allowing them, moreover, to operate their games in their clubhouses. Undoubtedly political protection of this sort was the real reason for the startling fact, brought out by the investigators, that out of 514 persons arrested in gambling raids in 1926 and 1927, only 5 were held for the Court of Special Sessions. Farley, Cruise, Perry and McQuade had accumulated an amazing amount of wealth within a relatively short time for men with small salaries, and their explanations for their rapid material progress were equally amazing. Sheriff Farley was finally removed from office by the Governor because his story that his bank deposits of over $360,000 came mostly from "a wonderful tin box" which he kept in his home somehow left too much to the imagination. The connection between the underworld, the district leaders and the courts now became clearer.[36]

Other minor officials also had much to explain. James J. McCormick,

Deputy City Clerk, was another who had an income beyond what one could expect from his salary. It was brought out that William J. Flynn, the Commissioner of Public Works in the Bronx, had used his official position to profit from certain land transactions; his activities so impaired the financial situation of Louis H. Willard, a rival, that Willard's wife committed suicide. One of the most interesting disclosures was that Democratic politicians, the eternal friends of the poor, had used the $10,000,000 relief fund appropriated by the city in 1931 as a campaign fund to reward deserving party members, thus depriving of relief many who really needed it.[37]

The most spectacular scandals that developed out of the Hofstadter inquiry dealt with the granting of permits, leases and franchises by the city. Seabury, remembering Tuttle's discoveries with regard to Doyle, Walsh and Vause, investigated city departments and bureaus possessing discretionary power to grant privileges. High on the list of agencies to be examined, of course, was the Board of Standards and Appeals. Seabury was able to do nothing with Doyle, who refused to co-operate with the committee, but Seabury's inspection of the Board of Standards and Appeals was not in vain. He found that during the years when George Olvany was head of the New Tammany, his law firm, Olvany, Eisner and Donnelly, made huge sums by taking an interest in certain cases pending before the Board. The firm did not handle these cases openly but used an intermediary lawyer who appeared in the official record. When the appeal was granted—and somehow it usually was when Olvany, Eisner and Donnelly were involved—the official practitioner would turn over the lion's share of the fee to the Olvany firm, practically always in the form of cash or cashier checks. Not all of the payments made to the firm went into the firm account; payments as high as $20,000 went into the individual account of one partner or the other. Olvany admitted that he sometimes talked to Chairman Walsh about cases, but only those already decided, or those in which he had no interest. When asked to produce his books and records, the former Tammany boss called attention to the fact that he was forbidden by law to do so unless his clients would sign a waiver of their privilege of having their affairs kept secret; but when pressed on this point, he admitted that he had not asked them to sign such a waiver. One of his partners, James F. Donnelly, testified that other records had been destroyed in 1928 when the firm had been reorganized. Nothing illegal could be proved against Olvany or his partners.[38]

It had been revealed in the Vause case that a steamship company had paid politicians to lease city piers. The Hofstadter investigation showed that the incident was not unique. Apparently Tammany had a policy of putting the squeeze on the companies. The North German Lloyd Lines, desperately in need of a pier, was kept dangling from about 1922 to 1930 until a $50,000 check was paid to William H. Hickin, president of the National Democratic Club, as a "lawyer's fee." Hickin deposited the check and shortly withdrew $45,000 in cash which promptly disappeared. There was little doubt that he had passed the money on to higher-ups—but who? Hickin could not be made to say.[39]

Playing a searchlight upon bus franchises granted by the city, the Hofstadter committee came upon some startling matters. It found, for one thing, that Borough President Lynch of Richmond had used his influence to obtain a franchise in his borough for the Thompkins Bus Company, owned by his intimate friend, Minthorne T. Gordon, although a rival, the Staten Island Coach Company, was a stronger firm and offered the city better terms. The franchise was granted on July 27, 1928. A week before this date, according to testimony, Gordon amply demonstrated his friendship for Lynch: he took over a newspaper in which Lynch was losing money and agreed to run it. Gordon also agreed to support the Borough President politically for which purpose he gave Lynch a $30,000 note.[40]

More startling was the information uncovered about the Equitable Coach Company, for its efforts to obtain a city-wide bus franchise cast a shadow on Mayor Walker himself. Senator John A. Hastings, one of Walker's intimate friends since his Albany days, organized the company along with a few other people in 1925. The senator owned a stock interest in the company and also drew, at first $1,000, and later $1,500 a month, from the company payroll for his services as a political contact man. Though the company was unknown and gave no real evidence of having the necessary capital to run buses, though another, and sounder, company gave the city superior terms in its application for a franchise, Walker, in July, 1927, jammed the Equitable Coach franchise through the Board of Estimate and subsequently tried to find financial backing for the company and help it in other ways. That in the end the franchise had to be cancelled because the company could not obtain financial support was not due to lack of effort on the Mayor's part. A day or so after Walker signed the franchise, he sailed for Europe with a $10,000 letter of credit bought for him by J. Allan Smith, the Equitable Coach's New York representative. Walker denied the implication that he had been bribed. He claimed that the letter of credit was for the benefit of members of his traveling party as well as himself; that all of them, for the purpose of paying for the letter, had made cash contributions to a common fund, his own share being $3,000; and that he never benefited beyond this amount. Why Smith should have bought the letter of credit is not clear. Smith testified that when he found out about the Walker trip he asked Hastings to be permitted to buy the letter so as to throw some business to the Equitable Trust Company, whose president was a friend of his. Smith said he received the $10,000 from Hastings; Hastings said he received it in turn from the late Senator Bernard Downing, a member of the party. Both Walker and Hastings admitted that they had frequent talks about the Equitable franchise before it was granted, but both of them deprecated the senator's usefulness in determining the outcome.[41]

The Hofstadter investigation had, indeed, brought in Walker, and this was not the half of it. It came out that J. A. Sisto, an investment banker heavily interested in one of the city's big taxicab companies, sent Walker $26,000 worth of bonds which represented the Mayor's profits in a stock transaction in which Walker had not invested any of his own money. It was pointed out that after the bonds were given, a Taxicab Control Board was set up whose practical effect was to limit entry into the taxi business —a definite advantage for the big companies—and that Walker had favored the law. Walker explained that the $26,000 in bonds were legitimate business profits, that although he put up no money and signed no commitment, he would have paid his share of the loss had there been any. He declared that, despite the legislation, no limitation had ever been imposed on cabs and called attention to the fact that, after receiving the bonds from Sisto, he had vetoed a bill which would have raised taxi fares.[42]

Ten of the bonds whose par value was $10,000 were debenture bonds of the Reliance Bronze and Steel Corporation, convertible into stock at the option of the holder. In 1931 this corporation received a $43,000 contract for traffic light standards on Fifth Avenue. The City Charter specified that a city official could be removed if found guilty of owning stock in a corporation doing work for the city. The Mayor said he had given the bonds to Mrs. Walker and that he was unaware of this contract.[43]

Paul Block, a newspaper publisher, was another one who enabled Walker to make stock profits without investing a dollar. He opened a joint brokerage account with the Mayor in 1927, and before it was closed in 1929, Walker made $246,000. Block said his only reason for doing this was his concern that the Mayor could not adequately live on his $25,000 a year salary, and no real evidence was produced to prove that there was any other reason. As in the case of the Sisto profits, Walker claimed that though he had made no contribution and signed no written agreement, he had agreed to make losses good.[44]

Then there was the matter of Russell T. Sherwood. From the early days of the Hofstadter inquiry, Seabury was unable to get Sherwood to appear before the committee. He avoided subpoenas with remarkable agility. First he went to Atlantic City; discovered there, he next turned up in Chicago; then in Mexico City, where he was married. Served there with an order of the Supreme Court of the State of New York requiring his attendance as a witness before the committee, he disobeyed, was adjudged in contempt by the court and fined $50,000. Sherwood was Walker's financial agent who made deposits and payments for him. Prior to the Mayor's election Sherwood had been a clerk in Walker's law office, where he had received $3,000 a year; in 1930 he took a bank job at $10,000 annually. From January 1, 1926, until the time he began his perigrinations, it was shown that Sherwood deposited almost $1,000,000 in several banks and brokerage accounts and more than $700,000 was in cash.[45]

The Mayor, incidentally, was not the only member of the Walker family to find himself in hot water as a result of the activities of the Hofstadter committee. The investigators discovered that the doctors who were given a monopoly of the city's workmen's compensation cases padded their bills and split their fees with Dr. William Walker, the Mayor's brother, though he had never been designated by the city to treat such cases.[46]

Seabury certainly had struck pay dirt. It was plain that Walker's foot had slipped. But to what extent? Was the Mayor guilty of accepting bribes? Legally the case for bribery was not conclusive. Walker unquestionably had accumulated huge sums of money, most of which he could not adequately explain. But did this involve the receiving of a recompense for official action? It is possible. The evidence presented, especially Sherwood's unusual behavior, is highly suggestive. But considering Walker's character there is another possibility. Walker appears to have been a happy-go-lucky, monetarily irresponsible individual rather than a scheming and grasping politician. He accepted gladly and unthinkingly money and gifts lavished upon him by his friends, a number of them wealthy men, and gave generously to other friends. Some of the rich men around him liked him for himself and expected nothing; others, like Block, wanted to bathe in his glamour.[47] Probably there were some who felt that for business reasons it would not hurt to become more friendly with the Mayor by doing him financial favors. For his part, Walker saw no reason why he should not accept his friends' liberality. Furthermore, he did not see why he should not use his position as Mayor to give his friends a hand when he could. It is this attitude rather than privilege selling which might explain the facts uncovered by the Seabury investigators. It is conceivable that it just never dawned on Walker that loose taking when coupled with favors to friends came perilously close to, and could easily be construed as, downright venality. Sherwood's mysterious actions and the vast sums he deposited do not prove that Walker took bribes. Perhaps Walker was afraid that if Sherwood were to testify he might disclose other examples of the Mayor's careless pecuniary habits which would do his cause more harm than good. In any case, whether or not he was personally dishonest, Walker's sin was big: he had betrayed his trust as Mayor.

Seabury's investigation of Walker before the Hofstadter committee—the climax of the investigation—took place on May 25 and 26, 1932. On June 8, he sent to Governor Roosevelt a statement of charges against the Mayor, accusing him of such malfeasance and nonfeasance "as to render him unfit to continue in the office of Mayor." Seabury, however, did not formally ask for Walker's removal, declaring that this decision was entirely up to the Governor. Roosevelt appointed two lawyers, Martin Conboy and J. E. Mack, to help him consider the charges and ordered Walker to answer them. The Mayor's reply contained a denial of any wrong-doing, a contention that many of the charges ought to be ruled out since they related to matters that occurred before he was re-elected and a counter-charge that the attack against him was motivated by political considerations. Beginning on August 11 and lasting for a number of days, Roosevelt held public hearings in the Executive Mansion on the charges filed against Walker. Once again the Mayor was examined, this time by the Governor personally. Roosevelt, who had recently become the Democratic candidate for President, was in a difficult political situation. If he removed Walker from office, he would alienate Tammany, which might seriously weaken his chance of winning New York State's important electoral votes. If he did not remove him, he would be accused of being weak and opportunistic which would also hurt his chances, and not just in New York. The eyes of the nation were on Albany. But Roosevelt was never forced to make a decision. On September 1, Jimmy Walker resigned as Mayor.[48]

It is possible to find fault with the Hofstadter investigation. While exposing some of the big fry, it was not able to do so in such a way as to lead to their conviction later, though one might argue that it did as well as it could have done. As is true of most such investigations in this country, the probers failed to show adequate interest in the bribe-givers. Yet whatever the shortcomings of the investigation, they were minor in comparison with its accomplishments. The inquiry filled in many gaps in the citizens' knowledge of Tammany rule. More light was thrown on the activities of district leaders and their relationship with the underworld, on one hand, and with the wheels of justice, on the other. Some politicians, it was seen, were making money by selling privileges and by extortion and in these practices had developed certain refinements; one was the use of an intermediary who was paid a "lawyer's fee." No investigation in the city's history, not even that conducted by the Lexow committee, probed so deeply or on so wide a front; no other single investigation during this period did so much to show the citizens the pervasiveness of corruption and looseness in the city government extending from the smallest politician to the Mayor himself.

One other investigation deserves brief mention. After an exposure of some malpractices in condemnation proceedings made by certain reform groups and Comptroller Charles W. Berry between 1927 and 1930, and after crusades by the *Evening Post* and *World-Telegram,* Walker, in the fall of 1930, found it advisable to have Leonard Wallstein designated special assistant corporation counsel to study the subject of condemning land in the city. Wallstein, a prominent New York lawyer, had been Mayor Mitchel's Commissioner of Accounts and was currently counsel for the Citizens Union.[49] His report on land condemnation issued early in 1932, after more than a year of investigation and study, pointed up wasteful methods and "honest graft." Statistical tables showed that on the average the city paid 67 per cent more than the assessed valuation of land it took, including interest in some cases. Unsalable land, it was disclosed, had been dumped on the city at fancy prices for the profit of politicians or other insiders. Organized groups of speculators had reaped large profits by buying up property shortly before the public announcement of its selection. A ring of sharp lawyers had established a practice of receiving advance tips from government insiders, soliciting trade from owners whose land was to be condemned on a percentage basis and winning huge amounts from indifferent judges and mildly protesting, perhaps conniving, representatives of the city. Wallstein linked Boss McCooey of Brooklyn with profit-making deals involving condemnation proceedings.[50] It might also be noted in this connection that the Hofstadter investigation brought out that the firm of Olvany, Eisner and Donnelly took an interest in condemnation cases and, in at least one case, found it quite remunerative.[51]

We have seen how between 1929 and 1932 the government of New York City was subjected to an intense scrutiny in the form of various investigations and what was revealed thereby. In the beginning, the investigations were limited in scope and the disclosures emerged in dribbles. Before long, the probes became broader, more systematic and more thorough; the trickles became a steady stream which turned into a flood. The scandals of the period had tremendous consequences for the city, and it is to these that we now turn.

5

Moving toward reform

THE SCANDALS of 1929–32 gave rise to one of the most powerful reform movements in New York's history. Where the scandals of the twenties had fallen on barren ground, the new scandals were more serious, their exposure was concentrated and the Mayor, himself, was involved. Taken as a whole, they convinced the people that the city government was shot through with corruption, incompetence, inefficiency and waste. This conviction, especially in the context of depression, stirred the civic conscience profoundly.

There can be no question that the depression which began in 1929 worked to encourage reform in New York as well as in other American cities. In the first place, it brought about a fundamental change in the national temper. Irritation, questioning and criticism replaced the complacency and indifference of the twenties; in the sphere of local government, the new mood scarcely disposed people to ignore or tolerate bad government. To some extent, the Depression also deflated the prestige of business values and made Americans more conscious of other values. Extremely important, moreover, was the fact that many citizens now financially hard-up regarded the money-making activities of politicians, not abstractly, but in a very personal way: they had been growing poor while politicians had been growing rich—and on their money!

In addition, in New York and some other places, the Depression, by producing a serious gap between expenditure and revenue, appeared to be pushing the government toward bankruptcy. Where this was true the local administration naturally came in for criticism. In New York's case, anyway, the criticism was not exactly unfair, for past machine practices and contemporary machine scandals played no little part in bringing the city to the brink of financial ruin. Briefly, New York's financial problem was this: During the twenties there had been a huge growth in the cost of city government and now, during the first years of depression, this cost continued to mount, in good part because of the need for relief expenditures. But at the same time as expenses were increasing, revenues were diminishing; many property owners could not pay their taxes; the amount of revenue derived from other sources—those listed under what is termed the General Fund—fell off because of the bad business conditions. The city, forced to borrow on the anticipation of tax collections, saw its temporary debt grow and at a time when conditions made the retirement of that debt impossible. Beginning in 1932, the high cost of government, the inadequate sources of revenue, the growing debt, along with the revelations of so much corruption and waste in the government, resulted in a loss of city credit. Some of the world's most famous bankers became reluctant to loan New York money for its current needs just when it was more than ever dependent upon borrowing since other sources of revenue were drying up. Through 1932 and 1933 the city was dangerously close to going under. In the end, it managed to stay afloat, but only at the price of an agreement with the bankers.[1]

The reform movement developed gradually in the period 1930–3. At first citizen resentment was voiced mainly, though not entirely, in nonpolitical terms. Later, in 1933, when an opportunity to overthrow Tammany presented itself and after the ground had been prepared in good part by the preceding nonpolitical activities, reform sentiment came to be expressed primarily in terms of politics.

The first rumblings of citizen discontent grew out of the Vitale dinner incident. It led to the investigation of the Magistrate by the New York Bar Association and his subsequent removal by the Appellate Division. Norman Thomas demanded a legislative investigation of the Magistrates' Courts, and Samuel Untermyer, prominent lawyer and Democratic statesman, endorsed the idea. Early in 1930 Republican leaders in the legislature, citing requests made upon that body for an investigation of the Magistrates' Courts, the unsolved Rothstein murder case and other alleged public scandals in New York City, pushed through a bill to investigate corruption in the city by creating a committee the members of which would be appointed by the Governor. This, however, was more a political move designed to embarrass Roosevelt in the coming gubernatorial election than the consequence of public pressure; and Roosevelt, equally foxy, vetoed it. The Ewald-Healy affair and Crain's failure to obtain an indictment from the grand jury created considerably more indignation. The Bar Association, Norman Thomas, Rabbi Stephen S. Wise of the Free Synagogue and others called on Roosevelt to investigate the Magistrates' Courts. The city's press put pressure on the Governor for action.[2] We have already noticed that as a result of the agitation the first Seabury investigation came into being.

As yet, however, indignation was neither widespread nor particularly strong, being limited to a handful of reformers and one or two newspapers. But in the fall of 1930 and the following winter, Kresel's disclosures of conditions in the Women's Court plus some additional drama changed the situation. The drama involved the murder of Vivian Gordon, on February 27, five days after she had become a witness in the vice inquiry, and the subsequent suicide a few days later of her fifteen-year-old daughter who had been appalled by the tragedy. The Women's Court scandals, even before the murder and suicide, were shocking many New Yorkers who had not been especially moved by the previous disclosures and were producing demands from different quarters for more thorough investigations. The Gordon affair staggered the city and set in motion the mobilization of the anti-Tammany forces.[3]

Civic organizations of all sorts, newspapers, churchmen, ordinary citizens, came up fighting. In early March the City Club, which had a long tradition of attacking Tammany district attorneys—it had brought charges against Croker's Asa Bird Gardiner in 1899 and Murphy's Edgar T. Swann in 1917—filed its charges against Crain which resulted in the second Seabury investigation. On March 17 a new reform group, the City Affairs Committee, organized in 1930 with the Reverend John Haynes Holmes as chairman, Rabbi Wise, Norman Thomas and John Dewey among the vice-chairmen and Paul Blanshard as executive director, filed charges with Governor Roosevelt in which it asked for Mayor Walker's removal. Though Roosevelt subsequently dismissed the charges, they helped to stimulate public discussion of civic conditions.[4]

Mostly, however, civic activity was directed toward obtaining a legislative investigation of New York City. The Citizens Union, the Society for the Prevention of Crime (the old Parkhurst society), the Board of Trade, the United Neighborhood Houses, a city federation of numerous settlements and neighborhood centers, and various women's organizations, like the Women's City Club, urged such an investigation strongly. So did a number of leading Protestant and Jewish religious leaders and their congregations; a subcommittee of the Greater New York Federation of Churches unanimously adopted a resolution calling for a thorough nonpartisan investigation. The *World-Telegram, Herald Tribune* and other newspapers joined in the demand.[5]

On March 12 William Jay Schieffelin, chairman of the Citizens Union, held a conference in his office. Nineteen citizens attended, some of them associated with reform groups, though at the meeting they represented only themselves. Out of the conference was born a citizens' committee, the New York Committee of One Thousand, with Schieffelin as chairman. Its purpose was to arouse and marshal public opinion in favor of a city-wide legislative investigation and to encourage citizens to testify in such an investigation without fear. A statement drafted by Henry Morgenthau, Sr. was adopted which demanded that the legislature bring about a thorough nonpartisan inquiry before it adjourned and asked the public to co-operate with the Committee of One Thousand.[6] The new group rapidly increased its membership and quickly became one of the most important rallying points for citizens demanding a legislative probe.[7] The public clamor for such an investigation could not be resisted and toward the end of March the legislature, which had been holding back, created the committee headed by Senator Hofstadter which, in its turn, made such a notable contribution to the development of reform.[8]

Though the high pitch of public indignation that followed the Gordon murder was short-lived, the civic conscience remained alert. During the next two years, under the spur of the Hofstadter and other revelations and a deteriorating economic situation, the anti-Tammany feeling deepened and merged with a general feeling of dissatisfaction with the status quo. Once started, citizen activity reflecting anger over civic conditions continued and increased. But while such activity in the days before the establishment of the Hofstadter committee had been mainly of a single kind, concerned with the creation of one investigation or another, action after that time assumed several different forms. There was, in the first place, activity in connection with the Hofstadter committee; civic groups and newspapers facilitated, defended and explained the work of the committee and in other ways did their best to maintain its effectiveness. Resentment over the financial plight of the city led to a second kind of effort. A third type involved criticism of the structure of government in the city and in the counties lying within the city, of the City Charter and the county system of government.

Conspicuous in the attempts to insure the success of the Hofstadter investigation was the Committee of One Thousand. After the inception of the legislative committee the Committee of One Thousand continued to function and add to its membership; by April, 1931, that membership included the names of many New Yorkers prominent at the Bar and in the worlds of religion, education, business and finance.[9] From the beginning one of the Committee's purposes had been to embolden witnesses to testify before the prospective legislative committee, and the practical consequence of this was to put the Committee of One Thousand into the business of opening up sources of wrongdoing for the Hofstadter investigators. In an effort to encourage people to come forward, the group, even before the creation of the Hofstadter investigation, had formed a special Lawyers' Committee to which citizens having grievances against the administration were invited to turn for guidance without charge. Maurice P. Davidson headed the special committee which included, among others, such people as William M. Chadbourne, Bernard S. Deutsch, Albert S. Bard, Stanley Isaacs, Walter M. Weis, Joseph D. McGoldrick, Dorothy Kenyon and Mrs. Rosalie Low Whitney. The Lawyers' Committee, whose membership quickly grew from 120 at the start to 200 in mid-April, operated through subcommittees, each of which, headed by an experienced lawyer, was given the task of investigating complaints involving a particular city department or subject. The result was that in the period before the legislative committee was able to get to work—during April, May, and June—the Lawyers' Committee became a depository for grievances. Though examination proved many of these grievances frivolous, there were many substantial ones; and a number of these Davidson eventually turned over to the Seabury probers. At the same time another committee of the Committee of One Thousand, headed by Mrs. Louis I. Dublin, prominent civic worker, was charged with gathering complaints from neighborhood agencies, especially settlement houses, so that any evidence of official maltreatment of the city's poorer people could be recorded.[10]

In other ways, too, the Committee of One Thousand helped the Hofstadter inquiry. When in the fall of 1931 Tammany, assisted by up-state allies, embarked on a desperate campaign to elect a sufficient number of assemblymen to enable the legislature to end the life of the Hofstadter committee and, in particular, tried to defeat a member of the committee, Republican Assemblyman Abbot Low Moffat, of the Fifteenth Assembly District, the Committee of One Thousand went forth to combat the threat. It sent out speakers to explain the work and findings of the investigation to the people and to appeal for the election of enough assemblymen to insure the continuance of the inquiry. What effect, if any, the citizens' committee had on the election is problematical, but Tammany's grand strategy failed and, though only one Republican was elected to the legislature from the city, that one was Abbot Low Moffat.[11]

The Committee of One Thousand was, of course, not the only civic group to expend energy in connection with the Hofstadter investigation. Much support for the inquiry came from the fiery little band of liberals and Socialists who made up the City Affairs Committee. While the group had concentrated on Walker's removal rather than on a legislative investigation in March, 1931, once the Hofstadter committee came into being, Paul Blanshard made it plain that the City Affairs Committee would back the inquiry and take a deep interest in its work. This it did and in different ways. Probably the most celebrated were the various attempts of the City Affairs Committee—usually without the aid of other groups—to have removed from office some of the politicians whom the Hofstadter investigators had shown up. At different times the Committee brought charges against such people as John Theofel, Democratic leader of Queens and Chief Clerk of Queens County Surrogate's Court, who had demonstrated before the investigators an abysmal lack of knowledge concerning his official duties; district leader James A. McQuade, Register and later Sheriff of Kings County; Dr. William H. Walker, the Mayor's brother, and the doctors with whom it was charged he split fees. Though not successful in bringing about the removal of any officials, the Committee's actions helped to keep them and the scandals surrounding them in the public eye.[12]

The second type of citizen activity developed in 1932, when indignation over the city's financial situation reached the boiling point. In February, a number of taxpayers, aroused by the high cost of government and the heavy burden of taxes, formed a Committee of Ten Thousand for the purpose of obtaining a more efficient and economical government. The committee was composed of members of various taxpayer and merchant associations, such as the Sixth Avenue Association, West Side Association of Commerce and Twenty-Third Street Association. Within a short time, however, this committee disappeared, apparently without doing very much. Perhaps one reason for its quick demise was that before long the Committee became more a merchants' pressure group for higher subway fares than a group concerned with the broader aspects of city finances.[13]

More significant was the Citizens Budget Commission. Organized in June, 1932, by prominent bankers, merchants and real estate men desirous of creating, not just a temporary, but a permanent body to keep an eye on city finances and work for budget reductions and tax relief, it has remained to this day one of the city's busiest reform groups. In its tactics and organizational setup, the Citizens Budget Commission resembled the municipal research bureaus. Emphasis was placed upon digging out and publicizing the facts relating to New York City's financial condition. A board of trustees directed the organization, but relied upon a paid staff of experts in public administration, public finance and research to do the work. Peter Grimm, president of the New York Real Estate Board, became chairman of the board of trustees and Harold Riegelman, active for many years in civic affairs, general counsel.[14] Throughout 1932 and 1933 the Citizens Budget Commission not only assailed the existing finances of the city, but made numerous suggestions for eliminating waste and reducing expenditures.[15]

Periodically the Charter, which dated from 1901, had been subjected to attack on one count or another; in 1907, 1911 and 1921 charter commissions had been appointed, but in each case the recommended charter had failed to secure the necessary approval of the legislature. From the time of the passage of the Home Rule Amendment and Law in 1923 and 1924 there had been, however, little organized criticism of the Charter until the time we are considering. Then the various investigations, especially that undertaken by the Hofstadter committee, together with the Depression, once again prompted discussion of the Charter's shortcomings.[16] The discussion, generally speaking, started in March, 1931, not only because it was a time of great fermentation, but because in his letter accepting the position of counsel to the Hofstadter committee, Samuel Seabury suggested that one purpose of the joint legislative committee, which had been granted extremely broad powers, should be to consider changes in the Charter.[17]

Some of those in favor of Charter revision looked upon the Charter as entirely responsible for the city's ills. This was not true, but to some extent the Charter undoubtedly had encouraged and facilitated looseness and waste. First of all, the Charter was long and confusing; more than 400,000 words in length, it dealt, not only with general principles, but with administrative and fiscal details.[18] Parts were archaic. Section 1227 forbade the citizens to "drive cattle, sheep, swine, pigs or calves through the streets and avenues of New York." [19] Then the structure of government provided for contained a number of weaknesses. The city had a bicameral Municipal Assembly which fostered buck-passing and irresponsibility. One house, the Board of Estimate, had not only legislative, but administrative, functions and spent much of its time on details. The other body, the Board of Aldermen, composed of sixty-five members elected from small districts, served no useful purpose, though it cost the taxpayers about $600,000 a year; and minority parties in the city were lucky to get one or two representatives on it. The Mayor had too big a job for one man. He had administrative, policy-making and ceremonial duties, each constituting a man-size job in its own right; as a result, his administrative and policy-making obligations usually suffered. Too many departments, boards and commissions existed with overlapping and duplicate functions. The borough presidents had both legislative and administrative duties; they both appropriated and spent money, with the result that log-rolling and waste were inevitable. Finally one of the worst features of the Charter, which worked to prevent its continual adjustment to changes in city life, was the difficulty in amending it. The voters themselves were powerless, initiative being left to the municipal legislature, which, of course, was not too enthusiastic about change.[20]

Critics of New York's Charter drew upon the experience of Cincinnati for inspiration and guidance. In the 1920's Cincinnati had been under the thumb of the Hynicka Republican machine, and civic conditions had been intolerable. Streets were impassable, city revenue inadequate, the police and fire departments undermanned, political job-holders numerous; so little confidence had people in their government that bond issues were continually defeated. A reform movement arose in the period 1924–6 and under the leadership of the City Charter Committee, a citizens' party, Cincinnati adopted a new form of government and threw out the machine. The new form of government entailed the establishment of a small city council entrusted with the power to make policy. Its members were elected at large by Proportional Representation. From among them, the council elected a mayor who had social duties. It hired a city-manager to carry out policy and administer the city. Since the adoption of the new plan, Cincinnati had become one of the best-governed cities in the United States.[21] This story of reform in Cincinnati was not lost upon New York's reformers. They sought and obtained the advice of Murray Seasongood, Henry Bentley and Mayor Russell Wilson, civic leaders in Cincinnati. Walter J. Millard, an expert on city government who had taken part in civic battles in numerous cities, including that of his own city of Cincinnati, enthusiastically lectured New Yorkers on the election of officials by Proportional Representation and the city-manager plan.[22] New York's Charter critics tended to embrace both ideas, to which they added others inspired by particular features of their city government.

Along with an attack on the Charter went an attack on county government in the city—or rather one should say county governments, for New York City had five counties, each coterminus with a borough, a subdivision of the city. In each county in the state, the state constitution provided that there be the office of county judge, district attorney, county clerk, sheriff and, except where this position had not previously existed, register. The county clerk in the counties lying within New York City had innumerable duties. Filing and preserving county records, issuing certain certificates, discharging the duties of clerk of the county court (except in Manhattan) and of the supreme court when it sat in his county—these were the most important. The sheriff, on the mandates of the courts of record in his county, made arrests on civil charges and served summonses and other papers. He was the custodian of the county jail for civil prisoners and possessed some vestigial powers involving criminal prisoners. The register was responsible for recording deeds, mortgages, chattel mortgages, land titles and conditional sales of personal property, and for furnishing certified copies of these documents. Other positions had been created by state law: a commissioner of jurors to supervise the selection of jurors, a commissioner of records to serve as keeper and preserver of records, a public administrator to administer the estates of dead persons under certain circumstances. The constitutional officers were all elected, whereas the commissioners of jurors, records and the public administrators were appointed, the method of appointment and the term of service varying widely.[23]

Despite the important-sounding nature of county offices, the truth was that in New York, as in other American cities, municipal government had long made most of them inefficient and costly vestiges which owed their preservation only to public apathy and the fact that they constituted lush fields of political jobs. Earlier in speaking of the sheriffs' offices, we saw one reason for county waste and inefficiency. There were others. Mandatory state laws, with few exceptions, fixed the salaries of county positions or allowed county officers to fix the salaries with only meager restrictions. No adequate central authority existed to supervise the various county establishments, making co-operation between them impossible and chaos inevitable. There was much duplication of work between the various county governments and between these and the city.[24]

For over half a century county government in New York City had been under criticism, and suggestions had been made for changing the system. Those attacking county government in New York generally had thought of reforming it by abolishing county offices through a merger with city offices, by consolidating the various county offices, or in both ways. (City Chamberlain Henry Bruère and Commissioner of Accounts Leonard Wallstein, after conducting a study of county government in New York City during the administration of Mayor Mitchel, reported, "The Constitution should be so amended as to permit the merger of the county governments with the city government and where that is not practicable, the consolidation of the several county establishments." [25]) Nothing had been done in any direction, however, when growing concern over machine politics and the city's budget in the early thirties once again focused attention on the county governments.

Agitation for reform of the Charter and county government was carried on mainly by civic groups, though it was not confined to them. One should note, however, that advocates of change did not always agree on what changes should be made or place the same emphasis upon the same proposal. The Citizens Union, Women's City Club, City Affairs Committee, Merchants Association of New York and Committee of One Thousand were among the chief organizations pressing for constructive reforms. Particularly active was the Committee of One Thousand. At its first formal meeting, Schieffelin advocated the adoption of the city-manager plan and the institution of a council whose members would be elected at large by Proportional Representation, and he continued to urge these proposals over the next two years. The committee created subcommittees for the purpose of surveying different parts of the city government with a view toward Charter and other innovations, and through such pamphlets as *Proportional Representation, The City-Manager Plan Is Coming!* and *County Government in New York City* attempted to educate the public on those topics.[26]

Discussion of the Charter and county government was notably advanced by the Hofstadter committee. In December, 1932, the committee, in line with Seabury's earlier suggestion, spent time considering proposals for reforming New York City's Charter and government. A number of prominent people, such as Nicholas Murray Butler, Al Smith, and Joseph V. McKee, then Acting Mayor, presented their ideas to the committee. At the end of the month, Seabury, in his final report to the committee, put forward his own recommendations on the subject and, in early January, the majority members of the committee sent a report to the legislature which contained other proposals. All the various plans, though differing from one another, were alike in that they entailed important, sweeping changes. All agreed that the complex structure of city government should be simplified by a consolidation of administrative departments. Most favored the establishment of a single, relatively small, legislative body for the city to be elected by Proportional Representation or some other method of insuring adequate minority representation. Some advocated the abolishment of borough government, though others would preserve some degree of it. Unanimously they regarded county government as unjustified and called for its abolition.[27]

One consequence of the Hofstadter committee's interest in governmental reform was that in early 1933 representatives of various civic and semi-civic organizations, such as the City Club, Citizens Union, City Affairs Committee, Committee of One Thousand, Society for the Prevention of Crime, Merchants Association, West End Association, Tax Protective League, Flatbush Tax Association, came together at a Civic Conference on Charter Revision for the purpose of reaching some common understanding as to Charter reforms to be proposed and acted upon. Richard S. Childs, father of the short ballot idea and the city-manager plan and president of the City Club, presided as chairman. At its first session, held on January 20, the conference passed two major resolutions, one calling upon the legislature to act on Charter revision for New York City at its current session, and the other empowering the chairman to create ten subcommittees to study various aspects of the different principal plans for Charter revision that had been made up to that time; the chairmen of these committees were to constitute a co-ordinating committee under the conference chairman. The reports of the subcommittees, after editing by the co-ordinating committee, were submitted to the conference at its second session on February 16 and adopted. Generally, the conference's recommendations followed in principle those found in most of the plans that had come out of the Hofstadter investigation, though only Charter revision, and not the problem of county government, concerned the conference. Representatives of the various groups who composed the conference, while not authorized to bind their organizations to anything adopted at the conference, agreed to submit its work to them for consideration.[28]

But in the end little of immediate importance came out of the agitation over the Charter and county government. Assemblyman Moffat introduced a bill in the legislature in 1933 to enable a certain number of qualified voters in a city in New York State to place a proposal for appointing a charter commission before the electorate by means of a petition; if the proposal carried, the work of the commission would be submitted to the voters for their approval at another election. The measure, after some rough going, passed the Assembly, where the Republicans had a majority, only to die in the Democratic-controlled Senate.[29] A series of eight bills, also introduced into the 1933 legislature by Moffat, designed to bring about a radical reorganization of county government in line with the thinking of the Hofstadter committee, also failed to pass.[30] Nor was the cause of Charter and county reform in 1933 aided by the fact that as the year advanced, reform energy became increasingly directed into political channels. In the end, a few innovations in the city government instituted by Tammany [31] constituted the only tribute to the activity of the advocates of Charter and county reform.

Nevertheless, the agitation we have been discussing was not without value. It strengthened the developing reform movement by contributing to it certain positive goals; partly for this reason, the reform movement came to stand *for* something, not simply *against* Tammany. And from the vantage of a later day it is clear that the demand for Charter and county reform at this time represented the ground-breaking phase of an effort destined to be of some significance for New York City.

Political action against the existing order began on a small scale in the fall of 1931 and for about a year remained subordinate to nonpolitical civic activity. The efforts of the Committee of One Thousand to elect enough assemblymen to insure the continuance of the Hofstadter investigation and especially to re-elect Assemblyman Moffat, a member of the investigating committee, has already been mentioned; but it is hard to evaluate the significance of the committee's role here. More notable was an attempt made, at the same time, in New York's Second Judicial District (of which Kings, Queens and Richmond were a part) to protest a bipartisan deal between Democrats and Republicans whereby twelve new supreme court justiceships, even before the bill creating them had been passed, were divided between the two parties, each party, furthermore, endorsing the other's candidates for the new positions. One of those nominated by both parties was Boss McCooey's son; another was Meier Steinbrink, Republican leader of Brooklyn at the time the deal was made. A small group of indignant men, led by James E. Finegan, a lawyer and a Brooklynite, formed a No Deal Judiciary Party, put up a ticket of four candidates and ran a campaign for their election. Though the bipartisan slate swept the field by a large margin, the No Deal ticket to some extent achieved its purpose.[32] These first instances of citizen political activity developed out of more or less specific fears or grievances and were disconnected. They had in mind particular objectives that were more limited than the overthrow of Tammany government, and, indeed, the No Deal ticket was directed as much against Republican politicians as Democratic ones.

In December, 1931, however, the Committee of One Thousand and the Citizens Union, probably with the example of the Cincinnati Charter Committee in mind, initiated a campaign which had as its aim the establishment of an independent ticket to contest the Tammany one in the 1933 elections. Both groups asked other civic organizations to help them acquire as many signatures as possible to a declaration which read: "I favor a change in the City Government and will support an independent ticket in 1933 provided the candidates meet with my approval." Schieffelin, head of both organizations, declared that after public sentiment for a political change had been rallied the next step would be the formation of a Committee of Seventy representing all boroughs and all classes of people to formulate the ticket and organize the campaign; he envisaged an independent citizens' organization as the instrument of political revolt rather than a fusion movement which would include the Republican Party. But this attempt to set in motion a political movement against Tammany died in early childhood; after February, 1932, we hear no more about it. In part it failed to develop into something important because the timing was bad—any movement looking toward the 1933 elections launched at so early a date was bound to be abortive—but another reason, no doubt, was the unconcealed opposition of Republican organization leaders and the fact that any reform movement which omitted them was not likely to be taken too seriously.[33] No political instrument had been created, no real political movement had been organized when Walker's resignation threw city politics into confusion and necessitated a special election for control of the city administration.

To speak of confusion is no exaggeration. Not until the Court of Appeals ruled in early October that an election for Mayor was necessary was it certain that one would be held in November.[34] And who would be the candidates? For the Democrats, as for their opponents, this was a source of trouble. Even before the court ruling the Democratic bosses in the city had become engaged in a struggle over the party's nomination. In the beginning all of the bosses, except Flynn, were for Walker's renomination. The former Mayor had apparently resigned in a mood of pessimism, convinced that Roosevelt would remove him anyway; but this mood had quickly passed, and Walker had decided to seek vindication by running for re-election.[35] Flynn's attitude toward renominating Walker was understandable. Walker could not run for Mayor without attacking Roosevelt for being "unfair," and Flynn, who, unlike the other four Democratic leaders, had enthusiastically supported Roosevelt's nomination for President and was deeply interested in his election, was strongly opposed to anything that might endanger the national ticket.[36] Besides, Walker's resignation had elevated Joseph V. McKee, a member of the Bronx machine, from President of the Board of Aldermen to Acting Mayor—and what political boss would give up such a good thing without a fight? Flynn hoped that there would be no election for Mayor in 1932 and that McKee could serve out the remainder of Walker's term—in fact, McKee brought suit to prevent the special election—but if there had to be a mayoral contest, the Bronx boss wanted Joseph McKee as the Democratic candidate.[37]

There was much to commend McKee, for the Acting Mayor was extremely popular. Though he had sat for seven years with Walker on the Board of Estimate, working closely with him and doing little to distinguish himself, McKee was acclaimed a civic hero after becoming Acting Mayor. Much of the press heaped praise upon him for making some obvious economies, riding to work in the subway, getting to work on time, presenting a serious appearance. Though McKee had never given the slightest sign of being free from the domination of political bosses, many independents hailed him as one of their own.[38] Clearly, the city had tired of Walker and was desperately looking for a savior to lead it forth from darkness.

In the end, however, the Democratic nomination went to neither Walker nor McKee. Either Walker changed his mind or, what is more likely, the Democratic chiefs changed theirs; in any case, Walker was counted out.[39] Tammany would have none of McKee for precisely the reason Flynn was so anxious for his nomination: McKee's election as Mayor would tremendously increase the Bronx boss's power and prestige and might easily destroy Tammany's domination of Democratic politics in the city.[40] Instead, the Manhattan organization and its satellites, without consulting Flynn, decided to nominate Surrogate John P. O'Brien. From the politician's point of view, the choice was ideal. O'Brien, a massive man with large brow and jaws and a protruding lip, had shown absolute loyalty to Tammany for over thirty years, for which he had been rewarded by promotions, the last, made by Murphy, giving him his bench position. As one of the two surrogates of New York County, he had accumulated a good record, for though of mediocre intellect, he possessed ambition and the will to toil. Prominent as a Catholic lay leader who made orations calling for a deeper religious spirit and higher moral standards, O'Brien was regarded as just the right man to offset the taint of Walker's public and private looseness.[41] Flynn was not happy about Tammany's choice, but at least it was not Walker, and Flynn thought it best to go along; above all, he wanted Democratic harmony for the state and national elections.[42] The truth was that Tammany had him over a barrel.

On their side, the anti-Tammany people were in a poor position to make a fight for the city administration for, as we have seen, they were totally unprepared. Even if they had not been, their chance of success in the fall of 1932 would have been slim. The Democratic label was at a premium; public attention was riveted upon the election of a President, not a Mayor; the knowledge that, no matter who won the mayoral election, the real showdown would have to take place anyway in 1933 did not encourage interest in the city contest.

Still a heterogeneous committee of independents, derived in part from the Committee of One Thousand and composed of such men as Schieffelin, Maurice P. Davidson, James E. Finegan, Joseph M. Price, whom we have met, and Raymond V. Ingersoll, Rufus McGahen and Ben Howe, whom we will see again, made an eleventh-hour attempt to effect a political revolt by means of a fusion movement. The committee talked with Samuel Koenig, leader of the Republican organization in Manhattan, who agreed to fuse with the candidate selected by the committee; Republican leaders were not averse to accepting an independent Democrat if need be.[43]

The group conferred nightly in an attempt to get a candidate for Mayor to run against Tammany. Seabury's name came up first, of course, but he was not interested, his friends declaring that he wanted nothing to interfere with the completion of his job as counsel to the Hofstadter committee. After the Democrats had nominated O'Brien, the independents asked the popular McKee to be the Fusion candidate, but he did not want that nomination. Then they thought of George McAneny. One of the city's outstanding citizens, a former president of the City Club, an incorporator of the Bureau of Municipal Research, McAneny had been elected Borough President of Manhattan in 1909; in 1913 running on Mitchel's ticket, he had been elected President of the Board of Aldermen. Davidson told this writer about the night they asked McAneny to run. McAneny was going to the opera and said he would meet them at the City Club after it was over and give them his answer. The committee got excited, drew up a statement of principles and began making plans for the campaign. When McAneny came, he had on his top hat, was obviously a bit tipsy, and after eyeing the group for a few moments burped, "No"—he would not run. Davidson and the rest were furious, but no amount of talking could change his mind. Finally McAneny suggested that General John F. O'Ryan, commander of the Twenty-Seventh Division during World War I and a former member of the Transit Commission, would make a good candidate. McAneny sent a committee over to his own suite at the Ritz-Carlton and ordered champagne to be opened for them. Then he and one other from the group went over to rouse the general, who was staying at the Hotel Lexington. They brought the prospective candidate over to the champagne party and worked on him until five o'clock in the morning. O'Ryan could not make up his mind and said he would give his answer at noon. He did; it was no. Once again, the members of the committee fumed, but little good it did them. They could not find a candidate—the slight chance anti-Tammany had of winning was an important reason—and the fusion effort blew up.[44]

The Republicans met and nominated their own candidate—elderly Lewis H. Pounds, who had been Borough President of Brooklyn in the time of Mayor Mitchel and State Treasurer; for twenty years Pounds had been actively identified with Republican politics in Brooklyn. The Socialists had already nominated Morris Hillquit. Political observers predicted O'Brien would win by 600,000 votes. He did, and the Democrats swept the city with record pluralities.[45]

Yet O'Brien's victory was not as convincing as it appeared. Ironically, the election demonstrated the depth of civic dissatisfaction, inspired anti-Tammany with hope and filled Tammany with consternation. For during the campaign, the *World-Telegram* spread the idea that voters should record their protest against machine government by writing in McKee's name for Mayor on Election Day,[46] and the results were astonishing. Notwithstanding the fact that it is more troublesome to carry a pencil and write in a name than to pull down a lever, that there is always subtle social pressure against taking too much time in the booth, that in many areas the atmosphere was cold to those wanting to write in a name, McKee pulled over 260,000 votes.[47] Nothing like this had ever happened before in New York City politics. If voters had thus acted at a time when those opposed to Tammany had been unable to organize effectively, when Democrats were sweeping to power everywhere, when the voters' main interest was on the presidential election, what would they do when presented with adequate political means for expressing their discontent?

6

The story of a fusion movement

McKEE'S WRITE-IN VOTE ignited a political fire, and the Acting Mayor immediately fanned it. Addressing the State Chamber of Commerce on November 16, McKee attacked Tammany rule, came out for a "decent regime" and called on his fellow citizens to begin organizing for revolt.[1] What lay behind McKee's speech was not clear. His friends declared that he had despaired of awakening his colleagues in the city administration to the critical state of city finances and felt that public opinion needed to be mobilized. Some, more critical, suggested that now that the election was over, Flynn might be preparing to break with the other Democratic bosses and back McKee independently in the next campaign. Most people, however, saw the speech as an announcement of McKee's willingness to assume the leadership of the good government forces.[2]

The first reaction to McKee's speech on the part of most of the anti-Tammany forces bordered on the hysterical, and those close to McKee described him as completely overwhelmed by the response. Anti-Tammany people tripped over one another in their haste to wrap him in the mantle of leadership. Groups like the Citizens Budget Commission, Citizens Union, City Affairs Committee, Committee of One Thousand, Young Men's Board of Trade hailed him as the apostle of a new deal in the city. A new group, the City-Wide Non-Partisan Committee, sprang up to support him. The newspapers were practically universal in editorial praise. (One newspaper cartoonist pictured McKee as a knight in armor spearing the Tammany dragon.) Most amazing of all, those practical politicians, Samuel Koenig, Frederick J. H. Kracke and Warren B. Ashmead, Republican leaders in Manhattan, Brooklyn and Queens, immediately approved the idea of McKee for Mayor in 1933.[3]

It did not take long for more prudent thoughts to set in. Should the movement tie itself irrevocably to McKee? Wasn't it too early to be talking about a mayoral candidate anyway? Republican State Chairman W. Kingsland Macy, while agreeing with most of the nice things said about the Acting Mayor, doubted the wisdom of committing the party so soon to a reform movement backing him. Important reform elements soon declared that the time was not ripe for a discussion of candidates.[4] Before long, the main interest shifted from McKee—though he was still regarded as the leading anti-Tammany candidate—to the means of bringing about a reform movement. In the end, the most significant result of the McKee boom of November was to set in movement certain groups whose activities were to be of great importance in the political developments of 1933.

One was the Republican Party. Interested in a fusion movement in 1932, Republican leaders became more eager than ever as signs multiplied pointing to an upheaval in 1933. W. Kingsland Macy was enthusiastically for fusion. Early in December, he appointed a Republican Mayoralty Committee, headed by former Governor Charles S. Whitman, to work along with other interested groups to bring about such a movement. Beginning with ten members, it was not long before the committee added a great many more; Dr. Nicholas Murray Butler, Frederic R. Coudert, Jr., George Z. Medalie, James R. Sheffield, George H. Sibley, Arthur Woods, William Ziegler were some of the prominent Republicans who served on it. The group received the support of the various county leaders. How serious the Republicans were about Fusion can be seen from the fact that Macy, Whitman and others stated that the Fusion candidate for Mayor should be an independent Democrat.[5]

Republicans in Manhattan anticipated fusion in yet another way, though this came later in 1933 and was not directly the result of the McKee excitement of November. For over twenty years, Samuel Koenig had run the Manhattan Republican machine and had been periodically accused of being a tool of Tammany Hall. Undoubtedly he had made his deals, but in 1933 he seemed to be staunchly for a fusion movement. Still many Republicans wanted to take no chances; they argued that at best Koenig was discredited in the public mind and that the Republican organization in Manhattan needed to regain the people's confidence if Tammany were to be beaten. Macy insisted that Koenig must go. Koenig refused to resign, with the result that a tremendous intraparty fight developed. Aligned against the county leader were some of the most important Republicans in the city—people like Elihu Root, Henry L. Stimson, Ogden L. Mills, George W. Wickersham, Charles Tuttle, George Medalie, Ruth Pratt— the Young Republican element, the *Times* and *Herald Tribune*. Supporting Koenig were most of the Republican district leaders in Manhattan. The anti-Koenig people formed the Organization of Regular Republicans for Change in the New York County Leadership and set to work in the assembly districts putting up insurgent slates of county committeemen. In the

September primary, one of the most exciting in years, the rebels, after a long period of agitation, succeeded in electing a majority of the county committeemen, thus dooming Koenig's rule. On September 28 the new committee met and elected as county leader Chase Mellen, Jr., a non-professional, a wealthy man with a family and personal history of public service.[6] No longer could there be any doubts about the loyalty of the Republican organization in Manhattan to Fusion.

Others besides the Republicans were propelled into action by the hub-bub over McKee. Maurice Davidson, who in addition to heading the Law-yers' Committee of the Committee of One Thousand was also chairman of its executive committee, called a conference of civic organizations in his office. He reminded them that only ballots could change civic conditions in the city and that there was need to create some political entity which would conduct a campaign against Tammany in 1933. While agreeing with him, none of the other civic groups represented, for one reason or another, was able to assume the responsibility of political organization; most were prohibited from engaging in political work by their constitutions and rules. The problem was thus shoved in the lap of the Committee of One Thousand, which promptly turned it over to the chairman of its executive committee, empowering him to select a committee to lay out the nucleus of a new political party. Shortly afterwards, Davidson called eight men into his office: Raymond V. Ingersoll, an independent Democrat who had been active in civic affairs and reform movements for more than thirty years; James E. Finegan; Bernard S. Deutsch, former head of the Bronx County Bar Association; Rufus E. McGahen, a member of the Committee of One Thousand and secretary of the Citizens Union; Joseph D. McGoldrick, Assistant Professor of Government at Columbia University; Russell Forbes, Associate Professor of Government at New York University; law-yers Charles G. Keutgen and Louis S. Lewis. Out of their conference in November was born the City Party.[7]

The immediate purpose of the new party was to provide a political instrument for the coming campaign which would unite citizens regardless of party labels, an agency which would extend into the assembly districts and "whether by itself or through the aid of a fusion with other groups and organizations" fight to bring good government to New York City. At the same time, however, the party had a more long-range objective. It hoped to be a permanent nonpartisan municipal political organization which would be available for many campaigns and which would offer a medium for intelligent civic action between campaigns.[8] The short-range and long-range aims of the new party, it may be recalled, were also those of the Citizens Union at the time of its formation in 1897.

Among other things, the City Party pledged itself to work for an honest budget which revealed the actual condition of the treasury; the discharge of political parasites, but the retention of efficient civil service employes with adequate pay; charter changes to promote democracy and efficiency;

a nonpartisan government for all the people, one in which the public welfare would take precedence over politics. Though advocating economy
and efficiency, the City Party was not an economy-oriented group. It
insisted upon a wide-visioned social program. It declared that while the
restoration of the city's financial structure was of immediate concern, the
ultimate object must be its moral and spiritual redemption.[9]

Theoretically the party was organized in a hierarchy extending from
the assembly districts at the bottom through borough committees to a central committee at the top; in practice, it was never able to organize in every
assembly district. Until after the election of 1933, nobody paid much attention to the source of authority. The founders elected Davidson chairman
of the Central Committee, and generally speaking, he appointed the other
officials. Not the Central Committee, however, but a smaller Executive
Committee headed by Davidson and composed of the party's most important officers made the real decisions. There was also an Advisory Council
whose members gave advice and lent the new organization the prestige of
their names.[10]

Many of the important officers were people we have come across before;
understandably some of the founders were among them. Ingersoll was
chairman and General O'Ryan vice-chairman of the Advisory Council.
Deutsch, Finegan and Keutgen were chairmen of the borough committees
in the Bronx, Brooklyn and Richmond. McGoldrick became party secretary, Ben Howe, director of organization, and Walter Weis, chairman of the
Law Committee.[11] In setting up the new party, its creators were not
unaware of the experience of the Cincinnati Charter Committee. Later,
in July, 1934, Davidson was to write to Henry Bentley, one of the founders
of the Charter Committee: "I may say that I wish to acknowledge now that
I benefited greatly from your wise counsel in organizing the City Fusion
Party. . . ." [12]

For much of 1933, until the real start of the campaign, the City Party
mainly concerned itself with organization and preparation. Davidson and
Howe were the busiest of men making speeches, issuing news releases,
trying to set up district organizations.[13] Thousands joined the new party,
particularly since it was not a full-fledged party within the meaning of the
state law, and membership in it did not conflict with enrollment in the
Democratic and Republican parties; at the beginning of April, Davidson
reported that there were between 40,000 and 50,000 members.[14] A
Speakers' Committee of the party was formed in February under the direction of Dr. A. B. Williamson, chairman of the Department of Public
Speaking at New York University, and the energetic Walter Millard prepared a detailed course on Proportional Representation for speakers so
that they would be able to engage in debate and answer any questions on
the subject. During this period the City Party also hammered O'Brien's
administration, especially as to its financial policies.[15]

Out of the political furor of November, 1932, came one other group which should be mentioned. Joseph M. Price, at the time chairman of the board of trustees of the City Club, called a meeting of civic leaders at the club on November 28 and organized what was later named the Independent Fusion Committee. Its object was to promote a fusion movement in 1933 by co-ordinating all the various groups anxious for reform. The committee started with eighteen members but eventually grew to fifty. A number of members—Charles C. Burlingham, Richard Welling, George McAneny, Raymond V. Ingersoll, Lillian Wald, for example—were veterans of 1913. Bernard Deutsch, Joseph McGoldrick, Lewis H. Pounds, Stanley Isaacs, Oswald Garrison Villard were also on the committee.[16] Despite its aim, however, the Independent Fusion Committee never became representative enough to serve as the real co-ordinator in a fusion movement, and it soon became just another element to be co-ordinated.

It had been obvious since the commotion over McKee in November, 1932, that those eager for reform in the city were thinking mainly in terms of a fusion movement—both Republicans and independent Democrats were very receptive to the idea—and in the spring of 1933 the attempt to select a fusion ticket began. On April 12, Joseph Price invited Whitman and Davidson to appoint from each of their groups a small committee which could join with a similar one from the Independent Fusion Committee and from any other interested organization for the purpose of picking a fusion slate. This was the origin of what might be called the Fusion conference committee, which during the spring and early summer assumed the task of choosing a common mayoral candidate. In practice, the conference group turned out to be much smaller and more informal than the one suggested by Price; its membership was flexible rather than rigid. The core of the group was composed of Price (representing the Independent Fusion Committee), Whitman (the Republican Mayoralty Committee) and Davidson and Ingersoll (City Party). Toward the end of its life, in late July, when the committee's work became increasingly difficult, J. Barstow Smull, who headed a Committee on Municipal Affairs of the State Chamber of Commerce, took part in its discussions, and at the very end, still others: Fulton Cutting, the old veteran of many civic wars and a member of Smull's committee; Rufus McGahen, representing the Citizens Union; former New York Supreme Court Justice Robert McC. Marsh, representative of the anti-Koenig Republicans; Cyrus C. Miller, another member of the Independent Fusion Committee. And always there was Seabury. Apparently he did not overtly take part in the work of the conference committee until late July and early August, but he was always in touch with its deliberations and made his opinions known. So immense was his prestige that his support was considered indispensable to any candidate chosen by the committee.[17]

In the spring of 1933, when the Fusion conference committee began its labors, McKee was still the leading choice for the anti-Tammany mayoral nomination. Then on May 3 McKee resigned as President of the Board of Aldermen, which position he had resumed after his stint as Acting Mayor, to become president of the Title Guarantee and Trust Company, with the declaration that the step marked his "complete elimination from politics and governmental office." Why he removed himself from politics is not clear, but one thing is: McKee had dropped a bomb on Fusionist plans and hopes. Where they had seen their best chance for victory, reformers suddenly found a disquieting political vacuum. They were dazed and bewildered; a spirit of defeatism hovered about the edges of the reform camp. Rather quickly, however, the situation adjusted itself. Certain independent Democrats and some Republicans attempted to fill the void by launching a movement to draft Al Smith for Mayor, a movement that quickly blew up when the former Governor issued a statement refusing to permit further consideration of his name. More important, Fusion leaders, recovering their equanimity, began a search for another candidate.[18]

The going was not easy. In the course of the next two and a half months, the Fusion conference committee offered the nomination to Seabury; Ingersoll; Richard C. Patterson, Jr., vice president of the National Broadcasting Company and former Commissioner of Correction under Walker; John C. Knox, United States District Judge for the Southern District of New York; Clarence J. Shearn, former New York State Supreme Court Justice and prominent attorney; Nathan Straus, Jr., one of New York's leading merchants and a man noted for his concern with city affairs; George V. McLaughlin, president of the Brooklyn Trust Company, who for a time had served as Police Commissioner under Walker. All were independent Democrats, for the committee recognized the wisdom of nominating a Democrat if possible. But for one reason or another all declined the nomination. Seabury was not interested in running for Mayor, and if he had not been boomed for this office as loudly as one might expect, it was because this fact was generally recognized by the anti-Tammany people. Perhaps he was unwilling to give up the status of a great lawyer and advocate of the public interest to take on the regimentation of a regular political position or, perhaps, as some believe, he had his eye on something bigger than City Hall. Ingersoll declined on the grounds of health, Patterson wanted to run, at first said yes, but later changed his mind when the board of directors of NBC asked him to choose immediately between a public career and a private one. Knox expressed a preference for the juristic life, and Shearn did not want the hardships of the Mayor's office. Straus refused, according to Davidson, because Governor Lehman was a Jew, and at a time of growing anti-Semitism in the world Straus did not want to lend credence to the notion that the Jews were trying to take over the government. McLaughlin, at a later date, said that he turned down the offer because he did not want to re-enter public life.[19]

One man, however, wanted to be Mayor, and throughout the spring and much of the summer of 1933, while the Fusion conference committee was looking for a candidate, he made no secret of his ambition. After his defeat for Mayor in 1929, Fiorello H. La Guardia had continued to represent East Harlem in Congress until he lost his seat in the Democratic landslide of 1932. Quickly recovering from a mood of pessimism, he threw himself into the race for Mayor. His political life was at stake. In bidding for the Fusion nomination, he possessed, as he had in his 1929 fight for the Republican nomination, an important club in his threat to run in the Republican primary if he were not made the candidate. This threat was not to be taken lightly, for obviously if the candidate selected by the Fusion leaders did not win the Republican primary his nomination would become worthless, and La Guardia was known as a two-fisted slugger. Sometimes he pushed his candidacy more or less subtly. In May he proposed a fantastic ticket, headed by Al Smith and containing such people as Norman Thomas and John P. O'Brien, and declared that unless a ticket substantially the same could be agreed upon, he, himself, would enter the Republican primaries with a full ticket. Most likely the real purpose of the suggestion was to call attention to the fact that La Guardia could throw a monkey wrench and that it would not be wise to ignore him. Behind the scenes La Guardia was more obvious. He pestered Davidson continually, said he didn't care who the Fusion committee was considering, he wanted to be the candidate and reminded Davidson of the Republican primary. Handicapping the former congressman in his quest for the nomination were a number of factors: conservative Republicans, as before, were opposed to him; he had lost in 1929; he was not an independent Democrat. But against these stood his popularity, especially with Italians, Jews and labor people, his campaign ability, his unquestioned hostility to Tammany.[20]

Moreover, a number of influential people favored La Guardia's nomination. Charles Tuttle and William Chadbourne, both important members of the Republican Mayoralty Committee, were for him, as was W. Kingsland Macy.[21] So was Adolf A. Berle, Jr., Professor of Corporation Law at Columbia who had been introduced to La Guardia in 1932 by Paul Kern, a former student of his who had gone to Washington on a fellowship the year before to do law research for the congressman. Berle was much impressed with La Guardia, wanted him for Mayor and in effect became his campaign manager. Probably more than any other person, Berle somewhat broke down the stereotype of La Guardia as a wholly impulsive individual by describing in important circles how careful he was in his facts and how diligent in his preparation. In the spring of 1933 Berle organized a committee which called on Seabury and persuaded him that La Guardia would make the best candidate. Seabury, in turn, convinced the influential Roy W. Howard, editor and part-owner of the *World-Telegram*.[22]

Despite the elements in his favor, La Guardia was not given too much consideration by the Fusion conference committee in its earlier sessions. At that time, the committee had a number of possible candidates, all independent Democrats and all less controversial. Though Seabury favored La Guardia, he would have backed those to whom the Fusion committee offered the nomination.[23] But toward the end of July, the situation changed, and La Guardia's candidacy was given more serious attention. The scarcity of potential candidates made the arguments against him appear less weighty than before. Moreover, as the field narrowed down, Seabury's enthusiasm for La Guardia mounted in proportion to his distaste for the remaining possibilities.

For in the end, it came down to either Robert Moses, General O'Ryan or La Guardia. Moses, father of New York State's admirable park system, was an independent Republican who had shown that he could be nonpartisan by serving as Governor Smith's Secretary of State. O'Ryan was an independent Democrat, conservative, dignified, highly respected and uninspiring, the kind so often put up by good government people in times of revolt. All the members of the Fusion conference group, except Seabury, preferred Moses or O'Ryan. Seabury was unalterably opposed to both. Moses he did not want because he felt that the proposed candidate was too friendly with Smith, that Smith would become his principal adviser and that consequently a real fight against Tammany would be impossible; perhaps, too, he objected to Moses' opposition to Proportional Representation. Seabury was against O'Ryan because he believed the general would make a weak candidate, was inexperienced in politics and was on record as approving a higher subway fare. Apparently also believing, rightly or not, that O'Ryan's candidacy was backed by the traction interests, Seabury strongly pushed La Guardia's nomination.[24]

This conflict over the nomination with Seabury on one side and the other members of the Fusion committee on the other constituted the most serious problem the budding Fusion movement had faced up to that time. Seabury charged the other Fusion leaders with insincerity in wanting to overthrow Tammany. They, in turn, resented his attitude and the obvious way he was throwing his weight around. On July 26 most of the conference members were on the verge of nominating Moses, but Seabury quit the group in protest; and Moses, who might otherwise have accepted the designation, declined it in order to preserve unity. With Moses out of the running, the majority then turned to O'Ryan. Hoping to get the jump on Seabury and pressure him into going along, and with the conservative Whitman leading the way, the majority met at the Lawyers' Club on August 1 and, without Seabury, named O'Ryan the candidate. The general was not averse to running, but in view of the muddled political situation, he deferred his decision. Instead of solving the problem, this move by the conference majority only exacerbated it. Seabury refused to endorse the nomination, denouncing it as "a complete and disgraceful sellout to Tammany," and La Guardia issued an ultimatum that, unless an agreement could be reached on a stronger and more acceptable candidate, he would run as an independent and enter the Republican primary. Rumblings against O'Ryan came from the ranks of the City Party and from the Republican Mayoralty Committee. Fusion had come apart at the seams.[25]

At this darkest moment reason prevailed. George Medalie, a member of the Republican Mayoralty Committee, lunched with Seabury and Roy Howard on August 2 and suggested that a new conference committee more representative of the various Fusion interests be created to supersede the older one. The other two men agreed with his idea and to the list of names for the proposed "get-together" committee that he had prepared. Charles C. Burlingham, a member of Price's group, was asked to be chairman of the new committee. A former president of the New York City Bar Association, an important figure in the reform movement of 1913, an eminent citizen deeply respected, Burlingham was just the man for the job. He accepted the assignment and, telephoning some of the other people on the list, called an organizational meeting for that very afternoon. Meeting with him in his office were Berle, Davidson and Finegan (the last two for the City Party), Robert McC. Marsh (anti-Koenig Republicans), Newbold Morris (the young president of the Republican Club in the Fifteenth Assembly District), J. G. Louis Molloy (one of Seabury's assistants in the Hofstadter investigation and head of the Knickerbocker Democrats, a new anti-Tammany Democratic organization) and Joseph Price (Independent Fusion Committee); Smull (Chamber of Commerce), though invited, could not attend. The new group scheduled a meeting to choose the candidate for the following evening at the Bar Association and invited some more people to join them at that time.[26]

Present at the Bar Association meeting on August 3, in addition to those who had been present in Burlingham's office, were Schieffelin, Seabury, Smull and a contingent from the Republican Mayoralty Committee. Whitman apparently had no intention of sending representatives, but that afternoon the Republican Mayoralty Committee had met, and with Tuttle and Stanley Isaacs taking the lead, pro-La Guardia members had forced the withdrawal of a resolution submitted by Whitman and other O'Ryan supporters recommending the general's nomination and had created instead a delegation to join the Burlingham group. The discussion at the Bar Association was fiery. Although there had been some talk about Bainbridge Colby, former United States Secretary of State, as a compromise candidate, the fight was still between O'Ryan and La Guardia. The action of the Republican Mayoralty Committee that afternoon had given the former congressman's chances a boost, Seabury and Berle vigorously spearheaded the La Guardia attack and, finally, a majority of the Burlingham committee recommended his nomination. Burlingham then telephoned O'Ryan, explained the situation to him and ventured to suggest that he withdraw in favor of La Guardia so as to give Fusion "the unanimity essential to success." Graciously O'Ryan did so.[27] The ordeal of picking a mayoral candidate was over. Seabury and La Guardia had won out.

The Burlingham committee, now possessing a good deal of prestige, continued to function until it filled in the rest of the ticket. It selected Bernard Deutsch for President of the Board of Aldermen and W. Arthur Cunningham, an officer of the Textile Banking Corporation and a Queens resident, for Comptroller. For the five borough presidencies it chose Langdon K. Post, former assemblyman, organizer of the Knickerbocker Democrats and, until a short time before, Assistant Federal Relief Administrator (Manhattan); Raymond Ingersoll (Brooklyn); Charles P. Barry, instructor in government at New York University and a member of the Bronx Executive Committee of the City Party (Bronx); George U. Harvey, Republican incumbent (Queens); Joseph A. Palma, automobile dealer and former member of the United States Secret Service (Richmond). The committee picked Jacob Gould Schurman, Jr., an assistant to Seabury in all three of his investigations, for District Attorney of New York County, and also selected candidates for less important positions. Since La Guardia was a Republican, the rest of the slate was composed mostly of independent Democrats; the only Republicans chosen for major positions, aside from La Guardia, were Harvey and Schurman. Opposition was raised to Harvey by some on the grounds that while Borough President of Queens, he had played along with Walker at times and had defended his administration; but Harvey was chosen, a tribute to political expediency. These names were later placed on the ballot by the Republican and City (Fusion) parties.[28]

In mid-September, a time when the Fusion campaign had just got under way, Fusion's chances looked bright. Not that victory was a sure thing. Tammany was well-entrenched, powerful and shrewd; and reformers had the unenviable knack of tripping over their own feet. Yet the Fusion people had important assets, and these tended to give them confidence; veteran foes of Tammany saw the outlook for La Guardia's election better than it was for Mitchel's in 1913. La Guardia was a strong candidate, and he had the support of Seabury. There was no doubt that the people of New York were in the mood for a political change. Aside from the fundamental factors previously noted, O'Brien and his administration were not popular, and, though there had been some talk in Democratic circles of shelving Mayor O'Brien in favor of a stronger candidate, in the end Curry had decided upon his re-nomination; and the other Democratic bosses, including Flynn, had agreed, though with something less than complete enthusiasm.[29]

Actually O'Brien's unpopularity was, to a large extent, undeserved. The Mayor was really a good-natured and likeable man and, in private among friends, he was often charming and witty. His intentions were good, and he worked hard. Mayor at a time when Tammany was forced to make a virtue out of necessity, O'Brien could boast of a number of significant accomplishments. He carried out some changes in governmental machinery and procedure in accordance with the recommendations of a Charter Revision Committee that he had appointed soon after his election, and most of them were sound. A few agencies of government—boards, bureaus or departments—were abolished or consolidated; the ineffective three-man Sanitary Commission was eliminated and replaced with a single commissioner (George McAneny was named as the first); a central Purchasing Department was created; an advance was made toward consolidating inspection of building plans and supervision over the construction of buildings; both an executive budget, which centered responsibility for the preparation of the annual expense budget in the Mayor, instead of the Board of Estimate, and a capital outlay budget, which made financial provision for future public improvements, were adopted.[30] The 1933 budget, by permission of the state legislature, was reopened and reduced 18 per cent from that of 1932 ($518,427,972 compared to $631,366,298) and salaries were cut $20,000,000, though this economizing came only as a result of pressure from the bankers and was open to criticism.[31]

Yet despite these achievements, O'Brien and his administration had become the objects of scathing ridicule and indignation. The Mayor's public personality, for one thing, was against him, for whatever charms he had in private usually evaporated when he appeared in his official role. Never a colorful man or one who could arouse enthusiasm, not physically or mentally agile, he easily became stereotyped in an age of growing anti-Tammany feeling as a lubberly character who always managed to put his foot in the bucket—a Mayor somewhat on the order of Hylan. The press did a good deal to build up this image, for when O'Brien became Mayor, a new crew of reporters, more critical-minded than the loyal group that had surrounded Walker, took over the City Hall assignment and early in the new Mayor's career decided that he was essentially a buffoon and did him the unkindness of reporting his statements in his own language, a treatment from which few public figures can escape unscathed.[32]

In dealing with the city's financial dilemma, moreover, O'Brien made enemies at every turn. Partly this was his fault. His budget slashing, though appreciated by many citizens, aroused much resentment in certain quarters because, obedient to the machine, the Mayor cut heavily such items as education, hospitals and relief, while failing to use the knife on a number of political jobs.[33] In good part, however, he was not to blame. If O'Brien had been rougher on political jobs, civil service employees still would hardly have taken kindly to the administration's pay cuts. The desperate plight of the city treasury necessitated additional taxes, but in view of the Depression and Tammany scandals, every attempt of the administration to raise revenue produced howls of anger from outraged citizens who would be adversely affected by the new taxes.[34] Even when the Mayor was given credit for his accomplishments, it was bestowed rather grudgingly since people generally recognized them as part of an eleventh-hour attempt by Tammany to retain power. Essentially O'Brien never had a chance; he was a Tammany Mayor at the wrong time.

How good Fusion's prospects were was clearly demonstrated in the Democratic primaries on September 19. The choices of the Democratic bosses had not gone uncontested, and the primary results were startling. While O'Brien won the contest for the mayoral nomination, by 180,000 votes, the combined vote of his opposition was over 130,000, an unusually large figure. Much more significant was the fact that Deputy Comptroller Frank J. Prial, who had the support of many civil service workers, ran as an insurgent for the Comptroller nomination and by 88,000 votes defeated John N. Harman, the choice of the county leaders and a protégé of Boss McCooey; the Brooklyn machine was not even able to carry its borough for McCooey's candidate. Furthermore, all the Democratic organizations except Flynn's suffered reverses of one sort or another. The Democratic leadership was stunned.[35]

How ironical that because of this very omen of Fusion victory, a situation developed in the early fall which quickly reduced Fusion's advantages and made the election more uncertain! For the day after the primaries, when the results were known, President Roosevelt, according to Ed Flynn, called him to Washington and suggested that Joseph McKee be urged to come out of private life and run for Mayor on a special ticket. According to the Bronx boss, the President promised to bless McKee's candidacy at the proper time.[36] Apparently there were two main reasons for Roosevelt's action. In the first place, while Roosevelt did not want Tammany to win, he did want the city to remain in Democratic hands, being afraid that a victory which would strengthen the Republicans in New York City would endanger the re-election of Governor Lehman in 1934 and his own re-election two years later. In the second place, with Tammany on the ropes, the situation presented the national administration with the chance of a lifetime to destroy Tammany's leadership in Democratic politics in New York, reduce the Manhattan machine to the status of just another county organization and, in general, gain control in New York City over the Democratic Party, whose components, excepting the Bronx organization, were still unfriendly to Roosevelt. Remembering 1932, the President may have been particularly concerned about New York City's delegates to the Democratic nominating convention in 1936.[37]

Flynn, who may also have seen in a McKee ticket a wonderful way of saving his county slate in a year in which Democratic success was doubtful,[38] quickly conferred with James A. Farley, the distributor of federal patronage, and together they laid the groundwork for a new ticket to be headed by the former President of the Board of Aldermen. They were considerably aided in their plans by the fact that, as soon as the results of the primaries were known and the rumor that McKee might run began to circulate, important business groups began to urge McKee's nomination. Despite the desires of others, McKee was at first reluctant to re-enter politics. But the pressure exerted by those interested in his nomination, most likely the tempting promise of help from Roosevelt and, no doubt, a certain amount of vanity finally broke down his resistance. On September 29, after a few days of inner wrestling, McKee announced his candidacy, and a short time later candidates for the other important offices were selected to round out the slate of what was called the Recovery Party.[39]

Two kinds of people became the backbone of the new party: professional politicians and wealthy conservatives. At the start, Flynn's machine naturally got behind the McKee ticket, and to this nucleus were added a number of Democratic district leaders in the other boroughs who felt that O'Brien could not win, but McKee could, as well as some remnants of Koenig's old organization. The conservatives were mainly businessmen and financiers who, though opposed to Tammany, had never been happy with La Guardia and welcomed the chance to back a candidate more to their liking. (Significantly, after McKee became a candidate, the New York State Chamber of Commerce voted to make him a member and dissolved the committee it had appointed to work with the Fusion movement.) Some of these conservatives were silk-stocking Republicans, though most of this species stayed with La Guardia. The bulk were rich independent Democrats who also had a thought to the political fortunes of the Democratic Party on the state and national levels. Nathan Straus, Jr. and George V. McLaughlin, both of whom had been offered the Fusion nomination, played conspicuous roles in the McKee movement. Straus became the Recovery Party's candidate for President of the Board of Aldermen, while McLaughlin served as chairman of McKee's Independent Citizens Committee. Other prominent people supporting the McKee ticket were bankers Henry Morgenthau, Sr. and Harvey D. Gibson, Averell Harriman, the railroad magnate, Frederic R. Coudert, Sr., international lawyer, and the venerable Fulton Cutting.[40]

McKee's entry into the mayoral race threw the political picture into confusion. What had shaped up as a relatively clear cut two-way contest between Tammany and anti-Tammany now became a complicated three-way race. Both the Tammany and Fusion camps lost strength by defections to the new party. Both were apprehensive and understandably bitter toward McKee. Tammany saw a glimmer of hope in the possibility that McKee's candidacy might somehow allow O'Brien to slip in as a minority winner—and it was true that Tammany's chances had improved—but this comforting thought was more than offset by the dismal one of what a McKee victory would mean to the Hall.[41] As for Fusion, its ranks had been broken, and history bore witness to how costly lack of fusion solidarity had proven in the past. The seriousness of the McKee threat to a Fusion victory could not be doubted. The former Acting Mayor was popular, his party was geared to attract independent Democrats and wrapped about the entire enterprise apparently was the magic name of Franklin Roosevelt, whose prestige in the fall of 1933 was immense.

The Fusion campaign was a heterogeneous affair marked by the participation of various groups and organizations. Of these, the most important were the Republican Party and the City Party, which at the end of August had changed its name to the City Fusion Party to emphasize its theme of union regardless of party labels. Though the activities of the two organizations were co-ordinated during the campaign, each kept its own identity, had its own campaign committee, raised and spent its own funds, made separate financial returns, arranged its own meetings and scheduled its own speakers (except in the case of big meetings), and occupied distinct offices.[42]

The members of the City Fusion Party—a good number of them young people—were among La Guardia's most enthusiastic supporters. Sporting with pride the party's button, which carried a picture of a four-leaf clover, many members circulated nominating petitions for the party's candidates and, afterwards, canvassed voters and distributed literature. Most of the party's workers were independent Democrats, for although it directed its appeal toward all groups of voters, in light of the existing political situation, it could hardly help but become the main vehicle of political expression for those independent Democrats favoring the Fusion cause. (Independent Democrats, however, also campaigned for La Guardia through other groups like the Roosevelt Democrats for La Guardia, the New Deal Democratic League for La Guardia and, especially, the Knickerbocker Democrats. Formed originally in the Tenth Assembly District in 1932 to elect Langdon Post to the Assembly over Tammany opposition, the Knickerbocker Democrats remained intact after Post's victory and spread to other assembly districts.[43])

A Fusion Campaign Committee on which the Republican and City Fusion parties had representation was set up to furnish co-ordination and direction. Burlingham was chairman, Tuttle and Davidson two of the vice-chairmen. David M. Heyman, a member of the Lewisohn Stock Exchange House, was made treasurer with the task of raising funds. The important job of campaign manager was entrusted to William Chadbourne, and an excellent campaign manager he proved to be, his fine sense of organization being matched only by his ability to soothe ruffled tempers. Time and again, Seymour Halpern, later a state senator and congressman but in 1933 a young man of nineteen serving as one of Chadbourne's secretaries, could hear his boss calming their explosive mayoral candidate. ("Now Fiorello," he would usually begin, a note of sweet reasonableness in his voice.) There were also on the Fusion Campaign Committee a sizable number of notable people who contributed the use of their names.[44]

Actually the work of steering the campaign was carried on by a small group composed of Seabury, Burlingham, Chadbourne, Paul Windels, La Guardia, and, occasionally, Berle and Roy Howard; some were not even members of the bigger Fusion Campaign Committee. Every day except Sunday they met for breakfast at Chadbourne's home to review developments and plan strategy. A lawyer and old friend of La Guardia, Paul Windels was one of the shrewdest and wisest figures in the inner circle, and though he limited his activity to giving advice, this was not an insignificant contribution. Paul Kern, La Guardia's former law researcher, now a young assistant law professor at Columbia, also helped to chart strategy at times, though he was not a member of the breakfast group. As he had been before, Seabury remained throughout the race the real leader of the Fusion movement; whether behind the scenes or campaigning, he exerted as much energy as if he, himself, were running for Mayor.[45]

Fusion strategy after the entry of McKee was to concentrate upon him as the chief enemy. Not that Tammany was forgotten, far from it, but the Recovery ticket was considered more dangerous to Fusion's success. At first the Fusion forces attacked the McKee candidacy as being just a stalking horse for Tammany, but soon this line was replaced by another: that McKee represented only the attempt of one boss (Flynn) to replace another (Curry) and that the bolt of some district leaders to McKee constituted but the "parade of the tin-box brigade" (Windels' phrase) from a weaker to a stronger candidate. While depicting McKee as Flynn's tool in an intraparty struggle, Fusion at the same time called attention to his link with Tammany and pointed up his record as a member of Walker's Board of Estimate, stressing such matters as the Equitable Coach Company affair and the "salary grab." La Guardia, it was emphasized, was the only candidate truly independent of machines and bosses, the only one, therefore, who could give the city real reform.[46]

A vital part of the Fusion offensive was its program for civic improvement which La Guardia publicized generally in piecemeal fashion. The Fusion mayoral candidate pledged himself to work for a number of changes, the most important of which were these: a nonpartisan administration in which jobs would be awarded according to merit, not politics; restoration of the city's credit through consolidations and the removal of political parasites—but no cuts to be made in the salaries of civil service workers; a new Charter which would deal only with general principles and which, among other things, would allow the people to initiate Charter amendments; unification and municipal ownership of the subways; improvements in the unemployment relief system; use of federal funds for slum clearance and the building of model multiple buildings under the auspices of a municipal housing commission; educational improvements, including the removal of politics from the schools; more playgrounds; better care of the poor's health, especially by speeding up the building of district health centers which had been allowed to lag; reform of the Magistrates' Courts.[47]

The Fusion program, which at once represented an indictment of Tammany government—what it had not done, what problems it had failed to wrestle with—and the Fusion blueprint for reform did not view reform as mainly a question of efficiency and economy. Efficiency and economy were there, but the emphasis was on service and welfare. That this was so was due to a number of combining circumstances: the social needs of the city, especially in an age of depression; the liberal spirit in the nation which in the thirties expressed itself in the view that government should be used positively to enrich the lives of its citizens; and most important, the fact that La Guardia and many other Fusion leaders were liberals. Because of this last point and the nature of the Fusion program of reform, a number of prominent liberals came out for Fusion; among them were Arthur Garfield Hays, Ernest Angell, Walter Frank, lawyers; Ernest Gruening, Norman Hapgood, Paul Kellogg, editors and writers; Carl Van Doren, Joseph Wood Krutch, Parker T. Moon, teachers and authors; Mary K. Simkhovitch, social worker; B. W. Huebsch, publisher. For similar reasons and because of a personal attachment many needle workers felt for La Guardia, several garment locals backed the Fusion candidate.[48]

Fusion, of course, hardly had free sailing. Both the McKee forces and Tammany attacked it, as well as one another, though the McKee assault was much more vigorous, a not surprising fact since the Recovery Party candidate counted heavily upon breaking into La Guardia's support. McKee charged La Guardia with being a demagogue, a "communist at heart," an unstable character whose administration, if elected, would result in chaos, the candidate of conservative Republicans who wanted a Fusion victory in order to help defeat Roosevelt in 1936, a tool of "Boss" Seabury who "dictated" the Fusion ticket. McKee put himself forward as the true political independent, the only unbossed candidate. Playing to independent Democrats, the Recovery Party did its best to underscore its reputed connection with the President at every turn, an approach apparent in numerous ways, ranging from the very name of the party and the display of Roosevelt's portraits at rallies to McKee's statement that "a vote for McKee is a vote for Roosevelt." McKee also advanced a program for the city's improvement which contained a number of important points; yet it is not without significance that there was more talk in it about finances and governmental changes and less about social services than in the Fusion program.[49] For its part, Tammany hit La Guardia for being "irresponsible" when he was President of the Board of Aldermen during Hylan's administration. It played up O'Brien's record while disavowing Walker's.[50]

The campaign was not, of course, just stratagems, charges and programs. It was men passionately engaged in winning an election. For Fusion it was, for example, the Fusioneers in action. An incongruous association of young Italian prizefighters and Park Avenue bluebloods—wealthy youths like Clendenin Ryan, Byrnes McDonald, Allan Stuyvesant and Cooper Schieffelin—the Fusioneers was organized mainly by Edgar Bromberger, an old friend of La Guardia, primarily to provide poll watchers in rough districts. Before election day the young men were plenty busy, organizing meetings, serving as advance agents and ushers in connection with La Guardia meetings, undertaking pre-registration canvassing and making themselves generally useful.[51]

Mainly, however, the Fusion campaign was La Guardia. His supporters had counted upon him for a dynamic campaign, and he did not disappoint them. He spoke at hundreds of meetings. Sometimes at night Seymour Halpern would accompany him into Harlem and listen to him speak in Spanish and Italian to the deep, full-throated response of the crowds.[52] Before an audience La Guardia possessed neither the poise nor the finesse that marked McKee's oratory, nor the friendliness that characterized O'Brien's. He was vehement and declamatory, the picture of a militant crusader. When he became excited, his eyes flamed, his dark hair became mussed and his underlip shot out in defiance. He pounded the rostrum and shouted until, at times, his voice broke. The crowds loved it, caught fire and cheered wildly.[53]

Political fever reached a heat not rivaled since the days of Mitchel. The newspapers took sides, adding to the intensity of the campaign; the *World-Telegram, Times, Herald Tribune* supported Fusion; the *Sun, Daily News* and Hearst papers, McKee.[54] Never before had so many New Yorkers registered to vote in a non-presidential election; the total was 2,324,389, over 750,000 more than had registered in 1929. In a straw poll conducted by the *Literary Digest,* more than 500,000 people sent in ballots. Occasionally the excitement generated spilled over into acts of violence: the wrecking of the interior of a south Brooklyn Democratic club supporting Fusion; the smashing of windows in some stores displaying La Guardia signs; the stoning of Democratic campaign trucks in the Bensonhurst section of Brooklyn; the accidental shooting of a ten-year-old girl while watching an O'Brien parade. As the campaign gathered momentum, Fusion's supporters left behind the depression that had come upon them at the time of McKee's entry and became highly enthusiastic. It was a period of intense idealism and immense hopes. Few among those working for a Fusion victory did not regard the campaign as the great crusade of the generation.[55]

The nation followed the political contest avidly; news about it rivaled NRA news from Washington as a topic of national interest. Editors thousands of miles from New York took sides, some for La Guardia, some for McKee—none for Tammany. Part of the interest was the result of the fact that many political reporters and observers insisted upon viewing the election as largely a fight between Roosevelt and the Republican Party. For the most part, however, people were simply fascinated, as they had been on similar occasions in the past, by the drama of their greatest city in political revolt. From across the sea, Europeans also watched with keen interest, though somewhat bewildered by all the turmoil since their own cities rarely suffered the same ordeal.[56]

For Fusion the climax to the campaign came on the night of November 2 at a huge rally in Madison Square Garden. In the afternoon airplanes flying over the city had advertised the meeting. Torchlight parades, starting in a dozen different quarters of the city after dark, had led the way to the Garden. Every seat in the arena was filled. An estimated 50,000 people unable to gain admittance jammed the area between Sixth and Ninth avenues. One of the most dramatic moments of the evening was the entrance of Seabury. He entered from a doorway behind the audience, but somehow his arrival became known simultaneously in all parts of the Garden. Men and women arose in their seats and faced the rear. They cheered and stamped their feet; they whistled and shrieked. From the balconies fluttered down a shower of tattered paper. When La Guardia arrived there was another tremendous ovation. Torn paper fell in such volume that the walls of the arena could be seen but dimly. The Fusioneers cheered until it seemed that the human larynx must fail. The stamping of feet sounded like an army marching. Rufus McGahen, sitting upstairs watching the crowd, felt a thrill shoot through him as he realized that the demonstrations were completely spontaneous and signalized the culmination of a movement that had been so long in developing. When the audience finally filed out of the Garden, after listening to speeches by La Guardia, Seabury, Post, Schurman and other Fusion candidates, several thousand of them stormed a Tammany rally in session at Times Square, tying up traffic for more than half an hour.[57]

Before the campaign came to an end, two things removed whatever chance McKee might have had. One was the injection of the issue of anti-Semitism. The other was the position that Roosevelt took with respect to the campaign. In one of his campaign speeches, Seabury, recalling his investigation of the city's administration of the first unemployment relief funds made when he was counsel to the Hofstadter committee, assailed Governor Lehman, along with the city administration, for failing to bring to justice those involved in the relief scandal. Whether Seabury was moved to include Lehman in his attack because he was angry about the Governor's inaction in the relief matter or felt that, by connecting Lehman and the city Democrats in this way, he might cut down Lehman's prestige, thereby enhancing Fusion's chances, or for whatever reason—the criticism of the popular Lehman, as other Fusion leaders immediately recognized, was a political error. McKee, obviously attempting to capitalize on Lehman's popularity, especially with the Jews, at once denounced Seabury's attack on the Governor as being shoddy; and to put La Guardia on the spot McKee sent him a telegram asking him to disavow Seabury. To escape from the trap, La Guardia hit McKee with brass knuckles. He sent back a scorching telegram asking the Recovery Party candidate if he was trying to "draw a red herring across the cowardly, contemptible and unjust attack" he had made and published against a great race. Thus La Guardia brought into the open the charge of anti-Semitism which had been whispered about McKee—and which, it was said, Tammany was planning to use—ever since the *Brooklyn Eagle* in November, 1932, had printed certain statements made by McKee in an article for the *Catholic World* in 1915. In this article, McKee, at the time a young teacher at De Witt Clinton High School, had complained that, although the Jews of New York City constituted only about 25 per cent of the population of the city, they made up more than 75 per cent of the city's high school enrollment, that the young Jews were embracing Socialistic thinking, that they were losing the religion of their parents and a code of absolute morality, and that to these people Christians would have to bow in future years, since education would give them an advantage in life. As he had in 1915, McKee in 1933 denied that he meant to be anti-Semitic and asserted that he did not criticize Jews, but only those "who abandoned Judaism." Actually, McKee's article was not an attack on the Jews as such but a conservative Irish Catholic's attack upon modern philosophy and secular education and a plea for more Catholic teachers to go into the educational system and for more Catholic children to take advantage of the city's high schools. Still it was not without anti-Semitic overtones, and its introduction into the campaign of 1933, at a time when Hitler's persecutions were alarming Jews everywhere, was political dynamite. Ed Flynn saw the writing on the wall.[58]

There was one slight hope left for McKee: perhaps Roosevelt would endorse him and give him real support. Although the President had been instrumental in launching McKee's candidacy, and though McKee's camp did everything possible to identify its cause with his—a connection which Fusion continually denied vehemently—Roosevelt's public position, from the start, had been one of "hands-off" local politics. Continually Flynn had asked Roosevelt to come out for McKee openly and, though met with evasions, had been confident that at the right moment the President would do so. But even after the issue of anti-Semitism made such action imperative, Roosevelt refused to publicly endorse McKee and his ticket; whatever he may have originally intended, the right moment for Roosevelt never came.[59] It is not hard to guess why. Being the politician he was, Roosevelt probably figured that his best policy was to do nothing. If he remained officially impartial, a McKee victory would rebound to his credit anyway, while the loss of prestige which a McKee defeat could entail would be kept at a minimum. Then, too, Roosevelt may have felt that it would be unwise to antagonize La Guardia, who was heart and soul for the New Deal and with whom he might be able to do business if elected; perhaps the President was influenced by the fact that most polls and surveys showed La Guardia leading.[60] Far from being inclined to rescue McKee from the dilemma in which the anti-Semitism issue had placed him, Roosevelt may have seen in it an excellent reason for maintaining his official silence.

On Tuesday, the seventh of November, the voters went to the polls. Tammany, which still had the racket mobs and control of the police, pulled out all the stops. During the campaign Dutch Schultz had handed over $12,000 to $15,000 of his racket money to Tammany for the election of its candidate for District Attorney. Now mobsters, trade-marked for their own purposes by identical pearl-gray fedoras, marched on the polling places south of Fourteenth Street in Manhattan, cracked skulls and took over voting machines. When Chadbourne protested upon finding 200 gangsters in one polling place in the Second Assembly District South, home of Tammany district leader Albert Marinelli, Chadbourne was arrested for disorderly conduct. That the thugs did not have things all their own way was largely due to the Fusioneers who, at the price of bloody noses, patrolled the streets and the polling places in an attempt to protect the sanctity of the ballot and encourage people to vote.[61]

Tammany's last-minute tactics could not stem the tide. As the results came in that night, it became apparent that once again, New York City had overthrown the machine. Fusion's victory, if incomplete, was decisive. La Guardia finally rolled up 868,522 votes to McKee's 609,053 and O'Brien's 586,672 to become a minority winner. Fusion won the other city-wide offices and the borough presidencies in all the boroughs except two, thus obtaining control of the Board of Estimate. But Tammany by a few thousand votes, a compliment largely to the activity of the men in the pearl-gray fedoras, maintained control of the office of District Attorney of New York County and that of Borough President of Manhattan. Using both the Democratic and Recovery Party lines, Flynn retained the Borough Presidency of the Bronx as well as his county offices, and most of the offices in the other counties remained in machine hands. The Board of Aldermen remained a Democratic stronghold.[62]

Fusion headquarters on election night was the scene of wild celebration. "As the returns piled up a La Guardia victory," wrote a *Times* reporter, "the smiles broadened, the shouting and cheering increased, and the hubbub welled into pandemonium." La Guardia's arrival increased the bedlam. "The tightly-packed crowd set up a roar of welcome and pressed forward as photographers' flashlights boomed. Thirty-five perspiring policemen struggled ineffectually for several minutes to clear a space for the Mayor-elect." Going into a side room, La Guardia made a brief radio address after which he once again returned to the crowd. "Everything was confusion. Crockery fell from tables to the floor. Shouts, cheers, handclapping and stamping of feet drowned out whatever Mr. La Guardia had to say to those nearest him." [63] After sixteen years, New York was to have a reform administration again.[64]

*

Part III
The Period of Reform

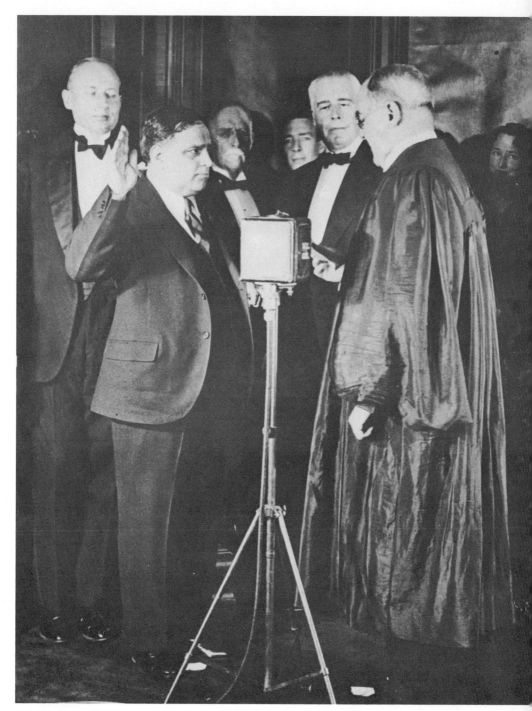

Ending sixteen years of Tammany rule on January 1, 1934, Fiorello H. La Guardia is sworn in as Mayor of New York City by Justice Philip J. McCook in the home of Samuel Seabury (center).

Aaron Burr, one of the first leaders of Tammany Hall

Mayor Fernando Wood

William Marcy (Boss) Tweed

Carmine De Sapio

William Jay Schieffelin

Dr. Charles H. Parkhurst

Samuel Seabury

The first Tammany wigwam, Nassau and Spruce streets, 1798

Tammany Hall, 1812-1867

Mayor James Walker, Grand Sachem John R. Voorhis, Judge George Olvaney and former Governor Alfred E. Smith in Tammany regalia at the laying of the cornerstone of Tammany Hall on Union Square at 17th Street, January 8, 1929.

The last Tammany Hall, built in 1929. There is now no building known as Tammany Hall. Instead Tammany operates out of an office on Madison Avenue.

John Kelly

Richard Croker

Charles Francis Murphy

Mayor William F. Havemeyer

Brown Brothers

Brown Brothers

Mayor William J. Gaynor

Mayor Seth Low

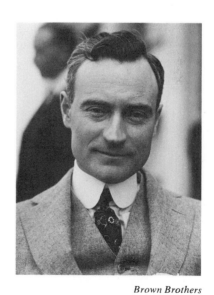

Wide World Photos

Brown Brothers

Mayor John F. Hylan

Mayor John Purroy Mitchel

Mayor Vincent R. Impellitteri

Ambassador to Mexico William O'Dwyer testifying before the Kefauver committee, December, 1951, about crime in New York City when O'Dwyer was Mayor.

The Robert F. Wagners, father and son.

Judge Samuel Seabury questioning Mayor James Walker during the Hofstadter committee investigation, 1932.

Herald Tribune-Steffen

Mayor La Guardia presiding at the Board of Estimate meeting of January 2, 1934. Around the table, left to right: James J. Lyons, Borough President of the Bronx; Samuel Levy, Borough President of Manhattan; Bernard S. Deutsch, President of the Board of Aldermen; Mayor La Guardia; W. A. Cunningham, Comptroller; R. F. Ingersoll, Borough President of Brooklyn; and George U. Harvey, Borough President of Queens.

The American Labor Party's rally for Mayor La Guardia in Madison Square Garden, October 31, 1937.

Herald Tribune, Acme and Kell Photos

President Franklin D. Roosevelt congratulating Mayor La
Guardia after commissioning him Chief of the Office of
Civilian Defense, May 22, 1941.

Mayor La Guardia and Budget Director
Kenneth Dayton at work on the city's budget,
March 21, 1939.

I. Haberman-New York Press Photographers Association

Mayor La Guardia dictating in the back of his limousine.

Mayor La Guardia talks with newly elected District Attorney Thomas E. Dewey at City Hall, November 3, 1937.

Brown Brothers

I. Haberman-New York Press Photographers Association

Picture of a mayor who has just skinned a Tammany tiger.

United Press International Photo

Mayor-motorman La Guardia taking the first city-managed BMT train out of Times Square station, June 1, 1940.

Brown Brothers

Air Raid Warden La Guardia reporting an "incident" at Fourth Avenue and 8th Street during New York City's practice daytime alert, October 22, 1942.

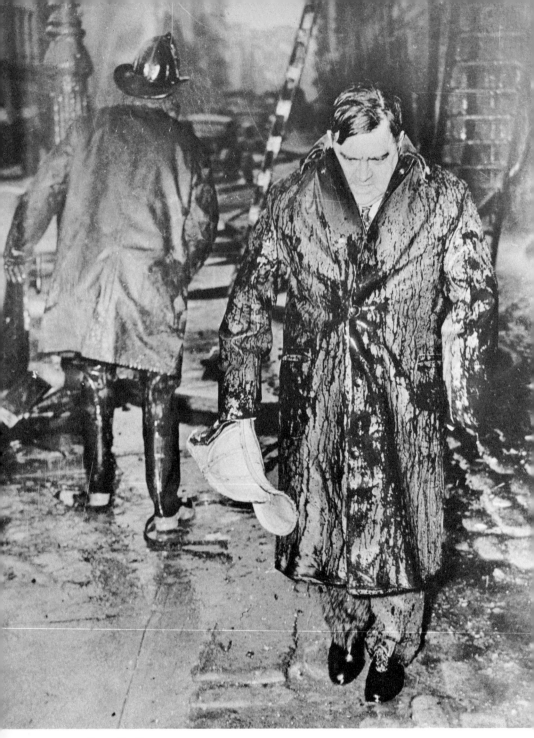

The world's most famous fire buff leaves the scene after overseeing the rescue of a fireman pinned beneath a beam.

Police Commissioner Lewis J. Valentine watches as Mayor La Guardia dramatizes his war against slot machines and slot machine racketeers, August 5, 1937.

Citizen La Guardia, with Mrs. La Guardia, leaves City Hall, January 1, 1946, after twelve years as Mayor.

7

Fiorello H. La Guardia

LA GUARDIA was the first Mayor of New York to rise from the ranks of the "new immigrants." He was born December 11, 1882, on Varick Street in New York City to Italian parents who had come through Castle Garden, the country's immigrant depot, three or four years before. His father, Achille, was the son of Don Raffaele La Guardia, an Italian government employee; according to one biography of Fiorello, Don Raffaele had served as one of Garibaldi's "Red Shirts," but this claim cannot be verified. Fiorello's mother, the former Irene Coen Luzzatto, was Jewish, being descended from two Jewish families with roots deep in the Italian past. Though Achille La Guardia had been baptized a Catholic, he broke with the Church in his teens and brought up his children as Episcopalians. An Italian-Jewish American, who was a Protestant— Fiorello La Guardia was an anomaly from the start.

Not alone because of his birth did Fiorello have upon him the impress of both the New World and the Old; he grew to manhood in the American West and in Europe. A short time after he was born his father, a musician, became a bandmaster in the United States Army, with the result that Fiorello spent most of his boyhood around Whipple Barracks, near Prescott, in what was then Arizona Territory. Here he went to school, learned to play the cornet, love Italian opera, and developed some deep-rooted attitudes that were to last him for life. When La Guardia was in his teens, the Spanish-American War broke out. His father, sent to Mobile with his regiment, fell a victim to the infamous "embalmed beef" and had to be discharged from the Army; he was already in poor health, and a short while later he died. Before his death, the family moved to Trieste and lived for a while with Fiorello's maternal grandparents; Achille was hoping to make a new start. Under the pressure of economic necessity, Fiorello obtained his first real job: in 1900, at the age of eighteen, he became a clerk in the American consulate in Budapest. Four years later he was promoted to Consular Agent in Fiume.

In 1906, feeling that "it was not good for a young and ambitious American to remain in that [the diplomatic] service too long at a time," [1] La Guardia resigned his consular post and returned to America in search of a better career. During the next few years, he worked as an interpreter on Ellis Island. He had studied Italian, German and Croatian in Europe; now he added Yiddish, French and Spanish. In the evening he attended New York University Law School. When he obtained his degree in 1910, he quit Ellis Island and began the practice of law, finding his first real clients among the men's clothing workers during their great strikes of 1912 and 1913. La Guardia fought picket and other cases for the union and addressed hundreds of meetings for the purpose of fostering solidarity between Italian and Jewish needle workers. The friendship and support that these activities won for him in Italian and Jewish labor circles was later cemented by his work in Congress.

La Guardia's real interest was not in law, however, but in politics. He joined the Republican Party because he could not stomach Tammany, his opposition to it dating from his boyhood days in Arizona, when he had read of the Parkhurst and Lexow disclosures in the pages of Pulitzer's *Sunday World*. His congressional district, the Fourteenth, stretched across Manhattan Island from the Hudson to the East rivers, taking in Greenwich Village and some of the tenement areas of the lower East Side. The Republicans had never elected a congressman from this district and had little hope of doing so; in fact, they had an "understanding" with the Democrats that they would put up only token candidates. One night late in the summer of 1914, La Guardia was in the clubhouse when his district leader shouted out: "Who wants to run for Congress?" Innocent of any "understanding" and anxious to get ahead, La Guardia said, "I do" and was made the candidate. Though he soon found out the facts of political life, he decided to make a fight anyway and using his knowledge of Italian and Yiddish concentrated his attack on the East Side. The result was astonishing. While La Guardia lost to his Democratic opponent, he did so by slightly less than 2,000 votes. The amazed Republicans, figuring that he might have a future in politics, rewarded him by having him appointed Deputy Attorney General of the State of New York. In 1916 he was once again given the congressional nomination, and this time the outcome was different. By campaigning vigorously, mobilizing the garment workers and letter carriers, pulling out the flophouse vote before Tammany did and keeping a good watch on the count, La Guardia won by a few hundred votes.

Hardly had he taken his seat in the House when his new political career was interrupted by America's entry into World War I. La Guardia voted for war and for a number of important war measures and then, without resigning his seat in Congress, enlisted in the Aviation Section of the Signal Corps. He served with distinction on the Italian front, rising from lieutenant to captain to major before his discharge and winning a number of decorations and citations. Returning to the United States, he was re-elected to Congress as a bipartisan Republican-Democratic candidate, the two parties having agreed to fuse in a number of districts that year in order to insure the defeat of Socialist candidates. But once again his term in Congress was cut short. In 1919 a special election had to be held for President of the Board of Aldermen to fill the vacancy caused by Al Smith's election to the Governorship the year before. The Republicans prevailed upon La Guardia to make the race. It was, as politicians remarked, a "queer year." A number of important ethnic groups resented the national Democratic administration because of the war and the peace treaties, and the Republicans accomplished an amazing feat: both La Guardia and Henry H. Curran, the Republican candidate for Borough President of Manhattan, were elected. La Guardia subsequently spent two stormy years on the Board of Estimate, usually in alliance with Hylan on the various issues to come before that body.

He expected to be the Republican nominee for Mayor in 1921—in that year he claimed that he had been definitely promised the nomination in 1919 if he were elected President of the Board of Aldermen. But La Guardia had crossed Republican Governor Nathan L. Miller on a few issues. And many Republicans had become disgusted with some of La Guardia's political traits: his tendency to go whooping off the reservation, his fiery antics, what they regarded as his radicalism and demagoguery. The Republican leaders gave the nod to Henry Curran. Wild with anger, La Guardia decided upon a fight to the finish; he entered the Republican primary against Curran. In what became a four-cornered race, the Republican machine easily put its candidate over, dealing La Guardia a crushing blow. Politically he seemed washed up. About the same time his baby daughter and wife died. At the end of 1921, La Guardia was a broken and beaten man.

To earn a living, he turned again to the law. Work, he discovered, kept him from remembering the past, and he plunged into it almost vindictively. Before long he rediscovered politics. Encouraged by Hearst, La Guardia began attacking Governor Miller and the GOP organization; in the summer of 1922 he startled the state by announcing that he would run for Governor as an Independent Republican candidate if Miller were renominated. Republican leaders suddenly found that La Guardia was not dead—he could not be elected, but he could bring about Miller's defeat—and they offered him the pipe of peace. Would he take the Republican nomination for Congress in the Twentieth District on the upper East Side of Manhattan? La Guardia would and did; and he had the last laugh. While Miller went down to defeat before Al Smith, La Guardia, after a bitter campaign, nosed out his Tammany rival. Once again he had won a congressional seat, and this time he was to keep it for a decade. In 1924 at the time of the La Follette third party, La Guardia bolted to the Progressive movement and was re-elected with Socialist help. After that, backed by the Gibboni, an organization of fervent Italian-Americans personally devoted to him, La Guardia took over control of the GOP organization in East Harlem and ran as a Republican.

Because of his achievements as Mayor, people have tended to forget about La Guardia's work in Congress. It is well to remember that long before he became Mayor, he had made a national reputation as a Representative. He attained distinction by his conscientious preparation, dramatics, insurgency and courage. He was one of the outstanding liberals in the House. During his first period in Congress, he fought the Espionage Act as dangerous to American civil liberties and opposed give-aways of war surplus to big interests at the expense of the public. During his second period, as a prominent member of the Progressive wing of the Republican Party, he opposed Prohibition, child labor, power monopolies and a national sales tax. He championed old age pensions, national unemployment insurance, employer liability laws, government operation of Muscle Shoals. He led the successful fight for the labor anti-injunction bill which bears his name and that of Senator Norris. In an age of political orthodoxy, La Guardia was a bold heretic, a New Dealer before the advent of the New Deal.[2]

Most men have complex personalities, but the one La Guardia brought with him to the Mayor's office was more complex than most. Indeed in certain ways it was paradoxical. There was, for one thing, a definitely unpleasant, if not nasty, side to the man, a side which made him extremely difficult to get along with. It was a side which his subordinates knew well. He could be and was autocratic, belligerent, overbearing, stubborn and opinionated. Impatient and irascible, he was given to violent outbursts of temper—and hell had no fury like one of Fiorello's tantrums. At times, he could be ill-mannered and even obscene; when he was Mayor he sent a letter to a newspaperman on the *World-Telegram* which it would be difficult to match for vulgarity.[3] And there were times when he showed a streak of pettiness and vindictiveness. In the spring of 1945 he split with Comptroller McGoldrick when the latter, against La Guardia's wishes, cast the crucial vote in the Board of Estimate to give the teachers a bonus in the 1945–6 expense budget. McGoldrick felt that the teachers deserved to get a cost-of-living bonus, the same as all other city employees, but La Guardia was opposed, essentially because he wanted to get even with the National Education Association which had criticized him a short time before.[4]

Yet there was a completely different side to La Guardia. He possessed a wonderful sense of humor and could be, when he wanted to, or when he was relaxing with his family and friends, positively charming and sociable.

Secretary of Interior Harold Ickes, commenting on the Gridiron Club dinner in December, 1937, noted that La Guardia, speaking without notes, was "sparkling and witty. He kept everyone laughing. And yet back of his wit were many barbs. He kidded the President and he especially kidded Jim Farley and Senator Wagner in connection with the [1937] New York mayoralty fight." It was a good speech, Ickes declared, done in good temper.[5] "Fiorello was lots of fun," Ickes wrote on another occasion, describing a visit with La Guardia. "He was lovely with his two young adopted children. We had several rounds of cocktails and then went to Henri's on Fifty-Second Street where we had a good dinner. Fiorello can always be depended upon to serve good food. . . ."[6]

Moreover, the "Little Flower" had a big heart. It was reflected at times in flights of sentimentality. It was seen in his genuine empathy and sympathy for the underprivileged. It came out in his unbounded love of children. "My greatest tribute to him [La Guardia]," said Stanley Howe, at the time Mayor La Guardia's chief secretary, "is that if the children of this city were its electors, the Mayor could be re-elected by their votes alone." [7] Probably he could have, for the children never had a better friend in City Hall. His deep affection for them explains, at least in part, that episode New Yorkers will remember as long as they remember La Guardia—his reading of the Sunday comics over the radio during a newspaper deliverers' strike which deprived readers of their papers. "When I wrote to you about skates," one little boy wrote the Mayor, who enjoyed corresponding with the younger set, "you were very kind to help me. Well, one day a gentle lady came to visit me. When she mentioned skates, I knew that you send [sic] her. But when she gave me that 5 dollar check, I was so supprised [sic] . . . Gee mister Mayor I so [sic] happy now that you convinced my mother that I could go skatting [sic]." [8] Within La Guardia there flowed a strong current of paternal feeling that was continually overflowing. And not just with regard to children. La Guardia loved to play father and give advice to adults. Especially he liked to counsel the mass of common people in the city; it was a basic reason for the little Sunday radio talks he made as Mayor.

Nor was this the only contradiction in his make-up. La Guardia was very much of a moralist and of the kind who was not only certain his side was right—as Ernest Cuneo, one-time law clerk to La Guardia, has pointed out—but was equally certain that no other answer was conceivable, except to crooks.[9] In his economic thinking he exhibited an almost childlike faith in the personal malevolence of "Them," the big capitalists and industrialists; "They" were as real to him, Cuneo notes, as the Bad Giant to a child of four.[10] He had a genuine and fierce hatred for graft and shady deals, corrupt politics, crime and gambling. Money-wise, New York never had a more honest Mayor; when, after his death, Newbold Morris and Marie La Guardia, the Mayor's second wife, opened his safe deposit box, Morris was astonished to discover that La Guardia's total investments consisted of $8,000 in war bonds.[11] With respect to drunkenness, divorce and sex, La Guardia could be moralistic to the point of prudishness; the harassment and eventual banishment of the burlesque theatres in New York which he carried out as Mayor was due, at least partly, to his Puritanism.[12]

At the same time, however, La Guardia did things which were clearly improper or amoral, where they were not immoral. To obtain ends he considered worthwhile or out of vindication, he was quite capable, as we have already discovered, of acting like a Machiavellian character. He helped the hotel waiters in a strike in 1934 by ordering the Health Department to investigate sanitary conditions in the hotels, a blackmail technique worthier of a machine, than a reform, administration.[13] In the fall of 1945 when Frank E. Karelsen, Jr., vice president of the Public Education Association, resigned from an advisory committee of the Board of Education and sharply attacked school conditions, La Guardia ridiculously attributed the attack to desperate attempts of politicians to once again profit from honest graft in connection with school sites and linked Karelsen's law firm with such activities twenty or so years before.[14] And Karelsen was not the sole victim of La Guardia's use of the smear.

Political behavior rarely flows from one well-spring, and this certainly seems to hold true in La Guardia's case. That he was governed in good part by idealism, that he sincerely wanted to make things better cannot be seriously gainsaid. Always, for example, he wanted to improve the condition of the needy immigrant, the laboring man, the little businessman. As a young consular agent at Fiume, when no political advantage could be derived from it, he instituted the practice, later adopted by the Immigration Service on a broad scale, of having the health of immigrants to the United States checked before their embarkation, instead of upon arrival, so as to reduce their disappointment and suffering.[15] At a time when it was not the most expedient thing for a young, aspiring lawyer to do, he joined the cause of the garment workers. Combining to produce his idealism, one feels, were several elements: his moralism, his humanitarianism, an enthusiasm for progress, a devotion to democracy. Mainly his crusading liberalism must be seen as an expression of this idealism.

And yet it would be absurd to say, after studying La Guardia's behavior, that he was motivated politically only by idealism. The accusation made by critics that he was opportunistic and demagogic must be adjudged as not wholly unfair. It is difficult to believe that as congressman and President of the Board of Aldermen he did not often play to the gallery. It cannot be doubted that his espousal of the New Deal and the cause of labor during his administration as Mayor was grounded in something more than sentiment and ideology, real as these were. Though he may have sincerely sympathized with the Jews in the 1930's, one is inclined to suspect that his bleeding heart for them may have been a trifle overdone in light of the fact that La Guardia was not above making anti-Semitic remarks, or remarks that could be so construed, to close friends in private;[16] in any case, a number of his anti-Nazi gestures must be tagged demagogic. Besides, other aspects of La Guardia's behavior, some of which we have noticed or will notice, strongly suggest another major source of his political actions.

What one is forced to conclude is that there was a good deal of the self-seeker in La Guardia; indeed a man who was a close friend of his, but who refuses to be identified, expressed the belief to the writer that La Guardia was as ambitious as any man ever was for success. Success, for him, did not mean money. It most assuredly did not mean social position; far from having a taste for the rich and influential like Mitchel, he tended to hold them in contempt.[17] Success for La Guardia meant essentially power and recognition—the attention of others, applause, fame and glory —and these ends he sought chiefly through politics with all the avidity of a first-class egotist. Without attempting any real psychological analysis of the man, an effort which would lead us into some very uncertain territory, it does seem, after talking to people who knew him well and reflecting on him, that at the root of La Guardia's egotism and quest for power and recognition lay a deep inferiority complex, the product apparently of several factors: the double social burden of being of Italian and Jewish descent, his short stature, possibly his limited formal education.

(Maurice Davidson told a wonderful story which illustrates La Guardia's concern with his stature. Davidson, for a time La Guardia's Commissioner of Water Supply, Gas and Electricity, went to City Hall one day to discuss with the Mayor the appointment of a confidential inspector whose job would be in a tough neighborhood. Davidson had picked out a big, husky fellow who had admirable qualifications. La Guardia wanted another man who was all right, but inexperienced and small. At one point in their conversation Davidson unwisely remarked of La Guardia's choice: "He won't do; he's too small." The Mayor turned white, sprang up from his desk and, unconsciously putting his hand inside his jacket in a manner made famous by a certain French general, screamed while jumping up and down: "WHAT'S THE MATTER WITH A LITTLE GUY? WHAT'S THE MATTER WITH A LITTLE GUY? WHAT'S THE MATTER WITH A LITTLE GUY?" [18])

Such an inferiority complex, incidentally, would help explain a good many other things about La Guardia. It would account for much of his aggressiveness. It would throw much light upon his definite flair for physical derring-do (as his connection with aviation during World War I), a trait he had in common with Theodore Roosevelt, one of his own few heroes.[19] It certainly would help us understand another, and very conspicuous, element in La Guardia's make-up: his almost psychopathic inability to take criticism of any kind. We have previously come across examples of this failing, but it was especially reflected in La Guardia's relations with the press of New York City during his administration as Mayor.

Though the New York City newspapers generally gave La Guardia good coverage, though few political figures received the continuous campaign support he received from them, the Mayor, in his turn, was suspicious of and antagonistic to the fourth estate. He deluded himself into thinking that, because they might take him to task now and then, the newspapers of the city were against him, that they had things "fixed" to prevent accurate news of his doings from reaching the citizens, that they emphasized the city's weak points instead of its strong points.[20] Because of this attitude La Guardia proved to be a real headache to City Hall reporters. For a reporter to ask the Mayor a pointed question was often to risk an outburst of temper and a tongue lashing; Paul Crowell of the *Times* said that he once saw La Guardia snatch a notebook from the hands of a stunned reporter, dash it to the floor and jump up and down on it.[21] The Mayor fought with several of the newspaper publishers of the city, often threatening them with suits; that they continued to support him politically was a tribute to his administration, not an expression of their personal love for him.[22] Nor, by the way, did he limit his attacks on publishers to those of newspapers. When *Fortune* brought out an extraordinarily fine issue on New York City in July, 1939, and one that generally boosted the city, La Guardia hit the roof because one article noted the presence of vice and gambling in New York. "Personally I think the article was lousy," he wrote Henry Luce, and then expanded, "There is a great deal of poison throughout the various articles." [23]

To return to our main point—as with most politicians, the animus behind La Guardia's political behavior has to be seen as the product of both idealism and self-interest. La Guardia, however, was more fortunate than many in that the demands of both generally run parallel. On both counts one feels, after discussing the matter with people who knew him well, he was intent on being an excellent Mayor, the best in the city's history.

There certainly can be no question that in addition to his fierce determination, he possessed certain invaluable assets for realizing such a goal, most of which we are not unfamiliar with. Extremely important, of course, was his tremendous energy and his capacity for and dedication to hard work. New York never had a Mayor who could match La Guardia in these respects. Once when he and Newbold Morris were in Radio City Music Hall, the Mayor, taking note of the Music Hall organist playing under a spotlight, whispered to Morris: "Newbold, that's how our city must be run. Like that organist, you must keep both hands on the keyboard and both feet on the pedals—*and never let go!*" [24] That was precisely the way La Guardia ran New York. Day and night, at least in his first eight years, he worked at his task, never letting go.

A typical day would find the Mayor driving to City Hall in the morning, lost in the back of his limousine behind a portable desk, going over his mail. On arriving at his office, he might begin dictating to two secretaries at once, then plunge into a series of fifteen-minute conferences with officials and delegations. After that he might dash off to dedicate a playground or unveil a statue, then perhaps drive across a borough or two to speak at a civic luncheon, dictating orders as he moved to a secretary who telephoned them back to City Hall. An hour later he might be back at his office to interview a line of people or discuss a problem with a deputy commissioner. In the evening he might have a dinner engagement, maybe several other kinds, too.[25] Relaxation he found in the companionship of his wife and two children and in an occasional baseball game and concert; true son of his father, music always meant a great deal to him.[26] But mainly life meant work at an unrelenting pace—one excellent reason, no doubt, why he was not always of sweet disposition.

He had the advantage of a first-rate mind. It was not the mind of an intellectual; La Guardia never was that. (McGoldrick doubts if he read a book during his entire administration and notes that he disliked reading reports.) But it was a quick, clear mind and in its ability to absorb material, positively brilliant. La Guardia could be briefed on a subject on which he knew little or nothing and then proceed to give as fine a speech on it as if he were an expert and to dramatize it in a way that the experts could not do.[27]

Drama, of course, could have been his middle name; few public officials have had La Guardia's flair for theater, a characteristic, one suspects, not unrelated to his desire for attention and applause. Who, but La Guardia, would launch an attack on racketeers in the artichoke business by leading a group of officials up to the Bronx Terminal Market early one cold December morning and, after having the police assemble an audience of shivering market concessionaires and their employees by blowing bugles in the old Hear Ye style, mount the tailboard of a truck and proceed to read a proclamation banning the sale of artichokes in the public markets? [28] And after a referendum was held to settle a long-standing boundary dispute between the Bronx and Mount Vernon and the residents of the area in dispute voted to remain in the Bronx, who, but La Guardia, would direct the Police Department band to serenade the seventy-four loyal Bronxites and hand out copies of a proclamation from the Mayor expressing his pride in their action? [29] (Even in his everyday relations with people, La Guardia continually exhibited his thespian skills. While impulsiveness was a conspicuous element in his character and many of his moods were genuine, he could also assume moods for the occasion—a mood of expansive charm, a mood of pleading harassment, a mood of fiery temper—and turn them on or off like lights.[30]) To La Guardia was granted that magic political gift of being able to infuse with color whatever he touched. Partly for this reason he was able to keep the voters interested, not only in his activities, but in the work of his administration.

Beyond this, La Guardia possessed a political adeptness akin to genius; he was one of the truly great political masters of his generation. His feel of the pulse of the electorate was unerring; always he understood its aspirations and needs. Good government, he recognized, was not only a good in itself; it was also good politics. A product of melting-pot America himself, he well knew the yearning of some of New York's minority groups for greater economic, social and political benefits. His consummate command of political skills, moreover, helped him in translating aspirations and programs into accomplishments.

His instinct for combat, a characteristic the reader can hardly have failed to observe, as truly marked La Guardia's actions after his election as Mayor as before and was as essential to his success, though what might be termed perverse manifestations of it often made life unhappy for the Mayor's friends and associates and was not otherwise to his advantage. Finally, though by no means least in importance, La Guardia had that indispensable quality—the ability to get things done. All in all, Fiorello La Guardia was in a number of ways well-equipped to be a great leader of urban democracy in an age of crisis.

*/8

Administration

THE MEN around the Fusion Mayor can be placed in one of three groups. It is important to keep in mind, however, that the position of an individual in this scheme tended to be more loose than fixed, that the people in a group were not necessarily on close terms one with the other and that not all of them were equally close to La Guardia or close in the same way. Closest to La Guardia generally, though not on all matters, was a somewhat heterogeneous circle of advisers—a group only in the loosest sense—whom La Guardia respected and to whose advice he would listen and sometimes act upon. At least at the start, the most important people here, all friends, were Seabury, Burlingham, Berle, Windels and Thomas D. Thacher, former federal judge and for a time Solicitor General under Hoover; Berle and Windels were also members of La Guardia's official family until his second term, the former as City Chamberlain, the latter as Corporation Counsel. With the passage of time, changes in relationship occurred. Between 1938 and 1944, Berle served as Assistant Secretary of State and for a while after that as United States Ambassador to Brazil, positions, of course, which removed him from contact with local affairs. Seabury and La Guardia may have become less intimate after around 1940, and Windels and La Guardia, though still on friendly terms, definitely drew apart during La Guardia's last term. Thacher and La Guardia became less close after Thacher's appointment to the Court of Appeals in 1943. Burlingham remained close to La Guardia to the end, always serving as an inspiration to him in many ways as well as a check on his sometimes ill-considered plans; from him the Little Flower would take a scolding, and from no one else in the world.

Other counselors included Edgar Bromberger, who also served in the administration as Deputy Commissioner of Sanitation, Magistrate, Commissioner of Investigation and Chief Magistrate; Victor F. Ridder, publisher of the *New York Journal of Commerce* and *New York Staats Zeitung* and prominent anti-Nazi German American; Dr. George Baehr, the Mayor's personal physician, a man much interested in public affairs; and, during La Guardia's last years in City Hall, William Reid, City Collector since the days of Walker, who became an influential adviser on tax matters. For a few years until the clergyman became too old, La Guardia turned to Monsignor York of the Brooklyn diocese to obtain the Catholic view; thereafter La Guardia consulted the Manhattan hierarchy.[1]

A number of mostly younger men, some of them fanatically devoted to La Guardia, who served him in one or another subordinate capacity constituted a second group. Included in this set in the early years of the administration and for much, if not all, of La Guardia's reign were Lester B. Stone, Paul Kern, Clendenin Ryan, Maurice G. Postley, David Marcus and Reuben A. Lazarus. A former reporter, Stone was at first La Guardia's secretary in charge of press relations, then Assistant Director of the Budget and finally, between 1941 and 1943, the Mayor's executive secretary. Kern, at first the Mayor's law secretary, was appointed to the city's Civil Service Commission in 1936 and later became its president; both Stone and Kern, the latter until he broke with La Guardia in the early forties, were on especially close terms with the Mayor. Clen Ryan, a Fusioneer in the '33 campaign, became La Guardia's confidential aide, serving in this capacity until 1939, when at his own request he was transferred to the Sanitation Department, where he subsequently became a deputy commissioner; at the end of 1939, he left Sanitation to head a newly created Department of Commerce. Postley, for whose ability La Guardia always had a high regard, was a former newspaperman who served as confidential food inspector in the Department of Health, secretary of the Department and, later, secretary to the Board of Education; from time to time, La Guardia pulled him into City Hall for special assignments. A graduate of West Point and a lawyer, David Marcus had been serving under George Medalie as an Assistant United States Attorney in the Southern District of New York when La Guardia in January, 1934, appointed him First Deputy Commissioner in the Department of Correction; in April, 1940, he became Commissioner of the Department. Whether as an assistant corporation counsel or as Assistant to the President of the Council, Reuben Lazarus, from early in the Fusion administration, served principally as La Guardia's legislative representative in Albany; in matters dealing with legislation, and particularly in the last eight years of the administration, nobody was closer to the Mayor.

From 1935 to 1940 when he served as La Guardia's appointment secretary, Stanley Howe was also part of this circle; he had begun his service under Fusion as First Deputy Commissioner of Public Welfare. Joseph Lilly and Louis M. Weintraub were important to La Guardia mainly in his second term. Lilly, originally a newspaperman, began his career in the city service in the Comptroller's office, where he was in charge of public relations. Heeding some ridiculous rumor about him, La Guardia had wanted him fired, but afterwards, realizing he had erred, he appointed him to the Tax Commission. They became friendlier, and Lilly came to write many of La Guardia's public statements. Weintraub, a friend of Paul Kern, while nominally in the Department of Investigation and the Corporation Counsel's office, served as La Guardia's chief researcher from about 1937 to 1941; he operated from a room directly beneath that of the Mayor at City Hall.[2]

The commissioners and other heads of agencies—those in the first group aside—as well as the rest of the Fusion members of the Board of Estimate fell into a third category. Among those in this group in the beginning were Police Commissioner John F. O'Ryan, Fire Commissioner John J. McElligott, Park Commissioner Robert Moses, Commissioner of Hospitals Sigismund S. Goldwater, Health Commissioner John L. Rice, Commissioner of Sanitation Thomas W. Hammond, Commissioner of Public Welfare William Hodson, Tenement House Commissioner Langdon Post, Commissioner of Accounts Paul Blanshard, Commissioner of Purchase Russell Forbes, Commissioner of Markets William Fellowes Morgan, Jr., Commissioner of Water Supply, Gas and Electricity Maurice Davidson, Commissioner of Correction Austin H. MacCormick, Commissioner of Licenses Paul Moss and Budget Director Rufus McGahen.

McElligott, who had spent twenty-eight years in the Department, was at the time of his appointment Fire Chief. Goldwater, who had been Mitchel's Commissioner of Health, was an expert in hospital construction and administration. Rice La Guardia took from New Haven, Connecticut, where he had compiled an enviable record as health officer. Colonel Hammond was an old Army man whose "aptitude and ability to handle men" La Guardia said he knew from a long acquaintance with him. Hodson, a professional social worker, had been serving since 1925 as executive director of the Welfare Council of New York City. Morgan, the owner of a refrigerating company and head of the National Fisheries Association, had long fought racketeering in the Fulton Fish Market; in this connection he had testified before Seabury in the Crain inquiry. MacCormick had been the head of the federal penitentiary at Chillicothe, Ohio. Paul Moss, the brother of B. S. Moss, a theatrical producer, had acted as La Guardia's business manager during the '33 campaign.[3]

Changes occurred in this group, of course, as they did in the others in the course of twelve years. After but nine months O'Ryan, who could not see eye to eye with La Guardia, resigned, and the Mayor appointed Chief Inspector Lewis J. Valentine to head the Police Department; Valentine remained in this position until the closing months of the administration. The end of 1936, for one reason or another, found new commissioners in Sanitation and in Water Supply, Gas and Electricity and a new Director of the Budget. By the end of 1945, with the exception of Parks and Licenses, all the top administrative posts under the Mayor showed a change in leadership, and in most cases, more than one. Moreover, the Fusion element on the Board of Estimate underwent changes, as we shall notice later. Here we will simply note that beginning in 1938 Joseph McGoldrick and Newbold Morris, respectively Comptroller and President of the Council (a new body which replaced the Board of Aldermen), became important members of La Guardia's team; they along with Robert Moses were probably the most influential people in the third category during the last eight years.[4]

With respect to his assistants, commissioners and the other Fusion officials, La Guardia was a tough taskmaster. He tried to drive them with the same intensity he drove himself. He tended to browbeat them in the same fashion in which he had bulldozed his little office staff in the days when he was a congressman. He shrieked, screamed and cursed at them, at times when others were present. Those who worked around him at City Hall came in for more of La Guardia's special treatment than the commissioners and other officials who saw him less often, but their lives were not easy. Perpetually he fired his commissioners, "absolutely and permanently, God damn you," and then the next morning demanded to know where they were. Incidentally, those officials who stood up to La Guardia, like Deutsch and Moses, made a surprising discovery—that that was the best way to get along with the Mayor.[5]

It wasn't all fire and brimstone. Occasionally La Guardia's sense of humor relieved tension. Once when a deputy commissioner in the Department of Markets resigned, La Guardia, without waiting for Commissioner Morgan's consent, appointed a successor, Matthew J. Diserio. Knowing that his commissioner was probably burning, the Mayor sent Morgan a telegram of assurance: "You will find Diserio's name on page 288 of the Social Register"; it was a dig at Morgan, whose name was in that listing. A short time later, La Guardia sent a second telegram: "My mistake, I mean the Bronx telephone book." Behind the humor was something deeper, but Morgan laughed heartily and his resentment dissolved.[6]

La Guardia had a great gag with his commissioners. In a stately box done up with ribbons, he kept a shiny shank bone of a sheep. Whenever some commissioner pulled a boner, the Mayor presented him with the bone; actually it was never really given away, but was returned to La Guardia who presented it again at the next opportunity. Once Fire Commissioner McElligott got it for getting burned with a Roman candle after proclaiming the Fourth of July was to be safe and sane.[7]

Among the commissioners themselves there was a good deal of *esprit de corps*. Fellowes Morgan declared that the other commissioners co-operated with him at all times and that it was "heaven to work with these men." When William Carey, a railroad builder, became Commissioner of Sanitation in 1936, he began to play host to the other commissioners at weekly Wednesday luncheons; the luncheons constituted an informal round table for the department heads, who otherwise seldom met as a group, and they practically all attended. La Guardia, himself, did not go to the luncheons preferring, instead, "kitchen cabinet" meetings of drinks and talk with his younger associates at his home on occasional Saturday afternoons.[8]

As a group, the department and agency heads appointed by La Guardia represented an unusual amount of ability and energy for an American city government. During the '33 campaign La Guardia had promised that they would be good. He had declared that they would be appointed on the basis of merit, not politics, that they would be experts—taken from outside New York if necessary—that they would be "career men" who had risen in the civil service. Throughout his administration he boasted that he had kept the faith. In good part he had.

True, La Guardia did make political appointments—a subject we shall discuss more fully later. True, only some of La Guardia's commissioners could really be labeled experts; Rice, Goldwater, Forbes, MacCormick, Moses, Hodson, Valentine and McElligott certainly fell under this heading —and Rice and MacCormick were taken from out of town. Only a few commissioners could be called career men.

Yet the undeniable fact is that more than any other Mayor in the city's history, La Guardia in making his top appointments placed merit before politics and picked experts and career men. (Incidentally, the selection of career men as administrators is not necessarily something to acclaim, as La Guardia found out in one or two cases: despite his technical knowledge, a man who has always taken orders as a subordinate may develop a timid habit of mind that unfits him for leadership; and one who has been party to the exploitation of the public for years may not be the best one to head a department.) Regardless of whether or not they had training for a particular position, La Guardia's top appointees were, on the whole, men of intelligence, energy and competency. His first appointees were generally more impressive than the later ones, especially those in his third term; but even later on, the departments and agencies were headed by able men and, in comparison to the usual machine appointees, extremely good ones. The kind of men La Guardia selected for the big posts represents one of his most outstanding accomplishments; without high quality administrators at the top, much of the gains of his administration would have been impossible.[9]

La Guardia, himself, was not the world's greatest administrator. This was true not only because he often created tension and resentment around him; he also fell down because he could not apportion his energy and time wisely and often got bogged down in trivia. Part of the trouble lay in his impulsiveness; like a child he tended to follow what interested him at the time. But much of his difficulty came from the fact that he found it hard to delegate power and responsibility; most likely he was motivated by a feeling that only he could do a task the way it should be done; perhaps, too, Fiorello was not uninfluenced at times by an unconscious desire to hog the spotlight on his administration.[10]

He began his first term by insisting that nothing should be done in his administration without him. This, of course, was impossible; work had to go on, commissioners had to act. What happened was that the administrative heads acted anyway, but God help them if they made the wrong decision. Gradually the Mayor gave in to necessity, but he never learned the art of efficient administration. He, himself, had to make out the dinner menu for the celebration of the Normandie's arrival on her maiden voyage. He personally had to lead a raid on an alleged house of prostitution in Brooklyn. The new City Charter which went into effect in 1938 contained a provision for the appointment of a Deputy Mayor by the Mayor for the purpose of giving the latter some relief from his chores. In La Guardia's hands this provision became a dead letter. Henry Curran, whom La Guardia first appointed Deputy Mayor, has written that in the beginning the Mayor turned over to him a few miscellaneous matters, but he got through with them in a month, and in the end, "the job came swiftly down to handling some of the mail and sitting for the Mayor in the Board of Estimate. That was all." [11]

And yet La Guardia must be given much credit as an administrator. After all, he was responsible for picking good people to serve under him. As Walker had set the tone of his administration, so La Guardia set the tone of his; and unlike the former, this administration bristled with energy and life. La Guardia's dynamic quality was one of the things that attracted many men of high calibre to the city's service. Everybody appointed by the Mayor knew that much was expected of him and that the Mayor was awake. Rufus McGahen tells the story of how one hot August afternoon he slipped away from his office to recline on the sands of Long Beach. He was lying dozing in the sun when a state trooper appeared, picked him out from all the people lying there and told him that the Mayor wanted him on the phone. La Guardia's first words were: "Where the hell are you? I've been looking for you for an hour." [12] Often, it is true, La Guardia went too far; he expected too much from his subordinates; he pushed them too hard. But not since Mitchel's time had a New York City administration been so alive.

New York's civil service, in the broad sense which encompasses all city employees, is divided into four main classes: exempt (or appointive), competitive (where applicants must take a competitive examination), noncompetitive (where only passage of a qualifying exam is required), labor (in which selection is by order of application). As striking as was the change brought about under La Guardia with respect to top flight positions (which form a part of the exempt class), the transformation which marked the rest of the civil service was even more impressive. Here, as in the top posts, there was a definite movement away from politics and favoritism toward merit as the basis for the selection of city personnel.

In the exempt positions below the top, as with the highest positions, the Fusion administration generally replaced Democratic politicians—district leaders, captains and workers—with abler individuals. In the Department of Investigation and Accounts, for instance, Blanshard got rid of the mediocre Tammany appointees and surrounded himself with energetic, intelligent and eager young men, the type Seabury had used in his investigations. The legal staff of the Corporation Counsel's office underwent a reorganization by which clubhouse hangers-on were supplanted with men with outstanding college, law school and practicing records, giving the city's Law Department a staff that could match that of any of the large private law firms. In the case of these and other agencies, Fusion took advantage of the Depression which, by curtailing private opportunity, brought into being a pool of capable young men for government service. A number of career men, a greater number than those appointed to the top spots, were made deputy commissioners in the departments. It is true that La Guardia when making appointments to the secondary exempt posts, as to the highest, was not uninfluenced at times by his personal liking for an individual or by political considerations. But, even then, the man appointed was usually competent and would not have been given the job had La Guardia not thought he was.[13]

With regard to the merit system, civil service in the narrower and commoner sense, something close to a revolution occurred. The percentage of city jobs in the competitive class, the heart of the merit system, was greatly increased, and in good part at the direct expense of the other classes. In 1933 54.5 per cent of city employees had taken competitive examinations for their jobs; in 1939 the figure was 74.3 per cent. During the same period, the percentage of jobs in the non-competitive class dropped from 17 to 14, thousands of positions being transferred to the competitive category; while the non-competitive class constituted a part of the merit system, qualifying exams, of course, were not as selective as competitive ones and were more easily open to manipulation. The percentage of positions in the labor class fell from 27 in 1933 to 11 in 1939. As for exempt jobs, the percentage dropped from 1 in 1933 to less than .5 in 1939 and to .3 during the fiscal year 1942-3—that is, from 853 jobs to 443 to 438. This reduction in exempt positions was more significant than the figures indicate, for the jobs were high-up, and their transfer to the merit system entailed important consequences in terms of governmental efficiency, the morale of rank and file employees, the strength of Tammany. Another reason for the growth of the competitive class was that thousands of relief and transit employees who had never been in the civil service were brought into the competitive category as a result of the extension of municipal functions.[14]

In other ways, too, the merit system was transmogrified. Under Tammany only the "faithful" were sought for civil service positions and advanced on the ladder—and not so much all the "faithful" as a particular group. Although civil service lists contained the names of individuals not of Irish extraction, Jews, Italians, Negroes and other minority peoples found it extremely difficult to enter the city's service, especially the Police and Fire departments. Loose and antiquated procedures enabled the machine to exercise control over jobs. The Civil Service Commission maintained no centers to dispense information about job opportunities; tips were simply dropped in the right places. Written examinations were almost exclusively the essay type which gave the examiner a maximum amount of discretion; scores were kept secret. Physical exams for policemen and firemen were farcical. Much of the equipment used in the tests was worthless, and the machines for measuring strength had their dials turned away from the candidates; only examiner Joe Ruddy, brother of a Tammany district leader, saw the score, and Ruddy's eyesight was influenced by certain considerations, one being money. Thousands of positions in the civil service were ungraded, with the consequence that promotional rights, if any, were uncertain. The system of rating the work of employees was ineffective. Salaries were subject to manipulation or arbitrary decision of department head or budget director.

Fusion, determined to bring merit back to the merit system, revamped procedures all along the line. The Civil Service Commission, making a definite attempt to seek out the highest type of eligibles for city jobs. established a public information bureau at its offices and took pains to publicize civil service information. Most written tests were changed to the objective, multiple-choice, short answer type; many of them were marked electrically. Candidates were permitted to see their papers after they were rated and compare their answers with a key. The Commission installed new equipment for physical exams with dials that candidates as well as examiners could see; much of the timing came to be done by electric eyes. (Joe Ruddy was found out and later sent to Sing Sing by District Attorney Thomas E. Dewey.) Fusion placed all but a negligible percentage of city employees in one of 46 classifications, adopted a better rating system and fixed and stabilized salary schedules and increments. Every city employee was encouraged to rise as high as his ability would allow by way of competitive examination and service ratings; the path upward, an employee now knew, could lead to some of the fatter salaried jobs that had once been in the exempt class and perhaps, as La Guardia showed in a few cases, to the very top itself. These changes not only helped to rejuvenate the merit system, but also brought an end to discrimination in the civil service against the non-Irish. With all individuals, regardless of background, given an equal chance to make the grade, the number of non-Irish in city employment increased.[15]

All of this does not mean that with respect to civil service Fusion was not open to criticism. Other improvements were needed—as the Citizens

Budget Commission pointed out in a study published in 1938—and they were not made. One was fuller co-operation and co-ordination between the city administration and the Civil Service Commission. Though the Civil Service Commission extended classification to ungraded jobs and even did a certain amount of reclassification as it went along, it never undertook the broad reclassification of positions and standardization of salaries which had become necessary; under La Guardia inequalities in titles and salaries continued to exist. While the new service rating plan was an improvement over what had been before, it might have been more effective had ratings been reflected in actual salary increments or reductions, instead of, as they were, only as percentages on promotional exams.[16]

La Guardia was not always true to the principles of the merit system. When relief, which had been an emergency city function, became a permanent one and the question of civil service status for temporary relief employees arose, the Mayor, for whatever reason, took a stand which brought him into conflict with the Civil Service Commission. The Commission insisted that the positions be filled on the basis of competitive examinations, while La Guardia wanted preference to be shown the temporary workers. In the first phase of the struggle, La Guardia advocated that the jobs be filled on the basis of qualifying exams given present workers, all subsequent vacancies to be filled by competitive tests. The Commission, headed at the time by James E. Finegan, stood firm and, despite court actions, sit-in demonstrations and picket lines organized by a group representing the temporary employees, carried out the competitive examinations; the Commission, however, did compromise to the extent of giving the old workers some consideration in the grading of papers, until this policy was disallowed by the courts.[17] Defeated on this broad front, La Guardia, a short time later, waged a second battle to freeze in their jobs over 100 provisional relief employees who were World War I veterans; but here, too, he was unsuccessful, his efforts being thwarted by the courts.[18] For his activities on behalf of the World War I veterans in Welfare, La Guardia was censured by the Civil Service Reform Association, which, for the most part, felt that his civil service record was exceptional.[19]

The Fusion civil service commissions did not exhibit a uniform quality. The first one, headed by Finegan, included the able Samuel H. Ordway, Jr., a long-time enthusiast of civil service, and Ferdinand Q. Morton, a Tammany appointee but a highly literate Negro who made a number of substantial contributions to the Commission. It did excellent work. In the spring of 1936 Ordway resigned, being replaced by Paul Kern, who at the start of 1938, after Finegan's resignation, became President of the Commission; La Guardia in March, 1938, appointed Wallace Sayre, secretary to the Commission, to fill the spot vacated by Kern. The work of the Kern-Sayre-Morton Commission during the years 1938–42 was generally also of a high standard. An investigation of the Commission by the Democratic-controlled Council in 1940–41 in the main fell flat on its face; the chief contribution of this political expedition was a maze of irrelevancies, misinterpretations and smears.[20]

At the same time, Kern was not without his faults. Though he was a belligerent liberal—and not a Communist, as the Democratic Councilmanic investigation implied—he had at times been taken in by Communist front organizations.[21] The Civil Service Reform Association, while praising Kern for intentions, zeal and energy, criticized him for engaging in American Labor Party politics (a practice which violated the spirit, if not the letter, of the Civil Service Law); for what it regarded as his lack of tact and decorum in the Councilmanic investigation; for what it termed his vilification of those who disagreed with his views; for "his arrogant and domineering manner in his relations with other department heads." Kern's behavior, the association charged, had the effect of discouraging department heads from co-operating with and making them lose confidence in the Civil Service Commission.[22]

During La Guardia's third term the Commission generally suffered in comparison with those of the Finegan-Kern period. In part this was because the great work had been done and World War II created difficulties. But if the view of the Civil Service Reform Association is accepted, La Guardia was also to blame for failing to keep the Commission strong. (He did not clarify the status of two commissioners, for example.) As a result the agency was hurt by uncertainty in policies and, at times, by conflicting directions; thus it was not able to enjoy the prestige it should have had with the departments and the public.[23]

Shortcomings, however, should not be allowed to obscure the extraordinary progress made by Fusion toward revitalizing the civil service. La Guardia firmly believed in the ideal of a real merit system in city employment and, though he did not always practice what he preached, he did much to achieve his ideal. Before La Guardia, few self-respecting people, if they could avoid it, chose city service as a career. The civil service reforms of the La Guardia period greatly raised the prestige of municipal employment and made it popular. In 1933 6,327 individuals applied for civil service jobs in New York; in 1939 the number was 252,084, a gain of 3,884 per cent. This amazing increase cannot be explained simply on the basis of the Depression, for in 1933 unemployment was also widespread and, besides, a substantial percentage of the applicants in 1939 were gainfully employed when they filed. Furthermore, as was true of La Guardia's appointees, the people who went into civil service tended to be of a finer type than those before them. And here, too, a new, unmistakable *esprit de corps* made its appearance. La Guardia once suggested that no achievement of his stood higher than civil service reform. None did.[24]

Changes in the field of personnel made it possible for Fusion to effectuate some other notable improvements in administration. First was a cleanup of graft, corruption and other discreditable practices that had flourished under Tammany. Mainly this work of house cleaning was carried out by the Department of Investigation and Accounts, which vigorously tracked down all clues uncovered by Seabury and followed up suggestions from the Mayor and complaints from the public. Blanshard brought to light a racket that had existed under Walker's regime whereby a group of fixers, including an inspector in the License Department, forced crippled and disabled men who sought newsstand licenses to pay from $1,000 to $7,000 for the privilege. Blanshard also spotlighted the fact that the Triborough Bridge Authority had fallen into the hands of political incompetents, one of whom, it was charged, had received a fee for obtaining a lease for quarters for the Authority. As a result, the Authority was reorganized with Robert Moses as chairman, a development that was greatly responsible for the subsequent brilliant success of the Triborough venture. With Commissioner of Purchase Forbes, Blanshard eradicated a fraud in the Purchase Department whereby unscrupulous coal merchants acting with Department testers cheated the city on coal deliveries. The Commissioner of Accounts uncovered what he termed the "meanest racket" at the City Home on Welfare Island for aged, friendless and destitute people. Not only were living conditions at the Home horrible, but the Tammany–appointed superintendent had grown rich by mulcting the inmates of their small savings. The superintendent was compelled to resign, a new one was chosen by civil service examination and before long a complete transformation of the Home was brought about. The investigations of Blanshard and his men during the first three years of the La Guardia administration resulted in the removal or resignation under fire of ninety-four public officials, criminal indictments against twenty-eight and the conviction of twenty; and nearly all of these officials were Tammany holdovers.[25]

Other officials also brandished the broom. Within a few weeks of taking office Commissioner MacCormick discovered that at the prison on Welfare Island certain prisoners, because of political influence, actually dominated their keepers; they lived like princes, committed crimes in jail and exploited fellow prisoners. Senior officials of the institution were dismissed and brought to justice. Comptroller Cunningham turned up various examples of curious city financing under Tammany, like the case in which some $28,750,000 owed to the city on assessments had not even been billed, let alone collected. La Guardia sent Bromberger into the Sanitation Department, a nest of graft and favoritism, with orders to scrub it clean; quickly he went into action, trying and firing a number of employees and getting rid of the grafters and special privilege boys. In the Department of Markets, which had been a dumping ground for Tammany heelers, Commissioner Morgan carried out a similar operation. The Law Department finally effectively smashed the old land condemnation racket.[26]

House cleaning accomplished, the La Guardia administration set itself the task of keeping the government clean. And, all things considered, it achieved in this respect a good measure of success; graft and corruption were held down. As had been generally true of New York reform administrations, La Guardia's administration saw an improvement in the Police Department, the Achilles' heel of city government. Valentine, at least for most of his reign, gave the Department outstanding leadership. He revived the defunct Confidential Squad to make sure no one took dirty money and cracked down on his men with a jarring discipline which was utterly impartial. In four and a half years, he busted 244 policemen, though most likely not all for graft-taking. (Though many officers naturally resented him, particularly those he routed from soft jobs to hard work, and an alarming number of policemen committed suicide because of the sudden change of direction, the rookies could take Valentine and like him.) Police corruption, for the most part, was kept under control; certainly the moral tone of the Department was incomparably higher than it had been in Walker's time.[27]

There was certainly some graft-taking in the La Guardia administration, but most cases were of the petty variety. Some clerks in the city morgue at Bellevue Hospital were discovered selling the best cadavers to certain medical schools. Some oil-burner inspectors in the Fire Department, as the Department of Investigation discovered in 1941, shook down businessmen. A number of elevator inspectors in the Department of Housing and Buildings were dismissed for bribery in 1941, and a year later a group of plumbing inspectors were discharged for the same reason. The Police Department was never free of petty graft, as Valentine admitted to Rufus McGahen, and there were other instances of it in the Fusion administration, too. The most elaborate and serious corruption involved police protection of gambling in Brooklyn. It was first exposed in April, 1942, through the efforts of special prosecutor John Harlan Amen and his grand juries. Seventeen policemen were found guilty and suffered penalties; and a slightly larger number, some of whom held high positions, filed for retirement. That was not the end of the graft-taking, however. As later events were to show, it was about this time that bookmaker Harry Gross began to make payments to the Brooklyn police.[28]

Compared with machine administrations, however, the La Guardia administration gave honest government; its achievement is especially impressive when one remembers how long it was in power. The reason for its success here is not hard to find. La Guardia demanded clean government. He applied stern pressure on the departments and insisted that every little complaint be investigated. Louis Yavner, for a time Commissioner of Investigation under La Guardia, said that under Fusion there was a greater uncovering of a smaller incidence of graft by the Department of Investigation than ever before.[29] How much in earnest La Guardia was about eliminating graft can be clearly seen from his handling of the Fire Department scandal in 1941. Though Commissioner McElligott was not involved in the corruption of the fire inspectors, the Mayor fired him anyway because the Commissioner had supported a deputy who had dealt a light sentence to one of the inspectors; voicing his regrets at having to part with McElligott, La Guardia declared that he would not condone petty graft, accused McElligott and his deputy of doing so and stated that no exceptions to his policy could be made.[30] Generally La Guardia's commissioners were as tough on corruption as their boss. City employees knew the attitude of the Mayor and his department heads and knew they were on the lookout for shady dealings. They knew that if they got caught they would be definitely finished and they thought twice. In addition, the creation of a new morale in the civil service worked toward honesty in government, even as honest government was a factor in the development of the new spirit.[31]

As La Guardia can be said to have given clean government, he also gave one that, on the whole, was strikingly efficient, effective, and in one sense economical. Improvements, savings, a surer sense of direction, and a firmer grasp of problems tended to characterize the executive agencies. The Department of Investigation and Accounts (after 1938 the Department of Investigation) had experienced a golden age from 1907 to 1917; during that period some excellent men held the office of Commissioner of Accounts, most notably John Purroy Mitchel and Leonard M. Wallstein. Then reaction set in; under Hylan and Walker the Department became largely ineffective. With La Guardia, it entered upon a second golden age. Throughout the Fusion period the Department's staff carried out a great deal of work, Walker's administration suffering by comparison. Under La Guardia a single examiner in one year questioned as many witnesses as had been examined by the entire Department during the last five years of Walker. The Department, in accordance with its purpose, conducted investigations, not only of wrongdoing, but of many other matters. Though necessity forced Blanshard to concentrate upon house cleaning and corruption, he also found time to conduct, among other inquiries, surveys of county government, the City Parole Commission, the Societies for the Prevention of Cruelty to Children, and to make certain consumer studies. The commissioners who followed him—William B. Herlands (1937–44), Edgar Bromberger (1944–5), Louis Yavner (July-November, 1945) —spent more time on the non-graft type of investigation, though they certainly did not ignore corruption. During these years, for example, studies were made of the administration of the human relations program in the New York City schools, the administration of relief in the city, anti-Semitic vandalism, ways to eliminate the meat shortage during the war. By weeding out graft, eliminating useless jobs and increasing efficiency, many of the Department's investigations saved the city money.[32]

Also reactivated was the Law Department; from a haven for politics and mediocrity under the machine, the office of the Corporation Counsel became a vigorous and successful department of government. In 1934 and 1935 the Department disposed of a tremendous amount of unfinished business from prior administrations and put its work on a current basis. One case, in which a judgment of $305,000 was won for the city from the New York Railway Company, had been lying around from ten to fifteen years, apparently forgotten by Tammany officeholders. While the average number of actions tried by the Law Department in the years 1924–33 was 599, the average tried in 1934 and 1935 was 1,378, an increase of 130 per cent; at the same time, the average amount recovered from the city per year in the period 1924–33 was $1,911,325, while for 1934 and 1935 it was $1,185,366. Among other accomplishments, the Department carried on an investigation, in co-operation with the Department of Taxes and Assessments and a specialized corps of utility engineers, which resulted in an increase of $203,000,000 in the assessment of the real property of certain utilities, underassessed for at least ten years, and a reduction of several points in the 1936 tax rate. As a result of litigation undertaken by the Department, the Court of Appeals ruled that the use of considerable areas in the beds of the streets for transformer vaults by utilities was not, as had been assumed, included in their franchises, but was an additional privilege for which the city could charge a rental; the ruling gave the city about $374,000 in additional revenue in 1936 and $462,000 in 1937.[33]

Though the new Purchase Department was created under O'Brien, the real work of organization and administration was undertaken by the La Guardia administration. La Guardia could hardly have picked a better man to head the job than Russell Forbes; an expert on government purchasing, he had, in fact, written the law establishing the new department. Forbes immediately came up against serious problems: the need to accumulate a staff and find office space, the necessity of purchasing for all departments immediately upon the assumption of office, further complicated by the exigency of having to buy material for work relief projects. Due to these difficulties, the new department for a time fell far short of maximum efficiency, many charges of delay being quite justified. For all that, the achievements of the Purchase Department even in its early years were not insignificant. Savings for the city were made, not only because the Department was able to buy in bulk, but because it increased competition among contractors. More than $50,000, for instance, was cut from the price of fuel oil in 1934 through increased competition; more than $27,000 was saved by letting a contract for printing the 1935 budget on a competitive basis with definite specifications for the first time in the city's history, although the same printer as before got the job. The Department greatly centralized the city storehouse system and modernized specifications of commodities bought by the city.[34]

From a picnic ground of political manipulation, the Department of Sanitation was metamorphosed into a first-class agency of government. It is doubtful if another department showed a more striking transformation in the morale of its employees. Fusion structurally reorganized the

Department, scrapped old equipment, purchased modern equipment and reduced the cost of operations; while in 1932 the cost per capita for street cleaning, collection and disposal service was $5.42, in 1935 it was $3.57, and the Department operated with 1,568 fewer men and 500 fewer trucks.[35]

The Board of Standards and Appeals, so conspicuously inadequate in the days of Tammany, developed an improved reputation. It was apparently held in higher regard by the courts, if one is to judge from sustaining decisions; out of 101 cases judicially reviewed in La Guardia's first three years, only 8 were reversed. To a great extent the higher prestige of the Board was due to the able work of the Corporation Counsel and his assistants who established basic legal principles as to zoning and clarified the Board's powers and the applicant's rights.[36] Nor were these the only areas of government which showed a more businesslike operation.

In certain ways, it is true, La Guardia could have given taxpayers more for their tax dollars. He could have, for example, improved the Police Department, possibly through a structural reorganization and surely by removing policemen from clerical and other non-vital work.[37] Perhaps in an age of fireproof construction and motorized equipment he should have consolidated fire districts. It is most likely that numbers of city employees were inefficient and not a few jobs useless.

But here, as with other aspects of administration, there is no mistaking the central fact: his shortcomings pale beside La Guardia's outstanding accomplishments.

9

Finances

IN THE FALL of 1932, the city's bankers, who had been showing increasing stringency in their demands, refused to make any more
loans to the city unless it agreed to make drastic cuts in the budget. The
result was that the new O'Brien administration freely used the ax on
expenditures. Securing the legislature's consent to re-open the 1933
budget, it reduced it 18 per cent from that of 1932, a reduction which
included a $20,000,000 slash in salaries. O'Brien received his loans, but
by the early fall of 1933, with his taxation program crumbling about him,
O'Brien was compelled to ask the bankers for additional help. This time
there was a showdown. Out of conferences among city officials, Governor
Lehman and the bankers, an agreement was reached between the city
and the clearing house banks—which the legislature subsequently legal-
ized—whereby the bankers consented to finance part of the government's
operating expenses through 1937, and the city, as a condition, accepted
certain limitations on its financial powers. The principal limitations were
two: the city could not raise the real estate levy above the current $429,-
000,000 (exclusive of the increase in debt service and the addition of
improvements to taxable property), and it had to carry a minimum
reserve of $50,000,000 to be held against taxes slow in payment or uncol-
lectable.[1] The so-called Bankers' Agreement saved the city from bankruptcy.

Still the problem of city finances was the most critical problem facing
the government when La Guardia came to office. In good part because
Tammany had not been able to bring itself to do a thorough job of cutting in the area of jobs and salaries, the 1934 expense budget totaling

$551,000,000 was unbalanced by about $30,000,000; actually the figure was higher, for O'Brien had reduced the apparent size of the budget by simply omitting certain necessary items, such as food, fuel and medical supplies for hospitals and taxes owed by the city to other communities for watersheds. The city had outstanding almost $500,000,000 in short-term obligations, of which about $200,000,000 represented revenue bills issued against tax collections (temporary debt). Because of these facts, the city was still burdened by a low credit rating which, among other things, prevented it from selling its long-term securities and barred it from federal loans and grants which were desperately needed to complete a number of highly expensive improvements; the new Independent subway system and a tunnel under the East River on which $62,000,000 had already been spent were two of them.[2]

During the campaign of 1933 La Guardia had made a number of promises dealing with the financial side of the city. Among them were ones to carry out the Bankers' Agreement and to balance the budget through sweeping economies which would be effected by consolidations and the elimination of political jobs. The budget, La Guardia said, would not be balanced by reducing the salaries of civil service workers or by resorting to new taxes, though he once declared that if he could not make up the entire budget deficiency through proper economies and added revenues became necessary, the sum secured from new revenues would surely not exceed that gained by savings. The end product, he promised, would be the restoration of city credit.[3]

No sooner did La Guardia move into City Hall than he swung into action on the fiscal front. To balance the budget the new administration needed, first of all, the permission of the legislature to reopen the 1934 budget. It also needed from the legislature authorization to cut through existing Charter provisions and override laws in order to bring about significant economies, new taxes, or both. On January 2, 1934, La Guardia sent to the legislature a drastic bill designed to allow the Mayor to balance the budget by cutting. The Economy Bill would give the Mayor power for a two-year period to abolish, consolidate or re-organize city and county offices, fix the compensation of city or county employees by executive order (certain employees excepted), and initiate, except in the case of certain judges, compulsory payless furloughs for one month a year. La Guardia, it will be noticed, immediately threw out the window his pledge not to reduce civil service salaries, a promise which, as the friendly *Nation* pointed out, never should have been made.[4]

Because of the financial emergency, the general expectation was that La Guardia's Economy Bill would be passed without delay. No expectation could have been more mistaken. Hardly had the bill been sent to Albany, than Governor Lehman attacked it for granting "full dictatorial powers" to the Mayor. Within a few days, however, the Governor and the Mayor worked out a compromise whereby the former agreed that if the legislature voted in favor of the bill all the powers which La Guardia had demanded would be bestowed on the Board of Estimate, which Fusion controlled, subject to a veto of the Municipal Assembly. Lehman now became a stout champion of the Mayor's program, but La Guardia's troubles had only begun. Civil service lobbies, obviously against anything which would result in a loss of pay for government employees, became a chief source of opposition to the Economy Bill. The Democrats in the Assembly constituted another; they were mainly worried about giving La Guardia a free hand in the county offices where he might run riot with political jobs, though they were not unmindful, too, of the political repercussions that might follow additional reductions in civil service salaries. Taking their cue from Ed Flynn, rather than Lehman, a significant bloc of Assembly Democrats for three and a half months refused to give the city an economy program. Four times the Economy Bill went down to defeat, though one concession after another was made to its opponents and President Roosevelt, especially on the last occasion, used his influence on its behalf. Lehman and La Guardia refused to give up, however; in early April the Mayor went to Albany to push the bill personally. Brought up for a fifth time, mutilated and emasculated, the bill finally passed, and the city was given a green light on budget reduction. The Economy Act gave the Board of Estimate power to put into operation payless furloughs, reduce salaries, with certain exceptions, and achieve reorganization in the agencies directly under the Mayor's control; power to bring about reorganization of county offices was denied. Immediately the Board of Estimate implemented those provisions of the Act relating to payless furloughs and salary reductions.[5]

The Economy Act, which, it was estimated, would result in reductions of from $11,000,000 to $14,000,000,[6] represented, in effect, an authorization to the city to save, not the full amount of the deficit, but half of it. If the budget were to be balanced, there was now only one way to do it, and La Guardia took it. He asked the legislature for and received from it a grant of additional taxes for a limited period. In May and June the Fusion administration placed a tax of 1/20 of 1 per cent on the gross income of most businesses, industries and professions, one of 1/10 of 1 per cent on the gross income of financial enterprises and renewed a 1½ per cent tax on the gross monthly receipts of utilities that O'Brien had used.[7] As a result of the Economy Act, other economy measures carried out by the city administration and the new taxes, La Guardia was able to balance the 1934 budget.

In keeping his promise, La Guardia, as we have observed, broke the one about reducing civil service salaries and possibly the one about taxes, though if he is judged on his more cautious statement on taxes, he fulfilled this pledge, too. It is interesting that while there was some opposition to La Guardia's new taxes from merchant and professional groups and from the utilities, no storm of protest developed such as had befallen

O'Brien's tax program and which La Guardia's advisers had privately anticipated; for this there were probably several reasons, not the least being that most citizens must have recognized that the Mayor had done his best to avoid new taxes in balancing the budget.[8]

With the passage and implementation of the Economy Act, the city's credit began to revive. On April 10, the day the economy machinery was put into motion, Comptroller Cunningham sold to a banking syndicate over $7,500,000 of 4 per cent special revenue bonds (short-term securities) at 3½ per cent cost to the city, the lowest since 1931; because of favorable opinion, the bankers were immediately able to offer the securities for resale. In June Comptroller McGoldrick sold a $3,000,000 issue of 60-day revenue bonds at an all-time low interest rate for short-term borrowings of ¾ of 1 per cent, while for the first time since 1931, the city's long-term 4 per cent bonds reached par. Because of the city's improved credit position the Fusion administration about the same time was able to get the bankers who financed the city under the Agreement to accept a reduction on the interest of revenue notes from 4 to 3 per cent, as well as a 50 per cent slash in the $50,000,000 reserve fund. By mid-August, the federal government, which had insisted that the city balance its budget as a condition for loans, was advancing cash funds for the construction of various capital projects, something La Guardia had greatly wanted and one of the principal reasons for his intense efforts to improve the city's financial situation. The first PWA funds were applied at once toward the completion of the Independent subway and the tunnel under the East River, as well as for the construction of a long-delayed Tuberculosis Pavilion at Bellevue Hospital.[9]

Improvement in New York's credit position continued in the years that followed. In 1935 Comptroller Taylor was able to carry out a series of refinancing operations, many involving the Bankers' Agreement, which saved the government millions in debt service. In contrast to 1933, when the city sold short-term securities for as high as 4 per cent, Comptroller McGoldrick in 1938 was able to issue $375,000,000 of revenue and special revenue bills at interest rates as low as .35 per cent.[10]

La Guardia thus made good on his promise to restore the credit of the city. It is true that he was not entirely responsible for this situation. An increase in real estate tax collections in 1934 over that of 1933 [11] was also a big factor in the revival of city credit; and for this the new administration was not responsible, except, perhaps, insofar as confidence in Fusion and its economic policies encouraged taxpayers to make payments. The Economy Act and the balanced budget, however, were principally instrumental in the development of a better financial situation in New York, and these accomplishments, in the main, were La Guardia's.[12]

The city's financial problems did not end with its emergence from the financial crisis of the early thirties. Though La Guardia continued to balance the budget all the years of his administration, making ends meet was not easy, and the city operated on a delicate budgetary equilibrium in an atmosphere of uncertainty.

The expense budget of 1935 was $553,432,600. Those of the next two years remained relatively close to this figure, the 1936 budget being smaller and the 1937 budget being larger. In 1938 the budget went up $30,000,000 to $589,980,577, only to decline in stages to $573,740,594 in the fiscal year 1941–2. Then in fiscal 1942–3, largely because of changes in budgetary accounting, the budget jumped to $769,214,273. During the next three fiscal years, it fluctuated, dropping to $742,205,823 in 1943–4, $729,640,922 in 1944–5 and rising to $755,410,335 in 1945–6.[13] Rising in one year and falling in another, the expense budget under La Guardia kept to a general upward movement. (La Guardia did not give economical government in the sense of the size of the budget.) To finance its budget, the city relied mostly upon the real estate levy and also on the General Fund, which until the early forties, with the exception of 1934, was made up of fees and charges, but no taxes. Basically the city's fiscal trouble was that rising expenditures continually threatened to outrun revenue from these sources.

The expense budget does not give the entire story of city expenses under La Guardia. It should be noted particularly that until the fiscal year 1942–3, when it was placed in the expense budget, the city's share of relief spending was figured in a separate budget; between 1935 and 1938, inclusive, New York spent an average of $64,000,000 a year for this purpose. Whereas O'Brien generally had met relief needs by borrowing, La Guardia insisted that relief be put on a pay-as-you-go basis and financed it by specially earmarked taxes. As a congressman La Guardia had been probably the biggest foe of a proposed national sales tax, but as Mayor he levied a city sales tax of 2 per cent (lowered in 1941 to 1 per cent) when he saw that he could not otherwise finance relief from current revenue. Other taxes were also specifically designated for the Special Emergency Relief Fund, though most were used for only part of the period covered by the separate budget. Among these taxes were one on the gross income of utilities, another on the gross income of financial and non-financial businesses, a tax on conduit companies, a compensating use tax (placed on tangible personal property purchased outside of the city and brought into the city in order to protect city merchants and prevent evasions of the sales tax) and a cigarette tax.[14]

Behind the rise in the expense budget during La Guardia's administration were several major factors. One was the introduction of new city services and the expansion of old ones. For one thing, the growth of municipal services entailed the construction of capital projects which brought about an increase in the large debt service item in the expense budget; although the city received much aid from federal funds, much of this money consisted of loans; and the city also had to resort to traditional long-term borrowing for financing public works.[15] New facilities, moreover, required funds for operation and maintenance. Because of the expansion of city services, both old and new, the number of government employees increased under La Guardia—from 86,364 in 1934 to 137,460 at the end of June, 1945 [16]—a development inevitably reflected in a rise in payroll and pension costs.

Furthermore, state legislation obliged the city to raise the salaries of certain groups of employees. Non-mandatory pay increases were also made by the city. Non-actuarial pension systems of long standing which covered some groups of employees constituted an increasing drain on the treasury. The city appropriated huge sums to meet debt service on its transit obligations because the five-cent fare, which the government adhered to, could not cover this cost.[17]

How censurable was La Guardia for the increased costs? It is clear, in the first place, that the city administration was not responsible for mandatory costs. Other expenses no administration could have avoided—for example, those resulting from expansion of existing services and some public construction, the consequences of a growing city and one in which population was shifting. But beyond these points was an undefined area involving an indeterminate percentage of expenses—an area of services and construction, non-mandatory salaries, subway financing—where real choice was possible. One's criticism of La Guardia for bigger budgets depends largely on the extent to which one values city policy in this area as against lower taxes and, quite likely, greater fairness to property owners.

The low tax point of view, as one would expect, was presented by real estate and business interests who paid the lion's share of taxes; throughout La Guardia's administration they kept up a running battle with him over budgets and taxes. Among other things, they generally held that city activity should be kept to what was absolutely essential and that the government should undertake a more conservative building program. They argued for a fare rise to make the subways self-supporting. Usually they could be found in opposition to pay increases for city employees. Rather typical of their view of salary rises was the complaint of Harold Riegelman, of the tax-conscious Citizens Budget Commission. Writing on city finances in 1938, Riegelman lamented that, though New York got along pretty well for four years under the Bankers' Agreement and not one of its essential services was pinched, as soon as the Agreement ended the city took the opportunity to raise the budget by several millions, in good part because of increases in salaries. Ignoring the fact that a number of pay increases were mandatory and that Riegelman's concept of city activity could be debated, it is plain that on his scale a smaller budget was more important than improving the condition of those who worked for the city.[18]

Unlike his critics, La Guardia did not have what was almost a fixation against pay rises; there were times when he favored and brought about salary increases for groups of employees. He supported the view that the subways should be subsidized. He was proud of the great increment in the physical wealth of the city represented by the construction of new schools, hospitals, health centers, parks, playgrounds, sewage disposal plants and other capital projects which took place during his administration and thought them worth an increase in the long-term debt. (Actually a reduction in the city's borrowing capacity under the State Constitution and then World War II forced the La Guardia administration in the late thirties and early forties to adopt a more conservative building program.) More broadly, he boasted of the expansion of city services which occurred under him and declared that this was done very economically.[19]

The burden of complaint of La Guardia's budgetary critics, especially property groups, was that real estate taxes were oppressively high. At a time when property values were declining, the tax rate, though rising and falling from one year to another, was moving generally upward, from $2.56 per $100 of assessed valuation in 1934 to $2.67 in 1945–6; high points of $2.84 and $2.89 were reached in the fiscal years 1940–1 and 1943–4.[20] Actually, however, the rising tax rate was not the main grievance of taxpayer groups. (And it might be pointed out that Cushman McGee, writing in 1940 on *The Finances of the City of New York* for R. W. Pressprich and Company, a member of the New York Stock Exchange, informed potential investors that the city's tax rate, which had hit $2.82 in 1939–40, was not excessive.)[21] What bothered property owners more was their conviction that the city was purposely over-assessing real estate to meet expenses.

It is difficult to evaluate the merits of this charge. At best assessing is a difficult job; it is hard for two people to agree on the value of a property. During the thirties and forties, a period of unstable values, the task of the assessor was especially troublesome. On top of this, the real estate interests and the city defined overassessment differently. The former, noting that the law stated that assessment was not to exceed "full value," equated this concept with current market value and called anything above it overassessment; since assessed values generally ran higher than market values, there was, if this view were accepted, widespread overassessment in New York City. The administration, however, held that under the city's Administrative Code, assessed valuation was to be based, not necessarily upon current market value, but upon what a parcel of real estate would sell for "under ordinary circumstances"; what the city contended was simply that the depressed values of the period did not represent property "under ordinary circumstances," a view which took much wind out of the charge of overassessment. The administration noted that in fact it had reduced assessed values, as indeed it had, though realty interests thought not nearly enough. There was some overassessment, the city conceded, but it denied that this was the rule.

All things considered, it is probable that the city assessed more property unfairly than it cared to admit, though less than the real estate people claimed. The courts, it should be observed, in a huge majority of certiorari suits brought by taxpayers to reduce assessments, found in their favor.[22] As to what degree unfair assessments of property represented a conscious, or even subconscious, attempt of officials to tailor tax yields to budgets, it is not easy to say. With the city's revenue from real estate constitutionally limited to 2 per cent of total assessed valuation (plus the amount needed for debt service) and with costs going up, it is most unlikely that city officials were uninfluenced by expenses in assessing property.[23]

Less convincing were charges made by the Mayor's budgetary critics that the administration's assessment practices and taxes injured the city by driving out industry. While a number of manufacturing firms left the city in the 1930's and 40's, this was by no means a general trend, and many other reasons, besides the city's financial policies, accounted for their departure.[24] A study of the relative over-all tax costs in three classes of manufacturing in New York and several other cities, undertaken in the early forties by Professor Harley L. Lutz of Princeton at the request of the Mayor's Business Advisory Committee, casts doubt upon the importance of New York's taxes in influencing businessmen to move. Comparing costs in New York with those in Baltimore, Boston, Bridgeport, Chicago, Newark and Philadelphia, Professor Lutz reported that the real estate tax, taken alone, showed practically insignificant differences in amount in the seven cities, that for most of the cities, including New York, taxes on manufacturing were predominantly state taxes and that state and local taxes did not in any case "differ sufficiently as among the seven cities and with reference to the particular industries studied, to justify in themselves any decision of corporate management to locate or refrain from locating in an otherwise desirable community." [25]

La Guardia, as much as his budgetary opponents, was concerned about the problem of making ends meet; moreover, he, too, felt that real estate taxes constituted a heavy burden on property owners, though he denied the administration was unjust to them. But his approach was different from that of his critics. Whereas they thought always in terms of cutting expenditures, the Mayor, declaring that he was practicing utmost economy, began during his second term to cast about for additional revenue as a means, not only of meeting expenses, but of relieving real estate of some of its load.[26] What made his task difficult was that New York, like other American cities, did not possess financial autonomy. The city, limited by the state constitution in the amount of revenue it could obtain from real estate and in its capacity to borrow, could hope to increase its revenue generally only in one or both of these ways: by obtaining a bigger share of state funds; by receiving authorization from the legislature to impose new taxes. For various reasons, the state had traditionally not been overly generous to the city. La Guardia had his work cut out for him.

The special relief taxes toward the end of La Guardia's second term began to produce a surplus of funds, and the Mayor's first serious efforts to secure additional revenue were directed toward obtaining permission from the state to use excess relief revenue for the expense budget. Slowly the state acquiesced. In 1940, the legislature, as compensation for transferring the proceeds of a bank tax from the city to the state—the state had also magnanimously appropriated the city's cigarette tax and part of its utility tax in this period—gave the city authority to use $4,500,000 of surplus relief funds for old-age assistance; but this was an arrangement for that year only. The next year the legislature gave the city more substantial help: the tax on the gross receipts of general and financial businesses was transformed at half its current rate into a general purpose tax estimated to bring in about $6,500,000 a year; in addition, the city was given permission to apply $4,000,000 of existing relief tax surplus to other welfare activities in fiscal 1941–2 and $3,000,000 of surplus funds to the reduction of debt service for three years. Finally, in 1942, Albany went the rest of the way and allowed the city to include home relief in the expense budget and place its remaining emergency taxes in the General Fund, where they could be used for any purpose.[27]

The addition to the General Fund which resulted from the legislation of 1941 and 1942 did not solve New York City's financial problem. The city did not gain much extra revenue by the new system, and costs quickly swallowed what increment there was. Moreover, an air of uncertainty hung over the new taxes, for they were authorized by the legislature on a yearly, not a permanent, basis. Throughout the rest of his administration La Guardia strove to wangle from the state the right to levy new taxes or increase old ones, but without success; the legislature, however, did give the city an increase in state aid at the end.[28] The quest of New York City for additional sources of revenue was just beginning in the La Guardia era. Inflation in the post-war period would magnify the city's dilemma and considerably embitter relations between the city and the state.

New York's financial troubles in the period 1935–45 should not be exaggerated. With adoption of the La Guardia financial program of 1934, the financial position of the city became basically sound. Despite annual struggles with the budget, the La Guardia administration, in the final analysis, was always able to close the gap between expenditure and revenue. The city's credit rating was high. Its temporary debt steadily declined throughout the period, reaching $41,000,000 (net) at the end of June, 1945. While its long-term debt rose from $1,897,481,000 (net) at the start of 1934 to $2,519,980,000 as of June 30, 1941, Cushman McGee advised readers that the resources of the city were ample to meet payments when due. And America's entry into World War II, by forcing the city to call a moratorium on public improvements, brought about a reduction in the funded debt; by June 30, 1946, it was down to $2,194,969,000 (net).[29] The war, it should be noted, also strengthened the city financially by compelling a curtailment in current expenditures resulting from a loss in government personnel and a shortage of materials and supplies. New York City in 1945 had left the desperate days of the early thirties far behind.

10

War against the underworld

BEFORE THE 1920's the criminal gangs of New York were independent groups of hoodlums, tied together by bonds of neighborhood and nationality, generally working for small change. They were principally made up of Irish, Italian and Jewish immigrants—and especially the sons of Irish, Italian and Jewish immigrants. First generation Americans separated by an immense gulf from the thinking and ways of their parents often found security and the means of adjusting to the American environment in street gangs. Sometimes the gangs evolved into avenues of self-advancement; if the offspring of the slums did not possess the advantages of capital or family connections, they might, at least, capitalize on the cohesiveness and aggressiveness of their gangs. Gangs became the means whereby some young men moved into politics and others, less moral, moved into crime. The slums of Manhattan, which also produced many great men, constituted in the first two decades of the twentieth century the biggest breeding ground for gunmen and racketeers this country has seen.[1]

On the lower East Side, the criminal gangs were predominantly Jewish and Italian. Among the more notorious were the Dopey Benny Fein gang, which included such characters as Irving (Waxey Gordon) Wexler, Louis (Lepke) Buchalter and Jacob (Gurrah) Shapiro; the gang of Paul Kelly (christened Paolo Vaccarelli) of which Johnny Torrio, later of Chicago fame, was a member; the Monk Eastman gang. The most infamous gang, and the one most powerful and dreaded, was the Mafia, a secret order of Sicilian origin founded in the United States by Ignazio (Lupo the Wolf) Saietta and composed of Italian-born gangsters. Preying primarily on their decent fellow countrymen in the United States, the members of the Mafia terrorized by bombing, blackmail and murder.

The head man in the Mafia reached the top after a violent struggle with rivals often involving murder. In New York City there were two bosses, one in Harlem and the Bronx and one in the downtown Manhattan and Brooklyn area. Ciro Terranova, czar of the artichoke industry, who was related by marriage to Saietta, was the boss in Harlem and the Bronx. The other crown in the period before the twenties shifted from one precarious head to another. In 1922 Giuseppe (Joe the Boss) Masseria finally became undisputed ruler of the Mafia in the downtown Manhattan-Brooklyn area by killing his chief competitor; he continued to rule throughout the twenties. One of his aide-de-camps was a young Sicilian-born gambler, gunman and narcotics peddler, Charles (Charlie Lucky Luciano) Luciana.[2]

Irish gangs, like the Gophers and the Hudson Dusters, mainly ruled the West Side. Out of this area came such notorious gangsters as Owen (Owney the Killer) Madden, a member of the Gophers, and the Diamond brothers, Jack (Legs) and Eddie. While the East Siders indulged in assorted illegal activities, including a simple kind of racketeering, the hoodlums on the West Side, growing up in an area of Hudson River wharves and New York Central freight yards, tended in their teens to become package and freight-yard thieves, whence they graduated to burglary and armed robbery.[3]

The period of World War I and the 1920's witnessed the transformation of New York's criminals to big-time status. The main reason for this development was Prohibition. Gangsters soon found that supplying the "spiritual" needs of a community which liked its liquor and was contemptuous of the attempt to enforce Prohibition was not only safe, but enormously profitable. There was scarcely an underworld character of importance who did not get into bootlegging to some extent, and most of them cleaned up. Big Bill Dwyer, a longshoreman from the 10th Avenue and 23rd Street sector of Manhattan's West Side, formed a syndicate with Owney Madden and Waxey Gordon, inaugurated wholesale corruption of policemen and Coast Guardsmen and, with his partners, made a fortune; in 1936 Dwyer was worth millions, owned racetracks in Ohio and Florida and played host to the horse-loving element of the socially elite. In 1925 Arthur Flegenheimer was a small-time hoodlum and occasional strong-arm boy for big runners. By the late twenties, through a combination of business talent and utter ruthlessness, Dutch Schultz had become the distributor of beer in Harlem and the Bronx and had a grab in other underworld activities; he had risen to the ranks of the millionaires.[4]

The underworld found other opportunities for big money at this time in the management-labor wars that marked the garment industry. At first management, and then also labor, employed characters like Dopey Benny Fein, Lepke and Gurrah to settle strikes; before long the gangsters had become racketeers with a hold on the industry that could not be shaken off. In professional gambling and the narcotics trade, the underworld found other sources of profit. Profits were used in good business fashion to make further profits in the same enterprise or other ones, the financial resources of the underworld continually growing bigger. Arnold Rothstein, for instance, was more than a professional gambler; he was a big underworld banker who used the fortune he accumulated from betting to buy stolen goods, finance a far-flung narcotics trade and put small-time hoodlums into the big time in rum and beer. (Usually, however, criminals in the twenties made their first big money in bootlegging and then siphoned off some of it into other activities.)[5]

Under the imminence and then actuality of Repeal, the bootleggers, in quest of new fields, turned in force to gambling and racketeering. In gambling, for example, Frank Costello, a one-time bootlegger, became a big-time operator by making slot machines his special preserve. He apportioned districts to operators, giving them a monopoly in their areas. Each operator had a corps of lieutenants who were responsible for regular routes and who undertook to place slot machines in stores, not infrequently by terrorizing their owners.[6]

Racketeering was the more important outlet, both from the point of view of the underworld and society, though it is well to note that the ending of Prohibition only tremendously accelerated a movement that had been steadily growing since the mid-twenties. In the early thirties, a wide variety of rackets, some old, many new, exercised a powerful stranglehold on the life of the city. A loan shark racket—shylocking—in which gangsters loaned money to small businessmen and others at fantastic rates of interest, securing payment by terror and beatings, was thriving; in 1935 Thomas E. Dewey noted that according to an exhaustive study made by the Russell Sage Foundation the gross income from this racket in New York City was conservatively $10,000,000 a year.[7] A "combination" in prostitution organized by Luciano was in operation; prostitutes were forced to hand over $10 a week, and madams and bookers were also made to pay up.[8] Dutch Schultz was the head of a numbers [9] racket; after having strong-armed the local policy bankers into joining an organization and paying for protection, he had strong-armed them out of their banks and had taken over their business.[10] (And the Dutchman made a good thing out of policy; Dixie Davis, his lawyer, once testified that the take from the numbers racket in New York City was as high as $100,000,000 a year.[11]) When Schultz became involved with Internal Revenue men between 1933 and 1935, Luciano, not expecting him to beat the rap, appropriated a big part of Dutch's numbers racket.[12]

Most racketeering was industrial racketeering, the "protection" of legitimate business. While variations existed, the typical industrial racket had these essential elements: a "trade association" created by the racketeers which businessmen were forced to join and to which they had to pay dues (though in some cases businessmen, hoping to keep competition down and prices up in defiance of anti-trust laws, organized the "association" and took in racketeers as partners for enforcement); a labor union under the control of the racketeers; a strong-arm squad. Sometimes the gangsters, in addition to forcing businessmen to pay a toll to a "trade association," fixed the prices they might charge for goods and services and limited their operations to specific areas or specific lists of customers. Generally the racketeers enforced their orders by threatening to bring their unions out on strike, but as supplementary discipline they resorted to sluggings, bombings, window smashings and, occasionally, murders.[13]

One of the most flourishing industrial rackets was the restaurant racket organized by Dutch Schultz, but actually run by his lieutenants; when the Dutchman ran into trouble with the federal government and Luciano muscled in on his numbers racket, Lepke took over the restaurant racket. Getting control of the waiters' and cafeteria workers' unions, Schultz and his men forced restaurant owners to join the Metropolitan Restaurant and Cafeteria Owners Association. The dues and other tolls to avoid strikes and stink bombs during rush hours were high and fancy: Lindy's, for example, paid over $6,000, the Brass Rail $5,000, Steuben's Tavern $17,000, the Foltes-Fischer chain almost $10,000. Profits from the racket reached $2,000,000 a year.[14]

The lords of industrial racketeering were the Gorilla Boys, Lepke and Gurrah; in 1936 it was estimated that each grossed more than $1,000,000 a year from rackets in industry. A big International Ladies' Garment Workers' Union strike in 1926, inspired by the Communists and involving a number of beatings, bombings and a few murders, launched Lepke and Gurrah into the big time. Obtaining control of the truckers' union, they forced garment jobbers and manufacturers to join associations under penalty of being assaulted, having their shops bombed with stink chemicals or explosives, their payrolls stolen and, most important, their goods not transported. The Gorilla Boys exacted tribute in terms of anything from $5,000 to $50,000 from jobbers and manfacturers for the simple service of permitting them to remain in business. In the years that followed, Lepke and Gurrah branched out into the fur industry, flour and bake-stuffs and motion picture theatres; they had a grab in the leather, millinery, handbag and shoe industries and with Luciano worked the cleaning and dyeing industry. A strange team, the Gorilla Boys—Lepke with his soft collie-dog eyes, almost apologetic manner and reputation for never losing his temper; Gurrah, loud, hulking, heavy-handed and aggressive. A strange team they were and seemingly invincible.[15]

There were plenty of other rackets in the city, too. Joseph (Socks) Lanza, a genial Italian labor leader, the economic and social leader of a thousand men, controlled the fish markets of downtown Manhattan, especially the Fulton Fish Market, as he had since the early twenties; he forced each seagoing fishing ship to pay $10 a load into his union's "benevolent fund," operated a "watchman's service" for the automobiles of retailers who came to the markets and decided whether a little vender could do business in the great open air pushcart market; some of the venders who were his friends had formed an alliance with him and were acting as "fences" for stolen fish. Ciro Terranova's artichoke racket was still going strong, now under the direction of another gangster, Joseph Castaldo, to whom Ciro had turned over the business in 1929; artichoke shippers and commission merchants sold only to the racketeer-controlled Union Pacific Produce Company because intimidated buyers would buy from no other source. The kosher poultry industry was under the thumb of a group of racketeers, the leader of whom was Arthur (Tootsie) Herbert. Using standard industrial racketeering methods, the racketeers maintained monopolies in feed, coops and trucking. Along the Manhattan and Brooklyn waterfront, labor gangsters dominating the International Longshoremen's Association extorted handsome profits as they had for years, both from their own longshoremen, dependent upon them for jobs, and the stevedoring and shipping companies, these last not entirely unhappy about the situation since the gangsters preserved discipline on the piers and kept labor costs down. In the thirties the big powers on the Brooklyn waterfront were Joe Adonis and Albert Anastasia.[16]

Aside from the more obvious evils connected with all these and other rackets, it should be noted that most of them added a staggering cost to the family budget, not only in New York City, but elsewhere in the United States, a situation that was particularly intolerable in a period of depression.[17]

More than the activities of the underworld were affected by the passing of Prohibition. Repeal also brought about a transformation in the gangster's methods of operation. Though the stature of the criminals rose in the twenties, their methods remained rooted in their small-time past. Independent gangs machine-gunned and bombed rivals for the supremacy of a territory; the underworld was a chaotic dog-eat-dog world in which the gun was the final arbiter of disputes, no man was sacrosanct and where the garish funeral became as much a part of the gaudy pattern of living of parvenu big shot gangsters as their $250 suits, penthouse apartments and morocco-bound libraries.[18]

As the twenties came to an end, a few of the wiser underworld figures —notably Capone in Chicago and Luciano, Costello and Lepke in New York—began to see that co-operation and understanding had more advantages than rugged individualism. The impending repeal of Prohibition served as a catalyst to such thinking, for it presented the ganglords with the problem of finding new enterprises and retaining their own power; they saw that in the new era mob operations would have to become streamlined; the Law would not be as co-operative as in the past, and internecine underworld warfare would only deplete the mobs and by creating publicity make all criminal activity difficult. In 1931 Luciano did something which greatly aided the development of the new approach. The Mafia was a clannish, old-worldish group with an isolationist psychology and limited vision for making profits; Joe the Boss was against combination with other groups. Luciano, leading a young Americanized group in the world of Italian crime which believed in co-operation with non-Italians and in big ventures, had his superior, Joe the Boss, murdered and the Mafia in the United States purged.[19]

A short time later a new order in the underworld came into being; understandings and working agreements took the place of gang rivalry. In a later day the Kefauver crime committee was to speak of a more or less loose, but close, personal and financial relationship between top level gangsters in different parts of the country.[20] But Burton B. Turkus, who as an Assistant District Attorney in Brooklyn in the early 1940's played a leading role in cracking Murder, Inc., has described the development of a much more formal underworld association based upon the confessions of killers in that organization. According to Turkus, John Torrio, capping the thinking of Luciano, Costello, Lepke and others, in 1934 outlined to the big lords of eastern crime a proposal for an eastern syndicate. His plan was accepted. A board of directors composed of the mob bosses— each one having equal power—was set up to handle all problems and disputes on the inter-mob level. In his own territory, each boss remained a czar, his business unmolested; to put an end to anarchy, no one could be ordered murdered in his territory without his approval. The ganglords created an enforcement arm to carry out board discipline or do murder jobs for a boss who preferred not to use his own men. They also set up a kangaroo court, composed of the bosses themselves, to hear charges against a high echelon gangster serious enough to warrant the death penalty; the decision of the court was final. Gangs agreed to interchange their political contacts. Before long the mobs from beyond the east—the Capone gang in Chicago, the Purple gang in Detroit, the Kansas City mob to mention a few—came to see the strength of the new union and flocked in, thus bringing into existence a national crime syndicate.

Because of their extraordinary skill in such matters, the work of enforcement all over the United States came to be entrusted to the Brooklyn chapter of the "combination" which the press later dubbed Murder, Inc. It included such base personalities as Abe (Kid Twist) Reles, Harry (Pittsburgh Phil) Strauss, Bugsy Goldstein, Happy Maione and Dasher Abbandando. Leadership was exercised by Albert Anastasia and his boss, Joey Adonis. Lepke, in particular, made good use of the Brooklyn mob's disciplinary service; during the thirties, he gave it orders for more than thirty murders.[21]

The key to crime's amazing good fortune in New York in the twenties and thirties lay, of course, in political protection; without protection the underworld cannot flourish, and machine politicians in Manhattan and Brooklyn saw to it that it received what it needed for a price. In Manhattan the principal protector of the underworld in the early twenties was probably Big Tom Foley whom we have already noted as the good angel for a group of bucketeers; more important, Foley carried on an alliance that Big Tim Sullivan had had with East Side Italian gangs in his day. After Foley died in 1925, Peter Hamill, his successor, carried on the tradition. When he died in 1930, the Italian gangsters decided to insure their contacts by ousting Harry C. Perry, leader in another East Side district, and putting in one of their own nationality, Albert Marinelli. Significantly when Lanza was indicted by a federal grand jury in the early thirties, Marinelli appointed him to a $3,600 job as an assistant clerk in the Second District Municipal Court. Does friendship of this sort help explain why the fish racketeer, though arrested seventeen times before his trouble with the federal government, never went to jail? [22]

Other Tammany district leaders, some of whom were implicated by the Hofstadter investigation in this connection, also shielded the underworld. Tom Farley, the leader whom Roosevelt removed as Sheriff, served, not only the professional gamblers, but Lepke and Gurrah and, though Farley never said so, this was the source of much of the money in his "wonderful tin box." [23] Most powerful of all the underworld's political contacts in the late twenties and early thirties was James J. Hines. A former blacksmith whose father and father's father had been Tammany election captains, Jimmy Hines, leader of the Eleventh Assembly District, was perhaps the strongest power in Tammany during this period. He was Dutch Schultz's chief political protector and, at one time or another, the protector of a host of other criminals, such as Owney Madden, Dwyer, Jack Diamond, Lepke, Luciano, Rothstein, Costello and Adonis.[24]

The underworld received dispensation through the police, the courts and especially the office of the District Attorney. We have already noticed that Seabury's exposure of disgraceful conditions in Crain's office raised a strong presumption in many minds that such conditions were not altogether without design. Crain's successor, William C. Dodge, chosen by Jimmy Hines and elected with the aid of Dutch Schultz's money and men, did not prove to be any more effective. Under Crain, a number of restaurant racketeers were indicted upon the insistence of some restaurant owners, but the case was postponed from one time to another until Dodge came in; then the case was ineffectually tried with the result that the defendants were acquitted and permitted to go on doing what they had been doing before their indictment—in fact, with greater ease, for the restaurant owners now saw there was no way out. One can cite other illustrations of Dodge's remarkable prosecuting ability, but nothing tells the story so well as a bit of testimony Schultz's lawyer, Dixie Davis, later gave at the Hines trial. Davis said that when a grand jury was moving toward the indictment of members of Schultz's policy gang, notably Davis himself, he told Hines that he ought to see Dodge about it. An Assistant District Attorney, Maurice G. Wahl, was "questioning too deeply," Davis told Hines, and Dodge ought to "get Wahl out of there." Hines talked to Dodge and Wahl was removed from the case. Subsequently Dodge asked

Davis some innocuous questions before the grand jury and let him go.[25]

Across the East River in Brooklyn the underworld also enjoyed good political ties. Here the identity of its political protectors generally remains shrouded in fog, but there can be no doubt of their existence. In 1938, at a time when Thomas E. Dewey was calling Joey Adonis Brooklyn's Public Enemy No. 1, the Brooklyn ganglord had a police record limited to one arrest—and no convictions—for disorderly conduct, an event that had occurred when he was sixteen years old. Since the early twenties Albert Anastasia had been literally getting away with murder; his only real jail penalty had been a rather short trip for carrying a gun. From June 11, 1930, when Abe Reles was picked up for murder the first time, until February 2, 1940, when he was taken off the streets for good, he was arrested on one or another charge, including six for homicide, on an average of once every seventy-eight days, excluding the time he spent in prison. But time after time he walked out free and clear, and Kid Twist, not the self-effacing type, boasted about the amount of "ice" he had to pay to stay out of jail.[26]

If anything, the reputation of the Democratic Brooklyn District Attorney's office, headed from 1931 to 1939 by William F. X. Geoghan, was less enviable than that of its Manhattan counterpart. Not only did the underworld make its influence felt, but the office was the subject of continual rumors of bribery. In 1933 racketeers arrested in connection with extortion in the Brooklyn laundry industry pleaded guilty only to receive suspended sentences from a judge who claimed his action represented his part of a pact with Geoghan. Responding to allegations of bribery, Governor Lehman ordered the Attorney General to supersede Geoghan. An Assistant Attorney General was specially appointed "to scrutinize all charges in the laundry business," and his investigation, though clearing all officials of improper conduct, brought about the indictment of 73 persons connected with the racket, many of whom were later convicted. Again in 1936, after the District Attorney failed to obtain an indictment of the suspects in the murder of one Samuel Druckman and it came out that the police, under authorization of the District Attorney's office, had even returned to the suspects their blood-stained clothing, Lehman ordered the Attorney General to supersede Geoghan with a special Assistant Attorney General. As a result an extraordinary grand jury indicted the suspected murderers, and they were later convicted; bribery of an Assistant District Attorney, a point at issue, could not be proven.[27]

In the underworld—and its protectors—Reform faced one of its greatest challenges.

From his first day in the Mayor's office, La Guardia, reinforced by his passionate hatred of crime, made war upon the underworld with all the power at his command. That power, it would be well to remember, was circumscribed: the Mayor, for instance, had no jurisdiction over the district attorneys and only limited, indirect control over some of the courts. La Guardia's main, but by no means only, weapon in this fight was the Police Department. Immediately upon becoming Mayor, he laid down the law to the police: "I have been told," he informed 200 ranking police officers, "that Fulton Street is considered the deadline for crooks. That deadline is now removed. It is replaced by the Hudson River on the west, the Atlantic Ocean on the south, the Westchester County line on the north and the Nassau County boundary line on the east. The crooks and the racketeers must be kept out. That is your job." To the consternation of some decent citizens, the administration instructed the cops to adopt a "muss 'em up" policy toward criminals.[28] With respect to the police, as well as other departments of the city, the advent of the Fusion administration dissolved the tie linking the underworld, the district leaders and the government.

Against gambling La Guardia conducted a crusade which few New Yorkers can have forgotten. When Fusion took over, slot machines constituted one of the most lucrative underworld enterprises in the city; a nickel machine in a reasonably good location would take in $20 a day, and at the start of La Guardia's administration, the Police Department admitted that there were between 25,000 and 30,000 such machines used for gambling in New York City. Because of the big take involved, because of the disorder, violence and terror that were part of the business and, most of all, because the machines ensnared young people into stealing, La Guardia at once set out to break up the slot machine enterprise and remove the machines from thousands of small shops, restaurants, candy stores and pool rooms. His path was not made easy by a federal court decision which restrained the police from interfering with slot machines unless it could be proven they were used for gambling. Nevertheless, La Guardia showed what an honest and determined Mayor and a freed Police Department could do. The police seized hundreds of machines. They raided a headquarters of the enterprise and confiscated important files and data. La Guardia, dramatizing his campaign, appeared at a police station and sat as a committing magistrate in a case. As if by magic, thousands of slot machines suddenly disappeared from stores.[29]

This was just the start. The Fusion administration fought the federal slot machine ruling to the United States Supreme Court and obtained a dismissal of the injunction. In co-operation with the state's Attorney General and various social agencies, it succeeded in getting an amendment to the state Penal Code, effective May 7, 1934, which sharpened the law's teeth against slot machines and made an even more effective drive against them possible. In the following weeks, the police seized and destroyed hundreds of machines. Before 1934 was out slot machines were dead in New York. Costello and his friends shifted their enterprise to Louisiana.[30]

La Guardia, however, was not soon done with gambling machines; no sooner were the slot machines driven out of the city than pinball machines took their place. Like the slot machines, they were placed on a commission basis in cigar stores, bars, grills and similar places. The average earnings of a pinball machine was between $35 and $40 per week, though the sum might reach $100 in some cases; conservatively speaking, the machines lured from the public between $20,000,000 and $23,000,000 per year. Chance, not skill, determined the outcome of a pinball game, and, despite the claim of owners that the machines were but amusement devices, it was well established that the usual kind of machine was used for gambling in contravention of the gambling laws. Also the pinball machines presented some of the same problems as had the slot machines—the industry was dominated by criminals and the machines exerted a demoralizing influence on youth.[31]

Beginning in 1934 La Guardia engaged in a ruthless drive against them. In 1939 the Police Department made 2,229 arrests in this connection, 84 per cent of which resulted in convictions; in 1940, the Department made 2,295 arrests, with 82 per cent convictions. Each year it confiscated and destroyed thousands of pinball machines. But by 1941 the campaign was only partially successful; Commissioner Herlands in a report to La Guardia on the subject admitted that, despite vigorous work by the Police Department, it had only seized about 20 per cent of the machines annually and that the devices "have continued to be widely used for gambling purposes." [32] Then in 1942 La Guardia's drive received two vital shots in the arm. In January Magistrate Ambrose Haddock, sitting as a justice in the Court of Special Sessions, removed what had been the great stumbling block in La Guardia's way by ruling that mere possession of a pinball machine was illegal and that it was not necessary for the government to show that it was used for gambling; by February 1, the administration had seized over 3,000 machines, had destroyed 448 of them—many being reduced to junk for the war effort—and had obtained convictions of operators in 420 cases. The War Production Board in March gave the administration's drive another boost when for war reasons it banned further manufacture of pinball machines.[33] Thus La Guardia licked the pinball machine as he had the slot machine before it.

As for other forms of gambling—policy, bookmaking, cards, craps, lotteries—the Fusion Mayor was no less sincere and vigorous in attempting to eradicate them. In radio speeches to the citizens of New York, he vehemently denounced the tinhorns. He pushed the police to crack down hard on them and, to a considerable extent, the police did. So zealous, in fact, was La Guardia in his attack on gambling that he sometimes invaded the personal rights of individuals, causing annoyance; once after the police had raided a private poker party, Magistrate Anna Kross chided them severely for "lawless law enforcement." Never did a New York City administration go so all-out against gamblers and gambling. La Guardia's efforts bore some fruit. He forced some of the city's big gamblers to move into New Jersey, and by keeping the gamblers under steady pressure, he made it harder for them to operate.[34]

Yet, aside from these accomplishments and the elimination of the slot and pinball machines, La Guardia failed in his gambling crusade. Commissioner O'Ryan could hardly have made a more ridiculous statement than one he made in March, 1934, when, after having given the police thirty days to wipe out policy and other forms of gambling, he announced that policy "is pretty well smashed." [35] With the exceptions noted, neither policy nor any other kind of gambling was ever destroyed by La Guardia's administration. To some degree, the administration was hampered by the handling of gambling cases in court. In March, 1935, La Guardia made public a report from Valentine showing the disposal of 7,093 policy case arrests in the Court of Special Sessions between February 1 and September 30, 1934; 30.7 per cent of those arrested were found guilty but given suspended sentences, 33.6 per cent were fined, while only 3.6 per cent received jail sentences; the maximum fine of $500 was imposed only once and the most common jail sentence was but ten days.[36] What was more important, despite some good police work against gambling, the gamblers, as we have noticed, were not unable to find some members of the force who would sell out the anti-gambling crusade: the tinhorns always found gambling profitable enough to pay huge amounts of ice while the police, their consciences tempered by a certain disrespect for vice laws, were never too far removed from temptation. Basically La Guardia could not completely win against the deep-rooted gambling urge. On one occasion during his last year in office, he declared that he had received "tens of thousands of letters" complaining about gambling with such accurate information that he could not help but wonder "what the police are doing." "Go on and act now," he admonished them, snapping his fingers vigorously. "Snap into it. Clean them out!" [37] At the end of almost twelve years this was a sad confession, and La Guardia must have known it.

The experience of the La Guardia administration with respect to prostitution, we might note, was rather similar. La Guardia put heat on the police to suppress the oldest profession and, though as a result of the Seabury investigation into the courts, the number of arrests seems to have fallen off for several years, the police were active in this area. Numerous arrests were made; the Investigating Squad of the Police Commissioner's office formulated a new plan to rid the city of notorious madams by the closest co-operation with FBI agents where any violation of the White Slave Act was found to exist; madams and prostitutes were forced to move about continually, as the experience of Polly Adler, New York's most notorious madam, attests.[38] For all that, prostitution continued under La Guardia. The *Fortune* article on vice in New York City in 1939, which angered La Guardia, stated that prostitution existed in the city, mainly in Manhattan; in Harlem it was prevalent and in the fashionable East Side midtown area, high class enterprises operated, generally through the technique of call girls.[39] Polly Adler, who ran the highest kind of brothel, stayed in business until she retired in 1945.[40] In 1943, a Brooklyn grand jury investigating lawlessness in that borough's "Little Harlem," the Bedford-Stuyvesant area, declared that "prostitution [in this section] is rife and evidence of the wide spread of venereal disease has been presented to us." [41] La Guardia, however, seems to have done better against prostitution than against gambling.

The Fusion administration showed the racketeers the same consideration it showed to the dealers in vice. Here there was a difference, however: city officials could not directly get at many of the racketeers, and the main contribution in the fight against racketeering was made by others. Nevertheless, the La Guardia administration's achievements in this area were not unsubstantial.

The administration struck out at racketeering in the public markets. As we mentioned earlier, La Guardia personally initiated a drive against the artichoke racketeers. He declared war on the Union Pacific Produce Company by issuing a proclamation forbidding the sale of artichokes in the city on the grounds that an emergency—namely the racketeering—existed. ("I want it clearly understood," he told the market concessionaires and their workers, "that no bunch of racketeers, thugs and punks are going to intimidate you as long as I am the Mayor of the City of New York.") [42] As La Guardia foresaw, by putting pressure on the artichoke receivers, the ban brought quick results. A few days later they signed an agreement at City Hall to sell directly to market dealers and retailers and not to the Union Pacific Produce Company, and the ban was lifted; the retail price of artichokes immediately dropped 25 to 30 per cent.[43] At the same time, the federal government, which throughout the thirties immensely helped local authorities in their fight against racketeering by prosecuting criminals for income tax evasions and violations of the Sherman Anti-Trust Act, got after the artichoke racketeers. It attacked the Union Pacific Produce Company for violating the anti-trust laws and, after various delays, convicted it and got four of the racketeers to plead guilty; Castaldo was given a suspended sentence in consideration of the fact that he had spent eleven months in jail for income tax violations.[44] Artichoke racketeering died, a victim of the combined efforts of the city and the national governments.

Even before this, Commissioner Morgan, who had old scores to settle, and his deputy, Big Mike Fiaschetti, a retired police captain who had won an Italian knighthood for smashing the Black Hand, informed the fish racketeers that a new age had dawned. The market officials revoked the permits of thirteen pushcart proprietors in the Peck Slip Fish Market, several for acting as "fences" for stolen fish; one of those whose license was taken away was a brother of Socks Lanza. A few days later Fiaschetti, accompanied by six uniformed patrolmen, conducted an early morning raid at the same market and drove out the self-appointed watchmen who had been intimidating truck drivers.[45]

Credit for catching up with Lanza, however, belongs to the federal government and District Attorney Hogan's office. Before La Guardia was elected Mayor, Socks and fifty-three other defendants, as a result of a federal grand jury investigation in 1933, had been indicted for conspiring to monopolize and restrain interstate trade in fresh water fish. Though he first won a mistrial, Lanza was convicted in 1935, and the following year, after his appeal was denied, he began serving a two-year sentence. In 1938 he was convicted of anti-trust violations in salt water fish, and six months were added to his term. The state in 1943 successfully prosecuted him, and a few other racketeers, for extorting money from a Teamsters' local; the court gave him seven and a half to fifteen years. As a result of these convictions, his power was broken.[46]

Morgan and Fiaschetti, along with Commissioner Blanshard, went after a racket that had established itself in Brooklyn's Wallabout Market purportedly under the aegis of district leader Frank V. Kelly's political club. A farmer was compelled to pay 50 cents to $1.50 for having his truck "watched" in spite of the presence of city patrolmen, and to hire from the same racketeer the carriers who took crates from the farmer's truck to the retailer's vehicle. Before La Guardia's first month in City Hall was out, the Department of Markets cleaned up this situation. The Department also put an end to other rackets involving the markets; though the administration fought a running battle against the poultry racketeers, other quarters proved more effective against them. By the close of La Guardia's first term, the problem of market racketeering had generally been beaten. A study of activities of the Market Department in subsequent years shows that the Department was not particularly concerned with racketeering.[47]

Against Dutch Schultz's policy racket the Fusion administration also struck a blow when Commissioner Blanshard discovered a fraudulent bail-bonding scheme that was connected with it. In order to more easily spring arrested policy collectors, certain professional bail runners had been coaching a number of small property owners to illegally pledge the same piece of property for more than one defendant. The evidence uncovered by Blanshard was so overwhelming that both Geoghan and Dodge were forced to undertake prosecutions, and these were unusually successful.[48]

Aside from the La Guardia administration's direct assault upon crime and vice, it also made invaluable contributions to the attack on the underworld undertaken by others in Manhattan and Brooklyn. This it did, not only by action, as we are going to see, but by its very presence, which served to reinforce the reform climate of opinion and inspire further efforts at reform.

The investigation that Blanshard's office conducted into bail-bonding had much greater consequences than the prosecution and conviction of some bondsmen. Revelations as to the extent and profitability of policy produced a demand in early 1935, especially from the Society for the Prevention of Crime, the old Parkhurst group, for the eradication of policy and other forms of vice. The Society, under the leadership of its president, Reverend George Drew Egbert, pastor of the First Congregationalist Church of Flushing, and its counsel, Samuel Marcus, was at this time enjoying somewhat of a renaissance. At the beginning of March, La Guardia announced an intensification of efforts against policy and under heavy pressure to do something, too, District Attorney Dodge appointed Marcus a special Assistant District Attorney and announced that everything would be done to get the higher-ups in the numbers game. From the first, however, it was apparent that Marcus and Dodge did not see eye to eye, and after a month of sporadic action which yielded few results, Dodge dismissed his special assistant with the explanation that though Marcus and the Society for the Prevention of Crime had promised to supply "valuable information," the appointment of Marcus had not "appreciably aided" the inquiry. Marcus retorted with a statement in which he spoke of "Judas Iscariot" and "Barabbas," and charged, what was not at all unlikely, that ever since accepting the appointment he had been handicapped by "disloyalty and chicanery of the highest type." [49]

Soon Dodge and the grand jury that had been impaneled in March to sift evidence of vice were also at loggerheads. Brighter and more determined than most grand juries, the March grand jury, led by its foreman, Lee Thompson Smith, a real estate executive, refused to let the District Attorney control the grand jury for his own purposes; instead it exercised the great powers that grand juries have, but seldom use, and "ran away." Suspecting the District Attorney's office of insincerity, the grand jury barred Dodge's assistants from its room and even the antechamber. When Dodge, in the face of demands from civic organizations that Governor Lehman appoint a special prosecutor, offered to remove himself from the investigation and name as special prosecutor a man chosen by the grand jury from a list of six, the grand jury refused to go along. Instead, on June 10 it gave a statement to the court. Calling some kinds of organized crime in Manhattan rampant, it asked the Governor to appoint a prosecuting attorney of outstanding capacity and public prestige to investigate with a special grand jury all forms of organized crime in New York County and their connection with law enforcement. Holding that its own usefulness was at an end, the grand jury asked to be and was discharged.[50]

Lehman acceded to the request of the March grand jury. He issued a call for an extraordinary term of the Supreme Court and a special grand jury to investigate vice, rackets and other crime in New York County and the relationship, if any, between them and law enforcement officials; the Governor named Justice Philip J. McCook, who had a reputation for honesty and courage, to preside. The post of special prosecutor Lehman offered to four outstanding Republican lawyers—Medalie, Tuttle, Thacher, Charles E. Hughes, Jr.—but each refused on the grounds that he had professional and public obligations which in justice and fair dealing could not be put aside. In a joint statement, the four urged the Governor to have Dodge appoint—this was the formal procedure—a young man whom the Bar Association had already endorsed for the position. His experience and ability, they said, pre-eminently qualified him for the work involved. After hesitating, for he questioned whether the young man was big enough, Lehman followed their advice and asked Dodge to make the appointment.[51] Thus came into existence one of the most important investigations in New York City's history, one whose consequences were to be of the greatest significance, not only with regard to crime in New York, but for city, state and national politics.

An Owosso, Michigan, boy whose grandfather was second cousin to the famous admiral, Thomas E. Dewey had grown up in his father's newspaper and print shop and had studied at the University of Michigan. Migrating to Manhattan in 1923, Dewey was not sure whether he wanted to be a lawyer or a singer. He studied law at Columbia, sang as a paid baritone soloist in a church and when he got his degree finally decided to stick with law. In his first years at the bar he was just another junior member in a big law office. Then early in 1931 while working on the preparation of a case for trial, he met George Medalie, whom Dewey's firm had retained as trial counsel in the case. Working with the young man, Medalie was impressed by his great energy and the thoroughness of his labors. When Medalie, on the last day of the trial, was named United States Attorney for the Southern District of New York, he asked Dewey to come along as his chief assistant. He put Dewey in active charge of preparing cases, and the office went after racketeers with energy that no local prosecutor had previously shown. After a long investigation, Dewey in 1933 obtained income tax indictments against Dutch Schultz and Waxey Gordon. When Medalie retired from office in 1933, Dewey temporarily became United States Attorney. At the time Lehman called him, however, he had retired to private practice and was doing well. He had a reasonable number of paying clients. On winter evenings he played indoor tennis two or three times a week or went to committee meetings of the Bar Association.[52]

Dewey had won the respect of others besides the elders of the bar. The underworld-Tammany alliance had grown to fear him, as is apparent from its reaction to his appointment. At the time the appointment was being considered, Dixie Davis told Jimmy Hines that Dewey was dangerous and said something ought to be done to prevent it before Dewey indicted all of them. Hines subsequently tried to do something but failed.[53] After Dewey was made special prosecutor, Dutch Schultz, who had already been burned by Dewey and as a consequence was in the process of losing his rackets, also tried to do something, and it proved to be the Dutchman's undoing. He decided that Dewey had to be rubbed out and tried to talk the members of the crime cartel into it. Lepke and Luciano, however, reasoned that to kill Dewey would create such an uproar that underworld business would be hurt everywhere and that the best strategy was simply to keep witnesses out of his reach. Their advice prevailed. When Schultz threatened to murder Dewey anyway in defiance of the syndicate's decision, the other ganglords, to protect themselves, decided it was time for Dutch to go. That is why Charlie Workman, one of gangland's most deadly executioners, strolled into a Newark, New Jersey, bar one night in October, 1935, and pumped bullets into Schultz and three of his aides.[54] Dewey thus caused the elimination of one mob boss without doing a thing, by simply being appointed.

From the start of his investigation Dewey received the wholehearted support of the La Guardia administration, an indispensable requirement for success. La Guardia told police officials and magistrates to give the special prosecutor complete co-operation. Valentine gave him a special squad of policemen and detectives too young to be tainted by corruption or disillusionment. The Mayor sent the special prosecutor various communications containing information he thought might help him in the investigation. The Board of Estimate unanimously voted a $122,000 appropriation for the inquiry; Democrat James J. Lyons, Borough President of the Bronx, denounced the investigation as "an extravagant use of the people's money" but voted for the appropriation anyway, declaring that he did so out of deference to La Guardia's recommendation. When Dewey later needed additional money, the Board did not fail him.[55]

Quickly setting to work, the young special prosecutor organized a staff of young, able, fervent, nonpolitical lawyers, accountants and investigators; among his top assistants were William Herlands, Barent Ten Eyck and Murray I. Gurfein, all of whom had served as Assistant United States Attorneys under him. Dewey set up headquarters in the Woolworth Building and took precautions to insure secrecy. He promised that no one who gave information would be molested; and he kept that promise, except in the case of one witness who refused police protection and was shot. Dewey's strategy followed from his goal. What he really wanted was to get the top men in the underworld, and to get them he knew that he needed the testimony of other criminals. He approached his job, therefore, with a cool, calculated willingness to bargain with small fry if they would give state's evidence against a master criminal. He knew, of course, that these witnesses could easily be attacked by defense counsel, but he felt that if the job were done thoroughly enough, if other evidence interlocked with the testimony of criminals, the case would be proved. Methodically, quietly, secretly and by dint of laborious research, Dewey and his staff prepared their cases. Seeing that an ancient New York law prohibiting a man from being tried for more than one specific crime at a time gave racketeers an out—they lived not by one intimidation, which might be hard to prove, but by hundreds—Dewey asked for, and the legislature instituted, a change whereby the courts could try an individual for any number of related offenses under the same indictment. Another law requiring the names of witnesses appearing before a grand jury to be written on the back of the indictment gave criminals the opportunity to reach witnesses before the trial. Dewey requested that this provision be changed, and again the legislature complied.[56]

In the fall of 1935, Dewey undertook his first prosecutions—against the loan sharks. By early December more than a score of the human leeches who loaned money at impossible rates of interest were convicted or had pleaded guilty; the sentences ranged from six months for individual operators to three, four or five years for leaders. Assigning two assistants to continue the search for loan sharks, the special prosecutor then quickly turned his attention to Luciano and his prostitution racket.[57]

Dewey had not wanted to get involved with prostitution. He didn't want his investigation to become just another prostitution exposé. ("Hell," he said at the start of his inquiry, "I didn't quit a good law practice to chase after prostitutes." [58]) What he mainly wished to do with the power Lehman had placed in his hands was to crack open industrial racketeering. But in the first few months of his investigation, he could not make a dent against this kind of racketeering. Businessmen were too afraid to testify; Lepke and Luciano had apparently given wise counsel. While in the midst of this dilemma, Dewey's assistants by diligent work uncovered Luciano's prostitution racket and gave Dewey an opportunity to get at one of gangland's biggest figures, and indirectly at some industrial racketeering, through prostitution. If Dewey could not get Lucky for his other rackets, he might convict him on compulsory prostitution. He jumped at the chance.[59]

It was a hard job. The madams, bookers and prostitutes were unhappy and tired of working for next to nothing and were glad of a chance to talk; but they were afraid. Dewey and his staff broke down their reticence and got them to testify against Luciano and the higher-ups in the racket. In the middle of May, 1936, Dewey put Luciano and the other big shots in the racket on trial. During its course, leaders in the political-criminal world moved heaven and earth to free Luciano. Polly Adler writes of how she was mysteriously brought to a meeting of men from all the biggest rackets in New York. They were deeply concerned about the Luciano trial and wanted to know if Polly could give some information that could be used to prove that the testimony given by the state's women witnesses was false; Polly could not help them.[60] The underworld paid a $2,500 bribe to a material witness who thereupon frustrated an important prosecution program by recanting a statement he had made to Dewey. Two of Dewey's aides reported attempts to corrupt them: in one case, one of Dewey's principal aides had been given assurance of being nominated and elected to the Supreme Court, or being paid $250,000 in cash as a forfeit in case the pledge failed, if he would "throw the case"; another aid was simply told that if he played ball he would find it lucrative. Luciano's friends worked in vain. On June 7 the jury found Luciano and the other racketeers guilty of compulsory prostitution. Justice McCook sentenced them to long terms in jail, Luciano getting from thirty to fifty years.[61]

The Luciano case was of tremendous importance for the Dewey investigation. In the first place, because notorious and sinister Luciano was the principal defendant and because of the nature of the charge itself, the trial created a good deal of public interest. The interest thus generated in the early part of the investigation carried over to a later time when Dewey's actions against certain industrial racketeers were exceedingly dull; the significance of these later cases might have been lost on the public if it had not still been under the spell of the Luciano trial.[62] Secondly, Dewey's victory over Luciano marked the first big crack in the wall of immunity which had surrounded the rackets in New York. The prestige of the young special prosecutor went up. He had actually sent one of the nation's biggest underworld figures to jail—and not for income tax evasion, either. More than likely Dewey's success made businessmen more inclined to talk about industrial racketeering.

In any case, in the summer of 1936, a year after the start of the investigation, Dewey finally found himself in a position to grapple with this problem. Governor Lehman placed two more special grand juries at his disposal, continued Justice McCook's term and named Supreme Court Justice Ferdinand Pecora to a special term to run concurrently with McCook's.[63] The grand jury that had been working with Dewey had seen witnesses afraid to testify and businessmen give evasive or mendacious answers. Accordingly, it recommended that a special body of citizens be formed in order to crystallize moral support for the work of law enforcement, insure provision of adequate protection for witnesses and convince businessmen to testify and that they would be adequately protected. Mayor La Guardia, to whom the grand jury's presentment was sent, appointed Harry F. Guggenheim, mining executive and former ambassador to Cuba, to head such a committee. The group, formally organized in the fall of 1936 as the Citizens Committee on the Control of Crime in New York, was patterned after similar groups in Baltimore, Chicago and Cleveland. Among its members were Lee Thompson Smith, foreman of the "runaway grand jury," Medalie, Raymond Moley and, after a time, Burlingham; William P. Beazell, former assistant managing editor of the *World* was made executive secretary.[64] In practice, the committee helped Dewey by aiding the families of key witnesses, the nature of whose services to the prosecution brought about loss of employment and savings and imposed other hardships on them. In addition, the committee took upon itself the task of keeping master-file records of complaints and arrests in New York City for felonies and grave misdemeanors and of the action taken in these cases by grand juries and the courts. These records gave a good view of the state of crime in the city; and, as we shall see, those relating to Brooklyn were to be of special importance. Begun as an aid to the Dewey investigation, the Guggenheim committee remained in existence for a number of years after the end of the inquiry, mainly concerning itself with reports on the state of crime in New York.[65]

Dewey's attack on industrial racketeering covered a wide front and continued for a number of years; from 1938 to 1942 Dewey carried on this work as District Attorney of New York County. In early 1937 he brought the restaurant racketeers to trial. For the first time, the story of the racket was told to the public by fear-filled witnesses whom Dewey persuaded or forced to testify. Seven men, three officials of the owners' "association," two officers of the waiters' union and two of the cafeteria workers' union, were convicted on counts of conspiracy and extortion and sent to the penitentiary and the racket was broken. This was the first time in the history of the country that a complete industrial racket had been placed on trial, and the blanket verdict rendered by the jury—it found every defendant guilty of every charge against him—represented a great victory for Dewey.[66] Not able to convict Tootsie Herbert and his fellow racketeers for their poultry activities, he succeeded in 1937 in indicting Tootsie and two others on the charge of stealing from the union treasury. The three pleaded guilty and were given substantial sentences. Their racket was smashed.[67]

In the early part of 1937 Dewey also began an investigation into the bakery-trucking and garment-trucking rackets. By the late spring and the summer he had gotten some garment racketeers to plead guilty and had convicted a few bakery racketeers. What was more important, the trail in both cases led unmistakably to the door of Lepke and Gurrah, and they were indicted for both rackets. About the same time the federal government sought to bring the Gorilla Boys to trial for violating the anti-trust laws with respect to the fancy fur industry; a short time later the United States also developed an interest in Lepke for his role in a conspiracy to violate the federal narcotics law. In the summer of 1937, the Gorilla Boys became fugitives. Gurrah surrendered to the federal government in April, 1938. Convicted on the anti-trust charge, he was sentenced to three years in jail and fined $15,000; in 1936 he had been convicted in an anti-trust action involving the rabbit skin trade and now also had to serve the sentence imposed in this case. After paying his debt to the federal government, Gurrah was brought to New York City at the end of 1942 to face charges of conspiracy and extortion in the garment and bakery industries. In 1943 he pleaded guilty to one count of extortion in the garment industry and in May, 1944, was sentenced to fifteen years to life. A broken, middle-aged man with a heart condition, Gurrah cried like a baby when sentenced.

The manhunt for Lepke undertaken by city and federal officials was one of the most intense and concentrated that the country has ever seen. For two years Albert Anastasia did an excellent job of hiding him in Brooklyn. Then in August, 1939, Lepke gave himself up to J. Edgar Hoover, apparently under the misapprehension that the federal government had agreed to a deal. There was none. The federal authorities convicted him on the narcotics charge, obtained guilty pleas from him on two indictments dealing with the rabbit fur industry, gave him a long jail term and turned him over to Dewey. Dewey promptly tried and convicted him for his flour and bakery operations; the state gave him thirty years to life.[68]

In 1937, at the same time as Dewey was striking out at the industrial racketeers, he also initiated a drive on the policy racketeers, once led by Dutch Schultz. In January he arrested seventy small fry connected with policy and converted them into witnesses. Then in July he struck against the big shots: Dixie Davis and eleven others were indicted as the current leaders of the policy racket. Davis and most of the others turned fugitive, but early in 1938 he and another leader, George Weinberg, were discovered in Philadelphia and, facing extradition, they returned to New York for trial. The trial as originally intended, however, was never held. For in the policy racketeers, Dewey found the means to get at the underworld's principal political protector in Manhattan. Though Hines's role had long been known, nothing could be proven against him. With Davis and Weinberg, however, Dewey had a good chance to make a case stick. They agreed to become the state's chief witnesses. When the policy trial opened in August, 1938, Hines had become the only defendant, charged with complicity in the numbers game and selling protection to the Schultz gang.[69]

The trial was top news across the country and was marked by fanfare and intense excitement. Not only was a Tammany giant on trial, but the proceedings emitted distinct political overtones; Dewey was being seriously considered for the Republican gubernatorial nomination. The principals at the trial worked to heighten interest: defense counsel Lloyd Paul Stryker, brilliant, a master of cross-examination, one of the greatest criminal lawyers in the country; Dewey, the youthful, dynamic and extremely capable prosecutor who had captured the imagination of the nation; and Jimmy Hines, in a sense Mr. Tammany, whose broad shoulders and heavy biceps, developed in his days as a blacksmith, blue flinty eyes, square reddened face and quiet voice conspired to impart an impression of strength and courage.[70] And once the trial began, there were sensational revelations.

Weinberg and Davis testified that Schultz and his gang had paid Hines to protect the policy racket—Weinberg said an average of $750 a week. They stated that in 1933 Schultz had contributed generously to Dodge's campaign fund through Hines. Davis' sister swore she delivered money from her brother to the Tammany leader. Max Steuer, Tammany adviser, reluctantly admitted that Hines had asked him to look into the possibility of getting an adjustment of Schultz's income tax trouble with the federal government. John F. Curry testified that Hines had asked him to name Dodge the candidate for District Attorney in 1933 and that when Tammany had controlled the Police Department Hines had asked him to transfer policemen; these requests, Curry said, he forwarded to the Police Commissioner and invariably they were granted. At last much of the inside story of what had been wrong with Manhattan justice was placed on the public record. Stryker, plainly worried, looked continually for a mistrial and finally won one from Justice Pecora. Dewey at one point asked a witness a question which linked Hines with the poultry racket. In the court's opinion, the question had prejudiced the case.[71]

The mistrial only delayed the outcome. Having lost the gubernatorial race against Lehman in 1938, Dewey, still District Attorney, brought Hines to trial again in the last week of January, 1939, this time before Judge Charles C. Nott, Jr. Gone were the vast crowds and great excitement; the show had lost its edge due to repetition and the absence of a political ingredient. In the course of the trial, George Weinberg committed suicide, but the court permitted his earlier testimony to be read into the second trial. At the end of February, the jury brought in its verdict: guilty. After appeals failed, Hines in October, 1940, began serving a four-year sentence. The conviction was another crushing blow to Tammany in a long series of defeats. New York City had proven to itself and to the world that a big politician could be caught and sent to jail. Hines's conviction represented the high-watermark of Dewey's work in Manhattan and, incidentally, gave a decided boost to his political fortunes.[72]

The job that Dewey did as special prosecutor and, later, as District Attorney was a remarkable one; up to the fall of 1937, when he ran on the Fusion ticket for District Attorney, he had compiled the amazing record of 72 convictions out of 73 indictments.[73] He broke the big rackets in Manhattan and sent numerous racketeers to prison, his success serving as a powerful commentary on William C. Dodge and the Tammany system. Credit for that success belonged to many: Governor Lehman, the special grand juries, the excellent, incorruptible judges, Mayor La Guardia and other city officials, the Dewey staff and, certainly not least, Dewey, himself. Intensely determined to do a good job, he did one by careful planning, shrewd calculation, hard work and by grace of a hair-trigger mind and high dramatic talent.

Dewey's achievement in Manhattan had significance for the prosecution of crime elsewhere. Believing that the whole of the United States was victimized by a super-mob loosely knit, but internally harmonious and co-operative, Dewey hoped from the outset of his work that the undoing of underworld leaders in New York might adversely affect the fortunes of their allies in other places and that other cities might be spurred to action by his example. When his success became apparent, civic and professional groups in other communities took heart and inaugurated measures to stamp out their local rackets. Out-of-town prosecutors asked him for advice.[74]

Tom Dewey started a new era in crime prosecution in Manhattan. After he became Governor in January, 1943, the standards he established were carried on by Frank S. Hogan, one of his assistants during the special investigation.

A special investigation in the late thirties and early forties also had significant consequences for Brooklyn law enforcement. The inquiry grew out of a series of circumstances in 1938. Charges of "fixing" involving members of District Attorney Geoghan's staff were once again made. The charges involved two different cases. In one case Assistant District Attorney William F. McGuinness was charged with accepting a bribe to "fix" a perjury case. In the other, Isidore Juffe, leader of a fur swindle in Brooklyn, who had been freed after arrest when Assistant District Attorney Alexander R. Baldwin stated that he was unable to find witnesses, told his aides that he had "paid plenty" to get off, and the story got into the newspapers; suspicion fell on Baldwin. In the midst of these happenings, La Guardia announced that the Guggenheim committee, which, it will be recalled, had begun to keep a master-file of felonies and serious misdemeanors and their disposition, had examined 14,000 cases in Brooklyn since July, 1937, and had found many irregularities. Viewing the congeries of events suspiciously, La Guardia at the beginning of October, 1938, ordered his Commissioner of Investigation, William Herlands, to examine charges of corruption of police and other officials in the Juffe case and to make a general inquiry into law enforcement in Brooklyn.[75]

The result was that once again La Guardia and his officials triggered an important anti-crime development. Despite Geoghan's attempt to thwart his investigation, Herlands found out enough damning information to petition Governor Lehman on October 10 to supersede Geoghan for the third time. After studying the Commissioner of Investigation's data, the Governor agreed to do so. He asked Attorney General John J. Bennett, Jr. to appoint John Harlan Amen to conduct an inquiry and created an extraordinary term. Since 1928 Amen, a slightly-built man with a wide smile and a kind of Yankee drawl, had been serving as a special Assistant United States Attorney. He was known as the "ace racket buster" of the federal government; in his last two years he had obtained 193 convictions in racket cases, with but one reversal on appeal. Plainly the youthful graduate of Harvard Law School was an ideal man for the task at hand.[76]

Two days after Geoghan's supersession, six volumes containing 7,200 permanent police records were stolen from the record room of the 78th precinct in Bergen Street. Commissioner Valentine personally conducted an intensive investigation and finally received information which implicated Lieutenant Cuthbert J. Behan, who was suspended and arrested. In the Governor's orders to Amen, the matter of the stolen records as well as the fur case were specifically cited as matters for investigation. In addition, Amen was given permission to investigate any and all matters affecting the enforcement of law in Brooklyn. These orders were far broader than those signed in the previous supersessions of Geoghan.[77]

The Amen inquiry was not supposed to be a Dewey investigation of Brooklyn. While Dewey had been given power to investigate racketeering and the relationship between crime and politics, Amen was authorized to inquire only into official wrong-doing and the theft of police records. In January, 1939, Amen's power was somewhat broadened to enable him to handle cases other than those involving official corruption if they constituted an integral part of corruption cases, but the focus still was on official dishonesty.[78]

As with the Dewey investigation, the Fusion administration completely co-operated with Amen's inquiry. Herlands turned over his findings to Amen and helped him when he could. Valentine, as he had done for Dewey, gave Amen a special, carefully selected police detail for his work. The La Guardia administration saw to it that the Brooklyn investigator received the appropriations he needed to do the job. As in Dewey's case, a hostile administration could have sabotaged the inquiry.[79]

The Amen investigation lasted four years, from 1938 to the end of 1942. It finally proved that corruption existed on Geoghan's staff. The inquiry discovered that McGuinness had been engaged in the practice of taking money since his appointment to the staff in 1931; after pleading guilty to accepting bribes, unlawful fees and a gratuity in specific cases, McGuinness was sent to Sing Sing. Assistant District Attorney Baldwin was acquitted by a jury of accepting a bribe in the Juffe case, but the case indirectly led to his disbarment on other grounds. As a result of the investigation, another Assistant District Attorney, Francis A. Madden, was also disbarred for a number of reasons, including bribe-taking.[80]

The investigation uncovered a corrupt bail-bonding scheme, similar to the one Blanshard had exposed a few years before. Certain individuals had been encouraging shady property owners to pledge their property illegally; many people were caught up in the scheme, including some police officers who supervised bailing at police station houses when the courts were closed. A number of individuals were indicted, many of them pleading guilty. Magistrate Mark Rudich was removed from the bench by the Appellate Division and subsequently disbarred for favoring a crooked bail-bond operator. Lieutenant Behan's apparent theft of police records was allegedly tied up with the crooked bail-bonding enterprise: he had wanted to hide his participation in the scheme from Herlands, who was getting too close. While acquitted of stealing the records by a trial jury, Behan was convicted in a departmental trial and dismissed from the force by Commissioner Valentine.[81]

Amen found that the system of selecting grand, special and trial juries in Brooklyn was so slipshod that criminals and others who had had trouble with the law sometimes sat on them; as a result of the exposure, the system was tightened up. An "abortion business" was uncovered which resulted

in criminal convictions, disbarments, disciplinary proceedings and suggestions for better law enforcement in this area.[82] We have already noted
that Amen's efforts led to the discovery that gambling was flourishing in
Brooklyn under police protection.

These and other findings of the Amen inquiry were not unimportant.
Yet they did not add up to anything comparable to Dewey's achievement.
Essentially this was because of the fact that Amen and Dewey conducted
different kinds of investigations. Amen, limited to cases of official corruption, was never in a position to get to the bottom of conditions in
Brooklyn. For example, his investigation into waterfront conditions,
(which would have struck oil) was taken out of his hands by the regular
prosecuting authorities. Moreover, within his assigned area, he found the
going rough. Bribery is not easy to prove, and it is usually found as the
consequence of an investigation into other matters, rather than as a result
of a specifically directed search. Because of its limited nature and limited
results and because it had to compete with pre-war and war news, the
Amen investigation never made the impact on the public it might have
made.[83]

Still the inquiry made enough of an impact to make Geoghan's renomination in 1939 impossible,[84] and this not so obvious consequence was the
most important of all for Brooklyn crime-fighting. For the Democrats,
instead, ran and elected County Judge William O'Dwyer, and subsequently
some of O'Dwyer's work as District Attorney was excellent. He appointed
Burton B. Turkus, a political independent, as Assistant District Attorney
in charge of the Felony and Homicide Section, and in the course of trying
to solve Brooklyn's two hundred unsolved murders, Turkus in 1940 uncovered Murder, Inc. and the national crime syndicate. Using the testimony
of Abe Reles and other members of the Brooklyn mob who turned state's
evidence, O'Dwyer sent Pittsburgh Phil Strauss, Happy Maione, Bugsy
Goldstein and Dasher Abbandando to the electric chair.[85]

Moreover, O'Dwyer's office finally solved the Joseph Rosen murder
of 1936 with sensational results. Rosen, an obscure Brooklyn candy store
owner, had formerly been a clothing truckman. A short while after
announcing his intention of seeing Dewey, he was riddled with bullets in
his candy store early one Sunday morning. Geoghan's office failed to solve
the murder despite much newspaper criticism. At one point, an assistant
prosecutor progressed sufficiently to say behind closed doors in the District
Attorney's office, "I think we're on the way to one of the greatest pinches
we've ever made." He was abruptly taken off the case. In fact, three different assistant prosecutors were assigned and called off one after the other.
When Reles talked, the mystery disappeared. Rosen had been one of those
ordered killed by Lepke. O'Dwyer's office accumulated enough evidence
to ask the federal government for a loan of Lepke—he was then serving
his narcotics sentence—so that it could put him on trial for the murder
along with two of his henchmen. In November, 1941, Lepke, Mendy

Weiss and Louis Capone were convicted and sentenced to die in the electric chair. Despite many appeals and delays of one sort or another by Lepke, he, along with the other two, was electrocuted in March, 1944. Lepke's death marked the first time a ganglord had been electrocuted, and it is the only case to date.[86]

When La Guardia left office in 1945, New York City was no longer in the grip of the underworld. The city had won its war against the slot and pinball machines, and while other forms of gambling had not been eliminated, they were under constant attack and forced to be on guard. Against vice, the Fusion Mayor had done his best and, if his success was not as brilliant as could be desired, the reasons went deeper than any personality or any administration. Most of the rackets that had plagued the city in 1934 had been smashed, thanks mainly to Dewey, as had the dread that had paralyzed the citizenry in the face of racketeering; one of the greatest legacies left to New York by the La Guardia period was the knowledge that the racketeers could be beaten. Gone from the New York scene in 1945 were some of the top figures in the underworld. Dutch Schultz had been executed by his own kind, Lepke Buchalter by the state. In jail were Charlie (not so lucky) Luciano and Gurrah Shapiro. Other criminals had transferred their operations elsewhere.

On the other hand, the underworld was far from beaten. While the crime combination had been subjected to devastating attack in New York, in 1945 it was still in operation, both in New York and elsewhere in the nation. In New York Frank Costello and Joey Adonis were still powers. The Brooklyn mob, while decimated, was not completely eradicated. Gamblers were raking in profits. Though racketeering was not as pervasive or as serious as in the thirties, it had certainly not disappeared. In the garment industry, for instance, David Dubinsky, head of the ILGWU, and others tried in vain to completely stamp it out. Waterfront racketeering went on in the same old way; aside from an investigation of the waterfront undertaken by La Guardia's Department of Investigation and Amen's abortive inquiry, nothing serious was done to tackle the waterfront problem. In 1951 the Kefauver committee was to report that "racketeers are firmly entrenched along New York City's waterfront with . . . resulting extortions, shakedowns, kick-backs from wages, payroll padding, gangster infiltration of unions, and large-scale gambling." Albert Anastasia, the committee noted, appeared to be the key to waterfront racketeering.[87]

Moreover, the tie that bound the underworld and politics had not been severed. In the thirties and forties, in fact, organized crime developed a greater influence in machine politics than it had enjoyed before. Frank Costello emerged in the forties as a power in Tammany Hall, and he was not the only underworld figure to interest himself in Tammany politics. In Brooklyn, Adonis and Anastasia were almost certainly still "fixed" politically, despite the change that had occurred in the District Attorney's office. While O'Dwyer did a first-rate job with respect to the ordinary killers in Murder, Inc., he never touched either Anastasia or Adonis, and this was not for lack of opportunity. A later chapter will have more to say about a number of these points.

11

The welfare city

W H E N   T H E   La Guardia administration came to power, New York City's physical and social needs, increased and aggravated by the Depression, were pressing for attention. The Fusion platform, it may be recalled, not unmindful of economy and efficiency, had stressed the intention of fulfilling these needs. In the campaign La Guardia had promised to work for such things as public housing and more playgrounds, for improvements in relief, education and the care of the poor's health. The new administration did not forget its pledges. This was not so apparent in the first few months because the city's critical financial situation held up many of the administration's plans. (The lack of visible results caused some of Fusion's friends to express doubts; the *New York Post* in May, 1934, for example, wondered whether La Guardia would remember that he was supposed to do more than just "economize" and remarked that so far his program was more in keeping with a McKee.[1]) Before long, however, it became obvious that the La Guardia administration was more than keeping the faith. In the end, none of Fusion's achievements were more substantial or more significant than those involving the physical improvement of the city and the increase of social benefits enjoyed by its people; nor, one is almost certain in saying, did any of La Guardia's other accomplishments make as deep an impression on the mass of citizens.

In thus coming to grips with the city's physical and social needs, the La Guardia administration followed in the tradition of New York City's reform administrations. Every administration in the city's past, of course, had had to concern itself to some extent with public works and social services; but as a rule machine administrations had acted, when they did act, more as a consequence of public pressure and the compulsion of events than as a result of intelligence, vision and a desire to better the community.[2] Yet to such a degree and on such a scale did the La Guardia administration interest itself in this area that the effort appeared, even when compared with previous reform administrations, almost as the charting of a new tack in municipal government. What was especially notable, the La Guardia administration realized more fully than had any American city government the thinking of those municipal reformers who conceived of good government largely in terms of positive programs in the interest of the masses. In doing this, however, the Fusion administration seems to have been influenced less by knowledge of one aspect of the municipal reform tradition than by the general liberal climate of opinion in the nation, with its emphasis on the expanding role of government; the extension of the function of government in New York City in the period was part of a larger movement which encompassed all levels of government in the United States.

No administration in the city's history built as many public projects or projects of such importance as did La Guardia's. Of course, it is true that no previous administration was in power so long, but there were more significant reasons for the achievement. Mainly it was the result of New Deal expenditures for recovery and relief. New York City received a liberal share of the billions distributed by the Federal Emergency Relief Administration, Civil Works Administration, Public Works Administration and Works Progress (Projects) Administration; by June, 1940, when 94 per cent of the PWA program in New York City had been completed (105 out of 116 projects), the city had received outright PWA grants of $115,938,000 and had borrowed an additional $136,086,000 under the program, acquiring in all more than $250,000,000 of construction funds; WPA money, including a relatively small appropriation made by the city, ran to about $145,000,000 a year, at least until 1938.[3] It must be borne in mind that the city financed or helped finance a number of projects in the traditional manner by means of its long-term bonds, but federal money was responsible for most of the city's huge construction program. La Guardia candidly recognized the debt New York owed to Washington. "All this [physical improvement] of course, would not have been possible even with the enthusiasm, ability and desire that could have been marshalled," he once wrote, "were it not that finances were made available by the Federal Government in many . . . instances." [4]

The Fusion administration, however, was not without a good deal of responsibility for the accomplishments. La Guardia, conscious of the importance of public works and relief to New York City and determined that the city should get as much of the federal bounty as possible, continually worked to advance the cause of the city in Washington. Smarting under campaign statements that only McKee would be able to obtain federal funds, La Guardia was hardly elected when he hurried to Washington to establish amiable relations with Secretary Ickes, the Great Dispenser. He succeeded—an achievement of no small dimensions considering the man he was dealing with. Not only Ickes, but Harry Hopkins, head of the FERA and afterwards the WPA, and, most important, the President showed friendship to La Guardia; one or two occasions aside, relations between the national administration and the city government were most cordial.[5] La Guardia's "in" with the administration could hardly have been without influence on the amount of federal money given New York City. Furthermore, New York's aggressive Mayor pushed his requests vigorously. It is true that federal funds would have gone to New York City whoever the Mayor had been, but it is unlikely that the city would have obtained as much New Deal money under another Mayor as it did under La Guardia.

For other reasons, too, the Fusion administration deserves credit for the construction that took place. La Guardia was greatly responsible for improvement in the city's financial position, a development that enabled the city to qualify for PWA funds. La Guardia claimed that because his administration was always ready with useful projects, it obtained federal money it otherwise would not have received, and very likely he was right. Anticipating the WPA program, the Mayor's Engineering Committee on Federal Projects met daily and prepared a list of worthwhile projects from a bigger list submitted by the city departments and borough presidents, with the result that New York was practically the only large city in the country to be ready with a comprehensive program for putting men to work when WPA came into existence in the summer of 1935, a fact that was probably not without influence on Roosevelt's decision to approve the liberal sum of almost $300,000,000 in WPA funds for the city.[6]

And it is important to note that the La Guardia administration made excellent use of the federal money it received—which might not have been true of a different administration. Fusion gave the taxpayers the most for their money in the form of valuable modern structures and other public works, some of them self-sustaining. Robert Moses became the administrator of much of the city's physical transformation, the Baron Haussmann of New York; in matters pertaining to planning and construction he had a powerful voice, not only because of the various positions he filled—Park Commissioner, head of the Triborough Bridge Authority, member of other authorities and of the City Planning Commission—but because of the influence he could exert in a more informal way. For giving Moses scope and backing, the latter even in the face of Roosevelt's displeasure at one point,[7] La Guardia deserves a good deal of praise. Arrogant, impatient, opinionated, contemptuous of those disagreeing with him, Moses was also brilliant, energetic and selflessly dedicated to the public service; most of all, he had a genius for getting important things done. It is unlikely that another man, even with a plethora of federal funds and a pool of WPA labor at his command, could have achieved for the city all that

Moses achieved. Aside from La Guardia, himself, it would be hard to name another public official in the history of New York who did as much to make the city a better place in which to live.

No listing of capital improvements constructed under La Guardia could omit his modern sewage disposal plants. Before La Guardia became Mayor, sewage emptied directly into the Hudson and East rivers and other bodies of water; in the summer a certain amount of chlorination was done near the beaches. It was left for Fusion to tackle this problem. With the aid of PWA funds, La Guardia erected a sewage treatment plant at Coney Island which practically eliminated the contamination of the bathing beaches in that area, and finished a disposal plant on Ward's Island in the East River. This was just the beginning. By 1945 the city had constructed an addition to the Coney Island plant, a City Island-Hart Island plant in Long Island Sound, a Bowery Bay plant, a Jamaica plant and a Tallman's Island plant; partially finished and in partial operation was the 26th Ward plant in Brooklyn. Altogether the modern plants, which cost approximately $58,000,000, put about 46 per cent of the city's sewage under treatment. Post-war plans of the La Guardia administration envisaged new projects and extensions to raise this proportion to 85 per cent.[8]

The refuse problem, it might be noted in passing, La Guardia for the most part handled without reliance upon capital improvements. When Fusion came to power, the city, while practicing incineration and land-filling, was still dumping much of its garbage and rubbish at sea. Time was running out for the city, however, for after a long legal battle the State of New Jersey had won a Supreme Court ruling forbidding New York from dumping garbage and rubbish in the ocean after June 1, 1933 (extended later to July 1, 1934) under penalty of paying a heavy fine to New Jersey. By completing the erection of two large incinerators and the modernization of two existing plants, La Guardia was able to meet the court's deadline.[9] While the La Guardia administration built one or two incinerators after that, it adopted a land-fill, rather than an incinerator, policy for garbage and rubbish; in fact, according to the Commissioner of Sanitation in the following administration, the city, which had operated 21 incinerators at the time La Guardia's land-fill policy was adopted, had only 4 in operation when La Guardia left office, 17 having been shut down. La Guardia's preference for land-filling over incineration was the cause of a running controversy during his administration. Commissioner Carey and others defended the policy as being cheaper than incineration, no more objectionable under proper safeguards (which Carey declared the Sanitation Department used) and in addition a good means to reclaim waste areas in the marginal sections of the city. Property owners in Queens, Richmond and, to a lesser extent, the Bronx, vigorously denounced the land-fill operations, however, claiming that liquid garbage leaked through the dikes of the fills polluting water and air, that odors in the summer were intolerable and that land-fills undermined property values; they insisted that garbage be separated from other refuse and incinerated in the city's plants. Under O'Dwyer the city reversed itself on incineration and adopted a program for building more incinerators, but the program fell behind and land-filling was carried on.[10]

The Fusion administration also constructed important market facilities. The Bronx Terminal Market, upon which Tammany had spent millions, but which was still unusable when La Guardia came to City Hall, was one of the city's choicest "lemons"; in 1933 the market showed a deficit of $75,000. La Guardia built 80 wholesale stores, a modern farmers' square and other improvements, rehabilitated float bridges to make water facilities available and encouraged merchants to use the market. Opened on April 27, 1935, the market showed a net operating profit of $192,000 for seven months of that year. Other steps followed in the modernization of food distribution in New York City. One of the most important was the enclosure of many of the city's open air pushcart markets. Traditional and colorful as they were, the pushcarts snarled traffic terribly and presented a sanitary problem, and La Guardia decided to put the peddlers off the streets. The first enclosed municipal retail market, built at Park Avenue between 111th and 116th streets, opened in the spring of 1936. By 1945 the city had 8 such enclosed markets (4 in Manhattan, 3 in Brooklyn, 1 in the Bronx) and was looking forward to the elimination of the 10 open air markets that remained. The enclosure policy, in addition to getting rid of traffic difficulties and insuring the distribution of cleaner food, had an important psychological effect upon the venders who, once transferred indoors, experienced a rise in status from peddler to merchant.[11]

Between 1934 and 1941 the Dock Department (since 1942 the Department of Marine and Aviation) made a number of physical improvements along the city's waterfront. The Department built fourteen new piers and put superstructures on four others. Three piers constructed—Numbers 92, 90 and 88 on the Hudson River—built at a total cost of $11,000,000 to accommodate the superliners *Normandie, Queen Mary, Queen Elizabeth* and *Rex* were 1,100 feet in length and had three-story superstructures and all modern conveniences.[12]

From the start of his administration, La Guardia agitated for a free port in New York Harbor—a place where foreign goods could be held for transshipment or rehandling without payment of duties; no such area existed in the United States. The most commonly suggested spot for a New York free port was a group of piers at Stapleton, Staten Island, built by Hylan at the close of World War I during a period of great shipping activity, but which since had fallen almost into desuetude. La Guardia got Representative Emanuel Celler of Brooklyn to introduce enabling legislation in Congress and made trips to Washington to argue for his project. As a result, Congress passed the Foreign Trade Zones Act of 1934, and under its authorization, the Secretary of Commerce in January, 1936, announced that New York City could operate a free port at Stapleton. The city transformed the Hylan piers into a foreign trade zone by enclosing and rehabilitating them with the aid of WPA funds. Opened in February, 1937, the nation's first free port, after a shaky start under municipal administration, soon proved successful when leased to a private corporation which was able to engage in certain necessary activities inappropriate to a city.[13]

In co-operation with the State Department of Public Works, various authorities and other agencies and with the assistance of federal, state and other funds, the city under La Guardia took great strides toward the creation of a comprehensive parkway and express highway system within the city limits. One of the most spectacular developments along these lines was the construction of the 10.68 mile Henry Hudson Parkway which, starting at 72nd Street, brought traffic from the West Side Elevated Highway to the Saw Mill River Parkway at the Westchester County line over a new Henry Hudson Bridge at Spuyten Duyvil. The East River Drive was developed along Manhattan's East River front; its upper end led into the newly built Triborough Bridge, a magnificent structure connecting Manhattan, the Bronx and Queens. To provide a free moving traffic belt around Brooklyn and Queens, the city built the splendid Belt Parkway from Owl's Head Park in Brooklyn to the Triborough Bridge Authority's Bronx-Whitestone Bridge, a distance of almost thirty-five miles. The Hutchinson River Parkway was constructed to carry the Belt and other arterial Bronx traffic from the Bronx-Whitestone Bridge through three and a half miles of attractive scenery into the county and state parkways of Westchester and Connecticut. To connect Manhattan's arterial highways with the Belt Parkway in Brooklyn, construction was begun in October, 1940, on the Brooklyn-Battery Tunnel (completed in 1950), and the Gowanus Parkway was built linking the Brooklyn entrance of the tunnel with Owl's Head Park. Nor were these the only improvements made within the city to facilitate motor transportation.[14]

The La Guardia administration advanced the Independent Subway system initiated by Hylan. Work was completed on the Eighth Avenue line, which had been opened in 1932, and La Guardia, using long-term city bonds because the project was ineligible for PWA funds, constructed a Sixth Avenue trunk line at a cost of $59,500,000; begun in March, 1936, the Sixth Avenue Subway was opened to the public in December, 1940.[15]

The city's only municipal airport when La Guardia became Mayor was the commercially unsuccessful Floyd Bennett Field. Acquiring the landing field of the Curtiss-Wright Corporation at North Beach, near College Point, at a cost of $1,300,000, the city bought some 130 acres of additional upland property and had the WPA "make" 323 additional acres by filling in shallow water places with ashes and develop the entire area into one of the country's finest airports; what was first called North Beach Airport and later La Guardia Field was opened in 1939.[16] Realizing that La

Guardia Field would not be big enough to serve the needs of New York in the coming air age, the Fusion Mayor in 1942 began construction of Idlewild—New York International Airport—on an immense stretch of land in the Jamaica Bay area of Queens; it was completed in 1948 under O'Dwyer.[17] Thus did La Guardia assure New York City's pre-eminence as an air transport center.

Most of these and other construction projects were the product of La Guardia's first two terms. By 1940, as we already have noted, the city had about reached the limit of its capacity to borrow for capital improvements. With improved economic conditions in the nation, federal spending was tapering off. On top of these developments came Pearl Harbor. By creating a shortage of labor, materials and funds for peace-time construction, the war put an end to all but a small part of the city's building program. During Fusion's last four years, efforts along this line mainly involved post-war planning. La Guardia, with the experience of the Depression in mind and believing, as did our foremost economists, that World War II would be followed by an unemployment crisis, inspired the City Planning Commission to advance a vast construction program to be undertaken at the end of the war; before La Guardia left office, the cost of the program had hit $1,250,000,000. La Guardia's program could not be entirely realized in the post-war era. Much of it was contingent upon generous federal aid; but the nation after the war, despite the gloomy prognostications, entered a period of full employment, and Washington did not embark on a spending program. Still many of the projects planned by Fusion in its last four years have since been brought into being.[18]

When Fusion took office, housing constituted the Number 1 physical and social problem in the city. As was true of other American cities, New York had in its midst disgraceful slums where the poor crowded together under shocking conditions. Though all boroughs suffered from slums and blighted areas, the worst housing conditions existed in Manhattan, notably on the lower East Side and in Harlem. During his campaign, La Guardia had promised to do something about housing. He had advocated slum clearance and the building of model multiple dwellings under the auspices of a municipal housing authority, its work financed by grants and loans from the federal government. Apartments would be built, he said, to rent at prices the poor could afford.[19]

When La Guardia moved into City Hall, circumstances favored the implementation of such a program; for purposes of recovery and relief the federal government was looking to spend millions, and the climate of reform of the day encouraged a wholesale attack on the housing problem. Early in January, 1934, Ickes sent a telegram to La Guardia promising PWA loans to a duly constituted New York City Housing Authority for the construction of low-cost housing projects; the Fusion Mayor jumped at the opportunity. The legislature was prevailed upon to pass quickly the Municipal Housing Authorities Law, and under its authorization, the Municipal Assembly in February created the New York City Housing Authority ". . . to promote the public health and safety by providing for the elimination of unsanitary and dangerous housing conditions, to relieve congested areas, and [for] the construction and supervision of dwellings and for the letting of apartments at reasonable rentals." La Guardia named Langdon Post, his Tenement House Commissioner, and four others to the new body, and a new era in municipal housing in America was launched.[20]

At the start the new agency was crippled by a lack of funds and credit; despite Ickes' promise, his excessive caution in releasing PWA funds prevented the immediate realization of the Authority's plans. The Authority, therefore, was forced to rely upon Yankee ingenuity in carrying out its job. It persuaded Vincent Astor, who owned the better part of a block of run-down tenements on the lower East Side, to accept $189,000 in Authority bonds for his property, though the property had an assessed valuation of $400,000. It borrowed money from Bernard Baruch on generous terms to pay for two tenements that divided the Astor holdings. Virtually penniless, the Authority decided upon an extensive remodeling job—with every third tenement torn down to allow space for light, air and recreation—rather than upon complete demolition and new construction. The money problem was solved through the co-operation of several relief agencies which did the actual work and by the expedient of using the proceeds from the sale of material salvaged from demolished buildings to meet the payroll of the Authority's small staff. On December 3, 1935, what was named First Houses was opened with rooms renting at an average of $6.05 per month. It was the first public housing project in the United States.[21]

After that the Authority's road was easier. The federal government began to play a more important role in 1936. With the Authority acquiring title to the necessary property and conveying it to the federal government, PWA began the construction of Williamsburg Houses in Brooklyn and Harlem River Houses in West Harlem, the first public housing built in New York City from the ground up; when completed these projects were leased to the Authority for operation. In 1937 the Wagner-Steagall Act established the federal government in the housing field on a more permanent basis by removing federal housing from the hands of the PWA and placing it under a United States Housing Authority. The Act empowered the new Authority to loan local public agencies up to 90 per cent of the money needed to build housing and to grant annual cash subsidies for the purpose of keeping rents in the projects within the means of low-income people. It gave local housing authorities the job of initiating, planning, constructing and operating the public housing in their own communities. Under this arrangement, the New York City Housing Authority built Red Hook and Kingsborough Houses in Brooklyn, Vladeck and East River Houses in Manhattan, Queensbridge and South Jamaica Houses in Queens and

Clason Point Gardens in the Bronx; the Authority, its credit rating more secure, was actually able to obtain most of its capital from private investors. Under the federal government's war housing program, the Authority put up the Edwin Markham Houses on Staten Island.[22]

Two further developments helped complete the public housing program in New York City. The New York State Public Housing Law of 1939, enacted under the authorization of a special housing amendment to the state constitution, spelled out a state low-rent housing program which, though differing in details, followed the broad pattern set by the federal government with local authorities as the actual operating agencies. By enacting an occupancy tax to provide subsidies for low-rent housing and agreeing to guarantee bonds of the Authority, New York City became the first American city to make wholly municipal aided public housing possible. Under these programs the Authority built the Vladeck City Houses and the Fort Greene Houses, respectively the first city and state subsidized public housing to be built anywhere in the United States. In all, the New York City Housing Authority in the La Guardia period built thirteen public housing projects, providing some 17,000 apartments. Practically all construction took place before Pearl Harbor.[23]

Several public officials were especially responsible for this advance on the housing front. La Guardia, of course, was indispensable; continually he gave the cause of public housing aggressive leadership. Secretary Ickes' assistance, belated as it was, was responsible for the initiation of federal housing. Without the co-operation of Nathan Straus, Jr., Administrator of the United States Housing Authority and a former member of the New York City Housing Authority, New York's program could not have got off the ground. Much credit, too, belongs to the hard-working, unpaid chairmen of the city's Housing Authority: Langdon Post (1934–7), Alfred Rheinstein (1937–9), Gerard Swope (1939–42) and Edmond B. Butler (1942–7).[24] And, of course, there was Robert Moses. Though for a time Moses' relationship to public housing was rather sketchy— public housing was essentially a New Deal innovation and La Guardia handled the Washington negotiations—Moses was always interested in it, particularly from the standpoint of recreation, and before long he became a power in this field too. Not only did Moses hold various influential positions, especially membership on the City Planning Commission, but he had more influence in Albany than did La Guardia. Moses came to play a powerful role in selecting sites for public, semi-public and, in many instances, private housing developments in the city and co-ordinating them with other improvements, including, of course, recreational facilities.[25]

Relations between some of these men, it might be noted, was less than harmonious. Ickes despised Post, whom he considered "a stuffed shirt without any stuffing," as well as Straus, whom he never felt was fitted for his job. Moses, though liking Rheinstein personally, at times clashed with him and had no fondness for federal handling of public housing. In December, 1937, Post broke with La Guardia over his desire to send a city representative to a conference called in Washington by Straus; the *New York Times* interpreted La Guardia's veto as an attempt to curry favor with Ickes at the expense of Straus. Two years later Rheinstein resigned from the Housing Authority when he became involved in a dispute with Straus and La Guardia tried to propitiate the federal official.[26] Despite personality and policy clashes, however, the work went forward.

Measured in terms of actual accomplishments, the record of the La Guardia administration in providing low-cost housing was rather meager; thirteen projects compared to the size of the problem represented hardly more than a drop in the bucket. (As for more and better housing for middle-income people, the city did little; city policy was limited to encouraging private groups, under the Redevelopment Companies Law of 1942, to construct middle-income projects, like Metropolitan Life's Stuyvesant Town, erected during the forties on Manhattan's East Side between 14th and 20th streets.[27]) Still when it is considered that public housing had hardly begun more than a decade before, that within that period the nation had fought a major war, that the New York City Housing Authority in 1945 had plans for fourteen additional low-cost developments at a total cost of approximately $124,000,000,[28] the La Guardia administration's achievement appears considerably more impressive. What was most significant of all, the city had made a start in the eradication of slums and the building of decent dwellings for people who, without government assistance, could not afford good housing. As had the state and federal governments, New York City in the La Guardia period had assumed a new responsibility to its citizens; that responsibility no administration after La Guardia's could repudiate.

One of the most amazing transformations under Fusion involved the city's recreational facilities. When La Guardia took over, the parks were in a deplorable condition; 20 per cent of the comfort stations were closed because parts of the plumbing were missing; fences, benches and other iron work were rusty from neglect. The zoos were filthy firetraps, and keepers had shotguns to shoot the animals in case of fire. Of the city's 119 playgrounds, most were dilapidated and inadequate; almost all were makeshifts, and rare indeed were chlorinated wading pools, sanitary field houses, play surfaces which could be cleaned, and adequate apparatus. Recreation was the province of five park departments, one in each borough, a system that hardly made for economical administration or the co-ordination of recreational development in the city. Political workers abounded in the departments.[29]

La Guardia determined to reorganize the entire metropolitan park program and co-ordinate it with programs under suburban and state jurisdictions. Furthermore, he wanted to bring Moses into his administration; but

Moses would come in only if a single park department was created with himself at the head and if at the same time he could retain his position as head of the state park system. Accordingly, the new administration at once obtained state legislation consolidating the five park departments into one city department and making it possible for the head of the state park system to act as city park commissioner and to hold additional unpaid city positions in the fields of planning, parks and public works.[30] In this rather simple manner, the machinery was created which was to enable Moses to outline, direct and co-ordinate a tremendous recreational development.

Moses immediately revamped the new Department of Parks. Establishing headquarters at the Arsenal in Central Park, he set about replacing political hacks with technical experts and restoring the morale of the Department's employees. By the spring of 1934 the city's parks were alive with workers who knew what they were doing.[31] This was only the start.

Using relief funds and labor, Moses began to improve the city's recreational plant all along the line. The Park Department rehabilitated the parks with unparalleled rapidity, redesigning and reconstructing many historic squares and parks in the older parts of the city. It extensively rebuilt the zoos in Central Park and Prospect Park. It increased the number of playgrounds to 381 in 1939 and 492 in 1945, and these were completely equipped, modern in every respect. It made major improvements at Orchard Beach in the Bronx and at Jacob Riis Park on the Rockaway Peninsula and carried out other important beach improvements in the 108th-73rd street area of Rockaway, where it replaced a blighted section with recreational areas and a shore parkway, and at Coney Island. The Department provided 17 outdoor swimming pools in congested neighborhoods, each the last word in modern construction; at the close of the swimming season, the pools were drained and converted into free outdoor play centers. While in 1934 the Park Department had 5 eighteen-hole and 3 nine-hole golf courses, in 1945 it could boast of 10 eighteen-hole courses, each being fitted out with a clubhouse, cafeteria, pro-shop and other accessories necessary for a pleasant round of golf. During the La Guardia period the Department added over 200 tennis courts to its recreational plant. Randall's Island in the East River was rid of its old, dilapidated hospital buildings and turned into a beautiful recreational area with a stadium seating 30,000 as its principal feature; since its opening in July, 1936, the stadium has been the scene of numerous track-meets, baseball games, college and high school football games, soccer, rugby and hurling matches and light opera productions.[32]

Moreover, under Fusion the Department of Parks increased its park acreage, from 14,827 acres in 1934 to 18,325 in 1944. In a few instances new land for parks was donated by philanthropic citizens, such as the Fort Tryon area presented to the city by John D. Rockefeller, Jr. Mainly the increment in the city's park land was the result of pushing out the bulkhead along the shore front, filling in swamps and reclaiming blighted areas. In

Manhattan Moses pushed out the bulkhead along the Hudson River in the course of constructing the Henry Hudson Parkway. In Brooklyn and Queens a tremendous area was filled in for the Belt Parkway. These and other Moses parkways, it should be noted, were built as beautiful shoe-string parks with footpaths, bicycle paths, in some cases waterfront promenades and with other facilities for passive and active recreation.[33]

Probably the most famous example of the "making" of park land was that of Flushing Meadow. When a group of distinguished citizens proposed that New York City hold a World's Fair in 1939, Moses flatly refused to go along unless Flushing Meadow in Queens, an area of marsh and refuse dumps, was selected as the site and the fair planned in such a way that at its conclusion the site would be available for a great new city park. And Moses had his way: he converted the disgraceful Flushing Meadow into one of the most beautiful settings any international exposition ever had, and when it was over, he converted it into Flushing Meadow Park, which at one time was the site of the United Nations General Assembly.[34]

In these and other ways Moses strikingly improved New York City's appearance and phenomenally increased the opportunities of its inhabitants for rest, relaxation and enjoyment.

In the early days of the Depression New York sought to meet the problem of relief for the unemployed by the traditional American method of private charity; public officials hesitated to modify provisions of state law and City Charter prohibiting the use of public funds for the relief of unemployed persons not in institutions—that is, for home or "outdoor" relief. But as the economic crisis deepened, it became evident that private relief was hopelessly inadequate. Accordingly, the New York State Legislature in September, 1931, passed the Wicks Emergency Relief Act, which permitted the state and the localities for a limited period (continually extended by subsequent legislation) to dispense public funds to unemployed people outside of institutions; communities had main responsibility, but the state offered reimbursement up to 40 per cent of their outlay. The act created a State Temporary Relief Administration. With respect to New York City, it set up a Home Relief Bureau and a City Commission Work Bureau; while these agencies were technically part of the state machinery, they were actually local bodies supervising the expenditure of much local money. Beginning in the spring of 1933, the federal government, through the creation of the Federal Emergency Relief Administration, undertook to grant $1 of federal aid for every $3 of state and local funds spent for relief, a development which made possible an expansion of New York's relief program. In November, 1933, the national administration, because of a sudden downturn in business and a rise in the relief rolls, created the Civil Works Administration as an emergency relief agency to put millions to work on "made-work" projects immediately; under this program the functions of the city's work relief body were taken over by the CWA, the Home

Relief Bureau being left with the job of dispensing "outdoor" relief. In January, 1934, there were approximately 121,000 home relief cases and 188,000 work relief cases in the city.[35]

Insofar as relief was a local matter, Tammany's handling of it in the period 1931–3 left much to be desired. The city made special appropriations for relief without the addition of new taxes, eventually financing them by borrowing, mainly through long-term bonds. Aside from other disadvantages, these methods could not provide enough money for the task at hand or place relief financing on anything more than a very insecure basis. Relief payments usually consisted only of a minimum food allowance; no regular rent allowance was included, rent generally being given only when a family was face to face with eviction; occasionally bags of coal, medical help and bundles of clothing were supplied. On a number of occasions the Home Relief Bureau was forced to close relief offices to new applicants. Also it had to practice a "skip system" whereby a person receiving an allowance for a two-week period might not receive another one until the next two-week period had elapsed. The Home Relief Bureau, moreover, gave relief only to individuals with families; single men received no assistance, except through the Municipal Lodging House, a form of relief repugnant to men who were normally self-supporting.

Relief under Tammany was not cash relief; the recipient was given relief orders, not money. Those who set up the relief system reflected the general sentiment of Americans at the time that public aid must be so hemmed about with restrictions that people would apply for it only as a last resort.[36] The non-cash policy also mirrored a lurking feeling, rooted so deeply in the national psyche that even the economic cataclysm of 1929 could not completely dispel it for a time, that the unemployed person was an irresponsible person. The system not only stigmatized the receiver, but made it impossible for him to buy economically, for food store owners and landlords, forced to wait for their money, discounted the orders. Certainly one of the worst features of Tammany relief was that the machine boys could not resist playing politics with it, both with respect to relief employees and recipients. In the course of his campaign, La Guardia struck out at Tammany for these and other failings in the relief system.[37]

Once in office, he proceeded to carry out a program of improvement. By basing relief financing on special taxes, he was able to correct most of the existing weaknesses. It was possible to regularize relief payments; no longer did offices have to close because of lack of funds; regular monthly installments replaced the "skip system." Relief was extended to single men. Allotments for food were progressively increased to meet rises in food prices. A regular allowance for rent was included in the relief payment, and home owners were allowed the equivalent of a rental allowance so that they could pay taxes and interest charges on their mortgages and save their homes; in May, 1937, the city's relief agency found it possible to increase rent allowances by approximately 20 per cent to meet an increase in rental costs. And not only rent, but provision for such necessities as light, fuel for heating and cooking, ice and household supplies came to be part of the regular payment. In 1933 a family of five received an average of $35.54 monthly in home relief—and this irregularly and for a limited purpose. In 1938 such a family received an average of $70 per month.[38]

While the family relief budget under La Guardia, as under Tammany, did not include a regular clothing allowance, provision being made from time to time as funds became available, sound financing permitted the Fusion relief body to spend much more substantial sums on the clothing needs of the poor than could be done in the past. In 1933 the annual expenditure on clothing for recipients was a mere $19,000; in 1934, 1935 and 1936 the average annual expenditure was $2,350,000. La Guardia's financing also made it possible to expand greatly, reorganize and improve the system of providing medical care to recipients in their homes. Whereas in 1933 approximately 30,000 families received medical care, three years later 220,000 families were cared for; had it not been for the better program of medical care, many of these would not have received needed medical treatment or would have further overburdened the crowded city hospitals, where the cost to the city would have been three times greater than the cost of treating the patient at home.[39]

Nor were these the only ways in which La Guardia strengthened the system. In early 1934 the legislature acknowledged the disadvantages of the non-cash policy by amending the Emergency Relief Act to permit local agencies to dispense cash, and La Guardia quickly took advantage of the authorization. The Home Relief Bureau in the spring of 1934 initiated the procedure of giving food allowances in the form of a negotiable check, and this system was extended to rent in May, 1935, and to coal in November, 1935; by 1936 the person receiving public assistance generally made purchases in the same fashion as any employed worker, a circumstance which enabled him to get the most for his dollar and freed him from some of the humiliation of being on relief.[40]

While the Mayor's office might listen to a plea by Marcantonio or another politician on behalf of some individual who felt he had been wronged in a matter of public aid or who aspired to a position on the relief staff, the Mayor seems to have intervened only to the extent of having the matter called to the attention of the proper people, perhaps with a request that something be done if possible; this writer has uncovered no evidence that La Guardia brought pressure to bear in favor of such people or contested the verdict of his appointees. Episodes of this kind aside, the La Guardia administration apparently eliminated political favoritism in the administration of relief and in the employment of relief employees.[41]

The CWA, after giving work to 197,000 New Yorkers during the first three months of 1934, came to a sudden end on March 31 with the result that work relief once again became a concern of the city; to handle this matter, the city set up the Works Division of the Department of Public Welfare, with the requirement that those employed on Works Division projects were to come from the home relief rolls. In June, 1934, most likely for efficiency reasons, La Guardia reorganized the entire relief set-up. The Home Relief Bureau and the Works Division were made branches of a new Emergency Relief Bureau, a six-man board appointed by the Mayor. William Hodson, Commissioner of Public Welfare, served as chairman and executive director of the new body until April, 1935, when he was replaced in these posts by Oswald W. Knauth, an outstanding business economist and a director of R. H. Macy & Company.[42]

(In 1935, the federal government discontinued the FERA and established the WPA with the object of giving work relief to as many employables as possible, leaving the entire field of home relief—henceforth to encompass only unemployables—to state and local authorities. Under this arrangement, the Works Division of the ERB dissolved into the WPA, and the ERB after that, with the exception of a few small work relief projects not federalized, became a home relief agency, doing the same thing as had the Home Relief Bureau in January, 1934, the state partially reimbursing the city for the ERB's cost. By 1936 it had become difficult to maintain the view that large-scale unemployment was but a short-term circumstance, and the legislature, reflecting the new sense of social responsibility to the unemployed that the Great Depression had evoked, amended the Public Welfare Law to regularize what the Wicks Act had been permitting on a temporary basis since 1931. Under the amended Public Welfare Law and the provisions of the new City Charter which empowered the Commissioner of what was now called the Department of Welfare to administer the Public Welfare Law, the ERB became superfluous. After December 31, 1937, it became the home relief division of the Department of Welfare.[43])

La Guardia's improvements in relief notwithstanding, no aspect of government during the Fusion period was more buffeted by the winds of controversy. The subject of relief administration seems to have attracted investigations the way a magnet does iron filings; there were inquiries by Mayor's committees, commissioners of investigation, a committee of the Board of Aldermen and a committee of the City Council, to mention only the most important.[44] A number of the investigations reflected the deep-seated suspicion with which many taxpayers viewed the disbursements of millions by the government for a purpose new to American experience; it was not easy to convince them that the administration of relief was being conducted in any but an inefficient and wasteful manner. Continual rumors of the presence of Communists in the ERB, Department of Welfare and the Workers Alliance (a union of relief recipients), and their influence on relief matters was a main factor behind a number of investigations. Rarely, if ever, were the inquiries free from the shadow of politics; often more than the shadow was involved.

What is the truth about relief administration in the days of La Guardia —about efficiency and economy, about the Communists? For all the inquiries, the answers to these questions are difficult. The investigations were usually conducted either by those who were friendly to the La Guardia administration's handling of relief or those who were not; and, not very surprisingly, the investigators generally seem to have ended by reinforcing their original predilections. These investigations can be used by students of the subject, but only with caution. Something, too, can be learned indirectly from inquiries and other happenings in O'Dwyer's time. Aside from this, information is skimpy. Any answers to the above questions must be sketchier than one would prefer.

From the point of efficiency and economy, the La Guardia administration's administration of relief was in certain ways praiseworthy. Under the direction of the able Charlotte E. Carr, who served as executive director of the organization from August, 1935, to August, 1937, the ERB generally kept administrative cost low. For much of 1935 the cost was in the neighborhood of 10 and 12 per cent of the relief dollar; with the advent of the WPA in August, however, the cost shot up and remained high for several months, for while transfers to the new agency greatly decreased the number on home relief, no corresponding reduction in personnel could be made until the transfer program had been completed. Before long, however, the ERB began to reduce its staff drastically, from more than 18,000 employees in November, 1935, to 12,500 in April, 1936, to 10,500 in September, 1936. This reduction, along with the closing of several relief stations, permitted a saving of several millions of dollars. In later years as relief cases dropped with improved economic conditions, the staff of the new Department of Welfare was reduced; as of June, 1945, the number of employees in the Department was 6,684. At the same time, the staff was improved in quality as a result of civil service examinations.[45]

But this is not the whole story. Early in O'Dwyer's administration, his Executive Committee on Administration presented him with a report sharply critical of the administrative and operating procedures in the Welfare Department, remarking that those procedures were mainly of long standing. The committee charged that lax administration in connection with the distribution of relief at local welfare centers resulted in inefficiency and waste in many cases; among other things, the committee complained that Welfare personnel did not all interpret the regulations in the Department's manual the same way and that the Department did not always keep proper records, maintain adequate control over special grants made at the centers, adequately check the income and financial requirements of those receiving relief or check effectively to determine to what extent they were employable. That there was certainly need for an administrative tightening in the Welfare Department was strongly suggested by the work of reorganization carried out under O'Dwyer by Commissioners of Welfare Benjamin Fielding and Raymond Hilliard.[46]

As for the matter of relief "chiseling," a major aspect of the economy question, no clear answer can be given. In March, 1935, at a time when the ERB, forced to concern itself with both home and work relief, was swamped with work, Hodson told an aldermanic committee that "chiseling" accounted for something like 10 per cent of the monthly relief appropriation, or $24,000,000 a year; he declared that he could save the money if he had a larger staff.[47] The situation undoubtedly got better as the caseload declined; but how much better exactly, one cannot say. In 1940, reporting on relief administration in the city, Herlands stated that few persons were improperly on the relief rolls—though he noted that in a large proportion of test cases, Welfare investigators had not done an adequate job in following leads relating to possible assets of the applicants,[48] a point which anticipated findings of the O'Dwyer Executive Committee on Administration. That committee, it should be noted, for all its criticism of slipshod procedures did not mention relief chiseling, a subject one feels might have been mentioned had it constituted a problem at the time.

That the Department of Welfare under La Guardia contained a sizable group of Communists and fellow-travelers inherited from the ERB is not open to doubt. The fact that O'Dwyer's commissioners flushed numbers of them out of the Department is proof enough. Even before O'Dwyer's time, any objective observer with but a modicum of acumen, would have been compelled to suspect strongly that talk about Communists in the Welfare Department was not just talk. For after Herlands in 1941 launched another investigation of Welfare, one specifically aimed at uncovering alleged Communist activities and proclaimed loudly that his investigation would be the most searching ever conducted by his department, the results were never published; the *New York Times* in 1947 declared that it had been reported without official confirmation that Herlands' report on the subject listed 600 employees of Welfare as suspected Communists, of which 200 were presently still employed.[49] While Communists were present in the school system and to a lesser degree in other areas of government during La Guardia's reign, nowhere do their numbers appear to have constituted so large a percentage of employees as in the Department of Welfare. (This would not be exactly surprising: relief, as a new service, provided opportunities for government employment to an extent not true in other fields, and the original relief staff was recruited from underprivileged areas.)

That the La Guardia administration did not do too much to prevent the Communists from entering the Welfare Department (or any other) or to get them out after they got in is also clear. The administration did not sympathize with communism. In an age in which most people (and especially most liberals) were not Communist-minded, the administration simply did not worry about the problem. It is true that until the end of the forties and early fifties, the government found it difficult legally to remove a Communist from a civil service position; yet it is not unfair to suggest that La Guardia might have worked for state legislation to correct this situation. Moreover, the main instrument of Communist activity in Welfare, at least in La Guardia's later years, was apparently the United Public Workers, Local 1 (CIO), the principal staff union; and the Department, especially in the light of the La Guardia administration's (and the O'Dwyer administration's) pro-labor attitude, hesitated to strike against the UPW until it could make a stronger case as to its being Communist-dominated; significantly when in February, 1950, the CIO expelled the UPW for being a tool of the Communist Party, Commissioner Hilliard soon afterwards ejected it as a recognized staff organization in the Department of Welfare.[50]

There is no question that the Communists propagandized among Welfare employees and relief recipients. How much influence they exerted in the Department is not easy to say. In 1948 Commissioner of Investigation John M. Murtagh, after examining 200 witnesses and analyzing a mass of data, reported that the UPW exerted an undue influence on policies within the Department. But it should be kept in mind that major policy was formulated in City Hall and by Department heads who do not appear to have been favorably inclined toward the Communist cause. Nor is there convincing evidence that undeserving persons were given relief because they were Communists or that staff workers were advanced for this reason. It does not seem that the often-made charge that the Communists and their friends dominated affairs in the Department of Welfare in the La Guardia period can be sustained.[51]

The Communists, it was also asserted, influenced the granting of relief through their control of the New York branch of the Workers Alliance. The Alliance was certainly radical and probably Communist-led; and Herlands, in his 1940 report on relief administration, admitted that often it did succeed in having relief complaints attended to. As a pressure group the Alliance was especially noisy, troublesome and persistent—Herlands declared that it presented five times more complaints than any other group —and officials, as Herlands pointed out, were naturally inclined to dispose of the most annoying cases first; with equally strenuous activity, Herlands held, another group or an individual could get the same amount of attention. That the Workers Alliance was thus probably able to ingratiate itself with the poor is something that many may deplore; yet it is not clear how the administration could have prevented this, especially since it is by no means certain that the Alliance did not often come to the aid of needy people to whom an injustice might otherwise have been done. As for the Workers Alliance or any other organized community group exercising domination over the administration of relief—this allegation, declared Herlands, was "entirely without justification." [52]

The Communist-in-Welfare issue has to be seen in perspective. There were Communists in this department, as there were in others, and the La Guardia administration can be censured for viewing their presence with complacency; it can be argued that the succeeding administration had to undertake the job of fumigation that was Fusion's responsibility. At the same time one has to remember that the temper of the times, especially during the Second World War, did not encourage an attack on Communists in government. It should be kept in mind that the number of Communists in the Welfare Department was small compared to the total number of employees in the Department, and their influence, as in other departments, was hardly as important as some of the administration's critics charged. One gets the impression that too often the Communist issue was the whip with which those who resented relief budgets flayed the administration.

Though the La Guardia administration's handling of the relief problem is open to criticism on some counts, it would be a great mistake to over-emphasize them in evaluating Fusion's performance in this area. The La Guardia administration, though certainly not unaided, was required in the 1930's to grapple with one of the gravest and most overwhelming problems of our contemporary history—the problem of alleviating mass distress, anxiety and degradation attendant upon the collapse of the American economic system. (Anyone finding it difficult to grasp the immensity of the problem might keep in mind that in March, 1936, at the peak of the relief caseload in New York City, about 1,466,000 persons, an excess of 449,000 cases, or approximately one out of every five New Yorkers, was dependent for support upon work relief or direct relief.[53]) Inheriting a system in which public assistance was uncertain, limited in scope, completely inadequate in amount and particularly humiliating in procedure and which was shot through with politics, La Guardia improved it in these and other respects to the benefit, not only of the unemployed, but the city as a whole. This was no mean achievement.

Humanitarian that he was, La Guardia made the health and medical care of New Yorkers, especially the poorer ones, prime considerations of his administration. In 1933 he assailed Tammany for political administration of the Health Department and called for a Department nonpolitically managed by experts in public health and disease prevention. He berated the O'Brien administration and previous Tammany administrations for failure to provide sufficient funds for the Department of Health, calling this a vicious type of economy; noting that O'Brien's economy moves had sacrificed health services to political jobs, La Guardia promised to make economies at the expense of political parasites, but "never at the expense of human life." [54] We have already noted that the Fusion Mayor immediately appointed Rice and Goldwater, two nonpolitical experts, to head Health and Hospitals. They and their successors, with the Mayor's backing, proceeded to administer their departments in the interest of the public and apparently without reference to political, or other improper, considerations. Inheriting a Department of Health budget of $4,594,044, La Guardia increased it to $5,860,477 before he left office. What was more striking, he increased the budget for the Department of Hospitals from $17,321,374 in 1934 to $36,216,072 in the fiscal year 1945–6, a rise of over 100 per cent.[55] While an increase in the size of a budget is not necessarily a reliable guide to an increase, not to mention an improvement, in service, in large part La Guardia's bigger Health and Hospital budgets were an indication of both.[56]

For twenty years one of the major aspirations of city health officials had been to bring the services of the Department of Health to the doorstep of the average citizen by means of district health centers; though committed to such a program, Tammany had made but slow progress toward carrying it out. The La Guardia administration divided the city into thirty health districts and undertook the erection of health centers; by the time the war forced a suspension of construction, the city had built fifteen up-to-date centers and had developed plans for the construction of similar facilities in the remaining districts in the city. The administration also erected a number of new baby health stations and better rehoused a score of others.[57]

Other advances accompanied the development of district health administration. Among other things, the Department of Health launched an intensive anti-syphilis campaign marked by a large increase in diagnostic and treatment facilities and by strong efforts to break down taboos surrounding the disease. The Department reorganized and strengthened its tuberculosis service and undertook, with the assistance of the WPA, X-ray surveys of many thousands of people, with the result that hundreds of new cases of tuberculosis were discovered. 1937 witnessed the establishment of an enlarged service for combatting pneumonia mortality: a special appropriation of $90,000 by the city enabled the Department to purchase anti-pneumococcic serum of various types; to appoint an individual of wide and noteworthy experience in the field as assistant director to head this service, as well as bacteriologists and other assistants; and to open typing stations in each borough for the production of therapeutic serum on a larger scale and for research on serum production. The infant mortality rate, a good gauge of the state of a community's health and of the effectiveness of its health program, was low during the La Guardia era; in 1942 it was 28.8 deaths out of every 1,000 live births, the all-time low for the city until 1946.[58]

To care better for the needy sick, the La Guardia administration, assisted by PWA money, added appreciably to the city's hospital plant. The administration completed, equipped and, in late 1935, opened Queens General Hospital with a bed capacity of 512. Adjoining Queens General it built the Triboro Hospital for Tuberculosis and on Welfare Island erected a new hospital for chronic diseases, later named Goldwater Memorial Hospital. It constructed a new women's pavilion at Harlem Hospital and made other major improvements totaling many millions of dollars at Bellevue, Kings County, Lincoln and other municipal hospitals. Before the war put an end to the city's hospital building and reconstruction program, hospital bed capacity, the fundamental index of a city's ability to serve its sick people, had been increased by some 8,000, bringing the city's total to 20,500. This did not mean that the city had solved its hospital problem, however. The city's institutions were overcrowded, and the Department of Hospitals was forced to receive more patients than it could satisfactorily handle.[59]

In 1944 La Guardia, who was a strong believer in all-inclusive medical insurance, submitted to the people of New York a plan for voluntary comprehensive health insurance based upon more than a year of study by a special committee named by the Mayor and headed by him. Under La Guardia's plan, any employee, including an employee of the city, who lived or worked in the city and earned up to $5,000 a year would be eligible as a member of a group to receive complete medical and surgical care for himself, his wife and all his children under eighteen; at least half of the cost of the program would be borne by the employer, the rest by the employee. If enough doctors signed up for the program, medical service would be provided by an "open panel" of doctors—the patient selecting any doctor—according to a system of fixed fees; otherwise the scheme called for the use of a "closed panel" of doctors on a salary basis. A non-profit corporation would administer the plan. The possibilities presented by the proposal for the practice of preventive medicine were enormous.[60]

Reaction to the idea—aside from the five county medical societies—was extremely favorable. In September, 1944, La Guardia, who hoped to have the plan in operation by January 1, 1945, announced that papers incorporating the HIP (Health Insurance Plan of Greater New York) had been filed with the necessary state officials. But for one reason or another HIP did not actually begin to function until March, 1947. As the insurance plan was finally set up, a member could select one of several groups of doctors affiliated with the program to supply him and his family with all but complete medical service; HIP paid the doctors' group a fixed sum per month for every individual under its care (regardless of whether service to the patient was actually rendered), the medical group dividing the payment among themselves.[61] Following a report in favor of city participation in HIP by a committee appointed by Mayor O'Dwyer to consider this matter, the Mayor committed the city to pay half of the membership cost of those city employees who enrolled in the program; the city thus became the biggest employer in HIP. By the end of 1947 the program had a total enrollment of 110,000; membership has steadily grown since. Forced to borrow its capital from private sources in its early days, HIP has since attained a stronger financial position and has paid off its loans.[62]

HIP was, and is, the most comprehensive medical insurance plan of its kind in the United States. In advancing the idea, La Guardia was quite conscious—and proud—of the fact that he was pioneering in the field of all-inclusive health insurance. As a matter of fact, according to Newbold

Morris, La Guardia thought that HIP is what he would be chiefly remembered for.[63]

In matters strictly educational, the New York City Board of Education is legally independent of the city government, responsible only to the state. At the same time, however, the Board is far from free of city control. Its members—in La Guardia's day there were seven—are appointed by the Mayor to seven-year terms (though members are removable only after a hearing on stated charges). While the state gives financial aid based upon pupil attendance in school and the city is required by law to set aside a certain amount of every tax dollar of assessed valuation for public education, the city determines the amount of funds it shall give to education above this minimum, and it can review the Board of Education's budget line-item by line-item.[64] Actually the state of the educational system in the city depends principally upon the city administration in power.

Under Tammany the educational system had suffered in many respects. The Board of Education, practically the same in membership under Walker as under Hylan, was composed of mediocrities, seven Democrats appointed as rewards for political service to the machine or to the Mayor personally. It was completely subservient to Tammany, and, despite its repeated assertions to the contrary, New Yorkers generally were aware that political favoritism and chicanery were rampant in the school system. Politics, rather than merit, was the key factor in determining appointment to high administrative posts. The political atmosphere surrounding the schools had corroded the morale of the teaching staff. It was difficult to believe that the Board of Education was ignorant of the operations of the condemnation racket with regard to school sites.[65]

The Board of Education, furthermore, devoted much time to routine administrative matters, the province of the Board of Superintendents— the Superintendent of Schools and the Associate Superintendents— appointed by the Board of Education for this purpose; the division of administrative responsibility on the Board of Superintendents between a chief superintendent and other superintendents was, in itself, a procedure which made for poor administration.[66] And the Depression and the city's financial crisis created additional trouble for the school system. Tammany cut the city's appropriation to the Board of Education for 1933 over $18,-000,000 from that of 1932 (from $97,715,609 to $79,240,592), a slash which in good part represented salary deductions for school personnel and which undoubtedly did not add to the morale of the teachers. By the time Fusion came to office, school construction had come to a dead halt.[67]

It might be expected that La Guardia, with his love of children and deep interest in their welfare, would closely concern himself with their education—and he did. During the campaign he had delineated a program looking toward the improvement of public education in New York;[68] as

Mayor he implemented part of it and was directly or indirectly responsible for other educational advances as well. Essential for any better school system, of course, was an improved Board of Education, and La Guardia soon brought one into being. As with his other top appointments, he generally named to the Board competent, conscientious, nonpolitical, high calibre people—people like Mrs. Johanna M. Lindlof, the first teacher member of the Board, James Marshall, Ellsworth B. Buck and Mary E. Dillon. La Guardia's appointees to the Board of Education, along with Superintendent of Schools Harold G. Campbell (1934–42) and John E. Wade (1942–7), formed a first-rate educational team, one that imparted a new, higher tone to the New York school system and provided it with enlightened leadership.[69]

(And while the Board of Education has never grown out of the habit of concerning itself with administrative matters that could better be handled by its professional staff,[70] an improvement in the administrative set-up was made toward the end of the Fusion period. In accordance with the recommendation of a legislative committee that had been studying the schools, the legislature passed a bill reorganizing the relationship between the Superintendent of Schools and the Associate Superintendents, making the latter in effect, not his equals as before, but his subordinates.[71])

La Guardia sought to eliminate politics, not only with respect to appointments to the Board of Education, but from the school system as a whole; political interference in the schools, Ellsworth Buck informed the writer, was one of the Fusion Mayor's pet peeves. That La Guardia, himself, interfered politically in the school system at times is perfectly true, as we shall note shortly (though doubtlessly he did not consider such action as political). Nevertheless, La Guardia and educational officials did much to substitute a standard of honesty and merit for political influence. The Board of Education eliminated honest graft with respect to school sites and instituted measures to prevent a recurrence of this practice in the future. By and large, promotions in the school system were made on the basis of qualifications for the job—with a consequent boost to the morale of teachers and other educational personnel—a development which in the opinion of Eugene R. Canudo, secretary to the Board of Education from 1943 to 1945, was probably Fusion's outstanding contribution in the field of education.[72]

In many other respects, too, La Guardia and the educational authorities furthered the cause of education. Following the re-establishment of the city's credit, and with the aid of the PWA, La Guardia resumed the construction of schools and by the fall of 1941 had built 92 new ones and a number of additions; while school construction was suspended during La Guardia's third term, the Board of Education made post-war construction plans totaling $130,000,000.[73] Between 1935 and 1938 the administration increased the city's appropriation for education steadily until in the latter year it stood at $97,797,957.[74] By keeping on teachers in the face of falling enrollment, La Guardia and the Board of Education did away with classes of 50 or more pupils, made a big reduction in the number of classes containing between 45 and 49 pupils and decreased the average class size; class size was reduced most impressively on the elementary level where the average went from 38.3 in October 1934 to 32.5 in March 1944. The La Guardia administration provided more classes for physically and mentally handicapped children, added units to the Board of Child Guidance and enlarged the Bureau of Reference, Research and Statistics. On the recommendation of La Guardia, the Board of Education in February, 1936, opened the High School of Music and Art in Manhattan as a place where the artist in artistically gifted children could be brought out and developed.[75] And these were not the only ways in which Fusion bettered the public school system.[76]

Yet for all this, in few fields was Fusion, and La Guardia in particular, attacked as intensely as in education—and by those who were generally friendly to the reform administration. The criticism, which marked La Guardia's last five or six years, boiled down to two major complaints: that La Guardia was interfering in school matters; that La Guardia and the Board of Education were not adequately meeting the educational needs of the city. Under the educational setup existing in New York City, it is manifestly impossible for the Mayor not to exert some influence on school affairs. La Guardia, with his inclination to get into every act and his feeling that things would not be done correctly unless he did so, undoubtedly played a larger role in educational matters than most Mayors. (Though Newbold Morris often told him that the Board of Education was mainly supposed to be a body independent of city control, La Guardia persisted in regarding education as very much his business and the Board of Education as a department under the city's jurisdiction.[77]) Perhaps it might be best to hold, as some do, that there is nothing wrong with the Mayor making his influence felt in school matters if the school system is thereby benefited, and that the charge of "political interference" is only justified when that influence is used in harmful or questionable ways. If this view is accepted, it must be said that La Guardia did not often exert political influence with regard to education. During his last few years as Mayor, however, he did on a few notable occasions throw his weight about to the disadvantage of the school system.

In the early part of 1943 the Fusion Mayor attempted to have the legislature pass a bill transferring the functions of the Board of Education's Bureau of Supplies to the city's Department of Purchase. A legitimate case could be made for the proposal; two investigations had discovered that the Bureau was inefficient in certain ways, and one inquiry, headed by Herlands, had advised that $500,000 could be saved if the Department of Purchase were permitted to absorb the work of the Bureau of Supplies. Considerable opposition to the scheme developed within the Board of Education, however. While the Board was not unaware of the possibility that Herlands' proposal might allow for a saving of money—though even this point was contested by the other investigation—the Board felt that the more important consideration was that it, and it alone, have control over school supplies; despite the intention of the bill to guarantee the Board's pre-eminent position in the matter of school supplies, the Board felt that as the proposal would work out in practice, its control would be weakened. Ellsworth Buck, President of the Board of Education at the time, Theodore F. Kuper, the Board's law secretary, and Superintendent of Schools Wade were especially active in opposing the bill. Toward the end of March, the City Council, apparently because of the attitude of school officials, voted not to recommend its passage to the legislature. La Guardia burned from the rebuff.[78]

About the same time, another issue further strained relations between La Guardia and the Board of Education. The Board, interested in filling the post of Director of Adult Education, a job which carried a salary of $7,500 a year, had been considering the appointment of Mark Starr, educational director of the ILGWU; Starr was the only one out of eighty candidates to survive all the required tests and was recommended by the Board of Superintendents and the Board of Examiners. Liberal elements were in favor of the Starr appointment. So apparently was La Guardia. The Board of Education, however, on two separate occasions refused to make the appointment. Ellsworth Buck declared that while he had high regard for Starr's capabilities, he felt that it would be unwise to appoint to the post at the time either a long-time protagonist or opponent of labor, and apparently enough other members of the Board of Education agreed with him.[79]

Following the affairs of the Supply Bill and the Starr appointment, La Guardia took the warpath against school officialdom. In April he made blistering attacks on President Buck for his part in the rejection of Starr (though the *New York Times* suspected that La Guardia was mainly peeved at Buck's failure to support the Supply Bill), at one point making the ridiculous statement that he would fire the President of the Board of Education the first time he got the chance. Shortly afterwards, La Guardia refused to reappoint Mrs. Lindlof to the Board of Education, though she was an outspoken liberal and champion of tolerance and democratic ideals; in her place the Mayor appointed Dr. George H. Chatfield, the Board's Director of Attendance, whom he caused to move to Queens for the occasion. La Guardia never gave any reason for his action against Mrs. Lindlof, but it is hard to believe that his recent conflict with the Board of Education was not in back of it. The *New York Times* suggested, and it was generally believed, that in refusing to reappoint Mrs. Lindlof, La Guardia was attempting to control the Board of Education.[80]

Other incidents contributed to the misgivings many were feeling with regard to La Guardia and the educational system. It was remembered that since his term on the Board of Education had expired in May, 1942, La

Guardia had kept Dr. Alberto C. Bonaschi on a day-to-day basis, instead of reappointing him or appointing another. Exerting his budgetary powers, La Guardia in April, 1943, without a word of explanation, cut from the school budget the line for Theodore Kuper, a man who in the opinion of the *New York Times,* had been a valuable member of the school system for eleven years. The *Times* suggested, probably correctly, that Kuper had incurred La Guardia's displeasure by properly carrying out his duties for the Board of Education in the matter of the Supply Bill. For reasons that are not entirely clear, La Guardia also cut from the budget an assistant superintendent of schools and for a time in the summer of 1943 held up the salary checks of three people newly appointed to administrative posts in the school system.[81]

La Guardia's actions elicited a storm of protest from teacher, parent, civic and other organizations, practically all of whom could normally be found in his corner; supporters of Mark Starr, almost without exception, resented La Guardia's browbeating of Buck, and leaders of the ALP, strong adherents of the Mayor though they were, expressed themselves as mystified and saddened by La Guardia's treatment of Mrs. Lindlof. In the summer of 1943 the New York High School Teachers Association and the Kindergarten-6B Teachers Association called upon the National Education Association to investigate La Guardia's behavior, which they regarded as a danger to the cause of free education. The NEA acceded to the plea and appointed an investigating committee composed of four prominent educators, two of whom had been president of the Association. After holding public and private hearings and conferring with teacher groups, school officials, laymen especially concerned with education and La Guardia, the investigating committee issued a report early in February, 1944. It accused City Hall of interference with the independence of the Board of Education and asserted that this interference had been injurious to the schools on various occasions, especially citing the events of 1942–3 that we have noted. The basis for most of the city's interference, the report declared, was the Board of Education's fiscal dependence upon the city; it recommended that the Board be guaranteed a bigger share of the tax dollar.[82]

Clearly on the defensive, La Guardia answered the NEA report with ridicule and invective. "No one on the NEA board," he declared, "has the mental capacity to grasp the magnitude of the school system of New York. . . ." Yet the inquiry was apparently not without its effect. In September, 1943, La Guardia appointed Dr. Bonaschi to the Board of Higher Education, a move probably not unrelated to the investigation.[83] While nothing was done to give the Board of Education a greater degree of fiscal independence, it does seem that after the time of the NEA inquiry La Guardia was more careful not to infringe upon the Board's domain.

Before leaving this subject, one important point must be underscored: while there is much to suggest that La Guardia in the period 1942–3 tried to dominate the Board of Education, there is little convincing evidence that he was successful. It is true that the Board of Education voted four to two to uphold the Mayor on Kuper's dismissal, but Kuper had a personality which irritated some of the members of the Board and made them not unhappy to be rid of him.[84] More indicative of the Board's attitude toward La Guardia's behavior was that a short time after the Mayor attacked Buck and Kuper and failed to reappoint Mrs. Lindlof, it unanimously re-elected Buck as its president.[85] The members of the Board of Education were too independent-minded to be dictated to; ironically, La Guardia could not boss the Board because of the very kind of men he appointed to it.[86]

Basic to the charge that the La Guardia administration was not adequately meeting the city's educational needs was the fact that, beginning with the budget for 1939–40, La Guardia tended to reduce somewhat the city's appropriation for education, reaching a low point of $90,010,529 in 1944–5. The decrease resulted in the elimination of teaching, administrative and clerical positions—though few, if any, employees were dismissed—and the curtailment in various degrees of such activities as day classes for adults, evening elementary and high schools and community and recreational centers.[87] (One of the most prominent casualties of La Guardia's retrenchment program in education, which also encompassed the budget of the Board of Higher Education, was the abolition in the early forties of Townsend Harris High School, a school for intellectually gifted boys under the supervision of the Board of Higher Education.[88])

La Guardia's position with respect to cuts in the educational appropriation was very clear. Enrollment in the schools was declining because of the low birth rate during the Depression, as was the amount of state aid to education, geared as it was to pupil attendance; New York City's school registration fell from a peak of 1,124,000 pupils in October, 1934, to 850,000 pupils in 1945.[89] "We cannot continue to spend the same amount of money on schools," La Guardia said, "when we have such a large drop in pupils." He insisted, however, that the city's appropriation had not decreased as much as the decline in enrollment and state aid warranted. He continually pointed out that registration was falling at a faster clip than a drop in teachers and that, despite his policy of not filling vacancies, class size was being reduced. He held, in short, that the city's financial contribution to education was adequate—at least once he said "generous." [90]

Teacher and parent groups had a different view. While recognizing the declining enrollment and diminishing state aid, they did not feel that the city should retrench because of it; in fact, they apparently felt that the less the state gave to education, the more the city should give. They believed that the city should take the opportunity to improve the quality of education, not only by not cutting, but by spending more. They accused the administration and school officials of not providing the type of education necessary for the welfare of the city's children and demanded increased services, more appointments, especially of teachers, and still smaller classes, finding justification for their demands in reports such as one by the New York City Sub-Committee of the Rapp-Coudert state legislative committee, which in the early forties investigated various aspects of education in the state, and the 1943 consultant report of Dr. George D. Strayer upon which the subcommittee's report was mainly based. The war, by preventing the construction of new schools or even proper maintenance and repairs with respect to old ones, and by creating personnel shortages, especially of teachers, intensified the antagonism between the La Guardia administration and its educational critics.[91]

In October, 1945, this conflict finally came to a head when most of the members of an Advisory Committee on Human Relations, which Superintendent Wade had set up a year before to help promote a program of racial tolerance in the schools, resigned *en masse,* the committee's chairman, Frank E. Karelsen, Jr., charging that school conditions were "chaotic and inexcusable," that nothing had been done to improve them despite repeated recommendations by the committee and that no sound human relations program could be established in the schools until there was a big improvement in the conditions under which school children received their education. Among other things, Karelsen demanded a complete teaching staff in every school, smaller classes, especially in tension areas, sufficient clerical and other help for school administrators, additional All-Day Neighborhood Schools and more attendance officers and child guidance and human relations counselors. Karelsen and a number of other people who had resigned from Wade's committee formed an Emergency Committee for Better Schools for New York's Children and asked Governor Dewey to order the State Department of Education to conduct a sweeping investigation of the city's schools. The Governor turned the request over to the Board of Regents, which in turn asked State Commissioner of Education George D. Stoddard to make a preliminary study of the school situation in New York City.[92]

La Guardia met Karelsen's criticism by attempting to link his name with honest graft practiced by Tammany in connection with school sites years before; he ordered Commissioner of Investigation Yavner to make a thorough inquiry into the events leading up to Karelsen's resignation from the Advisory Committee, an order replete with innuendo.[93] Soon, however, the Board of Education presented to Commissioner Stoddard a ninety-six-page rebuttal of the Karelsen group's charges, and the issue was intelligently drawn. Essentially the Board's position was that many of the Karelsen allegations were general and tended to create a false impression: that, while the school system was not free from fault, the Board was doing its best to correct deficiencies within the limitations of the budget and of circumstances caused by the war. Stoddard's report, which the Regents accepted in January, 1946, while not uncritical of the educational situation in New York, on the whole upheld the Board of Education's position. It tended to regard the school system as basically sound and the points of criticism as the growing pains of a giant which the Board of Education was aware of and was attempting to cope with as realistically as it could.[94]

There was much to be said for Fusion's educational critics in the running controversy which marked the last half of La Guardia's administration. The wisdom of La Guardia's decision to abolish Townsend Harris, intellectually the finest school in the city, is questionable. While the war made it difficult for the city to find and keep teachers, the shortage owed something, as the administration's educational critics claimed, to the shortsighted and callous policy of La Guardia and school authorities of trying to save money at the expense of teacher morale by continuing the policy, initiated by Tammany in 1931, of filling vacancies when they had to be filled, not with regular teachers, but with "permanent substitutes"; the permanent substitutes received lower salaries than regular teachers and no pensions and lacked the usual civil service protection. Not until 1945 did the Board of Education make regular appointments.[95] Beyond this, the school system did need the various improvements demanded by parent and teacher groups, and the educational budgets could be characterized as inadequate; even the sums asked for by the Board of Education represented, not what was needed, but what the Board thought it could get.[96]

The urgency of a need and the adequacy or inadequacy of a budget, however, are things often contingent upon one's point of view. As Charles Gilman, one-time auditor for the Board of Education, once observed to the writer, there never has been a time when the Board of Education has had enough money to do the educational job right.[97] It is also true that when it comes to funds for education, parents and teachers are a peculiarly insatiable lot. They were certainly right to badger La Guardia and the Board of Education for more good things for education—as they have done in the case of other administrations, before and since—but La Guardia may have been right, too, in drawing the line where he did, for to have granted their requests would have cost tremendous sums and as Mayor of New York he had to worry, not only about the needs of education, but about those of other departments and agencies and about keeping the city solvent; in La Guardia's view, when all things were considered, more money for the schools was just not available. The NEA report, it is important to note, whatever else it said about La Guardia, declared that he had made an honest effort to provide reasonable financial support for the schools.[98] And one should consider, too, that New York City's financial contribution to education steadily increased percentagewise in relation to the total educational appropriation (which also included state and federal money) in the years 1935–1944–5; and that the percentage of the city's funds spent for education in relation to the city's total expenditure generally rose between 1932 and 1942–3.[99]

Whether La Guardia or his educational critics were more correct in this controversy depends essentially upon what the true conditions in the schools were—and here there was no consensus even on the part of more or less impartial sources. One finds it hard, however, not to be influenced by the fact that the Stoddard report, which more than any other report on the educational situation in New York City focused on the complaints of La Guardia's critics, generally favored the administration's position.

La Guardia, probably because of his European heritage and experience, had a Latin "feel" for his city; he did not believe that poetry was a "frill." He dreamed of beer gardens along the Harlem River—a vision that was never realized—and of people dancing in Central Park—a vision that was. Especially he wanted to encourage art, music and cultural democracy in New York; he wished to make his city a "cultural" city to the same extent that various European cities were "cultural" cities.

His mind was fertile with schemes for stimulating cultural development. There was his plan for a High School of Music and Art, which we have already noticed. He once advanced a proposal—from which nothing ever came—for linking the city's radio station, WNYC, with the country's other non-commercial stations to form a new broadcasting system which would be devoted to educational and cultural activities; inter-station communication would be accomplished by short-wave. At another time he suggested that the Philharmonic Symphony Society, as a means of developing musically talented Americans and of assuring New York audiences the best in music, should copy a leaf from baseball's book and establish a musical minor league system from which talent could be perfected for New York City.[100]

La Guardia's most ambitious scheme for encouraging the arts was his plan for a municipal art center. Even before he entered the Mayor's office, he was understood to be anxious to establish a municipal music conservatory; realizing, however, that he must first deal with the state of the city's credit and that any expenditures for culture would be severely frowned upon by taxpayers until the financial crisis had been passed, he shelved his project for about a year. When in January, 1935, he took the scheme out of mothballs and made its implementation the central task of a newly created 118 member Municipal Art Committee, an art center had been added to the conservatory. The project continued to evolve, following in what was apparently its final form the lines of cultural centers in European cities. The proposed New York center was to contain, most notably, a huge auditorium adaptable to the various requirements of art and music, exhibition halls for the use of contemporary artists and a music library; space for the Museum of Modern Art and the museum part of the New York Public Library was to be provided. For five years La Guardia tried to realize this project, but difficulties cropped up—the reluctance of certain organizations which, it was hoped, would participate in the scheme to move to new quarters was a big one—and he was forced to give up; in February, 1940, he described the plan as the "one great setback in my administration." [101]

La Guardia's efforts to advance the arts in New York City, however, were not to be entirely frustrated. In the early forties Mecca Temple, headquarters of the Masonic Shriners, fell into the hands of the city for nonpayment of taxes; the city was unable to find a purchaser who would make a satisfactory bid. Newbold Morris, one of the Mayor's staunchest allies in his endeavor to improve the city's cultural life during La Guardia's second and third terms, gave him an idea: convert the building into a theatre of music and drama for the presentation of good programs at prices modest pocketbooks could afford. At first skeptical of the proposal, La Guardia soon got behind it. Morris organized a nonprofit membership corporation to take charge of the venture, and to it the Board of Estimate leased Mecca Temple, agreeing to accept as rent from the corporation a sum equivalent to the yearly taxes due from the building. While the project was not to be aided by a municipal subvention—the corporation had to be self-supporting or pass the hat if necessary—the city further helped the scheme by granting the corporation $65,000 to remodel the structure.[102]

In the reconverted Mecca Temple on the night of December 11, 1943, before a capacity throng that had come to hear the Philharmonic Symphony Orchestra, Mayor La Guardia dedicated an institution that quickly proved to be immensely popular with out-of-towners as well as New Yorkers; in its first two seasons, the New York City Center of Music and Drama, Incorporated, recorded more than a million paid admissions. Since its founding, its operas, light operas, dramas and ballets have added appreciably to the cultural life of New York; in a short time, the New York City Ballet has become one of the finest ballet companies in the world, widely acclaimed by European audiences and critics, not prone to cheer American contributions to culture. The City Center's popularly priced productions, furthermore, more than likely have helped educate many to music, drama and the dance who otherwise would have remained insensitive to these artistic mediums and partly on this account have worked to raise the cultural level of the population of the city—and probably, to an extent, that of people elsewhere. Under La Guardia, the government, though in an indirect manner, undertook to encourage the arts with consequences that few, if any, regret.[103]

The Fusion administration, as did other administrations during the New Deal period, displayed a new concern for the consumer; in various ways, the New York City government attempted to ease his problems. One big purpose of the La Guardia administration's war against the market racketeers was to cut the citizen's food bill. The Market Department in 1937 unleashed a crusade against weight-measure frauds that resulted in the apprehension of dishonest tradesmen at the rate of about a thousand a month; for a time at least, it became harder for gyppers to take advantage of the New York consumer.[104] Concerned about the hardships the Depression worked upon the people of the city, La Guardia established a Con-

sumers' Service in the Department of Markets to help housewives reduce
food budgets, while making meals more appetizing and nutritious. Every
day Consumers' Service gathered information as to what foods were most
in supply and disseminated this and other food information via the radio,
the lecture platform, newspapers, magazines and cooking schools. The
head of Consumers' Service, Mrs. Frances F. Gannon, a brisk, handsome
woman with bobbed white hair and pale blue eyes, conducted a campaign
to turn shoppers into intelligent buyers.[105]

In the mid-thirties, at a time when milk prices were very unstable, La
Guardia vigorously fought efforts of the milk companies to raise prices.
When in September, 1936, Borden and Sheffield, claiming that increased
costs made it necessary, raised the price of a quart of milk to health stations, which made distributions to the needy, from eight cents (a bargain
rate La Guardia had obtained from the companies in 1934) to nine cents
and increased the price to the general public, La Guardia blew up. Declaring that the one-cent hike to the health stations constituted "an unfriendly
act" and meant "war," he made an agreement with independent dealers
to supply the stations at the old eight-cent rate and also brought pressure
to bear to keep down the price to the general consumer; the big companies
returned to the old retail price, but the city continued to buy milk for the
health stations from the independents. Confronted with continual uncertainty as to the price of milk and with frequent milk emergencies, La
Guardia once proposed that the city construct a milk pasteurization plant
in the Bronx Terminal Market to serve as a "yardstick" for milk prices,
only to learn that the municipal government had no power to go into the
business of pasteurizing milk.[106]

Another scheme for a municipal yardstick was of somewhat greater
importance. La Guardia and Davidson believed that the city's 1934 contracts with the electric companies for providing street lighting and light
and power in public buildings were too costly to the city; when the bids
from the subsidiaries of the Consolidated Gas Company for 1935 were
seen to be even higher than the 1934 charge, the new Fusion administration decided to take bold action. On the day the city received the bids, it
rejected them and immediately pushed plans for the erection of a municipal
power plant which would supply some of the city's needs and serve as a
yardstick with respect to charges for electricity made upon it. Before long
the companies saw that they had made an error and bids were again
received, this time more favorable to the city: the companies guaranteed
the city a reduction of at least $1,725,000 based upon 1934 consumption.
Actually the city saved more than this on its 1935 electric bill. Further
revision of contracts in the next two years permitted the city to make
additional savings.[107]

While moving to reduce the cost of electricity to the city, La Guardia
did not forget the general consumer. In May, 1935, he announced that,
though the new rates offered by the companies no longer made it profitable

for the government to build a yardstick for its own purposes, the city would still build a power plant yardstick to enable the private consumer to save money. The plant, which would cost $45,000,000, would be erected on Welfare Island, he said, and would sell current to about 87,000 customers—and all classes of consumers—in Manhattan, Brooklyn, Queens and the Bronx in direct competition with the Consolidated Gas Company; according to the Mayor, it would sell electricity 40 per cent cheaper. To enable La Guardia to construct the plant in a way most favorable to the city, special legislation which had been introduced in the legislature before the capitulation of the Consolidated was kept alive. In December, 1936, Consolidated reached an agreement with the Public Service Commission to decrease rates to consumers in New York City at a total savings to them of $7,000,000 a year. There is more than a suspicion that the threat of La Guardia's power plant had something to do with the reduction.[108]

La Guardia never built his power plant. A majority of the members of the Board of Estimate were dubious of the soundness of putting the city into the power business and, for reasons that are not too clear (though one or two might be guessed at), the legislature would not go along; it refused to permit La Guardia to build a power plant by means of PWA funds or the bonds of a special authority which the city would not be responsible for. Actually La Guardia could have constructed the plant without special authorization from Albany—though the voters would have had to give him permission through a referendum—had he been willing to pledge the city's credit; but this he was not willing to do, probably because he was adverse to sacrificing more important capital projects for a power plant and did not want to be charged with adding to the tax burden for such a purpose.[109] It may have been, as Newbold Morris believes,[110] that La Guardia never really expected the legislature to co-operate with him in erecting the plant, that he simply used the project to club Consolidated. There is not much doubt, however, that had he been given the chance to build the plant on his own terms, he would have taken it.[111] Whatever was in La Guardia's mind, his proposal had the effect of benefiting the people of New York, both in their capacity as taxpayers and consumers.

New York City in 1934 had an extensive transportation system composed of streetcars, buses, elevated lines and subways, backbone of the system. Circumstances had brought into being three separate major rapid transit lines: the BMT (Brooklyn-Manhattan Transit Company); the IRT (Interborough Rapid Transit Company) and the IND (Independent System). The first subway, opened in 1904, ran northward from the old Post Office Building and was soon extended southward to Atlantic Avenue in Brooklyn; after having been dug by the city, it was leased to the IRT for operation under what came to be known as Contracts No. 1 and No. 2. Expanding rapidly and in need of additional subway facilities, the city in 1913, during the time of Gaynor, signed with private interests the so-called dual contracts—Contract No. 3 with the IRT and Contract No. 4 with the BRT (Brooklyn Rapid Transit Company)—for the construction and operation of two major subways. Under the terms of the contracts, the city, which undertook to furnish most of the money for the construction and equipment of the new lines (but which did not have enough borrowing margin at the time to finance the entire job), became exclusive owner of the lines and its equipment, but turned over operation of the subways to the two companies which agreed to run them in conjunction with elevated facilities they either owned or had leased and to pay the city, not a fixed rental as in the case of Contracts No. 1 and 2, but a percentage of the profits. The BRT, which soon went bankrupt, was succeeded by the BMT. In the 1920's there were demands for more rapid transit facilities, but the dual contracts were not popular, Hylan, the arch foe of the "interests," was in City Hall, and the city decided that this time it would both build and operate its own line; the result was the IND.[112]

With the years a multifarious transit problem had arisen to plague the city. One aspect of the problem was that for the companies, but even more for the city, the dual contracts had proven unfortunate. Despite some vigorous criticism of the contracts from the beginning as being unfair to the city, a good case could be made that, considering all the circumstances, the city and the companies had concluded a mutually advantageous deal. If private investors, rather than the city, were given first crack at profits, there were some understandable reasons for this, not the least being that the city, responsive to the popular temper, had insisted upon writing into the contract a provision prohibiting the companies from raising the fare above five cents, then the current price of a subway ride. What happened, however, was that even before the dual contracts went into operation, the First World War boosted the cost of labor and materials to such an extent that profits predicated upon a nickel fare became unrealizable. The result was that in 1918 the BRT, as we have just noted, fell into bankruptcy, and the IRT, additionally crippled in the years that followed by a decline in el traffic and, most likely, by competition from the city's new subway, experienced the same fate in 1932; while the BMT in 1934 was not in financial straits, its future did not appear bright.

The companies at least showed some profits; from the start the city knew only losses. From January 1, 1919 (when permanent operation of the new IRT line was begun) and August 1, 1920 (the date permanent operation of the BMT was started) until June 30, 1934, the city received only some $19,000,000 from the IRT as a result of Contract No. 3 and exactly nothing from the BMT as a result of Contract No. 4,[113] suffering a loss of over $183,000,000, a sum which represented the debt service on the city's IRT-BMT investment which the city was forced to provide out of real estate taxes. To meet the debt service on its IRT-BMT investment and on its own IND system, New York appropriated some $26,000,000 in its 1934 budget.[114] By making up the transit deficit through taxation, the city, in effect, undertook to subsidize the five-cent fare; this policy, not only added to the real estate tax load, but served to limit the city's ability to borrow under its debt limit and consequently its construction of new capital projects. Understandably the city would have been happy to melt this "frozen credit" through some revision of the dual contracts.

In other ways the transit situation was unsatisfactory. Conditions on the private subway lines were disgraceful because the companies were unable to finance improvements. The city, again because of the dual contracts, did not have enough of a say in planning and constructing additional rapid transit lines. It needed an easier and much cheaper method of removing the ugly els—which were clearly on the way out—and of restoring property values, facilitating the flow of traffic and making the city more beautiful than the procedure of condemnation allowed. The operation of the Independent Subway posed a serious difficulty: under the law the new subway eventually had to become self-supporting—which meant a fare higher than a nickel. But how would it be able to compete with the other lines in this case? And if the self-supporting provision were to be changed to permit retention of the five-cent fare on the new line, wouldn't the clean, modern IND further cut into the business of the private companies? (The very idea of competition among the lines was ridiculous.) For those who were concerned lest New York lose its nickel subway ride, there was much about the transit picture that was not reassuring.

One answer had come to be given to the series of problems that made up the city's transit predicament: *transit unification,* by which was meant the consolidation of all the subways and els—some would also throw in the privately owned buses and streetcars—into a single municipally owned and operated system. Unification would cancel the dual contracts. By permitting the substitution of one administrative and operating staff for three separate ones and by bringing about a reduction in fixed charges through the refunding of outstanding private, high-interest bearing securities with public or quasi-public, low-interest bearing, tax-exempt ones, unification, it was argued, would result in a decrease in the transit overhead and greater profits; eventually the city could cut down, though perhaps not eliminate, its budgetary appropriations to meet its IRT-BMT investment. Because of increased revenue from the lines and the city's greater financial resources, subway service would be improved. Unification, it was declared, would enable the city to extend rapid transit routes in a more orderly and economically sound fashion and to more easily eliminate the els. Unification would solve the problems presented by the operation of the IND; ruinous competition among the lines would be avoided. Those who wanted to preserve the five-cent fare held that only unification could save it.[115]

First suggested in 1919 by John H. Delaney, then Rapid Transit Construction Commissioner and later head of the city's Board of Transportation (after that body was created in 1924 to plan and construct new subways), unification received a concrete push in 1921 when the legislature created a Transit Commission composed of three members to be appointed by the Governor. In addition to the tasks of administering the dual contracts, regulating service on the BMT and IRT and performing a variety of other regulatory and quasi-judicial functions with regard to transportation, the Transit Commission was assigned the job of bringing about transit unification in New York City. The last business was hardly the easiest part of the Commission's work. Any plan for unification had to be acceptable, not only to various groups of private security holders—a fact that presented difficulty enough—but, after 1925, to the city; and city and Commission did not get along well. In its early years, the Commission was Republican-controlled and politics was doubtlessly responsible for some of the friction between that agency and the Hylan administration; that there were other, and more important, reasons for the disharmony, however, became clear after 1925 when the Commission became Democratic, and its relations with the city did not substantially improve. Much of the trouble probably was simply the result of feelings of rivalry engendered by the division of authority in the matter of unification. It seems also true that the Board of Estimate, much aware of the obloquy leveled at the dual contracts and afraid of making some unification deal which might turn into another political hot potato, was wary to the point of inaction.[116]

In 1931, after much work on a unification agreement had been done by Samuel Untermyer, who for a time served as special counsel to the Commission, and several tentative schemes had been suggested and, for one reason or another, discarded, the Transit Commission published a plan, basically that of Untermyer, fixing a total purchase price for the private lines at $489,000,000. The plan did not have the consent or approval of any of the transit companies. The Board of Estimate took no action on it. When Fusion came in, unification was right where it had been in 1931.[117]

La Guardia, who had made a campaign promise to bring about unification, immediately wrote off the 1931 plan as dead and struck out at the problem on two fronts. Believing that the Transit Commission only complicated the picture unnecessarily, he advocated and pushed at Albany a bill to eliminate the Commission by transferring its unification powers to the Board of Transportation and making the Commission, with respect to its other duties, the metropolitan division of the Public Service Commission. La Guardia also designated City Chamberlain Berle and Samuel Seabury as contact men to negotiate an arrangement between the city and the traction companies and their security holders; Seabury was named special counsel to the Board of Estimate in transit matters, a position which involved no fee. La Guardia's bill abolishing the Transit Commission failed to get through the legislature in 1934; nor, despite the Mayor's efforts, was any similar bill enacted during the next few years. Probably one excellent reason for La Guardia's failure here was that the Commission represented some choice political plums which neither the boys in the legislature nor the Governor were inclined to eliminate.[118] For a while, Seabury and Berle had somewhat better luck.

As a result of negotiations with the transit companies and their security holders, the city's representatives signed "memorandums of understanding" with the BMT and the IRT (respectively in February and November, 1935) for the purchase of their properties. Since the memorandums were but tentative agreements in need of development, Seabury and Berle next concerned themselves with drafting a definitive plan; this they presented to the Transit Commission in June, 1936. While differing on some points with the agreements contained in the memorandums, the final scheme was basically similar to them. At a gross price of approximately $436,000,000 —a figure somewhat higher than that contemplated in November, 1935, but lower than any previously proposed purchase price—the city would acquire the privately operated lines and then lease them for seventy-five years to a Board of Transit Control to which it would also lease its Independent Subway; the Board would undertake to operate all the lines as one system, pooling income from the lines to meet operating costs and fixed charges. Payment of the purchase price was to be effected through a refunding operation in which private securities would be exchanged for $110,000,000 of city bonds and about $303,000,000 of bonds of the Board of Transit Control, with the city assuming underlying mortgages on the BMT elevated lines. Estimates of revenue and profit were predicated on the assumption that the five-cent fare would be continued.[119]

The Seabury-Berle plan aroused hopes that unification was finally around the corner. Seabury and Berle had obtained the signature of every major private interest, something previously thought impossible; there was little doubt that this time the Board of Estimate, whose representative Seabury was, would go along. Only the consent of the Transit Commission was wanting. On May 9, 1937, despite the urging of the City Club, the Women's City Club and other groups that the plan be accepted,[120] the Commission flatly rejected it. Any unification agreement had to be based upon assumptions and compromises which could be challenged, as they could be defended, and the Transit Commissioners chose to challenge many of those contained in the Seabury-Berle plan. The Commission objected that the purchase price was too high, that adequate provision had not been made for certain labor costs, that the private interests still had prior claims to earnings, that the deal would result in a financial loss to the city with the consequent abandonment of the five-cent fare, higher taxes or both, that private interests would have too much say about the construction of new transit facilities, that, in short, the city would be better off under the dual contracts.[121]

Some, perhaps all, of the Commission's major objections may have had validity—after a searching study, the Citizens Budget Commission in the fall of 1936 raised some doubts as to how much the city would benefit from the Seabury-Berle plan [122]—yet the suspicion exists that the Commission did not arrive at its position entirely through the workings of disinterested logic. The rejection was caustic in tone and contained innuendoes as to the motives of the proponents of the plan. Though the city's representatives in presenting the proposal to the Commission had asked for—and in the opinion of the *Times* were entitled to [123]—a speedy decision, probably because they felt that they could not remain in accord with the private interests indefinitely, the Commission took almost a year, a period for consideration that may have been longer than necessary. When in the winter of 1936 the Board of Estimate sent a copy of the proposal to the Commission, its chairman, William G. Fullen, replied in a letter that belittled the Seabury-Berle accomplishment; he declared that the Commission was still waiting to hear from the city on the Commission's 1931 plan.[124] Did the Commission's opinion of the Seabury-Berle plan reflect in part, perhaps, ruffled feelings—its resentment at the city's initiative in the matter of unification and at La Guardia's attempts to have the Commission abolished? Did political considerations, particularly with respect to the 1937 mayoral election, have some influence on the thinking of the Democratic members of the Commission? Whatever the reason or reasons for the Transit Commission's rejection of the Seabury-Berle proposal, one point was incontestable: in three and a half years, unification had gone nowhere.

Slowly, however, it began to move forward again, this time as a result of a push from the Commission. Through its associate special counsel, Chester W. Cuthell, the Commission in August, 1937, began negotiations with the private interests; by November the negotiations had reached a point where the Commission felt the city should be represented, and it asked La Guardia to name one or more individuals to take part in further discussions. The city was scarcely in a frame of mind to entertain the suggestion. La Guardia turned down the Commission's request then and twice after that. From November, 1937, until the spring of 1938, the La Guardia administration took the view that the Commission's effort didn't amount to anything, that the Commission was just running around to avoid its abolishment; Seabury and Berle denounced the new plan the Commission was in the process of working up as a "hoax" and "another political document." As a result of the city's attitude, the unification negotiations between the Commission and the private interests bogged down because the private groups correctly felt that no agreement was possible as long as the administration and the Commission were at odds.[125]

This was the situation when in May, 1938, La Guardia suddenly changed his mind and decided to work with the Commission. Far from having been engaged in throwing up a smokescreen of activity, the Commission had been working in terms of a new approach to unification, and La Guardia apparently came to realize that there was merit in the new way, that it presented the only means of bringing about unification in his administration and that his best course lay in co-operating with the Commission. The Seabury-Berle plan and other plans before it had contemplated the use of bonds of a Board of Transit Control to pay the major part of the purchase price; because there was some doubt as to whether such bonds would be tax exempt, owners of private securities could claim that they were entitled to higher prices and higher interest rates than if the city were to use cash or its equivalent in city bonds as the sole purchasing medium and that they should exercise some influence on the city's transit policies. Everyone, of course, had recognized the desirability of using city bonds to buy out the private lines; the rub had been that the city's borrowing power in relation to its debt limit was too small to make the idea feasible. In rejecting the Seabury-Berle plan, however, Commissioner Reuben L. Haskell, the Transit Commission's lone Republican, had suggested that, at the State Constitutional Convention that was to take place in 1938, the city should seek to obtain a constitutional amendment excluding from the debt limit of the city the sum needed to purchase the properties of transit companies. It was this idea that lay at the heart of the new plan the Commission was trying to develop and which La Guardia now resolved to push.[126]

Results of the new relations between the city and the Transit Commission soon became apparent. La Guardia appointed a committee, consisting of himself, John Delaney, whom La Guardia had retained as chairman of the Board of Transportation, Newbold Morris and Joseph McGoldrick, to join with Transit Commissioners Fullen and M. Maldwin Fertig in negotiating with representatives of the BMT and the IRT and with representatives of the holders of securities in these companies; the negotiating setup made it certain that any deal agreed upon by the negotiators would be approved by the bodies or interests they represented. The city and the Transit Commission agreed to ask the Constitutional Convention for a debt exemption of $315,000,000, an amount, it was felt, which would take care of the bulk of the purchase price; introduced at the convention by Fertig, the amendment was passed by that assemblage and ratified by the voters of the state in November, 1938. With authorization of the exemption by the voters, the negotiations really got down to brass tacks.[127]

Out of the discussions came two agreements. According to the terms of one, the city would acquire the subway, elevated, trolley and bus property of the BMT for $175,000,000; by the terms of the other, it would purchase the subway and el facilities of the Interborough system for $151,000,000. The companies agreed to permit the city to condemn various antiquated els at their sale price, a price considerably lower than one that would come out of normal condemnation proceedings, so that the city could assess the cost upon property owners whose property abutted on the condemned lines, thereby avoiding spending any of its $315,000,000 for this purpose. The city would pay the combined purchase price of $326,000,000 by exchanging 3 per cent city bonds for outstanding securities of the BMT and IRT. Approved by the Board of Estimate and the Transit Commission, the agreements became operative (the IRT plan in November, 1939, the

BMT plan in February, 1940) after transit security holders had deposited stipulated percentages of various categories of securities.[128]

In early 1940 the legislature passed several measures necessary for the implementation of municipal operation; Albany conferred on the city, through the Board of Transportation, the right to operate the unified subway and surface transit facilities, made it clear that the Board of Estimate had control over the fare and limited the power of the Transit Commission to supervision over transit safety. (In 1943, after Dewey became Governor, the Commission was finally abolished, its various duties being taken over by the Public Service Commission.) [129] A demand by the Transport Workers Union (CIO)—that the city honor closed shop contracts it had with the IRT and BMT—threatened for a time to prevent a smooth transition to the new setup; the city was reluctant to do so since state legislation provided that after unification IRT and BMT workers were to be taken into the civil service, thus giving them the same status as IND employees, and civil service regulations precluded closed shop agreements. At the beginning of April, 1940, after about a year of contention between the TWU and the city in which the possibility of a transit strike always hovered in the background, La Guardia, John L. Lewis and other CIO officials reached an agreement whereby the Board of Transportation would take over the existing contracts, closed shop and all, holding in abeyance any ruling on what it felt was an illegal provision pending a decision by the courts.[130]

On June 1 and June 12, 1940, the city took formal title respectively to the BMT and the IRT systems and began municipal operations. The owner and operator of 781 track miles of subway and elevated lines, 437 track miles of street railway and 79 miles of bus routes representing a total investment of over $1,500,000,000, the city conducted the greatest municipal enterprise in America.[131] After twenty years of futility, the Fusion administration and the Transit Commission working together had realized the dream of unification.

Looking back on the twenties and thirties from the vantage point of our own day, it is not easy to understand why unification created the fuss it did or why La Guardia and other Fusion officials considered its enactment so desirable. For we know that unification did not usher in a transit millennium. It does not appear that subway service improved much with municipal operation. Though unified operation in its first year produced an operating profit of $28,000,000, profits dwindled after that and in the post-Fusion period became operating deficits, with the result that O'Dwyer raised the nickel fair to ten cents; save for one year, this action failed to check the rising tide of operating losses, and the city was unable to free itself from a mounting drain on its tax funds until the legislature in 1953, at the behest of Governor Dewey, created the New York City Transit Authority which, under a mandate to run the transit system on a self-supporting basis with respect to operation, promptly raised the fare to fifteen cents.[132] Even before the post-Fusion era, unification did not result in an improvement in the city's transit debt situation, and La Guardia in his budget message for 1944–5 felt compelled to recommend the adoption of a special tax— never enacted—for the purpose of wiping out the subway deficit (and improving transit facilities).[133]

Mainly this unhappy situation was not the consequence of unification. As the dual contracts had floundered on the shoal of the First World War, the unification deals ran aground on that of the Second; shortages of materials during the Second World War made it difficult for the city to improve the physical plant of the subways; more important, inflation during and after the war enormously boosted costs, especially that of labor. Though total revenue increased, total operating expenses climbed more sharply with the result that operating profit diminished and higher taxes or a higher fare became inevitable.[134]

At the same time, the way unification was actually carried out was not without some influence on the city's subsequent transit troubles. For one thing, while costs would have gone up anyway, administration of the unified system by an independent agency of one sort or another in all likelihood would have given more economical operation than that which marked the post-unification period. Such an agency would have been less sensitive than was the city, especially under O'Dwyer, to the demands of Mike Quill and other leaders of the TWU which not only were responsible for considerable wage hikes—much, if not all, of which could be justified in view of the rise in the cost of living—but, according to William Fullen, who later became a member of the New York City Transit Authority, a good deal of unjustified featherbedding as well.[135] An independent agency would have been quicker to raise the fare, though there are those who find in this fact an excellent argument against the creation of such a body. Also it is possible that the price paid by the city to the private interests to enable it to unify the transit system, though lower than that contained in the Seabury-Berle plan (a condition for which the Transit Commission, regardless of the reasons for its rejection of the Seabury-Berle proposal, is to be given credit) was too high; debt service on the purchase price was to be met out of transit revenues, and the greater the cost of this item, of course, the narrower the margin of profit—and the greater the chance that expenses would outrun revenues.[136]

These points, however, should not be permitted to obscure the great importance of unification to the city. Competition among the lines was eliminated and the problem of the IND solved. The city was able to remove most of the els with the consequence that adjacent property values were increased and the flow of traffic and the appearance of the city vastly improved. As sad as subway service was after unification, it was probably better than what would have been had there been no unification; the private companies had been making every effort to keep expenses to a minimum.[137] Unification finally made the city master in its own transit house. If preservation of the five-cent fare is to be considered a gain, unification and municipal operation, it should be noted, undoubtedly put off the rueful day when a higher fare became necessary. Among other reasons, the courts might well have permitted the IRT and the BMT (whose financial situation was deteriorating toward the end) to raise their fares. Not least significant, unification served to put all transit problems into one basket where they could be dealt with more easily.

(As to the question of whether the city couldn't have obtained a lower purchase price, one should keep in mind the obvious point that the city's negotiators always had to consider what the private interests would take. It has been argued that if the city could not have swung a better offer, it should have postponed unification until such time as it had a stronger bargaining position—indeed, perhaps, until the BMT had followed the IRT into bankruptcy. While the city may well have gotten a better deal had it waited, there is no telling how long it would have had to wait—negotiations with a bankrupt BMT, for example, might not have been as easy as some think—and in the meantime the city would not have been able to enjoy any of the advantages of unification. Besides, the city's bargaining position at the time was not weak; traffic on the lines was declining and city securities were carrying a 3 per cent interest rate, a rate attractive to investors. The city's bargaining position in the future might have been worse as well as better.)

The unification agreements, while far from ideal from the point of view of the city, presented the city with greater advantages than disadvantages. If the subsequent transit picture was not as bright as had been anticipated, this was chiefly the consequence, not of unification, but of events that were unforeseen and beyond the control of any city administration.

12

Changes in structure

1 9 3 3 H A D B E E N an indecisive year in the battle for Charter reform. It had been a frustrating year for the reformers: the Moffat Charter revision bill, as we observed in Chapter 5, had failed to pass the state senate. Yet for partisans of Charter reform the year had not been altogether unsatisfactory. In the spring of 1933 the city's Municipal Assembly, on the basis of power it enjoyed under the Home Rule Law,[1] passed a bill, which O'Brien promptly signed, enabling the Mayor, provided the voters approved in a referendum to be held at election time in November, to name a Charter commission of seventeen members; the measure would allow O'Brien to name the commission regardless of who was elected Mayor. The real proponents of Charter reform set themselves against this barefaced Tammany attempt to steal control of the Charter reform movement. They found their strongest ally in La Guardia. In the fall of 1933 the Fusion mayoral candidate, unable to elicit from O'Brien a promise that he would not appoint a Charter commission should the referendum carry, made defeat of the lame duck Charter part of his campaign, with the result that the voters in every borough defeated the referendum.[2]

And there was, of course, La Guardia's own victory at the polls to warm the hearts of the Charter reformers: La Guardia had pledged himself to fight for a new, modern Charter,[3] and a reform administration could be expected to encourage, rather than hinder, real Charter reform. (Indeed the Fusion victory seemed to stimulate even more interest in the subject of reforming the structure of government; in 1934 and 1935 practically every civic organization, as well as a number which were not, developed a blueprint for governmental reform.[4]) As before, the Charter reformers could count upon the support of Governor Lehman. Prospects for a new Charter at the start of 1934 were brighter than a year before.

The new year was hardly under way when the supporters of Charter reform resumed their drive in the legislature. Lehman launched the attack by devoting a major portion of his annual message to the need for modernizing local government. Specifically, he recommended that the legislature set up a Charter commission to draft a new Charter for New York City which would then be submitted to the city's voters, a somewhat different approach to the problem than that taken by the Moffat bill; presumably legislation for this purpose would take the form of an amendment to the Home Rule Law with respect to the city's Charter-making power. Legislative leaders agreed that Charter revision had to go through, but only after La Guardia's Economy Bill was disposed of in April did the legislature take up the subject in earnest. Difficulties soon cropped up. A number of Charter revision bills had been introduced. Which one should prevail? When the legislature decided to follow Lehman's suggestion, there arose what appeared to be a hopeless deadlock between Republicans and Democrats over the question of the Charter commission's personnel. Since the Republicans, co-operating with La Guardia's administration, still controlled the Assembly and the Democrats the senate, and especially since a two-thirds vote in each house was required for passage of the legislation, the complete concurrence of both parties was essential. A carefully balanced slate was finally worked out and agreed to by all the legislative leaders. Despite some last minute political shenanigans by the Democrats, which almost ruined everything, the Charter revision bill was passed.[5]

The bill created a somewhat cumbrous commission of twenty-eight members, a majority of whom were picked by the Democratic organizations. Still a majority of these were not of the kind whose decisions could be controlled, and the commission contained the names of some outstanding champions of real Charter revision. Richard Childs, Leonard Wallstein, Norman Thomas and Charles Tuttle were aboard. Al Smith was the chairman, Samuel Seabury the vice-chairman.[6] Despite the commission's defects, there was some chance that something good would come out of its labors.

It began well. The commission, which had also been given authority to deal with county reform, immediately recommended that the Governor call a special session of the legislature to pass an important constitutional amendment (of which more will be said later) and Lehman acceded to the suggestion. But before long the question of Charter revision was rending the commission. Smith, Seabury and a few others were in favor of drastic reforms, but the majority seemed to be bent on more moderate innovations. When, in opposition to Smith and Seabury, the commission voted to continue the Board of Estimate practically unchanged, only modify the Board of Aldermen, and showed a marked trend to restore to the borough presidents administrative and patronage powers which on the insistence of Smith and Seabury had been shorn from them, both men decided they had had enough. In early August, followed by a few other members, Smith and Seabury resigned to bring out into the open what they considered to be the fight for true reform. Charging that the commission contained members who had special interests to serve or who were committed in advance to preserving the status quo and that some members were doing their best to sabotage the new Charter, Smith, joined by Seabury, called upon Lehman to obtain a new law from the legislature creating a new, and smaller, commission whose members would be appointed by Mayor La Guardia or by him and the Governor.[7]

Not all men of good will shared the Seabury-Smith view of the commission. Childs, Wallstein and Thomas, to name a few, did not resign; indeed Childs became the new chairman of the commission and Wallstein the new vice-chairman. Childs denied that the commission was a politically-dominated group and pointed to the county reform amendment and the commission's decisions to recommend a smaller legislative body for the city, submit Proportional Representation to the voters and curb the borough presidents; he charged that Smith and Seabury desired to abolish the borough presidents entirely, a stand which ran in the teeth of borough sentiment. The city's civic front split down the middle on the issue of the Charter commission; at a meeting of twenty-four of the civic and semi-civic groups making up the Civic Conference, the participants voted twelve to twelve on the question of whether to disapprove continuation of the commission and urge the creation of a new one.[8]

Eventually Lehman decided to yield to the demands of Smith and Seabury; a desire to remove Charter reform as an issue in the approaching gubernatorial campaign was undoubtedly a big factor in his mind. With the assent of La Guardia, a bill was presented to the legislature amending the Home Rule Law so that the Mayor could appoint a Charter commission of nine members. Following a special home rule message by the Governor, the legislature in the middle of August unanimously passed the measure. It was expected that the new, smaller commission would prove to be a more cohesive body than the Smith commission, that it would be less given to internal bickering and less open to the charge of politics. By placing responsibility for the creation of a commission on the Mayor, the new law brought the attempt to revise the Charter more in line with the spirit of home rule.[9]

In January, 1935, La Guardia created a Charter Revision Commission with the appointment of nine prominent individuals. They were: Thomas D. Thacher, who was named chairman; Charles Evans Hughes, Jr.; Joseph McGoldrick; Frederick L. Hackenburg, a justice of the Court of Special Sessions who had served seven terms as a member of the Assembly, where he had established a reputation as an authority on Charter matters; Joseph M. Proskauer, noted lawyer, former justice of the Appellate Division, close friend of Al Smith; Thomas I. Parkinson, president of the Equitable Life Assurance Society and the New York State Chamber of Commerce and former dean of the faculty of Columbia Law School; Charles G. Meyer, president of the Cord Meyer Company (which had developed the greater part of Forest Hills, Queens), long a leading real estate figure; S. John Block, former state chairman of the Socialist Party, a man held in such esteem by non-Socialists that his repeated candidacy for judicial office had won the endorsement of the Citizens Union; Mrs. William P. Earle, Jr., executive secretary of the Women's City Club, former chairman of the Brooklyn League of Women Voters, a person who for many years had been active in civic and welfare work. Professor Joseph P. Chamberlain of Columbia, who had undertaken a similar role with the Smith commission, was appointed counsel to the new commission; Laurence A. Tanzer, civic leader and lawyer with long experience as a draftsman of laws pertaining to New York City, was named associate counsel.[10]

For about a year and four months, the Charter Revision Commission studied the problem of Charter reform. It held public hearings, private hearings (where city officials and experts of one sort or another were asked to testify) and executive sessions. As anticipated, it proved to be a more cohesive and harmonious body than the Smith commission. On April 27, 1936, the commission released its preliminary report containing the text of a proposed new Charter. In August, following the holding of public hearings which resulted in some changes in detail in the proposed Charter, the commission filed a copy of the final draft of its document with the City Clerk preparatory to the holding of a referendum on the question of adoption at the time of the fall elections.[11]

The new Charter was to be a short one running to about 40,000 words and simple enough for the average layman to read. The commission, in line with the opinion of all Charter reformers, had early decided to draft a Charter which would contain only fundamentals and to place the mass of laws, after compilation, codification and revision, in an Administrative Code. For the creation of the Administrative Code, the Board of Estimate in 1935 voted a special sum to the commission. Assistant Corporation Counsel Reuben Lazarus was named head of a special staff to undertake the job of revising, simplifying, consolidating and restating all provisions of law affecting the New York City government.[12]

The proposed Charter preserved intact the office of Mayor. The Mayor's already wide powers were not only to be retained, but augmented. The commission rejected a city manager for New York primarily because it felt, as did the proponents of the city-manager plan, that the efficacy of the system depended upon PR (Proportional Representation); and under the statute creating the commission, if the commission decided to recommend PR, the plan had to be submitted to the voters as a separate question; the commission felt it had to make a Charter which would work regardless of PR. To relieve the Mayor of routine duties, the position of Deputy Mayor was to be created and the Mayor given power to name the official. That unique feature of the city's government, the Board of Estimate, was to continue in its old form, and with the same apportionment of votes, as the city's policy-making directorate and the body having general control over city finances. As in the case of the Mayor, the Board would not only keep its old powers but assume new ones, such as those then exercised by the Sinking Fund Commission, an agency slated for abolition.

It was proposed that the much condemned board of sixty-five aldermen be transformed into a smaller City Council with more clearly defined legislative powers. The new body would become the Municipal Assembly with the sole power of initiating local laws, though the Council's legislative power would be limited by a provision requiring most local bills of any consequence to be approved by the Board of Estimate before going to the Mayor for his signature. The Council would retain the power of the Board of Aldermen to make reductions in the expense budget and, like the Board, could override the Mayor's veto of a cut by a vote of three-fourths of its membership. Two alternate ways of electing the councilmen were provided: by Proportional Representation, each borough serving as a district; by the normal plurality system of voting with state senatorial districts lying wholly within the city functioning as the councilmanic districts and with all boroughs, except Manhattan, receiving additional councilmen-at-large until such time as the legislature corrected the inequitable apportionment of senatorial seats that then existed.[13] The Bronx, Queens and Brooklyn were to receive better apportionment in the City Council than they enjoyed in the Board of Aldermen, especially if PR was adopted. (Believing that the voters should have a chance to say whether they wanted to use PR in the election of councilmen, the Charter Revision Commission in May, 1936, notified the Board of Elections that the question of PR would be submitted, along with that of the new Charter, to the electorate in November.)

The question of borough government and the role of the borough president, a point upon which the Smith commission had become impaled, was one of the toughest the Thacher commission had to face. The commission was subjected to pressure from two diametrically opposed sides: from those who wanted the office of borough president completely abolished and its powers conferred on city departments; from those who felt that the existing Charter did not allow sufficient decentralization and that many powers exercised by city departments should be transferred to the borough presidents. After prolonged study, the commission decided that neither position was sound and that the best policy was to steer to a middle course. The commission felt that each borough had an individuality of its own and that, in addition to its representation in the Council, it should continue to be represented by its borough president on the Board of Estimate. Nor would the commission strip the borough president of all his administrative powers, for it found a widespread belief that strictly local improvements paid for largely by assessments on the homes of local property owners should be entrusted to readily accessible local officials; the new Charter would preserve the powers of the borough president with regard to such things as the construction and maintenance of borough streets, bridges and tunnels, except those crossing navigable streams, and local sewers. At the same time, the commission proposed to take from the borough president powers he had over improvements of a more general kind, namely those dealing with public and private buildings, and bestow them on the city government.

If we discount PR, not an integral part of the new Charter, the most striking innovation proposed for the city government was the establishment of a City Planning Commission. The Commission would consist of the Chief Engineer of the Board of Estimate, a civil service employee, and six members appointed by the Mayor for terms of eight years, the terms expiring in such a way that normally only three appointments could be made in a Mayor's four-year term. The Commission would be given tremendous power over major public improvements and a strong voice with respect to financial planning. Its primary functions would be to make a Master Plan for the city, adopt zoning regulations—though the Board of Standards and Appeals would continue to grant dispensations—and prepare capital budgets and capital programs; generally recommendations of the Commission would take effect unless the Board of Estimate disapproved by a three-fourths vote. The Board of Estimate, which had been doing the planning for the city, had at times in the past unwisely added to the city's debt largely because the members of the Board were extremely sensitive to group pressures; the borough presidents, as we suggested earlier, had a say in appropriating funds for physical improvements which they themselves expended. By means of the ancient art of logrolling, the borough members of the Board were able to ingratiate themselves with influential constituents and advance their own political fortunes at the expense of the city as a whole. It was hoped that an independent, nonpolitical City Planning Commission would help eliminate extravagance and waste in the expenditure of capital funds while providing sounder municipal planning.

Despite all the talk of reducing the number of city departments, the Charter Revision Commission did not propose any real reduction; it came to the conclusion that mere increase in the size of a department as a result of the consolidation of functions provided no guarantee of more efficient government. Some old departments would be abolished or modified, however, and some new ones set up. The Department of Public Welfare would be replaced by a Department of Welfare which, under a change in the State Public Welfare Law, would be permitted to administer outdoor relief to the needy. In place of the Department of Plant and Structures, there would be a Department of Public Works, which would consolidate practically all the powers of the Department of Plant and Structures with the duty of the Department of Sanitation to plan and construct sewage disposal plants and that of the borough presidents to construct, maintain and repair many public buildings in their boroughs. Supervision over the planning and construction of private buildings was performed by a Department of Buildings in each of the five boroughs headed by an appointee of the borough president; the task of inspecting tenements after their completion fell, under the Multiple Dwelling Law, to the city's Tenement House Department. To dispel confusion, promote efficiency and impede the development of slums by co-ordinating under one roof supervision of the planning and construction of tenements with later inspection, the new Charter proposed the creation of a Department of Housing and Buildings, which would absorb the work of the five building departments and that of the Tenement House Department. A new Department of Finance headed by a City Treasurer, an appointee of the Mayor, would be created to take over the Comptroller's administrative functions of receiving and disbursing funds; the Comptroller would continue to audit, investigate and criticize the city's financial operations, be sole trustee of all trust funds held by the city and sell city obligations; the office of City Chamberlain would be abolished. The Department of Investigation and Accounts, while retaining broad investigatory powers, would give up the duty of making routine audits to the Comptroller and become simply the Department of Investigation.

The new Charter would institute a number of other innovations. Remembering the bleak days of the early thirties, the commission recommended a strengthening of the requirement for a tax deficiency appropriation in the budget. A gradual pay-as-you-go policy for smaller improvements, whereby each year 2 per cent more of the cost of such improvements would have to be financed from current revenue, was to be set up; the policy had actually been adopted years before, but, according to the Charter Revision Commission, had been "amended to death." The commission, with recent history in mind, proposed that any city official who refused to testify before a bona fide investigating body on the ground that his testimony would tend to incriminate him or who refused to waive immunity should lose his job and be ineligible for election or appointment to any office under the city government. Another provision, indicative of the pro-labor bias of the age, would require every contract granting a franchise for the performance of any public service to contain an agreement by the grantee to recognize the rights of its employees to bargain collectively. One of the most important changes would be a new method of amending the Charter so that the city government might more easily be kept responsive to the needs and wishes of the people; in addition to the existing method of amending the Charter by local laws (some of which had to be submitted to the voters), the new Charter would enable 50,000 qualified electors in the city to propose amendments on important matters by means of petition, such proposals then being submitted to referendums. These were the most important changes recommended by the Charter Revision Commission.[14]

Many people were sorely disappointed with the preliminary report. For all the talk of drastic changes, the Thacher commission had produced a document that entailed but moderate innovations and which seemed closer to the sort of thing the Smith body would have come up with than to the plans of the reform groups; the most radical change that might come out of the Thacher commission was the election of councilmen by PR, and this was not an organic part of the proposed Charter. Seabury attacked the commission for not abolishing the borough presidents and for not creating a strictly unicameral legislature elected by PR; to him the proposed Charter was "a step, although a very short step in the right direction." Smith apparently ignored the Thacher commission's handiwork; when in the fall of 1936 he finally got around to making a comment on it, it was to the effect that on the basis of a cursory examination of the document, some parts seemed desirable, others less so. La Guardia wrote Thacher of his unhappiness. "To say I am disappointed is putting it mildly. I had looked forward to a healthy, robust, normal child. Not even a puny incubator infant has been produced. Just a Caesarean delivery out of the belly of the old Charter, with a bit of unscientific plastic surgery inartistically applied. What a mess!" [15]

Rather quickly, however, those supporters of Charter reform who were dissatisfied with the Thacher commission's Charter came to back it. It seemed, after all, an improvement; and it was either the Thacher commission's Charter or nothing. In the summer of 1936 many civic leaders began to mobilize to get the voters to adopt it in the November election. A Citizens Charter Campaign Committee was set up with Judge Morgan J. O'Brien, former presiding justice of the Appellate Division, as chairman, George H. McCaffrey, research director of the Merchants Association, as vice-chairman and George B. Compton, who had been a member of the Smith commission, as director; the selection of Judge O'Brien, a former Grand Sachem of Tammany, to head the committee was undoubtedly a shrewd maneuver designed to counteract the influence of Democratic leaders with Democratic regulars.[16]

The central task of the pro-Charter forces was to educate the public. Women played a vital part in this work, notably through groups like the League of Women Voters, the Women's City Club and the American Women's Association. After being coached by George McCaffrey in training classes for speakers instituted by the Citizens Charter Campaign Committee, women speakers—by mid-October they numbered fifty—made the rounds of organizations presenting the case for the new Charter. Members of the Charter Revision Commission pitched in to assist their offspring; Thacher, Hughes and Mrs. Earle were especially active in explaining the new Charter to the voters, the last named frequently speaking as many as five times a day toward the end of the campaign, mainly in an effort to reassure the citizens of Brooklyn that the borough had nothing to fear from the new Charter. The pro-Charter people were greatly aided in their efforts by the support of the La Guardia administration, a generally favorable press and the co-operation of radio stations.[17]

Opposition to the new Charter came chiefly from four of the five borough presidents (only Ingersoll backed the new Charter), from various local taxpayer and trade organizations who objected to the new Charter's tendency to reduce the power of the borough presidents, from some labor people who mistakenly saw in the new document a threat to the worker's rights (notably his right to picket), from some groups of civil service employees laboring under an erroneous impression that some of the rights of their members would be endangered. The most important source of opposition was the Democratic organizations. If many reformers felt that the proposed Charter did not go far enough, the machine boys felt that it went entirely too far; they viewed with alarm such features of the new Charter as the substitution of a small Council for the Board of Aldermen (with the consequent loss of political jobs and, in the event of the adoption of PR, a lessening of organization control over nominations and elections), the consolidation of certain governmental functions (which would mean the loss of other jobs), and the penalty for officials who would not testify before investigating bodies.[18]

For quite a while the anti-Charter elements worked covertly. At first they tried to prevent a vote on the issue in the fall of 1936, believing that they could muster more strength at a special election than they could at the time of a presidential election. For this very reason, however, the Charter Revision Commission pushed for a vote on the proposed Charter in November and with success.[19] Next the opponents of the new Charter turned to the courts, and in the name of Edward J. Mooney, a Brooklyn truckman, brought suit contending that the act authorizing the creation of the Thacher commission was unconstitutional; upheld by the Supreme Court, the legal position of the anti-Charter forces was rejected by the Court of Appeals.[20] Not until within two weeks of the election did the forces opposing the new Charter come out into the open; the delay in swinging into action was probably due to overreliance on the Mooney case and the desire of Democratic politicians to insure the election of Democratic candidates for national, state and local offices before turning their attention to the Charter. Toward the end of October, representatives of more than fifty taxpayer organizations and some labor people who were against the new Charter formed the Home Rule League Against Proposed Charter to concentrate their opposition. The Democratic bosses, now confident that Democratic candidates would sweep the city by record pluralities, finally openly announced their hostility to the new Charter and ordered a concerted drive against it.[21] If leaflets that the writer has examined constitute any criterion, the anti-Charter people scraped the bottom of the barrel for arguments and based their campaign upon distortions, misrepresentations and exaggerations.[22]

They worked to no avail. In an age when voters were inclined to say yes to experimentation and innovation, the proponents of Charter reform were selling a "new Charter," something, moreover, that had long been demanded. The proposed Charter appeared to be a definite improvement over the existing one. The Charter reformers had the advantages of an early start, effective organization, important backing and enthusiasm. It was a presidential year. Not least important, because a proposition creating a three-platoon system and a shorter work day in the Fire Department was also on the ballot, firemen canvassed widely, asking voters to vote yes on all propositions so as to avoid making a mistake with respect to the three-platoon system.[23]

Nearly 1,000,000 people voted for the proposed Charter, 600,000 against. The proposition carried every borough except Richmond; its defeat there can be attributed to the fear of Staten Islanders of losing legislative strength in the new City Council and to the conservative reflex of small home owners.[24] In 1937 Reuben Lazarus' completed Administrative Code was enacted at an extraordinary session of the legislature convened for that purpose.[25] Most of the provisions of the new Charter became operative January 1, 1938.

It is not difficult to find fault with the new Charter. For all the agitation over Charter reform, the new structure of the government, as so many reformers had unhappily observed, was not too different from the old. The Board of Estimate has continued to share executive responsibility with the Mayor in many vital matters, a situation that in most administrations has encouraged inaction, inefficiency and buck passing; as important as are the Mayor's powers, he does not in many cases have sufficient authority to perform a job for which the public holds him responsible. By giving the Board of Estimate a prominent voice in the legislative process, the new Charter helped weaken the City Council. A good case can be made that the borough presidents, generally highly responsive to narrow political pressures, still retain too much legislative and administrative power.

Furthermore, a few of the features of the new Charter did not work out as well as had been expected. The pay-as-you-go provision, calling for a gradual transition to a policy of financing some of the city's physical improvements from current revenue, was so gradual and so limited that consultants to the Mayor's Committee on Management Survey reported in 1952 that the pay-as-you-go idea had not yet resulted in any substantial changes in the city's financial policy.[26] While the new Department of Housing and Buildings was an improvement over the previous setup in this field, a division of authority in the Department between the Commissioner on one side and the Deputy Housing Commissioner and five borough superintendents on the other proved unsatisfactory.[27] The position of Deputy Mayor, created to remedy what had been one of the big weaknesses of the government under the old Charter, never achieved the importance that was intended. Because of the pressure of other work on the City Planning Commission, the high turnover of staff in the Office of Master Planning and, most important, the contempt of Robert Moses for any over-all approach to planning, the Commission has never completed a Master Plan for the city.[28]

Yet the Charter reform of the La Guardia period was not unimportant; New York is better because of it. Among other things, the Charter is now short and comprehensible. The Council, whatever its faults, is superior to the Board of Aldermen in quality. Few would deny that the city has enjoyed wiser planning and has suffered less waste because of the presence of the City Planning Commission. The possibility of borough presidents spending funds that they help to appropriate as members of the Board of Estimate has been reduced. It can scarcely be doubted that the creation of the Department of Public Works and the Department of Housing and Buildings has resulted in more efficient government in these areas. Hardly least important, the people themselves now have the power to initiate important changes in the Charter; as we shall see shortly, they have used this power to further improve government in New York.

That many Charter reformers swallowed their disappointment and supported the new Charter so well in 1936 was due, in good part, to the fact that PR had a chance of becoming part of the new setup; no other single innovation proposed for New York City's government evoked as much enthusiasm among civic leaders and civic groups.[29] In PR New York's reform circle saw an excellent device, whose merit had been attested to by the experience of Cincinnati and other cities, for cutting down machine politicians to size and giving the average citizen a bigger say in the government. More specifically, reformers saw in PR a way of ending the complete domination of the city's representative body by the machine—a situation not reflective of the sentiments of the city's electorate—and giving minority parties and independents fair representation and of encouraging men of a higher type than the usual political nonentities to run for office. PR was also regarded as the best way of bringing about a more equitable representation of each borough in the city's representative body, something certainly needed.[30]

In the thirties PR was not a new idea for New York City's government; it had been suggested at least a generation before. The legislative commission which drafted the first Charter for Greater New York in 1896 viewed PR favorably, though it declined to include it in the Charter, holding that under the existing state constitution, it would be too risky to make PR a vital part of the Charter. Subsequent Charter commissions also considered PR and also expressed doubts as to its legality under the state constitution; they urged a constitutional amendment to remove any uncertainty. Interest in PR in the years before the thirties was sporadic, limited and rather academic. With the scandals of the early thirties came a new, more serious, look at this method of voting. Civic organizations, particularly stimulated by the fact that Seabury in his final report to the Hofstadter committee recommended it, took up the question of adopting PR and discussed it freely at their meetings. A number of civic groups formally endorsed PR. Public interest was aroused. It was obvious that any Charter commission would have to consider it again. To the professional politicians, this thought was most distressing, and they did their best to lessen the chances of PR's adoption by requiring, first of the Smith commission and then of the

Thacher commission, that if PR was presented to the voters, it be presented, not as part of the Charter question, but as a separate proposition; the assumption was that the demand for a new Charter was so great that PR, if included, might sneak in, but that if it were submitted separately, the voters would never accept it. The decision of the Thacher commission to give the voters of New York a chance to express themselves on PR in the fall of 1936 brought the movement to a head.[31]

Originally reformers thought of creating a single committee to fight for both the Charter and PR, but for tactical reasons two committees were established. There were conservatives who favored the new Charter but distrusted PR and "borough autonomists" and labor people who wanted PR but were against the new Charter. Furthermore, the members of the Charter Revision Commission, while unanimous on the question of submitting PR to the voters, were divided on the question of its adoption, and to afford the commissioners an opportunity of working as a harmonious unit for the new Charter a separate committee for that matter was desirable. Some of the leading members of the Citizens Charter Campaign Committee were also leaders of the Proportional Representation Campaign Committee, however; and so well were the two groups co-ordinated that for practical campaign purposes they worked as one. Dr. Henry Moskowitz, whose association with labor leaders and independent Democrats was undoubtedly a big reason for his selection, was made chairman of the PR Campaign Committee; Dr. George H. Hallett, Jr., executive secretary of the Citizens Union since 1934 and one of the nation's leading authorities on PR, was named campaign manager.[32]

The PR Campaign Committee waged an aggressive campaign to explain PR to the people and arouse their interest in its adoption. No details were overlooked. The reformers carefully thought out every angle of publicity, even to the creation of cartoons and comic strips. Every cultural, social and civic group that could be discovered was supplied with speakers, many of whom were women. Walter Millard, field secretary of the National Municipal League, did much work in the high schools stimulating discussions of PR among the students, who later talked things over with their parents. PR speakers put down every important fact bearing on audience reaction so that they knew exactly what point to emphasize and where work was needed. A sampling poll was used and progressively checked and analyzed; those on the inside of the PR campaign were actually able to predict the voting results quite accurately. As did the supporters of the new Charter, the pro-PR forces received La Guardia's blessing, much editorial support—most notably from the *Herald Tribune, World-Telegram, Daily News, Daily Mirror,* and *Post*—and generous contributions of time from radio stations.[33]

Perhaps to an even greater extent than was true in the case of the new Charter, the opposition to PR, which came mainly from Democratic politicians and certain conservative individuals,[34] failed to get moving. As did the opponents of the new Charter, those against PR apparently banked much upon a court test which went against them. The political considerations that caused Democratic politicians to delay their attack upon the new Charter also operated in the case of PR. According to George Hallett, the anti-PR forces were overconfident; they simply refused to believe that PR could win. When, apparently only within two weeks of election day, they finally opened a frontal attack, it didn't amount to much.[35]

The anti-PR drive would have had to have been something to have succeeded in 1936. Most of the factors that we previously noted as operating in favor of the adoption of the new Charter also worked to the advantage of PR. Furthermore, PR provided an automatic solution to the problem of the inequitable apportionment of seats in the city's representative body, and voters in Queens, Brooklyn and the Bronx were acutely aware of the unfair advantage enjoyed by Manhattan. The PR proposition carried by an even larger margin than did the one for the Charter, winning, as in the case of the Charter proposition, in every borough but Richmond.[36]

The form of Proportional Representation that New Yorkers had adopted for the election of their councilmen is technically known as the Hare, or single transferable vote, system. This is how it would work in New York: Each of the five boroughs would constitute a big councilmanic district. Candidates would be nominated, not by a primary, but by a petition containing at least 2,000 signatures. While PR ballots would contain no party emblems, they would have party or group designations; candidates would be listed on the ballot alphabetically, the names being rotated by election district to equalize the advantage of first place. A voter would indicate his preference for the candidates by marking the numbers 1, 2, 3, and so forth next to as many names as he chose. Each borough would elect a number of councilmen equal to the number of times the total number of valid votes cast in that borough contained a quota of 75,000 votes, with a remainder as large as 50,000 entitling the borough to an additional seat (the size of the Council thus being dependent upon the size of the vote at each election), and with the proviso, for Richmond's benefit, that every borough would have at least one councilman. The voters' first choices would first be counted—which might give one or two candidates 75,000 votes; each subsequent ballot showing a winning candidate as the first choice would be credited to the second choice marked on it, or, if he were elected, to the next choice indicated and so on. After this first count, the candidate with the lowest vote would be dropped, each ballot for him being transferred to the voter's next choice who could be helped by a vote. A new tabulation would be made and the process repeated until as many candidates as were to be elected received the quota, or until the number of candidates left in the race equaled the number of seats to be filled.[37]

The city's first elections to the new Council which was to meet in January, 1938, were scheduled for the fall of 1937. Recognizing the need of educating the voters as to PR voting, the civic organizations which had done so much to bring about the adoption of the system formed the Proportional Representation Joint Committee in July, 1937, to inform voters in a nonpartisan way about PR. (At the same time, the political clubs of all parties explained the system to their members.) On a more strictly political level, the reform set also worked to bring about the defeat of machine candidates for the Council and the election of anti-machine candidates. Mainly it did this through the Citizens Non-Partisan Committee, a group headed by Seabury and including many of the city's outstanding civic leaders which had been organized in the summer of 1937; formed originally to push for the re-election of La Guardia and a Fusion administration, the new group soon added the election of an anti-machine Council to its agenda. The Citizens Non-Partisan Committee endorsed a slate of thirty-three councilmanic candidates consisting of independents and nominees drawn from all anti-machine elements (with the exception of the Communists)—Republicans, American Laborites, City Fusionists and Socialists—nominated some of them itself and attempted to focus public attention on the lot.[38]

What a slate of candidates! New York had never seen its like in a contest for the Board of Aldermen. Endorsed, among others, by the Citizens Non-Partisan Committee were William Jay Schieffelin; B. Charney Vladeck, general manager of the Jewish *Daily Forward* and specialist in public housing; S. John Block; Mary K. Simkhovich, member of the City Housing Authority; Robert K. Straus, former deputy administrator of the NRA; Edward Corsi, Deputy Commissioner of Welfare and former Immigration Commissioner; Mrs. Earle; Frank S. Hackett, founder and headmaster of the Riverdale Country School in the Bronx. These and the other selections of the Citizens Non-Partisan Committee also received the support of the Citizens Union and La Guardia.[39]

Partly because of the efforts of the reformers, the elections produced a representative body completely new in the experience of New Yorkers. Out of 26 councilmen chosen, 13 were organization Democrats, 2 insurgent Democrats and 11 non-Democrats (5 American Laborites, 3 Republicans, 3 City Fusionists); [40] 4 of the 26 did not have the endorsement of one of the legal political parties. The percentage of seats that each group won was roughly equivalent to the percentage of votes the group received on the final count; the regular Democrats with 47 per cent of the vote got 50 per cent of the seats, the insurgent Democrats with 7 per cent of the vote got 8 per cent of the seats, while the ALP, Republican Party and City Fusion Party with 21, 8.5 and 10.5 per cent of the vote respectively got 19, 11.5 and 11.5 per cent of the seats. (Compare this to the last aldermanic election, for example, when the Democrats with 66 per cent of the vote filled 95 per cent of the seats, and the Republicans with 26 per cent of the vote won a mere 5 per cent of the seats.) The machine's iron control over the city's representative assembly had been broken—though the Democrats, after much trouble, organized the new Council—and representation given to shades of public opinion previously inadequately represented or represented not at all.[41]

The Council was novel for other reasons. Mrs. Earle, B. Charney Vladeck, Robert Straus, Charles Belous, a young lawyer from Queens, and one or two others constituted a finer type of representative than New York had been accustomed to, and, while most of the Council's Democratic members had been members of the Board of Aldermen, they were, by and large, among the more active and capable members of that body. The members of the first City Council, Charles Belous has observed, were as a group better educated (and more representative of occupations in the city) than had been the members of the Board of Aldermen. Very striking, too, was the apportionment of councilmanic seats among the boroughs. On the Board of Aldermen, Manhattan and Brooklyn held 24 seats apiece—though Brooklyn had the larger population—the Bronx had 8, Queens 6 and Richmond 3. With representation now geared to total valid votes in each borough, a more equitable apportionment resulted; Brooklyn received 9 seats to Manhattan's 6, while the Bronx and Queens obtained 5 each and Richmond 1.[42]

Again in the fall of 1939, 1941, 1943 and 1945, the citizens of New York chose their councilmen by means of PR. The size of the Councils varied, ranging from a high of 26 members (third Council) to a low of 17 (fourth Council). While the Democrats always won a majority of the Council, the anti-machine opposition was always well represented. In all but the second Council—and in the second Council if there were one or two Democratic defections—the minority was in a position to prevent the Democratic majority from overriding the Mayor's veto of laws (a two-thirds vote is required to override a veto).[43] The actual composition of the minority underwent some change with time: the City Fusion Party lost representation after the 1942–3 Council; the Communists gained a seat in 1941 with the election of Peter V. Cacchione and another in 1943 when Benjamin Davis, Jr. was elected; and, after it came into being, the Liberal Party won representation. Other women besides Mrs. Earle (who was continually returned to the Council) came to be elected, and the Negro community received representation, first with the election of Reverend Adam Clayton Powell, Jr. in 1941 and then with the election of Davis in 1943. Always the PR elections apparently produced Councils whose make-up reflected with relative accuracy the wishes of the electorate; certainly there was always a close correspondence between the percentage of seats a political group won and the percentage of votes it received on the final count.[44]

That PR accurately transcribed voter sentiment was hotly contested by PR's opponents. Their argument centered around two main charges: that PR failed to give a Fusion Council during the La Guardia regime; especially that it resulted in the over-representation of left-of-center groups, notably the Communists, and especially in the light of Republican representation.[45] Examination and reflection make this criticism of PR appear less sound than it looks at first glance. In Democratic New York, the anti-machine forces could only hope to elect a Fusion Council at the time of the mayoral elections, and in both 1937 and 1941 there were good reasons why they did not do so. Though it is clear from first choices that a small majority of the city's voters would have liked to have given La Guardia a friendly Council in 1937, they failed to make their desire effective. In a race in which there were many anti-machine candidates (carrying a wide variety of labels), the Democrats wisely put up relatively few candidates. Moreover, while regular Democrats kept on voting as long as they saw the party name, independents, with only limited guidance, quickly exhausted their ballots or perhaps in the case of independent Democrats began to vote for Democratic candidates.[46] In 1941, when the mayoral race was much closer and three boroughs elected Democratic presidents, a majority of all first choice councilmanic votes and a greater majority of final votes were cast for the Democratic candidates—a development not too surprising under the circumstances.[47] Nor should it be cause for wonder that liberal groups and the Communists did well in the PR elections and the Republican Party, considering that it is a major party, not so well; in 1945, for example, the American Labor Party, Liberal Party and Communists elected two candidates apiece, the Republicans three. The point that must always be kept in mind is the obvious, but often forgotten, one that PR pays off, not on the basis of a potential vote, as expressed in enrollment figures, for instance, but on the basis of the actual vote cast. What seems to have happened is that, regardless of party enrollment, many New Yorkers inclined toward liberalism and independency gladly welcomed the opportunity to support candidates put forward by minor political groups, including the American Labor and Liberal parties, whom they felt were more capable or more fully representative of their point of view than the candidates of major parties—something, of course, that was their privilege. Not the least significant reason the Republicans did not do as well as they might have, one suspects, is that organization leaders, for the most part, insisted upon running mediocrities, instead of more inspiring candidates of an independent and liberal stamp. That the Communists did well —in 1945 they received 9 per cent of the vote and 9 per cent of the seats—appears to have been due, not to the faulty operation of PR (or to the presence of so many Communists in New York), but to the fact that during an era of good feeling between the United States and Russia many people, indeed almost as an act of patriotism, played down the difference between communism and democracy and that the Communists were astute enough to pick candidates who made a wide appeal to certain minorities in quest of more adequate political representation; for example, Davis, an able Negro educated at Amherst and Harvard Law School, won the support of a good many non-Communists in Harlem during the period of Russo-American friendship as a well-equipped spokesman for the specific needs of the Negro community.[48]

As with the first PR election, subsequent PR contests resulted in a generally fair apportionment of delegates to the Council among the boroughs, though the actual number each borough obtained varied, of course, with the size of the vote.[49] Though through death and political defeat later Councils lost some of the high-grade people the first Council had known, the quality of the Council remained vastly superior to that of the Board of Aldermen; indeed, the calibre of the majority tended to improve with time, as the more incapable Democrats, under the stimulus of competition, were weeded out. After the 1941 elections the invaluable Stanley Isaacs joined the minority; though both he and Mrs. Earle were Republicans, neither obtained organization support until 1943, after they had won office as independents with minor party backing, an accomplishment that would have been impossible without PR.[50]

In certain ways, the PR Council was disappointing. It was charged that the councilmen were at times unruly, indulged in political horseplay and undertook silly excursions into national and international affairs. Critics asserted that, even when allowance was made for the limits placed on its power, the Council compiled what, on the whole, must be accounted a rather undistinguished record of legislation.[51] Much of this criticism was justified.

Yet critics of PR were not quite fair. There was much more about the Council that was valuable, and not all shortcomings were on closer view always shortcomings or were the fault of PR and the minority it allowed. Largely because of the presence of a substantial minority in the Council, the dispirited and perfunctory committee and other meetings of the Board of Aldermen gave way to animated sessions where issues were vigorously thrashed out; matters that would have quietly slipped by the old Board came under public scrutiny as a result of thorough debate. (Much of the unruliness that marked the Council was simply because of the very healthy fact that the minority now had a real voice and voting was no longer cut and dry in the manner of the Board of Aldermen.) While the Council's legislative record left much to be desired, this was not because of PR or the large minority, but because of the Democratic majority; and, as a matter of fact, the minority, through the pressure it could exert, was, in good part, responsible for much of the good legislation that was enacted. (That the Council did not compile a more enviable record of legislation owed much to the fact that, despite the views of the minority, the Democrats, influenced by their acquaintanceship with the Board of Aldermen, insisted upon construing the powers of the Council narrowly and that for most of the period La Guardia was in City Hall; significantly, after O'Dwyer became Mayor, the Council concerned itself more with broad legislation, with the result that the last PR Council from the point of bills enacted was, ironically, the best.[52]) Thus in the first Council, for instance, the aggressive minority, undaunted by the majority's inclination to set its pitch to trivia, introduced bills having a broader social and community significance—bills dealing with such things as consumers' problems, La Guardia's municipal power plant yardstick, public housing, relief and welfare financing, the reform of the firemen's and policemen's pension systems; and, though the minority could not get its bills passed, its active and militant attitude forced the majority, who undoubtedly would not have moved otherwise, into action with compromise measures.[53]

Furthermore, a sizable minority in the Council provided that body with a brake on bad legislation. This was most clearly seen in the first Council when the minority, though unable to bring about real county reform, did op the majority from passing a bill aimed at deflating the popular demand for such reform while keeping patronage intact; in the old days, passage of the bill would have been a foregone conclusion, but now the best Democrats, who could not stomach the plan, joined the anti-machine group, raised it temporarily to a majority and defeated the proposal. Always the fact of a healthy minority worked to keep the majority on its toes and to strengthen the hand of its better element. Certainly not the least important contribution of the PR Council was that it aroused public interest in the doings of the city's representative assembly (and not just in the beginning), something that had been conspicuously absent in the days of the aldermen.[54] Despite its failings and considering its limited powers, the truly democratic and generally able PR Council, with its vigorous minority, proved to be a most worthwhile city representative body—one that was in a much different class than the Board of Aldermen.

Critics of PR also attacked the system on other grounds—notably that it resulted in the overrepresentation of minor political groups, a point we dealt with before, that PR brought too many candidates into the field, that the count was too slow, that the cost of PR was too high, that PR stimulated ethnic and religious voting, that the voters never really learned how to use the system. Unquestionably there were too many candidates in the first PR election—232 in the city, 99 in Brooklyn alone—but friends of the new voting system predicted that as people saw that it was not so easy to win under it there would be fewer candidates, and they were right. The number of candidates successively dropped until there was a total of 65 in 1943—though 96 in 1945—and in the last three PR elections the ratio of candidates to councilmen elected averaged about four to one; [55] possibly the number of candidates was still too large for best results, but this situation did not constitute a fundamental defect of PR and could easily have been remedied by raising the number of signatures required on a nominating petition. The process of counting the PR ballots did take too long in 1937—final results were not known for a month—but there were extenuating circumstances: too many candidates were competing, the Board of Elections adopted a detailed plan for counting the ballots only a day before the elections (there is more than a suspicion that the machine-controlled Board was not just inefficient), canvassers were paid by the day instead of by the job, and some cases of fraud in the counting process in the Bronx delayed the count there for a time. Subsequently, when circumstances were different and the canvassing personnel were experienced, the count took an average of ten and a quarter days, which considering the number of New York voters and the use of paper ballots cannot be viewed as unreasonably long.[56] Closely related as it was to the number of candidates and the speed of the count, the cost of PR elections decreased as PR improved in those respects, falling from roughly $700,000 in 1937 to less than $300,000 for the following contests [57]—not an exorbitant price to pay for a vigorous Council. (Incidentally, the count could have been speeded up greatly and the cost lowered had the Board of Elections, in line with a suggestion of La Guardia, made use of PR voting machines; machines could have given the results in two days at most, and, while they would have increased the cost of elections at the start, in the long run they would have saved the city money by reducing the cost of canvassers and the rental for armories, where the count was conducted. Since the Board was not interested in increasing the attractiveness of PR voting, nor in creating technological unemployment among the "faithful" with regard to canvassing jobs, it is not surprising that it did not show much enthusiasm for this innovation.[58])

The vote transfers of PR ballots showed beyond all doubt that the electorate was influenced by race and religion in its voting. But this was hardly news. The same motives have operated under the traditional method of voting; melting-pot politics and "balanced" tickets were part of the old aldermanic system—as they continued to be in other areas of politics—representation on the basis of religion and nationality simply being taken care of in advance. (Nor is it entirely certain that there is something necessarily improper about such considerations, and no less of an authority than Edward J. Flynn had them in mind when he approved of the fact that "our whole system of government is based upon proportional representation" [59] —though the last thing he intended was a plug for PR.) Furthermore, it is very difficult to determine how much the factor of race or religion counted with the voter when he listed his preference under PR. If a Democratic Italian-American gives D'Angelo his first vote, Messeri his second vote and D'Ambroisia his third—all Democrats—is he mainly influenced by the fact that they are Italians or Democrats? According to Zeller and Bone, who made a study of PR in New York, while the extent of racial or religious voting was something of an unknown quantity and anybody could cite statistics to support his views, observations of transfers yielded much evidence that ethnic and religious factors took second place to party; the first studies, they said, indicated that many politicians had exaggerated the extent of ethnic voting.[60] Certainly it cannot be proven that PR accentuated (or diminished) prejudices and tensions.

That some voters found PR voting too complicated was true. Friends of PR admitted that a larger number of invalid ballots were cast in PR elections than had been anticipated, and the percentage remained higher in New York City than in other cities using the system. According to figures of the Commerce and Industry Association presented in the study by Zeller and Bone, the average percentage of invalid ballots in the five PR elections was over 11 per cent; if blank ballots are counted, the percentage of wasted votes was higher. There were also instances of alphabetical voting. On the other hand, there can be no question that PR accomplished its basic aim of substantially increasing the number of effective votes (in the sense of ballots cast for a winner) and reducing the number of wasted votes (in the sense of ballots cast for a loser) compared to that given by the plurality system. As to alphabetical voting, it should be remembered that the case of the citizen who simply votes according to first or prominent position on the ballot is evident under other systems of voting; under New York's PR system, furthermore, the problem was partly solved by rotation of names on the ballot. Nor, it should be noted, did PR voting, despite the difficulty it presented to some, lead to apathy. The Commerce and Industry Association pointed out that the total number of voters under PR compared very favorably with the total number who had voted for aldermen. Zeller and Bone noted that in some elections the number of ballots marked for councilmen exceeded those cast for borough president or comptroller. On the whole, they declared, the record showed that the voters used PR and were not discouraged from voting for councilmen because of it.[61]

Undoubtedly PR would have worked better in New York had the Council been a different kind of body. In PR cities, the Council usually exercises the most important powers of municipal government, the councilmen are the major local officials elected and the contests in which they are involved are the most exciting in municipal politics. None of this was true of New York, and the consequences were important. For one thing, the civic front, which needed money to do a better job of educating and informing the citizens about PR and of opposing machine candidates, found that funds were not easy to come by. Because of lack of money the Citizens Non-Partisan Committee, which continued to operate in subsequent PR campaigns pretty much as it had in 1937, was not able to nominate (and thereby give its distinct label to) all the candidates it endorsed.[62] And in part for this reason—though the nature of New York politics was also a factor—the Citizens Non-Partisan Committee never became, as did the Cincinnati Charter Committee, the one big opposition to the machine in PR elections. The result was that anti-machine votes were not as effective as they might have been, and Fusion did not do as well as it might have. Also had the Council been a more significant body, the public, no doubt, would have been more inclined to pay attention to the qualifications and voting records of individual councilmen, with a consequent gain for discriminate voting. These points and the shortcomings of the system previously indicated notwithstanding, PR as a device for giving better government did not fail in New York.

Efforts to get rid of PR began even before the first PR elections were held. Probably under the instigation of the Democratic organizations, two additional court actions were instituted in the early part of 1937, one in Manhattan, the other in Brooklyn, with the view of getting the courts to invalidate PR. But on June 2, 1937, the Court of Appeals finally put an end to this line of attack by ruling that nothing in the state constitution made the PR chapter of the New York City Charter unconstitutional. To surmount this difficulty, the Democrats, now joined by the Republican professionals, afraid of PR in upstate cities, successfully worked to get included in the revised state constitution of 1938 an amendment which would outlaw PR in every city in the state. This grand strategy completely failed, however, for in the fall of 1938 the voters of the state rejected the amendment by a ratio of nearly two and a half to one, not a single county out of the sixty-two in the state voting for it.[63]

In 1940 the city's Democratic machines tried again. This time they attempted to repeal PR using the new, popular method of amending the City Charter that the new Charter had provided. Through the president of the Bronx Chamber of Commerce, they filed a repealer petition bearing some 278,000 names. Support and opposition followed much the same lines as in 1936 and 1938. The Citizens Non-Partisan Committee took charge of the defense of PR. Civic organizations, labor groups and units of the Republican and American Labor parties distributed 1,000,000 pro-PR leaflets all over the city. Millard made speeches; six of the nine members of the Charter Revision Commission of 1935–6 issued effective statements on behalf of PR. By a majority of almost 225,000 ballots, New Yorkers voted to retain their system of preferential voting.[64] The supporters of PR hardly finished congratulating themselves when the Democrats came at them again—this time from a new direction. In 1941 the City Council adopted a local law abolishing PR; the law needed the approval of the Board of Estimate and then the voters, however, and it failed to clear the first hurdle.[65] Though continually defeated in their efforts to put an end to PR, the Democratic organizations had demonstrated in no uncertain terms how important such an achievement was to them. It was only a question of time before they would launch another attack.

That time came in 1947. New York's preferential system of voting, of course, had been in disfavor with people other than machine politicians— though the Democratic machines were the greatest opponents of PR and the instigators of action against it—and as the early forties gave way to the late forties an increasing number of citizens came to view it critically. The big reason for this was the election of first one and then two Communist councilmen. While there had not been too much objection to the presence of Communists in the Council during the war-time period of co-operation between the United States and Russia, the advent of the Cold War brought a reversal in the popular attitude. Not that the Communist councilmen, outnumbered as they were, could do any real harm, but many people greatly resented the fact that they held office and that they had an official sounding board for their nonsense. Inevitably popular anger became directed against the system of voting that permitted them to hold office; that two Communists should have been elected to the Council was taken by many as evidence that PR failed to reflect accurately the sentiment of the voters. The Democrats, sensing their opportunity, mobilized themselves for the big push.

They had plenty of help. The leaders of the city's Republican organizations, never happy about the fact that PR had deprived them of control over nominations, resentful of what they considered Republican under-representation on the Council and feeling, probably above all, that they could not permit the Democrats to exploit an anti-Communist issue, threw in their forces; because 1946 had been a Republican year and the city in 1947 was represented in the state senate by twelve Republicans as against thirteen Democrats, many Republicans, confusing the quirk of the moment with the march of history, as many of the politically-minded are often apt to do, felt that their party would gain more representation in the Council under the senatorial district system of elections. The Central Trades and Labor Council (a Democratic appendage), American Legion, Catholic War Veterans, Disabled War Veterans, Veterans of Foreign Wars, New York Board of Trade as well as many local chambers of commerce and property owners and taxpayer groups swelled the anti-PR ranks. To co-ordinate their activities, the anti-PR people created a Citizens Committee to Repeal PR, whose budget, according to its own sworn statement, was financed by the five Democratic organizations. The big circulation newspapers, a number of which had once backed PR, lent their support to the cause of repeal; of especial importance from the point of the independent vote was the editorial position of the respected and influential *Times,* which had never shown enthusiasm for PR and which had begun to view it suspiciously after the first Communist was elected to the Council in 1941. Officially the Catholic Church was neutral on the matter of PR, but as early as 1936 certain Catholic elements had opposed it, feeling it would lead to the election of Communists; and now it was no secret that much of the Catholic community was up in arms against the system.[66]

The most important civic organizations in the city, groups like the Citizens Union, City Club, Women's City Club and League of Women Voters, once again rushed to PR's defense. They were joined, among others, by the Liberal and American Labor parties, Americans for Democratic Action, the American Veterans Committee, the Commerce and Industry Association, the ILGWU and NAACP; the Communist Party, of course, could not be prevented from embracing PR with an unquestionably undesirable and unwanted hug. The PR elements formed a Keep Proportional

Representation Committee with Seabury as honorary chairman and Childs as chairman; the new committee took over the role once played by the Citizens Non-Partisan Committee, which, following a pattern not unusual to organizations of that kind, had risen, flourished and passed away, only to rise again under a new name. By no means did all Republicans line up solidly against PR; the New York Young Republican Club and the Young Women's Republican Club of New York refused to follow the lead of Thomas J. Curran, New York County Republican leader, and other Republicans spoke out in opposition to the party bosses on the issue. Harlem was especially strong for PR, afraid that the end of preferential voting borough-wide and the institution of plurality voting from senatorial districts might put an end to Negro representation. The *Herald Tribune, Post* and *PM* were the most important newspapers in the city to take PR's side.[67]

The 1947 campaign to repeal PR was one of the most dramatic and emotionally-charged campaigns ever waged in New York City over an issue that did not involve the election of candidates to public office. It was marked by scores of vigorous debates and forums held throughout the city under the auspices of local civic, veteran and business organizations, neighborhood rallies, much canvassing and the distribution of tons of literature; reputedly 25,000 copies of a pamphlet, *P.R. Exposed,* was distributed at one Tammany meeting. Against the claims for PR made by its supporters, the anti-PR forces advanced a number of charges, most of which have been suggested in preceding pages. The big point that anti-PR rode home, of course, was that of the Communists in the Council. PR, forced to swim against an emotional torrent let loose by a new mood in international relations, could not do the impossible. On election day it was drowned by almost 350,000 votes, one of the early casualties of the Cold War.[68]

The first elections to the Council under the senatorial district system, the alternate method of selecting councilmen provided by the Charter, took place in 1949. (In 1945 a local law, sponsored by Newbold Morris, had extended the term of councilmen from two to four years.) The Democrats won 24 out of the 25 seats to be voted for, failing only to beat Stanley Isaacs, who ran on the Republican and Liberal lines.[69] Four years later, the second councilmanic election under the senatorial district system produced a Council of 23 Democrats, Isaacs and Robert E. Barnes, a Queens Republican.[70] Harlem kept a representative in the person of Earl Brown, the Democratic, Republican and Liberal parties' nominee against Davis in 1949, but women representatives on the Council declined and then disappeared. Though senatorial districts had been reapportioned in 1943, borough representation was no longer as fair as before; in 1949 Brooklyn elected one councilman for every 88,000 voters, Queens one for every 118,000.[71] The choice of candidates has once more become the monopoly of district leaders (though, unlike aldermanic days, a few leaders, instead of one, now determine the candidates); Mrs. Earle didn't even try to run under the new setup. The calibre of the councilmen in the new Council taken as a whole is still much better than that of the aldermen, but it compares unfavorably with that of the PR Council—and especially if the Communists are excluded. Though the new Council has passed many important measures, it has shown little real initiative; it gives the general impression of being a rubber stamp of the Mayor and the Board of Estimate. The new system of elections has not prevented councilmen from indulging in foolish antics, and it is not clear to what degree the new Council has surpassed the old in the matter of dignified performance.[72] Nothing resembling recent disclosures that a few councilmen have violated conflict-of-interest provisions of the City Charter occurred during PR days.

There is much irony in New York's feat of burning down the barn to kill the rats: not long after repeal no Communist could have been elected in the city under PR or any other system.

To New York's civic leadership, the reform of county government was mandatory. Not only would it permit the elimination of tremendous waste and inefficiency, but the abolition of elective county offices would make for a shorter ballot and more intelligent voting, and the eradication of county political jobs would deal the machine a powerful blow. As with Charter reform, the Fusion victory of 1933 kindled the hope that county reorganization would finally move off dead center. And here, too, the first step away from dead center was taken by the Smith commission of 1934. The commission, as we noted earlier, had been given authority to consider county reform as well as Charter reform; hardly had it begun to function when it struck at the county problem. Smith wrote Lehman advising him to call a special session of the legislature to initiate the process for adopting a constitutional amendment which would make county reform possible. To be adopted, a proposed amendment to the state constitution must be passed twice by two different legislatures and then approved by the voters; the special session would enable the electorate to make its decision two years before it would normally be able to do so. Agreeing with Smith, Lehman called an extra session of the legislature for July, 1934.[73]

The proposed amendment submitted to the special session would authorize the city authorities to abolish all county offices, with the exception of those of judges, district attorneys and county clerks; the last, instead of being elected, would henceforth be appointed by the Appellate Division of the Supreme Court in their respective judicial districts and given the powers of commissioners of jurors and such other powers as local law might prescribe. The state, while effectuating a small amount of county reform directly, would leave the main task of reorganizing county government to the city itself, to be carried out through the Municipal Assembly or an equivalent institution which might replace it. Containing a provision for county home rule and the modernization of county government upstate, the amendment passed the legislature. In 1935 it was re-submitted to the legislature and again passed. In November, the voters approved the amendment by a thumping majority of more than three to one. Now it was up to the city to do something about the sheriffs, registers, public administrators, commissioners of records and, as some thought, commissioners of jurors.[74]

The city proceeded to do nothing. This was hardly surprising, for in 1936 and 1937 both the Board of Estimate and Board of Aldermen were in Democratic hands. In March, 1936, the two bodies set up a joint committee, headed by Alderman Murray Stand, ostensibly to draft legislation for the reform of county government, but actually to see that nothing of the sort was done, or that if legislation was advanced, it would be of a kind that might satisfy popular demand while preserving jobs. The committee first buried six bills proposed by Alderman Newbold Morris which would have given real reform. Then it seemed to lose interest in the county problem. It didn't even bother to hold perfunctory meetings; to questions about meetings of the committee, Stand gave what came to be a classic answer: "In due time." In the summer of 1937, a few months before the big city elections of that year, "due time" arrived. The committee was suddenly galvanized into action and bills presented which, while giving a little reform, would actually have created additions to the machine's patronage list. If the reformers were concerned, there was no cause; nothing happened.[75]

(The best the good government people could do in 1936 and 1937 was to keep the county issue in the public eye, exert as much pressure as possible on the machine boys and reap whatever advantage they could from the situation. La Guardia gave his instructions and in the summer of 1936 Commissioner Blanshard began to issue a series of reports on each county office, pointing out how much money could be saved through reorganization. That the Municipal Assembly, in spite of the county reform amendment, had failed to act on county reorganization was a strong argument advanced by the pro-Charter forces in 1936 for abolishing the Board of Aldermen by adopting the new Charter. Also in that year, Newbold Morris, as candidate for President of the Board of Aldermen, made use of the county reform issue, and in 1937 Fusion did likewise.[76])

With the advent of the PR Council and the new Fusion Board of Estimate in 1938, the proponents of county reform were encouraged to hope that the city would finally act under the 1935 amendment. In January Mrs. Earle sponsored five bills in the Council which followed the lines of the bills introduced in the Board of Aldermen by Morris two years before. The bills would abolish the commissioners of jurors and assign their duties to the county clerks, do away with the public administrators and assign their duties to the Comptroller, substitute one city-wide sheriff for the five county sheriffs and replace the various county registers and commissioners of records with one city-wide register. But the Democrats, in control of the Council, succeeded in bottling up the bills in committee for almost a year. In December, 1938, to bring matters to a head, La Guardia summoned a special session of the Council to act on the Earle bills. To the sheriffs, registers and other county officers, defeat of the bills was especially important because under a section of law which provided for their tenure their jobs would be secure for the balance of their terms should adoption of the bills be prevented in 1938, whereas passage of the bills before December 31 would automatically force them out of office at that time. The Council considered the Earle bills at a memorable session which began at 1:00 P.M. on December 20 and lasted until 8:20 A.M. on December 21. Several times it looked as if the meeting would be interrupted by fistfights. In the end, the Democrats, joined by two machine Republicans, sent the bills down to defeat, 17 to 9. Again the voters' mandate had been ignored.[77]

In 1939 the supporters of county reform tried a new approach. They decided to by-pass the Council and through the petition method of amending the Charter (to which the county offices in question were now subject as a result of the 1935 constitutional amendment), allow the voters to effect county reform themselves. A petition was circulated designed to accomplish the most important reforms sought by the Earle bills; in place of the existing sheriffs and registers, one city-wide sheriff and one city-wide register appointed by the Mayor from the civil service lists would be created. La Guardia, rather than the civic forces, took charge of the petition drive, with results that were not too happy. Running against time, the Mayor sent city employees into action gathering signatures, and this tactic was not only most improper, but unsound; a number of employees, not especially conscientious about their work, resorted to the copying of names and the like with the consequence that when, as was inevitable, the Democrats challenged the petitions, Supreme Court Justice Hofstadter voided them, finding that out of about 68,000 signatures, 20,000 were defective.[78]

The following year the petition movement was revived, but this time the civic groups were in the saddle, and there were no city workers. The Citizens Non-Partisan Committee, headed at the time by Thacher, and also involved, as we will remember, in an effort to stop a movement to repeal PR, spearheaded the county reform drive, which other civic agencies and numerous volunteers also participated in; the staff and facilities of the Citizens Union figured largely in the circulation of the petitions. In September the petitions were filed, whereupon they were again attacked by the Democrats. In the end, the story was the same. In good part because of technical defects in the petitions, the Court of Appeals voted four to three that they lacked a sufficient number of valid signatures to compel a referendum.[79]

Came 1941. Again the reform element began to circulate what had become its perennial petition—and with an eye to avoiding the technical irregularities that had hurt the past movement. The Citizens Non-Partisan Committee again led the way, operating with the staff and facilities of the

Citizens Union. More people than before were pressed into service. Tom Curran sent a letter to Republican workers and members of the Republican County Committee in his own district urging them to help with the campaign; other Manhattan Republicans also helped the cause. Campaign workers gathered a total of 92,000 names, 42,000 above the legal minimum.[80] That the machine could repeat its success of the previous two years considering this total was most unlikely. This time there would be a showdown.

The efforts of the partisans of county reform, as we noted above, had caused the Democrats to make gestures in that direction. The gestures continued after 1937. In early 1939, following the defeat of the Earle bills, Councilman John Cashmore of Brooklyn introduced three county reorganization bills which proposed to abolish the offices of register and commissioner of records, transferring their duties to the county clerks, and to abolish the elective sheriffs, transferring their duties to a marshal in each county appointed by the resident justice of the supreme court. (Cashmore declared that the Democrats would not back bills to abolish the commissioners of jurors because the state constitution already provided for the transfer of their duties to the county clerks, an interpretation that then, or soon after, apparently received the endorsement of all concerned.) [81] The bills, while not as bad as the Democratic bills of 1937, would not only not abolish the bulk of wasteful positions, but would transfer them to the protection of the courts, thereby removing them from control of the city— and increasing the extent of political pressure on the judges; it was Cashmore's proposals that the Council minority with Democratic help was able to defeat.[82] In 1940 the Democratic majority in the Council played a variation on the theme. Claiming to have revised the Earle bills, the Council approved measures which would have simply changed the method of selecting sheriffs and registers from election to appointment by justices of the City Court; this time La Guardia scotched the Democratic effort with a veto.[83] With the reformers again threatening to bring about real reform in 1941, the Democrats reverted to form; however, this time with the handwriting on the wall legible even to the most myopic, the Democratic proposals came closer to true reform than before. Council Majority Leader Joseph T. Sharkey introduced three bills providing for one city-wide elective sheriff in place of the five county sheriffs and the assumption by the county clerks of the work performed by the registers and commissioners of records of New York and Kings counties. All the bills were passed by the Council. One, that abolishing the offices of commissioners of records and transferring their duties to the county clerks, there was no argument about; approved by the Board of Estimate and signed by La Guardia, this measure, which did not require a referendum, dealing as it did with an appointive, and not an elective, office, went into effect as of January 1, 1942.[84] But Sharkey's other two measures, dealing with the sheriffs and registers, conflicted with the county reform petition, which, it will be recalled, called for one city-wide sheriff and one city-wide register appointed by the Mayor from civil service. What shaped up was a fight between half-way reform and full reform.

In this struggle, La Guardia did not endear himself to the city's civic leadership. For whatever the reasons, he was decidedly more tolerant of the Democratic compromise proposals than were the civic leaders: probably he saw in the Democratic bills a sure way of bringing about some important reform with a minimum amount of trouble—in a way, moreover, which would allow him to claim a greater share of the credit for reform than with the petition scheme. In the last days before the county reform petitions were filed, La Guardia tried to convince the reformers to abandon their plan and go along with the Democratic proposals. At one point he won over Seabury and Thacher, but Hallett and Eliot Kaplan, secretary of the Civil Service Reform Association, balked at the idea and talked the other two into holding to the original scheme. To La Guardia's anger, the petitions were filed. When the Sharkey bills dealing with the sheriffs and registers reached his desk he signed them. His argument was that, while the reforms advocated by the petition forces were much to be preferred, the petition might be invalidated again and it would be wise to take the Sharkey bills so that county reform would be assured a place on the ballot.[85] There is something to be said for this view. At the same time, as we have already noted, invalidation was not likely this time, and the presence of a few county reform proposals on the ballot might only serve to confuse the voters.

The city electorate in the fall of 1941 was confronted with three county reform propositions. Proposition No. 1 was the reform asked for in the petition. Proposition No. 2 was the Democratic proposal to abolish the registers and transfer their functions to the county clerks. Proposition No. 3 would abolish the county sheriffs for one city-wide elected sheriff. Under the Charter if all three propositions were to receive an affirmative majority, the one or ones receiving the largest vote would go into effect insofar as there was a conflict. La Guardia, Lehman and Lieutenant Governor Charles Poletti asked the voters to vote for all three so as to avoid confusion. But the reform element and the *New York Times* urged them to vote *Yes, No. No.* In the end, the citizens of New York turned out to be more discriminating than some of their advisers believed them to be; they approved Proposition No. 1 and defeated the other two.[86] For the reformers, who had struggled long and suffered much in this cause, it was a glorious triumph.

The new city-wide civil service Register and Sheriff took office January 1, 1942. Before long these offices exhibited an unmistakable new look. In the new sheriff's office, for example, the new, relatively small, high-grade civil service staff that replaced the old political appointees under the various sheriffs installed many improvements and brought about savings of approximately $1,000,000 as of June 30, 1945. Members of the Bar and other people who dealt with the new office commended it for the quality of its service. And in what must be considered the highest praise accorded the new sheriff's office, a few years after its establishment, Ed Flynn declared that it made for more effective and economical government and was an excellent reform.[87]

The county reform movement did not result in the abolition or reorganization of all of county government. No attempt was ever made to reform the offices of district attorney or county clerk, though a good argument might be made for inaction here. The city's power did not extend to one of the two commissioners of records in Manhattan, the Commissioner of Records of the Surrogate's Court; and in 1938 John J. Knewitz, Bronx Republican leader and Commissioner of Records in that county, shrewdly got the legislature to place his office under the Bronx County Surrogate's Court, where the city could not touch it.[88] The reformers did not push for the elimination of the public administrators; they felt that of all the county offices whose reform the constitutional amendment of 1935 left to the city, these most filled a function and that it was better to concentrate upon the other offices subject to change by the city.[89] Yet the reforms that were introduced—the changes with respect to the commissioners of jurors, sheriffs, registers and half of the commissioners of records—were real and significant. County reform was one of the great accomplishments of the La Guardia period.

Another area of government where structural reforms might have been expected was that of the Magistrates' Courts. In addition to exposing the rotten conditions in those courts under Tammany, Seabury, in the final report of his court investigation, had advanced definite recommendations for improvement, the central ones entailing structural rearrangements. He had advised that the existing Magistrates' Courts, Children's Court and Court of Special Sessions be abolished and their jurisdictions vested in a new Court of Special Sessions whose judges, after the passage of a Constitutional amendment, would be appointed by the judges of the Appellate Division, rather than the Mayor. The object of this proposal was to streamline the courts, eliminate jobs and remove the Magistrates' Courts from machine politics.[90]

But this suggestion of Seabury, as well as a number of his less sweeping ideas for court reform, never came to anything. Under O'Brien, the Children's Court was merged with the Family Court to create a new Court of Domestic Relations, thus removing the possibility of its becoming part of a different kind of merger. In 1934 Seabury and the Bar Association sponsored at Albany a Court Consolidation bill designed to abolish the Magistrates' Courts and Court of Special Sessions and replace them with a new Court of Special Sessions manned by a new and smaller group of judges appointed by the Mayor. (The idea of putting the appointment of magistrates, or their substitutes, in the hands of the Appellate Division never got off the drawing board.) The bill, presented as a measure of the La Guardia administration, passed neither in 1934 nor in subsequent years, however. (Where is the politician willing to cut court jobs?) This was the only scheme involving radical changes in the court system attempted in this period.[91]

In part, perhaps, failure to bring about a reorganization of the courts in question was the result of the extreme stubbornness of the professionals when it came to the courts and, with respect to a change in the method of appointing magistrates, the fact that a constitutional amendment would be required; still county reform had been faced with not too dissimilar obstacles. What seems to have been more important was that there was less unity and determination with regard to court reorganization among those who might be expected to be its friends than was true in the case of other reforms. A committee of the City Club, for instance, took exception to Seabury's ideas on court consolidation and the appointment of magistrates, and the Appellate Division, whose opinion on the matter naturally carried great weight, did not show much enthusiasm for being given the power of appointing judges, mainly afraid, undoubtedly, of being dragged into politics.[92] In truth, the wisdom of giving the Appellate Division the power of appointment as a means of minimizing political appointments was open to question; it could be, and was, the subject of conflicting opinion held by men of good will. In the end, the citizens of New York put their hope for court reform in the kind of magistrates it might be expected a reform Mayor would appoint and in the power he and they had to institute improvements of a less drastic sort. Indeed the very presence of La Guardia was probably a factor which worked against a legislative approach to the court problem.

In counting on La Guardia, the people were not disappointed. La Guardia in 1937 wrote, "Magistrates have been appointed by me without respect to politics and only with respect to honesty, competence and ability." [93] It was an overstatement. La Guardia did not always ignore politics, as in 1945, to take a notable case, when he rewarded some of the candidates on Morris' No Deal Party by appointing them to magistracies; yet to an amazing degree here, as elsewhere, he made merit the chief criterion for his appointments, took his selections from all political faiths, without the aid of clubhouse advice, and generally appointed to the Magistrates' Courts men of a higher calibre than had Tammany. (Occasionally, as part of his concept of "career advancement," La Guardia promoted men in city service with legal training to magistracies—a deputy police commissioner, for example, a fireman, an assistant engineer to the Board of Water Supply —though this was a debatable interpretation of "career advancement" and one that had varied results.) The judicial record of by far the greatest number of La Guardia's magisterial appointees was satisfactory where it was not outstanding. One reason for this is that when La Guardia appointed a judge, the one thing the appointee could invariably count on was that if a politician came into court and asked for a favor and the judge threw him out, City Hall would loudly applaud and, conversely, if the judge did not, La Guardia would roast him. Among other things, this meant that a judge always had a ready answer when someone asked him for a favor; he could blame his lack of generosity upon that man in City Hall.[94]

In other ways, too, the Fusion period witnessed an improvement in the Magistrates' Courts. Aroused by a committee of the Women's City Club, which after a survey of those courts in 1936 criticized the Women's Court, scene of some of the worst abuses in the past, for a lack of dignity, La Guardia had the physical appearance of the court altered into a more informal kind of place resembling the Children's Court. To put an end to "hippodroming tactics by lawyers" and to discourage the morbid listener, the judge's bench was replaced by a long table, and only the people seated around it could hear what was going on. New special Magistrates' Courts were created in an effort to afford the dispensation of better justice and to expedite proceedings. In 1935 an Adolescent Court, organized along informal lines, was opened in Brooklyn for the arraignment of all males between sixteen and eighteen charged with offenses, misdemeanors and felonies; before long another such court was established in Queens. A Wayward Minors' Court, whose name was later changed to the more appealing one of Girls' Term, was set up in 1936 to handle cases involving wayward girls formerly heard in the Women's Court. In line with a recommendation of Seabury, a Felony Court was created in 1936 in the four big boroughs to alleviate confusion and delay in the handling of both felony and minor cases. Chief Magistrate Henry H. Curran set up a Gamblers' Court in 1945 to better cope with bookmaking cases.[95]

In September, 1936, Chief Magistrate Jacob Gould Schurman introduced a uniform schedule of fines in the Traffic Court, another special Magistrates' Court. This action, not only simplified the collection of fines and speeded court procedure, something sought by Seabury, but served to restrict use of the suspended sentence, whose wide employment by magistrates in the days of Tammany had made the Traffic Court a happy hunting ground for the "fixer" and had threatened to undermine the entire system of traffic law enforcement. According to the system inaugurated by Schurman, magistrates could deviate from the schedule of fines if they wished and they could give suspended sentences, but the reason for so deviating had to be endorsed upon the outside of the complaint where all the world could read it. The results were immediate: in 1935 one-third of all convictions in traffic cases ended in suspended sentences; in 1937 sentence was suspended in only 2 per cent of convictions.[96]

To be sure there were areas where the improvement, if any, in the Magistrates' Courts was not too impressive. That the courts were not able to eradicate all bail-bond evils should be obvious from preceding pages. All the same, the Magistrates' Courts, and not only in the respects mentioned above, were transformed into a much improved judiciary under La

Guardia. The low tone that had marked the courts in the days of the Sea-bury inquiry became a thing of the past; the committee of the Women's City Club that had complained of conditions in the Women's Court in 1936 termed the Magistrates' Courts as a whole "businesslike and digni-fied." [97]

This betterment, it must be repeated, was not the consequence of any change in system; the La Guardia generation, which tried to improve other fields of government through structural reforms, relied upon the old setup and a reform Mayor when it came to the courts. It might be argued that despite its obvious shortcomings, this approach is the best one. In any event, the La Guardia generation did not experiment with another.

13

Politics

FOR TWELVE YEARS Reform remained in power, defying what had been an iron law of New York history—that it could not succeed itself. The success of Reform was the success of La Guardia who once elected became, to a degree that had not been true before, the central figure in the Fusion movement; in good part, and certainly in the public mind, he became the Fusion movement. At once symbol and leader, the Mayor elicited from the electorate, as did F.D.R., a political support that was in good part personal. The essential reason for La Guardia's success was the appreciation of the voters for the accomplishments of his administration, and especially for the service and welfare accomplishments. Moreover, La Guardia's administration, unlike that of previous reform administrations, carried no whiff of benevolent class government; partly at least, this was because of the fact that New York's first "new immigrant" Mayor was of common clay himself and instinctively democratic; probably, too, the absence of condescension on the part of Reform owed something to the note of aggressive equalitarianism which, as Eric Goldman has pointed out, set the liberalism of the thirties apart from earlier liberal movements.[1]

La Guardia was also aided by developments that were transforming traditional voting patterns in New York City. Under the stimulus of the Great Depression many people became conscious of politics and government who had rarely given them a thought before. The end of immigration, the political maturing of the "newer immigrants" and their children under the lash of hard times, the supersession of the old system of clubhouse relief by a broad public welfare program loosened the machine's hold on the immigrant blocs. Meanwhile the colleges and universities were raising the educational level of the New York citizenry. Young college graduates, especially second generation American Jews, had an alert interest in public affairs; in '33 they had furnished much of the powder and shot that beat Tammany. The consequence of these developments was a growth of independency in voting which La Guardia both contributed to and profited by.[2]

In a few ethnic and racial groups (the Italians, Jews and Negroes) and in organized labor, large and increasingly politically conscious, La Guardia found the mainstay of his strength; with them the Mayor carried on an unwavering political courtship—and one that assuredly was not free of demagoguery. While the Italians, Jews and Negroes were drawn to the Mayor by his general achievements, especially by his public housing, playgrounds, schools, health centers and other accomplishments of a social nature and by his policy of opening the doors of city service to all groups, they had, in addition, specific reasons for liking him. Though all newer American groups in the city probably got a vicarious satisfaction out of the rise of the "new immigrant" Mayor, the Italians, of course, were especially proud. The Jews were attracted by La Guardia's liberalism, as many of them had been even before he became Mayor, and by his anti-Nazi stand. More disinterested observers might readily criticize the Mayor for precipitating international incidents by refusing to license a German masseur on the grounds that this was reciprocation for alleged mistreatment of American Jews in Germany, and by declaring before the American Jewish Congress that the German Führer was a fanatic who menaced world peace and that he would like to see a figure of him placed in the chamber of horrors at the coming World's Fair. But to the Jewish people caught up in the thirties in a nightmare world, this was the voice of a good friend; to them, La Guardia, as did Roosevelt, became a symbol of anti-fascism.[3]

For the special problems of the Negro La Guardia showed a concern which did not go unappreciated. Bucking an ancient hostility between the police and the population of Harlem, he insisted that he would not tolerate police abuses here any more than in another part of the city, with the result that police treatment of colored citizens improved. He tried to help the Negro in other ways, too; he barred unions denying membership to Negroes from collective bargaining on the IND, protested a DAR ban on Marian Anderson, signed a statement urging employment of more Negroes in defense industries. In 1940, as a result of a nationwide poll conducted by the New York Public Library and the Association for the Study of Negro Life and History, La Guardia was cited, as one of five white persons, for distinguished achievement in the improvement of race relations during 1939; two years later the executive committee of the Harlem Children's Camp Fund presented him with a plaque in recognition of his work for Negro people. It is true that when the Metropolitan Life Insurance Company's Stuyvesant Town project was up for approval by the city in 1943, La Guardia sided with those approving a provision in the contract between the city and the company that would permit discrimination against Negroes; but the issue was complicated, and the very fact that La Guardia took the stand he did was testimony to the good works he had stored up with colored voters and their attitude toward him.[4] As a result of La Guardia's policies and actions, Tammany and the other Democratic machines, which had had most of the ethnic blocs in their hip pockets, found themselves left mainly with the Irish and the Germans, both of whom (and especially the latter) were steadily declining in political importance.

In 1933 La Guardia had received some support from organized labor, but it was not an especially important political factor. The next few years brought a change; labor, grown stronger and politically conscious, quickly became a vital ingredient in the La Guardia formula. It backed La Guardia principally because of his social program and because it would have been difficult for it not to have liked a Mayor who repeatedly cautioned the police against using clubs or pistols in dispersing groups of strikers or unemployed workers, who ordered all government printing to contain a union label, who vetoed an ordinance which would have permitted the city to purchase business machines from Remington Rand, Inc. because several labor organizations had protested that the company's policies were anti-labor, who, arriving on a visit to San Francisco in May, 1937, and finding his favorite hotel surrounded by pickets promptly refused to pass the picket line and declared, "I am entirely in sympathy with the hotel strikers and hope there is a speedy settlement." [5]

The relationship between La Guardia and Roosevelt furnished the Mayor another great political asset. La Guardia regarded the President with a respect and reverence he had for few, if any, other individuals. He saw too, of course, the practical wisdom of allying himself with Roosevelt. Every time F.D.R. ran for re-election, La Guardia vigorously campaigned for him in various cities. In 1936 the Mayor took a leading part in a conference of progressives called to aid Roosevelt during the campaign, and Vice President Garner said afterwards that La Guardia's presence at the conference had been a big help. Four years later La Guardia headed a committee of independent voters for Roosevelt, and, though Tom Corcoran really ran operations, La Guardia worked for F.D.R. night and day seven days a week throughout the campaign (and sent Louis Weintraub to Washington on a leave of absence to help the re-election drive). Though toward the end La Guardia felt somewhat embittered toward Roosevelt, mainly because he thought the President had let him down in the matter of a military appointment during the war, he still stuck by him, and it was La Guardia who planned the famous tour of New York City Roosevelt made in the rain during the campaign of 1944.

For his part, Roosevelt, who was fond of La Guardia and undoubtedly recognized his value to him, favored the Mayor during mayoral campaigns —to the irritation of the Democratic machines—by a stand of benevolent neutrality, when not by open endorsement. Though both men, generally speaking, appealed to the same elements in the electorate—for the same sort of needs and aspirations the President was attempting to satisfy on the national level, La Guardia was trying to meet on the local, and many Roosevelt voters would have voted for La Guardia anyway—the President's approval of La Guardia legitimatized his position with New Deal supporters, especially Democrats; they were able to view the Mayor as the representative of the New Deal in New York City. Furthermore, La Guardia's good standing at the White House aided him in bringing about many of his achievements, which, of course, were not unrelated to his popularity.[6]

Against these elements of La Guardia's political strength must be set off his alienation of many Republicans, in considerable measure an inevitable consequence of some of his political assets. Republicans naturally tended to resent the Mayor's continual support of F.D.R. and the New Deal; the conservative variety found much to criticize in the Mayor's labor record. Furthermore, though the Republican Party had been instrumental in putting La Guardia in office and keeping him there, he never supported a Republican candidate for top state or national office; the closest he came to doing so, according to one political writer, was in 1938 when he privately promised to be Dewey's campaign manager but ended by throwing his weight to Governor Lehman.[7] Again, Republican political leaders were angered by La Guardia's rather niggardly distribution of patronage and his unorthodox method of dispensing it—a point we shall come back to later. Still La Guardia always retained the staunch backing of a core of liberal, high-minded Republicans—people like Tuttle, Thacher and Medalie —who were not without influence in the party. To them the first consideration was always the preservation of the Reform administration, and their political activities on La Guardia's behalf were indispensable to the attainment of this goal.

In early May, 1934, only a few months after taking office, Comptroller Cunningham died. The courts soon ruled that an election to fill the vacancy had to be held in November. The decision threw the city political situation into confusion; a year after its big defeat, Tammany was to be presented with the opportunity of capturing the city's No. 2 public office and three votes on the Board of Estimate. The Democratic leaders designated Frank J. Taylor of Brooklyn, former Commissioner of Public Welfare, to run for the office. The elements that had backed La Guardia the year before rallied around young Joseph D. McGoldrick, an independent Democrat whom the Mayor had appointed to fill Cunningham's place temporarily. Notable among the groups supporting McGoldrick were the Citizens Union, the Knickerbocker Democrats and especially the Republican and City Fusion parties, which provided him with his two most important lines on the ballot.

The real issue in the election was whether or not the Fusion administration was to be given a vote of confidence, but it was complicated by a gubernatorial contest between Governor Lehman and Robert Moses. Democratic chieftains, plainly counting upon a sweep for Lehman to bring Taylor in, did everything possible to tie Taylor's campaign to Lehman's. While in the political circumstances of the time, they enjoyed an edge in the local contest, McGoldrick could not be counted out. He received strong newspaper support. The Central Trades and Labor Council, departing from its practice of endorsing only regular Democratic candidates, backed him because of La Guardia's "100 per cent co-operation," its president, Joseph P. Ryan, stating that he had worked hard for O'Brien, but La Guardia's policies had won him over. La Guardia campaigned for the Fusion candidate, though not so actively as he might have. (The Mayor clearly felt uncomfortable about the contest for, on the one hand, he was expected as a Republican to work for Moses, who, moreover, was a big man in his administration, and for McGoldrick, whom he had made Comptroller and whose election he wanted, while, on the other hand, he had no desire to injure Lehman or the New Deal.) McGoldrick, who entered the Democratic primary against Taylor, made a most impressive showing; right before the election a very large vote was indicated for him in many sections of the city considered strongly Democratic. But though the Fusion candidate made a remarkable race, Lehman brought home the bacon, as the Democratic leaders had figured. While many Democrats split their ticket, not quite enough did so to put McGoldrick over, and Taylor squeezed in with a plurality of less than 14,000. Had it not been for the candidacy of Socialist Harry Laidler, who received over 77,000 votes, McGoldrick would have won. Though it was little to boast about, Tammany had won its first victory against Fusion.[8]

1935 brought another skirmish between the Democrats and Fusion. For the post of District Attorney of Kings County, the Brooklyn Democratic organization renominated Geoghan, whose peculiar administration of the office has already been discussed. To oppose him, the Republican and City Fusion parties once again put up McGoldrick, who also received backing from the Citizens Union and various reformers. McGoldrick conducted a good, courageous fight. He challenged Geoghan to a public debate, which was refused. He charged that Geoghan's office had mishandled the Druckman murder case, declaring that it was only one of a series of shocking cases involving the miscarriage of justice in Kings County; he observed that various vicious criminals, like Abe Reles, Bugsy Goldstein and Pittsburgh Phil Strauss, had repeatedly "beaten the rap" in the county. Behind McGoldrick's charge that Geoghan was incompetent in office and did not destroy crime was the implication that politics and racketeering were linked in Brooklyn. The killing of Dutch Schultz during the campaign focused public attention on the gangster situation and helped McGoldrick.

Off-year elections, however, normally go to the machine, and the Fusion campaign of 1935 for District Attorney in Brooklyn was not as strong as the Fusion campaign for Comptroller a year before. There was, in the first place, little real fusion this time; while the City Fusion Party supported

McGoldrick, he remained pretty much dependent on the Republicans. Nor did the press in 1935 give McGoldrick the intense support it had given him in 1934, when it was caught up in the first flush of approval for the La Guardia administration and the office involved was a city-wide one. Lack of funds hampered the '35 campaign; McGoldrick did it all on $6,800, and there was no money to hire poll watchers or workers to get out the vote on election day. Moreover, La Guardia gave McGoldrick even less help than he did the year before. According to McGoldrick, the Mayor called him in early in the campaign and told him that the President did not want him to be a candidate. A while before, in August, a New Deal foe, Charles R. Risk, had won a special congressional election in Rhode Island which had been interpreted as a defeat for the New Deal, and both La Guardia and F.D.R. were afraid that a Democratic defeat in Brooklyn would be similarly construed. McGoldrick told La Guardia that he was already committed to the race and could not withdraw, and the Mayor responded by giving him no real support in the campaign, though he did come through with a belated endorsement. Geoghan was re-elected by a plurality of almost 150,000 votes. In other contests, too, the machine triumphed; in elections to the Board of Aldermen, thirteen Fusion aldermen were replaced by Democrats and the number of Fusion representatives on the Board reduced to three.[9]

The 1935 elections had hardly passed into history when the Fusion cause suffered a new, and particularly serious, reverse. Toward the end of November, Bernard Deutsch died. Timothy J. Sullivan, vice-chairman of the Board of Aldermen and Tammany leader in the Eighteenth Assembly District, automatically succeeded to the presidency of the Board; and with this development, not only the city's No. 3 public office, but control of the Board of Estimate fell into Tammany's hands. Less than half way through his term of office, fate again had cast La Guardia into the role of a minority fighter.[10]

A special election to fill Deutsch's position for the remainder of his term had to be held in November, 1936. Democratic leaders decided to nominate for the office, not Sullivan, but Sheriff William Brunner of Queens. (According to political observers, two reasons lay behind this move: a desire to assist the Queens machine which, because of internal dissension, was the weakest Democratic organization in the city, and a shrewd attempt by Tammany leaders to strengthen the Hall's bargaining position with respect to the Democratic mayoral candidate in 1937 by giving a lesser position to Queens in 1936.) Republican leaders and La Guardia, the most important voices to be heard in any such selection, got into a squabble over a Fusion candidate. In mid-July 1936, the Republicans, declaring that the Mayor had not responded to a slate of names they had submitted to him and that they had waited long enough, designated Newbold Morris as their nominee. Descended from one of New York's oldest and most distinguished families, Morris, a product of Groton and Yale, had become president of the Republican club in Manhattan's silk-stocking Fifteenth Assembly District in 1933. Becoming one of La Guardia's most enthusiastic admirers, Morris followed the Fusion candidate around during the great campaign of that year, sticking as close to him as Mary's lamb did to her. The experience opened his eyes: he saw parts of the city he had never visited and met new kinds of people; from the Fusion movement he gained a sense of direction which he had previously lacked. When La Guardia became Mayor, Morris was named an assistant corporation counsel and sent to Albany to work under Reuben Lazarus, who was keeping an eye on legislation affecting the city. In 1934, when the veteran Republican Joseph C. Baldwin resigned from the Board of Aldermen to run for the state senate, Morris was elected to his seat on the Board. The Republicans, in naming him their candidate for President of the Board of Aldermen in 1936, were very likely influenced by a feeling that Morris was a man La Guardia could not easily refuse to endorse.

But the Mayor did not want Morris; he retained suspicions of the Republican choice because of his Park Avenue address and the fact that Morris had blocked some of his bills on the Board of Aldermen. La Guardia's choice was A. A. Berle, Jr. Dismissing the Morris candidacy as a setup to let Tammany win and insisting that Republican leaders had told him that Morris could not be elected—accusations the Republicans ridiculed—La Guardia recommended Berle for the consideration of independent groups; the newly formed American Labor Party swung behind the Mayor. What saved the situation was that Berle declined to run. With his choice out, La Guardia eventually came around to Morris. Only the Republicans put Morris' name on the ballot that year; the ALP would not support a Republican (though it supported no one else for the office); while the City Fusion Party endorsed Morris, it failed, for some reason, to place his name on the ballot. From the start, Reform's prospects for success were not bright because of the simultaneous occurrence of the presidential election. How dim its prospects really had been was seen from the election returns; in the year of the great Roosevelt landslide, Morris was snowed under by more than 890,000 votes.[11]

In three successive years machine candidates had beaten representatives of Reform, but especially in 1934 and 1936 there were extenuating circumstances; and, in any case, everyone knew that the real test of Reform's political strength would come in 1937 when La Guardia—no one seriously thought otherwise—would be a candidate for re-election. The start of that year found him in a good position to repulse the machine's bid to recapture City Hall. Already he had compiled an enviable record of achievements and was extremely popular. The city's civic front was with him. The City Fusion Party, one of the two pillars of his political strength in the '33 campaign was enthusiastically behind him; while weaker than before, it was not insignificant, and the possibility existed that it might become more important under the force of circumstance. A new group, the Progressive

City Committee, which had been organized in 1936 as part of the Progressive National Committee Supporting Franklin D. Roosevelt for President, was interested in La Guardia's re-election. Led by Maurice Davidson, who had resigned as chairman of the City Fusion Party in 1934 and as Commissioner of Water Supply, Gas and Electricity in 1936, the Progressive City Committee included among its members such people as Louis S. Lewis, Jesse S. Raphael, Walter M. Weis—members or former members of the City Fusion Party—Richard Welling, Mary Simkhovitch, Samuel H. Ordway, Jr., Mrs. Bernard Deutsch, Dorothy Kenyon, Morris L. Ernst and Bruce Bliven.[12] Also solidly for La Guardia, and more important than either of these groups, was the new American Labor Party.

The ALP had been formed in the summer of 1936 as a medium through which organized labor and many Roosevelt supporters of shades from Socialist through independent liberal Democrat could support Roosevelt's campaign for re-election; while feeling a personal tie to F.D.R. and the New Deal, these elements could not endure Tammany and were not happy with the idea of voting for the President under the Democratic label. According to Warren Moscow, Sidney Hillman, representing the views of New York City's trade union leaders, sold the idea of a new party to the President with help from Mrs. Roosevelt and La Guardia; though Farley and Flynn had qualms about the idea, F.D.R. convinced them, and they helped the ALP get started. Backed by numerous trade unions, mainly CIO, but also AF of L, and composed chiefly of trade union members, the new party was led by union officials, notably by the leaders of the big apparel unions which formed the core of the party— Hillman (Amalgamated Clothing Workers), David Dubinsky (ILGWU) and Alex Rose (Hatters, Cap and Millinery Workers). When the smoke of the 1936 campaign had cleared, it was found that the ALP had given Roosevelt about 239,000 votes in New York City and overnight had become the leading minority party in the state. In the light of these results, it became obvious that the new party was not going to fold up and die because its usefulness to the Democrats was temporarily over. It quickly became clear that the party's next move would be to participate in the New York City mayoral race of 1937 and that the natural candidate for it to support would be La Guardia, close to the garment union leadership and rank and file and a leading spirit in the formation of the party. This, of course, was what Farley and Flynn had feared; and Roosevelt, who, as we have observed, liked the Little Flower and thought him politically useful may have had the development in mind when he overruled them.[13]

Decidedly less happy with the Mayor than these groups was the Republican Party. The organization in Queens was opposed to the Mayor's renomination, that in the Bronx was cold to it, while in the other big boroughs, Manhattan and Brooklyn, the machines were divided on the question.[14] The Republican attitude toward La Guardia presented him with his most serious political problem: while the Mayor might win re-election without the Republican line, it was not likely that he could do so; and the teachings of history, as we might recall, were very explicit on the need to fuse all big anti-Tammany groups, including most certainly the Republican Party, if the reform movement were to be successful. Yet La Guardia's chance of getting the Republican nomination again was by no means all dark; even here certain factors operated in his favor. He was the incumbent. His voting appeal was unquestioned. It was obvious that another candidate would not be acceptable to other groups, and a Republican candidate going it alone could not win. La Guardia might win anyhow as the candidate of the ALP, City Fusion Party, Progressive City Committee and perhaps some other groups; and if he did not, the onus of returning the Democrats to power would fall on the Republican Party. Furthermore, La Guardia had some very influential Republican support.

Not the least influential Republican in La Guardia's corner was Kenneth F. Simpson, who in September, 1935, had replaced Chase Mellen, Jr. as leader of the Manhattan Republican organization. Simpson, with his background of Yale College and Harvard Law School, listing in the Social Register, comfortable law practice and spacious brick home on East 91st Street, gave the appearance of being a political dilettante, but never were appearances so deceiving; the Republican leader was well-grounded in practical politics and beneath the cultured exterior he was as suited to the life as Jimmy Hines. A high-minded man and one who believed it was in the interest of the Republican Party to win, he favored Fusion and recognized the need to re-elect La Guardia; at the same time, he was intent upon driving the best bargain for himself and his organization in any Fusion movement. To further his ends, he executed a brilliant maneuver in the early part of 1937. Knowing that the clubhouse boys were denouncing La Guardia, he did not oppose them, but made the rounds of the clubhouses attacking La Guardia himself in language that the boys wanted to hear; by this means he prevented the development of a serious rival to La Guardia in the Republican Party as well as the crystallization of opposition to his own command around some leader.[15]

The movement to re-elect La Guardia and a Fusion administration got underway in the spring of 1937. Meeting at the Hotel Astor on March 31, the City Fusion Party adopted a resolution praising the La Guardia administration as one of the finest in the city's history and calling upon the Mayor to run again with a ticket composed of men of the quality of those who served on his ticket in 1933. Even before this, the party's leadership had appealed to members (and possibly others) for contributions; and in April, Ben Howe, the party's chairman, renewed the request, warning that only good organization, and not "Hallelujah choruses," could win for good government. About the middle of April, the Progressive City Committee asked the Mayor to run. And about the same time the New York Young Republican Club, after a bitter debate, adopted by a lopsided margin a resolution commending La Guardia's administration and endorsing him for re-election. When at the end of May Simpson gave out a statement which indicated that the Republicans might support a Democrat not too closely identified with Tammany or the New Deal for Mayor, Charles E. Hughes, Jr., Medalie, Thacher, Tuttle and a number of other prominent Republicans organized themselves to fight for La Guardia's renomination on the Republican ticket. In June the group began circulating a round robin urging La Guardia to be a candidate in the party primary. On a sweltering hot day in early July, La Guardia faced about a thousand cheering Republicans on the green sloping lawns of the Chisholm Mansion at College Point, which the Mayor was using as a summer City Hall, and accepted their petition to run. He indicated that he would accept other support as well in his bid for re-election.[16]

Simpson, still playing it cagey, did not immediately jump on the band wagon; he waited until the end of July to show his hand. Then, before La Guardia or Seabury's Citizens Non-Partisan Committee, which had been formed to back the Mayor and help select the rest of the Fusion slate in a manner similar to that of the Burlingham committee of '33,[17] could act on filling in a ticket, Simpson, repeating the Republican stunt of 1936, struck first. He put forward McGoldrick and Morris for the positions of Comptroller and President of the City Council—two good men and ones La Guardia would find it hard not to accept—and announced two lists of candidates, one for Borough President of Manhattan and one for District Attorney of New York County, from which he said the nominees for these positions had to be taken; he let it be known that many of the obstacles in the way of La Guardia's getting the Republican nomination would be removed if he went along.

As in the previous year, La Guardia bitterly resented the attempt to out-maneuver him in the naming of a ticket—it was reported, furthermore, that he again wanted to have Berle in one of the top spots—and he told his intimate advisers that he did not want the Republican nomination now; he would run as a candidate of the ALP with the endorsement of the City Fusion Party and other independent groups. Some of the Mayor's advisers, however, did not regard the Republican nomination so lightly, and, after a few days had elapsed and La Guardia had cooled off, a conference involving the Mayor, Simpson and Seabury was held, following which La Guardia accepted McGoldrick and Morris, as well as Stanley Isaacs, one of Simpson's choices, for Borough President of Manhattan.[18]

Simpson's victory did not insure La Guardia the Republican nomination, however, for though the Republican organization in Manhattan now rallied behind the Mayor, as did the rather unimportant organization in Richmond, important Republican elements remained opposed. Various conservative Republicans denounced the Mayor for catering to labor and for violating the canons of good Republicanism in other ways, most especially by supporting Roosevelt and the New Deal; and the Republican organizations in Queens and the Bronx put forward United States Senator

Royal S. Copeland, a Democrat, but of the anti-New Deal school, as their candidate for the Republican nomination. La Guardia's Republican supporters organized a primary campaign for him, William Chadbourne again serving as campaign manager. Of especial importance in this intraparty battle was the position of the Brooklyn Republican organization. Despite much anti-La Guardia feeling in the organization, for a long time it took no action, a tribute largely to the efforts of Paul Windels, who was very active in Republican politics in Brooklyn and who successfully maneuvered at a crucial county committee meeting to prevent the organization from adopting an anti-La Guardia position. Then a few days before the primary, Republican county leader John Crews, seeing a definite swing to La Guardia, came out for the Mayor, giving him a majority of the city's Republican organizations. La Guardia defeated Copeland, 82,000 votes to 46,000. In addition to the Republican nomination, La Guardia received that of the ALP, the City Fusion Party, and the Progressive Party (the Progressive City Committee in full political dress) where his selection was never in question. (Note, too, that to help La Guardia, the Socialists and Communists for the first time in their histories refrained from presenting candidates for Mayor, thus releasing their members from the obligations of party loyalty and permitting them to vote for the Mayor; the support of the Communists was hardly a blessing, and La Guardia immediately repudiated it.) [19]

Long before the Republican primary, the problem of forging the rest of the Fusion ticket had given Fusion partisans additional headaches. At the end of July the Citizens Non-Partisan Committee advanced a slate which it thought might be acceptable to the various Fusion interests. In addition to backing the Simpson-La Guardia candidates for Comptroller, President of the City Council and Borough President of Manhattan, it recommended William C. Chanler, First Assistant Corporation Counsel, for District Attorney of New York County and Isidore Nagler, vice president of the ILGWU, for Borough President of the Bronx and called for the renomination of Ingersoll, Harvey and Palma. McGoldrick and Isaacs aside, the candidates suggested by the committee dissatisfied one or another Fusion group; still, some progress was made toward harmonizing differences. Though the ALP was not in the beginning enthusiastic about Morris, suspecting that his labor views did not coincide with its own, or Ingersoll, who had voted for Landon and opposed Roosevelt's court plan, it finally endorsed both. Also solved was a conflict that developed between the Citizens Non-Partisan Committee and the Manhattan Republican organization over the nomination for District Attorney of New York County when the latter refused to take Chanler and insisted instead upon the selection of Irving Ben Cooper, whom it claimed had more experience in the field of criminal law. The man both groups actually wanted was special prosecutor Dewey, whose name had appeared on Simpson's list of desirable District Attorney candidates, but Dewey had quickly refused to run. In view of the split over the nomination, however, strong efforts were made to get Dewey to reconsider; according to Windels, while Dewey wanted to run, he was fantastically egotistical and demanded that the Fusion people agree to some ridiculous terms that they were unable to meet. Finally, about a half hour before the deadline for filing nominations, Simpson talked Dewey into taking the Republican nomination; the other Fusion elements also got behind him. His candidacy decidedly strengthened the entire Fusion ticket.[20]

Some differences were never composed. Borough President Harvey of Queens was a right-winger who could generally be counted upon to oppose progressive measures before the Board of Estimate; he was unsympathetic to the cause of labor and antagonistic to the ALP. Nevertheless, La Guardia, for what could only be reasons of sheer political expediency, endorsed Harvey for re-election and tried to bring about a fusion on the Republican candidate. But the ALP, understandably, would not touch Harvey, and, though he eventually received the City Fusion nomination by default, the Queens branch of that party seems to have pulled its weight for the Democratic candidate. In the Bronx the Republican organization of John Knewitz refused to back Nagler, the selection of the ALP, and put up its own candidate. La Guardia, who was for Nagler (who also received support from the Socialist and Progressive parties) charged in the campaign that Republican failure to fuse on Nagler was the result of a Republican-Democratic deal to keep the office of Borough President in Democratic hands, a decidedly likely possibility, for Republican-Democratic co-operation had been an open secret in the Bronx for years. Because Palma had made a deal with Tammany by which his followers supported Senator Copeland for the Democratic nomination for Mayor, apparently in return for Tammany help to the Richmond Borough President (who vainly hoped to win the Democratic as well as the Fusion nomination for that office), the ALP would not give Palma its nomination.[21] Altogether there was less fusion in 1937 than in 1933.

The Democrats also had their troubles in the summer of 1937. For a while there had been talk of getting Robert F. Wagner to run against La Guardia, but the Senator, telling Secretary Ickes that there was no issue between La Guardia and himself and that he would not lend himself to a move to pull Tammany's chestnuts out of the fire, refused to be drawn into the mayoral contest.[22] Finally a split occurred between Tammany and the other four county organizations which could only be resolved in a primary fight. For Mayor the Hall, still at odds with the Roosevelt administration, backed Senator Copeland, whose original sponsor reputedly was Al Smith, now in his anti-New Deal phase. The other four machines, allied with Washington and led by Flynn of the Bronx and Frank V. Kelly of Brooklyn, first designated Grover Whalen as their candidate and then replaced him, after straw votes showed him to be a poor choice, with Jeremiah T. Mahoney, who also received support from a number of Tammany district leaders. Mahoney, himself, was a Tammany district leader —a fact that, in all likelihood, was not unrelated to his selection by Flynn and Kelly—but he was decidedly the more refined sort. Friendly to the New Deal and to labor (Mahoney was state counsel for the AF of L), supposedly appealing to Jewish voters because he had argued against United States participation in the Olympic Games at Berlin two years before, possessed of a pleasant smile and a decisive manner of speaking—Mahoney, a big, impressive human specimen in excellent physical shape, was not without some assets as a candidate. A contest that was largely one between supporters and critics of the Roosevelt administration could have but one outcome in New York City: at the same time that La Guardia beat Copeland in the Republican primary, Mahoney beat him in the Democratic. Mahoney's victory represented a big defeat for Tammany; even were Mahoney to defeat La Guardia, the Hall could look forward only to an unhappy future, one in which it would find itself cut down to county size and brought into the New Deal camp on the same terms as the other county organizations.[23]

The mayoral campaign of 1937 differed in a number of interesting respects from the one of four years before. Now the race was a strictly two-way affair between the Democratic organizations and Fusion, with no third major candidate in the field to complicate the issue as had McKee in 1933. Organized labor now constituted a more significant political element. La Guardia was now the incumbent, and he had a record which could be compared against a definite Tammany record. While in 1933 La Guardia ran as the candidate of Fusion and voters tended to regard their choice as one between Tammany and Reform, in 1937 La Guardia ran as La Guardia with Fusion backing, and voters tended to be for or against *him*. Significantly, though Chadbourne again headed a Fusion Campaign Committee in 1937, both he and the committee were less important than in 1933; La Guardia actually ran his own campaign out of City Hall with the aid of some of his City Hall assistants. Yet, and somewhat ironically, despite his new importance, La Guardia in 1937 had to share star billing on the Fusion ticket with another candidate, something that did not occur in 1933. In the light of contemporary events, the popularity of the Fusion candidate for District Attorney of New York County and a feeling on the part of many that La Guardia's victory was a sure thing, Dewey's campaign attracted a good deal of attention.[24]

For Fusion there was one big issue in the campaign: was the city to retain good government or return to the Tammany spoils system? La Guardia proudly stood on his record. In addition to the traditional methods of campaigning, he adopted a unique technique to drive that record home to the voters. He released to the press, for the "benefit" of the opposition, twenty-nine "lessons" on good municipal government—on some days one "lesson," on other days more than one—dealing with different departments, agencies or areas of government and designed, as La Guardia put it in the first release, to "show clearly that more has been accomplished in more ways during the past four years than in a generation of Tammany before I took office on January 1st, 1934." [25] Most of the big papers in the city—only the Hearst press and the *Sun* were not in La Guardia's corner—helped Fusion keep the good government issue in the public eye.[26]

Unhappily for the Democrats, La Guardia's record *was* impressive. Mahoney kept looking around for something juicy to sink his teeth into but never found it. He criticized the rise in the budget and tax rate, calling the administration extravagant and expensive; charged La Guardia with demoralizing the police by restraining them from doing their duty, presumably a slap at La Guardia's strike policy; declared that the La Guardia administration had placed the sacrosanct five-cent subway fare in jeopardy; called the Mayor a clown and tried his best to tie him to the Communists, an approach he increasingly emphasized as the campaign advanced. Mahoney linked La Guardia and Lenin as stockholders in a Russian-American Industrial Corporation which he declared was a Communist organization, denounced the Mayor for not renouncing Communist endorsement (though the fact, as we noted, was otherwise), called the ALP a Communist group (though he was hard pressed to explain why his own party had accepted ALP aid a year before) and predicted the triumph of Americanism over Communism with his election. To support the Mahoney ticket, a former national commander of the American Legion announced the formation of an Anti-Communist Party with the declared aim of furnishing a vehicle whereby voters might specifically express their opposition to La Guardia's "red coddling" and "by which Republicans who believe in the principles of Abraham Lincoln, war veterans and citizens with respect for law and order may express their opposition to Mayor La Guardia and still remain independent." [27] It was perhaps with the intellectual bankruptcy of the Democrats uppermost in mind that Fusionists joyously sang to the tune of the popular "The Daring Young Man on the Flying Trapeze":

> Oh!
>> We'll get all the votes with the greatest of ease,
>> Mahoney Baloney is nothing but wheeze,
>> The heelers are howling—there's no graft to seize—
>> Good Government's now here to stay! [28]

The main prize over which both sides fought was the labor vote. La Guardia entered the race with a preponderance of labor backing. He had the support of the CIO unions which were affiliated with the ALP and had been endorsed by the State Federation of Labor and by Joseph Ryan, head of the International Longshoremen's Association and the Central Trades and Labor Council, which represented all the AF of L unions in the city; an AF of L committee for the re-election of La Guardia was formed, headed by George Meany and Ryan. Though labor had been predominantly Democratic for years, the Democrats were now in the position of trying to win back a defection: they concentrated upon the AF of L unions, where their only hope of success lay. Rather quickly Democratic efforts were rewarded by the shift of Ryan and his ILA to their side; despite Ryan's stand for McGoldrick in 1934, few really expected Ryan to stick with La Guardia until election day, for his group had long been part of the Tammany machine and some of his men were Tammany captains and workers. A labor committee favoring the Mahoney ticket was organized, and about the same time as the Anti-Communist Party was created, a Trades Union Party was brought into being, under the leadership of an ILA man, for the purpose of dispelling the impression that labor was solidly for La Guardia and providing yet another line for the Mahoney slate.[29] The Democrats also pressed Senator Wagner into service; despite appeals from some labor leaders that Wagner remain neutral in the campaign, the author of "labor's Magna Carta" worked at reminding labor people that the Democratic Party was their tried and true friend.[30]

Neither on the labor front, nor any other, did Mahoney's campaign result in much for him to cheer about. While some AF of L locals joined the ILA in support of him, the bulk of labor stayed with La Guardia. The Communist issue did not click as much as had been expected. Disappointing, too, were indications that the Republican vote for the Democratic mayoral candidate would not be as large as Democratic strategists had hoped and that many Republicans would swallow their dislike of La Guardia and vote for him in spite of his support of Roosevelt. While Farley and Lehman endorsed Mahoney the biggest Democrat of them all, the one in the White House, maintained a position of benevolent neutrality in La Guardia's favor. In the election districts Democratic canvassers reported an alarming trend: men and women who canvassers believed would vote Democratic almost automatically were going to vote for La Guardia because they believed he had been a good Mayor and did not wish to see a return of Tammany—and these Democrats were not of the kind who had deserted to the ALP. Test polls and information from well-informed and important sources indicated the re-election of La Guardia by a minimum plurality of 200,000 votes. It was generally believed he would sweep his city ticket into office; only the borough results seemed doubtful.[31]

The portents had been clearly read. Within three hours after the closing of the polls on election day, New Yorkers knew that La Guardia had broken the jinx that had hexed all previous reform Mayors in the city's history. The Fusion victory was tremendous, greater than the one four years before. La Guardia amassed a plurality of over 450,000, received about 60 per cent of the vote and carried every borough in the city; the Republican line accounted for roughly half of La Guardia's percentage of the vote, the ALP line for 21 per cent. With one exception, the rest of the Fusion city and borough ticket was swept into office, giving the administration 15 out of 16 votes on the Board of Estimate and emphatically putting an end to Tammany's control of that body; in the Bronx, thanks to John Knewitz, Borough President Lyons was re-elected. As previously mentioned, Fusion fell just short of controlling the new City Council. In Manhattan Dewey won a resounding victory which heralded the dawn of a new day in the District Attorney's office there, and both his victory and that of La Guardia in that borough entailed results that were nothing short of amazing. Some of those regarded as the strongest leaders in Tammany, Jimmy Hines for example, lost their districts to Dewey and La Guardia, while others, like Christie Sullivan and Marinelli in the Second Assembly District, managed to carry their districts for the Democratic candidates for District Attorney and Mayor by only the narrowest of margins. As battered as Tammany was in 1933, it was fortunate compared to its state after the 1937 elections. Appropriately, Deputy Police Commissioner Harold Fowler presented La Guardia with the skin of a tiger he had shot in India.[32]

As a result of his re-election, La Guardia became an even greater national figure than before, and he came to be mentioned as a possibility for all sorts of positions in the national government. During the next two years, with Roosevelt's intentions as to a third term anything but clear, La Guardia's name was brought up at different times for possible presidential or vice-presidential nomination, usually, but not always, in reference to a third party ticket. Indeed talk of this nature had begun even before his re-election, William Allen White in July, 1937, suggesting La Guardia as the Republican presidential candidate in 1940. When *Fortune* in 1939 conducted a poll to determine whom the voters wanted to see as the Republican standard bearer in 1940 (the poll was not limited to Republicans), La Guardia tied with Senator Arthur Vandenberg for second place behind Dewey. That the idea of running for President at least crossed La Guardia's mind is evident from a conversation Ickes reported he had with the Mayor at the end of 1938. La Guardia asked the Secretary if he thought he, La Guardia, could be nominated for President—by which party is not clear—and Ickes answered he did not think so. Whatever La Guardia's aspirations, in mid-May, 1940, before Roosevelt's decision as to a third term, La Guardia told 16,000 wildly cheering clothing workers that he would vote for F.D.R. if the President ran again—though possibly he had himself in mind as the presidential nominee of a third party, which he warned the Republican and Democratic parties would be formed should they both nominate "political palookas" for President. Apparently the Mayor was more serious about a vice presidential nomination; about two weeks before his speech to the clothing workers, he was reported to have lent tacit encouragement to a drive to obtain such a berth for himself on the ticket of either major party, indicating to close associates his belief that he would make a strong vice presidential candidate and that his independence of party lines left him free to join either side. As events turned out, the only role La Guardia played in the 1940 political scene was as one of Roosevelt's active supporters.[33]

La Guardia was also mentioned in the press in the 1940–41 period in connection with other high offices—various cabinet positions, a special mission to Latin America, the ambassadorship to Britain. (La Guardia effectively squashed the rumor as to the last by declaring that knee pants would not be flattering to his figure.) Apparently the nearest the Mayor came to a job of this level was when Roosevelt, at the end of 1940, indicated he would appoint La Guardia an executive assistant to the President, to serve as a liaison between the Chief Executive and a new defense setup. But, according to Ickes, when the President suggested this to the Stimson-Knox-Knudsen-Hillman defense group, he met with almost unanimous opposition and dropped the idea; the group felt that La Guardia would not work with the team, but would run all over the field with the ball. The Mayor did get two federal jobs. In the summer of 1940 he was appointed chairman of the American section of the Joint Permanent Defense Board, an agency set up to co-ordinate defense between the United States and Canada. In May, 1941, F.D.R. named him director of the new Office of Civilian Defense. Neither was the kind of position to force or induce La Guardia to give up City Hall. In the spring of 1941, with another mayoral campaign imminent, it was generally supposed that La Guardia would try to remain as Mayor.[34]

The political situation at the time—both similar to and different from the one four years before—contained elements both favorable and unfavorable to La Guardia's chances. At first glance it might seem that the odds were against the Mayor. The City Fusion Party, though it could still be counted upon, had progressively declined as a political force; it was now little more than a line on the ballot. Though the Progressive Party had been designed, according to Davidson, to be "a permanent body with a continuing educational program, in addition to having an immediate political function to discharge," it petered out soon after contributing about 28,000 votes to La Guardia's re-election. The Republican position with respect to the Mayor was again decidedly unclear; the Mayor's action in backing Roosevelt in 1940 had hardly enhanced his appeal to party members. The ALP was still important politically, but it was rent by serious internal disorders. In 1936 the Communist Party, by failing to poll 50,000 votes in the gubernatorial election, lost its official status as a party in the state at the same time as the ALP became a legal party. The ALP setup was just right for a militant group like the Communists and, instead of trying to regain their official status, the Communists enrolled in the new party *en masse,* giving it their great energy and fanaticism; by 1938 they controlled the ALP machinery in Manhattan. Though the non-Communist element of the ALP, which dominated the state organization and the other county organizations, could be counted upon to support La Guardia, the party's Communist clique in the spring of 1941 was as hostile to the "pro-war" Mayor as it was to the "pro-war" President; it was grooming Marcantonio to run against La Guardia.[35]

La Guardia, however, was in a stronger position than these facts indicate. His popularity was still high; his record in office after almost eight years was more impressive than ever. The threatening international situation worked in favor of another term. The Republican nomination was by no means beyond La Guardia's reach—and for the same reasons as in 1937. The big leaders of the ALP and most of the party's rank and file were, after all, on La Guardia's side. It was even reported that the President was trying to get him the Democratic nomination, though Democratic Party chieftains gave indications of not being happy with this idea.[36]

In March and April a third-term movement was launched by some of the Mayor's supporters. Percival E. Jackson, a Williams Street lawyer, organized a Citizens Non-Partisan Movement to Draft La Guardia for Mayor containing a number of prominent people, such as Marshall Field, Fannie Hurst, Bennett Cerf, Irving Berlin, Quincy Howe, Arthur Garfield Hays and Dorothy Kenyon; the committee circulated petitions exhorting the Mayor to run again. About the same time the City Fusion Party and the Citizens Union endorsed La Guardia for a third term. The Mayor took his time. In mid-June, the ALP's state executive committee urged La Guardia to run, and soon afterwards the German invasion of Russia brought the ALP left-wing to view the Mayor in a more friendly light; any question mark as to ALP support disappeared. Finally on July 21, after the Seabury-Thacher Citizens Non-Partisan Committee had endorsed La Guardia, McGoldrick and Morris for re-election and had begun working to obtain a Fusion nomination for them, La Guardia in a radio address declared his intention of seeking a third term. The possibility that he might get the Democratic nomination had disintegrated earlier when Flynn and other party leaders put down their collective foot (a development that friends of good government could well be happy about). What appeared likely was another alliance between the Republican Party and the ALP with the City Fusion Party, and perhaps some other group, giving Fusion additional support on the ballot.[37]

As before, however, the Republicans could not easily be counted in. With La Guardia's announcement, a struggle between La Guardia and anti-La Guardia Republicans, which had been going on behind the scenes, broke into the open. The Republican organizations again took sides; that in Manhattan, now led by Tom Curran, and those in Richmond and, this time, Brooklyn backed the Mayor, while the Republican machines in Queens and the Bronx withheld backing and finally rallied around John R. Davies, an extremely conservative Republican, who announced his intention of contesting La Guardia's nomination in the party primary. Davies, who had three times been president of the National Republican Club, was, in the opinion of the *New York Times,* an able man who knew what he wanted: to re-build the Republican Party on a conservative and old-fashioned basis. To Davies, La Guardia's main sins were his opposition to Republican state and national candidates and his interventionist attitude on foreign policy; Davies termed his candidacy a referendum on Roosevelt's foreign policy.[38]

Once again La Guardia's Republican supporters had their work cut out for them. Chadbourne was again conscripted as campaign manager. La Guardia headquarters were opened in all boroughs, county chairmen for the campaign were named and special committees of one sort or another set up. Nicholas Murray Butler, Medalie and Tuttle issued a statement in La Guardia's behalf stating that the issues of the campaign were good government and Tammany's defeat, not Roosevelt's foreign policies; and Dewey, Moses and Wendell Willkie declared for the Mayor. It was expected that La Guardia would win. He did, but his plurality of 20,000 over Davies was not as large as his plurality over Copeland in 1937; Republican professionals were credited with being in good part responsible for Davies' comparatively large vote.[39]

Before the primary, the rest of the Fusion slate had been hammered out by the various Fusion elements, the Citizens Non-Partisan Committee having helped the process in the manner of its performance of 1937. McGoldrick and Morris were renominated without trouble. For the spot of Borough President of Brooklyn, Fusion needed a new candidate, for Ingersoll had died in February, 1940. To run against Democratic candidate John Cashmore, who had been elected by the Brooklyn members of the City Council to fill Ingersoll's place in accordance with a provision of the City Charter, Brooklyn Republicans put up Justice Matthew J. Troy; this selection was endorsed by the ALP. The selection of a candidate for Borough President of Manhattan created difficulties of a special kind for Fusion. Though it was generally conceded that Stanley Isaacs had been a fine Borough President, he had made one mistake which caused an uproar and threatened to embarrass Fusion should he remain on the ticket: he had appointed Simon W. Gerson, an avowed Communist, to a confidential job. Fusion leaders decided that Isaacs would have to go and after much difficulty replaced him with Edgar J. Nathan, a member of the law firm of Cardozo and Nathan (once headed by the late Supreme Court Justice), a man active for many years in Republican politics and Jewish philanthropic and religious groups and a personal friend of Isaacs. Dewey decided he would not seek another term as District Attorney—most observers believed that the final factor which made up his mind was the uncertainty of his getting the ALP nomination from the left-wingers of the party who controlled the Manhattan organization—and when Tammany picked as its candidate Frank S. Hogan, one of Dewey's aides and a good man, Republican and ALP leaders endorsed the choice. Hogan was elected unopposed in November.[40]

In the Bronx and Queens, complete fusion on the top positions could not be attained. Knewitz again insisted upon running his own candidate against Lyons; the ALP nominated former Municipal Court Justice Matthew M. Levy. In Queens the ALP again refused to endorse Harvey, who this time, and apparently rather easily, received City Fusion support, though the Laborites now went along with Palma on Staten Island. (The Socialists and Communists this time put up candidates for Mayor, though the latter later withdrew their selection to aid La Guardia.) [41]

For their part, Democratic leaders, having resisted New Deal pressure for an endorsement of La Guardia, selected—and this time without an intraparty fight—O'Dwyer of Brooklyn to be the Democratic nominee for Mayor. O'Dwyer's rise provided another chapter in the voluminous immigrant success story. Arriving in America in 1910 at the age of twenty with only $25.35 in his pocket, this son of Erin had, within a generation, made the climb to county judge and district attorney via the rungs of hod carrier, clerk, plasterer, bartender, policeman, lawyer and magistrate. He was the logical choice for the Democrats in 1941. As District Attorney, O'Dwyer had made a national reputation as the man who broke up Murder, Inc. Having shown sympathy for the cause of the working man while on the bench, O'Dwyer was known as a friend of labor. Besides, he did not carry the burden of a Tammany label; he owed allegiance to the Kelly machine in Brooklyn. In 1941 the feeling was that he was a man of integrity and ability who had not allowed machine ties to interfere with efficient public service. [42]

Ostensibly the Fusion campaign of '41 was more disorganized than the two previous Fusion campaigns. No Fusion Campaign Committee existed as before, and the number of groups of one sort or another backing the Mayor seems to have been greater. In addition to the Republican, American Labor, City Fusion and United City parties which supplied Fusion with lines on the ballot (the United City Party was a campaign concoction of Berle, Henry Morgenthau, Sr. and the Affiliated Young Democrats to garner more New Deal votes for La Guardia by providing a replacement for the Progressive Party of four years before), the Fusion cause was backed by such groups as the Citizens Committee for the Re-election of Mayor La Guardia, Controller Joseph D. McGoldrick and Newbold Morris, President of the City Council, a letterhead and fund raising committee headed by Frank L. Polk, noted lawyer and former Corporation Counsel under Mitchel; the Independent Citizens Committee to Re-elect Mayor La Guardia, the new title of the Percival Jackson group; the All-American Committee for La Guardia, a committee representing nineteen foreign language groups headed by Edward Corsi; and the Citizens Non-Partisan Committee. Actually the campaign was, if anything, better organized than before, for as in '37 La Guardia really ran his own show and did his own co-ordination from City Hall with the help of his City Hall assistants, and he now had more experience doing it. [43]

In general, until the very end, the Fusion-Democratic battle of '41 was quite similar to the one four years earlier. Against La Guardia's record, spotlighted in different ways—which included a new set of "lessons" on good government, a comic book, a magazine resembling *Life* and another on the order of the *Reader's Digest,* all products of the busy City Hall group—the Democrats could do little. They tried a few maneuvers with but limited results. With some justification they accused La Guardia of being a part-time Mayor because of his defense duties. With no justification they again made the Communist Menace a central theme in their campaign and charged La Guardia with having sought Communist support, though the Mayor had promptly disavowed such support in no uncertain terms. O'Dwyer did his best to paint himself as an independent and New Deal kind of Democrat; he backed Roosevelt's defense program and foreign policies and promised to protect trade unions. The image of O'Dwyer, the New Dealer, was not especially effective, however. If one wanted a New Dealer, there was La Guardia, one of the originals. Anti-Roosevelt elements, having nowhere else to go, tended to move over to O'Dwyer's camp. Though Wagner and Lehman backed the Democratic ticket, the President, despite the attempts of Democratic leaders to dissuade him, this time openly endorsed La Guardia, and in unqualified terms; the Mayor and his associates, F.D.R. said, had given New York City the most honest and efficient municipal government of any within his recollection. As in 1937, labor, AF of L and CIO, generally sided with the Mayor.[44]

The campaign, unlike that of '37 and '33, was dull, and a mood of apathy engulfed the voters; registration was off about 34,000 from 1937 —a development that caused La Guardia's backers some concern. With the existing situation abroad, a municipal election hardly seemed like the most important thing in the world. (While beneath the surface of the campaign the isolationist-interventionist controversy agitated many voters, the issue found no expression in the campaign because both mayoral candidates endorsed the President's policies.) Probably more responsible for voter apathy was the feeling of many that La Guardia would be, more or less, automatically re-elected; though he was expected to be weaker than in 1937, it was felt that he would still win without too much trouble.[45]

One of those optimistic about La Guardia's chances was La Guardia, and it almost cost him the election. Usually during campaigns La Guardia had spells of pessimism in which he felt he wouldn't win, but in 1941 he exuded complete confidence. About a week before election day, he startled a campaign committee meeting by announcing: "Boys, we are going to win." That night he committed the great political *faux pas* of the campaign and almost became the chief figure in a Greek tragedy. The Court of Appeals, presided over by Chief Judge Irving Lehman, the Governor's brother, had ruled late in the campaign that a special election for State Comptroller which had been anticipated would not be held. La Guardia intensely disliked Governor Lehman—possibly because, while the Mayor in one form or another showed friendship to Lehman in his gubernatorial races, the Governor, unlike F.D.R., always endorsed the Democratic mayoral candidate against La Guardia—and now full of cockiness, La Guardia used this court decision as a jumping off point for a vehement attack on the Governor in which he gave a good demonstration of his unbridled tongue. Immediately La Guardia lost support from many who would normally support both men.

To the Democrats, in a state of political somnambulism, La Guardia's attack was a godsend. They came alive and hammered away at the theme that La Guardia's remarks showed how unworthy he was to be Mayor and that the public should rebuke him for his utterances where it hurt—at the voting machine. Frightened at the commotion he had caused, La Guardia's friends tried to get him to apologize or do something that would stop the criticism; Seabury, Burlingham, Windels and others begged him to take such action, but the more he was criticized the angrier he got. Finally he made a speech in which he said that he didn't call Lehman the names it had been said he called him—the choice epithets were references to political bosses. This was the nearest he would come to an apology.[46]

It turned out to be the closest New York City mayoral election since 1909. La Guardia's plurality was 132,000 votes; he received about 53 per cent of the vote—down 7 percentage points from 1937—the Republican and ALP lines contributing approximately the same percentage of his vote as in 1937. Elsewhere the Democrats also did better than four years earlier. Though Fusion retained control of the Board of Estimate, its vote there was reduced to twelve. Nathan and Palma were elected in addition to McGoldrick and Morris, but the other victorious borough presidential candidates were Democrats; Lyons was again re-elected as a result of Knewitz' repeat performance, Cashmore squeezed past Troy and Councilman James A. Burke finally put an end to the thirteen-year-old career of the controversial George Harvey. The Democrats won a comfortable majority of the seats in the Council.[47]

There can be no doubt that La Guardia's attack on Lehman was mainly responsible for his loss of strength from 1937. Significantly, as James A. Hagerty of the *Times* observed after the election, McGoldrick's plurality over his Democratic opponent was almost 21,000 votes greater than La Guardia's plurality over O'Dwyer.[48] McGoldrick believes that La Guardia easily lost a quarter of a million votes by his remarks and that he could have lost the election had they been made earlier in the campaign.[49]

No discussion of politics in the days of La Guardia would be complete without saying a few words about two other aspects of the political life of the time. One involves the honesty of elections. It will be recalled that while election frauds had decreased in the years immediately preceding La Guardia's election in comparison to what had been in the late nineteenth century and early years of the twentieth, they still figured, and not without consequence, in city politics. 1933 certainly showed that! With La Guardia's occupancy of City Hall, a significant change took place. The change was first noticeable in the 1934 election. Despite an enormous turnout of voters, no mass disturbance at the polls or incidents of hooliganism were reported. In spite of a bitter campaign and widespread belief that thuggery would keep policemen busy at the polls, the 1937 election was the cleanest and most orderly in the city's history up to that time; in the crowded tenement streets, one found no suggestion of intimidation of voters, and even in the Second Assembly District, where skull thumping was noted four years before, there was perfect peace. If anything, the 1941 election was marked by even more quiet; only three arrests took place at the polls, a new low record. All election dishonesty did not disappear in the La Guardia period; some registration irregularities usually cropped up during a campaign. But most dishonesty, and certainly that involving force or intimidation, disappeared. (With truth La Guardia could declare in 1945: "I promised in 1934 that we'd have quiet, orderly elections and that the children could roll their hoops outside the polling places. We've made good and there are no ambulances picking up the injured as there used to be.") There are those who believe that this achievement was Mayor La Guardia's greatest one.

The change from not unexpected violence, disorder and fraud did not come about because of the moral regeneration of politicians or the evaporation of the gorillas. It came about because of one essential development: La Guardia's election gave him control of the police force, and both he and Valentine insisted that the police do their job. Under this pressure and undoubtedly encouraged by an honest merit system, the police did remarkable work. In 1937, for example, hand-picked policing at possible trouble spots, with high ranking police officials actually touring their bailiwicks every minute the polls were open, made the difference. In 1937 and 1941 no campaign group did the work the Fusioneers did in 1933. There was no need for it.[50]

The second aspect has to do with the matter of nonpartisan and nonpolitical government. Speaking for the newsreels right after his inauguration at Seabury's home, La Guardia said, "I have just assumed the office of the Mayor of the City of New York. The Fusion administration is now in charge of our city. Our theory of municipal government is an experiment to try to show that a nonpartisan, nonpolitical local government is possible. . . ." [51] Throughout his administration La Guardia boasted that he had given the city such a government. How accurate was he?

"There is no Democratic or Republican way of cleaning the streets," La Guardia said,[52] and he meant not only cleaning the streets, but carrying on municipal government in general. He appointed Democrats, Republicans, American Laborites, City Fusionists and independents to office. If by nonpartisan government, La Guardia meant, as it seems, government not run by a political party and in which officials are chosen from all parties and none, he was certainly right about giving the city nonpartisan government. By nonpolitical government, La Guardia apparently meant, broadly speaking, government which operates in the public interest, in which that interest is not sacrificed to narrow political considerations. It should be clear from our previous discussion that La Guardia did generally, and in various ways, live up to this ideal. It should also be clear—and aside from some cases that might be debated—that at times La Guardia sacrificed the public for politics; his actions with respect to McGoldrick's candidacy for District Attorney in 1935 is a case in point. By nonpolitical government La Guardia, more narrowly, certainly had in mind the absence of political appointments, patronage and political activity on the part of city job-holders. This subject requires a brief word.

As we have already seen, La Guardia to an unusual degree placed merit before politics in making appointments; we have seen too how he made a real merit system out of civil service. At the same time one should under-stand that La Guardia's merit appointments not infrequently entailed politi-cal considerations, and it would be naive to think that he never made appointments in which politics figured as the major factor (though even here, it should be noted, the appointments do not generally seem to have worked against the public interest). With respect to top spots, it is difficult, for instance, not to term political the appointments of Frederick J. H. Kracke, the Republican leader of Brooklyn, as head of the Department of Plant and Structures, and of O'Ryan, who had stepped aside for La Guardia in the matter of the mayoral nomination. Where politics was an important factor in an appointment, the job concerned was usually not a top-flight one, however. La Guardia sometimes appointed Republican political figures to the courts and to small political jobs; Philip Sokol, now Deputy Commissioner and Counsel of the Department of Welfare, stated that he first got into welfare work through Republican politics and Edward Corsi—who, himself, became Deputy Commissioner of Welfare. After it came along, La Guardia gave the ALP some "recognition." Like Mayors before him, La Guardia, it might be mentioned, continued to pay off small political creditors by appointing them corporation inspectors. Appointed by the city, but paid for by the utility companies, the corporation inspec-tors, who are supposed to (but rarely do) inspect utility-made holes in the street are widely felt to constitute a group of choice political parasites.[53]

(In dispensing patronage, La Guardia, it should be pointed out, adopted a very interesting policy: he tended to by-pass the party leadership and deal instead with the elements in the party that were in opposition to it. In 1934 when Mellen was Republican leader in Manhattan, La Guardia wouldn't give him the time of day, but in 1937, after Mellen had been kicked out of the leadership because he hadn't been able to deliver jobs to the faithful, La Guardia refused to deal with Simpson and dealt with Mellen; he made him Deputy City Treasurer and put some patronage in his hands. This sort of thing La Guardia did in other boroughs and with the ALP, too; patronage went not to the Rose-Dubinsky leadership, but to the group headed by Marcantonio, whom the Mayor, moreover, was per-sonally fond of.[54] Presumably La Guardia felt that if any patronage were to be given by the Mayor, it should be given to prevent the organizations from becoming too strong (fearing, perhaps, that stronger political organizations would endanger him) and to build up followers more directly beholden to him. Republican leaders continually complained that La Guardia was stingy with patronage. He was, but what annoyed them even more was his way of handing it out.)

As for political activity on the part of officeholders, La Guardia had a standard policy that city employees—civil service or any other—must take no part in such activity. He ordered city officials to resign any post they might have in political organizations; accordingly, Commissioner of Plant and Structures Kracke resigned as head of the Brooklyn Republican organization and Davidson gave up the chairmanship of the City Fusion Party.[55] But it would be foolish to think that under La Guardia city employees never engaged in political activity. We saw earlier, for example, how the Mayor, himself, put city employees to work in 1939 gathering signatures for a county reform petition. When La Guardia's re-election campaigns rolled around, Fusion officials did not always act "nonpolitically"; in 1937, for instance, Corporation Counsel Windels, as we observed, maneuvered for La Guardia in Brooklyn, Deputy Commissioner Corsi boosted the Mayor at a City Fusion Party rally and Chamberlain Berle did the same thing at a Progressive City Committee luncheon.[56] During his career in the city service, Louis Weintraub, though officially in the Department of Investigation or the Law Department, wrote political speeches for the Mayor and undertook other chores that could hardly be termed nonpolitical.[57] President of the Civil Service Commission Paul Kern participated in ALP politics and was criticized for doing so, we may recall, by the Civil Service Reform Association. Yet here, as with respect to the other aspects of nonpolitical government we have been considering, La Guardia, while open to criticism, did not really do too badly considering the political facts of life in this country. Compared to his Tammany predecessors, he shone.

One final, though obvious, point: except as noted above, La Guardia assuredly never gave nonpolitical government.[58]

*

Part IV
From Yesterday to Tomorrow

14

Exit reform

LA GUARDIA made his reputation as Mayor in his first eight years in City Hall. In most respects he maintained good government during his third term; and he even took some steps forward: he concerned himself with post-war planning, for example, undertook an enlightened experiment in the field of social welfare by establishing the Bureau of Alcoholic Therapy in the Welfare Department to combat chronic alcoholism [1] and gave birth to HIP (Health Insurance Plan). Nevertheless, to some extent La Guardia fell down as Mayor during his last few years.

That he did so was due in part to the fact that he lost some first-class subordinates. La Guardia had been losing good men from early in his administration, but as time went on the trend increased; during his last years, his appointees, while usually good, were, generally speaking, not in the same class as the earlier ones. Some men La Guardia lost through death, such as Hodson, killed in a plane crash in 1943, and Leo Arnstein, his successor, who died a year later. Rice was forced out by ill-health in July, 1942. As time went on, what had happened during other periods of reform (and indeed happens to all administrations in America to some degree) happened to the La Guardia administration: some officials became tired of public service, perhaps found that the big challenge of the job had been licked and were drawn back to private life where the opportunities for making money are so much greater. This was true, for example, of Davidson, who got out in 1936, and Windels, who retired as Corporation Counsel at the end of La Guardia's first term. The war, when it came along, claimed the services of others, like Gerard Swope, Chairman of the Municipal Housing Authority, William H. Davis, another member of the Authority, William L. Gaud, an assistant corporation counsel, David Marcus and Joe Lilly. [2]

Then disputes of one sort or another between La Guardia and members of his team took their toll. The independent souls whom La Guardia gathered around him often reacted vigorously to his personality and, while most squabbles and fights were smoothed over, this was not always true. In cases where a quarrel did not lead directly to a resignation, it might, nevertheless, serve as a contributing factor. The first big man La Guardia lost through an argument was Police Commissioner O'Ryan, who handed in his resignation after only nine months of service. It was not too surprising that La Guardia and O'Ryan, both strong-willed and independent characters, should clash; almost from the beginning there were rumors that O'Ryan would resign. A major bone of contention between them was the policy of the police toward strikers. The liberal Mayor favored a broader concept of the right of workers to picket and demonstrate than did his Police Commissioner, who once, before an aldermanic committee, succinctly explained his position in these words: "My background has been military, and my training hasn't much to do with liberalism. I don't believe in times of emergency in letting crowds collect." [3] In addition to this difference, O'Ryan resented La Guardia's continual interference in his department. On one occasion, after O'Ryan had decided not to let the police discard their uniform coats in hot weather, La Guardia reopened the subject. Finally in September, 1934, matters came to a head. On primary day La Guardia, according to O'Ryan, abused him on the telephone because he had heard rumors of disorder in Harlem. The Mayor went over O'Ryan's head and ordered 1,400 policemen concentrated in the area. O'Ryan resigned with a blast that La Guardia had demoralized the police force with his meddling and had encouraged the Communists and other vicious elements by his strike policy. La Guardia retorted that O'Ryan's attack was "malicious and false" and dismissed it as "an ill-tempered, distorted and garbled narrative by a former police official." In 1937 O'Ryan campaigned for Mahoney. [4]

The following years brought other clashes within the administration which led to resignations. We have already mentioned that Langdon Post resigned as chairman of the city's Housing Authority in December, 1937, as a result of a dispute with La Guardia, as did Post's successor, Alfred Rheinstein, almost two years later. In April, 1940, Clen Ryan, who only a few months before had been made head of a new Department of Commerce, resigned his job reportedly because he resented what he regarded as the interference of La Guardia's labor adviser, Mrs. Henry Epstein, in his department. Ryan, however, said his dispute was not with the Mayor —though La Guardia, at least tacitly, seems to have approved of Mrs. Epstein's actions—and both men said nice things about each other. (In November, 1942, for other reasons, La Guardia dismissed Mrs. Epstein, who thereupon excoriated him.) [5] At the end of 1941, La Guardia and Commissioner Morgan reached the parting of the ways. La Guardia, as head of the Office of Civilian Defense, had named Morgan food co-ordinator of the city. He, in turn, had appointed to an important post under him a prominent woman, Mrs. Preston Davie, who did not meet with the approval of some other women; they complained to La Guardia, who asked Morgan to fire his appointee, something the Commissioner was loath to do. About the same time La Guardia insisted upon filling two or three vacant positions in the Department of Markets himself, though Morgan felt that after eight years in office he should be allowed to do this. Failing to get any satisfaction from La Guardia as to the points in conflict, Morgan handed in his resignation. Though in accepting it La Guardia said there was no "dispute," expressed regret at the Commissioner's going and praised him for his services, a short while later the Mayor announced "the discovery of some irregularities in the Department of Markets" and an inquiry by the Commissioner of Investigation into them, a move which led the *Times* to scold the Mayor for "cheap drama" and to recall that a similar move had followed Rheinstein's resignation; two months later, La Guardia, denying he meant any slur on Morgan, dropped the matter.[6] Early 1942 also witnessed a big fight between the Mayor and the Municipal Civil Service Commission which resulted in the ouster of Commissioners Kern and Sayre, a subject we shall have more to say about shortly.[7]

Without doubt, World War II was the basic reason why La Guardia's last years in office were not so brilliant as his earlier ones. In the first place, governing a great city in war time was not easy. Not only did appointees leave the city's service to undertake war work, as we have seen, but the war had a deleterious effect on the civil service. The city departments began to find their work hampered by the drafting of younger male employees and by the resignation of many employees to take more highly paid jobs in private industry or with the federal government; the number of resignations rose from 7,358 in the fiscal year 1941–2 to 15,712 in 1942–3, an increase of more than 100 per cent. Even retirements increased by more than 50 per cent, for many of the older employees found that if they retired from city positions and took less onerous work in private industry, their city pensions plus their new salary gave them a greater net income than before. At the same time, there was a considerable decline in the number of candidates seeking to take civil service exams and a notable increase in the number of those declining civil service appointments.[8] The manpower shortage, furthermore, was accompanied by a shortage of materials, supplies and equipment which added to the difficulties of the administration.

For a while, too, La Guardia, because of the war crisis, was overloaded with work. As energetic as he was, he couldn't serve as chairman of the American section of the Joint Permanent Defense Board and head of OCD and at the same time continue to function as the Mayor of the world's greatest city without easing up somewhere. His role as Mayor suffered. Had he not been too busy to talk things over with Morgan, the Commissioner might not have resigned, and it is possible that the disagreement that developed between Kern and La Guardia might not have become as serious as it did had the Civil Service Commissioner, who apparently tried to discuss the matter with La Guardia, not found him "too busy" with war work to talk over a "trivial case." During the campaign of '41, it might be recalled, the Democrats had assailed La Guardia as a part-time Mayor; that this charge was not just campaign oratory was seen after the election when supporters of the Mayor, like William Jay Schieffelin and the *New York Times,* strongly urged him to give full time to the Mayor's job.[9]

Though La Guardia denied he had neglected his city duties while holding down the OCD job and was disposed to hang on to what he had, circumstances soon solved the problem. La Guardia never liked his OCD position—he was induced to take it only after the right of attending cabinet meetings was conceded to him—and the job never liked him; before long he showed that he was not the man for it. Two months after he became Director of OCD, Ickes, who was friendly to him, wrote that La Guardia should not have taken the job, either on his own account or that of the country. Bernard Baruch, Ickes said, had told him that the Mayor was in the President's hair, that he was too spectacular to keep his feet on the ground; instead of working through the governors, La Guardia was setting up his own organizations in the states, and this was making the governors hot under the collar. F.D.R., Baruch said, had ruefully told him that at any rate he was glad he had not put La Guardia in the cabinet. Finally in February, 1942, La Guardia resigned as head of OCD, being replaced by James M. Landis, dean of Harvard Law School. It was the one job in his entire career in which he was unsuccessful.[10]

Finally, and most important, the war served to remove some of the luster from La Guardia's reign because of a deeper consequence it had upon the Mayor. Long before Pearl Harbor, La Guardia foresaw the probability of war with the Axis powers, and he wanted to play a part in it. With his love for the spotlight and his history of having served as an aviator at the front in the First World War, his response to war was bound to be romantic and ambitious. He wanted to be a general and sent overseas to do administrative work. Constantly he begged his friend Harry Hopkins to see what he could do. Hopkins felt certain that La Guardia could be of tremendous help to General Eisenhower in the Sicilian operation, and he urged Roosevelt to commission the Mayor. In early 1943 La Guardia was on the verge of being appointed a high army official (probably a brigadier-general) to govern the North African areas and, after it was invaded, Italy. On March 17, after a talk with the President, La Guardia wrote Hopkins a letter expressing intense excitement; he stated that Roosevelt had indicated he could be commissioned in April. La Guardia felt so sure of his appointment that he adjusted his pension, ordered his uniform and sought to designate a substitute Mayor of his own choosing by having an "emergency" law quietly introduced at Albany whereby various state, municipal and other officials, while on military leave, could appoint successors until they got back; the Ostertag bill was passed and law for two weeks before the Democrats realized what it was all about.[11]

Then suddenly the wheels stopped turning. Secretary of War Henry L. Stimson stated at a news conference in April that La Guardia had personally and patriotically offered his services to the War Department, but that he felt the Mayor was so useful in New York City that it would be very difficult to find any place in the army where he could be equally useful and that after talking the matter over with La Guardia it was decided to leave the matter open for the present.[12] In the months that followed, rumors cropped up from time to time that La Guardia would be given an overseas post. At the end of September, 1944, according to one news item, F.D.R. had virtually confirmed reports that La Guardia was to be commissioned in the armed services and sent to Italy in an administrative capacity; on a Friday Roosevelt said there was nothing on the reports then, but there might be something on them over the week-end. Perhaps with the election of 1944 imminent, the President was thinking of La Guardia's political support.[13] However that might be, as before, nothing happened over the week-end.

Nothing ever happened. La Guardia's war service was limited to civilian defense and making propaganda broadcasts to Italy;[14] he never got into uniform, and the job he might have had was given to Charles Poletti, former Lieutenant Governor of New York.[15] There never has been any clear answer as to why La Guardia was not commissioned; perhaps the explanation lies in a combination of reasons, rather than one. According to a dispatch from Rome to the *New York Times* in August, 1945, a high American officer who knew the Mayor well and had excellent connections in Washington (but whom the *Times* item did not identify) stated that the reason La Guardia's appointment did not come through in early 1943 was that the army balked at the topside political handling of what it regarded as a military problem. The upshot was that Washington put the matter squarely to General Eisenhower, then supreme commander in Algiers. Asked directly if he wanted La Guardia as a brigadier-general for service in Italy, Ike replied flatly "No," and that was that.[16] Another, and more widespread, explanation given for La Guardia's failure to obtain an army appointment—and presumably not just in 1943—is that Secretary Stimson was opposed to giving him one.[17] One former excellent newspaperman in New York told the writer that the Secretary was against the appointment only because he felt La Guardia would be a nuisance. But another extremely reliable informant has declared that the real reason Stimson put his foot down was that cagey old C. C. Burlingham, working behind the scenes and still wielding great influence, passed the word down to him that La Guardia was needed in New York City and that no one could take his place.[18] If this is the answer, or most of it, Stimson's statement of April, 1943, is seen to be more than just a polite way of brushing off the Mayor as one might be led to believe.

Whatever the real story, La Guardia's aspiration to become a general did not do him or his city any good. Some of his friends concede that it diverted his attention from municipal affairs. There are those who suspect that in an attempt to advance his personal ambition La Guardia in certain ways played false with the cause of good government; we shall come back to this matter in a few pages. Little doubt exists that La Guardia's personality was unpleasantly affected. His frustrations with respect to the overseas job when added to his disappointment with OCD, the difficulty of running the city during the war and perhaps his own failing health, filled his last years with bitterness. Irritable and arbitrary as he could be, he became even more so and even more sensitive to criticism during his last term.

It was in this period, it may be recalled, that dictatorial behavior on La Guardia's part provoked a controversy over education. It was in this period, too, that La Guardia's relations with the press, never of the best, took a marked turn for the worse. In early 1942 La Guardia, overworked and editorially battered because of OCD, told reporters he would not talk to them until they learned to quote him accurately. Then in September the explosion came. In a Sunday broadcast discussing the case of a little boy named George who had written in about a gambling place where his father generally lost his pay check, the Mayor asked little boys to keep him informed about "tinhorns" who were destroying the family happiness; he said he would not reveal the name of the child, but would send police to the gambling place. When the afternoon papers twisted his remarks to mean that the Mayor was urging youngsters to inform on their fathers, La Guardia turned purple with rage and denounced the papers over the air. Throughout the rest of his administration he remained at war with the press, apparently never losing a chance to take a swipe at it.[19] Though they are reluctant to say so, a few of La Guardia's supporters felt that toward the end of his term as Mayor he sometimes did things which bordered on the psychopathic. Seymour Halpern, for example, recalls that La Guardia fired an old loyal friend from a corporation inspector's job simply because Halpern had interceded for the man when learning that his position was threatened.[20]

Largely because of the effect of the war upon the Mayor and the city government, La Guardia's popularity with New Yorkers declined in his last years in City Hall. In June, 1941, a Gallup poll reported that 59 per cent of the voters in New York City were in favor of a third term for La Guardia, with but 26 per cent opposed and 15 per cent undecided;[21] apparently the Mayor had suffered but an insignificant loss in political strength from November, 1937, when he had been re-elected with 60 per cent of the vote. But during the '41 campaign, the Mayor's attack on Lehman cost him much support; and he finished the campaign, as we saw, with about 53 per cent of the vote. Shortly afterwards he was further pummeled by several developments—an attack on his handling of OCD, the intensification of his standing quarrel with the newspapers, his dispute with Morgan, his fight with the Civil Service Commission. By March, 1942, his popularity was way down; according to one political writer, if the Mayor were then up for re-election, he would be "a quick knockout," and this view, the writer claimed, was shared by a fairly wide sampling of La Guardia's friends and enemies.[22] This seems to have been La Guardia's low point, but he was severely criticized for other things afterwards, and compared with his first two terms as Mayor, his appeal was off. In the spring of 1945, with another mayoral campaign looming on the horizon, the *Daily News* ran a straw poll on mayoral candidates which ended with Jimmy Walker, of all people, leading the list with 40 per cent of the vote, O'Dwyer in second place with 30 per cent and La Guardia third with 25 per cent.[23] What was significant about the poll—and the *News* has a reputation for accuracy in the matter of polls—was not the vote for Walker; he was not a candidate and had no intention of being one, as most people undoubtedly knew; the vote for him might easily have been the means whereby New Yorkers in the absence of what they regarded as a compelling candidate indulged their nostalgia for the golden days of the twenties, before depression and war made life so much more complicated and trying. The significant thing was the vote for La Guardia in comparison with that of the other two.

What is particularly striking about the falling off in La Guardia's popularity during his third term is that it occurred, not just with respect to the general electorate, but with respect to civic and liberal elements that had formed his palace guard. Even before his second re-election, La Guardia had begun to make some of his most ardent supporters unhappy. In February, 1940, the Board of Higher Education, the body overseeing public college education in the city, by unanimous vote named Bertrand Russell, the eminent British philosopher, to a vacant professorship of philosophy at City College for a period beginning in February, 1941, and ending in June, 1942. Immediately some ecclesiastics and conservatives, scandalized by Russell's views on marriage and morals, let out a howl of protest. William T. Manning, Bishop of the Protestant Episcopal Church, greatly stimulated opposition by a letter to the press in which he denounced the appointment on the grounds that Russell was "a recognized propagandist against both religion and morality and [one] who specifically defends adultery." A taxpayer suit to void the appointment met with success, Supreme Court Justice John E. McGeehan declaring that Russell was not fit for his position because of his "immoral and salacious attitude towards sex" and that he was not legally qualified for it because he was not a United States citizen. The Board of Higher Education voted to appeal the decision. At this point, La Guardia, whom liberals had every reason to suppose would sympathize with the Board's position, effectively dismissed the issue by striking Russell's position from the new budget; Corporation Counsel Chanler advised the Board that he would not make an appeal. La Guardia's explanation that his actions were in line with his retrenchment policy of doing away with vacant positions was wholly unconvincing. Liberals were angry. The Mayor had not only taken the conservative side, but he had obviously interfered with the supposed educational independence of the Board of Higher Education to do so; and the only real reason for his actions seemed to be political expediency.[24]

Then in September, 1940, La Guardia, acting at the request of officers of the ILGWU and four employer associations that he pick an impartial "czar" of industrial and labor relations in the women's coat and suit industry, named Jimmy Walker to the $20,000-a-year post. La Guardia bore Walker no animosity—they had been on terms of personal friendship for twenty years—and representatives of labor and industry in the garment field expressed gratification at the choice. The job was not a city one, and a good case could be made that the well-liked Jimmy was admirably suited for it. But some civic people resented the selection. Seabury was especially irritated. He asserted that La Guardia had hurt the cause of good government by making the appointment and that it was done to get votes for the President. (Seabury seems to have taken the view of New York City Republican leaders at the time that the President, worried about the prospect of losing New York State in the coming election, was counting upon Walker's personal popularity to bring the city's large Irish vote, lukewarm to the President's third term nomination, back on the reservation. A more likely explanation for the appointment is the one advanced by Raymond Moley: Ed Flynn, who wanted to help Walker, apparently in need of a good job, got Roosevelt to ask La Guardia to make the appointment.)[25] The Walker episode was followed by other incidents to one degree or another dissatisfying to a number of La Guardia's staunchest supporters— La Guardia's unwillingness to go along with Borough President Isaacs in 1941, the Mayor's stand on the matter of county reform in the same year, his attack on Lehman, his conflict with the Civil Service Commission in early 1942, his behavior with respect to the educational system during his last years.

The dispute between La Guardia and the Civil Service Commission and subsequent developments—which might be labeled the Kern affair—created a minor uproar. The Kern affair developed out of circumstances following the enactment of county reform in November, 1941. The new offices of Sheriff and Register were to be run by civil service, and a question arose as to whether four employees in the old registers' offices, three of them, according to Kern, committeemen in the Kelly, Flynn and Sullivan (Staten Island Democratic) organizations, were without examination to be allowed into the competitive class of the civil service, a development that would confer permanent status upon them. The Municipal Civil Service Commission held that the four employees were in the exempt class. The State Civil Service Commission, to which the four appealed, ruled that because of their experience the four employees were to be re-classified into the competitive class. Apparently under the impression that it had La Guardia's support, the Municipal Civil Service Commission had fought the matter before the state commission; convinced that the ruling of the state commission was contrary to law and apparently still feeling that La Guardia was behind it, the Municipal Civil Service Commission now planned to fight the order in the courts.

Then, in January, 1942, things began to pop. The Corporation Counsel's office advised the Municipal Commission that it would not represent it legally; Chanler later said that La Guardia had told him that the action of the State Civil Service Commission was entirely justifiable. Kern, adamant, decided that since he was a lawyer he would represent the Commission himself. In court, however, Chanler argued that he alone had the right to represent the city's interest in the case and declared that he consented to the order under attack; the judge ruled in favor of Chanler and the four employees. Apparently Kern then tried to talk the matter over with La Guardia, only to get nowhere. Kern was incensed. On February 5 the Municipal Civil Service Commission issued a press release calling Chanler a politically-minded lawyer and declaring that his present attitude was not surprising in view of the fact that he had supported Ed Flynn's candidate for Mayor in 1933 against La Guardia. The Commission resolved to appeal the court decision and to institute an action against the Corporation Counsel ordering him to represent the Commission or to approve the designation of special counsel.[26]

La Guardia struck back quickly. The next day he suspended the entire Commission (Kern, Sayre and Morton), the Commissioners being informed of his action by newspapermen; upon learning that Morton had not assisted in the preparation of the news release, the Mayor lifted Morton's suspension. La Guardia's order asked the Commissioners to show cause why they should not be removed for "conduct unbecoming a Civil Service Commissioner and making a deliberately false statement concerning official matters and insubordination—all to the injury of Civil Service." The Mayor indicated to reporters that he had acted because he believed that no executive could permit one agency of government to attack another. Immediately upon suspending the Commissioners La Guardia stationed policemen and members of the Department of Investigation in the Commission's offices and denied the suspended Commissioners access to their records and papers. Two days later a public hearing was held in the Mayor's office. Kern's lawyer held that the charges were vague, that the notice for the hearing had been improper and hasty, that the Mayor had no power to remove the Commissioners in such a proceeding. Kern, himself, was bitter against the man he had once been so close to; he and La Guardia had come to the parting of the ways. He taunted the Mayor with selling out old friends, sarcastically declared that he was at a loss to understand La Guardia's sudden desire for "gracious etiquette" in his administration and called the charges the "hollowest kind of a pretext." According to Murray

Stand, La Guardia, far from happy in his role, had tears in his eyes. A few days later, the Mayor removed both Kern and Sayre from the Commission. La Guardia's action was later upheld in the courts.[27]

Then early in March, Kern, who had been implying all along that the reason given for the removal was not the real reason, let go a bombshell which the newspapers soon took up as "the Flynn paving block scandal." Kern charged publicly that twenty-seven city employees and a few thousand granite blocks belonging to the city had been used to decorate Boss Flynn's summer home at Lake Mahopac, New York. La Guardia, he said, had had information on the matter for nearly four months, for he, Kern, had told him about it on November 16, 1941. Since no action was taken, Kern said, he began his own investigation January 20, 1942. He said that after he had the facts in his possession he was assailed by many threats and entreaties to suppress his information on the grounds that since Flynn was chairman of the Democratic National Committee, it might embarrass the national administration in the midst of its war effort. At the time of the Commission's suspension, he declared, he had on his desk subpoenas for Flynn and Robert L. Moran, Bronx Commissioner of Public Works. His point was that the Flynn case was the principal cause of his dismissal from the Commission.[28]

The paving of Flynn's home with city blocks by city workers was not denied, but a number of other points made by Kern, as well as his interpretation of the events, were and vigorously. According to District Attorney Samuel J. Foley of the Bronx, who said he was investigating the matter, and Commissioner of Investigation Herlands, Kern had discovered the affair and told La Guardia, but La Guardia took action. He immediately directed Herlands to conduct a secret investigation which Herlands was doing when Kern disrupted and negated the inquiry by subpoenaing city employees who had worked on Flynn's estate. Herlands declared Kern knew on January 20 that the Department of Investigation had been actively working on the case since November 16, though he made no reference to this in his public statements and in general accused the former Civil Service Commissioner of sly innuendoes and trying to create an impression of something sinister. La Guardia asked that he be ousted as Mayor if Kern's charges of an attempted hush-up were true. Ed Flynn, who found himself in the middle of the controversy, scalded Kern. He charged that Kern knew, and knew long before he made his statement, that Flynn had no knowledge of, or responsibility for, the situation, but that Kern did not say so. He called Kern a cheap sniper who blamed the Bronx for the 1940–1 councilmanic inquiry of the Civil Service Commission and wanted to get even. Later, in his book *You're the Boss,* Flynn was to write that Kern's charges were an attempt to build up his case against La Guardia for the courts.[29]

Despite the objections of Kern and others that Foley was not the man to do the job because of his close friendship with Flynn, Foley presented the paving block case to a Bronx grand jury which proceeded to hear testimony from La Guardia, Kern, Herlands and others. Its presentment cleared everyone in the case. It found that, while the paving work had been done under Moran's supervision, Flynn had never expressed a desire that the work be done under city auspices without expense to him; that Herlands had begun his investigation in the middle of November, but it was made futile by Kern's action in calling witnesses; that a charge by Kern of conspiracy between La Guardia, Herlands and Flynn to suppress the Kern investigation was entirely without foundation and, in the opinion of the jury, never would have been made, but for the fact that Kern was greatly influenced by what he termed "his intuition." The presentment was immediately called a whitewash by Kern and others; but while it failed to answer satisfactorily all questions, there is no evidence that its basic findings were incorrect.[30]

What chiefly interests us about the Kern affair is the position taken at the time by civic organizations and some others usually friendly to La Guardia. When La Guardia clashed with the Civil Service Commission, old Richard Welling, president of the Civil Service Reform Association, sent a statement to the Mayor, authorized by the Association's executive committee, backing La Guardia's stand. It condemned the Municipal Civil Service Commission for its position in the dispute with the State Civil Service Commission, noting that in December, 1941, the Association had approved as lawful, reasonable and warranted on merit, the reclassification by the State Commission of some positions in the registers' offices and declared that it did not agree with Kern's characterization of the action of the state body as a dirty political steal or with his assertion that the Mayor and Corporation Counsel should have attacked it as such. But the Civil Service Reform Association stood alone. The consensus in the civic circle on the question of the four employees seems to have been that Kern was defending the merit system. This question, however, as far as most civic groups were concerned, was overshadowed by the one raised by La Guardia's suspension and removal of the Civil Service Commissioners. While the Mayor had the right to remove a Civil Service Commissioner for cause after a public hearing, the position held in general by civic leaders was that the cause was light, that the hearings had been inadequate and that the independence of the Civil Service Commission was at stake. When the Kern-Sayre case went into the courts, five organizations—the Citizens Union, City Affairs Committee, Women's City Club, League of Women Voters and Community Councils—filed a brief on behalf of Kern and Sayre. Furthermore, when the Flynn case was being aired, there was a tendency on the part of civic groups, while not condemning La Guardia, to agree with Kern's suspicions of Foley and to cry "whitewash" after the grand jury had handed up its presentment. The Citizens Union and others vainly tried to get Governor Lehman to supersede Foley in the Bronx investigation or have the case reopened after the presentment. Lehman was not without some good reasons for refusing, and an attempt of the

City Club to get the courts to air the case again also met with failure.[31]

That at least some liberals were critical of La Guardia for dismissing Kern and Sayre is suggested by George Britt's article "What Has Happened to La Guardia?" which appeared in the March 9, 1942, issue of the *New Republic*. Britt held that Kern was right in the civil service dispute with La Guardia and implied that for a man who served as the scapegoat in the politically-minded councilmanic investigation of the Civil Service Commission during 1940–41, an inquiry actually directed at the La Guardia administration, Paul Kern was most unfairly treated by the Mayor.[32]

To some of La Guardia's liberal backers, the Kern affair, some of the events before it that brought the Mayor under fire and La Guardia's dispute with educational officials after it, seemed to point to a rather sinister development: La Guardia was compromising with the foe and, as Kern charged, betraying his old friends. The foe, for one thing, was Ed Flynn, and the Mayor was suspected of playing with Flynn to advance his own ambitions, notably his quest for a generalship. The foe was also the conservatives, especially the ecclesiastical element, and here again La Guardia's actions were viewed as attempts to push himself ahead.[33] In 1943, when La Guardia failed to reappoint Mrs. Lindlof to the Board of Education, a meeting to pay her tribute was held. Speaking at the meeting, Mark Starr showed what was passing through the minds of some liberals when he said: "Unfortunately, our Little Flower is turning to poison ivy for many of the men and women who once were proud to serve with him to save our city from Tammany control. Does our Mayor think the favor of the clericals will endear him to the Italian people when he arrives as their self-nominated Garibaldi?" [34]

What was the truth? Was La Guardia really compromising himself? All we can say is that there is no real evidence that he courted either Flynn or church elements for the purpose of getting overseas. What we have comes down to intuitions. Whatever the truth, one thing is sure: some of La Guardia's most loyal supporters became strongly displeased with much of his behavior as time went on and came to share a view expressed by Councilman Stanley Isaacs at a Citizens Union luncheon in January, 1944. Isaacs, who always backed La Guardia, even after La Guardia refused to stand by him in 1941, declared that for half a dozen years New York had the finest administration ever seen in City Hall "but now it has slumped, retrograded." [35]

In early May, 1945, La Guardia, who had kept them guessing for months, announced on the radio that he would not be a candidate for a fourth term. It was his personal conviction, he said, that if he chose to run, he could be returned to office "without any trouble" and without the nomination of any regular political party. He did not so choose, however. As reasons for his decision, he listed a belief in rotation in office (had it not been for the emergency, he said, he would not have supported Roosevelt

in 1940 and 1944), a fear of growing stale in office or having his administration become satisfied and a desire not to become bossy ("they tell me
that I am sort of inclined that way at times"). He noted, too, that he
needed some rest. He declared that he had made his decision back in 1941
and had conveyed it to his friends at Christmas time, 1944, by means of a
symbol on his Christmas cards; the cards carried a photograph of Gracie
Mansion and in the lower right hand corner the number "814," which La
Guardia explained after the broadcast referred to Local 814 of the Furni-
ture Handlers Union, which would, presumably, move his belongings.[36]

Despite the Mayor's statement—and there is no doubt, at any rate, that
in the spring of 1945 he needed a rest—few felt or feel that it told the
story, or at least the entire story, of his refusal to run again. Other reasons
have been advanced to explain La Guardia's decision. Some believe that
his health was the real reason. Murray Stand, who had been very close to
him, said unequivocally that La Guardia did not run because he felt his
health would not permit him to serve another term, because he felt he
would die; and Newbold Morris in his book *Let the Chips Fall* has noted
that the Mayor in the spring of '45 was frequently in great pain. Perhaps,
too, as some have suggested, La Guardia did not seek another term because
he could foresee tremendous economic burdens for New York City in
future years—as, indeed, did occur—and he did not want them to dim his
earlier glory.[37]

Many feel that he really wanted a fourth term but declined to run
because he felt he could not get Fusion backing and, despite the boast contained in his statement, felt he could not win without it. (Had he decided
to run, the movers' symbol might simply never have been explained.) This
certainly was the view of Republican and Liberal Party leaders who were
very skeptical of La Guardia's official reasons for retiring. They maintained
there was no chance of La Guardia's obtaining either the Democratic or
Republican nominations and slight chance of his getting Liberal Party
endorsement, that he could not win re-election without at least one of these
nominations and must have known it. They thought he would change his
mind quickly enough if drafted by the Republicans and Liberals. This La
Guardia denied, but since the Republicans and Liberals never tested their
theory, we do not know.[38]

There certainly were good reasons why La Guardia could have believed
that he would not receive Fusion support. (That he recognized the difficulty
of getting the backing of certain elements that one would expect to figure
in a Fusion movement was suggested in his statement.) True, La Guardia
had always had difficulty getting the Republican nomination, but this time
the situation appeared different. All the Republican county leaders were
opposed to his renomination—though only three, those in Queens, the
Bronx and Richmond, openly said so. In the past La Guardia could count
on Manhattan, but in March, 1945, according to Tom Curran, 80 per cent
of the Republican district leaders in that county were against a renomina-

tion for the Mayor.[39] Curran, himself, had had a run-in with La Guardia in November, 1943, over responsibility for the election of Thomas A. Aurelio to the Supreme Court, during which the Republican leader accused the Mayor of being an ingrate to the Republican Party and the "most artful political dodger" the city ever produced.[40] Even supposing the Manhattan organization could be brought to back the Mayor, it was hard to see how this action could make any difference in La Guardia's chances for the Republican nomination, for while the Manhattan organization might carry the county for La Guardia in the primary, the vote would very likely not be sufficient to cancel out large anti-La Guardia majorities in the other counties; in 1941 La Guardia led Davies by only about 500 votes outside of Manhattan, and this time there was less support for him in Manhattan and more animosity to him outside. The consensus in political circles was that he could not win the Republican primary this time.[41]

Then there was the attitude of the new Liberal Party. It had been formed a year before as a result of the conflict within the ALP that we have noted. As time went on the Communist element in the ALP increased in strength; it took over control of one county organization after another in New York City, until the only real sanctuary left to the right-wingers was the gerrymandered state committee. Starting about 1943, Sidney Hillman, who, though not a Communist, believed in a united political front with them, came to join forces with the party's left-wing in opposition to the Dubinsky-Rose right-wing leadership, which was unalterably against any co-operation with the Reds. In 1944, when Hillman and the Communists won control of the state body in the spring primary, the right-wingers walked out and organized a new party. The presidential election of 1944 gave the Liberal Party about 320,000 votes in the state, much more than enough to raise it to the status of a legal party.[42] The vote also indicated the emergence in New York City of a significant new political group, one that would be important mainly because it provided a means whereby liberal Democratic voters who did not like to vote under the Democratic label could express themselves politically; this breed, whose support had made the ALP a powerful political factor, was becoming increasingly disenchanted with that party because of the growing power of the left wing within it.

Liberal Party leaders in the early part of 1945 indicated that they would not go along with La Guardia; in March, Alex Rose, party chairman, declared that the new party would try to bring about an "intellectually honest non-partisan administration," [43] and the implication was that the city did not then enjoy intellectually honest government. Liberal leaders were probably influenced in their attitude toward La Guardia by circumstances discussed earlier in this chapter, but the heart of their opposition was tied up with their rivalry with the ALP. At the time of the crucial 1944 ALP primary, La Guardia, whose main concern in the matter apparently was that the conflict between the two factions should not endanger the re-election of Roosevelt, had suggested that both groups support a joint slate for positions on the state executive committee, one that would represent a cross section of the rank and file of the ALP, but which would not contain any Communists. Hillman accepted La Guardia's formula for peace, or at least a truce; the right-wing would not. Believing, as they did, that compromise with the left was impossible and that La Guardia should espouse their cause, the right-wingers bitterly resented the Mayor's efforts. After the election Dubinsky declared that La Guardia's deliberate straddling of the issues between the two wings confused some ALP enrollees, kept others from the polls and was in large part responsible for the left-wing victory. He indicated that the ILGWU, which had spent good money for La Guardia in 1937 and 1941, and the Mayor were parting company.[44]

Moreover, various civic leaders and others who had consistently been for La Guardia were not encouraging. The City Fusion Party, which had previously boomed the Mayor for re-election, was cautious and noncommittal. In February leaders of the Citizens Union, several welfare organizations and other groups that had been traditionally friendly to the Mayor asked the Republicans to work with them on a Fusion ticket headed by someone other than La Guardia. True, leaders of the Citizens Union declared that while La Guardia had done some objectionable things in his third term, he had done some constructive things, too, and that before they would repudiate him publicly they would have to be assured of the nomination of a suitable substitute; their earnest desire to secure a replacement, however, was unconcealed. Reportedly the foremost civic leader in the movement to find a better candidate was George Hallett. Hallett began to find fault with La Guardia in 1941 at the time La Guardia rudely attacked Lehman. The Mayor's subsequent behavior did not reassure Hallett. Regarding the political situation of 1945, Hallett, at a later date, said: "Some of our people wanted to support him [La Guardia] for a fourth term, but thank God, he didn't run. If he had, and if we'd backed him, I'd have taken a long leave of absence." [45] Actually the only group La Guardia could count on in 1945 was the ALP.

What may have finally convinced La Guardia not to run was the failure of a boom for him launched in the spring of '45 by some of his old supporters, a number of whom, significantly, were apparently motivated less by real enthusiasm for the Mayor than by a belief that no other Fusion candidate could equal his popularity with the voters.[46] (Though La Guardia's popular following may have been something less than these people thought—the *Daily News* poll came out about a month after the boom—their thinking was not ridiculous; while La Guardia lost popularity in his third term compared to his first two, nothing in our previous discussion should be taken to mean that the Mayor did not retain the affection and support of large numbers of voters.) Following a meeting at Seabury's home in which more than a score of civic and political personalities participated—including, among others, Newbold Morris, Mrs. Earle, Baldwin, Childs, Chadbourne, Schieffelin and Kracke—forty-five Republicans signed a letter urging La Guardia's renomination by the Republicans and sent it to Republican leaders and state officials and to Governor Dewey; the main idea was to get Republican bigwigs outside of the city to bring pressure to bear on the city organizations in behalf of La Guardia. (La Guardia, himself, politely disassociated himself from the letter.) The strategy failed: upstate Republicans greeted the letter with coolness, the Republican state chairman declaring that the matter was up to the local leaders, and Governor Dewey, upon whom La Guardia's chances for getting the Republican nomination chiefly depended, gave the letter the silent treatment.[47] Within a short time it became evident that La Guardia had no support from those addressed by the forty-five; the boom for him was dead. It was not long after that La Guardia made his radio address declining to seek a fourth term.[48]

All this, of course, does not answer the question. La Guardia may well have refused to run, as we have indicated, for reasons which had nothing to do, or only a little to do, with the political developments we have been discussing. It is possible that La Guardia believed that if he chose to run he could be returned to office—if not "without any trouble," at least returned. He might have felt that with ALP support and an independent nomination under some name as the "Good Government Party"—and even, perhaps, in the end the backing of the Liberal Party, the bulk of whose rank and file were probably still for him—he could come in first.

With La Guardia's announcement, Democratic chances of electing a Mayor in the fall of 1945 increased. Not only did the Mayor's statement herald the retirement of a formidable vote-getter, it occasioned the dissolution of the old Fusion alignment (though, as we have indicated, that alignment would most likely have come to an end had La Guardia made a different decision) and brought about a significant addition to Democratic strength.

For with La Guardia out, the ALP and the Liberal Party sought an alliance with the Democrats. The Democrats could hope to win the support of only one of the two because of the animosity between them and because of their attitudes with regard to the mayoral candidate. Some of the ALP's most important leaders favored O'Dwyer, who was once again the leading candidate for the Democratic nomination; it was generally felt that if the Democrats chose him, they would have no difficulty in getting the ALP to endorse him, but if they should nominate some other candidate, they would not likely get ALP support. On the other hand, it was doubtful if the Liberal Party would take O'Dwyer; leaders of the new party professed that he was too closely identified with a political machine, but their real objection to him stemmed from the fact that O'Dwyer was close to Communist and pro-Communist elements in the ALP. For Mayor the Liberals had in mind Joseph McGoldrick, Supreme Court Justice Ferdinand Pecora or General Sessions Judge Jonah J. Goldstein.[49]

Finally Democratic leaders again decided to go with O'Dwyer, and a Democratic-ALP coalition came into being.[50] Perhaps the Democrats were influenced, at least to some degree, by the fact that in 1945 the ALP was more important than the Liberal Party. In any case, other considerations were involved in O'Dwyer's selection. In addition to his reputation as an excellent district attorney, he now had what, on paper at any rate, was a good service record. Entering the army in 1942 as a major, he had become after a series of promotions a brigadier-general and had been sent to Italy in 1944 to work with the Allied Control Commission; then in January, 1945, F.D.R. appointed him head of the War Refugee Board, according to one political writer in order to boost him politically.[51] Possibly, as was implied later, O'Dwyer's nomination was also promoted by elements in the underworld.

When it became evident that the Democrats and American Laborites would form an alliance, the Liberals, to maintain their political position, turned to the Republicans. The two groups worked out a common slate which they claimed represented the good government movement; it was subsequently backed by the City Fusion Party. Though it looked for a while as if the Republicans and Liberals would select McGoldrick as their mayoral candidate, they chose Judge Goldstein; McGoldrick was again nominated for Comptroller and Newbold Morris for President of the Council.[52] Goldstein, a product of the Jewish community on the East Side, had been a lifelong Tammany Democrat who had begun his political career in 1911 as secretary or clerk (Goldstein said secretary, others said clerk) to Al Smith, then majority leader of the Assembly. Goldstein received his first big political break at the time of the Seabury court investigation when Mayor Walker appointed him a magistrate to replace a jurist under fire. In 1936 Lehman appointed him to fill out an unexpired term of a judge of the Court of General Sessions, a position to which he was subsequently elected. In the minds of some, certain things made Goldstein mayoral timber. In the Court of General Sessions, where Manhattan's serious criminal cases are handled, Goldstein had won a reputation for humanitarianism. He had taken part in several fights against discrimination. He was active in Jewish charities. Primarily the Republicans and Liberals picked him because it was thought he could split the city's Jewish vote, normally Democratic; Liberal Party leaders sold the idea to Dewey and the Republicans.[53]

The nomination of Goldstein caused a deep resentment among certain good government people. Not only did he have a history of association with Democratic politics, but in 1945 he had been doing everything to get the Democratic mayoral nomination and, indeed, had been a leading contender for it right up until the time O'Dwyer was chosen. (Seabury, who had attempted to find another Fusion candidate after La Guardia bowed out but whose views Republicans and Liberals had not heeded, blasted Goldstein's selection as "a disgrace and an affront to the independent

voters of the City of New York" and declared that now there were two
Tammany tickets in the field.) [54] Soon a movement to form a new ticket
was under way. With an explosive statement, Morris had withdrawn from
the Republican-Liberal slate upon learning of Goldstein's nomination.
Asked then by mutual friends of his and O'Dwyer's to join the O'Dwyer
ticket and run for President of the Council, Morris wrote, "I thought about
this for about two minutes. . . . I realized I could not possibly support
O'Dwyer. I think it was at this point I decided to offer the voters of New
York an independent ticket." He talked things over with La Guardia and
they went to work to put together an independent slate.[55] In early August a
No Deal ticket was launched bearing La Guardia's endorsement, with
Morris as the candidate for Mayor and a number of relatively unknown
people in the other spots.[56] This account of the formation of the No Deal
ticket, it should be stressed, is Morris' version; most people this writer has
talked to about the matter do not credit Morris with having played so dominant a role in it. It is certainly true that he never would have run had La
Guardia not encouraged and helped him to do so. In a very real sense,
La Guardia made the decision to put the Morris ticket into the race. Why
he did so constitutes another big mystery in his career.

It is possible to accept (if not as the complete answer) La Guardia's
official reason for backing the Morris slate, which was essentially that he
regarded both the O'Dwyer and Goldstein tickets as politically controlled
and felt the need for a really independent ticket. It might be noted in this
connection that at one point in June when O'Dwyer was defying the political bosses with respect to the naming of his running mates, La Guardia
offered, through friends, to back O'Dwyer if he would reject the help of
Democratic leaders and run as an independent in the Democratic primary
or on an independent ticket; but O'Dwyer made up with the bosses and La
Guardia withdrew the offer. Perhaps, as Murray Stand believed, La
Guardia, who declared that the No Deal ticket was put in to win, really
thought it could, that his prestige was high enough to carry off the maneuver. It also could have been that La Guardia felt that though Morris had
little chance of winning, the effort should be made.[57]

Some reasons advanced to explain La Guardia's action are less flattering
to the Mayor. One common view, held, for instance, by Warren Moscow,[58]
is that La Guardia, who really wanted a fourth term but did not get the
support of Republican and Liberal leaders, got back at them by launching
a "spite ticket" to insure the election of O'Dwyer. There are those—and
they are former associates of La Guardia [59]—who have suggested to the
writer that at heart La Guardia wanted the Democrats to come back
because he felt that when they got through his own administration would
shine by comparison. These views are not far-fetched; La Guardia was that
egotistical.

Of one thing there is no doubt: the Morris ticket split the supporters of
Fusion. Davidson, Childs, the Citizens Union, the Citizens Non-Partisan

Committee, the *Herald Tribune* and *World-Telegram,* for example, backed the Republican-Liberal-City Fusion coalition; Herlands became Goldstein's campaign manager. Seabury, Morgan, Schieffelin, Rabbi Wise, the *Times* and the *Post* were among those supporting Morris. Between the two groups of former La Guardia supporters there was, as one might expect, a feeling of irritation. When, for instance, Morgan came out for Morris, he resigned from the Citizens Union and the Citizens Non-Partisan Committee with a biting letter which accused both groups of helping the Republicans put over a shrewd deal.[60] As weakened as Fusion had been by the alliance of the ALP with the Democrats, the Goldstein nomination and the Morris ticket crippled it even more.

The campaign of 1945 presented an interesting paradox. On the one hand, the three-cornered race was as elaborate, windy and vituperative a campaign as any in the city's history. Day and night the air waves reverberated with dozens of radio addresses and singing commercials. On the other hand, the public was singularly unresponsive to all the shouting. There was little enthusiasm for any candidate, except among the Morris people. There were no intense feelings of love or hate. Political rallies had rarely, if ever, been so poorly attended. Registration figures were down, to the lowest point since the departure of Walker. The public apathy seemed to assure what seemed to need no assurance: an O'Dwyer victory.[61]

In retrospect, the most noteworthy aspect of the campaign were certain charges made against O'Dwyer. Goldstein, whose main theme was that a Democratic victory would mean the return of graft and gangsterism, charged that every power in the underworld was behind O'Dwyer's bid for election and strongly implied that his nomination had been brought about by underworld leaders. He accused his Democratic rival of knowing Costello, Adonis and Irving Sherman, a shady character and a friend of Costello's; O'Dwyer, Goldstein said, had called at Costello's home during the war. Meanwhile, George J. Beldock, whom Dewey had appointed to fill O'Dwyer's place as District Attorney of Kings County when the latter resigned to run for Mayor, was making startling charges about O'Dwyer's work as District Attorney. After hearing Beldock and making an investigation, a Brooklyn grand jury handed up two presentments, one at the end of October, the other after the election in December, which strongly suggested that despite his good work against Murder, Inc., O'Dwyer had protected members of the underworld's top echelon—in particular, Albert Anastasia.

O'Dwyer, it was charged, had had a good murder case against Anastasia in March or April, 1940, based upon evidence that Reles could supply (O'Dwyer, indeed, termed it a "perfect murder case" before the grand jury); but though the Brooklyn prosecutor sent Kid Twist into grand jury rooms in Brooklyn and Sullivan County, New York, and even to California, he did not use Reles while he was in a singing mood to get the man whose approval, according to a report by Turkus, was necessary for the perpetration of an organized murder in Brooklyn. One night in November, 1941, after he had been in custody for about twenty months, Kid Twist was mysteriously killed by a fall from his hotel room, where he was supposedly being guarded by six policemen; the case went out the window with him.[62] Nor was anybody indicted in another case in which Anastasia was a principal suspect, that of the murder in 1939 of Peter Panto, a decent, independent-minded dock worker who in open meeting dared to denounce the gangsters who dominated his union, though O'Dwyer's office had some important information on the case. "We find," the grand jury said in its second presentment, "that every case against Anastasia was abandoned, neglected or pigeon-holed."

The Panto case, the grand jury noted, had caused both the Department of Investigation and John Harlan Amen to take a look at conditions on the Brooklyn waterfront. Amen tried to get the records of various union locals dominated by one Emil Camarada, who had threatened Panto. At this point O'Dwyer launched his own waterfront investigation, collecting the locals' books and in general interfering with Amen's inquiry. Amen bowed out; soon after, the new crusader abandoned his investigation, following a conference between him and Camarada. The stenographic notes of the testimony of a hundred witnesses examined by the District Attorney's office in the investigation were never transcribed.

Winding its way through this story of strange doings in the Brooklyn District Attorney's office was a name that New Yorkers were destined to become much more familiar with in the years ahead—James J. Moran. A florid giant of a man, Moran, who later characterized himself as having "a certain amount of gutter wisdom," first met O'Dwyer when he was an attendant and O'Dwyer a judge in Kings County Court. They became quite close; when O'Dwyer became District Attorney, he took Moran along as his chief clerk. Though he was not a lawyer, the grand jury observed, Moran was in complete charge of many important matters in the District Attorney's office; before the grand jury the police sergeant in charge of detectives in the District Attorney's office testified that the general feeling was that Moran was "practically the spokesman for the District Attorney" and that the police officers took their orders from him. The first presentment accused Moran of issuing orders for the withdrawal of certain "wanted notices" sent out by the Police Department for suspected criminals. Because his "wanted" card had been removed from police files, a waterfront hoodlum named Romeo, a man who might have testified against Anastasia in the Panto case, though apprehended by an alert policeman, was turned loose; soon after, his body was fished out of a river in Delaware.[63]

(The charges made in the fall of 1945 against O'Dwyer and his handling of the District Attorney's office were re-aired in later years before the Kefauver committee and the New York State Crime Commission, and additional information was uncovered. For instance, it came out that

Moran was well acquainted with certain underworld figures, including Costello; that Albert Tannenbaum, a member of Murder, Inc., had given Edward A. Heffernan, an Assistant District Attorney under O'Dwyer, a statement on February 7, 1941, that Mendy Weiss had told him that he, Anastasia and a man named James Ferraco had murdered Panto, that this statement was submitted to Moran, but nothing was ever done; that O'Dwyer did not proceed against Adonis, though O'Dwyer admitted Reles implicated Adonis in one case.[64])

O'Dwyer and his backers, as one would expect, acted to limit the effectiveness of these charges. Before Goldstein's attack, O'Dwyer, with much foresight, prevailed upon Irving Sherman to leave the city until after election day in order to be out of reach of the newspapers. Before the election O'Dwyer refused to testify before the grand jury. When the grand jury charges were made, the O'Dwyer forces brushed them off as a political smear. O'Dwyer replied to the grand jury's assertion that he had abandoned an investigation of racketeering on the Brooklyn waterfront by claiming that at the time mentioned he was more concerned with successful prosecution of members of Murder, Inc. than with an inquiry into alleged kickbacks on the waterfront.[65]

(Later, at the time of the Kefauver crime inquiry, O'Dwyer attempted to deal more with specific accusations. Yes, he said, he had known Joe Adonis, but "years ago." True, he had been very friendly with Sherman from about 1942 to 1945, but their friendship had cooled after that time. He admitted that he had gone to Costello's home in 1942, not to talk politics as had been implied, however, but merely to ask the gambler questions about war contract frauds in connection with work O'Dwyer was doing in the army. His explanation apparently for not pursuing steps to get an indictment in the perfect murder case was that he feared for the safety of a witness, a "delicate" little boy. As to why he did not use Reles against Adonis, O'Dwyer said that the idea of getting Kid Twist before a grand jury and asking him about Adonis just never occurred to him.[66])

The O'Dwyer forces had nothing to worry about; the charges made by Goldstein, Beldock and the grand jury made little dent on O'Dwyer's strength. Goldstein's charge of underworld interest in O'Dwyer's candidacy was poorly timed; it was made on Navy Day and did not get the public attention it might have otherwise received. Though the first grand jury presentment contained some serious charges, it represented only part of the grand jury's findings; and it came out only a week before election day. Of greater importance in minimizing the impact of the charges was the fact that they were made during a political campaign and irrespective of their truth or falsity, of course, were not divorced from politics; the same voter skepticism that had led New Yorkers to shrug off La Guardia's charges in 1929 once again operated. In the light of this skepticism, the image of O'Dwyer that many saw was the one that his supporters, as in 1941, had done their best to paint: O'Dwyer, the independent and Roosevelt Democrat. His election, declared his backers, especially the American Laborites, was essential for Dewey's defeat in the gubernatorial race of 1946 and for the election of a Democratic President in 1948.[67]

O'Dwyer received 57 per cent of the vote and won by a plurality of almost 700,000 votes, the largest in the city's history up to that time; with the exception of the borough presidency of Staten Island, he swept in a Democratic Board of Estimate. Goldstein, who despite his charges did not run a strong race, and Morris, who did, finished neck and neck, receiving 22 and 21 per cent of the vote respectively, the closeness of the race between them being principally the result of the defection of a large number of Republican voters from the former to the latter. The vote for Morris on the No Deal line was bigger than the vote for Goldstein on the Republican line, though Goldstein came in second because of the Liberal Party.[68] After twelve years, the Democrats had returned; an era had come to an end.

Looking back on the political failure of Reform in 1945, a few points appear clearly. The triumph of the Democrats was actually less impressive than it looked; and had the old Fusion alignment not dissolved it could have beaten O'Dwyer. The combined Republican, Liberal, ALP and Morris vote exceeded that cast for O'Dwyer on the Democratic line by over 220,000 votes; only the addition of ALP votes to Democratic ones gave O'Dwyer a majority of the total vote. It is also evident that once the ALP joined the Democrats, Reform was doomed; and the result could not have been different had the Liberal Party made an alliance with the Democrats. Indeed it is apparent that any split in the anti-machine front would have given the Democrats victory.

Was the breakup of Fusion inevitable in 1945? It could well be that no matter what, the ALP and the Liberal Party for their own reasons were determined to find themselves on different sides of the political fence that year. But a Fusion movement involving the Republican, American Labor and Liberal parties and enjoying City Fusion Party and civic leader support might possibly have come into being. Perhaps such a movement could have materialized had La Guardia done his best to bring one about. While the Mayor, as we have observed, could not likely have rallied such a movement around himself, it does seem, especially considering his influence in the ALP, that he might have been able to create one around Morris, or possibly someone else. Instead La Guardia made no attempt to prevent the ALP from backing O'Dwyer and in other ways completely abdicated responsibility for the continuation of Fusion government. (La Guardia's lack of effort toward effecting a strong Fusion movement is one of the big reasons for doubting his good intentions in 1945.) It is very possible that the man who more than any other realized the aspirations of the Reform movement, generally in a magnificent way, and was chiefly responsible for Reform's long life, paradoxically played a crucial role in its demise.

As they had done a dozen years before, on December 31, 1945, La

Guardia and a group of his close friends came together at Seabury's home to watch the clock tick out the end of the old year and the start of the new one. The mood was different this time. The Mayor was tense, and as twelve o'clock approached, he sat immobile, doubled up, as if in great pain. One of those present asserts an affliction of the mind and the soul troubled the Mayor, that he couldn't bear the thought of giving up all the power he had wielded for so long.[69]

His political career was behind him, and the road ahead was short. Only in a political sense had he retired; La Guardia could never really retire. In 1946 he started two series of radio broadcasts under commercial sponsorship. In one, which a dairy concern sponsored, he commented upon local affairs. In the other, sponsored by *Liberty Magazine,* he discussed the national scene—until, a few months after starting, *Liberty* released him from his contract because of alleged reckless and irresponsible statements. At the end of March, 1946, he succeeded Lehman as Director General of UNRRA, a post, in which, as the reader will not be surprised to learn, he became engaged in several controversies. In December, 1946, he resigned from the position after it had become evident that the United States and Great Britain, which had been supplying UNRRA with most of its money and food, would no longer support the organization. In April, 1947, complaining of poor health, La Guardia entered a hospital for treatment. In June he underwent an operation which, it was said, disclosed a condition of chronic pancreatitis. Released from the hospital in mid-July, he failed to show a good recovery; he lost weight and strength and, though continuing to work at writing for several hours a day, could not carry on his broadcasting. On September 16 he suddenly collapsed and sank into a deep stupor. On the 20th, the man who had been New York's greatest Mayor was dead of cancer at the age of sixty-four.[70]

Broadly speaking, the New York reform movement of 1933 was both similar to and different from past reform movements in New York and other cities. With respect to the rise of the movement—and here similarities with the past were greatest—once again corruption in government revealed by investigations gave rise to civic indignation and efforts at reform which culminated in a full-scale political revolt. As it generally had in New York since the late nineteenth century, the revolt took the form of a fusion movement. This time, however, the economic conditions of the period constituted an important contributing factor in the development of the movement. As to the fall of reform government, clearly a number of the developments which in the past had brought it to an end—the defection of lower-class people, for example—did not operate in the case of the 1933 movement. Still, it was the failure to maintain anti-machine solidarity (a solidarity, however, that had lasted for an unusual length of time) which assured the end of the reform movement of 1933, as similar failures had with respect to other reform movements before; and as had occurred before, too, the breakup of solidarity in 1945 was due essentially to the operation of partisan considerations. Perhaps La Guardia's personality and character may also have been responsible, at least in some degree, for the fall of the reform movement of his day—even as those of Low and Mitchel were not without effect upon the disintegration of the movements associated with them.

Some of the achievements of the reform movement of 1933 were similar to those of past movements. Yet so great in range and amount were the innovations and improvements that resulted from the movement of 1933 that the difference of degree from past movements seems to be almost one of kind; the achievements of the La Guardia administration, it should be remembered, constituted most, but not all, of the achievements of the movement. The La Guardia administration, moreover, had a distinct quality which distinguished it from past reform administrations. It was not only reformist in the traditional sense, but completely liberal and democratic, a development that owed much to the fact that the reform Mayor was an entirely different man than Havermeyer, Strong, Low and Mitchel. We shall see in the pages ahead that, as with some other reform movements before it, that of the La Guardia period had important consequences for government and politics in the city in the years that followed. It should be pointed out, too, that the reform movement of 1933 also influenced the quest for good government in other cities, notably San Antonio and Philadelphia,[71] even as New York in the thirties had been affected by Cincinnati and other places.

Altogether the reform movement of 1933 was the greatest in the city's history—and, almost surely one would not be wrong in adding, in the history of American municipal government.

15

New wine in old bottles

DURING THE LA GUARDIA and post-La Guardia periods, some important developments occurred in New York with respect to the machine, the forces of reform and related subjects that we want to examine in this chapter. These developments were influenced by the La Guardia administration, and more importantly in some cases, by significant economic and social changes that were occurring in the city.

One of the important trends of the thirties and forties in New York, as in many other cities, was a decline in the power of the political machine. Mainly this was the result of economic and social developments, most of which we have noted as being responsible for the growth of independency in politics in the La Guardia era. The ending of large-scale immigration struck at the bulwark of machine strength; while the quota system was established in the twenties, the political repercussions of the new immigration policy were not seriously felt until later. The Great Depression and the New Deal weakened the machine in various ways. For one thing, these events had the effect of making voters more concerned about issues and candidates and less about party labels. The government—federal, state and local—entered the social welfare field in a way that dwarfed and undercut the old charity methods of the politicians, while labor unions, their growth encouraged by government policies, soon began undertaking welfare activities of their own. The intimate bond that had existed between the lower-class voter and the district leader or precinct captain tended to dissolve. The economic-social legislation of the New Deal, together with the subsequent prosperity of the war years, brought into being a "new middle class" recruited from the ranks of the children of immigrants who had come to America in the period between 1900 and World War I. As these people rose in status, they generally moved to new neighborhoods, often to the suburbs, a development that did not work to the advantage of the machine.[1] The rising numbers of college-educated Americans—the percentage of 18-year-olds enrolled in colleges in the United States increased from 12 in 1930, to 18 in 1940, to 30 in 1955 [2]—contributed to the growth of political sophistication and the decline of the party organization; especially does this seem true of New York City, which can boast of a number of excellent four-year liberal arts colleges.

In addition, New York City's Democratic organizations were further debilitated by the fact that La Guardia deprived them of city jobs; during this period, they also lost most of their county sinecures. When the Democrats returned to power they discovered something else: the steady growth of civil service and professionalism in city employment had lessened the opportunities for dispensing patronage; many jobs were no longer political or could no longer be considered as such.

While all the city's Democratic organizations suffered a decline, that of Tammany was the greatest; the Tammany of the time of O'Dwyer and his successor, Impellitteri, was but a shadow of the pre-La Guardia organization. The Hall's decline was both absolute and relative with respect to the city's other Democratic organizations; during the La Guardia period, it lost its position as *the* machine in New York. Tammany underwent so pronounced a change because it was especially affected by at least most of the above developments and because it did not get on well with the Roosevelt administration.

(One reason Tammany, more than any of the other political organizations in the city, was hurt by the ending of immigration and the movement of people from older neighborhoods—and it was—was that these changes weakened Manhattan's census position in relation to that of the rest of the city, continuing a trend begun in the twenties; the percentage of the city's population living in Manhattan fell from 26.9 in 1930, to 25.4 in 1940, to 24.8 in 1950.[3] That these declining percentages entailed unfortunate consequences for Manhattan's political strength is seen from two other sets of figures, the percentage of voters in each borough enrolled in the Democratic Party in the city and the percentage of the Democratic vote cast by each borough in mayoral elections. In each instance the trend of the twenties continued, Manhattan's percentage of Democratic enrollees falling from 24.8 in 1929 to 21.5 in 1945 and its percentage of Democratic votes cast in mayoral elections decreasing from 26.8 in 1929 to 21.9 in 1945.[4])

After the 1933 election, Farley, continuing Washington's effort to destroy Tammany's special position in New York's Democratic family and to bring it into the New Deal camp, embarked upon a policy of using the vast power of federal patronage to wrench Tammany's allies away from it, build them up at the Hall's expense and promote dissension within Tammany with a view to forcing the selection of a Tammany boss who met with the approval of the national administration. Through Farley's influence,

James C. Sheridan and William T. Fetherston were installed as the Democratic leaders in Queens and Richmond, and Frank V. Kelly was able to succeed to the leadership of Brooklyn's Democratic organization after the death of McCooey in 1934; a new political combination was brought into being whose core was Flynn's machine in the Bronx and Kelly's in Brooklyn. In good part because he was *persona non grata* in Washington, John Curry was deposed by his district leaders in 1934—the first time in Tammany's history a leader of the Hall was ousted—and James J. Dooling, a district leader favored by Farley, chosen in his place. But the struggle was not over. Within a year Dooling and Farley were at odds. In 1937, as we have seen, the city's other Democratic organizations, backed by Farley, engaged in a bitter primary battle with Tammany; the outcome signalized the transference of hegemony in New York's Democratic Party from Tammany to the Flynn-Kelly combination. After that, and especially after the time of Christie Sullivan, the Hall apparently tended to get on better with the New Deal administration, though the relationship between Tammany and Washington never became a warm one.

This fight with the national administration cost Tammany dearly. As a result of the struggle the Hall was deprived of much federal patronage—even when its relations with Washington improved, it did not get many jobs—at a time when it could not afford to lose a political morsel. At the same time, Tammany suffered the disadvantage of having its Democratic rivals supplied with juicy federal plums. (Furthermore, Tammany, which had been opposed to Lehman's nomination in 1932, found itself in a not too dissimilar predicament with regard to state patronage.) Its anti-New Deal posture allowed the other Democratic organizations to crush it in 1937.

That Tammany experienced these troubles was the result of its leadership—also responsible, at least to a large extent, for other Tammany difficulties shortly to be discussed. Curry was but the first in a long line of mediocre and weak Tammany heads. The list includes Dooling (July, 1934–July, 1937), Christopher Sullivan (August, 1937–February, 1942), Michael J. Kennedy (April, 1942–January, 1944), Edward V. Loughlin (January, 1944–March, 1947), Frank J. Sampson (March, 1947–July, 1948) and Hugo Rogers (July, 1948–July, 1949). Such a far cry were these men from Kelly, Croker and Murphy that the term boss doesn't even fit them. Wiser Tammany leaders during the New Deal period would have done everything possible, as the leaders of other machines did, to identify their cause with Roosevelt (and Lehman). Events of the last few years indicate that, despite the shifts in population, far-sighted Tammany leadership might have preserved the Hall's leading position in Democratic politics in the city, though Tammany would no doubt have been forced to deal with the other Democratic machines more as equals.[5]

The decline of Tammany, it is important to note, was reflected in a change in the relationship between the Hall and the underworld. While the machine was growing poorer, gangland was wealthy and its leaders not unaware of the importance of political connections. The result was what one would expect: the balance of power in the ancient alliance tended to shift from the politician to the gangster.[6] The outstanding manifestation of the shift was that the underworld, instead of just buying protection as in the old days, came to install its own district leaders. (At the beginning of the thirties Albert Marinelli was made a district leader literally by the guns of Luciano's gorillas; soon it become routine in certain tough sections of Manhattan for underworld figures to make financial contributions and furnish manpower to those it favored as district leaders.) Underworld influence, moreover, extended to the county leadership itself. Marinelli, it was reported, controlled Christie Sullivan. And who can forget the connections of Frank Costello?

Costello, one of the kingpins of organized crime in America during the thirties and forties and later, testified before the Kefauver crime committee that he knew more than a dozen Tammany district leaders on a basis ranging from "friends" to "very close friends." But that was not the half of it. Years before it had been discovered that he had used his influence with his district leader friends to have Mike Kennedy elected head of Tammany; that Kennedy was not unappreciative was seen a year after the election when at Costello's behest Kennedy had Thomas Aurelio, a good friend of the gambler's, nominated for a position on the State Supreme Court. There can be little doubt that while Kennedy was leader Costello dominated the Hall, and Costello's influence does not seem to have waned appreciably in the half a dozen years following Kennedy's fall. Edward Loughlin was really a front man for Clarence Neal, district leader of the Sixteenth Assembly District and chairman of Tammany's committee on elections, and Bert Stand, Tammany secretary, both of whom were good friends of Costello's. Moreover, Costello was on good terms with district leaders Carmine G. De Sapio, Harry Brickman, Sidney Moses and Francis X. Mancuso; and every Tammany leader after Loughlin was chosen with at least the assent of this powerful group. Hugo Rogers, who took his orders from this group, and particularly from Mancuso, told the Kefauver committee at a private hearing that "if Costello wanted me, he would send for me." [7]

Also attesting to Tammany's plight was the ignominious alliance it formed in the forties with Vito Marcantonio, congressman from East Harlem and chairman of the ALP's New York County organization. Though he always denied he was a Communist, Marcantonio showed a consistent espousal of Communist causes and of Soviet foreign policy and was certainly closely linked to the Communists. Regarded as a protégé by La Guardia, Marc, according to Warren Moscow, became the only political leader in the city capable of giving out certain kinds of favors. He let the hungry Tiger in. (He let Republicans in, too, and, in fact, built up in East Harlem his own machine manned largely by Democratic and Republican professionals.) Furthermore, he could usually guarantee the election of anyone nominated by Neal and Stand for a Supreme Court justiceship by getting the ALP to endorse him.[8] In their turn, the leaders of Tammany saw to it that Marc received the Democratic nomination for Congress in 1942, 1944 and 1946 in addition to his ALP nomination. (The Republicans also endorsed him in 1942 and 1944.) When O'Dwyer became Mayor, he launched an attack on the leadership of the Hall, one purpose of which was to put an end to the Tammany-Marc alliance; and with the election of Sampson, O'Dwyer's man, as Tammany head, the alliance was dissolved.[9]

No discussion of the decline in power of Tammany and the other Democratic organizations in the city, of course, should be taken to mean that the machine had become unimportant. Election to high office without its support had become easier, but the machine still exercised an air-tight control over nominations; and with respect to elections to the judiciary and the lesser offices, which did not evoke much popular interest, receiving the Democratic nomination in most cases remained tantamount to being elected.

What pointed up the machine's continuing importance was the evidence —certainly with respect to Tammany—that regardless of any changes wrought in the machine by the passage of time, one thing had remained the same: the basic animus propelling the organization. This should be obvious from things already said and from certain facts brought out by the New York State Crime Commission in 1952. It became apparent from hearings before that body that several Tammany leaders had become wealthier than they cared to admit; they refused to disclose their incomes on the grounds that to do so might tend to degrade or incriminate them. (One district leader who declined to discuss his economic worth was asked if it was true that he had paid large sums for shoes; when he refused to answer, evidence was introduced to show that he had bought a pair of brown suede oxfords in 1946 for $153.) While the Commission was generally unsuccessful in uncovering the origin of this wealth, apparently one source was the sale of judgeships in a manner reminiscent of Walker days. One witness testified that William Connolly, leader in the Eighth Assembly District, South, offered him a municipal bench position in 1947 for $25,000 and that after he refused, the nomination went to another, who was elected; Connolly could not explain why in 1947, 1948 and 1949 he spent $10,000 more than was accounted for by his receipts. Other testimony implicated Angelo Simonetti, leader of a zone in the Thirteenth Assembly District, in similar dealings; and it is reasonable to assume that these were not the only cases of this kind.[10]

One final note on Tammany before leaving our present discussion. Until about 1942 there were very few Italian district leaders in Tammany —in fact, there seem to have been more Jewish ones, and there were never too many of these—and the Irish had little trouble in maintaining their traditional rule. But after 1942, the number, and particularly the influence, of Italian leaders increased quickly. (Probably one reason for this was that at a time when other Tammany politicians found it hard to come by campaign funds, Italian leaders received them from Italian underworld figures, who in addition to being motivated by what appeared to them as sound business reasons were very likely interested in giving a helping hand to fellow Italians.) In the forties Tammany was rocked by internal warfare, which while not entirely the product of an ethnic conflict—a struggle for power among district leaders had racked the Hall since Curry's time, and a number of Jewish leaders were part of what came to be known as the Italian bloc—owed much to a struggle between the Italians and the Irish for control of the Hall.

The struggle came to a climax during O'Dwyer's time. In 1947, having become fed up with what it regarded as discrimination against Italians in matters of patronage the Italian bloc, the leading figures of which were De Sapio, Mancuso, Sidney Moses and Brickman, deserted Loughlin, whom it had been supporting, and joined forces with O'Dwyer, also opposed to Loughlin, to enthrone Frank Sampson as leader of Tammany. The Italian group had no intention of staying with Sampson, however; it was determined to rule the Hall itself. In 1948, during the course of a fight with O'Dwyer over a nomination to the Surrogate's Court, the Italian bloc, by making promises of patronage to a small group of Negro leaders who held the balance of power, was able to win control of the Tammany executive committee and replace Sampson with Hugo Rogers, Borough President of Manhattan. Rogers was a compromise candidate—for the Italian bloc did not yet feel strong enough to elect its own leader, De Sapio—but he took his orders from the Italian group. A year later came the final push. Capitalizing upon the victory of Franklin D. Roosevelt, Jr. over the Tammany candidate in a special congressional election and subsequent demands for reform of the Hall, the Italian bloc, which was now more powerful, threw out Rogers and put in De Sapio. The scepter in Democratic politics in Manhattan thus passed from the Irish, who had held it for so long, to the Italians; another shift of a kind that Tammany had known before had taken place. In the other boroughs, however, the Irish remained in control.[11]

The Democratic administrations of O'Dwyer and Impellitteri showed the imprint of New York's experience with La Guardia as well as that of a number of other developments we have been considering in this chapter. La Guardia had accustomed New Yorkers to a standard of government that the Democrats, to some extent, had to adjust to; a more mature voting public was not inclined to put up with many of the old-time political shenanigans. Moreover, as a result of the decline of the machine, the growth of professionalism in government and a more sophisticated electorate, the Mayor, traditionally more community-minded than the machine politicians, found himself in a stronger position with respect to the political organizations. As in the relationship between the machine and the underworld, predominance in the relationship between the machine and the

Mayor tended to shift from the machine to the other component. It should be noted, too, that O'Dwyer, while certainly greatly beholden to the professionals for his career, was never as much a part of the machine as most previous Democratic mayors. For these reasons, the administrations of O'Dwyer and Impellitteri represented a decided improvement over Democratic government of pre-La Guardia vintage.

Honest and quiet elections did not pass with the La Guardia administration. Under O'Dwyer and Impellitteri, the old system of using top administrative positions to reward district leaders was, in general, not re-instituted; and the calibre of those appointed to public office, including the Magistrates' Courts, was on the whole higher than under Walker. Indeed O'Dwyer kept on some of La Guardia's appointees, Robert Moses, whom subsequent mayors also continued, being the most conspicuous. Finding themselves in the post-war period with a city suffering from various shortages and with an electorate that had come to expect much, O'Dwyer and Impellitteri continued to give construction and welfare the emphasis La Guardia had. A post-war construction program based upon the planning of the La Guardia administration was carried out, progress being made, among other things, in the building of schools and hospital facilities. Not only did the Democrats continue La Guardia's low-income public housing program; but to help the lower-middle-income family whose income ($3,500 to $4,500 a year) was too high to allow it into low-rent public housing, but too low to enable it to afford the lowest priced new private housing, the Democrats embarked upon a no-cash-subsidy housing program under which the City Housing Authority undertook to build self-supporting, partially tax-exempt, apartments. By the mid-1950's, New York, though still facing a serious housing problem, had made a striking achievement in public housing.[12]

Moreover, the Democrats, in other things beside housing, instituted improvements and broke new ground. O'Dwyer filled in the ranks of city employees depleted by the war and gave them a much-needed raise in pay. According to George Hallett, more progress was made in city planning under O'Dwyer than had been made under La Guardia. O'Dwyer reorganized the Welfare Department with the view of achieving more efficiency, and both he and Impellitteri undertook vigorous efforts to clean the Communists out of the Department.[13] Under O'Dwyer, a Department of Traffic and a Smoke Control Bureau were created to enable the City to better cope with the problems of traffic and air pollution, and a Division of Labor Relations was set up in an effort to minimize labor disputes. Under Impellitteri, the Smoke Control Bureau became a new Department of Air Pollution Control, and under Mayor Wagner the Division of Labor Relations became a Department of Labor. O'Dwyer was responsible for the establishment of the Mayor's Committee on Management Survey to conduct a comprehensive survey of the city's management needs; Impellitteri put some of the recommendations of this little Hoover commission into effect.

Because of increasing subway deficits, O'Dwyer abandoned a forty-four-year-old tradition in the city and raised the subway fare to a dime—an action that it is difficult not to account to his credit.[14]

Yet in spite of these creditable features, the administrations of O'Dwyer and Impellitteri were cruelly disappointing; in important ways Democratic government of the post-La Guardia period represented a definite regression. The story of the corruption that befouled the O'Dwyer administration, revealed chiefly by grand jury investigations, the Kefauver committee and the New York State Crime Commission between 1950 and 1952, is too well known to require much recounting. As a result of the work of Kings County District Attorney Miles F. McDonald and the confession of Harry Gross, one of the biggest bookmakers in the city, it was discovered that gambling, which La Guardia had been able to hold down during most of his administration, had increased during his last few years and had broken completely loose under O'Dwyer. Gross had paid huge amounts of "ice" to the police to be allowed to conduct his business, his pay-off totals in 1947, 1948 and 1949 reaching $3,000,000, exclusive of clothing and television sets sent to policemen and their families. Implicated were nearly 200 policemen, active or retired, from the lowest echelon to the highest, a few being close friends of O'Dwyer and his appointees. As a consequence of these revelations and others of police protection of gambling on Staten Island, a result of the work of the State Crime Commission, more than a hundred policemen resigned from the force, numbers were dismissed and a few were sent to jail. It was clear that the lightest charge that could be made against O'Dwyer was that he had been aware of the probability that corruption was rampant in the Police Department but had failed to take vigorous action against it. One grand jury was persuaded that the true purpose of the measures O'Dwyer did adopt "was to create an insulating zone of activity within his administration" which he hoped would fend off blows of criticism in the event police conditions were exposed.[15]

The Police Department was also disgraced by the announcement of the FBI in 1950 that the Department's crime statistics could no longer be considered sufficiently dependable for inclusion in *Uniform Crime Reports,* the official record of American crime. The police, it was apparent, had been indulging in the practice of not reporting all crimes, in order to save themselves work while keeping their record good. How spurious police statistics were was indicated by the figures on crime presented after the institution of partial reforms: reported cases of robbery, assault with gun and knife and larceny rose by 400, 200 and 700 per cent respectively, while reports of burglaries zoomed to a level thirteen times higher than that recorded in 1948 and 1949; additional reforms were followed by crime statistics that contrasted even more markedly with those noted before the adoption of any reforms.[16]

Then there were the activities of James J. Moran. Despite what the Brooklyn grand jury said about him in 1945, despite the fact that in 1946

District Attorney Hogan called O'Dwyer's attention to various rumors about Moran, on becoming Mayor O'Dwyer appointed Moran First Deputy Commissioner of the Fire Department; and in 1950, as he was getting ready to leave office, O'Dwyer named Moran to a life-time $15,000-a-year post on the Board of Water Supply. (O'Dwyer later declared: "I gave him the water-board job so he could educate his children. Tears streamed down Moran's face when I did it.") As First Deputy Commissioner of Fire, Moran placed on a business basis a racket, never completely eradicated under La Guardia, in which fire inspectors extorted money from installers of oil burners and refrigerators before granting them permits; the take from Moran's extortion scheme seems to have come to about $500,000 a year, Moran clearing up to $2,500 a week. Nor does it appear that this was Moran's only extra-curricular interest. Harry Gross declared at a Police Department trial that he gave Moran $5,000 in 1945 and $15,000 in 1949 as a campaign contribution for O'Dwyer. And John P. Crane, president of the Uniformed Firemen's Association, told the Kefauver committee that between 1946 and 1949 he gave Moran $55,000 in cash to assure the good will of the O'Dwyer administration with respect to legislation benefiting firemen. The Kefauver hearings, furthermore, revealed that between 1946 and 1950 Louis Weber, convicted policy racketeer, often called upon Moran in his office at the Fire Department; and, while the reason for these visits was never ascertained, there is a strong presumption in light of the Gross and Crane stories that Weber did not call on Moran to pass the time of day. Convicted in 1951 and 1952 of perjury in connection with his testimony before the Kefauver committee and of extortion in the Fire Department, and a few years later of federal income tax evasion, Moran was sentenced to a long stay in prison.[17]

It was not only in the matter of clean government that the Democrats fell down. If the appointments of O'Dwyer and Impellitteri were generally better than those of their Democratic predecessors, they were, for the most part, not so good as La Guardia's. La Guardia's nonpartisan approach went out the window; and in other respects, politics came to be more important, merit less important in appointment-making than in the days of Fusion. Before the Kefauver committee, O'Dwyer admitted that most of his appointments came from the Democratic county organizations and argued that since he was a Democrat he felt that he had an obligation to distribute patronage to the Democratic Party. Impellitteri seemed to feel the same way; soon after he was elected as an independent, he appointed Frank Sampson "patronage dispenser" and, aside from De Sapio, whom he would not forgive and whom he tried to starve to death politically, Impellitteri did business with the Democratic bosses.

Both O'Dwyer and Impellitteri, furthermore, put much store in personal friendships when it came to appointments. One obvious consequence of these practices is that a good number of appointees were at best mediocre. A few, appointed by O'Dwyer, were friends of Adonis and Costello. Not the least unfortunate result was that the hard-working civil service staff tended to become demoralized.[18]

Both O'Dwyer and Impellitteri failed to come to grips with a number of big problems facing the city. The greatest one confronting not only New York, but other American cities in the inflationary post-war period, was the financial problem of making ends meet in the face of steadily rising costs. Lacking financial autonomy, the city had to appeal to the legislature for additional sources of revenue, and this body, as usual in such matters, was not overly co-operative. O'Dwyer and Impellitteri got the worst of a fight with the Dewey administration. The Mayors, however, were not entirely the victims of circumstance. The impression was current that O'Dwyer and Impellitteri did not battle for additional state aid and new taxing powers for the city as vigorously as they might have; in some circles it was hinted that the Mayors, for reasons known best to them, were only shadowboxing. Impellitteri, in particular, pursued policies which hardly had the effect of creating sympathy for the cause of the city or of increasing its bargaining power with respect to Albany. His failure to carry out many of the important recommendations of the Mayor's Committee on Management Survey was only one way in which, instead of economizing, he was guilty of wasting. Instead of formulating a long-range, well-thought-out, financial program for the city, he continually presented last minute, patchwork budgets.[19]

Neither O'Dwyer nor Impellitteri tried to clean up the waterfront. O'Dwyer put on the phoniest kind of show. Announcing a full-dress investigation of the waterfront to discover why New York's port traffic had been ebbing away, he appointed as heads of a subcommittee on labor conditions on the docks two friends of his, W. J. McCormack, the stevedore tycoon, and Joseph P. Ryan, president of the International Longshoremen's Association, who, as anyone acquainted with the problem knew, should have been about the last two people named to such a group.[20] Under Impellitteri, New Yorkers complained loudly about dirty streets, unsafe parks, traffic congestion, lack of parking space, an undermanned Police Department and, most of all, the Mayor's failure to do anything about these conditions.[21]

Much of the reason for the generally unsatisfactory administrations of O'Dwyer and Impellitteri lay in the fact that, though the machine did not play quite the same role in their administrations as in those of previous Democratic Mayors, it was still much a part of them. Indeed, considering its weakened position, the machine did not do too badly under O'Dwyer and Impellitteri. Neither Mayor seemed to have adequately appreciated the subtle but definite fact that with respect to the machine the Mayor's position had grown stronger, or to have been inclined to take sufficient advantage of that fact to give the city better government; certainly they did not do so.[22]

Mainly the unhappy conditions New York experienced under O'Dwyer and Impellitteri were the results of shortcomings of O'Dwyer and Impellitteri. O'Dwyer, New York's 100th Mayor, presents a major enigma. A good-looking and charming Irishman, warm-hearted, friendly, intelligent and un-bigoted, he had another side which almost destroyed him. It was a side already strongly suggested to us by certain episodes in his pre-mayoral career. When Gross told about his payments to Moran, he added that Moran had invited him, along with seven other top bookmakers, to attend a meeting with O'Dwyer, a meeting Gross said he could not attend because of sickness but which Moran subsequently told him took place. Crane's story concerning his dealings with Moran contained the sensational statement that in October, 1949, during the mayoral campaign of that year, Crane had visited O'Dwyer at Gracie Mansion and personally handed him a red envelope containing $10,000 in cash. Whether or not O'Dwyer was personally corrupt—and both Gross's and Crane's stories, it must be kept in mind, were never substantiated—this certainly was true: O'Dwyer was weak on principle, integrity, moral courage, will-power and drive and suffered from certain defects of his qualities, such as his fondness for his friends. It is not necessary to assume O'Dwyer was personally dishonest to explain any of the unfortunate aspects of his administration.[23]

In 1945, in a frantic search to find a regular Democrat from Manhattan with an Italian name to run as the party's candidate for President of the City Council, Ed Loughlin came across the name Vincent R. Impellitteri in the "Little Green Book," the city's *Official Directory*. He thereupon set this unknown secretary to a State Supreme Court justice on the road to fame.[24] While Impellitteri was not wholly to blame for conditions in the city which irritated the citizens during his time as Mayor—the financial problem underlay a good deal of the trouble—he was not without much responsibility, and in addition to the matter of finances. Though personally likeable and well-intentioned, Impellitteri, like O'Dwyer, was basically a drifter, a passive character rather than a forceful, energetic personality, a fact that his numerous vacations in the Walker mode only served to underline; and he lacked the intelligence and vision for the nation's second toughest governmental job. Some men from undistinguished backgrounds, when placed by events in high positions, rise to the occasion. Impellitteri's tragedy was that he did not.

O'Dwyer and Impellitteri, like Hylan and Walker, were never cut out to be Mayor of New York. That they held this position during the post-war period, at a time when American cities needed especially fine leadership, only compounded the misfortune.

The reform front, as well as the machine, underwent changes in the La Guardia and post-La Guardia years. While the developments that occurred with respect to the reform community were not as profound or as striking as those relating to the machine, they were not unimportant. One was that the civic element, taken as a whole, experienced something of a decline in activity and importance in the La Guardia period and something of a revival in the days of O'Dwyer and Impellitteri.

That the civic front tended to lose momentum under La Guardia and regain it under his Democratic successors is not surprising; civic work has tended to be less vigorous during times when people have felt they have good government than at times when they have felt the lack of it. With regard to the weakening of the civic front in La Guardia's time, it should also be noted that La Guardia in another, and more direct, way had something to do with bringing it about: through his action in pillaging the civic organizations of some of their best people—for example, Rufus McGahen of the Citizens Union, Paul Blanshard of the City Affairs Committee—for service in his administration.[25]

In particular, the City Affairs Committee, the City Club and the City Fusion Party fell upon hard times during the Fusion period. The City Affairs Committee, though managing to stay alive through most of the La Guardia period, dissolved in the early forties, turning its good will and assets over to the Citizens Union; some of its members went into that organization.[26] ("It died," said the Reverend John Haynes Holmes, "because in the administration of La Guardia, we felt that our cause had been largely won." [27]) In the case of the City Club and the City Fusion Party, special factors, in addition to the circumstances mentioned above, were greatly responsible for what happened. The trouble experienced by the City Club was in considerable measure due to a decline in the club's non-resident membership, which created a serious financial problem for the organization. Non-resident members had been attracted to the club largely because of its clubhouse, which afforded them accommodations when in town; but time outmoded the club's facilities while providing better accommodations elsewhere in the city, and the non-resident members lost interest in the organization. In the mid-forties, the club, as part of a retrenchment program, gave up its clubhouse and moved to a modest suite in a midtown hotel. At the same time, the club's leadership was aging and new, younger leaders lacking.[28] Not least because of some light it may throw upon the problems of the civic party, the decline of the City Fusion Party is a subject that deserves more extended treatment.

The party emerged from the election of 1933 as a by no means inconsequential force in New York City politics. Though it was not a legal party, it was, if the vote it received is the criterion, the largest political group ever assembled in the city outside the Democratic and Republican parties. While actually a much smaller group, of course, the City Fusion Party was not a paper organization; if not organized in every assembly district or equally active in every district where it was organized, it was organized in many districts and some were particularly active. Thousands of enthusiastic, especially young, people were members, and they hoped for big things from it.[29] Quickly reaffirming its long-term purpose of serving as a permanent municipal party and civic group, the organization adopted a new charter establishing, at least in theory, democratic control.[30]

In 1934 the party was very active. It took a deep interest in the problems of the time facing the city, largely through committees, such as those on the courts, transit, education and legislation. It played an important role, as we have seen, in the Fusion campaign for Comptroller in that year. Charging that certain legislators had tried hard to sabotage the Fusion program in the city, City Fusion backed a number of Republican candidates for the Assembly and Senate whom it felt would carry out its policies and in some cases ran its own candidates for these bodies; it also endorsed some congressional and other candidates. And yet in 1934 the little City Fusion clubs, usually located over stores, were already beginning to die. After 1934, the party's decline was steady. It gave La Guardia only about 160,000 votes (roughly 7 per cent of his total vote) in 1937, by which time it had become a paper organization, and 63,000 votes (not quite 3 per cent of his total vote) in 1941. In elections after 1941, the party represented at most an insignificant line on the voting machine. In 1950 and 1953, when it did not even appear on the ballot, the remnant of what had once been a chief medium for Fusion victory endorsed the Democratic candidate for Mayor.[31]

In addition to the general factors that weakened other reform organizations,[32] the City Fusion Party was hurt by internal conflicts and some other problems. One conflict was that between party members who believed the party should receive patronage and those who believed it should not; some of those who favored patronage were sincere reformers, but many were band wagon jumpers who were in the party for what they could get.[33] The question of how much authority the party leadership should have with respect to the party's units and that of the advisability of going into state and national politics were other bones of contention within the organization.[34] The party was not helped by the fact that its leadership had but weak control over the use of the party name and emblem.[35] It suffered, too, from the establishment of the Progressive City Committee and especially the ALP, which competed with the City Fusion Party for the interest of politically-minded independent citizens.[36] Had all the big civic leaders in the city been members of the City Fusion Party, as Cincinnati's civic leaders were members of the Charter Committee in that city, the party would have been stronger, but this was not the case. Joseph Price, Richard Childs and others, recalling the early days of the Citizens Union, believed that a municipal party must become adulterated and that the best policy was to have no such party, but create one whenever needed.[37] Also there were La Guardia's actions.

In various ways the Mayor allowed—perhaps it would not be wrong to say encouraged—the new party to disintegrate. It was not only that he gave it hardly any patronage—a policy for which much can be said. In line with his general policy as to appointments, La Guardia forced members of his administration who were leaders in the party to give up their party positions, a move, according to Charles Belous, one-time chairman of the City Fusion Party in Queens, that helped to cripple the young party and which seems less justifiable.[38] What appears even less excusable was the Mayor's general unfriendliness to the new party; he was unkind, ungracious and unnecessarily tactless toward it; he snarled at people who helped put him in office. Writing to Stanley Howe in January, 1937, Belous complained that La Guardia had broken his spirit and that he had decided to resign as chairman of the City Fusion Party in Queens. Since becoming chairman, Belous declared, he had worked hard and sacrificed much. "Throughout all this time," he said, "I have not received as much as a word of thanks or kindness from the great infallible [La Guardia]. Instead, ridicule, disrespect and insult have been heaped on my head." At the slightest pretext, Belous declared, La Guardia threw the "bugaboo of patronage" in his teeth.[39] Belous was not the only one to lose interest in the City Fusion Party because of La Guardia's antagonism toward it.

Perhaps La Guardia's attitude toward the party was the result, or partly the result, of bending backward too far in an effort to be nonpartisan. (Jesse S. Raphael, a member of the party, in a letter to Maurice Davidson in November, 1934, held that the reason for "the indifference, if not antagonism displayed by the Mayor and many of the officials of the city toward the party" was that the administration had wrongly read Cincinnati's experience. Nonpartisanship in office was fine, he wrote, but New York's officials had not seen that "none of the city officials in Cincinnati have given up their active support of the 'Charter Committee' which stands for the independent movement in that city." [40]) Perhaps, as a few have suggested to this writer, La Guardia was motivated mainly by resentment and concern over the patronage-seekers in the new party—the presence of which constituted one important, and perhaps in La Guardia's mind crucial, difference between the organization and the Cincinnati Charter Committee. This writer's study of La Guardia leads to the feeling that the Mayor, to one degree or another, treated the City Fusion Party badly because he could not bear the thought of being beholden to it and was concerned lest it detract from his importance in the Fusion movement.

(Incidentally, political egotism probably explains, at least in good part, why La Guardia did not try some other way than that presented by the City Fusion Party—say by encouraging the formation of a new group more analogous to the Charter Committee in Cincinnati—to strengthen the Fusion movement as an entity apart from himself.[41])

It is easy to overemphasize this matter of the decline of the reform element in the Fusion period. Reformers, it should be kept in mind, continued to engage in a good deal of healthy civic activity. We have seen the part played by civic groups in the struggle for a new Charter, PR and county reorganization. Though it was not in the same category as the more permanent civic groups, the Citizens Non-Partisan Committee was certainly no sluggish organization. The Citizens Union remained as active as ever; its enrollment remained steady and, though it did not have as much funds as in the 1920's, this was not so much the result of a drop of interest in the organization as of the fact that it became a more liberal group and alienated the support of many wealthy conservatives.[42] The La Guardia period even witnessed the establishment of a new important civic organization: the Citizens' Housing and Planning Council.[43]

What ground the civic front lost in the days of Fusion it tended to regain in the post-La Guardia era. In the later period the La Guardia administration now had an effect which benefited the civic groups: the not-so-dim recollection of what municipal government could be like worked to promote dissatisfaction with O'Dwyer and Impellitteri and stimulated some citizens to take a more active interest in civic affairs. In 1950 the City Club was on the verge of disbanding. Attracted to this situation by an item in the *Times,* a group of younger people persuaded the club's board of trustees to take them in as members and give them a chance to make a go of the organization. With an assist from the O'Dwyer scandals, they succeeded in bringing additional new blood into the organization and keeping it alive. The club, it should be noted, played a leading part in criticizing the Police Department's crime reporting under O'Dwyer and bringing about a radical revision in the Department's reporting procedure. Two new civic groups made their appearance in the wake of the post-La Guardia investigations. In accordance with a recommendation of the Brooklyn grand jury that had been working with McDonald in investigating gambling that such a group be formed, Spruille Braden, former United States envoy to Argentina, and some others organized the New York City Anti-Crime Committee at the end of January, 1951, for the purpose of waging war on crime. The group undertook to employ trained investigators to dig up material pertaining to crime which it then turned over to the law-enforcing authorities. With the object of serving as a new civic watchdog, the City Affairs Committee (supposedly, but not actually, a rebirth of the old organization) came into being in 1952 with the Right Reverend Charles K. Gilbert, retired Bishop of the Protestant Episcopal Diocese of New York, as president. (However, the Anti-Crime Committee, despite a good record of accomplishments, was forced to suspend its operations after six years of work because of internal strife and lack of funds; and the City Affairs Committee, because of a disagreement that rent the organization, did not do much and within a short time went out of business.) Elsewhere in the civic circle, too, the O'Dwyer-Impellitteri period led to a quickening of life.[44]

Another development affecting the reform front in the La Guardia and post-La Guardia periods was that having to do with the ethnic make-up of the city's civic leadership. These years saw the continuation of a trend that had been in progress for a long time: the exodus of well-to-do and middle-class Protestants from the city to the suburbs. (According to one prominent sociologist, Dean Kenneth D. Johnson of the New York School of Social Work, the city's Protestant population, which accounted for 28 per cent of the city's total population in 1935 and 4 per cent of which was non-white, was down to 22 per cent in 1952, 8 per cent being non-white.[45]) As the number of Protestants declined, leadership in civic affairs came increasingly to be exercised by well-to-do and middle-class Jews.[46]

Finally, it is important to say a word about the effect of the ALP and the Liberal Party—basically the effect of the political maturing of organized labor—upon the quest for good government; while these two parties were not reform organizations, to a good extent they represented vital additions to the reform side. For a few years after the formation of the Liberal Party, the ALP remained the more important of the two. But in 1948 as a consequence of the ALP's decision to support Henry Wallace for President, the Amalgamated Clothing Workers, which was opposed to Wallace, pulled out of the ALP, leaving the Communists, who had been calling the tune anyway, in full control of the organization; and though the ALP polled more than 500,000 votes for Wallace in the state, it began to slither downhill after that. In 1954, ten years after the big split that resulted in the formation of the Liberal Party, the ALP, by polling less than 50,000 votes in the gubernatorial election of that year, lost its official party status and, incidentally, its name.[47] In 1949, the Liberal Party for the first time received a higher percentage of the total vote than did the ALP; after that the younger party always did better.[48]

Unlike most of the civic groups, the American Labor and Liberal parties made an impact on the fight for reform mainly in connection with elections. We have indicated in preceding pages something of their contribution to the cause of municipal reform. It may well be that the ALP, by its very presence, forced the Republicans to renominate La Guardia in 1937. In that year, it actually gave him his margin of victory, though this is not to say La Guardia would necessarily have lost the election had the party not been in existence. In 1937, as in 1941, the ALP polled two-thirds as many votes for the Mayor as did the Republicans. In 1945 and 1949, the Liberals joined the Republicans to form an anti-Democratic coalition (though in the first year the Liberals undoubtedly would have done better by the cause of municipal reform had they advanced a different mayoral candidate). As for the years immediately following 1949, it is likely that in one municipal contest (that for President of the City Council in 1951), possibly in more, the Liberal cause best represented the cause of good government. The real value of the ALP—in its early period—and the Liberal Party was that they offered avenues of expression to a growing number of independent-minded voters, thereby constituting a check upon the major parties.

At the same time, it must be emphasized that the two splinter parties at times acted in ways which worked against the interest of municipal reform

—or which at least placed them in a different corner from that of many supporters of municipal reform.[49] We have already observed that in 1945, following La Guardia's announcement that he would not run again, both the American Laborites and the Liberals preferred an alliance with the Democrats to taking part in an anti-Democratic coalition; and we have discussed the importance of the Democratic-ALP alliance for the election of that year. In 1949, though the Liberals again joined the Republicans, they insisted upon endorsing the Democratic candidate for Borough President of Manhattan, Robert F. Wagner, Jr.,[50] son of the famous senator, a move that tended to weaken the Republican-Liberal alliance. It is not clear that the action of the Liberals in forming a coalition with the Democrats in the mayoral race of 1950 was in the best interest of good government.

That the splinter parties did not always see eye-to-eye with others on the anti-machine side was not strange. The main concern of these parties was economic and social issues, their main field of activity state and national politics. When conflicts arose, as they were bound to, between the party's obligations (or what were thought to be its obligations) to its larger purpose and what was in the best interest of local government (or what many reformers considered was in the best interest of local government), the latter was naturally sacrificed to the former.

In 1949 a Fusion campaign was launched in an effort to defeat O'Dwyer, now seeking re-election. Headed by the veteran Samuel Seabury a Fusion Committee was formed containing a number of people who in one way or another had been associated with the La Guardia regime—people like Burlingham, Windels, Davidson, Isaacs, Morgan, Palma, Thacher, Mrs. La Guardia, Mrs. Deutsch; and partly through its efforts leaders of the Republican and Liberal parties agreed to coalesce on a city-wide ticket headed by Newbold Morris. But this fusion effort was far from being a real fusion movement; it was a synthetic affair which expressed no deeply felt grievance of the people. The corruption of the O'Dwyer administration was still beneath the surface; and Morris' charges that New York was wide-open to bookies, that the underworld dominated Tammany were generally regarded as so much political hot air. What was known were O'Dwyer's accomplishments, and the Mayor was extremely popular. Charles Belous, certainly no machine adherent, thought that O'Dwyer was a good Mayor, even after the performance of his predecessor, and that the Fusion campaign was unjustified. So did the voters who swept O'Dwyer back into office. While many things contributed to the Mayor's re-election, the basic factor simply was that New Yorkers saw no pressing reason for not returning to office a man whom they believed had done a pretty good job.[51]

1950, however, brought evidence of police corruption in Brooklyn (like Walker's, O'Dwyer's troubles developed in his second term), and with the scandals came a rise of civic indignation. Before the main scandals broke, on the last day of August, almost eighteen years to the day after the resignation of Walker, O'Dwyer quit as Mayor to become United States Ambassador to Mexico. (O'Dwyer did not give, nor has he ever given, a completely lucid explanation for his action.) Though O'Dwyer's departure occasioned a special election for Mayor, no fusion movement, even in name, developed to exploit the situation. The mayoral election coincided with those for Governor and United States Senator, and the Liberal Party allied itself with the Democrats to support a common ticket for all three big spots. The Democratic-Liberal coalition nominated Justice Ferdinand Pecora for Mayor. The Republicans named Edward Corsi as their mayoral candidate.

Yet popular feeling expressed itself. Stung by the fact that the Democratic-Liberal alliance had passed him over in selecting its nominee for Mayor, Acting Mayor Impellitteri, despite all sorts of pressures to cause him to change his mind, insisted upon running as an independent candidate. And Impy, as the press soon dubbed him, caught on. Many sympathized with him because he was an underdog and because they felt he had been given a raw deal. But also Impellitteri became the rallying point, not for the reform crowd, to be sure—which was generally confused and divided and not significantly involved in the campaign—but for a good number of independent-minded voters who wanted to protest against the police scandals and against bossism in the Democratic Party. Though these people were not reassured by the Acting Mayor's background, under the circumstances they were willing to take a chance on him. Impellitteri did his best to play to this vote. He called himself the "unbossed and unbought" candidate and promised to give the city an independent and businesslike administration.

The Acting Mayor won with more than 1,160,000 votes, 44 per cent of the total vote. His victory was a historic event in the politics of New York City. Not since the time of the Civil War had a Mayor been elected without the support of a major party; never before had one been elected with only a line on the voting machine behind him, on what Al Smith would have called a "Chinese laundry ticket." The election of Impellitteri was a monument to the growth of independent voting in the city. That the new Mayor subsequently failed to achieve good government shows only that hopes are not always realized.[52]

In the fall of 1951, the scandals that had begun to blossom a year before were in full bloom. The police graft investigation growing out of Harry Gross's confessions was still in the spotlight; police corruption on Staten Island was in the public eye. And once again the voters took the opportunity of a special election—that to fill Impellitteri's old job of President of the City Council—to voice their displeasure. The pattern of protest was not too dissimilar from that of 1950. Again the Republicans and Liberals failed to fuse on a candidate, this time because the only candidate they could have agreed upon, Congressman Jacob K. Javits, a Republican who had been elected with Liberal Party support, turned down the nomination.

The result was a three-cornered race among the Democrats, Republicans and Liberals. Waging his campaign on the links between crime and politics, however, the Liberal Party choice, independent Democrat Rudolph Halley, former chief counsel to the Kefauver committee, developed strong reform sentiment behind him, especially among independent Democrats. As a rule, the reform set and the old associates of La Guardia did not play a prominent part in the 1951 campaign—partly at least, it seems, because there was no one anti-machine candidate they could unite behind—but most of those who took an active interest in the campaign backed Halley. Like Impellitteri, Halley made history. Though it was an off-year election, though he was the candidate of a minor party (receiving, however, two additional lines on the ballot), Halley carried Manhattan, the Bronx and Brooklyn to win by almost 165,000 votes.[53]

In the spring of 1953 an attempt was made to bring about a fusion movement with respect to the mayoral election of that year which would depose Impellitteri and put someone better qualified for Mayor in City Hall. William Chanler, William Fellowes Morgan, James Marshall, Mrs. La Guardia, Davidson, Windels and others formed a new Citizens Non-Partisan Committee to serve as a co-ordinating group with regard to the Republican and Liberal parties, clearly the two essential components for any such movement. Representatives of the committee met with Charles Tuttle and other members of an Inter-County Republican Committee that had been appointed by the five Republican county chairmen in the city and with leaders of the Liberal Party. But the effort came to naught. The Republicans and Liberals could not agree on a mayoral candidate. Actually, as in 1951, the only person both could have accepted was Javits, but in May and early June when the Citizens Non-Partisan Committee and the Liberals were in favor of his nomination, the Republicans held back; and when at the end of June the Republicans finally came around, the Liberals had undergone a change of heart. Influenced by the views of the party's rank and file who were against a coalition with the Republicans and wanted Halley as the party's candidate, by a *Daily News* poll which showed the President of the City Council to be the people's choice for Mayor, by recollections of the voting pattern of 1950 and 1951, Liberal leaders decided they could go it alone with Halley and win. The Republicans nominated Harold Riegelman, general counsel to the Citizens Budget Commission, expert on city finances and Acting Postmaster in the city. Where they took any interest that fall, the reform people were destined to scatter their support among the chief candidates.[54]

Again, however, despite the absence of a fusion movement, the dissatisfaction that many felt with civic conditions did not go unrecorded. Within the Democratic Party, a movement developed to deny Impellitteri the party nomination. Led by De Sapio, the Mayor's political arch enemy, and Ed Flynn, both of whom were apparently much concerned about the popularity of Halley, the movement received the support of many independent

Democrats who wanted to get rid of Impellitteri, but desired to see the election of a Democratic Mayor. As their mayoral choice, De Sapio and Flynn put forward Borough President of Manhattan Wagner. Since Impellitteri had every intention of being the Democratic candidate and since his aspiration received the endorsement of the Democratic bosses in Brooklyn, Queens and Richmond, the result was the first Democratic mayoral primary fight since 1937. Before long, the struggle became mixed up with a fight between the conservative and liberal wings of the Democratic Party for control of the state organization, the former generally espousing Impellitteri's cause, the latter supporting Wagner's, a conflict from which Wagner could only hope to gain. On primary day, Borough President Wagner won a smashing two-to-one victory. While Wagner's triumph was largely the result of the conservative-liberal conflict and of the feeling of many Democratic regulars that he would make a stronger candidate than Impellitteri, it cannot be doubted that in part his victory reflected voter irritation with Impellitteri's administration.[55]

It must be said, however, that there was a decided limit to the public's interest in the mayoral race of 1953. Despite the fact that the primary fight was a bitter one, the citizens seemed indifferent to it, and only one-quarter of the city's enrolled Democrats bothered to vote. The regular campaign that followed was, if anything, marked by greater voter apathy. Undoubtedly the candidates had much to do with the lack of interest. Wagner was generally viewed as a pleasant fellow with a liberal record, the son of a loved and respected statesman (an image that must have had consequences for the primary, as for the regular, campaign). Riegelman, though in many ways the best-qualified candidate, was a conservative of the solid citizen type; moreover, he had the misfortune to run in a year when state legislation providing for a rent increase and for the creation of a city transit authority (which agency immediately raised the subway fare) made Albany a fighting word to many citizens of the city. Halley, as time went on, lost his appeal, coming to appear to many as a young man too much on the make. The candidates gave the impression of being second-rate thespians going through the motions of a shop-worn play. Some other candidate, especially one with Fusion backing, might have evoked more voter interest.

Undoubtedly, too, another factor was involved—a factor that in some degree would have worked to limit voter interest no matter who was running. Impellitteri's sins were not the dramatic kind; there was little or no graft or corruption. He could be charged only with giving the city mediocre leadership, of failing to deal intelligently and vigorously with pressing problems. While his failure in this respect was hardly unimportant and was resented, it was not the kind of offense which had traditionally raised the voters' hackles. And once Impellitteri was removed as a possibility, the emotional element, such as it was (particularly in light of the candidates running) went out of the campaign.

Under the circumstances that prevailed in the fall of 1953, Wagner's victory was scarcely surprising.[56]

From the above account, it seems clear that nothing that could really be called a reform movement occurred during the O'Dwyer-Impellitteri period;[57] events did not favor one. At the same time, there was not a little resentment over civic conditions, and that resentment was expressed effectively at the polls. There is a possibility—which in considerable degree would be the result of New York's experience with La Guardia—that the public had come to resent corruption in government more easily, that the civic conscience as to this matter had become more sensitive. Revelations of police-gambler tie-ups had hardly begun before voter reaction was registered—a quickness of response that must come as a surprise to anyone acquainted with the development of civic indignation in the past (though the matter is not clear, for corruption was but one reason, and possibly not the most important one, for Impellitteri's victory.) To what extent the public had grown more sensitive to other aspects of bad government was less clear. Certainly the electorate showed less compunction than ever about breaking traditional voting patterns to voice its irritation with conditions in the city; in this period, the growth of political independency reached a new high.[58] The development of independent voting, it should be kept in mind, while due mainly to other things, must be ascribed in part to the city's habit of supporting La Guardia.

16

Today and tomorrow

FINALLY IT IS IMPORTANT to attempt to tie up the past we have been discussing with the present and the future; not a little of the value of our study lies in the perspective it gives for viewing contemporary developments and making predictions as to future ones. Let us briefly consider the present state of the machine and reform camps and say a word about what the future is likely to hold for each.

The outstanding development in New York machine politics in the 1950's was the re-emergence, between 1953 and 1958, of Tammany Hall as the leading Democratic organization. Chiefly this was the result of the rise of Carmine De Sapio. De Sapio owed his growing political prominence to hard work, shrewdness, success and luck. In this period the first Tammany boss of Italian extraction showed himself to be the most capable head of the Hall since Charlie Murphy. He was largely responsible for Wagner's candidacy in 1953. When Wagner came to power, he recognized De Sapio, for purposes of patronage and political advice, as the dominant political leader in the city; and in February, 1954, in filling the position of Democratic National Committeeman held by Ed Flynn, who had died the summer before, the Democratic State Committee chose De Sapio—an action which both acknowledged the Tammany boss's new power and augmented it. De Sapio also wisely pushed the gubernatorial candidacy of Averell Harriman in 1954. When Harriman was elected, he named the Tammany boss Secretary of State in recognition of his political efforts and importance—the first time a Tammany chieftain was given a position of cabinet status.

Fortuitous events conspired to promote De Sapio's ascendancy. One such event was the death of Flynn, the city's leading Democratic politician; with Flynn around, the Tammany chief could not have moved as far and as fast as he did. Then Wagner's victory, while boosting De Sapio's stock, placed the Brooklyn, Queens and Richmond Democratic county leaders, who had supported Impellitteri, beyond the political pale. After Wagner moved to City Hall, both he and De Sapio waged war against them with results that further enhanced the Tammany chief's influence. In 1954, taking their cues from De Sapio and Wagner, the Brooklyn Democratic machine installed Joseph T. Sharkey, majority leader of the City Council, as county leader, and the Queens Democratic organization chose as its head James A. Phillips, secretary of the Comptroller's Department since 1946. Jeremiah A. Sullivan, leader of the Richmond Democracy, was reportedly granted an amnesty during a private session with De Sapio, presumably after acknowledging the error of his ways and promising to do the right thing in the future.[1]

Tammany's resurgence was helped by other things, too. Most of the money for political campaigns in New York City is to be found in Manhattan. That borough is the symbol of New York to the rest of the country and the world. There had been a long tradition of Tammany dominance in New York Democratic politics. In view of the loss of position suffered by the other big Democratic machines in the city, these Tammany assets assumed an extra importance.

The Hall's new hegemony did not mean that the Manhattan organization had the same voice of authority in the Democratic clan as it did in pre-La Guardia days. The census figures were still running against Manhattan.[2] But De Sapio's political weight was considerable; he was the *de facto* Democratic boss of the city. At the Democratic State Convention in August, 1958, he forced the nomination of District Attorney Frank Hogan for United States Senator, though Hogan was opposed by both Harriman and Wagner. Not since the time of Charlie Murphy had a leader of Tammany wielded as much naked political power as De Sapio did on that occasion.

An ancient Greek dramatist would well have understood what followed. De Sapio's blatant exhibition of power at the state convention set in motion a train of events which brought about a reversal in the fortunes of the Tammany chieftain and his organization. In November, 1958, while the Democrats were achieving impressive victories across the nation, Governor Harriman and senatorial candidate Hogan lost to Nelson Rockefeller and Kenneth B. Keating. Democratic Party liberals blamed De Sapio for providing the Republicans with the opportunity to exploit bossism as an issue. The liberals, led by Herbert H. Lehman, Mrs. Franklin D. Roosevelt and Thomas K. Finletter, former Secretary of the Air Force, mounted a drive to destroy De Sapio, the "image of bossism." (While De Sapio was winning with his candidates, and these were candidates the liberals supported, the Tammany leader, though the same image of bossism, had been endurable to the liberals and not infrequently the object of their praise.) In the 1959 primaries, the Village Independent Democrats entered the lists against De Sapio in his Greenwich Village district, and party liberals contested the control of De Sapio men in other areas in Manhattan. The Tammany boss retained his district leadership, but only by a squeak, beating his opponent by fewer than 600 votes. Elsewhere liberal candidates won seven districts and pressed De Sapio hard in five. In Harlem, Representative Adam Clayton Powell, Jr., who had defeated De Sapio's attempt to deny him the Democratic congressional nomination in the Sixteenth District the year before, led insurgents, not allied with the liberals, to victory in four districts. Neutral observers said that the Tammany leader had been given a bloody nose. The liberals landed other blows in the 1960 primaries. Their major triumph was that of William Fitts Ryan, an anti-De Sapio district leader on the upper West Side, who with Lehman's backing unseated De Sapio-supported Congressman Ludwig Teller in the contest for the Democratic nomination in the Twentieth Congressional District.

De Sapio's defeats once again cut Tammany down to size. Other county leaders in the city, especially Joseph Sharkey and Charles A. Buckley of the Bronx, the inheritor of Flynn's power, asserted themselves more. It was reported that Wagner undertook to accept recommendations directly from the other leaders without clearing them with De Sapio.

The Tammany of our time is in some respects not the Tammany of a decade ago. The executive committee that elected De Sapio to a new term as Democratic leader of New York County in 1957 differed greatly in membership from the one that first chose him in 1949. In addition to being smaller, the 1957 committee contained more college men and women and many younger members than the earlier group. Of the forty-one male district leaders in office in 1949, only fourteen remained in 1957, two having been elected to the judiciary, five having died and the others having fallen victim to the political wheel of fortune. Of the forty-one leaders in 1949, only eleven had attended college. Of the thirty-three leaders who comprised the executive committee in 1957, seventeen were college men, including three graduates of Ivy League institutions.

Some of the young college-educated leaders in the Hall, politically liberal, have proclaimed for themselves the goal of once and for all putting an end to Tammany's disreputable side, of turning Tammany into an organization truly representative of the Manhattan Democracy. In the decade of the fifties, eight so-called reform clubs elected district leaders. At this writing the reform element commands four and one-sixth votes out of sixteen in the Tammany executive committee. Increasingly the reformers have come to look upon the ending of De Sapio's rule as the *sine qua non* for achieving their objectives. While they are far from being able to take over the Hall, they could oust De Sapio or reduce his role to that of a figurehead were they to combine with Powell's Harlem group and with old-time Irish leaders who feel that Tammany has not been the same since it came under Italian domination. What the reformers would accomplish by engaging in this maneuver, however, is not clear.

In De Sapio's view, the reformers are, among other things, superfluous inasmuch as since 1950 he has been carrying out a program of reform within Tammany. According to De Sapio, the drive dates from Ferdinand Pecora's mayoral defeat, which made De Sapio realize that something had to be done to dispel the public's impression of him and his organization. (The Kefauver crime investigation and that of the State Crime Commission were probably not without effect on the thinking of the Tammany boss.) During the past few years he has led the public to believe that underworld influence in the Hall is a thing of the past. Some of the less prepossessing Tammany district leaders—Sidney Moses, Connolly, Brickman and Samuel Kantor—were forced out, and De Sapio has done his best to ridicule the charge that he, himself, was acquainted with underworld figures. Tammany provided for the direct election of district leaders by members of the party, abolished certain "synthetic" votes in the Tammany executive committee which permitted a county leader to remain in office after he lost the support of a majority of the district leaders, separated the election of women co-leaders in each district from that of the district leaders. De Sapio backed reforms like Permanent Personal Registration, pushed by most civic groups, and conducted post card surveys avowedly to ascertain the wishes of the voters on certain issues.

At the same time, De Sapio, under the guidance of public relations man Sydney S. Baron, undertook to create a new personal image. Forsaking the kind of English he had previously spoken, De Sapio studied the language. In place of loud, sometimes contrasting, attire, he took to wearing expensive dark suits and conservatively striped ties. He essayed the role of political lecturer at New York University—as part of a "Workshop in Practical Politics" conducted by Baron—where he contended that in recent years Tammany had come to symbolize enlightened democracy. In 1957 he became the author of an article in the scholarly *Harvard Law Record* in which he argued that a convention should be called to revise the New York State Constitution. Before 1958 De Sapio's efforts to establish new images of himself and Tammany met with some success. Some writers depicted the "new kind of Tammany boss" and his "new" organization in tones reminiscent of the "New Tammany" literature of the twenties. Many Democrats suspicious of De Sapio did not permit their suspicions to get the better of them.

It is not easy at this time to gauge the depth of reform that has taken place in the Hall. Possibly De Sapio has improved the moral climate of Tammany somewhat. There has not been any evidence that he has made money from hidden sources. It has not been proven that Tammany politicians are still doing business with criminals. The direct election of district leaders, the abolition of "synthetic" votes in the Tammany executive committee and the separate election of women leaders do represent gains for party democracy. Yet the Tammany boss is not quite the reformer and the Hall is not as reformed as De Sapio's press releases claim. It is a fact that he was aroused to action against Sidney Moses, Connolly, Brickman and Kantor only after they deserted him and sided with Impellitteri; moreover, he never tried to purge other leaders of questionable calibre who were not against him. He has resorted to the ancient device of re-districting to eliminate district leaders who were opposed to him, and there is no guarantee that he would not do so again if he were pressed and the opportunity presented itself. Democratic insurgents complained that at a meeting of the New York County Democratic Committee in 1959 the De Sapio forces included men who had no right to vote but who helped to shout down a resolution sponsored by the reform faction. A few recent scandals, particularly those involving the city's Title I program and the Bureau of Real Estate, make it clear that Tammany-connected individuals, mainly by way of honest graft, have been exploiting politics for their own profit.

What about present-day Democratic government in the city? The consensus of those informed about the city government is that in general Mayor Wagner made a better showing in his first term than he has since his re-election in 1957, when he defeated his Republican opponent, hotel man Robert K. Christenberry, by the largest plurality in the history of New York mayoral elections. To its credit, the Wagner administration, in line with recommendations of the Mayor's Committee on Management Survey, created the position of City Administrator with broad managerial powers, reorganized the Civil Service Commission to enable it to do a more effective job, undertook a reclassification of civil service positions which had long been needed, and introduced a new pay scale for city employees. The Wagner administration presented comprehensive fiscal plans to Albany calling for new taxing powers and more state aid for the city and fought hard for them. In 1960 Wagner won a major victory in this area when Governor Rockefeller and other Republican state leaders recognized the city's long-standing complaint that it was being short-changed by the state in the distribution of state funds to localities. Albany granted an immediate increase in state aid to the city, mainly for educational purposes, and promised to study the formula fixing the city's share of state aid allocations for education and the city's request that per capita grants made by the state be raised by at least 50 per cent.

The Fire Department seems to have been well run; by placing a new emphasis upon fire prevention, the Department brought about a striking reduction in the number of fires between 1953 and 1956. The Wagner administration has attempted to make the public more conscious of the litter problem, and the streets seem cleaner than under the previous administration; New York is far from a model of municipal cleanliness, however. The new accent on welfare—in the broad sense—given by La Guardia has been continued. The present administration has undertaken a huge school building program. It created a Commission on Intergroup Relations to work for the elimination of bias in the city and contributed to the enactment of the Sharkey-Brown-Isaacs bill making it illegal to refuse to rent private housing (except in the case of one or two family houses in groups of less than ten) to anyone because of race, creed or color. In the battle against slums, the administration has written into law improved standards of occupancy and has set in motion a twenty-block West Side rehabilitation project designed to stop the blight of a neighborhood in which much good housing is mixed with bad, without mass clearance and huge rebuilding.

As in the case of O'Dwyer and Impellitteri, Wagner has given a partisan, rather than a nonpartisan, administration. But this is an approach that is not without defenders among men of good will; and in connection with high level positions, the Mayor has largely exercised a free hand and has made a number of very good appointments; the quality of Wagner's top appointees is in general higher than that of those who served in the top posts under the two preceding Mayors. With respect to positions below the top level, where operating control often resides, the Mayor has more fully played the patronage game.

(Wagner and the party organizations have generally managed to remain on good terms, despite grumbling among Democratic leaders in the city that the Mayor has been more niggardly in dispensing jobs to the faithful than any of his Democratic predecessors. The machine apparently needs Wagner, and he, a party regular all his political life, seems to feel that he needs it. Apparently motivated by concern over his own political future Wagner has recently broken with De Sapio and given support to the Lehman-Mrs. Roosevelt reform faction in the Democratic Party. Before this, however, he was, not surprisingly, proclaiming the "forceful, dynamic, political brilliance" of De Sapio, "the stalwart friend of decency, honesty and integrity in government.")

The debit column of the Wagner record is a long one. Though the city under Wagner is better policed than in the days of Impellitteri, the Police Department, faced with an increasing number of major crimes and acts of juvenile delinquency, needs more men. Despite the enactment of anti-slum legislation and periodic widely-heralded drives against slum conditions, the war against bad housing in the city is a losing battle; enforcement of the housing laws has lagged because of a shortage of inspectors, corruption and, until recently, bad administration in the Department of Buildings and failure of the courts, with some exceptions, to mete out stiff sentences to violators. The need to provide middle-income housing constitutes one of the city's most serious problems, but implementation of the Mitchell-Lama Act, designed to encourage the building of such housing (by authorizing the city to lend builders up to 90 per cent of the cost of the housing and extend to them certain tax exemptions), was held up for a few years by a log jam that developed in the office of Comptroller Lawrence A. Gerosa.

Gerosa, who contended that his agency should not administer such a program, delayed approval of applications in the hope that the legislature would move the program to another agency.

It is true that under Wagner the city has made some gains in traffic reform, but the pace has been slow and hesitant; and with respect to the building of off-street parking facilities, the failure has been monumental. In early 1960 the City Administrator reporting to the Mayor on the effectiveness of the Department of Air Pollution Control found that there was "little evidence" of any basic improvement in the city's air contamination situation since the Department came into being in 1952 and that "the best that can be said is that the volume of pollutants would probably have been greater if there had been no control program." What he did not say was that chief responsibility for this situation lay with the Mayor for failing to give adequate budgetary support to the Department. Under Wagner New York has continued to borrow for things a city should not borrow for—needs that can reasonably be anticipated, such as the replacement of obsolete schools, the repaving of streets, cash to meet operating requirements—with the result that too much of the city's funds have had to go for debt service (more than 17 per cent of the 1960–1 executive budget) instead of for more constructive purposes. The Wagner administration has been criticized for holding to an investment policy that has cost the city large amounts of potential investment income and for undertaking to boost the income of a considerable number of city employees by increasing the government's contribution to employee pensions, rather than by raising salaries, an undesirable procedure inasmuch as pension arrangements are contractual under the state constitution.

Scandals, mainly in the second term, have sullied the administration. A major one concerned the operation of the Title I slum clearance program, in which municipalities are permitted to acquire substandard urban areas and sell them below cost to private and public developers, the federal government absorbing two-thirds of the markdown and the city one-third. In the case of one project, Manhattantown, politically-connected private developers, instead of building on the property the city turned over to them, contented themselves for five years with collecting millions of dollars in rents from undemolished slum properties and engaged in shady devices which enabled insiders to skim off profits from the Manhattantown corporation. Though a Senate committee hearing and the press revealed what was going on, the Wagner administration declined to recognize any scandal until further refusal became impossible. The vice-chairman of the Slum Clearance Committee, the agency entrusted with supervision of the Title I program in the city, was banker Thomas J. Shanahan, a top fundraiser for Tammany and close friend of De Sapio. In connection with another project, Shanahan's bank loaned money to a Title I sponsor who had deposited money in the bank and who Shanahan, in his capacity as the Slum Clearance official charged with checking the financial reliability of potential builders, had cleared for the development. Shanahan also approved as "tentative" sponsor for a mid-Harlem project one Louis I. Pokrass, an individual who had been linked in the Kefauver committee testimony to such underworld powers as Costello, Adonis and Meyer Lansky, under circumstances which make it impossible to believe that he was unacquainted with Pokrass' background. The project was never undertaken, however, possibly because the involvement of Pokrass became known.

The administration has been embarrassed by revelations in other quarters. Scandals involving theft, excessive rentals paid by the city to favored real estate firms, relocation frauds and outrageous padding of bills by private contractors for maintenance and repair of city property staggered the Bureau of Real Estate; the result was the arrest of the chief accountant of the Bureau and the resignation of a number of high officials in the agency including the director, the husband of De Sapio's secretary and De Sapio's personal choice for the job. The Department of Buildings, shaken by graft, corruption and maladministration, underwent two reorganizations. Stung by newspaper criticism, the administration brought about a reform of the City Housing Authority, which had neglected the vital problem of preserving the agency's huge housing investment. Officials in the Department of Markets were discovered protecting unscrupulous butchers and fuel dealers who gypped consumers out of millions of dollars a year. Investigations disclosed that the Department of Purchase suffered from glaring waste, inefficiency and corruption; Commissioner Joseph V. Spagna, who resigned, was charged by the State Investigation Commission with manipulating contract procedures to favor industrialist Fortune Pope, a long-time friend and a power in Tammany politics. Attracting much attention was the case of Manhattan Borough President Hulan E. Jack, who had permitted real estate operator Sidney J. Ungar, an intimate friend, also closely allied with Tammany, to pay a $4,400 bill for the remodeling of Jack's apartment—both men called the payment a loan—though Ungar was much interested in certain matters requiring the approval of the Board of Estimate. (Ungar admitted that he had agreed to pay for the remodeling because Jack was in politics and "probably could do favors for me.") As for gambling, indications are that bookmaking and policy are flourishing, protected to one degree or another by dishonest policemen.

The response of the Wagner administration to most of these scandals has tended to follow a pattern. Sometimes, as in the case of the Department of Markets, the initiative for investigation and reform has come from the Mayor's Office. More often the impulse has come from outside. Almost always the Mayor has played down the seriousness of the scandals, has avoided expressing a loss of confidence in high officials involved (Shanahan and Spagna are cases in point), has proclaimed his determination to root out all that is wrong and has ordered an inquiry, often by the City Administrator. Rarely have the investigations censured specific individuals; those carried out by the City Administrator have often been marked by vigorous criticism, but the criticism has always been of faulty systems, an approach which, while justifiable to a point, has had the effect of taking blame from the shoulders of responsible officials, placing it on impersonal structures and procedures. Reforms have usually followed the reports to the Mayor, but not always have they been as thorough as the situation requires. Too often one has been left wondering why the condition occurred in the first place.

Beyond the scandals and specific failures, there has been a failure of leadership in City Hall. Wagner has shown himself to be a stronger Mayor than O'Dwyer or Impellitteri. He knows the city government thoroughly, well understands the problems confronting the city and can discuss them intelligently. For the most part his trouble has not been in his plans and programs, which his press releases continually confuse with accomplishments. His trouble has mainly been in implementation—too often he has failed to act, and act decisively, in the public interest. "When in doubt, don't," his father had cautioned; and the Mayor, not infrequently in doubt, has followed the precept. Wagner has dawdled when action would involve him in controversy with other members of his administration or hurt a friend. (He has not given heed to a warning La Guardia once gave that you cannot be a good fellow and a good Mayor.) Often he has avoided making decisions when they might alienate a group of voters; few administrations have been more responsive to political pressures. Indeed behind the image of Wagner, the "good" Mayor, cultivated by the administration —it has devoted much attention to public relations—some critics discern, not a dedicated public servant whose first thought is the welfare of the city, but a political juggler whose main efforts have been directed toward balancing political interests to his own political advantage. That the Wagner administration has at times moved things forward in the city has been the result, in this view, of the happy fact that action in the public interest may also be good politics.[3]

And the future of the machine in New York? Here and elsewhere in the United States, the continuing increase in the number of college graduates and in the middle class, which seems assured, will almost certainly work to weaken the party organization; but for New York, at least, this is not apt to occur too quickly, for reasons to be suggested shortly. As for the spirit governing the machine, nothing has occurred to lead one to believe that any fundamental change has taken place or will soon take place—and this goes for Tammany, regardless of what elements may gain control. What is likely, however, is that the machine, which no longer has the same opportunities to bring about the advancement of its members and friends as it had before the 1930's, will see its opportunities here contract even more in the years ahead. It is probable, at least over the long run, that the public's expectations of government will continue to rise, professionalism in government will continue to increase and the position of the Mayor and other public officials will continue to become stronger in relation to the political organization, though to what extent any given official will take advantage of that fact to further the general interest is another matter. The money-making techniques of the politicians in the years ahead are most likely to be mainly of the more sophisticated sort which has steadily come in this century to replace the more obvious methods whereby politicians have battened at the public's expense; most graft will probably be "honest," involving cases of dubious ethics and propriety, and even when not so honest will, the chances are, be cleverly concealed.

Whether Tammany will once again assume command of Democratic politics in New York, and if so when, cannot be predicted. Such a development is not unlikely, as De Sapio has demonstrated, should the other boroughs neglect to push their advantages. Undoubtedly they will continue to benefit, as Manhattan will continue to suffer, from the movement of population within the city. If the Democrats in Queens, which borough has exhibited the greatest growth during the past generation, can ever overcome their endemic factionalism—as this is written they are under their third leader since Phillips—they could assume a new political importance in the next few years; in 1957 the potential Queens vote was 20 per cent larger than that in Manhattan. Once the bridge over the Narrows is built, Richmond should finally come of age as a member of the city's Democratic family.[4]

The Negroes and Puerto Ricans are bound to become more important in the political life of New York. Between 1940 and 1950 the Negro population of the city rose from 458,000 to 748,000 or about 60 per cent (as against a rise of 2 per cent for the white population), and the rate of growth since has remained rapid; by the end of the fifties, New York contained more than one million Negroes, one-eighth of the total population.[5] More spectacular has been the growth of a considerable Puerto Rican population in the city. Prior to 1945 there was comparatively little movement of people from Puerto Rico to the United States; in the first four decades of the twentieth century the net migration from the island averaged only some 2,000 to 3,000 persons per year. With the end of the Second World War, however, Puerto Ricans began coming to the mainland in large numbers, driven, as had been millions of other newcomers to America before them, by the hope of economic improvement; net migration from the island amounted to about 13,000 in 1945, 40,000 in 1946, 53,000 in 1951, 69,000 in 1953. The great bulk of migrating Puerto Ricans came to and settled in New York City; the number of New Yorkers of Puerto Rican birth or parentage soared from 246,000 in April, 1950, to perhaps 570,000 in May, 1957. It has been predicted that by 1970 there will be more than one million people of Puerto Rican descent in New York City.[6]

What effect the growing Negro vote will have on Democratic power in the city is not easy to say at this point. During the past few years Negro voters have represented an almost solid Democratic voting bloc in the city, but in the course of the national struggle over civil rights, the Democrats could lose some of their Negro support to the Republicans. A New York City Republican Party with considerable Negro backing would present a greater challenge to the Democrats than it does today. The Puerto Ricans are beginning to develop political consciousness; as low income people they will probably swell Democratic totals in the future. While machine politicians can no longer offer most of their old-time inducements as a means of corralling lower-class support, it is a safe bet that they will do what they can to cater to the needs and interests of these people. More broadly speaking, no city administration—Democratic or any other—will be inclined to treat the problems of these groups lightly.

It should also be expected that as time goes on the Negroes and Puerto Ricans will come to take more of an active interest in politics, including machine politics. (Already a Puerto Rican has been named district leader by the Democrats in Manhattan's Fourteenth Assembly District, East.[7]) Undoubtedly these people will use the political structure to attempt to advance themselves as others have done before them. It is not impossible that some day the Negroes and Puerto Ricans may assume the leadership of machine politics exercised by the Italians and Irish today.

An examination of New York's civic front at the present time reveals no striking developments from the situation that existed in the O'Dwyer-Impellitteri period. There may have been somewhat of a falling off in interest in civic work during Wagner's first term, when an air of complacency hung over the land and the Mayor was more highly regarded than he has been since. However that might be, the various civic organizations in the city are quite active today. Since February, 1953, the Citizens Union, the city's leading civic group, has presented over the radio a Sunday program, "Citizens Union Searchlight"—also on television since January, 1954—designed to acquaint New Yorkers with the leading issues and problems facing the city and its environs and with some of the most prominent individuals involved in these matters.[8]

The Wagner performance has prompted talk of a reform movement in 1961, but at this time, such a development is uncertain. In any case, reform movements will continue to mark the future as they have the past. While Americans appear to have grown less concerned with the accumulation of wealth, the ethos of the nation has not changed [9]; nor do we appear in this country to be on the brink of passing into a civilization whose underlying values are different from the ones we have known. In the foreseeable future, there will still be people who will turn to politics to realize the predominant goals of American life. And the majority of citizens, normally still too caught up in the business of achieving those goals in their own way to care too much about politics and government on the occasion when the politicians have overstepped certain bounds

(ambiguous and evolving though these be), will still respond to the dictates of their civic conscience and join with a hard core of more civic-
minded (but also self-seeking) citizens to demand better government.

In New York during the next few years, the tendency toward independent voting is likely to remain strong, thus facilitating the success of a
reform movement. Despite the political success of Impellitteri and Halley,
a fusion movement will probably remain the chief medium for effecting
reform, for it holds out the surest promise of victory. It is practically certain that such a movement will not get anywhere without the inclusion of
the Republican and Liberal parties—or, if the latter ever goes out of
existence, without the assistance of a party or group representing more or
less the Liberal point of view. (It can be safely predicted that the forging
of an agreement between the Republicans and Liberals, or their equivalent,
will be one of the hardest tasks confronting the supporters of fusion.) Nor
is it likely that the reformers—despite their minor role during the past few
campaigns—can be written off in the formation of a fusion movement
without great risk to its success. Indeed it is possible to argue that fusion
stands a better chance of being stronger when the reform element is in the
driver's seat.

No one can consider the future of good government in New York City
without taking into account the ominous shadow being cast upon that
future by the most pronounced sociological trend affecting American cities
today: the exodus of well-to-do and middle-class people from the city to
the suburbs in search of nicer neighborhoods, better schools for their children, easier parking, in general a more enjoyable life. In New York
between 1940 and 1950 at least 750,000 New Yorkers moved out of the
city, going mainly to Nassau and Suffolk counties on Long Island, Westchester, Connecticut and New Jersey. This migration from the city continued at a galloping pace in the fifties and, to one degree or another, is
destined to continue in the future.[10]

Unfortunately the kind of people moving to the suburbs are those most
likely to take an interest in community affairs. This means, for one thing,
that the base from which civic leadership has been recruited is shrinking
and that it will shrink even more in the years to come. (Incidentally, New
York's loss is suburbia's gain. According to an item in the *New York Times*
a few years ago, commuters forming a cross-section of a *Who's Who* in
the New York business and industrial world were becoming increasingly
active in the local government of communities in Fairfield County, Connecticut.[11]) And, more generally, this hegira to the suburbs—together with
the influx into the city of large numbers of lower-class people, a group
traditionally less concerned about the affairs of the city and more inclined
to acquiesce in machine rule—promises to weaken the city's defenses
against exploitation by politicians.[12]

It should not be assumed that the friends of good government in New

York cannot rise to the challenge to city government here outlined. But there can be little doubt that they will have their work cut out for them. They are not likely to succeed if in determination, political stamina, courage and the willingness to sacrifice, they are the inferiors of their predecessors in the struggle for better government.

Notes

PREFACE

1 *New York Times,* January 1, 1934.
2 "Joy Bells Ring in New York's New Deal," *Literary Digest,* January 13, 1934, 8.

1 / THE MACHINE TRADITION

1 Oscar Handlin, *The Uprooted: The Epic Story of the Great Migrations That Made the American People* (Boston, 1952), 209.
2 Roy V. Peel, *The Political Clubs of New York City* (New York and London, 1935), 35–36; Gustavus Myers, *The History of Tammany Hall* (second edition, revised and enlarged, New York, 1917), *passim.*
3 William L. Riordon, *Plunkitt of Tammany Hall* (New York, 1948), 75.
4 For example, one reason the Democrats nominated William J. Gaynor of Brooklyn for Mayor in 1909 was the opposition of the Brooklyn organization to the nomination of a distinctly Tammany man (Myers, *Tammany Hall,* 340).
5 The society chose Tammany, a Delaware chief whose exploits were legendary, and Columbus as co-saints. Both were considered one hundred per cent American. M. R. Werner, *Tammany Hall* (New York, 1928), ch. I.
6 Myers, 9–12.
7 *Ibid.,* preface vii, 20.
8 Joseph McGoldrick, "The New Tammany," *American Mercury,* September, 1928, 1–12.
9 Myers, *passim;* Werner, *passim.*
10 McGoldrick, "New Tammany," 5; Werner, 294–297; Peel, *Political Clubs of New York City,* 43; the classic description of the life of a district leader appears in W. L. Riordon's *Plunkitt.*

11 Werner, *passim*, especially note p. 293.

12 Lincoln Steffens, *The Shame of the Cities* (New York, 1904), 291; cf. Werner, 558.

13 On Tammany election manipulations in general, Werner, *passim;* Myers, *passim.*

14 Werner, *passim.*

15 Riordon, *Plunkitt*, 67.

16 In general, Werner, *passim;* Myers, *passim;* Harold Zink, *City Bosses in the United States: A Study of Twenty Municipal Bosses* (Durham, North Carolina, 1930), 125.

17 Note that the earliest Tammany braves did not let the grass grow under their feet. William Mooney, the founder of the Tammany Society, was removed in the 1800's as superintendent of the city's almshouse for appropriating city funds and supplies for his personal use, and other Tammany officials at this time were implicated for embezzlements and frauds of one sort or another (Myers, 23–25); the first Sachems collected money from gambling houses, dives and prostitutes and extorted money from prisoners in jail and in police court (Werner, 33); some early leaders grew wealthy through the opportunities for business which their government connections gave them (*ibid.*, 39).

18 Walter Chambers, *Samuel Seabury: A Challenge* (New York and London, 1932), 65–66, 94; Werner, 420.

19 Riordon, *Plunkitt,* 3–8, 111.

20 The discussion of the most prominent money-making techniques in different periods of Tammany history is based in general upon Werner, *passim* and Myers, *passim.*

21 Myers, *passim.*

22 Werner, *passim;* Myers, *passim.*

23 Werner, 26–29; Myers, 73, 191; Peel, *Political Clubs of New York City,* 252–256; Introduction by Roy V. Peel in Riordon, *Plunkitt,* viii.

Agreement seems to be lacking on when the Irish took control of Tammany. In *Political Clubs of New York City* (252), Peel states that the Irish did not secure domination until the late 1890's. But this date seems too late. McGoldrick's view ("New Tammany," 8) that the Irish enjoyed leadership since the days of Tweed appears to set the date too early, though it does seem that the average New York City politician in the 1860's, and perhaps for a while before, was an Irishman. Our feeling is that the triumph of the Irish—or any group—in Tammany cannot easily be pinpointed; it depends upon your criteria. In most cases control of the boss-ship is a good criterion, and I have used it in the discussion above and will use it again.

24 Werner, 303 ff.

25 Zink, *City Bosses,* 86–87.

26 Riordon, *Plunkitt,* 103 ff.

27 *Ibid.,* Introduction by Roy V. Peel, x.

28 *Ibid.,* 44.

For the above view of the old-time politicians I have generally drawn upon Werner, *passim,* Myers, *passim,* and the introduction by Peel in *Plunkitt.*

29 Myers, 266.

30 In general, Werner and Myers, *passim;* on Tweed, Werner, 104, 253–254; on Kelly, Werner, 277, Myers, 266; on Sullivan, Werner, 503, 509; on Croker, Werner, 304, 481 and Zink, *City Bosses,* 136; on Murphy, Werner, 483–484, 486, 564; on Plunkitt, "Plunkitt of Tammany and His 'Honest Graft,' " *Literary Digest,* January 3, 1925, 41–44.

31 John Jay Chapman, *Causes and Consequences* (New York, 1899), 42–43; *The Triumph of Reform: A History of the Great Political Revolution, November Sixth, Eighteen Hundred and Ninety-Four* (New York, 1895), introduction.

32 The above discussion of Tammany and the immigrants does not permit a more precise citation of sources. The following were used: Edward J. Flynn, *You're the*

Boss (New York, 1947), 10–11; Alfred E. Smith, *The Citizen and His Government* (New York and London, 1935), ch. 1; Myers, 57, 80–81, 94–95, 286; Werner, 424–428; Peel, *Political Clubs of New York City*, 252, 254, 258; Steffens, *Shame of the Cities*, 302; Lincoln Steffens, *Autobiography* (New York, 1931), 254–256; Chambers, *Seabury*, 104; McGoldrick, "New Tammany," 8; "Behind the Walker Case," *New Republic*, June 22, 1932, 140–141; "A Lesson from New York," *New Republic*, October 16, 1929, 228–229; Henry F. Pringle, "What's Happened to Tammany?," *Outlook and Independent*, May 15, 1929, 117; Norman Thomas, "Twisting Tammany's Tail," *Forum*, June, 1931, 337.

Incidentally, no one should get the idea that only the Democratic Party took up the practice of befriending the immigrants. In Philadelphia where the machine was Republican, for instance, the Republicans did what Tammany did in New York City, as is made clear in J. T. Salter, *Boss Rule: Portraits in City Politics* (New York and London, 1935).

33 Quoted in Werner, 336.

34 Myers, 68.

35 Werner, 153.

36 *New York Times*, November 12, 1933 (article by Gustavus Myers); *Independent Journal of Columbia University* (New York), November 1, 1933 (article by Joseph McGoldrick); interview with Joseph D. McGoldrick, May 31, 1951.

37 A number of general points were made in this chapter which do not admit of a more exact kind of documentation. In making them, I have drawn upon works already cited and others, among which the most important are the following: Harold Zink, *Government of Cities in the United States* (New York, 1939), 174 ff.; Robert S. Allen (ed.), *Our Fair City* (New York, 1947); Charles P. Taft, *City Management: The Cincinnati Experiment* (New York, 1933), chs. I–III; Constance McLaughlin Green, *Holyoke, Massachusetts: A Case History of the Industrial Revolution in America* (New Haven, 1939), ch. IX; Robert S. Lynd and Helen Merrell Lynd, *Middletown in Transition: A Study in Cultural Conflicts* (New York, 1937), ch. IX; William Bennett Munro, *Personality in Politics: Reformers, Bosses and Leaders—What They Do and How They Do It* (New York, 1924), 48 ff.

2 / THE REFORM TRADITION

1 *The Triumph of Reform: A History of the Great Political Revolution, November Sixth, Eighteen Hundred and Ninety-Four* contains a biographical index (372–397) which gives brief sketches of many of the people involved in the New York reform movement of 1894. Not all of these can be considered part of the city's reform element, but if the sketches are examined carefully, a good deal can be learned about New York's civic leaders. Statements in the text with regard to New York City are based largely upon this index. Broader generalizations are based in addition upon some of the works cited in note 36 of this chapter.

2 The tendency to have good government and to revolt against bad government appears to have been greater over the years in Cincinnati and Milwaukee, for instance, than in Boston and Philadelphia (the city Lincoln Steffens called "corrupt and contented"), though in recent times both cities seem to have changed. *Shame of the Cities*, chapter on Philadelphia; Robert S. Allen (ed.), *Our Fair City*, chapters on Philadelphia, Boston, Milwaukee; Taft, *City Management: The Cincinnati Experiment*, 8–15; *New York Times*, November 9, 1955.

3 *New York Times*, March 22, 1951.

4 Myers, *The History of Tammany Hall, passim;* Allan Nevins and Milton Halsey Thomas (eds.), *The Diary of George Templeton Strong* (New York, 1952), v. 1835–1849, 1850–1859, 1860–1865, *passim;* Allan Nevins (ed.), *The Diary of Philip Hone, 1826–1851* (New York, 1927), *passim.*

5 Citizens' Association of New York, *Reform in New-York City: Address to the People* . . . (New York, 1870); *idem, Address* . . . *to the Public* (New York, 1871); *idem, Report of the Work of the Association* . . . *1874* (New York, 1874). Also [James Parton], "The Government of the City of New York," *North American Review,* October, 1866, 459.

Unfortunately, for the reputation of the Citizens' Association, it was incredibly naïve about Tweed and his friends for too long. It may not have been just naïveté. It was discovered after the big exposures by the *New York Times* that one of the officers of the association, Nathaniel Sands, had received from Comptroller Connolly, a member of the Ring, $75,000 for alleged services in negotiating a city loan of some $15,000,000; Sands admitted this and resigned (Citizens' Association, Letters showing a portion of its work during 1870–1871 period (New York, 1871)). Besides, before this, in 1870, at least some of those on the famous committee of wealthy and respectable people which gave a seal of approval to the condition of the city's finances under Tweed were members of the association; it was charged that in return for this splendid co-operation taxes were not collected from certain wealthy people for 1868, 1869 and 1870, though it has also been alleged that the members of the committee were threatened with an increase in taxes if their report was not favorable (Werner, *Tammany Hall,* 207–208).

6 New York City Council of Political Reform, *Report for the Years 1872, '73, and '74* . . . *With Summary* (New York, 1875).

7 Frank Mann Stewart, *The National Civil Service Reform League: History, Activities and Problems* (Austin, Texas, 1929), *passim;* Civil Service Reform Association, *Report,* 1881 (New York, 1881); *idem, Report,* 1955 *(77th Annual Report to the Public,* New York, 1955); William Bennett Munro, "Dorman Bridgman Eaton," *Dictionary of American Biography,* V, 607–608; *Who Was Who in America,* 1 (1897–1942), "Godkin."

8 Richard Welling, *As the Twig Is Bent* (New York, 1942), 53 ff.; Commonwealth Club, Constitution ([New York], 1890).

9 Before long Roosevelt resigned to go to the New York state legislature, for one of the club's major tenets was that no member should hold public office (from a passage of a letter by Richard Welling quoted in M. A. De Wolfe Howe, *John Jay Chapman and His Letters* (Boston, 1937), 67). It might be noted that, according to Welling, Roosevelt had little patience with the other club members, who seemed to him to be a bunch of theorists; he wanted them in the Republican Party. (Welling, 41.)

10 Welling, 2, 41 ff.; William Jay Schieffelin, "Memoirs" (possession of the Schieffelin family); *Triumph of Reform,* biographical index.

The City Reform Club in 1892, it might be noted, successfully spearheaded opposition to a law which created a speedway in Central Park for the convenience of rich men and Tammany leaders who wanted to race their horses without having to go up into the wilds of the Bronx; because of mounting public pressure, the legislature was forced to repeal the bill in the same session in which it was passed. (Schieffelin, "Memoirs"; Welling, 52–53.)

11 Steffens, *Autobiography,* 215 ff. (quotation, 215); Charles H. Parkhurst, *My Forty Years in New York* (New York, 1923), ch. VII; Schieffelin, "Memoirs"; Werner, 348 ff.

12 Welling, 57–58; Schieffelin, "Memoirs"; City Club of New York, *The City Club of New York: A Brief Historical Sketch* (New York?, n.d.); article by H. H. Cur-

ran abridged in Joseph D. McGoldrick (ed.), *A Scrapbook of Politics* (mimeo., 1929); passage of a letter by Welling quoted in Howe, *Chapman*, 67.

13 Welling, 64–72, 91; *Triumph of Reform*, 149–152; *The City Club of New York: A Brief Historical Sketch.*

14 Walter Tallmadge Arndt, "A Quarter Century of Service: The Story of the Citizens Union . . . ," *Searchlight* (Citizens Union) December 14, 1922; Citizens Union, *The Citizens Union of the City of New York . . . What It Is. What It Does* ([New York, 1931]); Schieffelin, "Memoirs."

15 Luther Gulick, *The National Institute of Public Administration: A Progress Report* (New York, 1928), *passim;* William Bennett Munro, *The Government of American Cities* (New York, 1926), 428–429.

16 Women's City Club of New York, *Twenty Years of Achievement 1916–1936* ([New York, 1936]); Marguerite M. Wells, *A Portrait of the League of Women Voters at the Age of Eighteen,* The National League of Women Voters ([Washington, D. C.], 1938).

17 Parkhurst, *My Forty Years in New York,* ch. VII; especially see p. 117.

18 For example, see the pamphlet, *Why Vote at All in '72?* (New York, 1872).

19 "Criminal Degradation of New York Citizenship," 659–665.

20 Chapman, 3–18.

21 Edwin Lawrence Godkin, *Problems of Modern Democracy: Political and Economic Essays* (New York, 1896), "Criminal Politics"; *idem,* "The Problems of Municipal Government," American Academy of Political and Social Science, *Annals* (Philadelphia, 1894), 868–873.

22 Edmond Kelly, however, became a Socialist (passage of a letter by Welling in Howe, *Chapman,* 67).

23 John De Witt Warner, "Municipal Betterment in the New York City Elections," *Municipal Affairs,* September, 1901, 625–640; Chambers, *Samuel Seabury: A Challenge,* 96–98.

24 See, for example, New York City Council of Political Reform, *Report for the Years 1872, '73 and '74,* especially p. 5; Howard Crosby, "A Letter to the People of New York," *Forum,* December, 1886, 420–428; William Howe Tolman, *Municipal Reform Movements in the United States* (New York, 1895), Introduction.

25 There is a good deal of literature expressing the mechanism-oriented approach in New York. The following are a few examples: Union League Club, *Report of the Committee on Municipal Reform, Especially in the City of New York* (New York, 1867); Seth Low, *New York in 1850 and in 1890; A Political Study; An Address Delivered Before the New York Historical Society . . .* (New York, 1892); Alfred R. Conkling, *City Government in the United States* (New York, 1894), 208 ff.; Horace E. Deming, *The Government of American Cities* (New York, 1909). (Though the books by Conkling and Deming deal with American cities in general, not New York City, both men were active in the New York reform circle, and it is difficult to believe that they were not primarily motivated by conditions in their own city.)

26 Union League Club, *Report of the Committee on Municipal Reform,* 16; Citizens' Association of New York, *Reform in New-York City: Address to the People,* 12–15; New York Municipal Society, *Address, Certificate of Incorporation, Constitution, By-Laws* ([New York, c. 1875]); *Resolutions Adopted at the Mass Meeting Held at the Academy of Music, June 2d, 1886* (New York, 1886); [Committee of One Hundred], *Committee of One Hundred to the Citizens of New York* (New York, 1886).

27 *Report of the Committee on Municipal Reform,* 16.

28 See, for instance, William Scudamore, *Positive Program Progress,* Municipal Program Leaflet No. 7 ([New York, 1894]); Leighton Williams, *Municipal Reform:*

The Need of a Positive Programme, Municipal Programme: Leaflet No. 1 ([New York, 1894]); Tolman, *Municipal Reform Movements, passim;* but note especially p. 137.

29 Citizens Union, *The City for the People! Campagn Book of the Citizens Union* (New York City, [1897]); *idem, Platform of the Citizens Union, 1901* ([New York, 1901]).

30 Warner, "Municipal Betterment in New York City," 625–640; quotation from p. 629.

31 Welling, 59 (quotations); passage of a letter by Welling quoted in Howe, *Chapman,* 67.

32 Our last three paragraphs are based chiefly upon the following: Munro, *Personality in Politics: Reformers, Bosses and Leaders—What They Do and How They Do It,* ch. I; *idem, Government of American Cities,* 420–421, 428; Clifford W. Patton, *The Battle for Municipal Reform: Mobilization and Attack, 1875 to 1900* (Washington, D. C., 1940), 32; Chapman, *Causes and Consequences,* 55; Williams, *Municipal Reform: The Need of a Positive Programme,* 8.

33 Civic normality could also be disrupted by a great natural catastrophe which created a feeling of urgency, such as the tidal wave at Galveston in 1900, which killed 7,000 people, damaged $20,000,000 worth of property and led to the introduction of the commission form of city government; and the Dayton flood of 1913, which led that city to adopt the city-manager plan (Salter, *Boss Rule: Portraits in City Politics,* 220). This kind of disruptive force was rare, however.

34 The situation in Republican cities regarding fusion movements was completely reversed. There the Democratic Party was a chief ingredient, and the other fusion elements were mainly concerned with garnering as many Republican votes as possible. Note, for example, the situation in Cincinnati in Taft, *City Management,* 11, and elsewhere.

35 "Reform movement," of course, is one of those ambiguous terms which does not mean quite the same thing to everybody using it. I have used it—and will use it throughout the discussion—in two senses: mainly to mean the entire effort to throw out the machine; occasionally in a broader sense which includes a subsequent reform administration as well.

36 It is not possible to list all the material from which I have drawn for the general discussion of municipal reform movements. Much material dealing with New York City will be cited as we go along in this chapter. For other cities, the most important sources used were: Steffens, *Shame of the Cities;* Taft, *City Management;* Bayrd Still, *Milwaukee: The History of a City* (Madison, Wis., 1948); Roy Ellis, *A Civic History of Kansas City, Missouri* (Springfield, Missouri, 1930); Salter, *Boss Rule;* George Vickers, *The Fall of Bossism: A History of the Committee of One Hundred and the Reform Movement in Philadelphia and Pennsylvania* (Philadelphia, 1883).

37 A reform movement, it should be noted, is usually referred to by a year, the election year when it reached its climax; however, it should be kept in mind that at times the movement covered a greater period of time.

38 For 1844: Myers, 132–135; *Strong Diary* (1835–1849), 258; for 1853: Myers, 171–173; for 1857: Myers, 186–189; for 1861: Myers, 201; for 1863: Myers, 205.

39 Myers, 173.

40 *Ibid.,* 135–136.

41 *Ibid.,* 174.

42 *Ibid.,* 192.

43 *Ibid.,* 229–230, 240–244, 254; Werner, 206, 214, 217–232.

44 Myers, 254–255; *The City for the People! Campaign Book of the Citizens Union;*

New York City Council of Political Reform, *Report for the Years 1872, '73 and '74,* 31–32.

45 Myers, 252; Werner, 228, 230. Myers mentions Tilden as one of those prominent in the reform movement who was elected a Sachem of Tammany in 1872, but according to Alexander Clarence Flick, *Samuel Jones Tilden: A Study in Political Sagacity* (New York, 1939), p. 112, Tilden had been elected a Sachem as early as 1856.

46 Myers, 255–256.

47 *Ibid.,* 251, 256.

48 *Ibid.,* 274.

49 Quoted in Werner, 348.

50 *Ibid.,* 442–443; Myers, 278–279; Parkhurst, *My Forty Years in New York,* 141–145; *Triumph of Reform,* 13; Alvin F. Harlow, "William La Fayette Strong," *Dictionary of American Biography,* XVIII, 156.

51 Myers, 279; Steffens, *Autobiography,* 263–265, 275–281; Jacob Riis, "Tammany the People's Enemy," *Outlook,* October 26, 1901 (reprint); Citizens Union, *New York's Tenement Houses,* Pamphlet No. 4 (New York City, 1897); *idem, The City's Poor,* Pamphlet No. 5 (New York City, 1897); *idem, Merit System in the Civil Service,* Pamphlet No. 9 (New York City, [1897]).

52 Welling, 82.

53 Gregory Weinstein, *The Ardent Eighties and After,* third ed. (New York, 1947), 176; Schieffelin, "Memoirs."

54 Harlow, "Strong," 156.

55 W. T. Arndt, "A Quarter Century of Service: The Story of the Citizens Union." The vote in the election of 1897 was as follows:

Robert Van Wyck	233,997
Seth Low	151,540
Benjamin F. Tracy (Republican)	101,863
Henry George	21,693

The vote for George was a tribute to his memory (Myers, 282).

56 Werner, 456–457.

57 Alfred Hodder, *A Fight for the City* (New York, 1903), *passim;* Myers, 285–295; Werner, 469, 473; Chambers, *Seabury,* 72–73; Steffens, *Autobiography,* 431; *Triumph of Reform,* "Jerome" in the biographical index.

58 Myers, 303–305; Steffens, *Shame of the Cities,* 284; Joseph Coviello, "Seth Low as Mayor of New York City" (a master's thesis at Columbia University), *passim.*

59 "Letter to the Editor" of the New York *Herald,* April 12, 1903. The *Herald* stated that the writer, identified only as "Civicus," took a conspicuous part in the 1901 Fusion movement and that his letter represented the view of other influential reformers aware of its preparation.

60 Coviello, "Seth Low," 68.

61 Letter to the *Herald.*

62 Coviello, "Seth Low," 59.

63 Letter to the *Herald;* Myers, 303–304; Coviello, "Seth Low," 33 ff.

64 Letter to the *Herald.*

65 *Ibid.*

66 *Ibid.,* Werner, 492–493.

67 On the Fusion internal conflict in 1903 see the letter to the *Herald;* Coviello, "Seth Low," 62 ff.; Chambers, *Seabury,* 83–84.

68 Myers, 307–323; Chambers, *Seabury,* 84, 98–104; W. T. Arndt, "A Quarter Century of Service: The Story of the Citizens Union," 15–17. The vote in the election of 1905 was as follows:

McClellan	228,407
Hearst	224,929
William M. Ivins (Republican)	137,184

(Myers, 323.)

69 Myers, 324–341; Mortimer Smith, *William Jay Gaynor: Mayor of New York* (Chicago, 1951), ch. 4; Chambers, *Seabury,* 122–127. (Notice that the civic-minded Samuel Seabury supported Gaynor in this election.) In the mayoral election of 1909, this was the vote, ignoring minor parties:

Gaynor	250,378
Bannard	177,304
Hearst	154,187

(Myers, 341.)

70 Smith, *Gaynor,* 85; Louis H. Pink, *Gaynor: The Tammany Mayor Who Swallowed the Tiger* (New York, 1931), 155.
71 Smith, *Gaynor,* 73.
72 Mortimer Smith, "Mayor Gaynor—A Political Maverick," *American Mercury,* October, 1949, 469–476.
73 *New York Times,* February 16, 1943 ("Topics of the Times").
74 Smith, *Gaynor,* 177.
75 There is conflicting information on how much patronage Gaynor gave Tammany. One gets the impression from Smith (*Gaynor,* 81 ff.) that Gaynor was entirely independent in the filling of jobs, and Pink (*Gaynor,* 144) implies that the Mayor took some, though not many, names from Tammany. On the other hand, William H. Allen in his *Al Smith's Tammany Hall: Champion Political Vampire* (New York, 1928) states (p. 80) that Gaynor gave most of the patronage at his disposal to Tammany but made independent appointments too, and Gustavus Myers (*Tammany Hall,* 356) points out that Tammany appointees were numerous in the government. My view is much influenced by the information Myers presents.
76 Smith, "Mayor Gaynor," 473; Welling, 80.
77 Henry Hastings Curran, *Pillar to Post* (New York, 1941), 175.
78 *Ibid.,* ch. 11; Myers, 354 ff.; Charles C. Burlingham, *Nomination of John Purroy Mitchel for Mayor of the City of New York in 1913* ([New York?, 1943]); New York *Herald Tribune,* January 8, 1933 (article by Denis T. Lynch).
79 Munro, *Personality in Politics,* 24–25; [City of New York], *New York City's Administrative Progress 1914–1916. A Survey . . . Under the Direction of Henry Bruère, Chamberlain, City of New York* ([New York], 1916), 37, 55, 144 ff.; *New York Times,* July 16, 1917 (editorial); O. G. V. [Oswald Garrison Villard], "John Purroy Mitchel," *Nation,* July 13, 1918, 37; Myers, 400.
80 Stephen Wise, *Challenging Years: The Autobiography of Stephen Wise* (New York, 1949), 15.
81 Eda Amberg and William H. Allen, *Civic Lessons from Mayor Mitchel's Defeat* (New York City, 1921), 54.
82 The vote for Mayor in 1917 was as follows:

Hylan	313,956
Mitchel	155,497
Bennett (Republican)	56,438
Morris Hillquit (Socialist)	145,332

City of New York, Board of Elections, *Annual Report,* 1917 (New York, 1918). The discussion of the fall of the Mitchel administration is based upon the following: Emanie N. Sachs, "Being Human; A Great Mayor and What Happened to Him," *Century Magazine,* February, 1926, 385–398; Wise, *Challenging Years,* 14–15; Amberg and Allen, *Civic Lessons from Mayor Mitchel's Defeat, passim;*

"Mayoralty Campaign as Seen Three Months Off," *New York Times Magazine,* July 15, 1917, 5–6; Raymond V. Ingersoll, "The Recent New York City Fusion Campaign,"*National Municipal Review,* March, 1918, 187–189; Joseph M. Price, "Fusion Mistakes and a Way Out," *National Municipal Review,* March, 1918, 183–186.

83 I have not included as reform movements either the Locofoco movement of the 1830's aimed at the "purification" of Tammany or the famous mayoral election of 1886, in which Abram S. Hewitt triumphed over Henry George and Theodore Roosevelt, for these were fundamentally protests by labor against economic privilege, rather than demands for good government in the sense that I have been using the term.

It is necessary to add one further word about this listing of reform movements. It may occur to the reader that in the way I am using the term reform movement, it may not always be easy to decide when you have one; this is no problem where the term is used, as it often is, to mean only a political revolt that succeeds, a definition I find objectionable for a number of reasons, not least because it seems to imply that such revolts *must* succeed. The test according to the way I use the term can sometimes be only a subjective one. The mere statement by those involved in a political action that it is a reform movement does not, of course, make it one. One must examine the entire situation and from the various factors comprising it—some of them intangible—judge whether or not they add up to a serious effort to bring about reform. Obviously, in this case, disagreement over whether a certain complex of events is or is not a reform movement is possible. For this reason, there may be some who on one account or another will not be in entire agreement with my listing of New York City's reform movements.

84 Seth Low, *New York in 1850 and 1890;* George L. Rives, "The Mayor and the Revised New York City Charter," *North American Review,* October, 1901, 454–463.

85 Charles E. Hughes, "Home Rule Assured for New York City," *Review of Reviews,* October, 1925, 369–370.

86 W. Bernard Richland, "Constitutional City Home Rule in New York," *Columbia Law Review,* March, 1954, 311–337.

87 Wise, 21–22.

88 Seth Low, *New York in 1850 and 1890.*

89 Myers, ix.

90 *Government of American Cities,* 430–431.

3 / AN AGE OF TAMMANY

1 Gene Fowler, *Beau James: The Life and Times of Jimmy Walker* (New York, 1949), 82; William Bullock, "Hylan," *American Mercury,* April, 1924, 444; Nat Ferber, *I Found Out: A Confidential Chronicle of the Twenties* (New York, 1939), 43–45.

2 Bullock, "Hylan," 444–448; Ferber, 44.

3 Epexegeticus, "Sketches of American Mayors I: John F. Hylan of New York," *National Municipal Review,* March, 1926, 158–165; Ferber, 316; Fowler, 82–83, 182; Heywood Broun, "It Seems to Heywood Broun," *Nation,* March 21, 1928, 313.

4 Allen, *Al Smith's Tammany Hall: Champion Political Vampire,* 154; "The Smith-Hylan Battle," *Literary Digest,* September 12, 1925, 8–9.

5 Flynn, *You're the Boss*, 50–51.

6 Fowler, *passim;* Flynn, 51.

7 "Smith's Triumph Over Hylan and Hearst," *Literary Digest*, September 26, 1925, 8–9; "A 'New' Tammany to Rule New York," *Literary Digest*, November 14, 1925, 10–11.

8 Fowler, 198.

9 *New York Times*, August 9, 1929, September 15, 1932, April 18, 1933, October 14, 1934.

10 Fowler, *passim,* but especially chs. 8 and 9; Norman Thomas and Paul Blanshard, "Jimmy Walker," *Nation,* October 5, 1932, 300.

11 Fowler, *passim;* Thomas and Blanshard, "Walker," 300; Warren Moscow, "Prescription for the Ideal Mayor," *New York Times Magazine*, August 27, 1950, 66; Schieffelin, "Memoirs"; Wise, *Challenging Years: The Autobiography of Stephen Wise,* 16–18.

12 Thomas and Blanshard, "Walker," 300; Joseph McGoldrick, "Our American Mayors XII: 'Jimmy' Walker," *National Municipal Review,* October, 1928, 576.

13 Milton MacKaye, *The Tin Box Parade: A Handbook for Larceny* (New York, 1934), 265; *New York Times,* November 1, 1929.

14 Allen, *Al Smith's Tammany Hall, passim,* but especially note the Citizens Union quotation on p. 157.

15 Fowler, *passim.*

16 Allen, *passim;* McGoldrick, "Walker," 569.

17 Fowler, *passim.*

18 McGoldrick, "Walker," 569.

19 Epexegeticus, "Hylan," 162.

20 In the intraparty squabbles in the Democratic Party in New York City during the 1920's, the machine in the Bronx was closer to Tammany than were the other organizations. Bronx County had only a short time before been carved out of New York County, Tammany influence in the new county was still strong and Flynn had been appointed boss of the Democrats in the Bronx by Charles Murphy to make sure that relations between the two organizations remained harmonious. (Henry F. Pringle, "Roosevelt's Flynn," *Collier's,* October 12, 1940, 45.)

21 McGoldrick, "The New Tammany," *American Mercury,* September, 1928, 4; *New York Times,* August 25, 1934.
This drift of population from the older districts of the city to newer areas was not just true of New York City. In Philadelphia, for instance, the population of the first twenty wards, the oldest parts of the city, showed a decline between 1920 and 1930; in 1930, the area had 18.6 per cent of the entire population of Philadelphia as compared with 24.5 per cent ten years earlier. (Salter, *Boss Rule: Portraits in City Politics,* 60.)

22 City of New York, Board of Elections, *Annual Report,* 1921, 1929 (New York, 1922–1930).

23 "Al Smith and Tammany Hall," *New Republic,* October 10, 1928, 188–191.

24 On the new district leaders and the new refinement, see McGoldrick, "New Tammany," 3; Louis Seibold, "The Morals of Tammany," *North American Review,* November, 1928, 527–529; MacKaye, *Tin Box Parade,* 46–47; *New York Times,* November 12, 1933 (article by Gustavus Myers).
The direct quotation from Plunkitt is from Riordon, 65.

25 Allen, *passim;* Walter Davenport, "Tammany's Own," *Collier's,* March 4, 1933, 41–42; Ferber, 291–293.

26 Allen, 184, *passim;* Ruth Pratt, "Men Are Bad Housekeepers," *Harper's,* May, 1927, 687; "Two Years of Walker," *Searchlight* (Citizens Union), February, 1928; James E. Finegan, *Tammany At Bay* (New York, 1933), 122.

27 John Bakeless, "New York, the Nation's Prodigal," *Forum,* October, November, 1928, 602–603.

28 Bakeless, "New York," 601–602; Ferber, 283 ff.

29 Ferber, 132–142.

30 Allen, 166 ff.

31 *Ibid.,* 261–268.

32 *Ibid.,* 300–304.

33 Bakeless, "New York" is an excellent article on the cost of New York City's government at this time.

34 Pratt, "Men Are Bad Housekeepers," 682–688.

35 Bakeless, "New York," 611; Citizens Budget Commission, *Fiscal Facts Concerning the City of New York* [v. 1] (New York, 1940), 9, 31.

36 "Two Years of Walker," *Searchlight;* McGoldrick, "Walker," 569–570.

37 McGoldrick, "Walker," 570.

38 New York *Herald Tribune,* May 24, 1931; Thomas and Blanshard, "Walker," 300.

39 Henry F. Pringle, "Portrait of a Mayor-At-Large," *Harper's,* February, 1928, 314.

40 Citizens Union, *Searchlight,* 1918–1930 (New York, 1918–1930), various issues.

41 Civil Service Reform Association, *Report,* 1921–1929 (New York, 1921–[1929]).

42 City Club of New York, *Bulletin,* 1918–1929 (New York, 1918–1929), various issues; Women's City Club of New York, *Bulletin,* 1924–1928 (New York, 1924–1928), various issues.

43 Allen, 150.

44 Warren Moscow, *Politics in the Empire State* (New York, 1948), 10–11.

45 "Tammany from Smith to Walker," *New Republic,* May 8, 1929, 321.

46 For example, Seibold, "Morals of Tammany," 529; "Tammany from Smith to Walker," *New Republic,* 321.

47 See, for instance, "Civic Democracy," *Commonweal,* April 3, 1929, 609; Amos Pinchot, "Walter Lippmann II. 'The New Tammany,'" *Nation,* July 12, 1933, 36–37 (criticizes Lippmann's espousal of the "New Tammany").

48 "The Rise of Tammany," December 5, 1925, 22.

49 A good example of such thinking is that of the Gentleman at the Keyhole in "Top Sergeant," *Collier's,* November 22, 1930, 32.

50 New York *World,* April 26, 1929.

51 Pringle, "Portrait of a Mayor-At-Large," 317; *idem,* "What's Happened to Tammany?" *Outlook and Independent,* May 15, 1929, 117; Fowler, 239–240.

52 Fowler, 240.

53 Flynn, 55.

54 *New York Times,* April 9, 1929.

55 *Ibid.,* March 20, 1929.

56 Interview with William M. Chadbourne, March 22, 1951.

57 *New York Times,* February 27, 1929; New York *World,* March 3, 1929.

58 *New York Times,* April 20, 1929.

59 *Ibid.,* February 21, 27, 1929; New York *World,* March 3, 1929.

60 *New York Times,* March-May, 1929, various issues.

61 John Chamberlain, "Mayor La Guardia," *Yale Review,* September, 1939, 21–22; Lowell M. Limpus and Burr W. Leyson, *This Man La Guardia* (New York, 1938), *passim,* but especially ch. XII.

62 *New York Times,* July, various issues, August 2, 1929; Joseph D. McGoldrick, "Fusion Worse Confounded," *National Municipal Review,* September, 1929, 594.

63 The Gentleman at the Keyhole, "Broadway Isn't New York," *Collier's,* June 1, 1929, 45; "A Lesson from New York," *New Republic,* October 16, 1929, 229.

64 *New York Times,* September 9, 1929.

65 *Ibid.*, November 1, 1933.
66 *Ibid.*, November 1, 1929.
67 New York *World*, November 1, 1929.
68 "A Lesson from New York," *New Republic*, 229; "A Murdered Rothstein As Political Dynamite," *Literary Digest*, October 19, 1929, 70; *New York Times*, September 21, October, various issues, November 1–4, 1929.
69 *New York Times*, October 16, 23, 1929.
70 Fowler, 256.
71 *New York Times*, October 4, 1929.
72 Board of Elections, *Annual Report*, 1929.

4 / INVESTIGATIONS AND DISCLOSURES

1 William B. Northrop and John B. Northrop, *The Insolence of Office: The Story of the Seabury Investigations* (New York and London, 1932), 5; Fowler, *Beau James: The Life and Times of Jimmy Walker*, 270; "New York's Follies and Scandals of 1930," *Literary Digest*, July 26, 1930, 6; Alva Johnston, "The Scandals of New York," *Harper's*, March, 1931, 415.
2 Northrop, 3.
3 "Magistrate Vitale and the 'Murder Contract,'" *Literary Digest*, January 18, 1930, 10.
4 Northrop, 4.
5 Northrop, 6–7; Henry F. Pringle, "Tammany Hall, Inc.," *Atlantic Monthly*, October, 1932, 429; *New York Times*, March 15, 1931 (Sec. X).
6 Northrop, 5; Johnston, "Scandals of New York," 413–414; "New York's Follies and Scandals," 5–6.
7 Northrop, 7, 9–10, 125; "New York's Follies and Scandals," 5–6; *New York Times*, October 12, 1930 (Sec. IX).
8 *New York Times*, August 20, 1930.
9 Healy and Tommaney were tried twice, in November and December, 1930; the Ewalds were tried in January, 1931 (Northrop, 8–10).
10 *New York Times*, December 19, 1931.
11 Another incident which added little dignity to the courts was the mysterious disappearance, in August, 1930, of Supreme Court Justice Joseph F. Crater. He has never been seen since. At first his disappearance was thought to be connected with the Ewald-Healy affair; later other theories were developed, none completely satisfying. Though Crater vanished in August, his disappearance was not announced until a month later so that it did not figure in the agitation we are considering (Northrop, 10–11). The best account of the fascinating story of Crater's disappearance is Gordon Manning, "The Most Tantalizing Disappearance of Our Time," *Collier's*, July 29, 1950, 13–15.
12 *New York Times*, August 22, 26, September 24, 1930.
13 Chambers, *Samuel Seabury: A Challenge*, 3–15 and *passim*; Hickman Powell, "The Man Who Threw the Monkey Wrench," *American Magazine*, November, 1932, 78.
14 Chambers, *passim*; Powell, "Man Who Threw the Monkey Wrench," 82.
15 Chambers, 26–32 and *passim*.
16 *Ibid.*, 66, 176 and *passim*.
17 *Ibid.*, *passim*; City Club files.
18 Chambers, *passim*; MacKaye, *The Tin Box Parade: A Handbook for Larceny*,

297–298; Fowler, 276; "The Great Tammany Tiger Hunt," *Literary Digest,* April 18, 1931, 8; Powell, "Man Who Threw the Monkey Wrench," 78.

19 MacKaye, 142 ff.

20 *Ibid.,* 140–141.

21 *New York Times,* September 30, November 25, 26, 27, 1930; Northrop, 17–53; "New York Vice Ring," *Outlook and Independent,* December 10, 1930, 568–569. Eventually some of the policemen in the ring were sent to prison and others were dismissed from the force. A few of the bondsmen went to jail, a few had their licenses revoked. (Northrop, 17–53; Howard McLellan, "Tammany Fights a Triple Menace," *Review of Reviews,* October, 1931, 50.)

22 Northrop, ch. VI.

23 *Ibid.,* 71–80.

24 *Ibid.,* 81–99; "The Seabury Swath," *Outlook and Independent,* June 10, 1931, 163; "Ending Bargain-Counter Justice," *Literary Digest,* July 18, 1931, 7.

25 [State of New York], Supreme Court, Appellate Division—First Judicial Department, *In the Matter of the Investigation of the Magistrates' Courts in the First Judicial Department . . . Final Report of Samuel Seabury, Referee, New York, March 28, 1932* ([New York, 1932]).

26 See, for example, Emanuel H. Lavine, *The Third Degree: A Detailed and Appalling Exposé of Police Brutality* (New York, 1930).

27 Northrop, viii; Samuel Seabury, *In the Matter of the Investigation . . . of Charges Made Against Honorable Thomas C. T. Crain . . . Report and Opinion of Samuel Seabury, Commissioner* ([New York?, 1931]); *New York Times,* March 15, 1931.

28 Northrop, 116, 124; Fowler, 270.

29 Northrop, 116–121.

30 Seabury, *In the Matter of the Investigation . . . Crain . . . ,* 82–85.

31 *New York Times,* September 1, 1931.

32 Northrop, viii; *New York Times,* December 30, 1932.

33 Julian S. Mason, "The Scandals of New York," *Current History,* August, 1932, 528; interview with Phillip W. Haberman, Jr., March 8, 1951; Northrop, 297–299.

34 MacKaye, 299–300.

35 *New York Times,* January 22, 25, 1932; Northrop, 140–141.
    The Democrats, of course, were not friendly to the other investigations of the period either. John Curry and other Tammany politicians refused to testify in the Ward inquiry ("Silent Men of Tammany," *Outlook and Independent,* October 8, 1930, 215). At the time of the Women's Court disclosures, Walker defended the Police Department against "libel" (Northrop, 41), and throughout the course of the previous investigations, though periodically announcing his co-operation with the investigators, did his best to minimize their revelations (see, for example, *New York Times,* March 13, 1931). Crain hindered an attempt to examine grand jury minutes dealing with his activities against racketeers (Northrop, 117).

36 Northrop, 158–167, 234–235; *New York Times,* September 26, 1931, February 18, 25, 1932.
    Political protection of vice and crime in the twenties and early thirties was deeper and more pervasive than our discussion so far indicates. We shall see the truth of this later. Here we might simply note that such protection was the basic reason for what was one of the most deplorable situations in New York City; numbers of underworld figures, though arrested from time to time, continually escaped punishment. When Legs Diamond, the gangster, was shot in 1930, the newspapers pointed out that while he had been arrested twenty-one times for serious crimes, he had gone to prison only twice ("Gangland's Challenge to Our

Civilization," *Literary Digest,* October 25, 1930, 8), and Diamond's "luck" was not unique in this respect.

37 Northrop, 178–182, 236–248; Mason, "Scandals of New York," 532; Pringle, "Tammany Hall, Inc.," 431.

38 Northrop, 193–202; Pringle, "Tammany Hall, Inc.," 427–429; *New York Times,* June 12, November 20, 21, 1931.

39 Northrop, 183–192; Pringle, "Tammany Hall, Inc.," 430.
The Dock Department was also involved in steamship graft of one sort or another. T. F. Keller, Chief Engineer of the Department, committed suicide when due to testify before the Hofstadter committee. He had admitted receiving money from steamship companies and individuals doing business with the Department. (*New York Times,* July 11, 1931.)

40 Northrop, 204–210.

41. *Ibid.,* 249–263; Allen, *Al Smith's Tammany Hall: Champion Political Vampire,* 304–309; Pringle, "Tammany Hall, Inc.," 433; [State of New York], Joint Legislative Committee to Investigate the Administration of the Various Departments of the Government of the City of New York, *Hearing[s] . . . July 21, 1931 to December 8, 1932* ([New York, 1931–1932]), Fifty-Seventh Hearing, 8445, Sixty-Second Hearing, 9187–9188.

42 Northrop, 264–266; *New York Times,* May 13, July 29, 1932; Joint Legislative Committee, Sixtieth Hearing, 8877 ff.

43 Northrop, 265–266; Pringle, "Tammany Hall, Inc.," 433.

44 Pringle, "Tammany Hall, Inc.," 433; *New York Times,* May 28, 1932.

45 Northrop, 275–280; Pringle, "Tammany Hall, Inc.," 432.

46 Northrop, 272–274.

47 Fowler, 108, 190.

48 *New York Times,* June-September, 1932, various issues.
Would Roosevelt have removed Walker? Nobody really knows, but Raymond Moley, one of Roosevelt's advisers, thought so, and his belief was shared by Al Smith, Mrs. Roosevelt and apparently Walker, himself; not only did Jimmy resign, but upon doing so attacked Roosevelt for being "unfair." Moley believes Roosevelt would have removed the Mayor on the charge of nonfeasance, but not malfeasance. Mrs. Roosevelt is not sure on what charge the Mayor would have been removed, but remembers that her husband, who was fond of Jimmy, was vastly relieved when Walker resigned. There was undoubtedly another reason for Roosevelt's relief, too. On this subject see Raymond Moley, *27 Masters of Politics in a Personal Perspective* (New York, 1949), 210–211; Fowler, 326–327.

49 MacKaye, 54; Norman Thomas and Paul Blanshard, *What's the Matter With New York: A National Problem* (New York, 1932), 233; *New York Times,* February 1, 1932.

50 *New York Times,* February 1–4, 1932; Thomas and Blanshard, *What's the Matter With New York,* 233–234.

51 Joint Legislative Committee, Twenty-Second Hearing, 3587–3617 and *passim.*

5 / MOVING TOWARD REFORM

1 Harold Riegelman, *Finances of the City of New York* (Citizens Budget Commission, New York, 1938), 36–37; Finegan, *Tammany At Bay,* 14–17; William C. Beyer, "Financial Dictators Replace Political Boss," *National Municipal Review,* April, May, 1933, 162 ff.

The financial plight of New York City was experienced to a greater or lesser degree by Philadelphia and Chicago (Beyer, "Financial Dictators Replace Political Boss," 162 ff.).

2 *New York Times,* December 20, 23, 1929, January-August, 1930, various issues. The story of the development of New York City's reform movement is intertwined with that of the political maneuvering that took place between Republican politicians and Roosevelt in the period 1930–1932. Self-interest caused the Republicans to act in ways which usually had the effect of helping those in the city who wanted reform; self-interest made Roosevelt act in ways which often hampered those wanting reform. The Republicans who have always stood to gain by exposing corruption in Democratic New York City were particularly interested at this time in using city scandals to embarrass Roosevelt; before November, 1930, they wanted to prevent his re-election as Governor; after that the presidency was at stake. Revelations of corruption and misgovernment in New York City could hurt Roosevelt in two main ways. Anything that discredited the Democrats might embarrass the Governor by implication. Secondly, Roosevelt would be forced to take a stand with respect to the situation, and this would invariably make him enemies: if he came out vigorously against corruption and aided the good government people, he would most certainly alienate Tammany and probably the other Democratic organizations in the city; if, on the other hand, he looked the other way and played ball with the politicians who ruled New York City, he would incur the wrath of independents, not just in the city, but elsewhere. Roosevelt met the dilemma by attempting to propitiate both camps. He avoided taking the initiative, dragged his feet and often took refuge behind legal rationalizations; when this was not possible, he acted, but in a way which he hoped might minimize machine resentment. Naturally he irritated both sides. Probably he favored a cleanup of the city—he certainly said so (e.g., see *New York Times,* March 31, April 1 (editorial), 1932)—but this could not be done without political repercussions, and neither Roosevelt nor his opponents were primarily interested in the welfare of the city.

3 *Ibid.,* November-December, 1930, January-March, 1931, various issues.

4 *Ibid.,* March 18, April 29, 1931; Jonathan Mitchell, "New York—A City in Agony," *Outlook and Independent,* April 8, 1931, 500; City Affairs Committee, *The Fight for a Decent City: The Record and the Program of the City Affairs Committee of New York* (New York City, 1932).
Roosevelt's handling of these charges and those filed by the City Club against Crain illustrates his behavior with respect to the city scandals. In the case of the City Club charges, where circumstances hardly permitted any other course, the Governor, after conferring with Crain and Curry, quickly appointed Seabury as his commissioner. But when the City Affairs Committee brought charges against Walker, Roosevelt acted differently. He held them for a few days, then sent them to the Mayor, vacationing in California, asking him to reply promptly upon returning to New York ("Cleaning Up New York," *Nation,* April 8, 1931, 370). After reading Walker's answer, Roosevelt dismissed the charges without allowing the committee the rebuttal it desired (*New York Times,* April 29, 1931). It is true that the charges were general and did not concern malfeasance—the City Affairs Committee, without the power of subpoena, was not in a position to advance charges of this sort—but, for all that, they were not so irrelevant as to justify Roosevelt's dismissing them (*New York Times,* March 19, 1931, text of charges). For example, he might have referred them to the Hofstadter committee, which had come into existence. Tammany, however, had warned the Governor that to do so would constitute an unfriendly act (*ibid.,* March 26, 1931).

5 New York Committee of One Thousand, *The New York Committee of One*

Thousand, No. 1 (New York, 1931); *New York Times,* March, 1931, various issues; "The Churches' Part in the New York Revolt," *Literary Digest,* April 4, 1931, 22; "Will Tammany History Repeat Itself?", *Literary Digest,* March 28, 1931, 10.

Organized Catholic opinion with respect to civic conditions at this time, if formed, was scarcely articulate. An inspection of the *New York Times Index* shows no statement by Catholic religious leaders denouncing conditions in the city until the summer and fall of 1932, when the Reverend E. L. Curran and Monsignor John P. Chidwick deplored the civic situation (*Times,* August 20, September 24, 1932). On the lay level, the *Commonweal* was an important exception. In August, 1930, it criticized Walker for his disdain toward the developing scandals and, though at that time it tended to give Tammany a slight nod after noting both its good and bad points, by January, 1931, it no longer had any doubts that New York needed a good cleaning. Tammany, as we noted earlier, was dominated by Irish Catholics, the Hall, as the *Commonweal* pointed out on August 6, 1930, had been made by circumstances "the expression of reigning Catholic political consciousness" and there can be little doubt that a principal reason for Catholic behavior with regard to the city scandals was that the Catholic community was embarrassed.

6 New York *Herald Tribune,* March 13, 1931.

7 One scheme that the committee used to marshal citizens behind its banner was to send out hundreds of invitations to civic, business, patriotic and other groups interested in the welfare of the city asking each to appoint a committee of ten to serve as a subcommittee of the Committee of One Thousand. Scores accepted the offer, though some declined. Several large business associations refused to join claiming they were nonpolitical, but fear may have been a more basic reason. Schieffelin refused to reveal the names of some typical men and women who had agreed to serve on the subcommittees because many of them were afraid of Tammany reprisals. He, himself, received threatening letters from unknown sources, but regarded them as the work of cranks and refused a bodyguard. (*New York Times,* March 20, 1931.)

8 It might seem strange that the Republican-controlled legislature should have hesitated at all in voting such an investigation in view of what I have previously said about Republican strategy (Note 2 of this chapter) and the action of the legislature in voting an investigation of the city in 1930. But some Republicans in the early part of 1931 did not want an investigation. While W. Kingsland Macy, recently elected Republican State Chairman, and most Republicans in the legislature were in favor of one, William L. Ward, Republican boss of Westchester County, was not, and he had enough influence to block an inquiry. Why Ward was against a legislative investigation is not clear. Some thought that he did not want to disturb the status quo between Tammany and the Republicans, an action that might possibly endanger his own position (Mitchell, "New York—A City in Agony," 500–501). Another theory was that he was associated with the anti-Macy forces in the Republican Party which disliked the new chairman for his efforts to disentangle the party from the hold of the water power interests and that Ward's actions represented an attempt to weaken Macy's prestige and his hold on the state organization; the city investigation was Macy's pet project which he had been advocating for nearly two years before his election as state chairman (*New York Times,* February 9, 1931). Whatever Ward's reason, he became a thorn in Macy's side; in February, 1931, the Senate voted down a city inquiry (*ibid.,* February 19, 1931). But the state chairman refused to give up, and the civic pressure which developed out of the Vivian Gordon affair forced Ward's capitulation (*ibid.,* March 25, 1931).

9 In early April, 1931, the committee had 900 members; by the middle of the month, 1,200; by September, 1932, 2,260; and before it disbanded in December, 1933, the total had apparently reached 2,700 (*New York Times,* April 4, 17, 1931; memorandum in the Schieffelin collection of materials; Maurice P. Davidson, *The Redemption of New York. Address . . . November 20, 1938* [New York? 1938?]). Among the distinguished members of the Committee of One Thousand were such men as Dr. Nicholas Murray Butler, former Governor Charles S. Whitman, Bishop William T. Manning, the Reverend Harry Emerson Fosdick and the Reverend John Haynes Holmes (*New York Times,* April 17, 1931).

10 *New York Times,* March-June, 1931, various issues.

The Committee of One Thousand, incidentally, had no monopoly on the business of collecting grievances. The *Brooklyn Eagle* established a Public Relations Service Bureau to which readers were urged to send specific instances of oppression of citizens or other irregularities on the part of city officials, city departments or the courts. The *Eagle* planned to turn such information over to the Hofstadter committee. (*Brooklyn Daily Eagle,* April 9, 1931.)

11 *New York Times,* October 28, November 4, 1931.

12 *Ibid.,* March 26, 1931, March 18, 27, August 8, 1932.

13 *Ibid.,* February 12, March 26, April 19, August 8, 1932.

14 *Ibid.,* June 13, July 11, 1932; I. Berger, "The Property Owner and the Citizens Budget Commission," *Real Estate News,* September, 1932, 300.

15 For example, *New York Times,* August 7, September 21, October 31, 1932, March 11, August 24, October 4, 6, 1933.

16 Russell Forbes, "Charter Reform in New York City," *National Municipal Review,* April, 1933, 169; "Charter Revision Proposal for New York by Queens [County] Chapter [of the New York State Society of Professional Engineers] and New York University," *American Engineer,* March-April, 1934, 19.

17 New York *Herald Tribune,* May 24, 1931.

18 Forbes, "Charter Reform in New York City," 168.

19 New York *Herald Tribune,* May 24, 1931.

20 League of Women Voters of the City of New York, Municipal Affairs Committee, *Brief on Charter Revision for the City of New York* (mimeo., [1935]); Forbes, "Charter Revision in New York City," 169.

21 Henry Bentley, "When Citizens Unite," *Survey,* October 1, 1931, 19–21; Richard S. Childs, *Civic Victories: The Story of an Unfinished Revolution* (New York, 1952), 164.

22 Maurice P. Davidson, *The Redemption of New York City;* New York Committee of One Thousand, *Walter J. Millard* ([New York?, c. 1931]). Note that Seabury in February, 1932, went to Cincinnati to study the city-manager plan and other aspects of the Cincinnati experiment. He conferred with Bentley, Wilson and City Manager Clarence Dykstra and made a speech at a dinner of the Cincinnati Charter Committee (*New York Times,* February 27, 28, 1932.)

It might be added that the example of Milwaukee and Detroit, both of which were then enjoying good government, made an impression upon New York's reformers, though these cities had less influence than did Cincinnati. All three cities were used by New York's reform element to call attention to what an aroused citizenry could do; see, for instance, the following publications of the Committee of One Thousand: *Milwaukee Gangless,* No. 3 (New York, 1931); *Detroit Rules Itself,* No. 6 (New York, 1931); *The Redemption of Cincinnati,* No. 10 (New York, 1931).

23 "County Government Reorganization," *Searchlight* (Citizens Union), January, 1933, 6–7; Henry Bruère (City Chamberlain) and Leonard M. Wallstein (Com-

missioner of Accounts), *Study of County Government Within the City of New York and a Plan for its Reorganization. Prepared for the Constitutional Convention, 1915* (New York, 1915), 10–12; *New York Times,* June 10, July 8, 1934.

In New York City, commissioners of records existed only in New York, Kings and Bronx counties; New York County had two—one for the County Clerk's office, the other for the Surrogate's Court.

24 New York State Constitutional Convention Committee, *New York City Government, Functions and Problems* (New York, 1938), 219; Bruère and Wallstein, *Study of County Government,* 1 and *passim; New York Times,* June 10, 1934.

25 Bruère and Wallstein, *Study of County Government,* 3.

26 *New York Times,* 1931–1933, various issues; "County Government Reorganization," *Searchlight,* 6–8; Merchants' Association of New York, *Report by Special Committee on Reorganization of City Government* (mimeo., [1933]); *The New York Committee of One Thousand* and the pamphlets of that organization listed in the text, respectively No. 9 (New York, 1931), No. 13 (New York, 1932), No. 8 (New York, 1931).

The Republicans, Socialists and even Democrats also concerned themselves with the subject of Charter and county reform. Though some Republican politicians were indifferent to the problem, an important group of Republicans composed of such men as James Marshall, Charles S. Whitman, Jacob Gould Schurman, Jr. formed a Republican Committee on Charter Revision and early in 1933 issued a report recommending sweeping changes, among which were the establishment of a common council to be elected from the boroughs by PR, limitation of borough government and the effective consolidation of city departments. *Report of the Republican Committee on Charter Revision* (mimeo., [1933]).

The Socialists, with their conviction that changes of this kind were superficial and even misleading, remained rather indifferent to them, with the exception of PR, which they favored (*New York Times,* October 31, 1931, December 17, 1932, January 5, 1933). As for the Democrats, Mayor-Elect O'Brien in November, 1932, saw fit to appoint a Charter Revision Committee to make a study of the Charter and advance recommendations for its revision (*ibid.,* November 26, 1932); the move constituted one of the best commentaries on the efficacy of the agitation over Charter and county reform. While O'Brien's committee made a number of worthwhile suggestions, they did not involve fundamental changes in structure, but dealt mainly with the reorganization of bureaus and departments, a development that was hardly surprising. *Preliminary Report of Charter Revision Committee Appointed by Hon. John P. O'Brien, Mayor . . . January 2, 1933* ([New York, 1933]).

27 [State of New York], Joint Legislative Committee to Investigate the Administration of the Various Departments of the Government of the City of New York, *Hearing[s] . . . July 21, 1931 to December 8, 1932,* Sixty-Sixth Hearing; State of New York, *idem, In the Matter of the Investigation of the Departments of the Government of the City of New York . . . Final Report of Samuel Seabury* ([New York?, 1932]); *New York Times,* December, 1932, various issues, January 10, 1933.

28 *Reports Adopted by the Second Session of Civic Conference on Charter Revision, February 16, 1933* ([New York?, 1933]); New York *World-Telegram,* January 21, 1933.

Among the recommendations adopted by the conference were the creation of a small single legislative body to be elected from the boroughs by PR; consolidation of departments; the retention of borough governments, but a limitation on their powers (in this respect the conference was not as radical as some other proponents of governmental reform); stronger powers for the Mayor. Neither the conference, nor the major plans of the December-January period advocated replacing the Mayor with a city manager; the conference declared that the city-manager plan came "too sharply in conflict with traditional political values and modes of thought to make possible its adoption at this time."

29 *New York Times,* March-April, 1933, various issues.
There were two general ways in which New York City could get a new Charter. The legislature could enact one for the city by means of special legislation, which under the Home Rule Law required an emergency message from the Governor followed by the concurrent action of two-thirds of the members of each house. Since the time of the Home Rule Law, the Board of Aldermen and the Board of Estimate acting as the Municipal Assembly could initiate action in one of two ways. It could prepare a Charter, adopt it as a local law and then submit it to the voters for approval. Or it could adopt a local law providing for a referendum on the question of whether a commission should be set up to draft a new Charter, said law containing such details as the number of members that would be on the commission, whether they were to be elected or appointed and the manner of appointment; if the voters agreed to the proposal, the work of the commission would be submitted to the electorate for its approval at another election. (City of New York, *Official Directory,* 1936.) The proponents of Charter reform could not make use of any of these methods in 1933. It was impossible to obtain favorable action from two-thirds of the members of each house of the legislature (as Moffat and others who attempted to bring about the enactment of a new Charter quickly discovered), primarily because of the Democratic majority in the Senate; Democratic legislators from New York City, it need hardly be said, were not enthusiastic about governmental reforms for the city. Tammany thoroughly controlled the Municipal Assembly. The Moffat bill was put forward as a means of circumventing the road blocks in the path of Charter reform. A general measure applying alike to all cities in the state, which could be passed by a simple majority in each house, it had a better chance of clearing the Senate than a bill creating a new Charter for New York City.

30 Citizens Budget Commission, *The Cost of the Administration of County Government in the City of New York* ([New York], 1934), 235–245; *New York Times,* February 27, 1933.

31 See chapter 6, p. 104 for the Tammany innovations.

32 *New York Times,* September-November, 1931, various issues. Each of the four No Deal candidates received over 100,000 votes, and McCooey and Steinbrink ran behind the rest of their ticket. City of New York, Board of Elections, *Annual Report,* 1931 (New York, 1932).

33 *New York Times,* December, 1931–February, 1932, various issues (quotation from *Times,* December 27, 1931); *Christian Science Monitor,* December 28, 1931.

34 *New York Times,* October 7, 1932.

35 Fowler, *Beau James: The Life and Times of Jimmy Walker,* 325–328; *New York Times,* September 6, 7, 1932. One reason Walker may have resigned—perhaps the chief one—was that if he had been removed, he could not technically have run again ("Jimmie Walker Beats the Boot," *New Republic,* September 14, 1932, 112).

36 It should be noted here that, from being Tammany's closest ally, the Bronx machine in the early 1930's became its chief rival in intraparty affairs. Aside from their disagreement over national politics and the mayoral nomination, Tammany (supported by the Democratic organizations in Brooklyn, Queens and Richmond) and the Bronx machine differed over the gubernatorial nomination in

1932. Flynn backed Herbert H. Lehman, Roosevelt's choice, while the other Democratic leaders were either opposed to or unenthused about this nomination (*New York Times,* October 3–5, 1932).

37 Flynn, *You're the Boss,* 128; *New York Times,* September 13, 1932.

38 "New York Amazed by Its New Mayor," *Literary Digest,* September 24, 1932, 9; Edward Levinson, "Joseph V. McKee, Reformer?," *Nation,* December 21, 1932, 605–606.

39 It is not entirely clear why Walker was not renominated. Fowler in *Beau James* sees Walker making the decision. According to this account, the former Mayor, who had sailed for Europe after his resignation, declined to run after a period of much inner turmoil, and not definitely until engine trouble on the ship returning him to America made it impossible for him to reach New York in time for the mayoral nominating convention which had been made necessary by the special circumstances (331–332). But it seems more probable that the real decision was made by the bosses. If they had wanted him to run, it is unlikely Walker would have refused; nor would he have had to be at the convention in person. Certainly there were important reasons why they might have refused him the nomination. (1) In all probability, Walker's selection as candidate would have split the Democratic Party in New York City, and Tammany leaders could not have failed to recognize this fact and certain possible unpleasant consequences for them. A Tammany victory in the municipal election would be put in jeopardy. The Democrats might lose the New York gubernatorial election and the presidential election, and though Tammany politicians had little love for either Lehman or Roosevelt, they preferred their election to that of the Republican candidates. Besides, suppose Roosevelt won anyway, without their help? Many in the Manhattan organization had vivid recollections of how the Hall had been cut off from federal patronage in the days of Wilson, and they were not looking for history to repeat itself. In short, there were many considerations which might have made Tammany prefer harmony to conflict. (*New York Times,* September 4, 1932, contains a good analysis of the problem facing Tammany.) (2) Al Smith thought that Walker was through politically (Fowler, 325), the former Governor still carried some weight in the Hall, and in any case, there were probably other Tammany politicians who shared his opinion. (3) Important Catholic opinion was opposed to Walker's renomination. This was made quite evident when Monsignor John P. Chidwick in a funeral oration on the occasion of the death of Tammany district leader Martin G. McCue praised McCue highly for his years of honest service and his faithfulness to his wife in a way which left little doubt as to the clergyman's view of Walker. According to important sources, the churchman's sermon, given before an audience made up largely of Tammany leaders and their wives, was a principal reason Tammany put thumbs down on Walker; Curry had long been friends with Chidwick, and following the sermon, the Tammany executive committee gave the boss a vote of confidence (*New York Times,* September 24, 1932). Schieffelin writes in his memoirs that after the Chidwick sermon, Tammany leaders sent the returning Walker a wireless: "True to our promise, we offer you the nomination as Mayor. Be sure that you decline."

40 There seems no reason to question Flynn's interpretation of the situation presented in *You're the Boss,* 128–129.

41 "Fusion Baits the Tiger in New York," *Literary Digest,* September 2, 1933, 7; "Tammany Mayor Decides to Seek Reëlection," *Newsweek,* July 8, 1933, 10; Allen Raymond, "From Playboy to Pietist," *North American Review,* January, 1933, 4–11.

42 Flynn, *You're the Boss,* 129–130.

43 Maurice P. Davidson, *Foundations of Fusion* (mimeo., [1934], Davidson collec-

tion of materials); interview with Maurice P. Davidson, January 26, 1951; *New York Times,* September 6, 1932.

44 *New York Times,* September 5–9, October 8, 1932; interview with Davidson, January 26, 1951.

The attempt to organize a fusion movement for the mayoral election was not the only political action undertaken by independents in the fall of 1932. Once again a judicial deal between Democrats and Republicans produced an organized protest. This time Tammany and the Republican organization in Manhattan nominated a common slate for three out of four Supreme Court vacancies in the First Judicial District (New York and Bronx Counties). Aron Steuer, the son of Max Steuer, famous lawyer and close friend of Tammany leaders, and Samuel H. Hofstadter, Republican chairman of the famous investigating committee, were two of the three mutually endorsed. To express their resentment, a group of Bar leaders formed an independent ticket composed of George W. Alger, chairman of the cloak and suit industry, and Bernard S. Deutsch, former president of the Bronx County Bar Association. The Bar group, subsequently known as the Independent Nominating Committee, received the enthusiastic support of the Committee of One Thousand and many independents. Though Steuer and Hofstadter won over the independent slate by a two-to-one margin, the protest vote exceeded all expectations; Deutsch received 294,406 votes, Alger 289,864. *New York Times,* September 30, October-November, 1932, various issues; City of New York, Board of Elections, *Annual Report,* 1932 (New York, 1933).

45 *New York Times,* September 16, October 9, 31, November 9, 1932; Board of Elections, *Annual Report,* 1932. The final canvass gave O'Brien 1,056,115 votes; Pounds 443,901; Hillquit 249,887.

46 See, for example, New York *World-Telegram,* November 7, 8, 1932.

47 The vote for McKee was actually larger, for many votes were discounted for technical reasons. Originally, the official canvass gave McKee a total of 241,432 votes, but it was soon discovered that many election frauds had been perpetrated; in a number of election districts, O'Brien's total had been increased at the expense of Hillquit, sometimes at that of Pounds as well, and a good many write-in votes for McKee had been simply thrown out. A recount gave McKee 262,649 votes. (*New York Times,* January-March, 1933, various issues.)

6 / THE STORY OF A FUSION MOVEMENT

1 *New York Times,* November 17, 1932.

2 New York *Herald Tribune,* November 18, 1932.

3 *Ibid.; New York Times,* November 19, 26, December 9, 1932; Levinson, "Joseph V. McKee, Reformer?," *Nation,* December 21, 1932, 605.

4 *New York Times,* November 23, December 27, 1932.

5 *Ibid.,* December 5, 9, 27, 1932, January-March, 1933, various issues.

6 *New York Times,* New York *Herald Tribune,* January-September, 1933, various issues.

7 Davidson, *The Redemption of New York City;* interview with Maurice P. Davidson, May 22, 1950.

8 Raymond V. Ingersoll, *The City Party* (radio address printed by the City Party, [New York?], 1932).

9 The City [Fusion] Party, *Statement of Purpose and Declaration of Principles of the City Party* ([New York?], 1932).

10 Interview with Davidson, March 27, 1951.

11 The City [Fusion] Party, *The City Party* ([New York?], 1933), leaflet; stationery of the City Fusion Party (Davidson collection of materials).

12 Copy of a letter from M. P. Davidson to Henry Bentley, July 20, 1934 (Davidson collection of materials).

13 City Party News Releases, January 4-June 24, 1933 (Davidson collection of materials).

14 *New York Times,* April 1, 1933. Joseph McGoldrick states that, while hundreds unquestionably filled out membership cards, City Party membership figures must be taken with caution because the party engaged in the practice of encouraging people to form groups and join up in units and when such groups came in they usually gave their own figures which the party accepted (interview with Joseph D. McGoldrick, April 11, 1951).

15 City Party News Releases, February 11-June 13, 1933.

16 Charles C. Burlingham, *Nomination of John Purroy Mitchel for Mayor of the City of New York in 1913; idem, Nomination of Fiorello H. La Guardia for Mayor of the City of New York in 1933* ([New York?], 1943); *New York Times,* November 29, 1932, January 16, February 8, 1933.

17 *New York Times,* April 13, May-August, 1933, various issues, but especially May 10, July 22, August 2; interview with Davidson, December 9, 1950.

18 *New York Times,* May 4–15, 1933 (quotation, May 4); "McKee Chooses Not to Run," *Literary Digest,* May 13, 1933, 7.

19 *New York Times,* May-July, 1933, various issues; New York *Herald Tribune,* October 12, 1933; interviews with Davidson (December 9, 1950), Paul Windels (February 6, 1951), Adolf A. Berle, Jr. (May 25, 1950).

20 *New York Times,* April-July, 1933, various issues; interview with Davidson, December 9, 1950; Limpus and Leyson, *This Man La Guardia,* 353 ff.

21 Interviews with William M. Chadbourne (March 22, 1951) and Charles H. Tuttle (March 20, 1951); *New York Times,* July 29, 1933.

22 Paul J. Kern, "Fiorello H. La Guardia," *The American Politician,* J. T. Salter, ed. (Chapel Hill, N. C., 1938), 43; interviews with Paul Kern (May 10, 1951) and Berle (May 25, 1950); Burlingham, *Nomination of La Guardia.*

23 Interview with Davidson, December 9, 1950.

24 MacKaye, *The Tin Box Parade: A Handbook for Larceny,* 327; Burlingham, *Nomination of La Guardia; New York Times,* July 27–29, 1933; Cleveland Rodgers, *Robert Moses: Builder for Democracy* (New York, 1952), 229.

25 Burlingham, *Nomination of La Guardia; New York Times,* July 27-August 2, 1933 (quotation, August 2); Rodgers, *Moses,* 229.

26 Burlingham, *Nomination of La Guardia; New York Times,* August 3, 1933.

27 Burlingham, *Nomination of La Guardia* (quotation); Schieffelin, "Memoirs"; *New York Times,* August 2–5, 1933.

28 Burlingham, *Nomination of La Guardia; New York Times,* August 8–18, 1933.

29 *New York Times,* June 16-August 18, 1933.

30 New York *World-Telegram,* December 31, 1932; *New York Times,* January 21, March 25, April 12, 19, May 7 (II), 24, June 20, August 20 (II), 25, October 22, 1933.

31 *New York Times,* January 7-February 16, 1933.
    At the end of September, 1933, O'Brien's administration was to reach the agreement with the bankers which staved off city bankruptcy (*ibid.,* September 29, 1933) for which it deserves some credit; in the light of the circumstances at the time, however, it is hard to see what other course the city administration could have pursued. The Bankers' Agreement is discussed in chapter 9.

32 MacKaye, *Tin Box Parade,* 323.

33 *New York Times,* February 9–13, 1933.

34 *Ibid.,* June-September, 1933, various issues.

35 *Ibid.,* September 20, 21, 1933; "New York's Revolt Against the Tammany Old Guard," *Literary Digest,* September 30, 1933, 8.
   The defeat of Koenig in the Republican primary was also an indication of which way the political wind was blowing.

36 Flynn, *You're the Boss,* 133, 136.

37 See, for instance, *New York Times,* October 11, 23, 1933; "Hands Off, Mr. Farley!," *Nation,* October 4, 1933, 367.

38 Richard H. Rovere, "Profiles: Nothing Much to It [Edward J. Flynn]," *New Yorker,* September 8, 1945, 30; Moscow, *Politics in the Empire State,* 134–135. But see also note 62 of this chapter.

39 *New York Times,* September 22-October 6, 1933; Flynn, 133.

40 *New York Times,* September-October, 1933, various issues; interview with Chadbourne, March 22, 1951.
   La Guardia, it should be noted, received much more support from conservative-minded anti-Tammany elements in 1933 than in 1929. This change appears to have been due less to a different opinion of the man than to a greater interest in reform.

41 *New York Times,* September 30, October 1, 1933.

42 Interviews with Davidson, December 9, 1950, March 27, 1951; *New York Times,* August-October, 1933, various issues.

43 Interview with Davidson, March 27, 1951; *New York Times,* September-October, 1933, various issues.

44 Interview with Davidson, March 27, 1951; interview with Seymour Halpern, May 11, 1951; *New York Times,* August 29-September 1, 1933; stationery of the City Fusion Party used in the 1933 campaign.
   Unlike most other Fusion campaigns in the past, the one in 1933 was not directed by a citizens committee with a number in its name (like the Committee of Seventy of 1894), though this was hardly of great importance. The Committee of One Thousand had not assumed quite the same role as the other numbered committees that had appeared previously; among other things, however, it had given birth to a municipal party which played a vital part in the Fusion campaign. In the fall of 1933 the Committee of One Thousand was practically defunct, and in December its assets were turned over to the Citizens Union (*New York Times,* December 22, 1933).

45 Interviews with Chadbourne (March 22, 1951), Windels (February 6, 1951), Halpern (May 11, 1951); "Fusion Baits the Tiger in New York," *Literary Digest,* September 2, 1933, 7.

46 *New York Times,* October, 1933, various issues; interview with Windels, February 6, 1951.

47 *New York Times,* October-November, 1933, various issues, especially November 5.

48 *Ibid.,* October 12, November 2, 1933.
   La Guardia also received the backing of some other labor elements, but he did not receive as much official union support in 1933 as he was to obtain later in the thirties. Some garment locals backed Charles Solomon, the Socialist candidate for Mayor. The traditionally Democratic Central Trades and Labor Council, headed by Joseph P. Ryan, surprised no one by endorsing O'Brien. (*Ibid.,* October-November, 1933, various issues, especially October 11, 30, November 2.) Organized labor, it should be kept in mind, was not as politically important in New York City as it was soon to become.

49 *Ibid.,* October-November, 1933, various issues (McKee's statement, October 25).

50 Tammany's main attack was leveled at the hated McKee ticket. Among other things, Tammany charged McKee with voting for waste when President of the Board of Aldermen and accused him of attempting to ride into office on the coat-tails of Roosevelt and Lehman. It carried on war against the Recovery Party by dismissing from public office Democratic district leaders who had gone over to McKee and by trying to initiate a revolt against Flynn's machine in the Bronx. On the Tammany campaign, see *ibid.*, October-November, 1933, various issues. The Socialists also assailed La Guardia, as they did everyone else in the field, and, perhaps, gave him more than his share, for they were aware that he was popular with people who usually voted for them. As one would expect, they presented a more radical municipal program than either La Guardia or McKee. (*Ibid.*)

51 *Ibid.*, October 5, 1933; interviews with Edgar Bromberger (November 27, 1954) and Halpern (May 11, 1951).

52 Interview with Halpern, May 11, 1951.

53 S. J. Woolf, "On the Stump With Three Contenders," *New York Times Magazine,* October 22, 1933, 6–7.

54 *New York Times,* September 30, October 8, 1933; New York *Herald Tribune,* October 25, 1933; New York *Daily News,* November 1, 1933; New York *Sun,* October 27, 1933.

55 "La Guardia Leads, McKee's Percentage Climbs," *Literary Digest,* October 28, 1933, 7; "Latest Ballots Swell La Guardia's Lead," *Literary Digest,* November 4, 1933, 7; City of New York, Board of Elections, *Annual Report,* 1929, 1933 (New York, 1930–1934); *New York Times,* October 31, November 1, 3, 1933.

56 Albert Shaw, "New York City Votes a New Deal," *Review of Reviews and World's Work,* December, 1933, 13; "La Guardia Leading in the Digest Poll," *Literary Digest,* October 14, 1933, 7; Charles W. Thompson, "The New York Fight Begun," *Commonweal,* August 11, 1933, 360.

57 *New York Times,* November 3, 1933; interview with Rufus E. McGahen, April 19, 1951.

58 *New York Times,* October 13–17, 1933 (quotation of La Guardia, Oct. 15; quotations of McKee, Oct. 14, 17); Joseph V. McKee, "A Serious Problem," *Catholic World,* May, 1915, 208–214; Paul Blanshard, "La Guardia Versus McKee," *Nation,* October 25, 1933, 476; Flynn, *You're the Boss,* 137.

59 *New York Times,* October, 1933, various issues; Flynn, 136.

60 The *Literary Digest* poll showed that, while McKee kept gaining in percentage from one week to the next, La Guardia always led the way. Incidentally, the *Digest's* prediction as to the order of finish was accurate, but it gave La Guardia and McKee substantially higher percentages and O'Brien a much lower one than those candidates actually received. (*Literary Digest,* October 14-November 4, 1933.) For other polls, see *New York Times,* September-October, 1933.

61 "The Tammany Drama," *Newsweek,* September 12, 1938, 13–14; New York *Herald Tribune,* September 8, 1935; Moscow, *Politics in the Empire State,* 120–121; interview with Bromberger, November 27, 1954.

62 Board of Elections, *Annual Report,* 1933.
La Guardia received 446,833 votes on the Republican line and 421,689 votes on that of the City Fusion Party. Despite the enthusiastic predictions of McKee's supporters, their candidate failed to carry a single borough. O'Brien's vote was the big surprise, for he did better than most observers had figured. To some extent the Mayor's good showing was the result of election frauds. But mainly it represented a personal tribute to O'Brien, for in the last few days of the campaign, the crowd suddenly discovered something decidedly winning in the Mayor's personality. "It was noted," declared the *Literary Digest* ("La Guardia's Victory

Crowns the Digest Poll," November 18, 1933, 7), "that he was a clean fighter, dignified, earnest, and very human."

Statistically speaking, Flynn did win in the Bronx because of his control of both the Democratic and Recovery Party lines. From this fact, it has sometimes been stated or implied (cf. Rovere and Moscow, note 38 of this chapter) that (1) to win in this way was the reason, or a reason, why the Recovery Party was launched and that (2) if it had not been for the Recovery ticket, Flynn would have lost. These points, however, should be kept in mind: as to (1), we cannot discover the motivation for an action simply by examining its effects, and in the present case, the evidence we have indicates that the McKee ticket was not established, or at least primarily established, on account of Flynn's concern over his Bronx offices; and as to (2), Tammany retained all its county offices in the election without the aid of the Recovery Party, and it is not impossible that in the Bronx, an overwhelmingly Democratic area, Flynn would have won his offices anyway had there been no Recovery ticket.

63 *New York Times,* November 8, 1933.

64 It should be noted before leaving the 1933 election that the combination of bad government and the Depression also produced successful reform movements in other cities that year. For example, the Vare machine in Philadelphia suffered a stunning defeat as did the machines in Pittsburgh, Cleveland and Bridgeport. ("Turning Out the Ins," *New Republic,* November 22, 1933, 33; Charles W. Thompson, "Meaning of the Elections," *Commonweal,* December 1, 1933, 124.)

7 / FIORELLO H. LA GUARDIA

1 Fiorello H. La Guardia, *The Making of an Insurgent. An Autobiography: 1882–1919* (Philadelphia and New York, 1948), 60.

2 The above sketch of La Guardia is based upon the following: La Guardia, *The Making of an Insurgent, passim;* Limpus and Leyson, *This Man La Guardia, passim;* Arthur Mann, *La Guardia: A Fighter Against His Times, 1882–1933* (Philadelphia and New York, 1959); Chamberlain, "Mayor La Guardia," *Yale Review,* September, 1939, 17–22; Arthur Garfield Hays, "La Guardia for Mayor of New York," *Nation,* July 19, 1933, 71; Blanshard, "La Guardia Versus McKee," *Nation,* October 25, 1933, 476; *New York Times,* November 8, 1933; New York *World-Telegram,* October 18, 1933.

3 The individual who gave this information, until recently one of the outstanding political reporters in New York, prefers to remain anonymous; I believe him to be completely reliable.

4 *New York Times,* April 27, May, various issues, 1945; interview with Joseph D. McGoldrick, July 15, 1954.

5 Harold L. Ickes, *The Secret Diary of Harold L. Ickes: Volume II, The Inside Struggle, 1936–1939* (New York, 1954), 271.

6 Harold L. Ickes, *The Secret Diary of Harold L. Ickes: Volume III, The Lowering Clouds, 1939–1941* (New York, 1954), 47.

7 *New York Times,* April 12, 1939.

8 Alfred S. [last name unintelligible] to La Guardia [no date, but around August 11, 1942] (The Personal Papers of Fiorello H. La Guardia, Municipal Archives and Records Center, New York City).

To an indignant parent who once wrote the Mayor criticizing him for failing to keep an appointment with a group of school children at City Hall, La Guardia sent a lengthy letter of apology, explaining that an unfortunate mix-up had occurred as a result of a hectic schedule. At the end, he said: "Frankly I would not write at such length if the same blunder had happened to a committee of adults, but as it is a case of children I feel very bad about it." (La Guardia to George A. Saxton, May 18, 1940, La Guardia papers.)

9 Ernest Cuneo, *Life With Fiorello* (New York, 1955), 17.

10 *Ibid.*, 34–35.

11 Newbold Morris (in collaboration with Dana Lee Thomas), *Let the Chips Fall: My Battles Against Corruption* (New York, 1955), 213.

12 Interviews with McGoldrick (July 15, 1954), Charlotte E. Carr (October 20, 1954); Cuneo, *Life With Fiorello*, 78–79.

13 *New York Times*, February 21–24, 1934.

14 *Ibid.*, October 28, 29, 1945.

15 La Guardia, *The Making of an Insurgent*, 53–60.

16 I was given this last piece of information by individuals who were extremely close to La Guardia, but who do not wish to be quoted.

17 La Guardia was a most unpretentious man. For years as Mayor, he lived with his wife and two children in a modest apartment near Fifth Avenue on 109th Street, a humble section of the city, until the neighborhood changed. When the Negroes and Puerto Ricans moved into the area, La Guardia, afraid for his children, but also afraid of the political repercussions if he moved, shrewdly got the city to take over the old Gracie Mansion, remodel it and present it to the Mayor as the little White House of the city, thus solving the dilemma. (The Gracie Mansion story was told to me by a man who was one of La Guardia's close friends.)

18 Interview with Davidson, October 27, 1953.

19 Cuneo, *Life With Fiorello*, 113–115.

20 *New York Times*, 1934–1945, various issues; letter from Arthur Hayes Sulzberger to La Guardia, December 21, 1935 (La Guardia papers).

21 *New York Times*, March 27, 1946.

22 Interview with McGoldrick, July 15, 1954.

23 La Guardia to Luce, July 18, 1939 (La Guardia papers).

24 Morris, *Let the Chips Fall*, 118.

25 "For Job No. 3," *Time*, August 2, 1937, 14.

26 Chamberlain, "Mayor La Guardia," 24; *New York Times*, 1934–1945, various issues.
   Music lover that he was, La Guardia venerated Toscanini. Once he was asked to make an exception and allow a car to park at Times Square. "What?" he screamed. But when told that it was Toscanini's car, he instantaneously mellowed. "Toscanini," he said, "can park anywhere he wants in my city." And that night Toscanini's car was parked alone in front of the Hotel Astor. (Interview with Charlotte E. Carr, October 20, 1954.)

27 Interviews with Louis M. Weintraub (August 6, 1953) and McGoldrick (July 15, 1954).

28 Interview with William Fellowes Morgan, Jr., April 23, 1951; *New York Times*, December 22, 1935.

29 *New York Times*, June 25, 1936.

30 "Mayor La Guardia's New York," *Fortune*, July, 1939, 93; interviews with Weintraub (November 23, 1953), Paul Blanshard (December 29, 1953), Mrs. Fiorello H. La Guardia (June 30, 1954).

8 / ADMINISTRATION

1 Limpus and Leyson, *This Man La Guardia*, 390; interviews with Paul Windels (March 30, 1955), Edgar Bromberger (November 27, 1954), Mrs. Fiorello H. La Guardia (June 30, 1954); Moscow, *Politics in the Empire State*, 212–213; letter from Joseph D. McGoldrick to me, August 29, 1956.

2 *New York Times*, 1935–1945, various issues, June 12, 1948; Limpus and Leyson, 390; interviews with Joseph D. McGoldrick (July 15, 1954) and Louis M. Weintraub (August 6, 1953).

3 City of New York, *Official Directory*, 1934; *New York Times*, 1934, various issues (quotation, May 28); *Who's Who in America*, 1932–33, "Goldwater"; *Who's Who in America*, 1934–35, "Rice," "Hodson"; Limpus and Leyson, 378.

4 *New York Times*, 1934–1945, various issues; interview with McGoldrick, July 15, 1954.

5 Various interviews; Limpus and Leyson, 385; "Mayor La Guardia's New York," *Fortune*, July, 1939, 94 (quotation); John Palmer Gavit, "La Guardia—Portrait of a Mayor," *Survey Graphic*, January, 1936, 56.

6 Interview with William Fellowes Morgan, Jr., July 7, 1954.

7 Interview with Morgan, April 23, 1951.

8 Interview with Morgan, April 23, 1951; "Mayor La Guardia's New York," *Fortune*, 96, 204.

9 Interviews with Weintraub (August 6, 1953), Paul Blanshard (December 29, 1953).

10 That La Guardia had such a desire is not hard to believe. McGoldrick told me that La Guardia tried to discourage his commissioners from talking to newspapermen and insisted that all administration news releases emanate only from City Hall. To get too much publicity, McGoldrick declared, was a good way for an appointee to get into trouble with the Mayor. (Interview, July 15, 1954.)

11 Information about La Guardia as an administrator has been obtained mainly from interviews, especially those with McGoldrick (May 31, 1951) and Rufus McGahen (April 19, 1951); Curran, *Pillar to Post*, 346–348.

In connection with Curran's statement it should be noted that La Guardia did not consider his responsibility of attending meetings of the Board of Estimate too important and after the adoption of the new Charter generally left it to his Deputy Mayor to represent him and cast his vote at Board meetings. La Guardia's persistent absence from meetings of the Board was repeatedly criticized by its Democratic members and by individuals and organizations attending its meetings. (*New York Times*, January 4, 1946.) The criticism was not without justification; La Guardia's practice, not only constituted an affront to citizens who wanted to present their views at such meetings, but tended to demean somewhat the Board of Estimate.

12 Interview with McGahen, April 19, 1951.

13 Various interviews, especially one with Paul Blanshard, December 29, 1953; Rebecca B. Rankin (ed.), *New York Advancing: A Scientific Approach to Municipal Government . . . 1934–1935*, F. H. La Guardia, Mayor ([New York], 1936), 142.

14 City of New York, Civil Service Commission, *Report*, 1933–34 (*Problems and Progress of 1934: 50th and 51st Annual Reports*, New York, 1934); idem, *The Balance Sheet: a Merit System Progress Report, 1933–1940* ([New York, 1940]); idem, *Report*, January 1940 to June 30, 1942 (*57th Report*, [New York?], 1943); idem, *Report*, July 1, 1942 to June 30, 1943 (*58th Report*, [New York?], 1944);

Civil Service Reform Association, *Report,* 1937 (New York, 1937); "Mayor La Guardia's New York," *Fortune,* 204; interview with Paul Kern, May 10, 1951.

15 Civil Service Commission, *The Balance Sheet;* Burton S. Heath, "Investigation by Innuendo," *Survey Graphic,* October, 1941, 498, 499, 502; Citizens Budget Commission, *Civil Service in the City of New York* . . . (New York, [1938]), 96; interview with Samuel H. Ordway, Jr., December 10, 1953.

16 Citizens Budget Commission, *Civil Service in the City of New York,* 84–101.

17 *New York Times,* 1936–1939, various issues.

18 *Ibid.,* 1940–1941, various issues.

19 Civil Service Reform Association, *Report,* 1941 (New York, 1941), 11–12.

20 *New York Times,* 1934–1945, various issues; various interviews; Civil Service Reform Association, *Report,* 1936–1942 (New York, 1936–1942); Heath, "Investigation by Innuendo," *passim.*

21 Heath, "Investigation by Innuendo," 538.

22 Civil Service Reform Association, *Report,* 1939, 1941, 1942; quotation, *Report,* 1942.

23 Civil Service Reform Association, *Report,* 1945 (*The New York Civil Service in 1944. 67th Annual Report,* New York, 1945).

24 Interview with Ordway, December 10, 1953; Civil Service Commission, *The Balance Sheet,* 16; Charles Belous, *Faith in Fusion* (New York, 1951), 31; Gavit, "La Guardia—Portrait of a Mayor," 11; "Mayor La Guardia's New York," *Fortune,* 204.

25 Harold Seidman, *Investigating Municipal Administration: A Study of the New York City Department of Investigation* (New York, 1941), 104; Paul Blanshard, *Investigating City Government in the La Guardia Administration. A Report of the Activities of the Department of Investigation and Accounts 1934–1937* (New York, 1937), *passim.*

26 *New York Times,* January-April, 1934, various issues; "La Guardia to Date," *Nation,* February 7, 1934, 146; interview with Bromberger (November 27, 1954); interview with Morgan (April 23, 1951); Rankin, *New York Advancing* . . . *1934–1935,* 143; Moscow, *Politics in the Empire State,* 25.

27 "Nineteen Thousand Cops," *Fortune,* July, 1939, 168; various interviews.

28 City of New York, Department of Investigation, *Annual Report,* 1938 (*First Annual Report,* New York, 1939), 24; *New York Times,* January 18, May 9, 1941, March 9, December 1, 1942, May 8, 1952; interview with McGahen, April 19, 1951; John Harlan Amen, *Report of Kings County Investigation 1938–1942* ([New York, 1942]), 123–125.

29 Interview with Yavner, May 7, 1951.

30 *New York Times,* May 9, 1941.

31 Interviews with McGahen (April 19, 1951), Yavner (May 7, 1951).

32 Seidman, *Investigating Municipal Administration, passim;* Blanshard, *Investigating City Government, passim* (for specific economies, the result of the Department's work, see, for example, pp. 51, 134–136, 107–109); interview with Yavner, May 7, 1951.

33 Rankin, *New York Advancing* . . . *1934–1935,* 142–144; *idem* (ed.), *New York Advancing, World's Fair Edition, The Result of Five Years of Progressive Administration in the City of New York, F. H. La Guardia, Mayor* . . . (New York, 1939), 102.

34 Rankin, *New York Advancing* . . . *1934–1935,* 322 ff.; telephone conversation with McGoldrick, June 29, 1956.

35 Rankin, *New York Advancing* . . . *1934–1935,* 249 ff.; *New York Times,* August 28, 1936.

36 *Rankin, New York Advancing* . . . *1934–1935,* 205.

37 See in this connection *The New York Police Survey: A Report for the Mayor's Committee on Management Survey* (New York, 1952).

9 / FINANCES

1 *New York Times,* September 29, 1933.
2 "For Job No. 3," *Time,* August 2, 1937, 14; Joseph McGoldrick, "Now That Election Is Over," *Nation,* November 22, 1933, 592; Rankin (ed.), *New York Advancing: A Scientific Approach to Municipal Government . . . 1934–1935, F. H. La Guardia, Mayor,* 50, 55–56, 58.
3 *New York Times,* October 4, 11, 12, November 5, 1933; New York *Herald Tribune,* November 1, 1933.
4 *New York Times,* January 3, 1934; "La Guardia Economy Bill," *Nation,* February 28, 1934, 232–33.
5 *New York Times,* January-April, 1934, various issues (quotation from Lehman, January 6); "La Guardia's Economy Bill an 'Incubator Baby,' " *Literary Digest,* April 14, 1933, 8; "The Mayor Who Refuses to Take a Licking," *Literary Digest,* February 17, 1934, 8.
6 *New York Times,* April 6, 11, 1934.
7 *Ibid.,* April-June, 1934, various issues.
8 *Ibid.*
9 *Ibid.,* April 11, August 13, 1934; Rankin, *New York Advancing . . . 1934–1935,* 54, 56.
10 Rankin, *New York Advancing . . . 1934–1935,* 28 ff.; *idem, New York Advancing, World's Fair Edition, The Result of Five Years of Progressive Administration in the City of New York, F. H. La Guardia, Mayor . . . ,* 204–205.
11 *New York Times,* May 2, November 3, 1934.
12 William H. Allen in *Why Tammanies Revive: La Guardias Mis-Guard* (New York, 1937) minimizes La Guardia's responsibility in restoring city credit. Allen holds that the city's credit would have been restored no matter who was Mayor because of the economies forced on the city by the Banker's Agreement (pp. 55, 63). Yet city credit remained low under O'Brien and significantly only began to revive when additional economies, for which La Guardia had struggled vigorously and unrelentingly for months, were authorized by the legislature and initiated by the city.
13 City of New York, *Budget,* 1935–1945–46.
  The expense budget of the city, it should be pointed out, is not its total budget, which includes such items as state and federal aid.
14 Cushman McGee, *The Finances of the City of New York* (New York, 1940), 208; Citizens Budget Commission, *Fiscal Facts Concerning the City of New York,* V. 2 (New York, 1947), Table 27 and footnotes; Rankin, *New York Advancing . . . 1934–1935,* 71; *idem* (ed.), *New York Advancing, Victory Edition, Seven More Years of Progressive Administration in the City of New York, 1939–1945, F. H. La Guardia, Mayor* (New York, 1945), 355; *New York Times,* November, 1934, various issues.
15 Provision for capital projects was made in the capital outlay budget (since 1939 the capital budget), but actual expenditures were figured in the expense budget as debt service. The capital (outlay) budget rose from $90,300,000 in 1936 to $292,-000,000 in 1937; after that it declined until it reached $36,300,000 in 1943; toward the end of World War II, it climbed sharply again, to $197,000,000 in 1945

and $225,000,000 in 1946. (City of New York, *The City Record: Official Journal of the City of New York,* 1936–1946, various issues. With the exception of the last, figures include amendments to the budget.)
The first capital outlay budget was submitted by La Guardia in 1936. Though the law providing for one had been passed under O'Brien, it had been suspended until 1936, first because low city credit made borrowing impossible and later because generous federal grants under the Public Works Program made it unnecessary. (Rankin, *New York Advancing . . . 1934–1935,* 60–61.)

16 La Guardia began by cutting the number of city employees from 90,798 to 86,364. But after that the number rose steadily, except for the war years when there was a drop. City of New York, Civil Service Commission, *Report,* 1933–34–July 1, 1943 to June 30, 1945 (New York [and New York?], 1934–1945). Figures do not include teachers and some others.

17 *New York Times,* 1935–1945, various issues; Riegelman, *Finances of the City of New York,* especially 21–27; "Mayor La Guardia's New York," *Fortune,* July, 1939, 206.

18 *New York Times,* 1935–1945, various issues; William Church Osborn, *City Finances; an Address at the Annual Dinner of the [Citizens Budget] Commission, February 27, 1936* ([New York, 1936]); Citizens Budget Commission, *Save New York City: A Short and Long Range Program to Stabilize the Finances of the City of New York* (New York, 1940); Riegelman, *Finances of the City of New York.*

19 *New York Times,* 1935–1945, various issues; *Message of the Mayor of the City of New York to the Board of Estimate Submitting the Executive Budget,* for the Fiscal Year 1941–42 ([New York], 1941).

20 Citizens Budget Commission, *Fiscal Facts Concerning the City of New York,* [V. 1], V. 2, Table 14.

21 McGee, 9.

22 State of New York, Joint Legislative Committee on Assessing and Reviewing, *Assessing and Taxation Needs in New York State Being the Final and Summarizing Report* (Albany, 1943), 51. According to McGoldrick, however, judges tended to favor property owners, and in areas where judges held that property was overassessed, they sometimes awarded owners high prices in condemnation cases (interview, June 29, 1954).

23 On the assessment issue: *New York Times,* 1935–1945, various issues; McGee, 9–10; Joint Legislative Committee, *Assessing and Taxation Needs in New York State;* Pearl Bernstein Max, *Municipal Dollars and Sense* (League of Women Voters of the City of New York, [New York?], 1947); various interviews.

24 In December, 1935, Comptroller Taylor commissioned a Special Representative, Charles E. Murphy, to inquire into reports that manufacturers were leaving New York City on a large scale. Murphy found that, though 476 firms had left New York between 1931 and 1935, it was definitely not true that there was a general exit of manufacturing establishments from the city. (It should be noticed that this period did not coincide with La Guardia's administration.) According to Murphy's survey, racketeering in business and labor, high transportation costs and other reasons, as well as high rents and taxes, were responsible for the departure of the firms. (Charles E. Murphy, *Report to Hon. Frank J. Taylor, Comptroller of the City of New York, on Industrial Survey of New York City, First Phase,* December 30, 1936 (New York, [1936?]), *Second Phase,* March 30, 1937 (New York, [1937]), *Third Phase,* June 30, 1937 (New York, [1937]). A few years later, in 1943, a committee appointed by Governor Dewey to study employment and business conditions in New York City, headed by John W. Hanes, former Undersecretary of the Treasury, painted a somewhat less favorable picture of the city's manufacturing position, to which the La Guardia administration took strong exception; because of a number of reasons, including high taxes and assessments, the Hanes

Committee declared, the city was declining in manufacturing. There is evidence, however, that the committee did not do a particularly thorough job of investigation and analysis, and much of its data was based on the Census of Manufacturers of 1939, which might well have been dated. (*New York Times,* April 12, 13, 1943.) While some firms undoubtedly continued to leave the city, it is difficult to see how one could talk about the decline of manufacturing in New York about this time. In November, 1944, the Consolidated Edison Company reported that between January and June 1944 the city made a net gain of 182 manufacturing concerns (*New York Times,* November 9, 1944).

25 *Report on Relative Tax Costs Within Seven Selected Cities for Three Groups of Manufacturing Industries to the Department of Commerce, New York City . . .* (New York, 1944).

26 *Message of the Mayor of the City of New York to the Board of Estimate Submitting the Executive Budget,* for the Years 1938–1945–46 [exact title varies slightly] ([New York], 1937–1945), especially that for the fiscal year 1941–1942; *New York Times,* January 2, 1940 (La Guardia's address to the Council).

27 *New York Times,* 1937–1942, various issues.

28 *Ibid.,* 1943–1945, various issues.

29 McGee, 277–278; Rankin, *New York Advancing, Victory Edition,* 312; Frederick L. Bird, *The Municipal Debt: A Description, Analysis and Appraisal of Debt Policy and Administration of the City of New York,* Technical Monograph Number One, Finance Project, Mayor's Committee on Management Survey ([New York, 1952]), Table 9.

10 / WAR AGAINST THE UNDERWORLD

1 Craig Thompson and Allen Raymond, *Gang Rule in New York: The Story of a Lawless Era* (New York, 1940), 3.

2 *Ibid.,* 3–5, 14–17, 23–25; Burton B. Turkus and Sid Feder, *Murder, Inc.: The Story of "the Syndicate"* (New York, 1951), 74 ff.

3 *Gang Rule,* chs. 1, 2.

4 *Ibid., passim.*

5 *Ibid.; Murder, Inc.,* 334–335.

6 *New York Times,* March 18, 1951 (article by Warren Moscow); Mayor [Fiorello H.] La Guardia, *Lessons on Good Municipal Government* (mimeo., [1937]), News Release for October 29, 1937.

7 *New York Times,* December 4, 1935.

8 Hickman Powell, *Ninety Times Guilty* (New York, 1939), *passim.*

9 In the numbers game or policy, a person bets that he can guess a number. In the early thirties, the numbers upon which policy bets were paid consisted of three digits computed from the betting odds on pari-mutuel machines at various race tracks. Though the odds were a thousand to one against a bettor hitting the three digits on the nose, many people, especially poor people, were fascinated by the game because the pay-off was at six hundred-to-one and bets as small as a penny were taken. (*Gang Rule,* 320–321.)

10 *Gang Rule,* 320.

11 Blanshard, *Investigating City Government in the La Guardia Administration. A Report of the Activities of the Department of Investigation and Accounts, 1934–1937,* 51 ff.

12 *Murder, Inc.,* 128–131.

13 *Gang Rule,* ch. 10; "Fight Against Fear," *Time,* February 1, 1937, 16.

14 *Gang Rule*, 252 ff.; "Fight Against Fear," *Time*, 16; *Murder, Inc.*, 131.

15 *Gang Rule, passim; Murder, Inc.*, 332–333, 346; *New York Times*, October 27, 1936.

16 *Gang Rule, passim; New York Times*, December, 1952–January, 1953, various issues.

17 Lepke and Gurrah's racket in flour and bake-stuffs, for example, added $1,500,000 a year to the cost of trucking the flour alone (*Gang Rule*, 245).

18 *Gang Rule*, ch. 5.

19 The description of the development of the new order in the underworld is based in general upon *Murder, Inc.*, Introduction and especially ch. 4, but I have also drawn from *Gang Rule*, especially ch. 12, and Frederic Sondern, Jr., *Brotherhood of Evil: The Mafia* (New York, 1959), 81–82, 105–106.

20 United States Congress, Senate, Special Committee to Investigate Organized Crime in Interstate Commerce, *Third Interim Report*, 82nd Congress, 1st Session (Washington, 1951), 1–2.

21 *Murder, Inc., passim*. While Turkus uses the term "Murder, Inc." to include the national crime syndicate, I am following the practice of most writers in limiting it to the Brooklyn gang of killers.

22 *Gang Rule, passim*.

23 *Ibid.*, 244.

24 *Ibid.*, ch. 6, 328.
The close bond between Tammany politicians and the underworld was pointed up at the Democratic national convention in 1932. At the Drake Hotel in Chicago, Hines shared quarters with a follower and Frank Costello, Albert Marinelli bunked in an expensive suite with Luciano and ex-sheriff Tom Farley roomed with Dutch Goldberg, adviser to the rackets, and another man, a friend of Farley, Lepke and Gurrah. (*Ibid.*, 244.)

25 *Ibid.*, 258, 338.

26 *New York Times*, November 1, 1938, December 14, 1952 (article by Ira Henry Freeman); *Murder, Inc.*, 55–56, appendix.

27 Amen, *Report of the Kings County Investigation, 1938–1942*, 4 ff.

28 *New York Times*, January 2, 1934 (quotation), January 27, November 2, 1935.

29 *Gang Rule*, 380; "New York Mayor's War on Slot-Machines," *Literary Digest*, March 3, 1934, 9; La Guardia, *Lessons*, News Release for October 29, 1937.

30 La Guardia, *Lessons*, News Release for October 29, 1937; *New York Times*, April 19, May 8, 1934, March 22, 1951.

31 City of New York, Department of Investigation, *Report from Commissioner of Investigation William B. Herlands to Honorable Fiorello H. La Guardia, Mayor, the City of New York on the Operation of Pinball Machines in the City of New York, December 17, 1941* ([New York, 1941]), *passim*.

32 *Ibid.*, 1–2, 12, 13.

33 *New York Times*, January 22, February 2, March 17, 1942.

34 *Ibid.*, 1934–1945, various issues (Magistrate Kross's statement, October 19, 1936); Special Committee to Investigate Organized Crime in Interstate Commerce, *Third Interim Report*, 142.

35 *New York Times*, March 6, 1934.

36 *Ibid.*, March 11, 1935. 3.8 per cent of the defendants failed to appear; 7.7 per cent were acquitted or discharged on the recommendation of the District Attorney; 9.4 per cent had been initially discharged by magistrates, and records were not available in 11.2 per cent of the cases.

37 *Ibid.*, February 5, 1945.

38 Polly Adler, *A House Is Not a Home* (New York and Toronto, 1953), *passim;* Report September 5, 1939 from the Commanding Officer, Investigating Squad to the Police Commissioner (The Personal Papers of Fiorello H. La Guardia).

39 "Vice in New York," *Fortune*, July, 1939, 48, 54, 60.

40 This is apparent from her account in *A House Is Not a Home*.

41 *New York Times*, November 16, 1943.

42 *Ibid.*, December 22, 1935.

43 *Ibid.*, December 29, 1935, January 1, 1936.

44 *Ibid.*, January, 1936–July, 1937, various issues.

45 Limpus and Leyson, *This Man La Guardia*, 399; *New York Times*, February 2, 6, 1934.

46 *Gang Rule*, 268, 271; *New York Times*, November 15, December 2, 1935, March 8, 19, 1938, January 5, 30, 1943.
Excerpts from the report of the State Division of Parole on parole violation charges against Lanza at the time of the famous Lanza parole case in 1957 (Lanza, apparently because of political influence, had been released following his arrest for violating parole) suggest that the last statement in the paragraph might have to be modified. Confidential information obtained from a person familiar with Fulton Fish Market operations alleged that Lanza "through his family and combination, continues to control the Fulton Fish Market." Another source said of Lanza's influence: "He has always been the boss in the fish market. He is still the boss; if you send him back for ten years he will still be the boss. (*New York Times*, May 10, 1957.)

47 Rankin (ed.), *New York Advancing: A Scientific Approach to Municipal Government . . . 1934–1935, F. H. La Guardia, Mayor*, 280; New York *Herald Tribune*, January 27, 1934; La Guardia, *Lessons*, News Release for October 29, 1937; *New York Times*, 1938–1945, various items and articles about the Department of Markets, including those containing information about the Department's annual reports.

48 Blanshard, *Investigating City Government*, 51 ff. Geoghan prosecuted and convicted 43 bondsmen; Dodge prosecuted 18 and convicted 14.

49 *New York Times*, March, various issues, April 1, 2, 1935 (quotations on Marcus' dismissal, April 2).

50 *Ibid.*, May-June, 1935, various issues.

51 *Ibid.*, June 28, 29, 30, 1935.

52 "Fight Against Fear," *Time*, 14; Powell, *Ninety Times Guilty*, 47–48.

53 *New York Times*, September 1, 1938. Davis testified at the Hines trial that Hines talked to Dodge about not appointing Dewey; but Dodge told Hines, said Davis, that if Lehman wanted the appointment he was going to obey him.

54 *Murder, Inc.*, ch. 6.

55 *New York Times*, July 9, 19, 1935, October 7, 1937; "Fight Against Fear," *Time*, 15; La Guardia papers (communications from La Guardia to Dewey).

56 *New York Times*, July, 1935, various issues; George Britt, "Racket-Rider Thomas E. Dewey," *Digest*, October 30, 1937, 15; Powell, 49–51; Beverly Smith, "The Hand in Your Pocket," *American Magazine*, November, 1936, 83.

57 *New York Times*, December 4, 1935; "Fight Against Fear," *Time*, 15.

58 Quoted in Powell, 51.

59 *New York Times*, June 14, 1936 (article by Russell Owen).

60 Adler, 296.

61 *New York Times*, June 8, 9, 1936; Powell, 311 ff.

62 Robert I. Center, "The Halt of Racketeering," *Atlantic Monthly*, October, 1937, 448–449.

63 *New York Times*, July 8–10, 1936.

64 "Can Crime Win?," *Literary Digest*, August 22, 1936, 4; *New York Times*, August 16 (article by Charles Bayer), October 22, 1936, November 8, 1943.

65 *New York Times*, 1938–1943, various issues. The committee appears to have

issued its last report in 1943 (for the year 1942); there is no mention of the committee in the *New York Times Index* after 1943.

66 *New York Times*, January-June, 1937, various issues, especially March 26.

67 *Ibid.*, January 8-August 18, 1937, various issues; La Guardia, *Lessons*, News Release for October 29, 1937.

68 My account of Lepke and Gurrah in the late thirties and early forties is based upon the *New York Times*, 1936–1944, various issues, and *Murder, Inc.*, 352, 355.

69 *New York Times*, January, 1937–August, 1938, various issues.

70 *Ibid.*, August 28, 1938 (article by Russell Owen), January 29, 1939 (article by Craig Thompson); *Gang Rule*, 138.

71 *New York Times*, August-September, 1938, various issues; "The Tammany Drama," *Newsweek*, September 12, 1938, 13–14.

72 *New York Times*, January, 1939–October, 1940, various issues; "Hines Conviction Puts Dewey in GOP Forefront Again," *Newsweek*, March 6, 1939, 11–12.

73 George Britt, "Racket-Rider Thomas E. Dewey," 14.

74 "Fight Against Fear," *Time*, 16; Center, "The Halt of Racketeering," 457; *New York Times*, January 11, 1938.

75 Amen, *Report*, 8–9; *New York Times*, October 3, 1938.

76 Amen, *Report*, 9–11; Webb Waldron, "City Watchdog," *Survey Graphic*, March, 1939, 210; *New York Times*, October 30, 1938 (article by Robert S. Bird).

77 Amen, *Report*, 10–11.

78 *New York Times*, January 7, 1939.

79 *Ibid.*, 1938–1941, various issues; Amen, *Report*, 12, 14.

80 Amen, *Report*, 48 ff., 84–86, 93 ff.

81 *Ibid.*, 56 ff.

82 *Ibid.*, 34 ff., 79 ff.

83 *Ibid.*, 16 ff.; interview with John Harlan Amen, May 3, 1954.

84 Amen, *Report*, 230.

85 *Murder, Inc.*

86 *Ibid.*, 361–362, chs. 13, 14.

87 *Ibid.*, 106; *New York Times*, October 30, 1945, April 24, 1952; Special Committee to Investigate Organized Crime in Interstate Commerce, *Third Interim Report*, 132 (quotation).

11 / THE WELFARE CITY

1 New York *Post*, May 16, 1934.

2 This is not to say that Tammany did not at times make a creditable record in certain kinds of construction, such as the building of piers and schools.

3 *New York Times*, March 20, 1938 (article by William R. Conklin), June 16, 1940.

4 Rankin (ed.), *New York Advancing, World's Fair Edition, The Result of Five Years of Progressive Administration in the City of New York, F. H. La Guardia, Mayor* . . . , xvi.

5 *New York Times*, 1934–1945, various issues; Harold L. Ickes, *The Secret Diary of Harold L. Ickes: The First Thousand Days, 1933–1936* (New York, 1953), 126.

6 *New York Times*, November 7, 1934; Rankin (ed.), *New York Advancing: A Scientific Approach to Municipal Government* . . . *1934–1935, F. H. La Guardia, Mayor*, 72.

7 Roosevelt intensely disliked Moses, apparently because of a conflict that had developed between the two men when both were working under Governor Smith (see Frank Freidel, *Franklin D. Roosevelt: The Ordeal* (Boston, 1954), 219–220).

In a spirit of pettiness, the President ordered Ickes to put pressure on La Guardia to force Moses out as head of the Triborough Bridge Authority; the Authority was getting PWA funds for its work. Not wishing to lose Moses or antagonize Washington, La Guardia, beginning in February, 1934, adopted a masterful policy of evasion; he refused to fall in line even after Ickes refused to approve PWA projects for New York City (November, 1934) and declined to honor requisitions for funds for pending projects (January, 1935). The newspapers came to the aid of La Guardia and Moses: they roasted Ickes so severely for what was obviously an improper use of federal funds that the affair almost became a national issue. In March, 1935, the national administration backed down. New York kept its Moses, and the flow of federal money was resumed. (*The Secret Diary of Ickes: The First Thousand Days, passim.*)

8 *New York Advancing . . . 1934–1935,* 16, 73–74; *New York Advancing, World's Fair Edition,* 34; Rankin (ed.), *New York Advancing, Victory Edition, Seven More Years of Progressive Administration in the City of New York, 1939–1945, F. H. La Guardia, Mayor,* 186.

9 *New York Times,* March 18 (article by George S. Saper), June 28, 29, 1934.

10 *Ibid.,* 1935–1946, various issues (statement of O'Dwyer's Commissioner of Sanitation, June 29, 1946); Rodgers, *Robert Moses: Builder for Democracy,* 178.

11 *New York Advancing . . . 1934–1935,* 274–277; *New York Advancing, World's Fair Edition,* 103, 105; *New York Advancing, Victory Edition,* 210; *New York Times,* April 27, 1935; interview with William Fellowes Morgan, Jr., April 23, 1951.

12 *New York Times,* November 2, 1934, October 19, 1941; *New York Advancing, World's Fair Edition,* 36.

13 *New York Times,* February 2, 1936 (IV, p. 2 and article by R. L. Duffus), 1937–1938, various issues; Morris, *Let the Chips Fall: My Battles Against Corruption,* 135.

14 *New York Advancing . . . 1934–1935,* 72; *New York Advancing, World's Fair Edition,* 24 ff.; *New York Advancing, Victory Edition,* 43–44; Rodgers, 105 ff.

15 *New York Times,* January 2, March 24, 1936, December 15, 1940.

16 *New York Advancing, Victory Edition,* 48; *New York Times,* December 2, 1939.

17 *New York Times,* April 10, 1942, July 1, 1948.

18 *Ibid.,* 1942–1945, various issues; Rodgers, 138–139.

19 *New York Times,* November 3, 1933.

20 City of New York, New York City Housing Authority, *Annual Report,* 1954 (*Twentieth Annual Report,* [New York], 1955), includes quotation; *New York Advancing . . . 1934–1935,* 194; *New York Times,* February 14, 1934.

21 New York City Housing Authority, *Annual Report, 1954; New York Times,* December 8, 9, 1934, December 4, 1935; *New York Advancing . . . 1934–1935,* 196.

22 New York City Housing Authority, *Annual Report, 1954; New York Advancing . . . 1934–1935,* 196; *New York Advancing, Victory Edition,* 81–82.

23 New York City Housing Authority, *Annual Report, 1954.*

24 *New York Times,* 1934–1947, various issues.
During the entire period he was chairman of the New York City Housing Authority, Post also served as Tenement House Commissioner. Rheinstein served as Commissioner of Housing and Buildings—which office replaced that of Tenement House Commissioner—until a few months before he resigned as head of the Housing Authority.

25 Rodgers, 141–148.

26 Ickes, *The Secret Diary of Harold L. Ickes: Volume II, The Inside Struggle, 1936–1939, passim* (quotation, 215); Rodgers, 145–147; *New York Times,* December 2–4, 1937, October 9, 12, 1939.

27 Citizens Housing and Planning Council of New York, Inc., *1953 Directory of Large-Scale Rental Housing in New York City* ([New York?], 1953).
Under the New York Redevelopment Companies Law, passed in 1942 and amended in 1943, a city may condemn property and sell it to a redevelopment corporation for the construction of middle-income rental housing. The city may exempt from taxes for a period not over twenty-five years that part of the value of the project which exceeds the assessed valuation of the land and buildings existing in the area just before the project was undertaken. The statute limits the return on the investment to six per cent for interest, amortization, depreciation and dividends. A contract between the developer and the city fixes the rentals and other conditions applicable to the construction and management of the project.

28 *New York Advancing, Victory Edition*, 79.

29 Rodgers, 83; *New York Advancing . . . 1934–1935*, 127, 129.

30 City of New York, Department of Parks, *12 Years of Park Progress* ([New York?], 1945), 5; Rodgers, 79–80.

31 Rodgers, 83–84, 87; *New York Advancing . . . 1934–1935*, 127.

32 *12 Years of Park Progress, passim; New York Advancing, World's Fair Edition*, 28, 109–110, 112–113; *New York Advancing, Victory Edition*, 40–42.

33 City of New York, *Official Directory*, 1934, 1944; *12 Years of Park Progress*, 13–14; Rodgers, 87.

34 Rodgers, 112–117.

35 City of New York, Emergency Relief Bureau, *Final Report to the Honorable F. H. La Guardia, Mayor, June 6, 1934–December 31, 1937* (mimeo., [1938]); *New York Times*, September 19–21, 1931, December 5, 1933.
In addition to the home relief cases, there were also about 12,000 cases in homeless shelters who received direct relief (ERB, *Final Report*).

36 See especially *New York Times*, February 18, 1934 (article by William H. Matthews).

37 On Tammany's system of relief and La Guardia's criticism, *New York Times*, 1931–1933, various issues; *New York Advancing . . . 1934–1935*, 344–345; ERB, *Final Report*.

38 ERB, *Final Report; New York Times*, February 10, 1935 (article by R. L. Duffus).

39 ERB, *Final Report*.

40 *New York Times*, February-May, 1934, various issues; *New York Advancing . . . 1934–1935*, 345.
The Emergency Relief Bureau, however, continued to issue vouchers to those recipients who showed themselves to be incapable of self-management by using relief allowances for purposes other than those for which they were intended; the percentage of those on voucher relief was negligible. (ERB, *Final Report*.)

41 The Personal Papers of Fiorello H. La Guardia; interviews with Charlotte E. Carr and Philip Sokol (presently Deputy Commissioner and Counsel of the Department of Welfare), October 20, 1954.

42 *New York Times*, 1934–1935, various issues; *New York Advancing . . . 1934–1935*, 343.

43 *New York Times*, 1935–1937, various issues; ERB, *Final Report; New York Advancing . . . 1934–1935*, 344.
The Department of Public Welfare carried out an important program of aid to various dependents, including children, old people, the blind, disabled veterans, the families of deceased veterans and the homeless; much of this program was considerably strengthened by the Social Security Act of 1935. The new Department of Welfare carried on this work along with its new function of dispensing outdoor relief to the unemployed.

44 *New York Times*, 1934–1941, various issues.

45 *Ibid.*, 1935–1941, various issues; City of New York, Civil Service Commission, *Report*, July 1, 1943 to June 30, 1945 (*59th Report*, New York, 1945).

46 *New York Times*, 1947–1948, various issues.

47 *Ibid.*, March 23, 1935.

48 *Ibid.*, March 6, 1940.

49 *Ibid.*, March 3, 1941; October 18, 1947; May 16, 1948.

50 *Ibid.*, February 17, March 10, 1950; interview with Sokol, October 20, 1954.

51 *New York Times*, March 14, 1941, October 18, 1947, May 16, June 4, 1948; interview with Sokol, October 20, 1954.

52 *New York Times*, 1937–1941, various issues, especially March 6, 1940 (Herlands' report).

53 ERB, *Final Report*.
There were at the time roughly 218,000 cases of direct relief—189,000 cases of home relief, 14,000 cases of home relief supplemented by work relief, 15,000 cases in homeless shelters—and 231,000 cases of work relief.

54 *New York Times*, October 22, 1933.

55 City of New York, *Budget*, 1934–1945–46.
Though the budgets of the Department of Health and the Department of Hospitals generally rose under Fusion, for various reasons the Health Department budget for 1935, 1940–41 and 1942–43 was smaller than that of the previous year and the 1942–43 Hospitals budget was slightly lower than the one for 1941–1942.

56 It is true, however, that the rising budgets in the two departments also reflected other factors: for example, the general price rise which occurred during World War II, the loss to the Health Department after 1943 of valuable WPA assistance which had to be made up and salary increases for low-paid workers. *Message of the Mayor of the City of New York to the Board of Estimate Submitting the Executive Budget*, for the Years 1935–1945–46 [exact title varies slightly] ([New York], 1934–1945).

57 *New York Advancing . . . 1934–1935*, 223 ff.; *New York Advancing, World's Fair Edition*, 56; *New York Advancing, Victory Edition*, 148; *New York Times*, October 22, 1933.

58 City of New York, Department of Health, *Health for 7,500,000 People: Annual Report . . . for 1937 and a Review of Developments from 1934 to 1938* (New York, 1938), 104–105, 156 ff., 172 ff.; *New York Advancing, World's Fair Edition*, 55; *New York Advancing, Victory Edition*, 148.

59 *New York Advancing . . . 1934–1935*, 233, 234; *New York Advancing, World's Fair Edition*, 63–64; *New York Advancing, Victory Edition*, 157; *New York Times*, May 3, 1940, March 9, 1942.

60 *New York Times*, May 1, September 4, 5, 1944; "Health and Fiorello," *Time*, September 25, 1944, 44, 47.

61 The plan as established thus followed the "closed panel" idea, the doctors in the program receiving what might be called retainers. The term "closed panel," however, is rather an unfortunate one in that it may easily lead to misconceptions. It should be kept in mind that while a member of the plan can only utilize the services of doctors associated with the program, he can select his general physician from out of the medical group of his choice and change his personal doctor within the medical group or transfer to another medical group if he wishes.

62 *New York Times*, 1944–1947, various issues; information from the Health Insurance Plan of Greater New York.

63 *New York Times*, May 1, 1944; interview with Morris, June 30, 1954.

64 There is also a Board of Higher Education in the city in charge of New York City's four-year colleges (City College, Brooklyn College, Hunter College, Queens

College) and community colleges (Staten Island Community College, Bronx Community College and Queensborough Community College). Its members are likewise appointed by the Mayor and its funds are mainly supplied from the city treasury under budgetary controls similar to those that operate with respect to the Board of Education and city departments and agencies.

65 New York Committee of One Thousand (Allen Raymond), *New York's Public School System* (No. 5, New York, 1931).

66 George D. Strayer, Director of Survey, *Report of the Survey of the Administration and Financing of the Schools of the City of New York Submitted to the New York City Sub-Committee of the Joint Legislative Committee on the State Education System* (68 ff.) in the *Interim Report of the New York City Sub-Committee of the Joint Legislative Committee on the State Education System Transmitted to the Legislature March 8, 1943* (Albany, 1943).

67 City of New York, Board of Education, *Total City, State-Federal Appropriations for the Years 1921 to 1953–54. Operating Budget* ([New York?, c. 1954]), chart; *New York Advancing . . . 1934–1935*, 111.

68 *New York Times*, October 27, 1933.

69 Various interviews; *New York Times*, 1934–1945, various issues.

70 See, for instance, Mayor's Committee on Management Survey, *Modern Management for the City of New York*, V. II (Report of the Mayor's Committee on Management Survey, New York [1953]), 458.

71 *New York Times*, March 20, 1944.
According to Truda T. Weil, La Guardia's adviser in educational matters at the time the legislation was passed, La Guardia, despite a definite campaign pledge to the contrary, was for some reason not in favor of the centralization of administrative power in the hands of the Superintendent of Schools (telephone conversation with Truda Weil, September 17, 1954).

72 Interviews with Buck (July 8, 1954) and Canudo (July 19, 1954); *New York Times*, July 16, 1943 (editorial).

73 *New York Times*, 1935–1941, various issues (especially October 5, 1941), November 7, 1943, June 18, 1946.

74 *Total City, State-Federal Appropriations. . . . Operating Budget*.
The Board of Education's total appropriation in 1938 was $152,505,464.

75 *New York Advancing . . . 1934–1935*, 108, 118, 124; *New York Times*, February 1, 1934, June 25, 1936, April 2, 1941, April 3, 1944; *Message of the Mayor of the City of New York to the Board of Estimate and the City Council Submitting the Executive Budget*, for the Fiscal Year 1945–46 ([New York], 1945).

76 In the realm of higher education, the La Guardia era saw the creation of Queens College (1937) as a fourth municipal college (*New York Advancing, World's Fair Edition*, 144). Brooklyn College, which had been operating from rented quarters in the Borough Hall section of Brooklyn, was, with the help of federal money, provided with a campus and college buildings between 1935 and 1937. *Brooklyn College Bulletin* (College of Liberal Arts and Sciences), 1955–56.

77 Interview with Morris, June 30, 1954.

78 *New York Times*, January-March, 1943, various issues; Strayer, *Report*, 73; interview with Buck, July 8, 1954.

79 *New York Times*, April 12, 30, 1943; interview with Buck, July 8, 1954.
It was guardedly charged by some at the time of the Starr affair that La Guardia, for his own reasons, really didn't want Starr to be appointed and exerted his influence successfully against him (*New York Times*, May 21, 1943). I have been unable to uncover credible evidence to support this position.

80 *New York Times*, April-May, 1943, various issues, June 12, 1954.
Chatfield's appointment was La Guardia's second "carpetbagger" appointment from Queens; Mrs. Lindlof was not really a Queens resident at the time La Guardia

appointed her as the Queens representative (*New York Times,* May 6, 1943). La Guardia's "carpetbagger" appointments represented a disservice to the idea of borough representation on the Board of Education.

81 *Ibid.,* May-September, 1943, various issues.

La Guardia's elimination of the position held by Assistant Superintendent Joseph M. Sheehan probably had its basis in the fact that Sheehan was a political character for whom the legislature once passed a special law giving him a higher salary than the other assistant superintendents; nonetheless, La Guardia's action represented undue interference in educational matters. The reason La Guardia held up the checks of three administrative assistants is more clouded. In one case, that of Truda T. Weil, the Mayor publicly stated that he considered her a lame duck whom the Board of Education was trying to put into a new job; Miss Weil had been Mrs. Lindlof's confidential secretary. (While La Guardia may well have believed the lame duck charge, he may have been more influenced by Miss Weil's connection with Mrs. Lindlof.)

Sheehan, nearing retirement age, retired rather than fight. La Guardia changed his mind about the three appointees; in the case of two, he soon directed that their salaries be paid, and after an interview with Miss Weil, the other appointee (during which he probably discovered that she was really a person of ability), he made her his adviser in educational matters with the title and salary of administrative assistant and gave her a desk in City Hall.

82 *New York Times,* April-July, 1943, February, 1944, various issues; "Blooming Little Flower," *Newsweek,* September 27, 1943, 76; National Education Association of the United States, *Interferences With the Independence of the New York City Board of Education* (Report of an Investigation by the National Commission for the Defense of Democracy Through Education, Washington, 1944).

83 *New York Times,* February 7, 1944 (also the source of the quotation).

84 Interview with Canudo, July 19, 1954.

85 *New York Times,* May 12, 1943.

86 Councilman Stanley Isaacs charged La Guardia with also interfering with the Board of Higher Education on many occasions, specifying the case of the abolition of Townsend Harris High School, an event we shall presently consider. The Chairman of the Board of Higher Education, Ordway Tead, denied that La Guardia had anything to do with the Board's vote on this issue, asserting that he (Tead) personally favored the abolition and influenced other members of the Board as much as he could. It is perhaps suggestive, however, that Tead had no comment when asked if, in his opinion, La Guardia interfered with the Board generally speaking. (*Ibid.,* March 9, 1945.)

87 *Ibid.,* 1939–1945, various issues; *Total City, State-Federal Appropriations. . . . Operating Budget.*

In 1944–1945 the total appropriation for the Board of Education was $134,712,722. The La Guardia budget for education for the fiscal year 1945–1946 showed an increase of over $5,000,000 from that of the previous year and marked the start of a new upward trend in educational appropriations.

88 *New York Times,* 1941–1942, various issues.

While the desire of La Guardia to achieve savings seems to have been a factor in the abolishment of Townsend Harris, one tends to suspect that this was not the only, nor perhaps the most important, consideration involved. La Guardia, it appears, hoped to save mainly about $300,000 a year, the cost of running the school (though the cost of improving it was probably also a factor). But Dr. Robert Chestney, director of Townsend Harris at the time of the abolition, raised an interesting point which causes one to pause. He observed that since most of the $300,000 went for teacher salaries and since the Board of Higher Education had promised to try to place displaced Townsend Harris teachers in other teaching positions, the city would not save too much money. More significant, perhaps, in the abolition of Townsend Harris is something that Newbold Morris once told me: La Guardia did not believe in homogeneous education for the intellectually gifted (interview, June 30, 1954).

89 Strayer, *Report*, 74; *New York Times*, December 23, 1945 (article by Benjamin Fine).

During the period immediately preceding 1934–1935, enrollment in the elementary schools was slowly declining, but enrollment in the junior high, senior high and vocational high schools was rising so rapidly that the total enrollment of the schools continued to rise. After 1935, however, though registration in vocational high schools continued to increase and that in senior high and junior high schools kept moving upward until 1938 and 1939 respectively, total school enrollment fell steadily. (Strayer, *Report*, 74.)

90 *Message of the Mayor of the City of New York to the Board of Estimate Submitting the Executive Budget*, for the Fiscal Years 1940–41—1944–45 (quotation from the *Message* for the Fiscal Year 1942–43).

91 *New York Times*, 1940–45, various issues.

92 Frank E. Karelsen, Jr. to Superintendent of Schools John E. Wade, October 17, 1945 (mimeographed copy of the letter); *idem, New York City School System. Speech Over Station W.J.Z., November 10, 1945* (mimeo., [1945]); *New York Times*, October 18, 28 (article by Benjamin Fine), December 21, 1945.

93 *New York Times*, October 28, 1945.

Yavner, after making an inquiry, issued a report on the Karelsen advisory committee in December 1945. Far from settling anything, the report, which criticized Karelsen for weak and inadequate leadership of the committee, only provoked further controversy, the Karelsen side regarding it as a "whitewash" and a "one-sided, political document." Yavner said nothing about Karelsen and the matter of school sites. (*Ibid.*, December, 1945—January, 1946, various issues.)

94 *Ibid.*, December 23, 1945 (article by Benjamine Fine), January 19, 1946.

The Board of Regents declined to investigate the situation further.

95 *Ibid.*, February 20, 1939, January 31, 1945.

While the Mayor's Committee to Survey the Situation of Substitute Teachers, headed by A. A. Berle, Jr., reported (*ibid.*, February 20, 1939) that the practice of filling vacancies with substitutes had been stopped by the Board of Education, this does not seem to have been the case (see *Interim Report of the New York City Sub-Committee . . . State Education System . . .* , 39).

96 Interview with Canudo, July 19, 1954.

97 Interview with Gilman, July 9, 1954.

98 *Interferences With the Independence of the New York City Board of Education*, 29.

99 *Total City, State-Federal Appropriations. . . . Operating Budget;* Strayer, *Report*, 466.

100 Warren Moscow, "Prescription for the Ideal Mayor," *New York Times Magazine*, August 27, 1950, 66; *New York Times*, January 7, 1935, January 13, 1937, February 7, 1940.

101 *New York Times*, 1935–1940, various issues (quotation, February 7, 1940); interview with Newbold Morris, June 30, 1954.

102 Morris, *Let the Chips Fall*, 161 ff.; *New York Advancing, Victory Edition*, 267, 269.

103 *New York Times*, December 12, 1943; *New York Advancing, Victory Edition*, 269.

The establishment of the City Center did not cause La Guardia to forget his bolder scheme. "Some day," he declared in the course of dedicating the City Center, "the great Art Center will be housed in a magnificent structure and will combine all the activities originally planned." (*New York Times,* December 12, 1943.) The Lincoln Square project promises to fulfill La Guardia's prophecy.

104 *New York Times,* 1937, various issues, especially May 30 (VI).

105 *New York Advancing . . . 1934–1935,* 282–283; *New York Advancing, Victory Edition,* 211; *New York Times,* January 1, 1939.

106 *New York Times,* May 15, 1934, February 21, September 6, 9, 22, November 14, 1936.

107 *New York Advancing . . . 1934–1935,* 296; *New York Times,* December 28, 1937.

108 *New York Times,* 1935–1936, various issues, especially May 13, 1935, December 17, 1936.

109 *Ibid.,* 1935–1939, various issues.

110 Interview, June 30, 1954.

111 That La Guardia had a good deal of enthusiasm for municipal power and retained it even after the defeat of his yardstick scheme is suggested by an item in the *New York Times,* August 17, 1945, reporting a prediction made by La Guardia at a luncheon of employees of the Department of Water Supply, Gas and Electricity. The Mayor prophesied that within fifteen years the city would be supplying electric light and power to consumers then served by private companies. This is one prediction of La Guardia that proved to be incorrect.

112 Charles L. Craig, *Problems of the New Administration. Speech . . . January 2, 1934* ([New York?], 1934); *New York Times,* May 15, 1938 (article by Paul Crowell).
The Independent Subway was operated by the Board of Transportation, a city agency of three men appointed by the Mayor.

113 During the same period both transit companies made profits of over $91,000,000 (Citizens Budget Commission, *Transit Unification Aspects and Effects . . .* (mimeo., [1935])).

114 Citizens Budget Commission, *Fiscal Facts* [V. 1], Table 51.
Had the earnings on the IRT and the BMT warranted the payment to the city of its share of the operating income, the city in the fifteen year period would have received $281,000,000 more than it did (*Transit Unification Aspects and Effects*).

115 Material for the past few paragraphs has been drawn mainly from the following: Citizens Budget Commission, *Transit Handbook: An Analysis of the Rapid Transit Problem in New York City* ([New York], 1934), *passim; Idem, Transit Unification Aspects and Effects;* City Club of New York, *Unification in a Nutshell* (New York, [1937?]), leaflet; *New York Times,* November 26, 1935, February 13, 1936, May 15, 1938 (article by Paul Crowell).

116 *New York Times,* February 20, 1938 (article by Warren Moscow), November 20, 1938 (article by Paul Crowell).

117 *Ibid.,* November 20, 1938 (article by Paul Crowell).

118 *Ibid.,* 1934–1937, various issues, especially January 16, April 18, 1934, July 17, 1937.

119 *Ibid.,* November 2, 1935, June 19, 23, 1936, May 10, 1937.

120 See, for example, City Club of New York, *Unification in a Nutshell;* Women's City Club of New York, *The Tale of Topsey Transit: A Primer for Subway Sardines* ([New York], 1937).

121 *New York Times,* May 10, 1937.

122 Citizens Budget Commission, *Studies on Transit Unification in the City of New York,* Oral Statement Before the Transit Commission . . . by Harold Riegelman . . . October, 1936 (mimeo., [1936]).

123 *New York Times,* June 23, 1936.

124 *Ibid.,* February 5, 1936.

125 *Ibid.,* 1937–1938, various issues, especially March 9, May 16, 1938.

126 *Ibid.,* May 10, 1937, May 8, 15, November 20 (article by Paul Crowell), 1938.

127 *Ibid.,* May-November, 1938, various issues, February 19, 1939 (article by Kenneth Campbell), July 2, 1939 (article by Paul Crowell).

128 *Ibid.,* 1939–1940, various issues; interview with Joseph D. McGoldrick, June 29, 1954.

129 *New York Times,* March-April, 1940, various issues, March 29, 1943.

130 *Ibid.,* February 19, 1939 (article by Kenneth Campbell), February 25 (article by Paul Crowell), April 3, 1940.
The agreement between La Guardia and the CIO leaders only temporarily settled the closed shop issue. When the city took over the private lines, the contracts had a year to run, expiring on June 30, 1941. During this period the administration urged the union to make a test case of the questionable provision, but it was unwilling to do so, and La Guardia, firmly opposed to a closed shop for civil service employees and annoyed by the TWU's attitude, set himself against continuing the contracts. In June, 1941, the union threatened a strike and the city prepared for an emergency. Then a few days before the expiration date of the contract Germany invaded Russia, and the Communists who were in real control of the union called off the strike; the whole affair blew over. After that time, the TWU transit workers worked without a contract. (Interview with McGoldrick, June 29, 1954.)

131 *New York Times,* February 25 (article by Paul Crowell), June 2, 13, 1940.
Unification, it should be understood, did not involve all transit facilities in the city; a number of surface transit lines remained in private hands.

132 City of New York, Board of Transportation, *Report . . . of the New York City Transit System for Five Years Ended June 30, 1945* ([New York?, 1945?]), 135; *New York Times,* 1948–1953, various issues.

133 *New York Times,* April 2, 1944.

134 Board of Transportation, *Report,* 31 ff., 135; interview with Morris, March 23, 1951.
As a consequence of inflation, the cost of miscellaneous materials and supplies to the Board of Transportation was 14.5 per cent higher in 1944–1945 than in 1940–1941, while that for labor, exclusive of pensions, was 35.4 per cent greater in 1945–1946 than in the fiscal year ending June 30, 1940, the last fiscal year before unification (Board of Transportation, *Report,* 31, 37).

135 Interview with William G. Fullen, July 27, 1954.

136 It has been argued too that the city's negotiators, who suggested what subsequently became the purchase price after calculating what price would permit an operating profit on the basis of a five-cent fare after most expenses were paid (interview with Morris, June 30, 1954), did not adequately anticipate future expenses. The city's representatives, however, could not be expected to base their calculations on speculation on an uncertain future; one should especially keep in mind in this connection that the unification deals were reached before the outbreak of World War II.

137 Abraham Dollinger, "Father Knickerbocker, a Transit Magnate: A Short History of Unification" (type., 1940, Municipal Reference Library), 14.

12 / CHANGES IN STRUCTURE

1 For a better understanding of this and some other points to be made in this chapter, the reader is advised to review note 29, Chapter 5—the part discussing the ways the city could obtain a new Charter.

2 *New York Times,* April-November, 1933, various issues.

3 *Ibid.,* October 13, 1933.

4 In addition to those put forward by civic organizations, plans of governmental reform in New York City were advanced, for example, by the City Fusion Party, a group of New York University faculty members and the Queens County Chapter of the New York State Society of Professional Engineers. See City Fusion Party, *Plan of City Fusion Party for Revision of New York City Charter* (mimeo., [1935]) and "Charter Revision Proposals for New York by Queens [County] Chapter [of the New York State Society of Professional Engineers] and New York University," *American Engineer,* March-April, 1934, 6, 18–24.

5 *New York Times,* January-May, 1934, various issues; "A Charter Commission Created for New York City," *National Municipal Review,* May, 1934, 268.
On the last evening of the session, the Democratic majority leader in the Senate presented the Charter measure only to see fellow Democrats rise and amend it from the floor by adding a name that was supposed to be omitted—Frank J. Prial. The Democrats then passed the amended bill, sent it to the Assembly and promptly adjourned the Senate so that the Republicans would have to take the amended bill or nothing. At first the Republicans in the Assembly were inclined to take nothing, but after Lehman called La Guardia at 2:30 A.M. and won his consent to the new arrangement, they passed the bill in the expiring moments of the Assembly amid scenes of turbulence, according to the *Times* reporter covering the event, seldom seen in a legislative body anywhere at any time.

6 "A Charter Commission Created for New York City," *National Municipal Review,* 268–269; League of Women Voters of the City of New York (Lucille J. Buchanan), *The New York City Charter Commission of 1934* (mimeo., [1934]).

7 *New York Times,* June-August, 1934, various issues.

8 *Ibid.,* August, 1934, various issues.

9 *Ibid.*

10 *Ibid.,* February 4, 21, 1935, April 27, 1936; New York City Charter Revision Commission, *Preliminary Report and Draft of Proposed Charter for the City of New York . . . April 27, 1936 . . .* (New York City, 1936), 2.

11 New York City Charter Revision Commission, *Preliminary Report,* 1–2; *New York Times,* May-August, 1936, various issues.

12 George Britt, "New York's Charter," *Digest,* October 16, 1937, 15; *New York Times,* June 21, 1935, December 16, 1936.
In 1936 a Board of Statutory Consolidation, consisting of the Mayor, Comptroller, President of the Board of Aldermen and Corporation Counsel, took over the responsibility for codification from the Charter Revision Commission; Lazarus and his staff continued to do the real work. (*Times,* December 16, 1936.)

13 The legislature reapportioned senatorial seats in 1943; this was the first such reapportionment since 1917.

14 For our discussion of the proposed Charter, we have drawn upon the following: Laurence A. Tanzer, *The New York City Charter Adopted November 3, 1936 With Source Notes, a History of the Charter and an Analysis and Summary of Its Provisions . . .* (New York, 1937); "Support the Home Rule Charter," *Searchlight* (Citizens Union), September, 1936, 6–13; Charles Evans Hughes, Jr., *Speech on the Proposed New York City Charter at the Stated Meeting of the Association of the Bar of the City of New York, October 20, 1936* (mimeo., [1936]); *New York Times,* April-November, 1936, various issues; New York Herald Tribune, August 23, 1936; Britt, "New York's Charter," 15; Department of Investigation, *First Annual Report,* 11.

15 *New York Times,* April 27 (quotation from Seabury), October 31, 1936; La Guardia to Thacher, April 27, 1936 (The Personal Papers of Fiorello H. La Guardia). By the time of the public hearings on the proposed Charter in May, La Guardia

had mellowed. While criticizing certain parts of the document and stating that "it is not the Charter that I would have written," he expressed gratification for the work of the Charter Revision Commission and declared that he realized that in a city like New York everybody could not agree on everything in a Charter. New York City Charter Revision Commission, *Minutes, February 6, 1935–August 14, 1936* (mimeo., [1935–1936]), Public Hearing, May 7, 1936.

16 *New York Times,* April 21, 26, May 3, October 18, 1936; William Jay Schieffelin, "P. R. and New Yorkers," *Survey Graphic,* July, 1937, 385.

17 *New York Times,* September-October, 1936, various issues; *Brooklyn Daily Eagle,* November 29, 1936; George H. McCaffrey, "Proportional Representation in New York City," *American Political Science Review,* October, 1939, 844.

18 *New York Times,* October 22, 24, November 1, 2, 1936; *Bronxboro* (the official publication of the Bronx Board of Trade), May-November, 1936; William D. Patterson, "A Body Blow for Tammany," *Nation,* December 26, 1936, 759–760. Conservative in the manner of political machines and probably more concerned with state and national politics, the city's Republican organizations, it might be noted, took no action on either the new Charter or PR in the fall of 1936.

19 *New York Times,* April 28, 29, July 16, August 18, 1936.

20 *Ibid.,* October 2, 1936; New York *Herald Tribune,* October 11, 1936; Tanzer, *New York City Charter,* 525–529.
The constitutionality of the act creating the Charter Revision Commission was challenged on the grounds that the legislature had illegally delegated its powers. The Court of Appeals held, however, that the act in question did not involve a delegation of power by the legislature but was an amendment to the Home Rule Law passed properly in accordance with the provisions for enacting special local laws.

21 *New York Times,* October 22, 24, November 1, 1936.

22 See, for example: Home Rule League Against Proposed Charter, *Defeat a Bad Charter. Vote NO Without Fail* (New York, [1936]); Joint Committee Technical Civil Service Employees, *Fellow City Employees* ([New York?, 1936]). Municipal Reference Library.

23 Britt, "New York's Charter," 15.

24 The exact figures on the vote were 952,519 for the adoption of the new Charter, 603,072 against, a majority in favor of the new Charter of almost 350,000. City of New York, Board of Elections, *Annual Report,* 1936 (New York, 1937).
Richmond, where the proposition lost by better than two to one, had three aldermanic seats out of sixty-five; it was to have one councilman out of about twenty-five under the new system. It should be noted that at the same time the borough rejected PR and a proposal for a State Constitutional Convention.

25 Rankin (ed.), *New York Advancing, World's Fair Edition, The Result of Five Years of Progressive Administration in the City of New York, F. H. La Guardia, Mayor* . . . , 164. It was necessary to have the Code submited to the legislature because a number of state laws were involved in the codification (*New York Times,* December 16, 1936).

26 Mayor's Committee on Management Survey, *Modern Management for the City of New York,* V. II (Report of the Mayor's Committee on Management Survey), 86.

27 Toward the end of 1955 the Wagner administration remedied this situation by bringing about the enactment of legislation investing the commissioner of what now became the Department of Buildings with plenary power (*New York Times,* November 23, December 9, 1955).

28 *Ibid.,* August 14, 1953; Rodgers, *Robert Moses: Builder for Democracy,* 129–135; interview with George H. Hallett, Jr., March 31, 1951.

29 See, for example, "A New City Charter," *Searchlight* (Citizens Union), February, 1935, 2–3.

30 See, for instance, the arguments for PR in Proportional Representation Campaign Committee, *"P. R." Means Proportional Representation. It Also Means People's Rule* (New York, [1936]).

31 McCaffrey, "Proportional Representation in New York City," 841–842; *New York Times,* January 31, 1930.

32 Schieffelin, "P. R. and New Yorkers," 385; McCaffrey, "Proportional Representation in New York City," 844; stationery of the Proportional Representation Campaign Committee (possession of George H. Hallett, Jr.).

33 Schieffelin, "P .R. and New Yorkers," 385; McCaffrey, "Proportional Representation in New York City," 844; *New York Times,* November 3, 1936.

34 For example, a good segment of the Chamber of Commerce of New York State opposed PR. New York *Herald Tribune,* September 28, 1936; Chamber of Commerce of the State of New York, Research Department, *Proportional Representation: What It Is and How It Works in New York City. A Study and Summary Prepared for the Committee on Law Reform,* second edition, revised ([New York?], 1947), 4.

35 *New York Times,* September-November, 1936, various issues; Tanzer, *New York City Charter,* 8, 529–530; Home Rule League Against Proposed Charter, *Defeat a Bad Charter. Vote NO Without Fail* (the League was also against PR); telephone conversation with Hallett, December 10, 1954.

36 PR won by a majority of 367,969, 923,186 people voting for the proposition, 555,217 against (Board of Elections, *Annual Report,* 1936). The new Charter, it will be observed, received a larger yes vote than did PR.

37 Tanzer, *New York City Charter,* chapter 43 of the Charter.

38 McCaffrey, "P. R. in New York City," 846–847; *New York Times,* September 27, 1937; "New York's First Use of P. R.—A Study in Contrast," *National Municipal Review,* January, 1938, 55.

39 Citizens Non-Partisan Committee, various press releases, 1937 (New York Public Library); *New York Times,* October 21, 26, 1937.

40 Ten of the eleven non-Democrats elected had received the endorsement of the Citizens Non-Partisan Committee ("New York's First Use of P. R.," *National Municipal Review,* 55).

41 "New York's First Use of P. R.," *National Municipal Review,* 52–55; George H. Hallett, Jr., *P. R. Has Accomplished Its Purpose. A Radio Address . . . Wednesday, December 1, 1937, Station WEVD . . .* (mimeo., [1937]); *Idem, Answers to the 17 "Reasons" for Abolishing P. R. Advanced by the Citizens' Committee to Repeal P. R.* (mimeo., [1947]), 11; Frederick Shaw, *The History of the New York City Legislature* (New York, 1954), 196.

42 "New York's First Use of P. R.," *National Municipal Review,* 56; Belous, *Faith in Fusion,* 48–50; Hallett, *P. R. Has Accomplished Its Purpose.*
   The extent of unfair apportionment with respect to the city's representative assembly that existed prior to PR and what PR did to that inequality can be clearly seen from the following: after the aldermanic campaign of 1935, the last one, the average alderman from Manhattan represented 69,000 people, the average alderman from Queens, 240,000; the first PR election seated 1 Manhattan councilman for every 90,000 voters and 1 Queens councilman for every 87,000 voters (Shaw, *History of the New York City Legislature,* 234).

43 The composition of the Councils with respect to the number of Democrats and non-Democrats was as follows:

1940–41 Council	14 Democrats	7 non-Democrats (6 actually, since Alfred E. Smith, Jr., elected as an independent, voted with the Democrats)
1942–43 Council	17 Democrats	9 non-Democrats

      1944–45 Council   10 Democrats   7 non-Democrats
      1946–49 Council   14 Democrats   9 non-Democrats
City of New York, Board of Elections, *Annual Report,* 1939, 1941, 1943, 1945 (New York, 1940–1946).

44 George H. Hallett, Jr., "The Second Use of P. R. in New York City," *National Municipal Review,* December, 1939, 880–881; *Idem,* "New York's Third P. R. Election," *National Municipal Review,* December, 1941 (reprint), 1–3; "New York City's Fourth Use of P. R.," *National Municipal Review,* December, 1943, 619–620; "P. R. in New York Prevents Landslide," *National Municipal Review,* January, 1946, 44–45; Shaw, 196.

Three women were elected in 1941, two in 1943 and two in 1945 (City of New York, Board of Elections, *Annual Report* for these years).

45 See, for instance, *New York Times,* October 27, 29, 1947 (editorials).

46 *New York Times,* December 5, 1937 (article by Warren Moscow); "New York's First Use of P. R.," *National Municipal Review,* 55; City Affairs Committee, *The Councilmanic Race—1939* ([New York], 1939).

47 "Proportional Representation—Success or Failure?" *Political World,* December, 1941, 10.

Moreover, what PR's critics completely ignored in this line of attack was the obvious point that without PR Fusion would have done much worse than it did.

48 Hallett, "New York's Third P. R. Election," 3; "Proportional Representation—Success or Failure?" *Political World,* 10; "New York City's Fourth Use of P. R.," *National Municipal Review,* 619; "P. R. in New York Prevents Landslide," *National Municipal Review,* 44–45.

Though some opponents of PR charged that the Communists gained an advantage under it through "bullet voting," it is hard to see how this could be. A "bullet vote" is a vote cast for first choice only, without using the second, third and other choices permitted. Since a PR ballot is never even looked at for second choice till the fate of the first choice is decided, it can make no difference to the first choice whether later selections are marked or not. In fact, "bullet voting" is simply foolish voting; if the first choice is defeated, all "bullet votes" for him are wasted instead of being transferred to someone else the voter would like to help.

49 In 1939, for example, the vote for the Council, not as large as in 1937, gave a Council composed of 7 representatives from Brooklyn, 5 from Manhattan, 4 each from Queens and the Bronx and 1 from Staten Island (City of New York, Board of Elections, *Annual Report,* 1939).

50 Interview with Hallett, March 31, 1951; "New York City's Fourth Use of P. R.," *National Municipal Review,* 620.

51 See, for instance, *New York Times,* October 27, 1947 (editorial).

52 Among the laws passed by the last Council were ones providing for rent control at a time when Congress had relaxed controls, creating a Smoke Control Bureau to grapple with the serious problem of air pollution and establishing a Traffic Commission to deal with the growing problem of traffic congestion.

53 Belous, 60; Shaw, 213 ff.

54 George H. Hallett, Jr., "The Case for P. R.," *American Scholar,* Spring, 1943 (reprint), 168; Belous, 56–57; Shaw, 226–227.

55 Shaw, 189 (incl. n.5); Belle Zeller and Hugh A. Bone, "The Repeal of P. R. in New York City—Ten Years in Retrospect," *American Political Science Review,* December, 1948 (reprint), 1142; Willam Jay Schieffelin, "Proportional Representation: Does It Work? The Experiment in New York—Two Views," *Vital Speeches,* December 15, 1937, 154.

56 Shaw, 189 (incl. n.4); McCaffrey, "P. R. in New York City," 848; New York *Herald Tribune,* November 14, 1937; Hallett, "Second Use of P. R. in New York City," 884–885.

57 Shaw, 189 (incl. n.4).

58 New York *Herald Tribune,* November 14, 1937; Sophia A. Olmsted, *Remarks on the P. R. Election in Concluding the New York University Forum Hour on the Subject of Proportional Representation . . . Wednesday, December 1, 1937, Station WEVD . . .* (mimeo., [1937]); Schieffelin, "Proportional Representation: Does It Work?," 154.

A picture of one kind of PR voting machine, developed by IBM, appears in the Citizens Union *Searchlight,* September, 1936 (Special Charter Number). Another type is shown in the New York *Post,* February 7, 1939.

59 Flynn, *You're the Boss,* 222.

60 Zeller and Bone, "Repeal of P. R. in New York City," 1140–1142.

61 *Ibid.,* 1142–1144.

62 Telephone conversation with Hallett, December 10, 1954. It might be noted that after the first PR election, the executive secretary of the Citizens Union also became the secretary of the Citizens Non-Partisan Committee, and this group subsequently operated out of the headquarters of the Citizens Union.

63 Tanzer, *New York City Charter,* 14–15, 530–559; Belous, 44; George H. Hallett, Jr., "New York P. R. Ban Defeated in Every County," *National Municipal Review,* January, 1939, 69–70.

The voters in the fall of 1938, exhibiting an unusual degree of voting discretion, defeated three out of nine State Constitutional amendments; the amendment prohibiting PR was the worst beaten of all.

64 George H. McCaffrey, "New York Repulses Attack on P. R.," *National Municipal Review,* December, 1940, 829; Citizens Union, *Annual Report,* [1940] (New York, [1940?]).

The vote was:

| For repeal | 567,165 |
| Against repeal | 788,640 |

Again Richmond was the only borough to vote against PR, though PR did much better here this time than in 1936. City of New York, Board of Elections, *Annual Report,* 1940 (New York, 1941).

65 Chamber of Commerce of the State of New York, Research Department, *Proportional Representation,* 13.

66 Zeller and Bone, "Repeal of P. R. in New York City," 1128–1131; *New York Times,* November 2, 1936, 1947, various issues.

67 Zeller and Bone, "Repeal of P. R. in New York City," 1128–1131, 1138.

68 *Ibid.,* 1144, 1146; New York Times, 1947, various issues; Chamber of Commerce, Research Department, *Proportional Representation,* 18 ff.; Keep P. R. Committee, *DANGER* ([New York?, 1947]), leaflet.

PR, aided somewhat by the three-platoon question in 1936, was somewhat handicapped in the 1947 campaign for repeal by the fact that a soldier bonus amendment, which most veteran organizations were pushing, and three popular housing questions also appeared on the ballot (Zeller and Bone, 1137, 1146).

The vote on repeal was:

| For | 935,222 |
| Against | 586,170 |

Every borough voted for repeal. City of New York, Board of Elections, *Annual Report,* 1947 (New York, 1948).

69 *New York Times,* March 13, July 19, 1945; City of New York, Board of Elections, *Annual Report,* 1949 ([New York?], 1950).

70 *New York Times,* November 4, 1953.

71 Shaw, 245.

72 See, for instance, *New York Times,* January 21, 1955 (editorial), March 27, 1957.

73 *Ibid.,* May-July, 1934, various issues.

74 *Ibid.*, July, various issues, October 23, 1934, November 6, 1935.
75 *Ibid.*, March 10, 1936, July 21, 1937; New York *Herald Tribune*, December 20, 1936; City Affairs Committee, *The County Reorganization Amendment: A Challenge to Democracy* ([New York], 1940).
The Democratic bills of 1937 dealing with county reform provided for the consolidation of the offices of register, commissioner of jurors and commissioner of records in the office of county clerk (though it was doubtful if many jobs actually would be eliminated in the process). The duties of the sheriffs and the city marshals would be merged in each county and transferred to a new borough marshal to be appointed by the Supreme Court in each county; the creation of the borough marshals would remove from the Mayor's appointment list more than 80 positions (city marshals) and place them with the Supreme Court. (*New York Times*, July 21, 1937.)
76 New York *Herald Tribune*, September 13, December 20, 1936; *New York Times*, October 28, 1937; Blanshard, *Investigating City Government in the La Guardia Administration. A Report of the Activities of the Department of Investigation and Accounts, 1934–1937*, 9 ff.
77 *New York Times*, January 26, November 30, December 7, 22, 1938; *New York Advancing, World's Fair Edition*, 162.
78 *New York Times*, 1939, various issues; telephone conversation with Hallett, December 2, 1954.
79 Citizens Union, *Annual Report*, [1940]; interview with Hallett, March 31, 1951; *New York Times*, October 30, 1940.
80 Interview with Hallett, March 31, 1951; Citizens Non-Partisan Committee, *County Reform: Why We Need It and How to Get It* ([New York], 1941); *New York Times*, March-July, 1941, various issues.
81 *New York Times*, January 17, 1939. The new system whereby the county clerks were appointed by the Appellate Division and assumed the duties of the commissioners of jurors seems to have gone into effect as of January 1, 1940; at least this was true with respect to Kings County. Kings County, County Clerk, *Annual Report*, 1940 (Brooklyn, [1941]).
Cashmore also stated that the Democrats would not introduce bills dealing with the public administrators because they were recognized as officers of the courts (and beyond the reach of the city). *New York Times*, January 17, 1939.
82 The Council actually passed one of Cashmore's bills, that transferring the duties of the commissioners of records to the county clerks (*New York Times*, February 22, 1939), but it died at this stage of the enactment process.
83 *Ibid.*, August 9, 1940; Paul Blanshard, "A Battle Lost, A War to Win," *National Municipal Review*, December, 1940, 779.
84 *New York Times*, July-September, 1941, various issues.
85 Interview with Hallett, March 31, 1951; *New York Times*, August 15, September 5, 1941.
86 *New York Times*, October 27-November 6, 1941; interview with Hallett, March 31, 1951.
The vote on the three propositions was:

Proposition No. 1	509,284 Yes	228,019 No
Proposition No. 2	306,454 Yes	379,617 No
Proposition No. 3	316,159 Yes	390,397 No

(City of New York, Board of Elections, *Annual Report*, 1941.)
87 Rankin (ed.), *New York Advancing, Victory Edition, Seven More Years of Progressive Administration in the City of New York, 1939–1945, F. H. La Guardia, Mayor*, 305, 308, 337–338; Richard S. Childs, "First Civil Service Sheriff," *National Municipal Review*, June, 1948 (reprint), 3–4; Flynn, *You're the Boss*, 25–26.
88 *New York Times*, March 20, 1938.

89 Telephone conversation with Hallett, December 10, 1954.

90 Seabury also made the following proposals: centralize all Magistrates' Courts in a borough in one building; reduce by one-half the number of assistant clerks and attendants in the Courts and tighten up civil service regulations; simplify the collection of fines; institute a cash bail-bond of $10 to $25 for persons charged with minor offenses; permit immediate arraignment before a judge, thus eliminating booking at station houses; abolish the Magistrates' Homicide Courts and establish special courts for all felony cases; include a family term in the new Special Sessions Court insead of making the Family Court part of another proposed court; create a central probation bureau to serve all criminal courts to replace the existing numerous separate systems; strictly observe the laws defining the circumstances under which a policeman may make an arrest; require judges to certify the accuracy of the records of trials held before them; inaugurate a public defender system whereby the Appellate Division would appoint attorneys designated by the bar associations and the Legal Aid Society to represent poor defendants, paying them from out of the public treasury. (*New York Times*, March 28, 1932.)

91 *Ibid.*, March 24, April 28, 1933, 1934–38, various issues.
As to Seabury's less radical court recommendations (see note 90), we have just noticed what happened to the Family Court; aside from one or two proposals whose adoption will be referred to in the text, the reduction of court personnel and extension of civil service and the centralization of the Magistrates' Courts in the Bronx and Manhattan in one building, none of the other suggestions were carried out. The need of poor defendants for adequate legal assistance was met somewhat by the Legal Aid Society which in the late thirties expanded its activities in the criminal field. Interviews with Judge Jacob Gould Schurman (December 7, 1954) and Edgar Bromberger (November 27, 1954); information from the Legal Aid Society.

92 *New York Times*, March 29, August 8, 1932.

93 La Guardia, *Lessons on Good Municipal Government*, News Release for October 20, 1937.

94 Various interviews, especially those with Joseph D. McGoldrick (May 31, 1951), Eugene R. Canudo (July 19, 1954), Schurman (December 7, 1954) and Bromberger (November 27, 1954); *New York Times*, 1934–45, various issues; Belous, 38.

95 *New York Times*, July 6, September 2, 1936, January 27, 1938, May 11, 1945; Rankin (ed.), *New York Advancing: A Scientific Approach to Municipal Government . . . 1934–1935, F. H. La Guardia, Mayor*, 148–149; *New York Advancing, Victory Edition*, 284; [City of New York], City Magistrates' Courts, Probation Bureau, *The Wayward Minors' Court: A Pamphlet of Essential Information* ([New York, 1939]); interview with Schurman, December 7, 1954.

96 Interview with Schurman, December 7, 1954; *New York Advancing, World's Fair Edition*, 175; *New York Times*, January 27, 1938.

97 *New York Times*, July 6, 1936.

13 / POLITICS

1 Eric F. Goldman, *Rendezvous With Destiny: A History of Modern American Reform* (New York, 1952), 371–372.

2 Moscow, *Politics in the Empire State*, 52–53; Salter, *Boss Rule: Portraits in City Politics*, 256–260; New York *Herald Tribune*, February 18, 1934; interview with Paul Kern, May 10, 1951.

3 *New York Times*, 1934–1937, various issues; P. Stuyvesant, "La Guardia Will Be Re-elected," *New Republic*, July 14, 1937, 268.

La Guardia's remark about Hitler and the chamber of horrors created such a storm in the German press and government that Secretary of State Hull had to send Germany a formal apology; then La Guardia repeated his attack and Hull had to do the job all over again (*Times*, 1937, various issues). Despite the apologies of the State Department, Roosevelt, according to Ickes, made it plain at a cabinet meeting that he would have liked to have seen a gold medal pinned on La Guardia's lapel (Ickes, *The Secret Diary of Harold L. Ickes: Volume II. The Inside Struggle, 1936–1939*, 90).

4 *New York Times*, 1936–1943, various issues; conversation with Lester B. Granger, Executive Director, National Urban League, April 23, 1957.

The Stuyvesant Town project was approved by the Board of Estimate 11 votes to 5, the majority apparently upholding the contention of Robert Moses that the terms then offered by the city represented the "minimum inducements" necessary to attract private capital to the task of slum clearance (*Times*, June 4, 1943). According to Newbold Morris, who as President of the City Council cast three votes against the project (Borough President Edgar J. Nathan of Manhattan cast the other two negative votes), neither he (Morris), nor La Guardia knew of Stuyvesant Town's intended policy of racial restriction in the beginning. When they found out, Morris opposed the project believing that an important principle was at stake. La Guardia, though he did not argue with Morris, went along with the plan. He felt that he was committed to Moses and the Metropolitan, that, after all, the project would house many people and that this gain could not be overlooked. According to Morris, La Guardia also felt that since he had the Negroes in his camp anyway he could get away with it. (Interview with Morris, June 30, 1954.)

5 *New York Times*, April 8, 1934, December 17, 1936, May 21, 1937 (quotation), September 21, 1947.

Conservative critics condemned La Guardia's pro-labor actions as a pernicious form of demagoguery, one that hurt the public especially by the promotion of lawlessness and the destruction of property. That La Guardia was politically motivated in his treatment of labor, it would be ridiculous to doubt, but to hold that he was only so motivated and that a genuine sympathy for the cause of the working man played no part, or but a minor part, in his thinking would be equally ridiculous—as we have observed earlier. That he sacrificed the public interest to labor does not seem to have been generally true. It is true that a big taxi strike in the early months of 1934, thought to have been encouraged in the first instance by an unguarded remark dropped by the Mayor, resulted at one point in rioting and lawlessness which caused injury to people and damage to property, basically because La Guardia gave the strikers considerable leeway in picketing and demonstrating; Police Commissioner O'Ryan, who disagreed with La Guardia's liberal strike policy, charged in September, 1934, that the Mayor's attitude had encouraged the Communists and other vicious elements to exploit the strike (and one of hotel workers) for their own ends, and this is not improbable. Yet La Guardia's liberal interpretation of the right to picket and assemble did not often embarrass him, and even in the case of the taxi strike there was something to be said for his actions: he had acted upon the assumption that the strikers if allowed a broad leeway to strike and demonstrate would not cause violence, and a grand jury investigating the subsequent rioting observed that this policy had worked fairly well in a previous case. (O'Ryan, himself, told an aldermanic committee in April, 1934, that the strikers might have lived up to expectations and intimated that in that case La Guardia's policy would have been vindicated.) With respect, not only to his strike policy, but to his labor policy in general, a good case can be made that La Guardia's stand at this time in the city's history was more in keeping with the public welfare than that of a Mayor less sympathetic to the cause of labor would have been; through an age of labor turmoil, New York City remained free of wholesale bloodshed.

It should be kept in mind, furthermore, that La Guardia could be tough with workers and labor leaders if he felt they threatened the public interest. On the occasion of a mass demonstration of relief workers, that easily could have been Communist-inspired, the police seized Congressman Marcantonio and twelve other leaders when they attempted to lead a parade for which they had no permit and held them for a time in protective custody—an event which caused the liberal *New Republic* (February 26, 1936, 62–63) to criticize the La Guardia administration. At another time, La Guardia locked leaders of striking building trades employees in a room at City Hall and had the heat turned off to let them know at firsthand the effect of their strike on many thousands in the city. It should be particularly noticed that La Guardia continually fought the demands of Mike Quill and the TWU for a closed shop and for the same kind of collective bargaining rights enjoyed in private industry; the Mayor refused to recognize the right of the civil service transit workers to engage in a strike or be bullied by Quill's perennial threat to call one. While much of the TWU's wage demands in the period 1941–1945 were eventually met by the city, La Guardia did not easily come across and what appears to be true is that he regarded the transit workers, not highly paid in an era of growing inflation, as another group of a class of low-paid city workers whose pay he would adjust when the money became available; the most significant raises the transit workers got came as part of a bigger adjustment for other employees too. (This discussion has been based mainly on the *New York Times,* 1934–1945, various issues, December 3, 1946.)

6 *New York Times,* 1936, 1940, 1944, various issues; Moscow, 27; Ickes, *The Secret Diary of Harold L. Ickes: Volume III. The Lowering Clouds, 1939–1941,* 335; interviews with Louis M. Weintraub (August 6, 1953), Paul Windels (March 30, 1955) and Joseph D. McGoldrick (June 29, 1954).

7 Moscow, 27.

8 On the election for Comptroller in 1934: *New York Times,* May-November, 1934, various issues; interview with McGoldrick, April 11, 1951.

The vote for Comptroller was:

Taylor	831,390
McGoldrick	815,561
Laidler	77,695

McGoldrick carried Brooklyn and Queens. City of New York, Board of Elections, *Annual Report,* 1934 (New York, 1935).

9 The account of the election of 1935 is based upon the following: *New York Times,* September-November, 1935, various issues; New York *Herald Tribune,* October 18, November 1, 1935; interview with McGoldrick, May 31, 1951.

The vote for District Attorney of Kings County was:

Geoghan	362,249
McGoldrick	215,105

City of New York, Board of Elections, *Annual Report,* 1935 (New York, 1936). With respect to La Guardia's and Roosevelt's view of the District Attorney contest, it is ironic to note that after the election some observers saw in Fusion's defeat a slap at the President's WPA and at La Guardia, who was prominently connected with it. (See "Washington Notes; A Setback for La Guardia," *New Republic,* November 20, 1935, 44.)

10 New York *World-Telegram,* November 22, 1935.

The Democrats on the Board of Estimate now had 9 votes—those of Taylor, Sullivan, Borough President of Manhattan Levy and Borough President of the Bronx Lyons—to Fusion's 7 (or 6, for Harvey could not always be counted on to back the administration). As a matter of fact, Democratic control of the Board of Estimate did not prove to be too great a trial to the Fusion administration. In the first edition (1936) of *New York Advancing,* La Guardia wrote (p. 18) that in major matters the Board co-operated in carrying out the La Guardia program and that the best of relations existed between the Mayor and the Comptroller.

11 The past two paragraphs are based on the following: *New York Times,* July-October, 1936, various issues; Richard H. Rovere, "Good Citizen: Newbold Morris," *New Yorker,* October 28 (p. 28), November 4 (pp. 28–31), 1944; Morris, *Let the Chips Fall: My Battles Against Corruption,* ix, 58–60, 104.

The vote for President of the Board of Aldermen was:

Brunner	1,687,765
Morris	797,469

(City of New York, Board of Elections, *Annual Report,* 1936.)

12 M. P. Davidson, *Progressives in Public Office. Speech Over W.A.B.C., August 16, 1937* (mimeo., [1937], Davidson collection of materials); interview with Maurice P. Davidson, December 9, 1950; *New York Times,* December 7, 1936.

13 Moscow, 104–107; Hugh A. Bone, "Political Parties in New York City," *American Political Science Review,* April, 1946, 277; *New York Times,* July-December, 1936, various issues, October 10, 1937.

The New York trade union leaders, it may be noted, had been working for Roosevelt's re-election through Labor's Non-Partisan League, a nationwide organization that was conceived of as an arm of the Democratic Party, but they preferred to support the President through a separate party; the ALP was originally set up as a branch of Labor's Non-Partisan League.

The Knickerbocker Democrats had been quite active in 1934 (*New York Times,* 1934, various issues; New York *Herald Tribune,* February 18, 1934), but by the time the 1937 campaign rolled around, the organization had faded away. Some of the members of the group may have gone into the ALP (telephone conversation with J. G. Louis Molloy, May 4, 1955).

14 *New York Times,* February, 1937, various issues.

15 Noel F. Busch, "Profiles: Boss Without Cigar [Kenneth F. Simpson]," *New Yorker,* October 28, 1939, 21–27; interview with McGoldrick, May 31, 1951; Moscow, 75.

16 *New York Times,* January-July, 1937, various issues; letter from Ben Howe to Louis S. Lewis, April 20, 1937 (Davidson collection of materials).

17 The Citizens Non-Partisan Committee, it should be noted, differed in important ways from the Burlingham committee of 1933. Aside from the fact that the Citizens Non-Partisan Committee never concerned itself with a mayoral selection, being from the start ardently for La Guardia's re-election, the committee, less truly representative of the various Fusion elements than the Burlingham committee had been (representatives of Republican political leaders and the ALP were not on it) and confronted, as we shall see in a second, by the maneuvering of Simpson, never played the dominant role in the organization of a Fusion slate that the Burlingham committee had played in 1933.

18 The past two paragraphs are based upon the *New York Times,* July, 1937, various issues.

Simpson soon proceeded to justify his support of La Guardia to the Republican faithful. Making the rounds of the clubhouses again, he this time declared on the subject of La Guardia: "Yes, he is an S.O.B. and all the things we have been saying are true, but he is *our* S.O.B., and we must stick with him for the good of the party." (Interview with McGoldrick, May 31, 1951.)

19 *New York Times,* August-September, 1937, various issues; interview with Windels, February 6, 1951; Limpus and Leyson, *This Man La Guardia,* 407–410; City of New York, Board of Elections, *Annual Report,* 1937 (New York, 1938).

The exact results of the La Guardia-Copeland primary fight were:

La Guardia	81,680 votes
Copeland	46,410 votes

(Board of Elections, *Annual Report,* 1937.)

20 *New York Times,* July-August, various issues, October 10, 1937; interview with Windels, March 30, 1955.

21 *New York Times,* September-October, 1937, various issues.

22 Wagner told Ickes that F.D.R. had asked him to run but said that he thought the President did so only because he had been strongly urged. When Wagner refused, F.D.R. laughed and said: "Well, Bob, I bet three to one that you would not run." Wagner also confided to Ickes that he hoped Senator Copeland would run because he believed La Guardia would beat him handily. (*Diary of Ickes: II,* 162–163.)

23 *New York Times,* July-October, 1937, various issues; New York *Herald Tribune,* September 19, 1937; Max Lerner, "Tammany's Last Stand," *Nation,* September 11, 1937, 256; "Perplexing Primary," *Time,* September 27, 1937, 13.

24 Interviews with McGoldrick (May 31, 1951) and Weintraub (August 6, 1953).

25 La Guardia, *Lessons on Good Municipal Government.* Louis Weintraub, who headed the Mayor's research staff at the time, stated that, though the *Lessons* were written for a political purpose, they were based upon accurate information (interview with Weintraub, November 23, 1953). This appears to be so.

26 Various New York City newspapers at the time.

27 *New York Times,* October, various issues (quotation, October 4), November 2, 1937; "La Guardia Wins Again," *Literary Digest,* November 13, 1937, 6.

28 "Gone With the Breeze" (1937 Fusion campaign song, Davidson collection of materials).

The song continued:

> Republican, Fusion and Labor,
> The City Progressives as well,
> We'll make a clean sweep throughout Greater New York,
> For the whole of our ticket is swell!
>
> Oh!
> We'll get all the votes with the greatest of ease,
> The Tammany Tiger is gone with the breeze,
> No longer can racketeers do as they please,
> La Guardia's here now to stay!

29 Mahoney thus received three lines on the ballot to La Guardia's four.

30 *New York Times,* October, 1937, various issues.

31 *Ibid.,* October-November, 1937, various issues; "Tiger Skin," *Time,* November 15, 1937, 16.
As in 1933, F.D.R. handled the New York situation cagily. One reason possibly was that he wasn't too sure who would win; Flynn had informed him that his own polls indicated a Mahoney victory (*Diary of Ickes: II,* 233–234).

32 *New York Times,* November 3–5, 1937; "Tiger Skin," *Time,* 15–16.
The results of the mayoral election were:

La Guardia	1,344,630 votes
Mahoney	890,756 votes

La Guardia's total vote broke down this way:

Republican Party	674,611
ALP	482,790
City Fusion Party	159,556
Progressive Party	27,673

(Board of Elections, *Annual Report,* 1937.)

33 *New York Times,* 1937–1940, various issues; *Diary of Ickes, II,* 545.

34 *New York Times,* 1940–1941, various issues; *Diary of Ickes, III,* 398.

35 Will Chasan, "Can Tammany Come Back?," *Nation*, April 19, 1941, 465–466; Moscow, 108–109; Bone, "Political Parties in New York City," 278–279; Maurice P. Davidson, *Address at Cooper Union Rally, September 23, 1937* (mimeo.?, [1937]), quotation (Davidson collection of materials).

36 *New York Times*, March-May, 1941, various issues; Chasan, "Can Tammany Come Back?," 466.

37 *New York Times*, March-July, various issues, August 13, 20, 1941.

38 *Ibid.*, July-September, 1941, various issues.

39 *Ibid.*, September, 1941, various issues.
   La Guardia received 63,246 votes in the primary, Davies 43,426. While in the 1937 contest with Copeland La Guardia carried every borough, but one, and only lost the Bronx by about 150 votes, in the 1941 primary he lost both the Bronx and Queens, the first by around 1,500 votes, the second by over 3,000. (Board of Elections, *Annual Report*, 1937; *New York Times*, September 18, 1941.)
   After the primary, Davies made plans to run as an independent, but he eventually had to withdraw from the race because he could not get a sufficient number of signatures on his nominating petition (*Times*, October 2, 8, 1941).

40 *New York Times*, June-August, various issues, November 5, 1941.

41 *Ibid.*, June 5, July-August, various issues, October 11, 1941.

42 *Ibid.*, July 20, 1941 (article by Warren Moscow), August 20, 1950; Robert G. Spivack, "New York's Mayoralty Race," *New Republic*, July 9, 1945, 43; Lester Velie, "William O'Dwyer—The Man Who Won't Come Home," *Collier's*, August 21, 1953, 33.

43 *New York Times*, September-October, 1941, various issues; telephone conversation with McGoldrick, June 4, 1957; George Britt, "La Guardia Will Win," *New Republic*, October 20, 1941, 499.

44 See note 43.

45 *New York Times*, September 13, October 12 (article by James A. Hagerty), 1941; Moscow, 235.

46 Interviews with Weintraub, August 6, November 23, 1953; *New York Times*, October 28-November 3, 1941; Moscow, 235.

47 City of New York, Board of Elections, *Annual Report*, 1941.
   La Guardia received 1,186,518 votes to O'Dwyer's 1,054,235.
   La Guardia's vote broke down this way:

Republican Party	668,485
ALP	435,374
City Fusion Party	63,367
United City Party	19,292

48 *New York Times*, November 6, 1941.

49 Interview with McGoldrick, May 31, 1951.

50 My discussion of the honesty of elections under La Guardia is based upon the *New York Times*, 1934–1945, various issues (La Guardia's statement, November 7, 1945) and various interviews.
   While a group called the Fusioneers supported La Guardia in 1937, it was very insignificant and did not do the sort of work the Fusioneers of 1933 did (*Times*, June 25, October 1, 1937). There is no mention of Fusioneers in the *New York Times Index*, 1941.

51 *New York Times*, January 1, 1934. It should be noted that La Guardia, with characteristic egotism, ignored the contribution of previous New York reform administrations, especially that of Mitchel, in the matter of nonpartisan, nonpolitical government.

52 Interview with Murray W. Stand, April 4, 1955.

53 Interviews with McGoldrick (May 31, 1951) and Philip Sokol (October 20, 1954);

New York Times, 1934–1945, various issues; New York *Evening Journal,* June 14, 1934; telegram from Marcantonio to La Guardia, October 16, 1939 (The Personal Papers of Fiorello H. La Guardia).

54 Interviews with McGoldrick, May 31, 1951, July 15, 1954.

55 *New York Times,* March 11, September 25, 1934, October 9, 1935; interview with Davidson, May 22, 1950.

56 Allen, *Why Tammanies Revive: La Guardias Mis-Guard,* 26; *New York Times,* April 1, 18, 1937.

57 Interview with Weintraub, August 6, 1953.

58 I must say that I cannot help but wish that La Guardia had not talked about non-political government. The term is an ambiguous one, and it undoubtedly encourages some people to believe that government can be run without regard to political considerations of any kind. To encourage people to believe this is to muddy their thinking as to the relationship between politics and government and to create an impossible standard for judging reform government that only invites disillusionment with it.

14 / EXIT REFORM

1 Rankin (ed.), *New York Advancing, Victory Edition, Seven More Years of Progressive Administration in the City of New York, 1939–1945, F. H. La Guardia, Mayor,* 178.

2 *New York Times,* January 26, July 16, 20, 1942, February 17, 1943, August 15, 1944; interviews with Davidson (December 9, 1950) and Windels (March 30, 1955); telephone conversation with Joseph D. McGoldrick, June 29, 1956.

3 *New York Times,* April 10, 1934.

4 *Ibid.,* September 26, 1934. For the story of La Guardia-O'Ryan relations, *ibid.,* February-September, 1934, various issues, October 16, 1937.

5 *Ibid.,* April 6, 7, 1940, November 3, 5, 1942.

6 *Ibid.,* December, 1941–March, 1942, various issues (quotations, December 28, 1941, January 26, 27 (editorial), 1942); interview with Morgan, July 7, 1954.

7 It should be kept in mind in connection with breaks between La Guardia and his subordinates that many of them remained on terms of friendship with the Mayor after they got out of government service. Morgan did, for instance.

8 City of New York, Civil Service Commission, *Report,* July 1, 1942, to June 30, 1943, 3.

9 *New York Times,* December 20, 30 (editorial), 1941, February 10, 1942 (editorial). The quotations are from the editorial of February 10.

10 *Ibid.,* January, various issues, February 11, 1942; Ickes, *The Secret Diary of Harold L. Ickes: Volume III, The Lowering Clouds, 1939–1941,* 572–573.

11 *New York Times,* March, 1943, various issues, March 2, 1944, September 21, 1947; Robert E. Sherwood, *Roosevelt and Hopkins: An Intimate History* (New York, 1948), 724–725; Rodgers, *Robert Moses: Builder for Democracy,* 232.

12 *New York Times,* April 9, 1943.

13 *Ibid.,* September 30, 1944, August 23, 1945.

14 *Ibid.,* October 26, 1942. That La Guardia's broadcasts helped to boost Italian morale was attested to by the residents of one Italian town after liberation. One man who had listened to them despite warnings had been sent to jail. (*Ibid.,* October 3, 1943.)

15 Sherwood, *Roosevelt and Hopkins,* 725.

16 *New York Times,* August 23, 1945.

17 For example, Sherwood in *Roosevelt and Hopkins* (p. 725) holds to this view. Warren Moscow has stated that it was the opposition of both General Marshall and Stimson that stymied La Guardia's chances (*Politics in the Empire State*, 28).

18 Neither informant wishes to be identified.

19 "Little Caesar: La Guardia and the Press," *Time*, October 5, 1942, 58, 60; *New York Times*, 1942–1945, various issues.

20 Interview with Halpern, May 11, 1951.

21 *New York Times*, June 6, 1941.

22 George Britt, "What Has Happened to La Guardia?," *New Republic*, March 9, 1942, 323.

23 *New York Times*, May 22, 1945.

24 *Ibid.*, March-October, 1940, various issues (quotation from Manning's letter, March 1; from McGeehan's decision, March 31).
   According to Newbold Morris, La Guardia, who knew the liberals were on his side, saw in the Russell incident a chance to win over the church groups (interview, June 30, 1954). It is also possible that La Guardia, with his puritanical streak, may not have been uninfluenced in his actions by a personal dislike of the Russell appointment.

25 *New York Times*, September 5–7, November 1, 2, 1940, December 20, 1941; Moley, *27 Masters of Politics*, 212.
   To some extent, Seabury may have been influenced in his attitude toward the Walker appointment by the fact that he was supporting Willkie in the presidential campaign.

26 *New York Times*, December 25, 26, 1941, January 31, February 6, 7, 1942; City Affairs Committee, *The Civil Service Commission and the Mayor* (New York, 1942).

27 *New York Times*, February 7–10, 17, July 14, 1942, January 8, 1943 (quotation from La Guardia's suspension order, February 7; quotations from Kern's remarks, February 10); City Affairs Committee, *The Civil Service Commission and the Mayor;* interview with Murray Stand, April 4, 1955.

28 *New York Times*, March 9, 10, 1942.

29 *Ibid.*, March 9, 10, 14, 1942; Flynn, 170.

30 *New York Times*, March 31, April-May, various issues, 1942.
   The Citizens Union made much of the fact that though someone (or ones) was (were) obviously guilty of violating laws, no action was taken by the jury; but the jury's position was simply that while certain violations had occurred they did not warrant an indictment.
   According to newsmen and others in whom I have faith, Ed Flynn was really blameless. The story as told to me by one very reliable former newspaperman (who does not wish to be identified) is that a gardener or decorator, hired by Mrs. Flynn in her husband's absence to improve the Lake Mahopac home, found some Belgium paving blocks, not worth very much, stored in the Bronx. She went to Moran and asked if she could use them, and the Bronx Commissioner of Public Works, thinking he would be doing the boss a big favor, sent them up to Mahopac with a crew of workers to do the job. Indeed it is hardly credible that Flynn, wealthier than any other county leader in the state (Moscow, *Politics in the Empire State*, 89), would risk so much for what amounted to a few hundred dollars' worth of city property and city labor.
   Many informed people believe that La Guardia had been looking to get rid of Kern, feeling that the Commissioner had become too much of a political liability to him because of his leftist activities. As that might be, the question of why La Guardia actually fired Kern when he did remains. It is entirely conceivable that La Guardia was sufficiently provoked by Kern's actions in connection with the civil service question to fire him on that account alone, though whether the

Mayor was justified in doing so is debatable. The Flynn case could have figured in the ouster. But how? Did La Guardia resent Kern's interference in the case because he was trying to hush it up—to ingratiate himself with Flynn—or because he saw in Kern's action in launching an investigation of the matter another example of what he regarded as insubordination, and one that could unjustifiably place the administration in an embarrassing light?

31 *New York Times*, February-June, 1942, various issues.

32 Nor is it without significance that even the *New York Times*, which throughout the Kern affair generally sided with La Guardia, was not without criticism of the Mayor. Kern's behavior was certainly insubordination, the *Times* said at the time of the suspension of the Commissioners (although it declared that the merits of the civil service controversy more broadly speaking were open to argument). Yet La Guardia was blamed for what the newspaper considered hasty action and another unhappy display of irascibility similar to that shown in the Morgan case shortly before; like the Morgan case too, the outcome might have been different, it felt, had La Guardia taken the time to quietly talk things over with his appointee (February 10, 1942). Later, when the Flynn case broke, though the *Times* believed it absurd to charge the Mayor with collusion in wrong-doing, felt that Herlands really did investigate and that Kern "went off half-cocked," it declared that La Guardia may well be criticized for not telling Kern how he was handling the case and commented that it would be in line with the Mayor's recent record to charge him with high-handedness in his relations with his subordinates (March 11, 1942).

33 Britt, "What Has Happened to La Guardia?," 324–325.

34 *New York Times*, May 21, 1943.

35 *Ibid.*, January 9, 1944.

36 *Ibid.*, May 7, 1945.

37 Interview with Murray Stand, April 4, 1955; Morris, p. 204.

38 *New York Times*, May 7, 8, 10, 1945.

39 *Ibid.*, March 22, 25, 1945.

40 Before election (November, 1943), it was discovered that Aurelio had obtained the Tammany nomination through the good offices of Frank Costello. Both the Democrats and the Republicans, who had also nominated Aurelio, repudiated him, but they could not remove his name from their lines on the ballot. The Democrats supported the ALP candidate, Matthew M. Levy, but the Republicans ran one of their own, George Frankenthaler, under an independent label. Aurelio won, any chance of defeating him having gone out the window when the opposition to him split its vote. After the election, La Guardia blasted the Republicans over the radio, charging that their move was responsible for Aurelio's victory. Replying, Curran attacked La Guardia and defended the Republican action; he said the Republicans had backed Frankenthaler because Alex Rose of the ALP had broken a pledge that a candidate on whom all could agree would be nominated. *New York Times*, August 29, 30, 31, September-November, various issues, 1943. Quotation from Curran's attack on La Guardia, November 16.

41 *Ibid.*, March 22, 1945.

42 Moscow, 111–113; Bone, "Political Parties in New York City," *American Political Science Review*, April, 1946, 278–280; *New York Times*, May 20, November 10, 1944.

43 "New York May Ring Own Curfew on La Guardia in November Vote," *Newsweek*, April 2, 1945, 44.

44 *New York Times*, March 23, 24, 31, 1944.

45 *Ibid.*, January-April, 1945, various issues; New York *Herald Tribune*, February 5, 1945; Dwight MacDonald, "Profiles-Cit [George H. Hallett, Jr.]," *New Yorker*, August 22, 1953, 36 (quotation from Hallett).

46 Oswald G. Villard wrote in April, 1945, that among a small group of La Guardia supporters headed by Seabury there was unhappiness with the Mayor. Yet if you talk to them about the coming mayoral race, Villard declared, they ask: "Who could you put in his place who has such a large popular following?" ("Mr. La Guardia and the Union," *Christian Century,* April 11, 1945, 462–463.)

47 Outwardly friendly, there was no real love between La Guardia and Dewey. Warren Moscow wrote in March, 1944, that while the Governor's office could not be said to have ever worked against a La Guardia measure for personal reasons, neither had it ever exerted itself to enact one of La Guardia's measures (*New York Times,* March 21, 1944). Probably the basic reason the two men did not enjoy a closer relationship was that they were both egotists of a high order; La Guardia could never stand another New York official getting publicity. Dewey, furthermore, could not have been unaffected in his attitude toward La Guardia by the fact that in his big political battles for the Governorship and the Presidency (1944) the Mayor did not support him.

48 *New York Times,* April-May, 1945, various issues; New York *Herald Tribune,* April 12, 1945.
   It is also possible that Roosevelt's death might have somewhat influenced La Guardia not to run again. Though relations between La Guardia and Roosevelt were a bit strained at the end—not only did La Guardia feel somewhat bitter about his failure to get overseas, but in early 1945 the Mayor clashed with the national administration over the hour for a national wartime curfew on places of entertainment ("New York May Ring Own Curfew on La Guardia," *Newsweek,* 44)—as long as Roosevelt was President, there was always a good possibility that La Guardia would receive some sort of aid from him. Truman presented a different situation: he was politically regular and, moreover, had been sharply critical of La Guardia when his appointment as a general had been under consideration (*Times,* September 21, 1947). In the spring of 1945 all political parties agreed that the President's death and Truman's accession meant that La Guardia could expect no help from the White House in 1945 (*Times,* April 14, 1945).

49 *New York Times,* May 9, 10, 13, 18, 1945; telephone conversation with McGoldrick, January 20, 1958.

50 *New York Times,* June, 1945, various issues.
   In addition to backing O'Dwyer, the ALP supported the Democratic candidates for Comptroller, President of the City Council and the borough presidencies of Manhattan, Brooklyn and Queens (*ibid.,* November 7, 1945). The Democrats endorsed some ALP candidates for the Council (Bone, "Political Parties in New York City," 281).

51 Spivack, "New York's Mayoralty Race," *New Republic,* July 9, 1945, 43; *New York Times,* January 28, 1945.

52 *New York Times,* June 5–9, July 29, 1945; Moscow, 117.

53 Spivack, "New York's Mayoralty Race," 42–43; interview with James A. Hagerty, July 17, 1953.

54 *New York Times,* May 8, 22, June 9, 1945; quotation from Seabury, June 9.

55 Morris, *Let the Chips Fall,* 206–207.

56 *New York Times,* August 5, 1945.

57 *Ibid.,* June 13, August 8, 1945; interview with Stand, April 4, 1955.

58 *Politics in the Empire State,* 28.

59 These people do not wish to be identified.

60 *New York Times,* August-October, 1945, various issues; New York *Herald Tribune,* September 16, October 27 (editorial), 1945; New York *Post,* October 30, 1945 (editorial).

61 Robert G. Spivack, "New York's Mayoralty Election," *New Republic,* October 29, 1945, 567; *New York Times,* November 4, 1945 (article by James A. Hagerty).

62 In 1941 the death of Reles was termed a suicide (*New York Times*, March 22, 1951). Ten years later a Brooklyn grand jury, again looking into the Reles case, declared that Reles had died while trying to escape from police custody. Judge Samuel Leibowitz was unwilling to accept the jury's findings and said he was keeping the door open for future evidence (*ibid.*, December 22, 1951).

The escape theory as to Reles' death has never gone down too easily for one reason: Reles' life would not have been worth two cents if he had gotten away; the underworld was very anxious to see him.

63 The discussion in the last few paragraphs has been based upon the following: *New York Times*, October 18, 19, 24, 30 (first grand jury presentment), December 21 (second grand jury presentment), 1945, May 8, 1952; New York *Herald Tribune*, October 1, 1945; Fulton Oursler, "The Remarkable Story of William O'Dwyer," *Reader's Digest*, May, 1952 (reprint).

64 *New York Times*, May 2, 1951, December 19, 1952.

65 *Ibid.*, October 30, November 4, 1945; New York *World-Telegram and The Sun*, August 15, 1951.

66 United States Congress, Senate, Special Committee to Investigate Organized Crime in Interstate Commerce, *Hearings*, 81st Congress, 2nd Session, 82nd Congress, 1st Session (Washington, 1950–1951), Part 7, Hearings of March 19, 20, 1951.

67 *New York Times*, November 4, 1945 (article by Hagerty).

68 *Ibid.*, November 7, 8, 1945.

The vote for Mayor was as follows:

O'Dwyer	Democratic Party	867,426
	ALP	257,929
	Total	1,125,355
Goldstein	Republican Party	301,144
	Liberal Party	122,316
	City Fusion Party	8,141
	Total	431,601
Morris		408,408

(City of New York, Board of Elections, *Annual Report*, 1945.)

Upon the reasonable assumption that not more than 100,000 of the votes for Morris came from independents and Democrats, it seems that about as many Republicans voted for Morris as for Goldstein. The extent of the Republican defection from Goldstein showed clearly in the returns from Manhattan's 9th A.D., the one sure Republican district in the city (whose boundaries closely resembled those of what had once been the 15th, silk stocking, A.D.); Morris carried it—the only A.D. in the city not won by O'Dwyer—by a plurality of 2,984 over O'Dwyer and 4,233 over Goldstein. (*New York Times*, November 8, 1945). The Republican vote in the city came to 15 per cent of the total vote, the lowest Republican percentage in a New York mayoral contest since 1917.

Incidentally, the Liberal-Republican strategy with respect to the Jewish vote did not work out. Jewish Democrats tended to stick closely to O'Dwyer, or, if of a more independent mind, to back Morris (*Times*, November 4, 1945, article by Hagerty). The Jews in New York have not shown the same political clannishness as some other groups, say the Italians, and have voted solidly for Jews only of the Lehman calibre; Goldstein did not fill the bill. (Moscow, 117–118.)

69 This person does not wish to be identified.

70 *New York Times*, 1946–1947, various issues.

71 In May, 1939, as a result of a reform movement, Maury Maverick was elected Mayor of San Antonio on a Fusion ticket. That New York's Fusion movement

played a part in the thinking of Maverick, and presumably other San Antonio reformers, is evident from a letter written by Maverick to La Guardia (February 20, 1939, The Personal Papers of Fiorello H. La Guardia) in which the Texan asked for advice on the matter of a Fusion campaign; La Guardia advised him (La Guardia to Maverick, March 7, 1939, La Guardia papers). According to Richardson Dilworth, presently Mayor of Philadelphia, La Guardia's work in New York definitely influenced the growth of a reform spirit in Philadelphia which led to a reform movement there in 1951 ("How Clean Government Came to Philadelphia." Address at the Sixtieth Anniversary Dinner of the City Club of New York, May 27, 1952).

15 / NEW WINE IN OLD BOTTLES

1 Samuel Lubell, *The Future of American Politics* (New York, 1952), especially chs. 3, 4.

2 *New York Times,* May 23, 1955.

3 In 1920, Manhattan had had 40.6 per cent of the city's population, Brooklyn, the runner up, 35.9 per cent; by 1930 Brooklyn had become the most populous borough with 36.9 per cent of the city's population. After this its percentage also began to decline, falling to 36.2 in 1940 and 34.7 in 1950. That part of the city showing the greatest population gain was Queens; its percentage of the city's population rose from 8.3 in 1920 to 15.6 in 1930 to 17.4 in 1940 to 19.7 in 1950. Similar percentages for the Bronx, the other big borough, are: 13 (1920), 18.3 (1930), 18.7 (1940), 18.4 (1950). These percentages are based upon population figures for the boroughs given in *The World Almanac and Book of Facts,* 1936, 1955 (New York, 1936–1955).

4 During the same period the percentage of Democratic enrollees in the city living in Brooklyn went from 33.8 to 35.7, that of those living in the Bronx and Queens went from 19.7 to 20.9 and from 18.3 to 19.3 respectively. In the 1929 mayoral election, Brooklyn cast 32.7 per cent of the Democratic vote, the Bronx 18.4 per cent, Queens 11.9 per cent; in the 1945 election the same boroughs cast respectively 33.8, 18.6 and 22.7 per cent of the Democratic vote. The percentages used here and in the text are based upon enrollment figures and election returns given in the City of New York, Board of Elections, *Annual Report,* 1929, 1945.

5 Our discussion in the last few paragraphs is based upon the *New York Times,* 1934–1945, various issues; Moscow, *Politics in the Empire State,* 127.

6 It appears that something like this shift occurred in Brooklyn too, but the picture there is far from clear. The Kefauver committee showed that Joe Adonis was a man of such importance in Brooklyn that leading politicians came to his restaurant to eat, though it was in an out-of-the-way, run-down neighborhood. Testimony indicated that Adonis gave financial assistance to various political leaders. (United States Congress, Senate, Special Committee to Investigate Organized Crime in Interstate Commerce, *Third Interim Report,* 139–140.)

7 Before the New York State Crime Commission in 1952, Irving Daniel Neustein, a former Tammany district leader, testified that in 1945 Costello wanted to get him out as district leader; Neal passed the word to Neustein's captains, who thereafter refused to support Neustein. Around Democratic headquarters, Neustein said, Costello was often referred to as "the boss."

My discussion of the machine-underwold relationship is based on the following: *New York Times,* 1934–1945, various issues, November 26, 1950 (article by Warren Moscow), November-December, 1952, various issues; United States Congress, Senate, Special Committee to Investigate Organized Crime in Interstate Commerce, *Hearings*, 81st Congress, 2nd Session, 82nd Congress, 1st Session, Part 7, Hearings of March 19, 20, 1951; *Idem, Third Interim Report*, 109 ff., especially 121–124 (Rogers' statement: 111); New York State Crime Commission, *Second Report . . . March 9, 1953* (Albany, 1953); Lerner, "Tammany's Last Stand," *Nation*, September 11, 1937, 255–256.

8 One court nomination Marcantonio could not deliver was that involving Aurelio. Two of Marcantonio's lieutenants put up Aurelio's name at the ALP nominating meeting, but at that time the Dubinsky-Rose faction was still in control of the party and they overrode Marcantonio's choice and selected Matthew Levy. (Gus Tyler, "The Roosevelt or the Tiger," *New Republic*, May 16, 1949, 9.)

9 Moscow, 98–100, 126; Richard H. Rovere, "Vito Marcantonio: Machine Politician, New Style," *Harper's*, April, 1944, 394–398; Tyler, "The Roosevelt or the Tiger," 10; *New York Times*, May 1, 1947.

Tammany's decline was symbolized in 1943 by the sale of the Tammany Hall building, erected at Union Square in the salad days of Walker, to Local 91 of the ILGWU. The Tammany Society, the patriotic and social group, moved to the National Democratic Club; the political Tammany took up offices on Madison Avenue. ("Tammany Twilight," *Newsweek*, September 6, 1943, 62–64; *New York Times*, September 23, 1943.)

10 *New York Times*, November, 1952, various issues; New York State Crime Commission, *Second Report*.

11 *New York Times*, 1942–1949, various issues.

For the discussion above, I roughly calculated the number of Irish, Italian and Jewish district leaders in Tammany by noting names. While this procedure obviously leaves something to be desired, it is the only one possible, and I feel that it provides a not too unreliable index for our purpose. For the names of district leaders, I have relied upon *Political Almanac: "The Unofficial Directory of the City of New York"* (New York, 1938) and a few issues of the *New York Times* in which the names of Tammany district leaders appeared in connection with the election of a county leader.

12 *New York Times*, 1946–1953, various issues; City of New York, New York City Housing Authority, *Annual Report, 1954*.

By 1955, a little over twenty years after it had been set up, the New York City Housing Authority had become the nation's largest landlord. It had completed nearly 80,000 apartments in 71 projects, with more apartments in the process of construction and on the planning board. It was responsible for the clearance and redevelopment of 500 acres of city slums involving the demolition of 55,000 slum apartments and the development for public housing of 500 acres of substantially vacant land, mostly in outlying sections. (*Annual Report, 1954*.)

13 How successful O'Dwyer and Impellitteri were in this flushing-out operation is not entirely clear. While numbers of Communists or suspected Communists were removed from the Welfare Department during their administrations (*New York Times*, May 4, 1951), the Wagner administration later reported that cases of questionable loyalty had been uncovered there (*ibid.*, September 22, 1955).

14 *New York Times*, 1946–1954, various issues; interview with George H. Hallett, Jr., March 31, 1951; "An Appraisal of the Impellitteri Record," *Searchlight* (Citizens Union) May, 1952; "An Appraisal of the Impellitteri Record: May, 1952–April, 1953," *Searchlight* (Citizens Union), May, 1953.

15 *New York Times*, 1949–1954, various issues; New York County, Court of General Sessions, *People of the State of New York Against John M. Murtagh, Defendant. Report of the Third November, 1951, Grand Jury . . .* ([New York?, 1952]).

16 *New York Times,* 1950, various issues; *The New York Police Survey: A Report for the Mayor's Committee on Management Survey,* 34–35.

17 *New York Times,* 1951–1952, various issues, July 1, 1955; Lester Velie, "William O'Dwyer—The Man Who Won't Come Home," *Collier's,* August 7, 1953, 21 (O'Dwyer's statement on Moran); *Idem,* August 21, 1953, 34.

18 *New York Times,* 1946–1953, various issues; "An Appraisal of the Impellitteri Record"; "An Appraisal of the Impellitteri Record: May, 1952-April, 1953"; interviews with Hallett (March 31, 1951) and Richard S. Childs (February 9, 1951).

19 *New York Times,* 1946–1953, various issues; "An Appraisal of the Impellitteri Record"; "An Appraisal of the Impellitteri Record: May, 1952-April, 1953."

20 Mary H. Vorse, "The Pirates' Nest of New York," *Harper's,* April, 1952, 36–37; *New York Times,* 1951–1953, various issues.
   In 1953 serious measures were taken for the first time against crime on the docks, but this was not the city's doing. New York State and New Jersey set up a bi-state Waterfront Commission with vigorous powers to initiate reforms (*New York Times,* June 27, 1953). The AF of L finally expelled the corrupt ILA and chartered a new union to take its place; the new union, however, eventually lost out to the ILA (*ibid.,* 1953–1954, various issues).

21 *New York Times,* 1951–1953, various issues.

22 O'Dwyer's failure to take a stronger line with the political organizations was pointed up by his actions with respect to the Tammany leadership during his administration. Though he began by attempting to reform, or at least control, the Hall and succeeded with the help of the Italian bloc in having Sampson installed in place of Loughlin, he lost momentum after that and ended by giving up the fight; though he fumed when Rogers was elected and objected to De Sapio, he eventually settled down to a working relationship with both. (*New York Times,* 1946–1951, various issues.)

23 *New York Times,* 1949–1952, various issues; Velie, "William O'Dwyer," *Collier's,* August 7, 21, 1953; Court of General Sessions, *People . . . Against . . . Murtagh . . . ;* various interviews.

24 *New York Times,* September 10, 1950, March 22, 1951.

25 Various interviews.

26 Interview with Hallett, October 30, 1953.

27 Letter from Holmes to me, April 6, 1954.

28 Interview with Walter M. Weis, April 27, 1951; *New York Times,* February 8, 1950.

29 *New York Times,* November 18, 1933, November 13, 1935 (letter to the editor from George Boochever); interviews with Weis (April 27, 1951), Joseph D. McGoldrick (April 11, 1951), Maurice P. Davidson (March 27, 1951).

30 The new charter called for the election of a county committee in each borough by the party's members. The county committee would then elect a county executive committee which would, in turn, elect representatives to a city executive committee. Voting was to be by PR. (*New York Times,* December 18, 1933; copy of a letter from Maurice P. Davidson to Henry Bentley, July 20, 1934, Davidson collection of materials.)
   That democratic control was not achieved in practice for the most part is learned from Davidson's letter to Bentley. Brooklyn was the only borough, according to Davidson, which adhered to the letter and spirit of the charter at the time of the party's unofficial primaries in the spring of 1934. (The primaries could only be unofficial since the City Fusion Party was not a legal party.) There the party was reorganized. For one reason or another, the other boroughs refused or neglected to hold primaries so that when the new city executive committee met "it was necessary to accept delegations which were appointed by the [old] county executive committees . . . and let it go at that."

31 *New York Times,* 1934–1953, various issues; City of New York, Board of Elections, *Annual Report,* 1937, 1941, 1945, 1949, 1950 (New York [New York?], 1938–1951); City Fusion Party, Various desk sheets of the party (notes of the week's happenings) covering the period February 3-June 9, 1934 (Davidson collection of materials); interview with McGoldrick, April 11, 1951.

32 With respect to the loss of good people suffered by civic organizations on account of appointments to the La Guardia administration, it should be noted that Davidson, McGoldrick and Mrs. Lucile Kraft, the City Fusion Party's paid secretary, all ended up in the city administration, the last as secretary to the Water Department.

33 New York *World-Telegram,* February 3, 1934; *Daily Mirror,* April 15, 1934; various interviews.
Davidson gave his view of the situation in his letter to Bentley, July 20, 1934. "It was necessary for me to stand firmly against the onrush of patronage seekers, band wagon jumpers and a host of people some of whom seemed inspired by good motives, but many of them [*sic*] with a very narrow [and] crude political outlook." He was not in the strongest position for this task, however, because he, himself, had received a job in the La Guardia administration. The letter indicates that Davidson and the other party leaders were not in favor of control by the general membership of the party and made the changes in party mechanism noted hitherto because the pressures for change were too great to be resisted. Control by the rank and file they feared would turn the party over to the patronage seekers. Davidson apparently felt that the best way to preserve the party in its purity was for the leadership to appoint its own successors.

34 *New York Times,* 1934, various issues; interview with Davidson, January 5, 1951.

35 Because no law assured the party's executive committee control over party nominations, various aspirants to elective office could, and did, file nominating petitions entitling them to the name and emblem of the City Fusion Party; an aspirant had only to file a valid petition before anyone else. At one point, the City Fusion Party leadership was able to get a law through the legislature giving it control over party nominations, but Lehman vetoed it. In 1937 the party leadership attempted to achieve the same end through litigation, basing its case on provisions in its own constitution. It won but a partial victory: the Court of Appeals ruled that when the party filed a valid nominating petition for a candidate, that candidate was to be given the party's nomination regardless of who filed first, but in cases where the party did not file a valid petition, the first person who did so could use the party's name and emblem. (Telephone conversation with Weis, September 5, 1957.)

36 That the Progressive City Committee, which had, in general, the same goals as the City Fusion Party, would hurt the latter was foreseen by Ben Howe, City Fusion chairman at the time of the Committee's formation. He was definitely hostile to the new group. Invited by Welling to attend the keynote luncheon of the Progressive City Committee, he declined, declaring that he was "entirely out of sympathy with the movement" believing it "the most ridiculous political blunder that it has ever been my experience to meet." He said he could not see what the new organization was trying to do unless it was to "parallel and weaken the City Fusion Party." Welling wrote back "the more the merrier," adding, "I am still loyal to you." (Copy of a letter from Howe to Richard Welling, April 8, 1937; copy of a letter from Welling to Howe, April 9, 1937 (Davidson collection of materials).)

37 Interview with Rufus E. McGahen, April 19, 1951.

38 One can understand La Guardia's appointment policy in the case of the old-line political clubs, says Belous (*Faith in Fusion,* 75), but the City Fusion Party was a different kind of group. The City Fusion Party leaders who went into the La Guardia administration were highly principled persons who had no use for the machines and had gone into politics in order to destroy them. If La Guardia could not trust

these officials to serve without divided allegiance, he should not have appointed them. I tend to agree.

39 Belous to Howe, January 4, 1937 (The Personal Papers of Fiorello H. La Guardia).

40 Raphael to Davidson, November 26, 1934 (Davidson collection of materials).

41 And political egotism probably explains in part La Guardia's trouble with Republican Party leaders in the city. One wonders whether La Guardia had to be quite so nasty to them as he was to safeguard good government. Since he did give some patronage, he might have given it to them, instead of their rivals. He might have tried to be friendlier, perhaps had them over to lunch once in a while and, without sacrificing substance, made them feel appreciated and important—which, after all, is what many people want who go into politics.

Much of our discussion of La Guardia's relations with the City Fusion Party and related subjects is based upon various interviews.

42 Interview with Hallett, October 30, 1953.

43 The group was formed in 1937. Citizens Housing and Planning Council of New York, Inc., *1953 Directory of Large-Scale Rental Housing in New York City.*

44 Various interviews and conversations with members of the City Club of New York; *New York Times,* 1950–1956, various issues.

45 *New York Times,* October 27, 1954.

46 The prevalence of Jewish people in New York's civic circle today is obvious from a glance at the listings of officers in the outstanding civic groups.

47 *New York Times,* November 3, December 18, 1954; Moscow, 118. The party lost its name because the legislature in 1954 had passed a law prohibiting a political party in the future from using such words as "American," "United States," "New York" in its title, exceptions being made only to existing parties, which category the ALP now ceased to fall into.

48 City of New York, Board of Elections, *Annual Report,* 1949 and subsequent years.

49 We are not considering here the ALP after 1945; after that time the party lost meaning for municipal reform.

50 *New York Times,* August 6, 1949.

51 *Ibid.,* 1949, various issues; New York *Herald Tribune,* 1949, various issues; Belous, *Faith in Fusion,* 5–6, 101–102.

In this campaign—as in all subsequent ones, municipal or otherwise—the ALP ran its own candidate. The vote for Mayor was as follows:

O'Dwyer:			1,266,512
Morris:	Republican Party	570,713	
	Liberal Party	373,287	
	City Fusion Party	12,069	
	Total		956,069
Marcantonio:	ALP		356,626

(Board of Elections, *Annual Report,* 1949.)

52 On political developments in 1950: *New York Times,* 1950, various issues. The vote for Mayor was:

Impellitteri:	Experience Party		1,161,175
Pecora:	Democratic Party	711,358	
	Liberal Party	223,993	
	Total		935,351
Corsi:			382,372
Paul L. Ross:	ALP		147,578

(City of New York, Board of Elections, *Annual Report,* 1950.)

53 *New York Times,* 1951, various issues.

The vote for President of the City Council was:

Halley:	Liberal Party	583,176	
	Independent Party	54,138	
	City Fusion Party	20,997	
	Total		658,311
Joseph T. Sharkey:	Democratic Party		495,011
Henry J. Latham:	Republican Party		435,699
Clifford T. McAvoy:	ALP		102,136

City of New York, Board of Elections, *Annual Report,* 1951 ([New York?], 1952.)

54 *New York Times,* April-November, 1953, various issues; William C. Chanler, Chairman of Citizens Non-Partisan Committee, to members of the committee, July 28, 1953 (mimeographed copy of the letter).

55 *New York Times,* June-September, 1953, various issues.
Wagner received 350,477 votes to Impellitteri's 181,295 (*ibid.,* September 17, 1953).

56 *Ibid.,* August-November, 1953, various issues.
The vote for Mayor in 1953 was:

Wagner:			1,022,626
Riegelman:			661,591
Halley:	Liberal Party	428,688	
	Independent Party	38,416	
	Total		467,104
McAvoy:	ALP		53,045

City of New York, Board of Elections, *Annual Report,* 1953 (New York, 1954). Wagner, it should be noticed, was a minority winner, his vote being exceeded by the combined vote for Riegelman and Halley. This fact suggests that, despite the public apathy, a majority of the electorate did not want a Democratic administration in City Hall. It also encourages one to believe that Javits, running as a Fusion candidate, would have won the election.

57 Concerning the identification of reform movements, the reader's attention is called to the second paragraph of note 83 in Chapter 2.

58 In June, 1953, James A. Hagerty of the *New York Times* estimated that approximately 700,000 voters in the city were regular Democrats, not more than 400,000 on the outside were regular Republicans and that a potential 2,000,000, the remaining number of voters, constituted an element to which party loyalty meant little or nothing (*Times,* June 28, 1953).

16 / TODAY AND TOMORROW

1 Frank Kelly died in 1946. From that time until the selection of Sharkey, the following headed the Brooklyn Democratic organization: John Cashmore (1946–1950), Francis J. Sinnott (1950–1952), Kenneth F. Sutherland (1952–1954). In Queens, Phillips replaced James A. Roe who had served as Democratic leader since 1938, succeeding Sheridan. In Richmond, Sullivan had taken over from Fetherston in 1941. (*New York Times,* 1938–1954, various issues.)

2 A special census of New York City conducted in 1957 found that between 1950 and 1957 Manhattan suffered a decrease in population of 166,032, a decline of 8.5 per cent. While the population in Brooklyn decreased by 135,742 (5 per cent) and that in the Bronx fell off by 26,910 (1.9 per cent), the number of people living in Richmond increased by 20,465 (10.7 per cent) and the number living in Queens went up by 211,733 (13.7 per cent). *New York Times,* October 9, 1957.

3 The discussion of the machine in the last few years and of the Wagner adminis-

tration is based upon various New York newspapers, especially *New York Times,* 1954–1960; "A New Kind of Tiger," *Time,* August 22, 1955, 12–15; Robert L. Heilbroner, "Carmine G. De Sapio: The Smile on the Face of the Tiger," *Harper's,* July, 1954, 23–33; Robert Bendiner, "The Provincial Politics of the Empire State," *Reporter,* May 12, 1960, 21–23; Fred J. Cook and Gene Gleason, "The Shame of New York," *Nation,* October 31, 1959; City Club of New York, *The Wagner Record: One Year Later* ([New York], 1955); off-the-record interviews and conversations.

4 *New York Times,* 1957–1960. The Republican organizations in Queens and Richmond should also gain in position with respect to the Republican Party in the city. In both boroughs the Republicans and Democrats should continue for some time to be more evenly matched in political strength than they are in the other boroughs.

5 Mayor's Committee on Management Survey, *Modern Management for the City of New York,* V. II (Report of the Mayor's Committee on Management Survey), Appendix B; Oscar Handlin, *The Newcomers: Negroes and Puerto Ricans in a Changing Metropolis* (New York Metropolitan Region Study, Cambridge, Mass., 1959), 49.

6 Columbia University, Bureau of Applied Social Research, *Puerto Rican Population of New York City* (mimeo., 1954); *New York Times,* October 27, 1954, January 17, 1955, May 31, 1957.

Dean Kenneth D. Johnson of the New York School of Social Work, who made the prediction as to the Puerto Rican population in 1970 referred to in the text, estimated that by that year the Puerto Rican and non-white population (the non-white category is composed mainly of Negroes, but also of Asians and some others) will make up 28 per cent of the census of the City of New York (*Times,* October 27, 1954).

7 *New York Times,* March 23, 1954.

8 Citizens Union, *Annual Report* [1953] (New York, 1954).

9 Success for most Americans seems to have come to mean the attainment of a comfortable, secure and leisurely existence rather than a wealthy one. On this subject, see, for example, D. W. Brogan, "Unnoticed Changes in America," *Harper's,* February, 1957, 27–34; William S. White, " 'Consensus American'— A Portrait," *New York Times Magazine,* November 25, 1956, 14.

10 *New York Times,* August 9, 1953, June 7, 1960.

11 *Ibid.,* November 28, 1954.

12 It should be kept in mind that the building of the bridge over the Narrows between Brooklyn and Staten Island is likely to reduce to some extent the exodus from the city; many middle-class families will probably move to suburban-like Richmond, which, of course, will keep them in the city.

Bibliographical Note

This book has been based mainly upon interviews and conversations; newspaper items and articles, especially in the *New York Times;* collections of papers and materials of certain individuals; government and semi-government reports; reports and other writings, printed and unprinted, of private organizations and individuals; books and magazine articles. These materials have already been mentioned in the notes, and I do not feel much is to be gained by noting them again in a formal bibliography. It might be helpful to students of La Guardia and the La Guardia era, however, to say a word about the collections of papers and materials used in this study and about books pertaining to La Guardia and the La Guardia period. Most, but not all, of these books have been cited in the notes.

COLLECTIONS OF PAPERS AND MATERIALS

The Personal Papers of Fiorello H. La Guardia are to be found in the Municipal Archives and Records Center, 238 Williams Street, New York City. The collection consists of letters, speeches, reports, radio addresses, press releases and other materials contained in 123 file drawers, along with almost 250 scrapbooks of newspaper clippings and photographs. The materials deal mainly with La Guardia's mayoralty. There is an Index of Personal Subject Files covering the period January, 1934– December, 1945. The William Jay Schieffelin collection, in the possession of the Schieffelin family, consists mainly of three sets of typewritten reminiscences, which I have referred to in the notes as the "Memoirs." One set is a copy of Schieffelin's reminiscences in the Columbia University Oral History Project. The collection contains newspaper clippings, letters and other materials in envelopes. It should be noted that the collection deals with other aspects of Schieffelin's life aside from his role as municipal reformer—his interest in various humanitarian causes, for example. The Maurice P. Davidson collection, probably now in the hands of his family, contains various materials pertaining to the Fusion movement of 1933 and the City Fusion

Party, principally newspaper clippings, pamphlets, leaflets, speeches (some not printed), stationery of the City Fusion Party, City Fusion Party news releases (January–June, 1933) and desk sheets (February–June, 1934) and some letters.

BOOKS DEALING WITH LA GUARDIA AND THE LA GUARDIA PERIOD

Fiorello H. La Guardia, *The Making of an Insurgent. An Autobiography: 1882–1919* (Philadelphia and New York, 1948) is the only volume of a projected autobiography. Naturally La Guardia presents himself in a favorable light, but the book contains a good deal that is valuable. It tells us much, directly and indirectly, about the kind of man La Guardia was and why he held some of the attitudes he did. Arthur Mann, *La Guardia: A Fighter Against His Times, 1882–1933* (Philadelphia and New York, 1959) is volume one of an intended definitive life of La Guardia. Scholarly and competently written, it is the best biography of the Little Flower for the period before La Guardia became Mayor. Lowell M. Limpus and Burr W. Leyson, *This Man La Guardia* (New York, 1938) carries La Guardia's life through his re-election in 1937. While it contains important information about La Guardia, Limpus and Leyson is marked by grave defects: too much hero worship, lack of proportion (less than 50 of the 420 pages deal with La Guardia's mayoralty), the absence of documentation and, especially, numerous inaccuracies. Jay Franklin, *La Guardia: A Biography* (New York, 1937) is an unsatisfactory job by an admirer.

Aside from the biographies, La Guardia is the chief figure or an important figure in several books. Paul J. Kern's "Fiorello H. La Guardia" in J. T. Salter, ed., *The American Politician* (Chapel Hill, N.C., 1938) is a readable, though somewhat superficial, sketch; in 1938 Kern was extremely enthusiastic about La Guardia. Ernest Cuneo, *Life With Fiorello* (New York, 1953) is a memoir by a La Guardia partisan, covering mainly the period 1931–1932, when Cuneo served as law clerk to La Guardia. La Guardia is also treated rather uncritically in Newbold Morris (in collaboration with Dana Lee Thomas), *Let the Chips Fall: My Battles Against Corruption* (New York, 1955), the story of Morris' public career through the early 1950's. Robert Moses, *La Guardia: A Salute and a Memoir* (New York, 1957), is, as Moses suggests, "a series of reminiscences loosely strung together on the rope of memory"—which, incidentally, is not devoid of some of Moses' pet prejudices. Rexford G. Tugwell, *The Art of Politics as Practiced by Three Great Americans: Franklin Delano Roosevelt, Luis Muñoz Marín, and Fiorello H. La Guardia* (Garden City, New York, 1958), is not without some insights into La Guardia but has to be used with much caution. The author is given to making inaccurate (wild would not be too strong a word in some cases) statements in discussing La Guardia and his mayoralty. Howard Zinn, *La Guardia in Congress* (Ithaca, New York, 1959), is a first-rate account of this aspect of La Guardia's career.

A few books focus more directly on the La Guardia administration. William H. Allen, *Why Tammanies Revive: La Guardias Mis-Guard* (New York, 1937), attacks the administration for what Allen regards as "preventable errors, violated pledges and dodged opportunities." Some of Allen's criticism is sound, but much of it is unfair in that it ignores too much the realities of political life. No student of the La Guardia era can disregard the three editions of *New York Advancing* edited by Rebecca B. Rankin, former Librarian of the Municipal Reference Library (*New York Advancing: A Scientific Approach to Municipal Government . . . 1934–1935, F. H. LaGuardia, Mayor*, New York, 1936; *New York Advancing, World's Fair Edition, The Result of Five Years of Progressive Administration in the City of New York, F. H. La Guardia,*

Mayor . . . , New York, 1939; *New York Advancing, Victory Edition, Seven More Years of Progressive Administration in the City of New York, 1939–1945, F. H. La Guardia, Mayor,* New York, 1945). These books present reports by the different city agencies of the functioning of the city government under La Guardia and the achievements of the La Guardia administration. (The first edition of *New York Advancing* deals more with Fusion achievements, the other two more with the workings of the city agencies.) While containing valuable information about the La Guardia administration, the *New York Advancing* books do not tell the entire story; they tell what La Guardia accomplished, but not about where he fell down. In *Faith in Fusion* (New York, 1951) Charles Belous recounts his role in the Fusion movement of the La Guardia era and expresses his faith in Fusion as the best way of maintaining good government. Though lacking perception and depth and containing some errors, the book furnishes some important information about the La Guardia period.

Index